Hands-On
CHEMISTRY ACTIVITIES
with REAL-LIFE APPLICATIONS

NORMAN HERR

JAMES CUNNINGHAM

JOSSEY-BASS
A Wiley Imprint
www.josseybass.com

Published by Jossey-Bass
A Wiley Imprint
989 Market Street, San Francisco, CA 94103-1741   www.josseybass.com

Jossey-Bass books and products are available through most bookstores. To contact Jossey-Bass directly call our Customer Care Department within the U.S. at 800-956-7739, outside the U.S. at 317-572-3986 or fax 317-572-4002.

Jossey-Bass also publishes its books in a variety of electronic formats. Some content that appears in print may not be available in electronic books.

Library of Congress Cataloging-in-Publication Data

Herr, Norman
    Hands-on chemistry activities with real-life applications : easy-to-use
    labs and demonstrations for grades 8–12 / Norman Herr, James Cunningham.
        p.   cm. — (Physical science curriculum library ; v. 2)
        Includes index.
        ISBN 0-87628-262-1
        1. Chemistry—Experiments. 2. Chemistry—Study and teaching (Secondary)
I. Cunningham, James B. II. Title. III. Series.
QD43.H47   1999
540'.78—dc21   98-38898

Printed in the United States of America

FIRST EDITION
PB Printing 10 9 8

DEDICATION

To my wife, Roberta, our children Christiana, Stephen, and John,
and my parents Herb and Betty Herr.

NORMAN HERR

To the memory of my father, Edward Cunningham,
and my mother, Veronica Cunningham.

JAMES CUNNINGHAM

ABOUT THE AUTHORS

Norman Herr is a professor of science and computer education at California State University, Northridge. He received his Ph.D. from the University of California, Los Angeles, and has worked as a chemist, college science instructor, and consultant for the College Board's Advanced Placement program. He previously served as Chair of the Science Department at Maranatha High School in Sierra Madre, California. Dr. Herr has written numerous articles in the field of science education and has co-authored *Hands-On Physics Activities* with James Cunningham.

James Cunningham is a professor of science and computer education at California State University, Northridge, where he serves as Chair of the Department of Secondary Education. He received his Ph.D. in Science Education from Syracuse University and previously served as Chair of the Departments of Science and Mathematics at Brainbridge Island and Trout Lake high schools in the state of Washington. Dr. Cunningham is author of *Teaching Metrics Simplified* and co-author of *BASIC for Teachers* and *Authoring Educational Software*. He is also co-author of *Hands-On Physics* with Norman Herr.

ACKNOWLEDGMENTS

We are grateful to Dr. Margaret Holzer in the Chemistry Department at California State University, Northridge, for serving as technical editor for this resource, and to Connie Kallback and the staff at Prentice Hall for their editorial expertise. Thanks to Al Squatrito for information on the planimeter and Zedcor® Inc. for use of 18 clip art illustrations. In addition, we wish to thank the science teacher candidates at California State University, Northridge, for field testing the activities and offering suggestions for improvement. We also wish to express deep gratitude to our families for their support and encouragement while this book was being written. Graphics contained in this resource were created by Norman Herr using *Claris Draw®*.

ABOUT THIS RESOURCE

Hands-On Chemistry Activities With Real-Life Applications contains over 300 intriguing investigations designed to engage students in a genuine pursuit of science. Because of the favorable response to *Hands-On Physics Activities,* the authors used the same approach and philosophy in writing this resource. This hands-on, inquiry-based approach to teaching and learning science follows recommendations set forth in the National Academy of Sciences' *National Science Education Standards* and the National Science Teachers Association's *Scope Sequence and Coordination Project.*

Activities included in this resource provide meaningful interactions between students and their world in a manner encouraging sound scientific reasoning. Many of the activities produce unexpected or dramatic results that capture student interest. Each set of investigations is preceded by a concise introduction to relevant concepts, providing students a foundation on which to build their understanding. This resource contains more than 450 illustrations and 100 tables to guide students and teachers in carrying out the activities. To stimulate student reasoning, thought-provoking questions are included after each set of activities. Following each student section, material developed especially for the teacher explains concepts in greater detail, answers questions, and provides directions for presenting activities as impressive classroom demonstrations. Interesting and practical applications of scientific principles and concepts are introduced throughout the resource, helping students understand the relevance of science to their everyday lives.

The authors have made every effort to include activities that can be carried out safely with materials commonly found in the students' everyday environment. Some require materials found in the typical science classroom, or inexpensive equipment available from scientific supply houses. Activities have been successfully implemented and tested in the classroom by experienced and novice science teachers.

Although every effort has been made to design activities that can be carried out safely, the authors emphasize that chemical investigations may involve hazards. Consequently, teachers and students must pay particular attention to all recommendations concerning safety, printed in italics throughout this resource. Whenever dealing with chemicals, it is essential to wear protective clothing and eyeware. Some activities, while dramatic, may be dangerous and should be performed only by the instructor as indicated in the resource. If you have reservations regarding safety, do not carry out an activity.

As students perform the investigations described in this resource, they will become engaged in the processes of science, and will acquire knowledge and understanding of basic science concepts and the relevance of these to their everyday lives.

Norman Herr, Ph.D.
James Cunningham, Ph.D.
California State University, Northridge 1998

CONTENTS

UNIT TWO: MATTER
79

UNIT FOUR: THERMODYNAMICS AND KINETICS
347

5.7 CRYSTALS AND CRYSTALLIZATION 568

APPENDIX
593

A.1 UNITS, QUANTITIES, AND CONVERSIONS 594

A.2 LANGUAGE OF CHEMISTRY 600

A.3 SAFETY 611

A.4 CHEMICAL PROCUREMENT AND PREPARATION 616

UNIT ONE

Measurement

1.1 Language of Chemistry

1.2 Units of Measurement

1.3 Measurement

1.1 LANGUAGE OF CHEMISTRY

More scientific research is published in English than any other language, making English the "language of science." Scientists around the world learn English so they can keep abreast of current research and share their findings with others. Unfortunately many have a difficult time learning English and scientific terms because they do not understand the structure of this rich, but complex, language.

The English language has developed over the centuries as the languages of the native peoples of the British Isles have melded with those of conquering and immigrating peoples. The Romans invaded England in AD 43 and occupied the country until approximately AD 400. During this time their Latin language blended with the native Celtic languages. As the Romans left, the Anglo-Saxon tribes from northern Germany, Holland, and Denmark began immigrating (AD 450–550), bringing with them their Germanic language which gradually became the backbone of English. The word "English" comes from "Angleish," the language of the Anglo-Saxons.

The English language gained many new terms following the Norman Conquest of 1066. In that year, William, the Duke of Normandy (William the Conqueror) sailed across the English Channel from what is now France to the southeastern coast of England. Within a few months his troops defeated the English, and William became the new King of England. In the years that followed, many people migrated from Normandy bringing with them their Latin-based language.

The Norman conquest of England opened the door for communication with the rest of Europe. Religious, cultural, and scientific scholars came to England, bringing with them a wealth of knowledge that they expressed in the scholarly languages of Latin and Greek. These terms were quickly adopted by the English, and as new scientific concepts developed, they were expressed using Latin and Greek words.

Today, scientists continue to assign names using Latin and Greek roots. Because classical Greek and Latin are no longer spoken (they were replaced by modern Greek and Italian), the meanings of such roots do not change. Living languages like English are dynamic and subject to change. For example, the word "run" in English can have more than 25 basic meanings such as "to move quickly," "to flee," "a sequence," "a creek" or "a ranch." Next year a new meaning of "run" may be introduced just as we have recently seen new slang meanings introduced for such words as "cool," "awesome," "bad," and "radical." By contrast, the meanings of classical Latin and Greek roots don't change because these languages are no longer spoken in everyday communication. For example, the Latin word "curr" meant "run" (to move quickly) one thousand years ago and should mean the same thing 1000 years from now. Thus, when scientists wanted to describe the movement of electrons, they introduced the term "electrical <u>curr</u>ent," and when computer developers wanted to give the name for an object that could move quickly across the screen they gave it the name "<u>curr</u>sor." These words were developed to have specific meanings that won't be subject to as much change as common words.

A knowledge of Greek and Latin root words can greatly enhance your understanding of scientific terms and provide you with a better understanding of English and other European languages. Approximately 50% of all words in the English language have Latin roots, many of which are shared by Spanish, French, Portuguese and Italian. It is very helpful to understand these roots when learning one of these languages or when learning English if one of these Latin (Romance) languages is your native tongue. In this chapter we will examine chemical "nomenclature," the study of names commonly used in chemistry. By understanding a few roots and rules, you will be able to understand a significant amount of the language of chemistry.

1.1.1 NOMENCLATURE: ELEMENTS

Concepts to Investigate: Nomenclature, root words, etymology, periodic table.

Materials: Periodic table; suggested: dictionary, book of baby names, root word books.

Principles and Procedures: Do you know what your name means? The vast majority of names are rooted in history and have a meaning that is often forgotten as the name is passed down from generation to generation. Confer with relatives, baby name books or other resources to determine the meaning of your first, middle and family names.

The names given to the elements give clues about their properties, or after whom or where they were named. Helium derives its name from the Greek word "helios," meaning "Sun" because the first evidence of its existence was obtained by analyzing the spectrum of sunlight. The word "hydrogen" comes from the Greek words "hydro," meaning water (as in hydroelectric, hydrolysis, etc.) and "gene," meaning beginning (as in Genesis, gene, genetics). Thus the word hydrogen means "water former," an appropriate name for a substance that forms water when it combusts:

$$2H_2 + O_2 \rightarrow 2H_2O$$

Astatine is a highly reactive element with a very short half-life. The chemists who first studied this element derived its name from the Greek word *astatos,* meaning "unstable." The noxious gas bromine's name was derived from the Greek word *bromos* that means "stench," reflecting its unpleasant odor. Examine the periodic table (Figure A) and see how many names for which you can determine the meaning.

Questions

(1) What are the meanings of your first, middle and last names?

(2-15) Examine the periodic table and try to determine the name(s) of the element(s) described.

(2) Named for the university where many of the transuranium elements were synthesized.

(3) A sequence of three elements named after a series of three planets.

(4) A spectral analysis of this element shows that it emits a very strong indigo (blue-violet) colored line.

(5) This element was named after a cleaning compound, which was found to contain large quantities of it.

(6) This element was known in ancient times. It was mined originally on the Mediterranean island of Cyprus from which the element obtained its Greek name *cuprum.*

(7) This element was named in honor of two famous French chemists: Marie Curie and her husband Pierre Curie.

(8) This element was named from the Latin word *fluere* meaning "to flow" because its compounds are often used as a fluxes in metallurgy.

(9) Chemists described this element as cryptic (meaning hidden) because it is a colorless, odorless, and tasteless gas with a concentration of only about 1 part per million in the atmosphere.

(10) The ancient Romans made water pipes out of this metal, and the terms "plumbing" and "plumber" were derived from its original Latin name.

(11) This is the only element in the d-block that has not been isolated from the Earth's crust. It derives its name from the fact that it had to be synthesized by technical means.

(12) Chemists Robert Bunsen and Gustav Kirchoff were examining the spectral emission of an ore known as lepidolite when they discovered a dark ruby-red spectral line never seen before. The element they subsequently discovered derived its name from the color of its spectral emission line.

(13) This element is strong, corrosion resistant, and has many uses in the aerospace and defense industries. It derives its name from the mythological Greek Titans who were extremely strong.

(14) Frenchman Paul-Emile Lecoq named the element he discovered after the ancient Latin name for his homeland.

(15) The original Latin name of this element was *hydrargyrus,* meaning liquid (*hydr-,* as in hydrant, hydrate) silver (*arg-,* as in *argentum* the Latin word for silver, or *argentite* for the mineral silver sulfide). Known also as "quick silver," the symbol of this element reflects its original Latin name.

(16) The symbols of most elements correspond to their common names, but there are a number of notable exceptions including copper (Cu), gold (Au), iron (Fe), lead (Pb), silver (Ag), mercury (Hg), and tin (Sn). Can you explain why the symbols of these elements don't match their names?

PERIODIC TABLE OF THE ELEMENTS

1	2	3	4	5	6	7	8	9	10	11	12	13	14	15	16	17	18
1 H Hydrogen 1.008																	2 He Helium 4.003
3 Li Lithium 6.941	4 Be Beryllium 9.012											5 B Boron 10.81	6 C Carbon 12.011	7 N Nitrogen 14.007	8 O Oxygen 15.999	9 F Fluorine 18.998	10 Ne Neon 20.179
11 Na Sodium 22.990	12 Mg Magnesium 24.305											13 Al Aluminum 26.981	14 Si Silicon 28.086	15 P Phosphorus 30.974	16 S Sulfur 32.06	17 Cl Chlorine 35.453	18 Ar Argon 39.948
19 K Potassium 39.098	20 Ca Calcium 40.08	21 Sc Scandium 44.956	22 Ti Titanium 47.88	23 V Vanadium 50.942	24 Cr Chromium 51.996	25 Mn Manganese 54.938	26 Fe Iron 55.847	27 Co Cobalt 58.93	28 Ni Nickel 58.69	29 Cu Copper 63.546	30 Zn Zinc 65.39	31 Ga Gallium 69.72	32 Ge Germanium 72.59	33 As Arsenic 74.92	34 Se Selenium 78.96	35 Br Bromine 79.904	36 Kr Krypton 83.80
37 Rb Rubidium 85.468	38 Sr Strontium 87.62	39 Y Ytrium 88.906	40 Zr Zirconium 91.224	41 Nb Niobium 92.906	42 Mo Molybdenum 95.94	43 Tc Technetium (98)	44 Ru Ruthenium 101.07	45 Rh Rhodium 102.906	46 Pd Palladium 106.42	47 Ag Silver 107.868	48 Cd Cadmium 112.41	49 In Indium 114.82	50 Sn Tin 118.71	51 Sb Antimony 121.75	52 Te Tellurium 127.60	53 I Iodine 126.905	54 Xe Xenon 131.29
55 Cs Cesium 132.905	56 Ba Barium 137.33	57 La Lanthanum 138.906	72 Hf Hafnium 178.49	73 Ta Tantalum 180.948	74 W Tungsten 183.85	75 Re Rhenium 186.207	76 Os Osmium 190.2	77 Ir Iridium 192.22	78 Pt Platinum 195.08	79 Au Gold 196.967	80 Hg Mercury 200.59	81 Tl Thallium 204.383	82 Pb Lead 207.2	83 Bi Bismuth 208.980	84 Po Polonium (209)	85 At Astatine (210)	86 Rn Radon (222)
87 Fr Francium (223)	88 Ra Radium 226.025	89 Ac Actinium 227.028	104 Rf Rutherfordium (261)	105 Db Dubnium (262)	106 Sg Seaborgium (263)	107 Bh Bohrium (262)	108 Hs Hassium (265)	109 Mt Meitnerium (266)	110 Uun Ununnilium (269)	111 Uuu Unununium (272)	112 Uub Unumbium (277)						

Lanthanide Series

58 Ce Cerium 140.12	59 Pr Praseodymium 140.908	60 Nd Neodymium 144.24	61 Pm Promethium (145)	62 Sm Samarium 150.36	63 Eu Europium 151.96	64 Gd Gadolinium 157.25	65 Tb Terbium 158.925	66 Dy Dysprosium 162.50	67 Ho Holmium 164.930	68 Er Erbium 167.26	69 Tm Thallium 168.934	70 Yb Yterbium 173.04	71 Lu Lutetium 174.967

Actinide Series

90 Th Thorium 232.038	91 Pa Protactinium 231.036	92 U Uranium 238.029	93 Np Neptunium 237.048	94 Pu Plutonium (244)	95 Am Americium (243)	96 Cm Curium (247)	97 Bk Berkelium (247)	98 Cf Californium (251)	99 Es Einsteinium (252)	100 Fm Fermium (257)	101 Md Mendelevium (258)	102 No Nobelium (259)	103 Lr Lawrencium (260)

Key:

1	← atomic number
H	← symbol
Hydrogen	← name
1.008	← atomic mass

A

1.1.2 NOMENCLATURE: COMPOUNDS

Concepts to Investigate: Nomenclature, binary compounds, ionic compounds.

Materials: Photocopy of Figure B, scissors.

Principles and Procedures: In William Shakespeare's *Romeo and Juliet,* the daughter of the Capulet family falls in love with the son of her family's archenemies, the Montagues. Distressed by the hatred between their families, Juliet asks: *"What's in a name? That which we call a rose, By any other name would smell as sweet."* Although this line of reasoning may have worked well for Shakespeare, it does not work well for anyone learning chemistry, or any other science for that matter.

In chemistry, names are descriptive and meaningful and help communicate ideas the same way a cartographer's map helps describe a newly discovered island. Chemists assigned meaningful names to the 109 elements and have established logical rules for naming compounds composed of these elements. Chemists are not free to name a new compound anything they want any more than a cartographer is free to draw a map with any borders he or she desires.

Binary compounds: Compounds composed of only two elements (such as $NaCl$, SO_2, HBr, and H_2O) are known as binary compounds. Binary compounds are named by placing the name of the element with the positive oxidation state first, followed by the element with the negative oxidation state. When writing the formula of a compound composed of a metal and a nonmetal, the symbol for the metal (oxidized element) always precedes the symbol for the nonmetal (reduced element). The name of the nonmetal component generally assumes the suffix -ide. For example, a compound of copper and sulfur would be known as copper sulfide, or a compound of chromium and oxygen would be known as chromium oxide. In certain binary compounds composed of nonmetals, two or more compounds may form. For example, nitrogen and oxygen combine to form N_2O, NO, NO_2, N_2O_4, and N_2O_5. To differentiate one compound from another, the following Greek prefixes are used: (1) *mono-,* (2) *di-,* (3) *tri-,* (4) *tetra-,* (5) *penta-,* (6) *hexa-,* (7) *hepta-,* and (8) *octa-.* For example, the compound NO_2 would be correctly named nitrogen dioxide.

Ionic compounds: Ionic compounds form as a result of the attraction between positively charged ions (cations), and negatively charged ions (anions). In ionic compounds, the total positive charge must equal the total negative charge. For example, the singly charged cation ammonium NH_4^+ will combine in a one-to-one ratio with the singly charged bromide Br^- anion to form ammonium bromide: NH_4Br. By contrast, three bromide ions (Br^-) are required to balance the chromium (III) cation Cr^{3+} when forming chromic bromide ($CrBr_3$). Table 1 lists common cations and anions.

The following activity is designed to help you visualize the ratios in which ionic compounds form. Make four photocopies of Figure B and cut all of the individual ion symbols apart. Cations (light circles) combine with anions (dark hexagons) in such a way that there is no net charge. For example, combine one aluminum (charge +3) with three bromides (charge −1) to produce neutral aluminum bromide ($AlBr_3$). Ratios other than 1:3 will not produce a neutral product, and therefore do not occur in nature. To answer the questions below, move the ion symbols around to balance charge and determine appropriate formulas for the compounds listed.

Upon examining Table 1, you will notice that certain metallic elements form more than one ion. For example, iron may carry a +2 charge or a +3 charge. To differentiate these, we apply a Roman numeral after the metal ion for clarification. For example, Fe^{2+} is known as the iron (II) ion, while the Fe^{3+} ion is known as the iron (III) ion.

$\overset{+}{H}$ $\overset{+}{Ag}$ $\overset{+}{K}$ $\overset{+}{Na}$ $\overset{-}{Cl}$ $\overset{-}{OH}$ $\overset{-}{Br}$ $\overset{-}{ClO_3}$

$\overset{+}{NH_4}$ $\overset{++}{Ca}$ $\overset{++}{Mg}$ $\overset{++}{Zn}$ $\overset{-}{HCO}$ $\overset{-}{CN}$ $\overset{-}{NO_3}$ $\overset{-}{HSO}$

$\overset{++}{Sn}$ $\overset{++}{Ni}$ $\overset{++}{Ba}$ $\overset{++}{Fe}$ $\overset{-}{NO_2}$ $\overset{--}{O}$ $\overset{--}{S}$ $\overset{--}{Cr_2O_7}$

$\overset{+++}{Fe}$ $\overset{+++}{Cr}$ $\overset{+++}{Al}$ $\overset{++++}{Sn}$ $\overset{--}{SO_3}$ $\overset{--}{SO_4}$ $\overset{---}{PO_4}$ $\overset{----}{Fe(CN)_6}$

$\overset{+}{H}$ $\overset{+}{Ag}$ $\overset{+}{K}$ $\overset{+}{Na}$ $\overset{-}{Cl}$ $\overset{-}{OH}$ $\overset{-}{Br}$ $\overset{-}{ClO_3}$

$\overset{+}{NH_4}$ $\overset{++}{Ca}$ $\overset{++}{Mg}$ $\overset{++}{Zn}$ $\overset{-}{HCO}$ $\overset{-}{CN}$ $\overset{-}{NO_3}$ $\overset{-}{HSO}$

$\overset{++}{Sn}$ $\overset{++}{Ni}$ $\overset{++}{Ba}$ $\overset{++}{Fe}$ $\overset{-}{NO_2}$ $\overset{--}{O}$ $\overset{-}{S}$ $\overset{--}{Cr_2O_7}$

$\overset{+++}{Fe}$ $\overset{+++}{Cr}$ $\overset{+++}{Al}$ $\overset{++++}{Sn}$ $\overset{--}{SO_3}$ $\overset{--}{SO_4}$ $\overset{---}{PO_4}$ $\overset{----}{Fe(CN)_6}$

$\overset{+}{H}$ $\overset{+}{Ag}$ $\overset{+}{K}$ $\overset{+}{Na}$ $\overset{-}{Cl}$ $\overset{-}{OH}$ $\overset{-}{Br}$ $\overset{-}{ClO_3}$

$\overset{+}{NH_4}$ $\overset{++}{Ca}$ $\overset{++}{Mg}$ $\overset{++}{Zn}$ $\overset{-}{HCO}$ $\overset{-}{CN}$ $\overset{-}{NO_3}$ $\overset{-}{HSO}$

$\overset{++}{Sn}$ $\overset{++}{Ni}$ $\overset{++}{Ba}$ $\overset{++}{Fe}$ $\overset{-}{NO_2}$ $\overset{--}{O}$ $\overset{-}{S}$ $\overset{--}{Cr_2O_7}$

$\overset{+++}{Fe}$ $\overset{+++}{Cr}$ $\overset{+++}{Al}$ $\overset{++++}{Sn}$ $\overset{--}{SO_3}$ $\overset{--}{SO_4}$ $\overset{---}{PO_4}$ $\overset{----}{Fe(CN)_6}$

B

Table 1: Common Ions

Common Cations		*Common Anions*	
aluminum	Al³⁺	acetate	$(C_2H_3O)_2^-$
ammonium	NH_4^+	bromide	Br^-
barium	Ba^{2+}	carbonate	CO_3^{2-}
calcium	Ca^{2+}	chlorate	ClO_3^{2-}
chromium(III)	Cr^{3+}	chloride	Cl^-
cobalt(II)	Co^{2+}	chlorite	ClO_2^-
copper(I)	Cu^+	chromate	CrO_4^{2-}
copper(II)	Cu^{2+}	cyanide	CN^-
hydronium	H_3O^+	dichromate	$(Cr_2O_7)^{2-}$
iron(II)	Fe^{2+}	fluoride	F^-
iron(III)	Fe^{3+}	hexacyanoferrate(II)	$Fe(CN)_6^{4-}$
lead(II)	Pb^{2+}	hexacyanoferrate(III)	$Fe(CN)_6^{3-}$
magnesium	Mg^{2+}	hydride	H^-
mercury(I)	Hg_2^{2+}	hydrogen carbonate	HCO_3^-
mercury(II)	Hg^{2+}	hydrogen sulfate	HSO_4^-
nickel(II)	Ni^{2+}	hydroxide	OH^-
potassium	K^+	hypochlorite	ClO^-
silver	Ag^+	iodide	I^-
sodium	Na^+	nitrate	NO_3^-
tin(II)	Sn^{2+}	nitrite	NO_2^-
tin(IV)	Sn^{4+}	oxide	O^{2-}
zinc	Zn^{2+}	perchlorate	ClO_4^-
		permanganate	MnO_4^-
		peroxide	O_2^{2-}
		phosphate	PO_4^{3-}
		sulfate	SO_4^{2-}
		sulfide	S^{2-}
		sulfite	SO_3^{2-}

Questions

(1) *Binary Compounds:* Name the following compounds: KF, CaI_2, AlN, HCl, H_2S, NO, Li_2O, $MgCl_2$, Na_2S, HgO.

(2) Using the appropriate ion labels, determine the formulas for the following substances:

    (a) tin (II) fluoride (stannous fluoride; also known as Fluoristan, the active ingredient in Crest® toothpaste.)

    (b) tin (IV) oxide (stannic oxide; used to polish glass and metals)

    (c) tin (IV) chloride (stannic chloride; used to stabilize colors in soaps)

    (d) iron (III) oxide (ferric oxide; a form of rust, used as a red pigment in paints)

    (e) magnesium hydroxide (used in antacids and laxatives such as milk of magnesia)

    (f) zinc oxide (used in some sunblocks to absorb ultraviolet light and protect the skin)

    (g) sodium hydrogen carbonate (sodium bicarbonate; baking soda, used to deodorize refrigerators and as a leavening agent to help bread rise)

(h) calcium phosphate (one of the main components in bone; used in fertilizers to provide plants with phosphorous)

(i) sodium nitrite (kills bacteria; used to preserve such foods as frankfurters, corned beef, and tunafish)

(j) ammonium phosphate (used by fire fighters to retard the spread of forest fires)

(k) silver cyanide (used as a source of silver when electroplating silver-plated objects)

(l) sodium hydroxide (used in drain cleaners to cut grease and open clogged drains)

1.1.3 CHEMICAL TERMINOLOGY: UNDERSTANDING THE LANGUAGE OF CHEMISTRY

Concepts to Investigate: Nomenclature, terminology, root words.

Materials: Recommended: root-word book, dictionary.

Principles and Procedures: The longest word in the English language is *pneumonoultramicroscopicsilicovolcanoconiosis.* Although the 45-letter giant may appear quite incomprehensible at first, look again and see if there are any roots inside it you can recognize. For example, you may see the word "microscopic" or "volcano" buried amidst the rest of the letters. Although scientific terms may seem very confusing, they are actually logical and relatively easy to decipher if you know the basic roots from which they are derived. We will now analyze the roots in *pneumonoultramicroscopicsilicovolcanoconiosis* in an effort to understand what the word means. To illustrate the everyday usage of these root words, we will give examples of words in the English language in which they are incorporated.

- *pneumono-* refers to the lungs or air (e.g., pneumonia is a disease of the lungs; pneumatic brakes are air brakes)
- *ultra-* above, beyond (e.g., ultraviolet light has an energy above visible light; ultrasound refers to sound with a frequency higher than 20,000 Hz, the upper limit of human hearing)
- *micro-* small (e.g., a microchip refers to a small computer chip; microorganisms are small organisms like bacteria and protozoans)
- *scop-* view (e.g., a telescope views things that are far away; an arthroscope provides doctors with an internal view of joints)
- *silic-* the element silicon (e.g., silica dioxide, the main ingredient in sand; silicone resins used in insulating electrical wires)
- *volcan-* volcano, fire (e.g., volcanos appear to spit forth fire; vulcanization is the process of treating rubber with tremendous heat, pressure, and sulfur in a manner reminiscent of the conditions in a volcano)
- *coni-* dust (e.g., conidia are dust-like fungal spores)
- *-osis* disease or condition (e.g., tuberculosis, a disease of the lungs caused by the tubercle bacillus; osteoporosis, a disease in which the bones become excessively porous and fragile)

After examining these root words, we might predict that pneumonoultramicroscopicsilicovolcanoconiosis is a lung *(pneumono-)* disease *(-osis)* with welts resembling volcanos *(volcano-)* caused by the inhalation of extremely *(ultra-)* small *(microscopic-)* particles of silicaceous *(silico-)* dust *(coni-).* Notice that the name for the disease provides us with much information about it. Once you know the meaning of some basic root words, it is possible to understand the meaning of a wide range of scientific terms. Table 2 lists many of the common root words used in chemistry and provides examples of chemical terms that make use of these terms.

Table 2: Root Words Frequently Used in Chemistry

root	L	meaning	example	explanation
-ane	-	single covalent bond	alkane, propane	alkanes have only single bonds
-ene	-	double covalent bond	alkene, polypropylene	alkenes have one or more double bonds
-ion	L	process	fusion	the process of combing or fusing nuclei to form a heavier nucleus
-oid	G	like, form	metalloid	some properties are like those of metals
-yne	-	triple covalent bond	alkyne, ethyne	alkynes have one or more triple bonds
a-	G	not, without	amorphous carbon	carbon without crystalline shape
acid	L	sour, sharp	hydrochloric acid	acids stimulate the sour taste buds
alkali	Ar	soda ash, alkali	alkali lake	alkali lakes have very high mineral content
allo, -io	G	other, different	allotrope	one of the two or more forms of an element that have the same physical state
alpha	G	1st letter of Greek alphabet	alpha particle	designated by the letter "alpha"
amin	N	ammonia	amine, amino acid	an ammonia base in which one or more of the three hydrogens is replaced by an alkyl group
amph, -i, -o	G	double, on both sides	amphoteric, amphibian	amphoteric species react either as acids or bases
anti	G	against, opposite	antiseptic	substance that works against microbes
aqua	L	water	aqueous solution	water-based solution
baro	G	pressure	barometer, bar	barometer measures pressure
beta	G	second letter of Greek alphabet	beta particle	designated by the letter beta
bi	L	two	binary compounds	compound made of two elements
bio	G	life	biochemistry	chemistry of living systems
carb, -o, -on	L	coal, carbon	carbohydrate	compound made of carbon, hydrogen, and oxygen $(CH_2O)_n$
chem-	G	chemistry	chemical kinetics	the kinetics of a chemical reaction
co, -l, m, -n	L	with, together	coefficient, colligative	number that appears with a formula in a chemical equation
com	L	with, together	compound	a compound results when elements combine with each other
com	L	with, together	composition reaction	a reaction where molecules are assembled together
conjug	L	joined together	conjugate acid, conjugal	acid formed from its conjugate base by the addition of a proton
cosm, -o	G	the world or universe	cosmic rays, cosmos	high energy rays from space (the cosmos)
cry, -mo, -o	G	cold	crystal	crystals form when solutions are cooled
de	L	down, without, from	decomposition, denature, dehydrate	a reaction in which materials are broken down

root	L	meaning	example	explanation
dens	L	thick	density, dense	density is a measure of how "thick" a fluid is (how much mass per unit volume)
di	G	separate, double, across	disaccharide	two monosaccharides tied together
dis	G	separate, apart	dissociation	separation of ions when dissolving
duc, -t	L	lead	ductile	the state of being able to be pulled or led through a small opening to produce a wire
e	L	out, without, from	evaporation	the process of vapor leaving from the surface of a liquid
ef	L	out, from, away	effervescence	rapid escape of gas from a liquid in which it is dissolved
electr, -i, -o	G	electrode	electrolyte	something that dissolves in water to give a solution that conducts an electric current
elem	L	basic	elements	a substance that cannot be broken down into more basic substances by normal chemical means
empir	G	experienced	empirical	based upon experience or observation
en	G	in, into	endothermic	a reaction which "takes heat in"
equ	L	equal	equilibrium	a dynamic condition in which two opposing reactions occur at equal rates
erg	G	work	energy, erg	energy is the ability to perform work
exo	G	out, outside, without	exothermic	exothermic reactions give heat to the outside environment
ferr, -o	L	iron	ferromagnetism	strongly attracted to a magnet, like iron
fiss, -i, -ur	L	cleft, split	fission	the splitting of nuclei
flu	L	flow	fluids	gases and liquids are defined as fluids because they flow
fract	L	break, broken	fractional distillation	distillation in which the components of a mixture are broken down and separated by different boiling points
gamma	G	3rd letter of the Greek alphabet	gamma rays	high energy electromagnetic waves identified by the Greek letter gamma
gen	G	bear, produce, beginning	gene	a section of a DNA chain that codes for a particular protein that the organism can produce
glyc, -er, -o	G	sweet	glycogen, glycolysis, glycolipid	a sugar- (glucose-) based monomer that stores energy in animals
graph, -o, -y	G	write, writing	graphite	form of carbon used in the pencil "leads" we write with
halo-	G	salt	halogens	halogens (e.g., F, Cl, Br) are often found in salts (e.g., NaF, NaCl, KBr)

(continued)

Table 2: (Continued)

root	L	meaning	example	explanation
hetero-	G	other, different	heterogeneous mixture	a mixture whose properties and composition differ from point to point
hom, eo, -o	G	same, alike	homogeneous mixture	a mixture whose properties and composition are the same throughout
hybrid	L	a mongrel, hybrid, combination	hybrid orbital	orbitals produced by the combination of two or more orbitals of the same atom
hydr, -a, -i, -o	G	water	hydrolysis	the breaking of bonds using water
hyper	G	over, above, excessive	perchloric acid (note: "hyperchloric" has been shortened to "perchloric")	the oxidation state of chlorine in hyperchloric (perchloric) acid is above what it is in chloric acid
hypo	G	under, beneath	hypochlorous acid	the oxidation state of chlorine in hypochlorous acid is below the oxidation sate of chlorine in chlorous acid
im	L	not	immiscible	not mutually soluble (not miscible)
in	L	in, into	intrinsic physical properties	properties inherent to a substance, and not upon the amount present
iso	G	equal	isomers	compounds that have the same molecular formula, but different structures
kilo	G	thousand	kilogram	1000 grams
kine	G	move, moving, movement	kinetic energy	energy of motion
lip, -o	G	fat	lipoprotein	fatty acid combined with protein
liqu, -e, -i	L	fluid, liquid	liquefy	the process of becoming a liquid
lys, -oi, -is, -io	G	loose, loosening, breaking	hydrolysis	the breaking apart of a substance by an electric current
macr, -o	G	large, long	macromolecule	macromolecules are large organic molecules
malle, -o, -us	L	hammer	malleable	ability to bend and change shape when hit by a hammer
mer	G	part	polymer	made of many parts
mer, -e, -i,-o	G	a part	dimer	made of two parts
met, -a	G	between, change	metabolism	reactions that change biochemicals from one form to another
meter	G	measure	calorimeter	measures heat energy (calories)
mill -e, -i, -o	L	one thousand	milliliter	one thousandth of a liter
misc	L	mix	miscible	when two solvents dissolve (mix evenly) in each other
mon -a, -er, -o	G	single, one	monomer	single molecular units that can join to make a polymer
morph, -a, -o	G	form	amorphous sulfur	sulfur without definite crystals or shape
neo	G	new, recent	neoprene	a synthetic (new) rubber
neutr	L	neither	neutral	neither positive nor negative

Table 2: *(Concluded)*

root	*L*	*meaning*	*example*	*explanation*
nom, -en, -in	G	name	nomenclature	system of assigning names
non	L	not	nonpolar	does not have polar characteristics
nuc, -ell, -i	L	nut, center	nucleus	center of the atom
oct, -i, -o	L	eight	octet rule	tendency to acquire a total of 8 electrons in highest energy level
orbi, -t, to	L	circle	orbital	electrons may go around the nucleus in patterns known as orbitals
oxid	F	oxygen	oxide	compound containing oxide ion (O^{-2})
photo		light	photochemical smog	air pollutants transformed by sunlight
polar, -i	L	of the pole, polarity	polar covalent	one pole of the bond has a more negative character, and the other a more positive character
poly	G	many	polymer	many molecules bound together to make a new molecule
pro	G	forward, positive, for, in front of	proton	positively charged particle
quant	L	how much	quantum	refers to a given amount of energy
radi, -a, -o,	L	spoke, ray, radius	radioactive	produces rays of electromagnetic energy
sacchar, -o	G	sugar	monosaccharide	single sugar unit
sal, -i	L	salt	salinity	referring to the amount of salt in solution
solu-	L	dissolve	solubility	refers to the tendency to dissolve
spect	L	see, look at	spectator ions	ions that "watch" but are not involved in the reaction
super	L	above, over	superheated	retaining liquid properties beyond the normal boiling point
syn	G	together, with	photosynthesis	molecules are put together with energy derived from light
therm, -o	G	heat	thermochemistry	the study of changes in heat energy accompanying chemical and physical changes
thesis	G	an arranging, statement	hypothesis	a testable statement
tran, -s	L	across, through	transition elements	elements that you pass through when going from the left to right side of the periodic table
un	L	not	unsaturated	bonds that are not saturated
vapor, -i	L	steam, vapor	vaporization	the process of making a vapor
vulcan	L	fire	vulcanized	vulcanized rubber has been treated with heat

Questions

(1) In Table 3 you will find 20 terms and 20 definitions. Analyze the roots in each word, and then match the definitions to the terms. Refer to Table 2 when necessary.

Table 3: Identifying Words Based upon Their Roots

(a)	aqua regia	(1)	A binary compound consisting of carbon and a more electropositive element, especially calcium.
(b)	barograph	(2)	A corrosive, fuming, volatile mixture of hydrochloric and nitric acids, used for testing metals and dissolving platinum and gold. Also called nitrohydrochloric acid.
(c)	carbide		
(d)	conduction		
(e)	cryogen	(3)	A device which records pressure.
(f)	deliquesce	(4)	A liquid, such as liquid nitrogen, that boils at a temperature below about 110 K ($-160°C$) and is used to obtain very low temperatures; a refrigerant.
(g)	dosimeter		
(h)	effluent		
(i)	electrophoresis	(5)	A medical condition in which the blood is carrying abnormally low levels of oxygen.
(j)	ferredoxin		
(k)	fissionable	(6)	An instrument that measures and indicates the amount of X-rays or radiation absorbed in a given period.
(l)	hypoxia		
(m)	isotope	(7)	Any of a class of carbohydrates, such as starch and cellulose, consisting of a number of monosaccharides joined by glycosidic bonds.
(n)	macroscopic		
(o)	microradiography		
(p)	photophosphorylation	(8)	Any of a group of iron-containing plant proteins that function as electron carriers in photosynthetic organisms and in some anaerobic bacteria.
(q)	polychromatic		
(r)	polysaccharide		
(s)	thermodynamics	(9)	Atoms with same atomic mass but different atomic numbers.
(t)	thermometry		

(10) Capable of having its nucleus split.

(11) Having or exhibiting many colors or wavelengths.

(12) In this reaction, the light-dependent transfer of electrons in photosynthetic cells is coupled to the creation of ATP from ADP.

(13) Large enough to be perceived or examined by the unaided eye.

(14) Liquid waste from industrial processes, especially such liquid waste that is released into a river or other waterway.

(15) Measurement of temperature.

(16) Physics that deals with the relationships between heat and other forms of energy.

(17) Process in which an X-ray photograph is prepared showing minute internal structure.

(18) The migration of charged colloidal particles or molecules through a solution under the influence of an applied electric field usually provided by immersed electrodes.

(19) The transmission or conveying of something through a medium or passage.

(20) To dissolve and become liquid by absorbing moisture from the air.

(2) *Bi-* is the Latin root for two. A binary compound is any compound made of two elements. Understanding this helps us understand non-scientific English terms as well. For example, a *bicameral* legislative system is based on two legislative branches (known as the Senate and the House of Representatives in the United States), *bicentennial* refers to the <u>second</u> hundred years, *biceps* are muscles with <u>two</u> heads (attach-

ments), *bicuspid* is a tooth with <u>two</u> points or cusps; and a *bicycle* is a <u>two</u>-wheeled vehicle. For each of the terms listed in Table 4, identify at least two other words in the English language that use the root with the same meaning.

Table 4: Examples of Common Words That Use Roots

Chemical Term	Root	Meaning	Other Words That Use This Root
equilibrium	*equ-*	equal	equation, equilibrium, equal, equator, equate, equidistant
thermochemistry	*therm-*	heat	
compound	*com-*	with, together	
calorimeter	*meter-*	measure	
polymer	*poly-*	many	
monomer	*mer-*	part	
radioactive	*radi-*	ray, radius	
superheated	*super-*	above, over	
hydrolysis	*hydr-*	water	
graphite	*graph-*	write, writing, picture	
chemosynthesis	*syn-*	together, with	

(3) Table 5 shows the root words used to identify magnitude. The terms in bold type are frequently used in chemistry.

Table 5: Expressing Order of Magnitude

Power	Decimal Representation	Prefix	Symbol
10^{18}	1,000,000,000,000,000,000	exa	E
10^{15}	1,000,000,000,000,000	peta	P
10^{12}	1,000,000,000,000	tera	T
10^{9}	1,000,000,000	giga	G
10^{6}	1,000,000	mega	M
10^{3}	**1,000**	**kilo**	**k**
10^{2}	100	hecto	h
10^{1}	10	deka	da
10^{0}	**1**		
10^{-1}	0.1	deci	d
10^{-2}	**0.01**	**centi**	**c**
10^{-3}	**0.001**	**milli**	**m**
10^{-6}	**0.000 001**	**micro**	**m**
10^{-9}	**0.000 000 001**	**nano**	**n**
10^{-12}	0.000 000 000 001	pico	p
10^{-15}	0.000 000 000 000 001	femto	f
10^{-18}	0.000 000 000 000 000 001	atto	a

Use the data from Table 5 to answer the following questions:

(a) There are _____ micrograms in a milligram.

(b) A micrometer is _____ times as large as a nanometer.

(c) There are _____ milliliters in a liter.

(d) There are _____ microliters in a liter.

(e) There are _____ milliseconds in a minute.

(f) A kilogram is composed of _____ grams.

(g) A millimole contains _____ times more atoms than a nanomole.

(h) A centigram is 1/_____ of a gram

FOR THE TEACHER

1.1.1 NOMENCLATURE: ELEMENTS

Discussion: Table 6 shows the etymology of the names of the elements. You may wish to photocopy this list and share it with your students so that they can see that names and terms in science are meaningful. Once they understand some basic root words, they will be able to predict and or/understand the meanings of new words by inspection and comparison. For example, once they know that *chloros*- means "green," it will be easier for them to remember that chlorine is a green gas; chlorophyll, a green pigment and chlorella, a unicellular green algae. An excellent resource for studying the meanings of the roots of scientific words is the *Dictionary of Word Roots and Combining Forms* by D.J. Borror (Mayfield Press, Palo Alto, CA 1960).

Table 6: Etymology of the Names of the Elements

Element		Z	Year	Meaning
Actinium	Ac	89	1900	Greek: *aktis*, ray
Aluminum	Al	13	1825	Latin: *alumen*, substance with astringent taste
Americium	Am	95	1944	English: *America*
Antimony	Sb	51	1400s	Greek: *antimonos*, opposite to solitude
Argon	Ar	18	1894	Greek: *argos*, inactive
Arsenic	As	33	1200s	Greek: *arsenikon*, valiant
Astatine	At	85	1940	Greek: *astatos*, unstable
Barium	Ba	56	1808	Greek: *barys*, heavy
Berkelium	Bk	97	1949	English: University of California *Berkeley*
Beryllium	Be	4	1797	Greek: *beryllos*, a mineral
Bismuth	Bi	83	1400s	German: *bisemutum*, white mass
Boron	B	5	1808	Arabic: *bawraq*, white, borax
Bromine	Br	35	1826	Greek: *bromos*, a stench
Cadmium	Cd	48	1817	Latin: *cadmia*, calamine, a zinc ore
Calcium	Ca	20	1808	Latin: *calcis*, lime
Californium	Cf	98	1950	English: State and University of *California*
Carbon	C	6	prehistoric	Latin: *carbo*, coal
Cerium	Ce	58	1804	English: The asteroid *Ceres*, discovered 1803
Cesium	Cs	55	1860	Latin: *caesius*, sky blue
Chlorine	Cl	17	1808	Greek: *chloros*, grass green
Chromium	Cr	24	1797	Greek: *chroma*, color
Cobalt	Co	27	1735	Greek: *kobolos*, a goblin
Copper	Cu	29	prehistoric	Latin: *cuprum*, copper
Curium	Cm	96	1944	French: Marie and Pierre *Curie*
Dysprosium	Dy	66	1886	Greek: *dysprositos*, hard to get at
Einsteinium	Es	99	1952	German: *Albert Einstein*
Erbium	Er	68	1843	Swedish: *Ytterby*, town in Sweden where discovered
Europium	Eu	63	1900	English: *Europe*
Fermium	Fm	100	1953	Italian: Enrico *Fermi*
Fluorine	F	9	1886	Latin: *fluere*, to flow
Francium	Fr	87	1939	French: *France*
Gadolinium	Gd	64	1886	Finnish: Johan *Gadolin*, Finnish chemist
Gallium	Ga	31	1875	Latin: *Gaul*, or France

(continued)

Table 6: *(Continued)*

Element		Z	Year	Meaning
Germanium	Ge	32	1886	German: *Germany*
Gold	Au	79	prehistoric	Anglo-Saxon: for gold; symbol from Latin *aurum* for gold
Hafnium	Hf	72	1922	Latin: *Hafnia*, the city of Copenhagen, Denmark
Helium	He	2	1895	Greek: *helios*, the sun
Holmium	Ho	67	1879	Latin: *Holmia*, the city Stockholm, Sweden
Hydrogen	H	1	1766	Greek *hydro genes*, water former
Indium	In	49	1863	Latin: *indicum*, produces an indigo-blue spectrum line
Iodine	I	53	1811	Greek: *iodes*, produces a violet-like *spectrum line*
Iridium	Ir	77	1804	Latin: *iridis*, rainbow
Iron	Fe	26	prehistoric	Anglo Saxon: iren, symbol from Latin *ferrum*
Krypton	Kr	36	1898	Greek: *kryptos*, hidden
Lanthanum	La	57	1839	Greek: *lanthanien*, to be concealed
Lawrencium	Lw	103	1961	English: Earnest *Lawrence*, inventor of cyclotron
Lead	Pb	82	prehistoric	Anglo Saxon: *lead;* symbol from Latin: *plumbum*
Lithium	Li	3	1817	Greek: *lithos*, stone
Lutetium	Lu	71	1905	Latin: *Lutetia*, ancient name of Paris
Magnesium	Mg	12	1774	Latin: *magnes*, magnet
Mendelevium	Md	101	1955	Russian: Dmitri *Mendeleev*, devised periodic table
Mercury	Hg	80	prehistoric	Latin: *Mercury*, messenger; *Hydrarygus*, liquid silver
Molybdenum	Mo	42	1782	Greek: *molybdos*, lead
Neodymium	Nd	60	1885	Greek: *neos*, new and *didymos*, twin
Neon	Ne	10	1898	Greek: *neos*, new
Neptunium	Np	93	1940	English: planet Neptune
Nickel	Ni	28	1750	German: *kupfernickel*, false copper
Niobium	Nb	41	1801	Greek: *Niobe*, mythological daughter of Tantalus
Nitrogen	N	7	1772	Latin: *nitro*, native soda and *gen*, born
Nobelium	No	102	1957	Swedish: Alfred *Nobel*, inventor of dynamite
Osmium	Os	76	1804	Greek: *osme*, odor of volatile tetroxide
Oxygen	O	8	1774	Greek *oxys*, sharp, and *gen*, born
Palladium	Pd	46	1803	English: planetoid *Pallas*, discovered 1801
Phosphorus	P	15	1669	Greek: *phosphoros*, light bringer
Platinum	Pt	78	1735	Spanish: *plata*, silver
Plutonium	Pu	94	1940	English: *Pluto* the planet
Polonium	Po	84	1898	Polish: *Poland*, country of co-discoverer Marie Curie
Potassium	K	19	1807	English: *potash;* symbol Latin *kalium*
Praseodymium	Pr	59	1885	Greek: *Praseos*, leek green and *didymos*, a twin
Promethium	Pm	61	1947	Greek: *Prometheus*, fire bringer in Greek mythology
Protactinium	Pa	91	1917	Greek: *protos* first
Radium	Ra	88	1898	Latin: *radius*, ray
Radon	Rn	86	1900	Latin: comes from *radium*
Rhenium	Re	75	1924	Latin: *Rhenus*, Rhine province of Germany
Rhodium	Rh	45	1804	Greek: *rhodon*, a rose
Rubidium	Rb	37	1860	Latin: *rubidus*, red
Ruthenium	Ru	44	1845	Latin: *Ruthenia*, Russia
Samarium	Sm	62	1879	Russian: *Samarski*, a Russian engineer
Scandium	Sc	21	1879	Scandinavian: *Scandinavia*
Selenium	Se	34	1817	Greek: *selene*, moon
Silicon	Si	14	1823	Latin: *silex*, flint
Silver	Ag	47	prehistoric	Anglo-Saxon: *siolful;* symbol Latin: *argentum*
Sodium	Na	11	1807	Latin: *sodanum* for headache remedy; symbol Latin: *natrium*

Table 6: *(Concluded)*

Element		Z	Year	Meaning
Strontium	Sr	38	1808	Scottish: town of *Strontian*, Scotland
Sulfur	S	16	prehistoric	Latin: *sulphur*, sulfur
Tantalum	Ta	73	1802	Greek: *Tantalus* of Greek mythology
Technetium	Tc	43	1937	Greek: *technetos*, artificial
Tellurium	Te	52	1782	Latin: *tellus*, the earth
Terbium	Tb	65	1843	Swedish: *Ytterby*, town in Sweden
Thallium	Tl	81	1862	Greek: *thallos*, a young shoot
Thorium	Th	90	1819	Scandinavian: *Thor* from Scandinavian mythology
Thulium	Tm	69	1879	Latin: *Thule*, northerly part of habitable world
Tin	Sn	50	prehistoric	Latin: Etruscan god, Tinia; symbol Latin: *stannum*
Titanium	Ti	22	1791	Greek: Greek mythology, *Titans* first sons of the earth
Tungsten	W	74	1783	Swedish: *tung sten*, heavy stone, symbol German: *Wolfram*
Uranium	U	92	1789	English: Planet *Uranus*
Vanadium	V	23	1830	Scandinavian: goddess *Vanadis* of mythology
Xenon	Xe	54	1898	Greek: *xenos*, strange
Ytterbium	Yb	70	1905	Scandinavian: Ytterby, a town in Sweden
Yttrium	Y	39	1843	Scandinavian: Ytterby, a town in Sweden
Zinc	Zn	30	prehistoric	German: *Zink*, akin to *Zinn*, tin
Zirconium	Zr	40	1824	named for the mineral, *zircon*

Answers: (1) Encourage students to ask their parents and/or examine books of baby names. Most public libraries have books of baby names used by expectant parents to name their children. (2) Berkelium (after the University of California, Berkeley). (3) Uranium (element 92, named after Uranus), Neptunium (93, named after Neptune), and Plutonium (94, named after Pluto). (4) Indium, named for the indigo-colored spectral line it emits. (5) Boron, named after the chemical borax (sodium tetraborate decahydrate) that contains boron. Boraxo® is a common household cleaner made largely of borax. (6) The symbol for copper (Cu) is derived from its ancient name *cuprum*. (7) Curium. (8) Fluorine. (9) Krypton. (10) Lead. The symbol Pb is derived from the Latin *plumbum* for lead. (11) Technitium. (12) Rubidium. (13) Titanium. (14) Gallium. (15) Mercury; *hydrargyrus* (Hg). (16) These elements were identified long before English became the dominant language of science. The symbols are derived from the Latin names given these elements by the alchemists: *cuprum* (Cu), *aurum* (Au), *ferrum* (Fe), *plumbum* (Pb), *argentum* (Ag), *hydrargyrus* (Hg), and *stannum* (Sn).

1.1.2 NOMENCLATURE: COMPOUNDS

Discussion: We suggest that you make photocopy transparencies (make certain the transparency sheets are compatible with your photocopy machine) of the ion labels and then cut out the individual ions, sort them, and place them in appropriately labeled envelopes. You can then demonstrate to your class the ratios in which ions combine using an overhead projector.

Prior to the Roman numeral method of differentiating ions with different charges, chemists used the suffixes *"-ic"* and *"-ous"* to differentiate oxidation states. The suffix *"-ic"* always indicates the higher of the two common oxidation states. Thus, in chloric acid ($HClO_3$) chlorine has a higher oxidation state (+5) than in chlorous acid ($HClO_2$), where the oxidation state is +3. A compound with a higher oxidation state assumes the name *per-* (shortened version of *hyper-*) as in perchloric acid ($HClO_4$) where the oxidation state is +7. Finally, a compound with a lower oxidation state assumes the name *hypo-* as in hypochlorous acid HClO where chlorine has the oxidation state of +1. It is left to the teacher's discretion when to introduce this aspect of chemical nomenclature.

Answers: (1) Potassium fluoride, calcium iodide, aluminum nitride, hydrogen chloride, hydrogen sulfide, nitrogen monoxide, lithium oxide, magnesium chloride, sodium sulfide, mercury (II) oxide (2) (a) SnF_2; (b) SnO_2; (c) $SnCl_4$; (d) Fe_2O_3; (e) $Mg(OH)_2$; (f) ZnO; (g) $NaHCO_3$; (h) $Ca_3(PO_4)_2$; (i) $NaNO_2$; (j) $(NH_4)_3PO_4$; (k) AgCN; (l) NaOH

1.1.3 LANGUAGE OF CHEMISTRY

Discussion: We suggest that you write the word *pneumonoultramicroscopicsilicovolcanoconiosis* on the board or overhead. You can then ask students if they can see any root words. As you write the root words and their meanings, students will understand the value of root word analysis in deciphering difficult terms.

Answers: (1) a-2; b-3; c-1; d-19; e-4; f-20; g-6; h-14; i-18; j-8; k-10; l-5; m-9; n-13; o-17; p-12; q-11; r-7; s-16; t-15. (2) See Table 7. (3) (a) 1000; (b) 1000; (c) 1000; (d) 1,000,000; (e) 60,000; (f) 1000; (g) 1,000,000; (h) 100.

Table 7: Common Words That Use the Same Roots as Chemical Terms

Chemical Term	Root	Meaning	Other Words That Use This Root
equilibrium	*equ-*	equal	equation, equilibrium, equal, equator, equate, equidistant
thermochemistry	*therm-*	heat	ectotherm, endotherm, BTU, thermometer, geothermal, hypothermia, isotherm, thermal, thermostat, thermodynamics, thermocouple
compound	*com-*	with, together	company, comparable, companion, compose, compare, compassion, compromise
calorimeter	*meter-*	measure	kilometer, meter, millimeter, micrometer, nanometer, ammeter, altimeter, barometer, odometer, speedometer, thermometer, voltmeter
polymer	*poly-*	many	polygon, polygraph, polynomial, polysaccharide, polystyrene, polyunsaturated, polyvinyl chloride
monomer	*mer-*	part	polymer, conglomerate, bicameral, isomer, merge, immerse, mermaid
radioactive	*radi-*	ray, radius	radius, radial, radiology, radiation, irradiate, radiator, radium, radiation
superheated	*super-*	above, over	superlative, superb, supersonic, supercharged, supercool, superficial, superhighway, superimpose, superintendent, superior, supernatural, superstar, superscript, supernova, supervise
hydrolysis	*hydr-*	water	carbohydrate, dehydrate, hydrant, hydraulics, hydra, hydroponics, hydroelectric, hydrofoil, hydrocephaly, hydrogen
graphite	*graph-*	write, writing, picture	photograph, biography, cardiograph, choreography, calligraphy, graph, lithograph, geography, oceanography, paragraph, phonograph, photograph, seismograph, telegraph
chemosynthesis	*syn-*	together, with	synergy, synonym, sync, synchronize, synthesize, syncopate, synapse, geosynchronous

Applications to Everyday Life

Vocabulary development: One of the best ways to build your vocabulary is by studying those root words commonly used in the English language. For example, if you know the meaning of the root *super-* (above, over), you know something about the meaning of more than 100 words in the English language, for example, super, superb, supercharge, superconductivity and superficial.

Learning other languages: An understanding of root words is helpful when learning other languages that share those root words. Table 8 shows the similarity of words among the languages spoken in Western Europe. A mastery of Latin root words will greatly aid those trying to learn the Romantic (Latin) languages (French, Spanish and Italian).

Table 8: Similarities of Terms in Different Languages

English	*French*	*German*	*Spanish*	*Italian*
chemistry	chimie	Chemie	química	chimica
solution	solution	Lösung	solución	soluzione
oxygen	oxygène	Sauerstoff	oxígeno	ossigeno
reaction	réaction	Reaktion	reacción	reazione
laboratory	laboratory	Laboratorium	laboratorio	laboratorio
science	science	Wissenschaft	ciencia	scienza

Naming new discoveries, concepts and inventions: To talk about a discovery, concept or invention, it is important to first give it a name. The name should be descriptive, such as automobile (auto- self, mobile- movable–an invention that propels itself), laser (**l**ight **a**mplification by **s**timulated **e**mission of **r**adiation) or modem (a device that **mod**ulates and **dem**odulates signals for transmission on phone lines). Although chemists have synthesized elements 104–109, there is disagreement over what to call them. Table 9 shows the names given by IUPAC (the International Union of Pure and Applied Chemistry) and the ACS (American Chemical Society). The table indicates that IUPAC and ACS wish to honor different individuals with the naming of these elements. For example, element 106 has been named Rutherfordium (after Ernest Rutherford, the scientist who explained radioactivity) by the IUPAC, but Seaborgium (after Glen Seaborg, the nuclear chemist who helped isolate and identify elements 94–102) by the ACS. Until the controversy is settled, many chemists are using the Latin name for one-hundred-six: unnilhexium (*un,* 'one'; *nil,* 'zero'; *hex,* 'six'; *-ium,* the standard suffix applied to all new chemical elements). Thus, *unnilhexium* means the one-hundred-sixth element.

Table 9: Naming New Elements

	Temporary		*IUPAC*		*ACS*	
104	Unnilquadium	Unq	Dunbnium	Db	Rutherfordium	Rf
105	Unnilpentium	Unp	Joliotium	Jl	Hahnium	Ha
106	Unnilhexium	Unh	Rutherfordium	Rf	Seaborgium	Sg
107	Unnilseptium	Uns	Bohrium	Bh	Nielsbohrium	Ns
108	Unniloctium	Uno	Hahnium	Hn	Hassium	Hs
109	Unnilenium	Une	Meitnerium	Mt	Meitnerium	Mt

1.2 UNITS OF MEASUREMENT

An accurate and consistent system of measurement is the foundation of a healthy economy. In the United States, a carpenter pays for lumber by the board foot, while a motorist buys gasoline by the gallon, and a jeweler sells gold by the ounce. Land is sold by the acre; fruits and vegetables, by the pound, and electric cable, by the yard. Without a consistent, honest system of measurement, world trade would be thrown into chaos. Throughout history, buyers and sellers have tried to defraud each other by inaccurately representing the quantity of the product exchanged. In the Bible we read that the people of Israel were commanded to not ". . . use dishonest standards when measuring length, weight or quantity" but rather "use honest scales and honest weights . . ." (Leviticus 19:35–36). From ancient times to the present there has been a need for measuring things accurately.

When the ancient Egyptians built monuments like the pyramids, they measured the stones they cut using body dimensions every worker could relate to. Small distances were measured in "digits" (the width of a finger) and longer distances in "cubits" (the length from the tip of the elbow to the tip of the middle finger; 1 cubit = 28 digits). The Romans were famous road builders and measured distances in "paces" (1 pace = two steps). Archaeologists have uncovered ancient Roman roads and found "mile"-stones marking each 1000 paces (mil is Latin for 1000). The Danes were a seafaring people particularly interested in knowing the depth of water in shipping channels. They measured soundings in "fathoms" (the distance from the tip of the middle finger on one hand to the tip of the middle finger on the other) so navigators could easily visualize how much clearance their boats would have. In England distances were defined by the King's body features. A "yard" was the circumference of his waist; an "inch," the width of his thumb; a "foot," the length of his foot. English farmers, however, estimated lengths in something they could more easily relate to: "furlongs," the length of an average plowed furrow.

As various cultures emigrated to England, they brought with them their various measurement systems. Today, the English or Customary system reflects the variety of different measurement systems from which it originated. There are, for example, many units in which distance can be measured in the Customary system, but they bear no logical relationship to each other:

1 statute mile = 0.8688 nautical miles = 1760 yards = 320 rods = 8 furlongs = 5280 feet = 63,360 inches = 880 fathoms = 15,840 hands

Many English units are specific to certain professions or trades. A sea captain reports distances in nautical miles and depths in fathoms, while a horse trainer measures height in hands and distance in furlongs. Unfortunately, most people have no idea what nautical miles, fathoms, hands or furlongs are because they use only the more common measures of miles, yards, inches.

Early English settlers brought the Customary system of measurement with them to the American colonies. Although it is still widely used in America, scientists prefer to use the metric system. Unlike the English (Customary) system, the metric system did not evolve from a variety of ancient measurement systems but was a logical, simplified system developed in 17th– and 18th–century Europe. The metric system is now the mandatory system of measurement in every country of the world except the United States, Liberia and Burma (Myanmar).

In 1960, an international conference was called to standardize the metric system. The international System of Units (SI) was established in which all units of measurement are based upon seven base units: meter (distance), kilogram (mass), second (time), ampere (electrical current), Kelvin (temperature), mole (quantity), and candela (luminous intensity). The metric system simplifies measurement by using a single base unit for each quantity and by establishing decimal relationships among the various units of that same quantity. For example, the meter is the base unit of length and other necessary units are simple multiples or submultiples:

1 <u>meter</u> = 0.001 kilo<u>meter</u> = 1000 milli<u>meters</u> = 1,000,000 micro<u>meters</u> = 1,000,000,000 nano<u>meters</u>

Table 1 shows the SI prefixes and symbols. Throughout this resource, we use the metric system of measurement.

Table 1: SI Prefixes and Symbols

Power	Decimal Representation	Prefix	Symbol
10^{18}	1,000,000,000,000,000,000	exa	E
10^{15}	1,000,000,000,000,000	peta	P
10^{12}	1,000,000,000,000	tera	T
10^9	1,000,000,000	giga	G
10^6	1,000,000	mega	M
10^3	1000	kilo	k
10^2	100	hecto	h
10^1	10	deka	da
10^0	1		
10^{-1}	0.1	deci	d
10^{-2}	0.01	centi	c
10^{-3}	0.001	milli	m
10^{-6}	0.000 001	micro	m
10^{-9}	0.000 000 001	nano	n
10^{-12}	0.000 000 000 001	pico	p
10^{-15}	0.000 000 000 000 001	femto	f
10^{-18}	0.000 000 000 000 000 001	atto	a

1.2.1 THE IMPORTANCE OF UNITS

Concepts to Investigate: Fundamental units, derived units, factor labels, dimensions.

Materials: None.

Principles and Procedures: When crossing the border to Canada, American motorists are often surprised to see speed limits of "90" or "100." If they don't realize that Canadians measure speed in kilometers/hr while Americans measure in miles/hr (1.00 mile/hr = 1.61 kilometers/hr; 60 miles/hr = 97 km/hr) they may soon be in for trouble with the law. If, for example, an American motorist accelerates until her speedometer (measured in miles/hr) reaches "100," she will be traveling 38 miles/hr over the posted speed limit of 100 km/hr since a speed of 100 km/hr is equal to only 62 miles/hr. As this example illustrates, measurements without units are meaningless and may lead to serious misunderstandings. Everything that can be measured must be expressed with appropriate units.

Units in everyday life: We use units every day, often without even realizing it. In the statements that follow, you will find a wide variety of interesting facts, but each is missing a crucial piece of information—the dimensions (units)! All the statements are meaningless until you supply the appropriate units. On the basis of your experiences, try to match the appropriate units from the list provided.

carats	grams/mL	kilowatt-hours	milligrams
cm	inches	liters	pounds
degrees Celsius	kcal (Cal)	megabars	stories
degrees Fahrenheit	kilograms	miles	tons
feet	kilometers	miles per hour	yards

(a) America's tallest building (Sears Tower in Chicago) is 110 ___ high.

(b) The Empire State Building in New York is 1250 ___ high.

(c) The Nile is the world's longest river. It is 4180 ___ long.

(d) The Amazon River in South America is 6296 ___ long.

(e) The coldest temperature ever recorded was −128.6 _____ in Vostok, Antarctica, in 1983.

(f) The highest recorded temperature in the United States was in Death Valley, California, when the mercury reached 57 _____!

(g) The world record rainfall occurred in Cherrapunji, India, where 1042 ___ of rain fell in one year.

(h) The largest recorded hailstone to ever fall landed in Coffeyville, Kansas, in 1979. It had a diameter of 44.5 _____ !

(i) The longest punt in NFL history was by Steve O'Neal of the New York Jets. He kicked the football 98 ____.

(j) The largest seed in the world is that of the coc-de-mer coconut tree, which may weigh as much as 40 ____!

(k) The world's largest meteorite is located in Southwest Africa. It weighs 650 _____ .

(l) The most popular soft drink in the world is currently Coca Cola®. More than 210 million _____ were consumed each day in 1990.

(m) The largest diamond in the world was mined from South Africa in 1905 and weighs 3106 _____ .

(n) Earth is the densest of the nine planets, with an average density of 5.515 _____.

(o) The world's fastest aircraft is the *Lockheed SR-71 Blackbird*, clocking a record speed of 2,193.67____.

(p) The largest gold nugget ever found had a mass of 100 _____!

(q) One large chicken egg contains an average of 274 ____ cholesterol.

(r) A 16-year old male requires an average of 2800 ____ of energy per day while an average 16-year old female requires only 2100 ____.

(s) The United States produces and consumes more electric energy than any other nation. Each year the United States produces over 2500 billion ____.

(t) The largest pressure ever developed in a laboratory was 1.70 _____, used to solidify hydrogen in 1978.

Questions

(1) Why is it essential that all measurements be accompanied by appropriate units?

(2) Individuals who travel to regions of the world with poor sanitation are warned to filter or boil their water before drinking it to remove deadly water-born pathogens that cause diseases such as cholera or typhoid. If you were traveling in a region known to have a polluted water supply, would you drink water that your host said had been heated to 100 degrees for five minutes? Explain.

1.2.2 UNITS IN CHEMISTRY

Concepts to Investigate: Fundamental units, derived units, SI (International System) units.

Materials: Optional: dictionary, encyclopedia, chemical handbook.

Principles and Procedures:

Fundamental and derived units: There are only 26 letters in the English alphabet, yet with these 26 letters it is possible to construct all of the words in the English language. Similarly, there are seven "letters" in the "language of measurement" from which all units of measurement are derived. These seven "letters" are *distance, mass, time, electric charge, temperature, amount,* and *luminous intensity* (see the first seven entries in Table 2). These are known as the *fundamental units* because they cannot be expressed in a simpler fashion. All other units are derived from these seven units.

Distance is a fundamental unit, because it can be expressed in no simpler terms. However, volume is a derived unit because it is expressed as the cube of distance. For example, when measuring the volume of a box you multiply its length by its width by its height. The resulting volume is expressed as a cube of distance (d^3), such as cubic feet or cubic centimeters. Density is also a derived unit because it is expressed as the ratio of mass/volume, where volume itself is a derived unit expressed as a function of distance cubed. Thus, we can express density (a derived unit) in terms of fundamental units as mass divided by distance cubed (m/d^3).

In 1960 the 11th General Conference on Weights and Measures adopted the International System of measurement (SI) and assigned base units for each physical quantity. Table 2 shows some common physical quantities and their SI units. The first seven (bold type) are the seven fundamental units while the remaining units are derived from these.

SI multiple units and non–SI-units: Some of the most commonly measured quantities in chemistry are distance, mass, time, temperature, volume, density, pressure, amount, concentration, energy, velocity, molarity, viscosity, and electric charge. All of these quantities can be measured in a variety of different ways. For example, distance can be measured in centimeters, nanometers, miles, inches, feet, fathoms, Ångstroms, microns, kilometers, yards, light-years, femtometers and mils. Different units are used to measure different things. For example, interstellar distances are measured in light-years (e.g., the distance between our Sun and the next nearest star Proxima Centurai is 4 light-years) while intermolecular bond lengths are measured in Ångstroms (e.g., the distance between hydrogen and oxygen in water is 0.958 Å)

Unfortunately, those unfamiliar with the variety of units used to measure distance might assume that all of these units represent different physical quantities, when in fact they are all used to measure distance. Although groups like the International Union of Pure and Applied Chemists (IUPAC) and others have recommended that all quantities be measured in SI units (e.g., meters) or multiples of SI units (e.g., femtometers, nanometers, micrometers, millimeters, centimeters, kilometers), many other measurement units continue to be used (e.g., miles, inches, feet, fathoms, Ångstroms, microns, yards, light-years, mils).

The left hand column in Table 3 lists some of the most commonly measured quantities in chemistry and the middle column lists the SI units. Table 4 provides a list of other units that are used in the measurement of one of these eight quantities. Examine each of these terms and try to determine which quantity it measures (distance, mass, time, etc.). Place these units in the table adjacent to the quantity you believe they measure. After classifying the units, consult a dictionary, encyclopedia, chemistry text or other resource to determine if your classification is correct.

1.2.3 PROBLEM SOLVING (DIMENSIONAL ANALYSIS)

Concepts to Investigate: Problem solving, dimensional analysis (factor-label method, unit analysis).

Materials: None.

Principles and Procedures: Cardiovascular diseases (diseases of the heart and blood vessels) are the leading cause of death worldwide. To address this problem, biomedical engineers have designed various artificial hearts, which surgeons may some day routinely implant in patients whose own hearts are failing. Before implanting such a device in a patient, a surgeon needs to have an idea of how long it might be expected to work before needing to be replaced. If an artificial heart is capable of pumping at least 17,000,000 pints of blood before failure, how long will it probably last in a patient whose average heart rate is 72 beats per minute, and average stroke volume (the amount of blood pumped with each stroke) is 70 mL?

When faced with such a problem, people usually resort to their calculators and punch in sequences such as the following:

$$(17,000,000 \times 473 \times 70)/(72 \times 60 \times 365) = ?$$
$$(70 \times 72 \times 60 \times 365)/(17,000,000 \times 473) = ?$$
$$(17,00,000 \times 473 \times 72)/(70 \times 60 \times 365) = ?$$

Each one of these includes the correct numbers, but which equation yields a correct answer? Actually, all are incorrect because they do not specify units (a dimensionless product is meaningless) and illustrate errors in logic (the calculations will yield incorrect numbers because they are not set up correctly). Fortunately, such errors can be avoided using a technique known as dimensional analysis.

Dimensional Analysis (also known as factor-label method and unit analysis) is the single most powerful technique in solving problems of this kind. Dimensional analysis allows you to set up the problem and check for logic errors before performing calculations, and allows you to determine intermediate answers enroute to the solution. Dimensional analysis involves five basic steps:

(1) **Unknown:** Clearly specify the units (dimensions) of the desired product (the *unknown*). These will become the target units for your equation.
(2) **Knowns:** Specify all *known* values with their associated units.
(3) **Conversion factors and formulas:** Specify relevant *formulas* and all *conversion factors* (with their units).
(4) **Equation:** Develop an *equation* (using appropriate formulas and conversion factors) showing that the units of the left side (the side containing the known values) are equivalent to the units of the right side (the side containing the unknown). If the units are not equal, then the problem has not been set up correctly and further changes in the setup must be made.
(5) **Calculation:** Perform the *calculation* only after you have analyzed all dimensions and made sure that both sides of your equation have equivalent units.

Let us illustrate dimensional analysis using the problem of the artificial heart.

(1) <u>Unknown (target units)</u>
We want to determine the number of *years* the heart can be expected to beat.

(2) <u>Known values</u>
The artificial heart is projected to pump at least *1.7×10^7 pints* of blood
The average heart rate is *72 strokes/minute*
The average stroke volume is *70 mL/stroke*

(3) <u>Conversion Units</u>
There are *473 mL/pint*
There are *60 min/hr*
There are *24 hr/day*
There are *365 day/yr*

(4 & 5) <u>Equation and Calculation</u>

$$\frac{1.7 \times 10^7 \text{ pints}}{} \left|\frac{473 \text{ mL}}{\text{pint}}\right| \frac{\text{stroke}}{70 \text{ mL}} \left|\frac{\text{min}}{72 \text{ strokes}}\right| \frac{h}{60 \text{ min}} \left|\frac{1.0 \text{ d}}{24 \text{ h}}\right| \frac{y}{365.25 \text{ d}} = 3.0 \text{ years}$$

We can now analyze the dimensions to ensure that our problem is set up correctly before performing the calculation. The only way that we can get equal units on the left and right side is by dividing by the stroke volume, heart rate, and time conversion factors. Notice that when dividing, you simply invert and multiply. The units of the unknown (the target value) are years. Since all of the units on the left side of the equation except "years" cancel, the problem is set up correctly and we can perform the calculation and determine that the heart may be expected to pump a little more than three years.

In addition to ensuring that your problem is set up correctly, dimensional analysis also yields other answers enroute to the final solution. In this problem, the first calculation indicates how many milliliters of blood the heart may pump while the second indicates the number of strokes the heart may be expected to perform. The third product indicates the number of minutes the heart may be expected to operate, while the fourth and fifth calculations indicate this same time converted to days and years.

$$\frac{1.7 \times 10^7 \text{ pints}}{} \left|\frac{473 \text{ mL}}{\text{pint}}\right| \frac{\text{stroke}}{70 \text{ mL}} \left|\frac{\text{min}}{72 \text{ strokes}}\right| \frac{h}{60 \text{ min}} \left|\frac{1.0 \text{ d}}{24 \text{ h}}\right| \frac{y}{365.25 \text{ d}} = 3.0 \text{ years}$$

8.0×10^9 mL blood
1.1×10^8 strokes
1.6×10^6 minutes
2.7×10^4 hours
1.1×10^3 days
3.0 years

Another example may help indicate how useful this technique is. Let's say that a painter is painting a fence 300 meters long and 2.0 meters high with paint that costs $23.00 gallon. If a gallon of paint covers 60 square meters, what does it cost to paint the fence?

The unknown in this question is the cost of painting the fence. Thus, our answer on the right side of the equation must have units of dollars ($). Looking at the known information, we see that the only thing which has the unit "dollar" in it is the cost of the paint ($23.00/gallon). Knowing that the answer must be expressed in units of dollars, we start off by multiplying by $23.00/gallon to keep dollars ($) in the numerator. All that is necessary at this point is to cancel out the units of "gallons" in the denominator. We know that a gallon covers 60 square meters (1 gallon/60 m²), so we must multiply by this value to cancel gallons. Now we are left with square meters (m²) in the denominator that can be canceled if we multiply by the length (300 m) and height (2.0 m) of the fence. All of the units on the left cancel except dollars ($), indicating that we have set the problem up correctly and the calculation can now be made.

$$\frac{\$23.00}{\text{gallon}} \; \frac{\text{gallon}}{60 \, m^2} \; \frac{300 \, m}{} \; \frac{2.0 \, m}{} \; = \; \$230$$

Questions

(1) Analyze the units in each of the following equations and determine the units of the answer.

    (a) The product of density (g/mL) and volume (mL) =

    (b) The product of concentration (mol/L) and volume (L) =

    (c) The product of pressure (N/m²) and area (m²) =

    (d) The quotient of mass (g) divided by volume (mL) =

    (e) The product of velocity (m/s) and time (s) =

(2) Dimensional analysis can be used to solve most word problems, regardless of the subject. Solve the following problems using dimensional analysis.

    (a) Calculate the number of seconds in the month of December.

    (b) Linoleum flooring is sold in one foot squares. Approximately how many squares must be ordered to cover the rooms in a school if each room is 1300 square feet and there are 10 rooms per floor and 3 floors in the building?

    (c) How many donuts can you buy with $23.00 if they cost $3.00/dozen?

    (d) A light year is the distance light travels in one year. *Sirius* (the dog star), the brightest star in the sky, is approximately 8.6 light years from Earth. How far (in km) from Earth is it if light travels 3.0×10^8 m/s?

    (e) The density of lead is 11.3 g/cm³. What is the mass of a block of lead 20.0 cm high, by 30.0 cm long by 15.0 cm deep?

FOR THE TEACHER

Scientific notation and significant figures: When dealing with very large or small numbers, it is best to use scientific notation. Scientific notation is a method that simplifies the writing of very small and very large numbers and computations involving these. In scientific notation, numbers are expressed as the product of a number between 1 and 10 and a whole-number power (exponent) of 10. The exponent indicates how many times a number must be multiplied by itself. Some examples follow: $10^1 = 10$, $10^2 = 10 \times 10 = 100$, $10^3 = 10 \times 10 \times 10 = 1000$.

Exponents may also be negative. For example, $10^{-1} = 1/10 = 0.1$. Also, $10^{-2} = 1/100 = 0.01$ and $10^{-3} = 1/1000 = 0.001$. Following are some examples of numbers written in scientific notation:

$30 = 3 \times 10^1$ $150 = 1.5 \times 10^2$ $60{,}367 = 6.0367 \times 10^4$

$0.3 = 3 \times 10^{-1}$ $0.046 = 4.6 \times 10^{-2}$ $0.000002 = 2 \times 10^{-6}$

Writing a number in scientific notation involves successively multiplying the number by the fraction 10/10 (which is equal to 1). Multiplying a number by one does not change the value of that number. For example:

$$142 = 142 \times \frac{10}{10} \times \frac{10}{10} = 1.42 \times 10^2$$

It is certainly not necessary to use the above formal procedure to write a number in scientific notation. After some practice your students will be doing it in their heads. You may wish to explain scientific notation as follows: to write 142 in scientific notation, move the decimal point two places to the left (which is dividing by 10^2), and multiply by 10^2 to get 1.42×10^2. To write 0.013 in scientific notation, move the decimal point two places to the right (which is multiplying by 10^2), and divide by 10^2 to get 1.3×10^{-2}.

Computations involving numbers written in scientific notation are easy to perform. To multiply numbers written in scientific notation, multiply the whole-number parts and add the powers (exponents). To divide numbers written in scientific notation, divide the whole-number parts and subtract the power (exponent) of the demoninator from the power of the numerator. Following are some examples:

$$(3 \times 10^4) \times (5 \times 10^3) = 15 \times 10^7$$

$$\frac{6 \times 10^8}{3 \times 10^3} = 2 \times 10^5$$

$$(5 \times 10^2) \times (2 \times 10^3) \times (1.5 \times 10^{-4}) = 1.5 \times 10^2$$

$$\frac{6 \times 10^{-2}}{2 \times 10^{-4}} = 3 \times 10^2$$

Scientific notation makes it possible to unambiguously indicate the number of significant digits in a measurement. Suppose a student reports a measurement of the mass of a reagent as 230 g. How many significant digits are contained in this measurement? We don't know! The digits 2 and 3 are obviously significant, but what about the zero? Is it just a place holder or did the student actually estimate the mass to the nearest g? Scientific notation can help the student and us answer this important question. Carefully inspect the following:

$$230 = 2.3 \times 10^2$$

$$230 = 2.30 \times 10^2$$

The first measurement 2.3×10^2 indicates that there are only two significant digits in the measurement. That is, the student did not measure to the nearest gram—the zero is only a place holder. The second measurement 2.30×10^2 indicates that the student did measure to the nearest gram—the zero is a significant digit.

1.2.1 THE IMPORTANCE OF UNITS

Discussion: It is very common to forget to include units when recording measurements or performing calculations. Remind your students that measurements without units are meaningless, and encourage them to "catch" you whenever you have omitted units. If students try to catch your mistakes (real or planned), they will be much more aware of their own.

This activity is designed to help students understand the importance of units and recognize their use in everyday life. Students are asked to supply units for various measurements where they have been purposely omitted. Some of the questions are designed in a seemingly contradictory fashion to help students recognize the importance of always using units. For example: question "a" states that "The world's tallest building (Sears Tower in Chicago) is 110 ___ high," while question "b" states that "The Empire State Building in New York is 1250 ___ high." This seeming contradiction is resolved if you realize that the heights of these buildings are measured in different units (stories versus feet).

Answers: (Activity): (a) stories, (b) feet, (c) miles, (d) kilometers, (e) degrees Fahrenheit, (f) degrees Celsius, (g) inches (h) cm, (i) yards, (j) pounds, (k) tons, (l) liters, (m) carats, (n) grams/ml (o) miles per hour, (p) kilograms, (q) milligrams, (r) kcal (Cal) (s) kilowatt-hours, (t) megabars. (1) There are many different ways to measure any particular quantity and it is essential to use the correct unit to avoid confusion and unwieldy numbers. For example, mass can me measured in grams, centigrams, kilograms, milligrams, micrograms, atomic mass units, carats, ounces, slugs, tons or metric tons. (2) Hopefully, before you drink, you would ask your host whether it was heated to 100 degrees Celsius or Fahrenheit! Water at 100 degrees Celsius boils (at atmospheric pressure), while water at 100 degrees Fahrenheit is only slightly above body temperature.

1.2.2 UNITS IN CHEMISTRY

Discussion: Fundamental and derived units: Students and teachers have a common tendency to omit units when performing scientific calculations. This bad habit may result from the fact that many of us have learned mathematics in a "dimensionless" environment where the problems do not involve real-life measurements. Encourage the teachers at your school to employ units when teaching mathematics so students will be accustomed to using them when studying science.

An understanding of fundamental units can help you and your students discover and understand relationships between various terms and quantities. Every derived unit is composed of fundamental units. For example, acceleration can be expressed in terms of velocity and time. By examining the units of acceleration (m/s²), you can see its relationship to velocity (m/s) and time (s) :

$$a = \frac{m}{s^2} = \frac{m}{s} \times \frac{1}{s} = velocity \times \frac{1}{time} = \frac{velocity}{time}$$

Thus, by examining the units (dimensional analysis), it becomes clear that acceleration is the ratio of velocity to time. This discovery is consistent with the definition of acceleration as the change in velocity per change in time.

A second example may further help show the value of dimensional analysis: A farad is a measure of electrical capacitance (the ability to store charge) and can be expressed in fundamental terms as:

$$\frac{C^2 \cdot s^2}{kg \cdot m^2}$$

where C represents charge in coulombs, s represents time in seconds, kg represents mass in kilograms, and m represents distance in meters. If we know how a quantity may be expressed in fundamental terms, we can discover relationships between it and other quantities. For example, knowing the fundamental units of capacitance *(C)*, potential difference *(V)*, and charge *(Q)*, we can see the relationship between them:

$$C = capacitance \qquad\qquad farad = \frac{C^2 \cdot s^2}{kg \cdot m^2}$$

$$V = potential\ difference \qquad volt = \frac{kg \cdot m^2}{C \cdot s^2}$$

$$Q = charge \qquad\qquad coulomb = C$$

An examination of the fundamental units, shows that capacitance is very similar to the inverse of potential difference:

$$capacitance:\ \ C = \frac{C^2 \cdot s^2}{kg \cdot m^2} \qquad\qquad inverse\ of\ potential\ difference:\ \ \frac{1}{V} = \frac{C \cdot s^2}{kg \cdot m^2}$$

If we multiply the inverse of potential difference (1/*V*) by charge (*Q*; measured in coulombs, C), then the units are the same as capacitance:

$$\frac{1}{V}Q = \frac{Q}{V} = \frac{(C) \cdot C \cdot s^2}{kg \cdot m^2} = \frac{C^2 \cdot s^2}{kg \cdot m^2} = C$$

Thus, by examining the fundamental units of capacitance, charge and potential difference, we have discovered a basic physical relationship: capacitance is equal to ratio of charge to potential difference *(C = Q/V)*.

This example indicates how an analysis of fundamental units can elucidate important relationships. It also illustrates the confusion students may experience when solving problems. Notice that C represents coulombs, while *C* represents capacitance. Students are frequently confused when the same letter is used to represent different things. Fortunately, there are standards (Appendix 2-1) for the designation of symbols and these should be introduced to students before confusion arises.

SI multiple units and non–SI-units: This exercise is designed to show students the variety of units that may be used to measure the same quantity. When students see the complexity of terms, they will hopefully understand the value of using SI units whenever possible.

Table 5: SI and Non–SI-Units

Quantity	*SI Units*	*Other Units*
distance	meters	centimeters, nanometers, miles, inches, feet, fathoms, Ångstroms, microns, kilometers, yards, light-years, femtometers, mils, astronomical units
mass	kilograms	grams, centigrams, kilograms, milligrams, micrograms, atomic mass units, carats, ounces, slugs, tons, metric tons
time	seconds	hours, days, minutes, centuries, decades, millennia, nanoseconds, milliseconds
temperature	kelvin	degrees centigrade, degrees Celsius, degrees Fahrenheit, degrees Rankine
volume	cubic meters	milliliters, cubic centimeters, liters, bushels, gallons, cups, pints, quarts, pecks, tablespoons, teaspoons, cubic yards, barrels, board feet
density	kilograms per cubic meter	grams per milliliter, grams per cubic centimeter, grams per liter, pounds per cubic foot, ounces per gallon
pressure	newtons per square meter	pascals, kilopascals, bars, millibars, dynes/cm², bayres, torrs, millimeters Hg, centimeters H_2O, atmospheres (atm), pounds per square inch (PSI)
energy	joules	joules, kilojoules, ergs, dynes, calories, kilocalories, kilowatt-hours, British thermal units, therms, electron volts

1.2.3 PROBLEM SOLVING (DIMENSIONAL ANALYSIS)

Discussion: Dimensional analysis is a very powerful tool for solving problems and can be used in every discipline where calculations are made using measured values. In this section we have introduced some simple examples, but it is up to the teacher to illustrate this technique repeatedly when solving problems before the class. Students will learn by example, and if you are not consistent with using units and dimensional analysis, they will not be either. Dimensional analysis has saved many teachers embarrassment when solving problems in class, because the teacher can check units to determine if the problem setup is correct or incorrect before proceeding with a calculation. Insist that students include dimensions and perform dimensional analysis when solving problems. Another example of dimensional analysis may help illustrate its usefulness in chemistry:

Determine the volume of dry hydrogen collected over water at 27°C and 75.0 cm Hg as produced by the reaction of 3.0 g zinc metal with an excess of sulfuric acid.

(1) *Unknown:* The unknown quantity (V_2) is the volume of gas at standard temperature and pressure and has units of *liters of hydrogen*. Note that the unit is not merely liters, but *liters of hydrogen* as distinguished from other substances.

(2) *Knowns:*

Starting mass of zinc: 3.0 g Zn

Temperature: $T_2 = 27°C = 300$ Kelvin

Pressure: The gas pressure (750 mm Hg) is the sum of the vapor pressure of water at 27°C (27 mm Hg; see Appendicies 1-5 and 1-6)) plus the vapor pressure of hydrogen. 750 mm Hg = 27 mm Hg + P_2 $P_2 = 723$ mm Hg.

(3) *Equations and conversion factors:*

The balanced equation for this reaction is

$$Zn + H_2SO_4 \longrightarrow ZnSO_4 + H_2$$

Thus, the mole ratio of zinc to hydrogen is: 1 mole zinc/1 mole hydrogen

The gram-atomic weight of Zn is: 65 g/mole

Standard temperature; $T_1 = 273$ K

Standard pressure; $P_1 = 760$ mm Hg

At standard temperature and pressure the molar volume of a gas is 22.4 liters/mole

Combined gas law:

$$\frac{P_1 V_1}{T_1} = \frac{P_2 V_2}{T_2} \qquad V_2 = \frac{V_1 T_2 P_1}{T_1 P_2}$$

(4) *Connecting path (dimensional analysis):* The equation to be used is

$$\frac{V_1 T_2 P_1}{T_1 P_2} = V_2$$

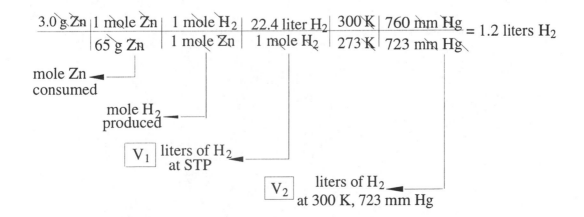

(5) *Calculation:* The calculation is done only after an analysis of the dimensions ensures that the left and right sides of the equation have equivalent units. In this case, the answer is 1.2 liters of hydrogen.

The student must make sure that all units (dimensions) are canceled appropriately to leave just the desired unit, which in this case is *liters of hydrogen* gas. You will notice that what may seem like a rather complex problem is reduced to a simple series of multiplications and divisions. Virtually all of the problems encountered in secondary science classes may be reduced to a simple "straight line format," which helps students structure their thinking as they solve problems. With a little practice your students will find the factor-label method is easy and convenient to use and is a help in eliminating errors. If the desired unit does not appear in the final answer, your students can be sure that something is amiss and can immediately proceed to locate any errors in logic. Students may not be familiar with the "straight-line method" for setting up problems and might not realize that the vertical lines replace the parentheses in a standard algebraic setup.

Many students get confused when dividing by fractions because they fail to specify units and/or do not clearly specify the order of operations. For example, when a student writes down the problem 3/4/5, he or she will get 0.15 if three-quarters is divided by 5, or 3.75 if 3 is divided by four-fifths. Such confusion can be eliminated by using the straight line technique and requiring that fractions not be expressed in the numerator or denominator:

ambiguous expression: 3/4/5   clear expressions: $\dfrac{3}{4\,|\,5}$ or $\dfrac{3\,|\,5}{4}$

Answers: (1) (a) g; (b) mole; (c) N; (d) g/mL; (e) m

(2a) $\dfrac{31\ \text{days}}{\text{December}}\ \bigg|\ \dfrac{24\ \text{hr}}{\text{day}}\ \bigg|\ \dfrac{60\ \text{min}}{\text{hr}}\ \bigg|\ \dfrac{60\ \text{sec}}{\text{min}}\ =\ \dfrac{2{,}678{,}400\ \text{seconds}}{\text{December}}$

(2b) $\dfrac{1\ \text{tile}}{1\ \text{ft}^2}\ \bigg|\ \dfrac{1300\ \text{ft}^2}{\text{room}}\ \bigg|\ \dfrac{10\ \text{rooms}}{\text{floor}}\ \bigg|\ \dfrac{3\ \text{floors}}{\text{building}}\ =\ \dfrac{39000\ \text{tiles}}{\text{building}}$

(2c) $\dfrac{12\ \text{donuts}}{\text{dozen}}\ \bigg|\ \dfrac{\text{dozen}}{\$3.00}\ \bigg|\ \$23.00\ =\ 92\ \text{donuts}$

(2d) $\dfrac{8.6\ \text{lt-years}}{}\ \bigg|\ \dfrac{365\ \text{days}}{\text{lt-year}}\ \bigg|\ \dfrac{24\ \text{hr}}{\text{day}}\ \bigg|\ \dfrac{60\ \text{min}}{\text{hr}}\ \bigg|\ \dfrac{60\ \text{sec}}{\text{min}}\ \bigg|\ \dfrac{3.0\times10^{8}\ \text{m}}{\text{sec}}\ \bigg|\ \dfrac{\text{km}}{1000\text{m}}\ =\ 8.13\times10^{13}\ \text{km}$

(2e) $\dfrac{11.3\ \text{g}}{\text{cm}^3}\ \bigg|\ 20\ \text{cm}\ \bigg|\ 30\ \text{cm}\ \bigg|\ 15\ \text{cm}\ \bigg|\ \dfrac{\text{kg}}{1000\ \text{g}}\ =\ 102\ \text{kg}$

Applications to Everyday Life

Business: Everything that is bought or sold has dimensions. A land investor needs to know if a tract is measured in acres, hectares, square feet or square miles. A commodities broker needs to know if soy beans are priced by the bushel, peck, kilogram, liter, cubic foot or cubic yard. A building contractor needs to know whether a developer has given him an order for concrete in cubic yards or cubic feet. It would be nearly impossible to run a successful business without knowledge of the units of the trade.

Retooling: In the 1980s, much of the American automobile industry switched from the English system of measurement to the metric system of measurement. Changing the measurement units required a massive amount of retooling. For example, where a one-inch bolt was previously used, a 2.5-cm bolt was substituted. Because of the slight differences in size, it became necessary to buy new tool sets to work on these cars. However, the effort put the U.S. automobile industry in a more favorable position internationally and economically. Many other industries in the United States either have made the change or are making the change.

Home economics: Recipes always specify measurements in units. You need to know whether your recipe is measured in tablespoons, teaspoons, cups, quarts, gallons, milliliters or liters! When cooking dinner, it is essential that you know whether directions were written for a stove calibrated in Celsius or Fahrenheit. When comparing the rates of competing long distance phone carriers, it is necessary to know the unit on which the billing rate is set.

Monetary systems: Each country has its own monetary system. Although countries may use the same unit, it may have a different meaning. A Canadian dollar is not worth the same as an American dollar, neither is a Japanese yen worth the same as a Chinese yuan. The full name of the unit should be specified whenever doing calculations. In other words, it is necessary to specify an American dollar, not just a dollar.

Measurement: It is important that you know the meaning of the units by which something is measured. On business reports you may hear the price of a particular commodity quoted. Although they may say that it costs $1000 per ton, the question remains—are they quoting the price per long ton (1.016 metric tons), per short ton (0.97 metric tons), or per metric ton? To understand the world around us, it is necessary to know how items are measured, and what the units they are measured in represent.

1.3 MEASUREMENT

Measurement is the process of gaining quantitative information about the physical world. The science of measurement is closely linked to the development of technology because more advanced technologies demand better systems of measurement. For example, while a farmer may be satisfied knowing the length of a furrow to within one meter, an electronic engineer may require a tolerance of one nanometer (billionth of a meter) when designing an integrated circuit on an advanced computer microprocessor. The demand for improved systems of measurement is found in nearly all technological fields and has been accentuated by major scientific endeavors such as the American space program.

Between 1966 and 1968, Americans landed a series of seven probes on the Moon to photograph and study the lunar surface in preparation for the first manned expedition. In 1967, Surveyor 3 landed in an ancient crater known as the Sea of Tranquillity and sent back data indicating that it would be a suitable landing site for a manned mission. On July 16, 1969, Neil Armstrong and Edwin Aldrin became the first humans to set foot on the surface of the Moon. They traveled over 400,000 kilometers through space and landed within walking distance of the Voyager 3 craft with only ten seconds of fuel remaining. Imagine what would have happened if NASA scientists had inaccurately measured the thrust of the Saturn V rockets, the mass of the payload, the distance to the Moon, the location of Voyager 3 craft, the gravitational field of the Moon, the rate of fuel consumption, the speed of the Apollo 11 craft, the orbit of the Moon around the Earth, the astronauts' rate of oxygen consumption or the radio frequency of the communication gear! Had scientists inaccurately measured any of these, or thousands of other variables, the most dramatic human exploration in history would have ended in sheer disaster.

All measurements are merely comparisons to a standard measure. The most universal system of measuring length in the ancient world was the cubit (approximately the length from the elbow to the extended middle finger), and "cubit" sticks were often checked for accuracy against the royal granite cubit block in Egypt. Today, we no longer standardize measures against cubit blocks, or meter steel sticks, but rather against physical phenomenon that we believe change even less than granite or steel. The meter, for example, is currently defined as the length of the path traveled by light in a vacuum during a time interval of 1/299,792,458 of a second, where a second is defined as exactly 9,192,631,770 periods of radio radiation emitted as a result of gyroscopic precession of the outermost electron in undisturbed cesium atoms! Although these definitions do not help us gain an intuitive understanding of their magnitude, they are invariant and thus serve as excellent standards for measurement.

All measurements are approximations. Suppose we use the two metric rulers shown in Figure A to measure the length of a metal rod. The bottom ruler is graduated (marked) in centimeters while the top is graduated in millimeters. Using the cm-ruler we can see that the length of the rod is between 2 and 3 centimeters and the best we can do is estimate that the length of the rod is about 50% of the distance from the 2 centimeter mark to the 3 centimeter mark. Our best guess at the length is 2.5 centimeters. The first digit of our answer is certain (it is clearly more than 2 and less than 3), but the second digit, an estimate, is uncertain. Using the centimeter ruler we measure the length of the rod to two significant digits (one measured, plus one estimated).

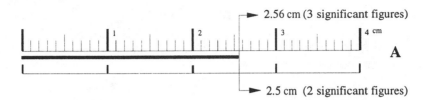

Using the millimeter-ruler, we can see that the end of the rod is about 60% of the distance between the 2.5 and 2.6 marks. Using this ruler we estimate the length of the rod to be 2.56 centimeters. The first two digits of the answer are certain (it is clearly more than 2.5 and less than 2.6) but the last digit is an estimate and is uncertain. Using the millimeter ruler we measure the length of the rod to three significant figures (two measured, plus one estimated). Whenever you make measurements, make sure that you include only significant digits: all measurable digits, plus one estimated.

1.3.1 LENGTH: ESTIMATING AND MEASURING

Concepts to Investigate: Length, units, approximations, direct measurement, indirect measurement, estimating, optical illusions, significant digits.

Materials: Meter stick, mm ruler.

Principles and Procedures: Linguists say that people are fluent in a language when they start thinking in that language. For example, an English-speaking person is considered fluent in Swahili (the language of Eastern Africa) when he or she actually thinks in that language. Linguists suggest that the best way to become fluent in a new language is to immerse yourself in a culture where you must use that language to communicate. Thus, although it may be helpful to learn Swahili by listening to tapes, reading books, and taking classes, the best way to become fluent is to live in Kenya, Tanzania or Mozambique where you must speak Swahili to be understood.

Many Americans learn the English system of measurement from childhood, but never become fluent in the metric system because they have never had to use it to communicate. When they report their height, they report it in inches, and when they report their weight, they do so in pounds. If asked their height or weight in metric terms, they generally do some calculations in their heads to convert English units to metric units. In this activity you will be asked to think purely in metric terms, without first thinking in English terms and then converting to metric. By developing some common benchmark measures of length in metric units, it will be easier to become fluent.

Part 1: Estimating length: To think in metric units, it is helpful to have some easy-to-remember "benchmark" measures with which to compare. Use a meter stick and a ruler with millimeter divisions to find common objects that are approximately 1 millimeter, 1 centimeter and 1 meter in length. For example, the tip of a sharpened pencil may be approximately 1 mm in diameter, or the width of one of your fingernails may be approximately 1 cm. Identify the items you have chosen in the spaces provided in the Table 1.

Table 1: "Benchmarks" for Length

Metric Unit	Approximately the Same Length as This Common Item:
millimeter	
centimeter	
meter	

Using these "benchmarks," estimate the following distances in the appropriate metric units. After you have written your estimates, measure the distances and calculate the percentage error for each: [(estimate − measured)/(measured)] × 100%. Enter your answer in Table 2.

Table 2: Estimates of Length

	Your Estimate	*Your Measurement*	*Percent Error*
length of room	(m)	(m)	%
width of room	(m)	(m)	%
your height	(cm)	(cm)	%
height of door	(cm)	(cm)	%
length of pencil or pen	(mm)	(mm)	%
thickness of 50 sheets of paper	(mm)	(mm)	%

Part 2: Measuring distance: Look at the illustrations in Figure B and then answer the questions in the first column of Table 3. Now measure each length as accurately as possible and record your measurements in the appropriate boxes in the middle of the table. Draw

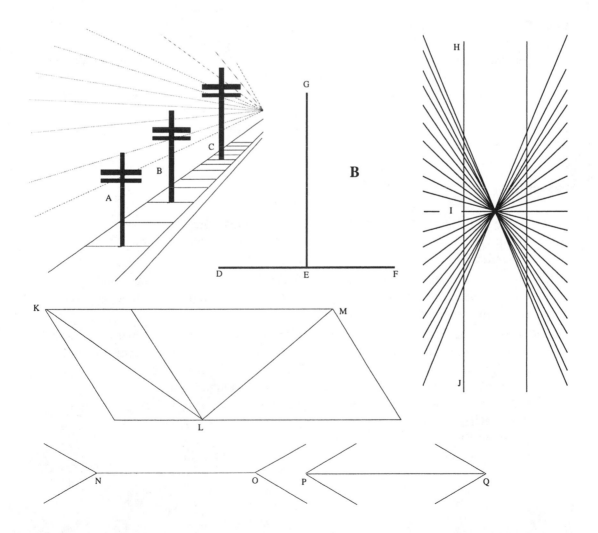

Table 3: Estimating and Measuring Distance

Assumption Based on Observation	Measurement to the Nearest Tenth of a Millimeter			Conclusion Based upon Measurement
Which appears the tallest? A B C	Pole A	Pole B	Pole C	Which pole is the tallest? A B C
Which line appears longer? DF GE	DF	GE		Which line is longer? DF GE
Do the tracks appear parallel? yes no	width at H	width at I	width at J	Are the tracks parallel? yes no
Which line appears longer? KL LM	KL	LM		Which line is longer? KL LM
Which line appears longer? NO PQ	NO	PQ		Which line is longer? NO PQ

conclusions based upon your measurements and put the answers in the final column. Were your original assumptions correct? Why or why not?

Part 3: Indirect measurement of distance: Suppose we wish to measure the thickness of one page of a book. It is impossible to measure the thickness of a page directly with your ruler because the thickness is much less than the distance between the mm markings. However, we can obtain an indirect measurement. Use a ruler to measure the thickness of all the pages together (not counting the back and front covers). Divide the result by the total number of sheets. For example, if a book of 800 pages length (400 sheets) has a width of 40 mm, then the thickness of one sheet is 0.10 mm (40 mm/400 sheets). Compute the thickness of sheets in this book and compare them with those from another book of your choice. Chemists must often use indirect measurement to determine such things as the mass of a molecule or the length of a chemical bond.

Questions

(1) A chemistry student measures the width of a platinum electrode with a millimeter ruler and reports that it is 9.0000 mm. The teacher says the student's measurement is impossible. Why?

(2) Did your conclusions based upon direct measurement in part 2 agree with your predictions based solely on observation? Why is it important to make direct measurements in science whenever possible.

(3) Polyethylene is a polymer (a long chain of smaller molecules known as monomers) used in the manufacture of many plastic containers. If you see a recycle symbol (Figure C) with the number 2 or the letters HDPE, then the container is made of high density polyethylene. Suppose a chemist has determined that a single polymer strand of polyethylene measuring 0.07 millimeters in length is composed of 100,000 monomers. Using the principal of indirect measurement, how long would you estimate each monomer to be?

C

Table 4: Formulas for Surface Area of Regular Shapes

Rectangle A = length × width	length / width (rectangle)	*Circle* A = π × radius²	radius (circle)
Trapezoid A = height × 1/2 × (base 1+ base 2)	base 1 / height / base 2 (trapezoid)	*Triangle* A = 1/2 × base × height	height / base (triangle)

1.3.2 AREA: ESTIMATING AND MEASURING

Concepts to Investigate: Area, measuring area of regular and irregular surfaces, indirect measurement, optical illusions.

Materials: Metric graph paper, centigram balance, scissors.

Principles and Procedures: Chemists are very interested in surface area because it is one of the key factors that determines the rate at which a chemical or physical reaction proceeds. The larger the surface area of contact between two reactants, the faster the resulting reaction. For example, when making hot cocoa, you *stir* the cocoa powder into the water or milk to separate the cocoa particles from each other and place them in contact with the water or milk so they can dissolve. Stirring increases the surface area of contact between the cocoa and the milk. In a similar manner, a snow-making machine at a ski slope sprays out an aerosol of water rather than a stream of water so the tiny water droplets will be in direct contact with the cold air and freeze more rapidly.

Part 1: Surface area of regular objects: The surface area of regular planar surfaces can be calculated using standard formulas such as those shown in Table 4. Verify these formulas by drawing these shapes on millimeter graph paper and then counting the number of millimeter squares in which the majority of the square is inside the figure as shown in Figure D. If the formulas are correct, the number of square millimeters counted inside the boundary of the object should be nearly equivalent to the value obtained by formula.

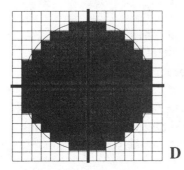

D

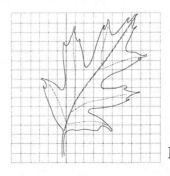

E

Part 2: Indirect measurement of irregular surface area: The surface area of an irregular shaped two dimensional object can be estimated by counting the number of squares within its boundary as illustrated in Figures D and E. This technique provides an estimate, but it is rather tedious and time consuming. In this activity you will perform a less tedious and more accurate indirect measurement of surface area (Figure F). Measure the dimensions of a plain sheet (without holes) of photocopy or drawing paper and calculate its area. Weigh the paper on the most sensitive balance available (sensitivity of 0.01 grams or better) and calculate the area to mass ratio. Now trace the irregular shape to be measured (a leaf, the palm of your hand, etc.) onto the paper and cut out and weigh the trace. Multiply the mass of the cutout by the area/mass ratio for the paper to indirectly measure the area of the object, and record your calculations in Table 5. If you do not have a sensitive balance, you may wish to carry out the process using heavy cardboard.

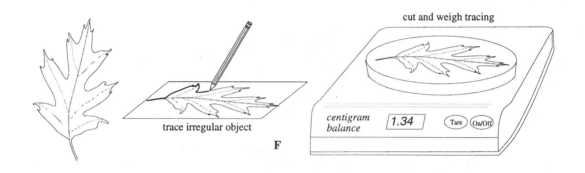

trace irregular object

F

cut and weigh tracing

centigram balance | 1.34 | Tare | On/Off

Table 5: Indirect Measurement of Surface Area

Object	Estimated Area (Number of Boxes Enclosed)	Indirectly Measured Area
leaf	mm²	mm²
hand	mm²	mm²
your figure	mm²	mm²

Questions

(1) For regular planar objects, is the value determined by counting squares more or less accurate than the value obtained by calculation? Explain.

(2) Why is it advantageous to use heavy posterboard or cardboard instead of paper when determining the area of an irregular object if you do not have a sensitive scale?

(3) For irregular planar objects do you think the weight is more accurately measured by counting the squares or by indirectly measuring the area by massing the cutout and multiplying this value by the area/mass ratio for the paper?

1.3.3 VOLUME: ESTIMATING AND MEASURING

Concepts to Investigate: Volume of regular objects, volume of irregular objects, volume formulas, displacement method for measuring volume, incompressibility of liquids.

Materials: Centimeter graph paper, paper clips, pennies, cardboard, plastic wrap or aluminum foil, 1 liter plastic soda bottle, two 50 mL burets, isopropyl alcohol.

Safety: Isopropyl alcohol is flammable and must be kept away from flames. Like all organic solvents, it should be used only in a well-ventilated area.

Principles and Procedures:

Part 1: Units of volume: The volume of a solid, liquid or gas is the amount of space it occupies. A variety of SI units are used to indicate volume depending upon the size of the object measured. The volume of a house may be measured in cubic meters (m^3), while the volume of an automobile fuel tank is measured in liters (L) and a soda can in milliliters (1 milliliter = 1 cubic centimeter (cm^3)).

This activity will help you discover some important relationships among the various metric units of volume. Cut three 10 cm × 10 cm squares from centimeter graph paper and paste them onto stiff cardboard cut as shown in Figure G. Fold the cardboard on the dotted lines and securely tape the edges to form a cube (no top) with inside dimensions 10 cm by 10 cm by 10 cm. Line the inside of the box with a clear plastic bag so it will hold water. The volume of a regularly shaped container such as your box is easy to compute. Simply multiply the length by the width by the height: 10 cm × 10 cm × 10 cm = 1000 cm^3 (1000 cubic centimeters). A volume of 1000 cm^3 is also called one cubic decimeter (1 dm^3). Note that the term *cubic centimeter* (cm^3) is derived from the fact that it is the volume of a cube with sides of length 1 cm (1 cm × 1 cm × 1 cm = 1 cm^3 = 1 mL).

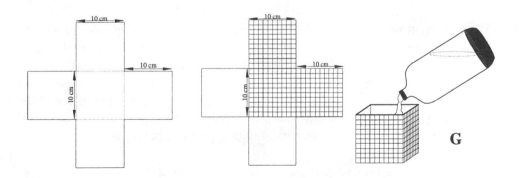

Obtain a one-liter plastic bottle such as those used to hold drinking water and other beverages. You have seen one-liter bottles of soda in the supermarket and have probably noticed that the liquid level in the bottle is generally about 5 millimeters below the top because this is the actual 1-liter line. Fill the bottle with water to this point, and then carefully pour the water into the plastic-lined box. What is the approximate volume of the box in liters?

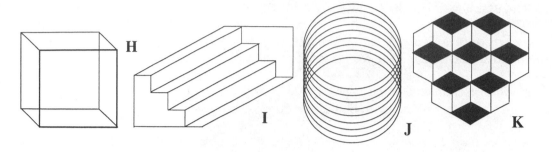

Part 2: Calculating volume: Figures H-K illustrate optical illusions, pictures that play tricks on our perception. Examine the cube (Figure H). Is the area within the darker lines the outside or inside of the cube? It depends on the orientation of the cube seen by your mind. Keep looking and you will see the cube flip back and forth between these two orientations. Inspect the stairs and hollow tube shown in Figures I and J. In which direction does the staircase run? (right side up, or upside down?) In which direction does the tube in Figure J run; up or down? Keep looking at each figure and you will see each reverse! Try blinking if you can't see both ways. How many stacked boxes do you see in Figure K? Are the black squares the tops or bottoms of the boxes. Are there six or seven boxes?

It is not possible for you to make direct computations of the volumes of these figures because they are displayed in only two dimensions and presented at oblique angles. We will therefore provide linear dimensions and ask you to calculate volumes.

(a) Find the volume of the cube (Figure H) assuming the dimensions of its sides are 23.0 cm. (b) Find the volume of the staircase (Figure I) assuming that each step is 14.4 cm high, 160.5 cm wide and 29.2 cm deep. (c) If the radius of each of the circles at the end of the tube (Figure J) is 4.00 cm and the length of the tube is 5.10 cm, what is the volume? Since the tube is in the shape of a cylinder, its volume is computed by multiplying the area of one end (the base; $A = \pi r^2$) by the length. (d) What is the total volume of all the boxes in Figure K (six or seven as you see it!) given that the length of an edge is 12.5 mm? Record these values in Table 6.

Part 3: Measurement of volume by displacement: Chemists must often determine the volume of small or irregular objects. For example, a forensic chemist (one who works with law enforcement officials to help solve crimes) might be asked to determine the manufacturer of a bullet recovered from a crime scene. Knowing that different manufacturers use different alloys with different densities, the chemist may first determine the volume of the bullet so that he or she may then mass it and ascertain the density (density = mass/volume). How would you determine the volume of an irregular object such as a bullet?

Copyright © 1999 by John Wiley & Sons, Inc.

Table 6: Apparent Volumes of Illusions

	Volume (cm³)	Volume (mL)	Volume (L)
(a) Cube	cm³	mL	L
(b) Stairs	cm³	mL	L
(c) Cylinder	cm³	mL	L
(d) Blocks (6)	cm³	mL	L
(d) Blocks (7)	cm³	mL	L

In this activity you will be asked to measure the volume of some small irregular objects such as a penny, a paper clip, and a tack using indirect measurement and water displacement. Fill a graduated cylinder partially with water and carefully record the volume to the nearest 0.1 mL. When reading volumes, always report the value at the bottom of the meniscus (the curved surface at the air/fluid interface) as shown in Figure L. Place 50 or more paper clips in the cylinder and lightly tap the glass until no air bubbles remain attached to the paper clips. Record the final volume. The difference between the two volume measurements

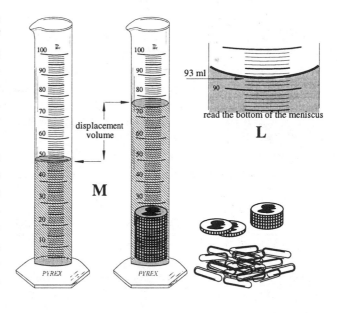

is the volume of 50 paper clips (Figure M). Therefore, you can determine the volume of one paper clip simply by dividing this volume by 50. Repeat with tacks and pennies and enter your findings in Table 7.

Part 4: The case of the vanishing volume; or 2 + 2 = 3: A liquid is defined as a form of matter that flows, has constant (fixed) volume and takes the shape of its container. The object was placed in a cylinder containing water, and the water flowed around it. Since water is relatively incompressible (maintains a fixed volume), the change in volume in the cylinder was equivalent to the volume of the submerged object.

When you apply pressure to a liquid, its shape may change, but not its volume. This principle is used in automobile brakes. When the driver presses on the pedal, brake fluid flows through the brake line, transmitting pressure to the brake shoes. If the brake fluid were compressible, the fluid would compress and less force would be transmitted to the brake shoes, rendering the design useless.

Table 7: Measuring Volume by Displacement (mL)

	Original Volume (V_1)	Final Volume (V_2)	Displacement Volume ($V = V_2 - V_1$)	Quantity of Object (n)	Volume of Single Object (V)
paper clips					
thumbtacks					
penny					

(a) Fill two 50 mL burets to the 25.0 mL mark with water. Slowly drain 25.0 mL of water from one buret into the other and read the final volume to the nearest tenth of a milliliter (Figure N). Record the final volume to the nearest tenth of a milliliter in Table 8. (b) Repeat procedure "a" using isopropyl alcohol in both burets. (c) Finally, fill one 50 mL buret to the 25.0 mL mark with water and another 50 mL buret to the 25.0 mL mark with isopropyl alcohol. Slowly pour 25.0 mL of water from the water buret into the alcohol buret and carefully read the final volume to the nearest tenth of a millimeter.

Do all of the mixtures add up to 50.0 mL? Did the volume of any of the mixtures decrease or increase significantly (by more than 1%)?

Table 8: Vanishing Volume?

(a) 25.0 mL Water + 25.0 mL Water	(b) 25.0 mL Alcohol + 25.0 mL Alcohol	(c) 25.0 mL Water + 25.0 mL Alcohol
mL	mL	mL

Questions

(1) Complete the following:
  (a) $1 \text{ dm}^3 = ? \text{ cm}^3$ (d) $1 \text{ m}^3 = ? \text{ cm}^3$
  (b) $1 \text{ mL} = ? \text{ cm}^3$ (e) $2 \text{ km}^2 = ? \text{ mm}^3$
  (c) $100{,}000 \text{ mL} = ?\text{L}$

(2) Explain how indirect measurement can be used to find the volume of a drop of liquid too small to be measured directly.

(3) Given the following formulas, determine the volumes of the objects illustrated in Figures O through R.

  Rectangular Prism (Box) $V = L \times W \times H$
  Cylinder $V = \pi \times R^2 \times H$
  Cone $V = 1/3 \times \pi \times R^2 \times H$
  Sphere $V = 4/3 \times \pi \times R^3$

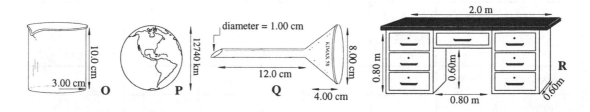

(4) A liquid is defined as a form of matter that flows, has constant (fixed) volume and takes the shape of its container. Which of these characteristics seems not to hold true upon mixing of alcohol and water? Explain.

1.3.4 MEASURING MASS

Concepts to Investigate: Mass, weight, relative error, indirect measurement, atomic mass measurements.

Materials: Wooden dowel, three small "eye" hooks, two large plastic cups, 1000 mL graduated cylinder (or dm^3 box constructed earlier), marbles, spring scales graduated in pounds or ounces, marking pen, adhesive tape, string, unpopped popcorn, rice, dry beans.

Principles and Procedures: Mass is the amount of matter in an object. Weight is the force (pull) of gravity on an object. Mass and weight are related, but they are not the same. The mass of an object remains the same even if it is moved to the top of a mountain (where the gravitational field strength is slightly less than at sea level) or into deep space (where gravitational field strength is approximately zero). The weight of that same object, however, would be slightly less at the top of the mountain and virtually zero in deep space because weight is dependent upon gravitational field strength!

In the International Metric System (SI) the kilogram (kg) is the unit of mass. Other units of mass derived from this are the gram (g), the centigram (cg), and the milligram (mg). The newton, N, is the SI unit of force or weight. One kilogram weighs about 9.8 newtons or 2.2 pounds on Earth. A common D flashlight battery weighs about one newton. The following is a chart which shows the SI units for mass and the weight that these masses would have on Earth.

A spring scale such as a traditional bathroom scale is used to measure weight. When you step on the scale, the spring compresses (or extends, depending on its design) due to the force of gravity on your body. On the Moon, the same scale would show your weight to be approximately one-sixth of that on Earth because the Moon's gravitational force is only about one sixth as strong as the Earth's.

A double pan balance is used to measure mass. The object to be massed is placed on one pan and then known masses are placed on the other pan until the beam balances. The mass of the object is the sum of the known masses. On the Moon the double pan balance would show your mass to be the same as that on Earth because the force of gravity is the same on the reference pan as on the unknown pan.

Part 1: Construction and use of a double pan balance: In this activity you will construct a double pan balance (Figure S) and use this to mass some common objects. Obtain a meter stick or wooden dowel and attach a hook in the center as well as one at each end as shown. Using a hole puncher, punch holes in two large plastic cups and suspend these with strings from the hooks. Before you can mass anything, you must be certain that the balance is "zeroed" (perfectly balanced). Add small pieces of tape to the outside of the higher cup until

Table 9: SI Masses and Their Weights on Earth

Mass	Mass in Grams	Weight in Newtons	Weight in Pounds
1 kg	= 0.1000 g	9.8 N	2.2 lbs
1 g	= 0.001 g	0.0098 N	0.0022 lbs
1 cg	= 0.00001 g	0.000098 N	0.000022 lbs
1 mg	= 0.000001 g	0.000009 8 N	0.0000022 lbs

equilibrium is reached. You can determine the accuracy of your balance by measuring an object of known mass. Place a known mass in one cup, and slowly add water with a pipet or straw until it is perfectly balanced. Pour the water into a graduated cylinder and record the volume. Since the density of water is 1 g/mL, the numeric value of the volume in milliliters is the same as the mass in grams. Calculate the relative error of your measurement by subtracting the measured mass from the known mass (the mass measured using a commercial balance, Figure T), dividing this value by the known mass and multiplying the quotient by 100%. What is the relative error of your measurement? Does your double pan balance appear to accurately measure mass?

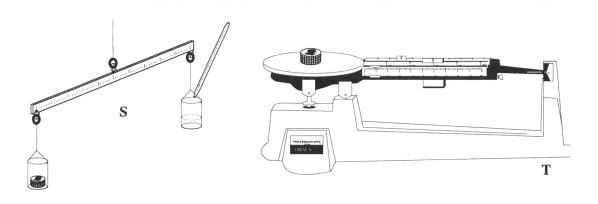

Part 2: Indirect measurement of mass: In chemistry books you frequently see statements such as: "the mass of a carbon 12 atom is 1.9924×10^{-23} grams." How can chemists make such statements when the most sensitive balances in the world (ultramicrobalances) are only able to measure to within a few micrograms (1×10^{-6} g)? Chemists are obviously not able to directly weigh an individual atom, but they can weigh a large quantity, and if they know approximately how many atoms are present in the sample, they can calculate the average value of one atom. Such form of measurement is known as indirect measurement and is frequently used in chemistry. In this activity you will use your double pan balance to indirectly measure the average mass of a grain of rice, a bean, a popcorn kernel or another small object.

Pour out exactly 100 mL (100 g) of water into one cup. Carefully add kernels of popcorn in the other cup until the cups are balanced. At this point, the total mass of the popcorn is 100g. To determine the average mass of a single kernel, divide 100g by the number of kernels. Repeat this procedure with dry rice and beans. Calculate class averages for the masses of these objects.

Part 3: Thinking metrically: Linguists say that a person is fluent in a language when he or she can "think" in that language. A person fluent in Japanese can think in Japanese terms rather than thinking in the native language, and then translating thoughts into Japanese. All countries of the world except the United States, Liberia, and Burma (Myanmar) have adopted the metric system as their official measurement system, and consequently children growing up in these countries learn to think in metric terms. Americans, however, grow up in a world where English units predominate, and consequently think in English terms. When they read that an object has a mass of 5 kilograms, they may mentally convert it to 11 pounds to understand its relative magnitude. To become fluent in the metric system, it is essential to think in metric terms rather than converting to English. To do this, it is important

Table 10: Thinking Metrically

Mass	Object with Approximately the Same Mass	Object of Unknown Mass	Estimated Mass	Measured Mass	Relative Error of Estimate
1 g	thumbtack	pencil	g	g	%
10 g		this book	g	g	%
100 g		can of soda	g	g	%
1 kg		2 liter soda bottle	g	g	%

to develop some common reference standards. For example, if you know that a thumbtack has a mass of approximately 1 gram, then you can easily imagine that a mass of 15 grams is roughly equivalent to the mass of 15 thumbtacks. Using your double pan balance or a commercial balance, find common household items that have a mass of approximately 1 gram, 10 grams, and 1 kilogram. After you have developed a set of reference masses, use these to estimate the mass of a pencil, this book, a can of soda, and a 2-liter soda bottle. Measure the masses of these and determine the relative error of your estimates. Complete Table 10.

Questions

(1) In 1988 Leonid Taraneko set the world weight lifting record by lifting 475.0 kg. Complete Table 11 to determine if you could lift this 475.0 kg mass on the Moon or in deep space. (0.4536 kg/lb)

Table 11: Mass and Weight

	Earth	Deep Space	Moon
Mass	475.0 kg	kg	kg
Weight (pounds)	1047 lb	lb	lb
Weight (newtons)	4655 N	N	N

(2) Explain why a double pan balance is used to measure mass, while a spring is used to measure weight.

(3) Could your double pan balance be used to accurately measure mass on Mars? In deep space?

1.3.5 DENSITY OF SOLIDS

Concepts to Investigate: Density, relative density (specific gravity), intrinsic properties, non-destructive testing.

Materials: Part 1: Pre-1982 pennies, post-1982 pennies, graduated cylinder; Part 2: Metals to serve as unknowns (U.S. and foreign coins, sections of metal pipe, nails, tacks, ball bearings, etc).

Principles and Procedures: Why do some things float, and some things sink? When asked this question, many people suggest that things "lighter" than water float, while things "heavier" than water sink. If this is the case why do logs float, while pebbles sink? Surely logs are much "heavier" than the pebbles, and yet they float while pebbles sink! Clearly, it is not the mass or weight of an object that determines if it will sink or float.

The buoyancy of an object (its capacity to remain afloat) is not dependent upon its mass, but rather upon its density (mass to volume ratio). If an object has a density greater than water (more mass in the same volume), it will sink, and if it has a lower density than water (less mass in the same volume), it will float. Stated in another way, if the weight of water displaced by an object is less than the weight of the object, then object will sink. If the weight of water displaced is equal to the weight of the object, the object will float. The density of an object can be determined by dividing its mass by its volume.

Part 1: Non-destructive testing: Hiero II, king of Syracuse (a region of Greece) during the 3rd century BC, commissioned the production of a gold crown, but then suspected that the goldsmith may have defrauded him by substituting a less precious metal in the interior of the crown. Hiero II then commissioned a man by the name of Archimedes to determine if the crown was made of pure gold, but demanded that he not damage or disassemble the crown. In other words, Archimedes had to answer the king's question by developing a non-destructive test for composition.

According to tradition, Archimedes is said to have placed a block of pure gold equal to the mass of the crown in a container and filled it to the brim with water. He then removed the gold and placed the crown in the container and noticed that water overflowed. He concluded that the goldsmith had cheated the king because the crown had the same mass as the gold object, but it had larger volume and caused the water to overflow. Archimedes showed that the goldsmith had partially substituted a metal other than gold when fashioning the crown because its density (mass/volume ratio) was less than gold!

Originally, American pennies were made of 95% copper and 5% zinc. In the late 1970s the price of copper rose so dramatically that Congress feared the copper content in pennies would be more valuable than one cent and that people would hoard the copper coins and melt them down and sell the copper. Consequently, a bill was proposed in Congress to reduce the copper content of pennies. In this activity, you will use the same basic principle Archimedes used to determine if Congress passed the bill and put it into effect.

Collect approximately 50 pre-1982 U.S. pennies and 50 post-1982 pennies (do not use 1982 pennies). Determine the mass of both sets of pennies. Determine the volume of each group by the method of water displacement shown in Figure M in 1.3.3. Calculate the density of the pre-1982 and post-1982 pennies by dividing their mass by their volume. On the basis of your results, does it appear that the bill was enacted?

Table 12: Identifying a Substance by Its Density

	mass	*volume*	*density*	*likely identity*
Unknown 1				
Unknown 2				
Unknown 3				

Part 2: Identifying a substance by density: Density is an intensive physical property of matter, meaning that it does not depend upon the amount of matter present. Thus the density of one drop of water is the same as the density of a glass full. Intrinsic physical properties like density, boiling point, melting point, ductility, malleability, color, crystal shape and refractive index can be used to identify substances. In this case you will use density to identify the composition of certain unknown metals provided by your instructor.

Fill a graduated cylinder approximately one-third full with water and record the level of the meniscus to the nearest tenth of a milliliter (Figure L in 1.3.3). Record the mass of the cylinder and water to the nearest tenth of a gram. Add enough metal shot, rods, or coins until the water level is near the top of the graduations and measure the volume and the mass as before. The mass of the metal is the difference between the first and second weighing, and its volume is the difference between the first and second volumes. Report the mass, volume, and density of the unknowns in Table 12. Compare these values with those in Table 13 and predict the content of the unknown metals.

Table 13: Densities

Substance	*Density at 20°C (g/mL)*	*Substance*	*Density at 20°C (g/mL)*
0.91	ice	8.90	nickel
1.00	water	8.96	copper
2.70	aluminum	10.5	silver
7.14	zinc	11.35	lead
7.87	iron	13.6	mercury

Questions

(1) When identifying a substance, chemists are concerned only with intrinsic properties, not extrinsic. Explain.

(2) Using a handbook, table or computer software, examine the density data for a particular family of elements. Describe the relationship between atomic number and density within a family.

(3) According to your data, does it appear as though the U.S. mint changed the composition of pennies in 1982? Explain your reasoning.

1.3.6 DENSITY OF LIQUIDS

Concepts to Investigate: Density gradient, specific gravity.

Materials: <u>Part 1</u>: Vegetable oil, glycerol, corn syrup, liquid detergent, isopropyl alcohol; <u>Part 2</u>: Food coloring, flask, overhead transparency or note card; <u>Part 3</u>: Plastic drinking straw, modeling clay or paraffin, sand, beaker, glycerin, olive oil, milk, salt.

Principles and Procedures:

Part 1: Density gradient: The following household liquids vary in density from about 0.9 g/mL to about 1.4 g/mL: vegetable oil, glycerol, water, corn syrup, detergent, and isopropyl alcohol. In this activity you will be attempting to rank them in order of increasing density. Use a mechanical pipet or eye dropper to place a small amount of one fluid onto the surface of another (Figure U). To avoid turbulence, you should release the liquid from the pipet as slowly as possible, preferably down the side of the test tube. If the fluid sinks, then it has greater density than the fluid in which it has been placed, but if it floats, it has a lesser density. Repeat the procedure with other pairs of liquids until you believe you have established a density ranking. Once you have done so, use the pipet to construct a six-tier density gradient in a test tube as shown in Figure V. If your density scale is correct, there will be only minimal mixing of the liquids. Label the fluids in the diagram.

Do the following to calculate the densities of each of these liquids. First, determine the mass of a dry graduated cylinder. Pour the first liquid into the cylinder, measure its volume, and determine its mass. The mass of the fluid is the difference between the mass of the full cylinder and the mass of the dry cylinder. The density is simply the mass divided by the volume ($D = \frac{m}{V}$). Calculate the density of each fluid and compare your values with the density gradient. Is the densest fluid on the bottom and the least dense fluid on top?

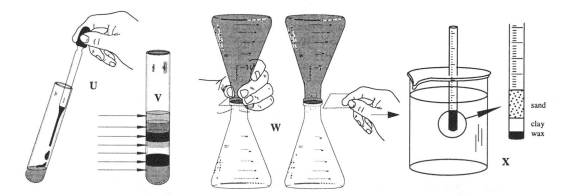

Part 2: The effect of temperature on density: Place a couple of drops of blue food coloring in each of two identical Erlenmeyer flasks. Fill the flasks to overflowing with cool tap water, mixing to distribute the food coloring evenly throughout. Repeat the procedure with two flasks of warm tap water, but this time add red food coloring. Place a plastic square cut from an overhead transparency on top of one of the warm flasks and carefully invert the flask and place it on top of a cool flask (Figure W). Carefully remove the sheet and watch for mixing. Repeat the procedure, but place the remaining cool flask on top of the warm one. Which fluid has a greater density, the warm water or the cool water?

Part 3: Specific gravity: Buoyancy is dependent upon the density of a fluid. The denser a fluid, the greater the buoyant force per unit volume displaced. Since the density of ocean water is 1.025 g/mL, while that of fresh water is only 1.000 g/mL, an equal displacement of salt water will produce a greater buoyant force than fresh water. For this reason, boats float slightly higher in salt water.

Since the buoyancy of an object is dependent upon the density of the fluid in which it is floating, it is possible to make an instrument that measures fluid density on the basis of how high the instrument floats. Such an instrument is known as a hydrometer and can be constructed from a plastic drinking straw as illustrated in Figure X. Seal one end of a straw by plugging it with modeling clay and paraffin (hot candle wax) as shown. Hold the straw upright in water while you pour a small amount of sand into the open end of the straw. Add enough to stabilize the straw, but not enough to sink it! Carefully note the water line and mark this as 1.00 with a fine tipped permanent marker, since the density of water is 1.00 g/mL. To provide another reference point, float the hydrometer in olive oil and mark the level as 0.92. The density of olive oil is 0.92 g/mL, or 92% the density of water, so we say it has a specific gravity of 0.92. The specific gravity is merely the ratio of a substance's density relative to water. Using these two points, you should be able to generate an approximate scale of specific gravity. Using your hydrometer, determine the approximate specific gravity of glycerin and milk. If you do not have these liquids, you may still observe how the hydrometer works by slowly adding salt to the beaker and watching the hydrometer rise.

Questions

(1) Assume that a cylinder was filled with mercury (a liquid metal with density 13.6 g/mL), water (1.0 g/mL) and maple syrup (1.4 g/mL). Which fluid would occupy the bottom position, and which the top? Describe what would happen to each of the following items if placed in this cylinder: a block of pine wood (0.8 g/mL), a lead fishing weight (11.4 g/mL), a copper coin (8.9 g/mL), a gold ring (19.3 g/mL), and a block of ebony wood (1.2 g/mL).

(2) In part 2 you probably noticed the development of a purple color. What is the temperature of the purple water relative to the red and blue?

(3) If you have ever gone diving in a lake or ocean, you may have noticed the temperature drop dramatically as you go down only 1 or 2 meters. Explain.

(4) Plankton are small or microscopic organisms that float or drift near the surface of ocean or lake waters. They are the base of the aquatic food chain, and therefore extremely important to all other aquatic life. Plankton depend upon nutrients, which typically are denser than water and sink. If water is undisturbed, it is possible for so many nutrients to sink to the bottom that plankton can no longer live, and thus no other aquatic life as well. Fortunately, changes in temperature can cause a mixing of water that brings nutrients back up to the surface. Explain.

(5) Hydrometers are used to determine the density of water in car radiators. Since density varies as a function of the amount of anti-freeze (ethylene glycol) added, it is possible to determine the percentage of antifreeze in the radiator and the temperature at which it would freeze. Knowing the specific gravity of ethylene glycol to be 0.958, would a radiator containing fluid with a specific gravity of 0.976 or 0.989 be better prepared for cold weather? Explain.

1.3.7 DENSITY OF SOLUTIONS

Concepts to Investigate: Density, concentration.

Materials: Part 1: Green and ripe tomatoes; Part 2: Cans of diet and regular soft drinks.

Principles and Procedures: Many of us enjoy maple syrup on our pancakes, French toast or waffles. This syrup comes from the sap of maple trees in the Northeastern United States and Southeastern Canada. Native Americans learned how to collect the sweet sap of the sugar maple by cutting the bark and then collecting the sap that drains out of the wound in the late winter and early spring. Early colonists in these regions learned how to make syrup and sugar from this sap by boiling off the water. Millions of liters of maple syrup are produced in this manner each year and sold throughout the world. Maple tree farmers sell the sap to refiners, who measure the sugar content of the sap on the basis of density. The denser the sap, the greater the sugar content and the more syrup or sugar can be made. This principle is true for other solutions as well: the more dissolved solutes, the denser the solution. You will use this principle to investigate the quantity of dissolved solutes in fruits and soft drinks.

Part 1: Separating ripe from green tomatoes: Approximately 75% of the entire American tomato crop is processed into juice, canned tomatoes, sauces, pastes, and catsup. Before tomatoes can be processed, the green tomatoes must be removed so only the ripe ones will remain for processing. The ripeness of a tomato can be determined not only by color, but also by density. When tomatoes are placed in water, they either float or sink depending upon their ripeness (Figure Y). Which are denser, green or ripe tomatoes? Place ripe and green tomatoes in an aquarium or sink filled with water and determine which are denser. Most tomatoes are separated by machine rather than by hand. How would you design a machine to separate green from ripe tomatoes?

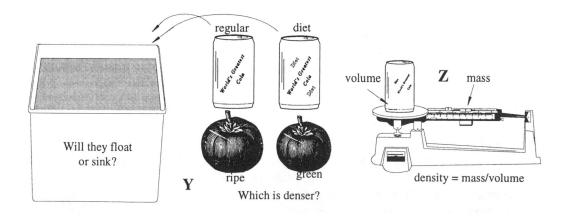

Part 2: Diet vs. regular soft drinks: Do you get "more" for your money when purchasing regular soft drinks or diet soft drinks? Examine the labels of regular and diet varieties of the same soft drink. In most situations they have exactly the same volume (e.g., 355 mL), but not the same mass. Place cans of diet and regular soft drink (of the same brand) in an aquarium or large pail of water and observe what happens (Figure Y). Which soft drink has the

greater density? Calculate the densities (Figure Z) of the regular and diet drinks by determining the mass of the fluid (the difference in mass between a full and empty can) and dividing by the volume (printed on the side of the can). Which has greater density?

Questions

(1) Which have greater density, ripe tomatoes or green tomatoes? Which has more dissolved solutes?

(2) Draw a simple design for a machine that can be used to separate green tomatoes from ripe ones.

(3) Which have greater density, regular or diet soft drinks? Which has more dissolved solutes?

(4) Examine the "nutrition facts" label on the side of the regular and diet soft drink cans. What dissolved solutes do they list? Which is the main solute that contributes to the difference in density between the two drinks?

(5) What is the density of the regular soft drink and the diet soft drink?

1.3.8 DENSITY OF SOLUTIONS: THE MYSTERY OF THE STRAIT OF GIBRALTAR

Concepts to Investigate: Density, salinity, concentration, currents.

Materials: Non-iodized salt, egg, food coloring, cake pan, tape, overhead transparency, paper punch, pepper, food coloring.

Principles and Procedures: The Mediterranean Sea (Figure AA) is a great expanse of water that stretches from the Atlantic Ocean on the west, to Asia on the east, and separates the African and European continents. Its name means "sea between lands" (*med-* means middle: e.g., median, *terra-* land; e.g., terrestrial). Historians have referred to this sea as the "incubator of Western Civilization" because the major civilizations of ancient Egypt, Israel, Phoenicia, Greece, and Rome had their beginnings on the shores of this sea. Prior to the development of the Suez Canal in 1869, the only link between the Mediterranean and the oceans of the world was through the Strait of Gibraltar, a 13 km (8 mi) wide strip of water connecting the western Mediterranean with the Atlantic Ocean.

When the Phoenician explorers and traders first sailed through the strait in approximately 800 BC, they noticed a very strong current coming into the Mediterranean from the Atlantic. As later sea-faring people traveled through the Strait of Gibraltar, they also noticed a very strong current, approaching two meters per second in certain areas. As cartographers developed accurate maps of the Mediterranean, it became apparent that it was not connected to the ocean through any other points except the Strait of Gibraltar. This raised a very perplexing question: how can the water continually flow one way into the Mediterranean? Some people hypothesized that there was a major underwater "drain," and others hypothesized that the cartographers had simply not found another strait similar to Gibraltar where the water flowed out of the Mediterranean and into the ocean. What do you think? Try these activities and then generate your own hypothesis.

Part 1: Salt water vs. fresh water: Dissolve a couple of tablespoons of salt into a Erlenmeyer flask or similar container. Put a drop of food coloring into the salt water to distinguish it from fresh water. Fill another container with fresh water and cover the top with a note card or a small square of plastic cut from an overhead transparency. Carefully invert the fresh water on top of the salt water and remove the card or square (Figure BB). Observe the containers for two minutes. Is there much mixing between the fresh and salt water? Repeat the process placing the container with the salt water on top of the fresh water (Figure CC). On the basis of these observations, which appears to have a higher density, fresh water or salt water?

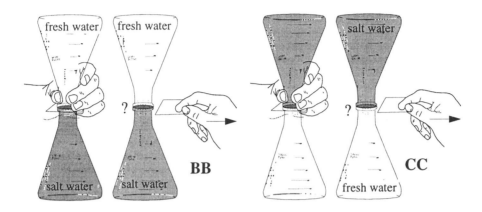

Part 2: Salinity and buoyancy: If the density of an object is less than the density of the fluid in which it is placed, the object will float. If the density of the object is greater than the density of the fluid, it will sink. Archimedes' principle states that an object is buoyed by a force equivalent to the weight of the water it displaces. Knowing this, what will happen to a ship or fish as it moves from saltwater to freshwater or vice versa? Place a fresh egg in a beaker of tap water, and record its position. Slowly stir salt into the beaker until the egg rises and is suspended above the bottom of the beaker but below the surface of the water (Figure DD). What should be

DD

added to raise the egg to the surface? What should be added to cause the egg to sink to the bottom once again? Try it!

Part 3: Solving the mystery of the Strait of Gibraltar: Oceanographers have determined that the Mediterranean Sea loses three times as much water from evaporation as it receives from the rivers that flow into it. As water evaporates from the sea, salts are left behind, and the sea becomes saltier, but not as salty as it would be if there was no outflow of salty water. By making a model (Figure EE) of the Mediterranean Sea and the Strait of Gibraltar, it may be possible to solve the mystery. Construct a dam in the middle of the pan using plastic cut from an overhead transparency or similar divider. Using a paper punch, cut one hole near the

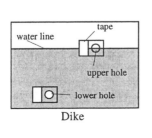

Dike

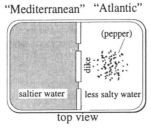

top view

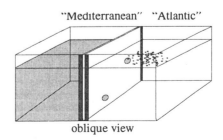

oblique view

EE

top right of the divider (for surface currents) and one near the bottom left (for deep currents) as illustrated. Attach small pieces of paper to the ends of each of two pieces of Scotch tape to serve as non-sticking tabs. Seal the holes with the sticky part of the tape, and then position the divider in the middle of the pan using duct tape or other strong water-resistant tape. Identify one side of the cake pan "Mediterranean" and the other side "Atlantic." Dissolve approximately five times as much salt in one beaker as in the other. The amounts are not critical, but the beaker representing the Mediterranean should have substantially more salt. Alternatively, you may simply use tap water for the Atlantic and very salty water for the Mediterranean. Add green food coloring to the beaker with the saltier solution. Slowly pour the saltier solution into the Mediterranean side while simultaneously pouring the less salty solution into the Atlantic side so as not to put excessive pressure on the dike. Add pepper to the surface of the "Atlantic" side. Carefully remove the tape from the dividers and observe the movement of the food coloring and the pepper. Which way does the salty water travel? The less salty water? On the basis of your observations, can you explain why sailors must always contend with a strong in-flowing current at the Strait of Gibraltar?

Questions

(1) Which has higher density, salt or fresh water? Explain.

(2) Major cargo ships sail up the Saint Lawrence Seaway from the Atlantic Ocean to the Great Lakes. If their ballast tanks are not adjusted, will the ships ride higher or lower when they move from the ocean to the fresh water seaway?

(3) What is your solution to the mystery of the Strait of Gibraltar? How can water apparently flow into the Mediterranean Sea, but not out?

(4) An estuary is the region in which the water from a river mixes with the tidal waters of the ocean. Estuaries are very rich ecosystems, supporting a wide variety of plant and animal life. Would you expect halophytic ("salt-loving") organisms to live closer to the surface or bottom of the water? Explain.

(5) Oil drillers often flood oil wells with salt water to increase production. Why?

1.3.9 DENSITY OF GASES

Concepts to Investigate: Density, density of gases.

Materials: Part 1: Candle, matches, baking soda, vinegar, beakers; Part 2: Aquarium or sink, bubble solution, bubble wand or wire ring.

Principles and Procedures:

Part 1: The mystery of Lake Nyos: Lake Nyos in Cameroon, West Africa (Figure FF), sits in the crater of an ancient volcano, much the same as Crater Lake in Oregon. In August of 1986, large bubbles of a colorless, odorless gas started bursting from the surface of the lake, and within a short time more than 1700 people living on the shore of the lake died. Scientists determined that the gas coming from the lake was simply carbon dioxide, a naturally occurring gas that normally constitutes only 0.03% of the atmosphere. Carbon dioxide is essential for life on Earth, as it is the gas that plants use in photosynthesis. Unfortunately, when carbon dioxide concentrations are too high, the oxygen needed for respiration is displaced and suffocation may occur. How did the carbon dioxide at Lake Nyos build up to fatal levels? Why didn't it simply rise out of the crater and leave the people unharmed?

Attach a candle to a can lid using molten wax or a hot nail pierced through the lid as shown in Figure GG. Place the candle upright in an empty beaker that is deeper than the candle. Place an identical candle on the table top outside the beaker. Light both candles.

Produce carbon dioxide gas by reacting sodium hydrogen carbonate (baking soda) and acetic acid (the active ingredient in vinegar):

$$NaHCO_3 + HC_2H_3O_2 \longrightarrow Na^+ + C_2H_3O_2^- + CO_2 + H_2O$$

Add approximately 50 mL of baking soda to a 100 mL of vinegar in a 500 beaker and observe rapid bubbling. The carbon dioxide collects in the beaker and can then be poured into the beaker containing the candle as shown. Do not pour the carbon dioxide directly on the flame, but rather inside the beaker next to the rim (Figure HH). How long does it take to extinguish the candle? Prepare a fresh batch of carbon dioxide and repeat the procedure with the other candle (Figure II), pouring the carbon dioxide an equal distance from the flame. Does the flame go out? Why or why not? Is the density of carbon dioxide greater or less than air?

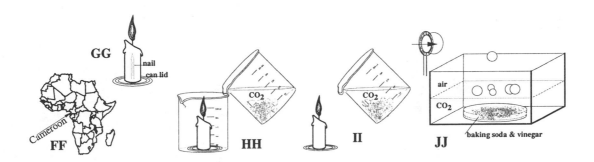

Part 2: Floating bubbles on carbon dioxide: If carbon dioxide is indeed denser than air, then it should be possible to hold it in an open beaker just as water can be held. Pour approximately 200 mL of vinegar on approximately 100 g of baking soda that is resting on the

bottom of an aquarium or plugged sink. After the bubbling has stopped, use a child's bubble wand to blow bubbles over the container so that they gradually fall into it. Do not blow into the container as this will disturb the carbon dioxide present. If the carbon dioxide is denser than air, then the air bubbles should float upon the invisible layer of carbon dioxide just as wood floats on water (Figure JJ).

Questions

(1) We breathe carbon dioxide with every breath we take, and we get carbon dioxide in every carbonated soft drink, so why did the people at Lake Nyos die when the carbon dioxide was released from the lake?

(2) Air is composed of 78% nitrogen (N_2) and 21% oxygen (O_2). Calculate molecular weights of these two gases and carbon dioxide (CO_2) and suggest a reason why the carbon dioxide might have a greater density than air.

(3) "Dry ice" is the common name for solid carbon dioxide. It sublimes (goes directly from solid to gas) at room temperature, and you may see condensation trails descending off the block. Dry ice is frequently used for special effects in stage shows. Knowing that humans cannot breathe air containing 10% or more carbon dioxide, what special precautions should be made when using dry ice?

(4) Would fire extinguishers that produce carbon dioxide gas be more effective in fighting ground fires or ceiling fires? Explain.

(5) Some fire-extinguishers designed for fighting electrical fires contain halon 1301 (bromotrifluoromethane, $CBrF_3$) because it does not cause short circuits or damage electrical equipment. Does halon sink to the ground or rise to the ceiling when released from the fire extinguisher?

FOR THE TEACHER

1.3.1 LENGTH: ESTIMATING AND MEASURING

Discussion: Help your students understand that there is always some uncertainty in every measurement due to the limitations in the construction and reading of measuring instruments, and they must therefore never report greater precision than their measuring instruments allow. They should report only significant digits (those that can be measured, plus one estimated digit), and always include units in their measurements. Following are some general rules concerning significant digits:

- digits other than zero are always significant
- zeros between two other significant digits are always significant
- zeros used for the purpose of locating the decimal point are not significant
- zeros used after a number to the right of a decimal point are significant

Examples:

346 — three significant digits
5.67×10^8 — three significant digits
564.7 — four significant digits
0.00529 — three significant digits
23.50 — four significant digits
7.03 — three significant digits

In a computation involving significant digits, the result should express no greater precision than the least precise measurement used in the computation. That is, the answer cannot claim precision greater than that of the least precise measurement used to compute it. (1) in addition and subtraction the answer may contain only as many decimal places as the least precise measurement used in computing the answer; (2) in multiplication and division the answer may contain only as many significant digits as the least precise measurement used to compute the answer.

Examples:

$321 + 12.4 + 8.72 = 342$ $\qquad$ $0.0195 \times 1200 = 23$

Answers: (1) The smallest value that you can report with a millimeter ruler is the nearest tenth of a millimeter (0.1 mm). The student's "measurement" of 9.0000 indicates that he/she measured to the nearest tenth of a micron, implying 1000 times more precision than exists. (2) The figures in this activity are classic optical illusions created by an unorthodox use of perspective, and as a result, the conclusions drawn from observation generally do not agree with those drawn from direct measurement. Direct measurement allows for an objective, accurate assessment that is not possible by simple observation. (3) Answer: 0.07×10^{-3} m/L $\times 10^5$ monomers = 0.7 nm/monomer.

1.3.2 AREA: ESTIMATING AND MEASURING

Discussion: An explanation of significant digits is found in the previous activity. If you have not introduced this concept to your students, it would be appropriate to do so at this time.

Students may notice that there is no simple formula for computing the area of an irregular planar figure, a problem that has confronted people for centuries, especially geographers who were trying to make surveys and maps. In response to this need, an ingenious instrument called a planimeter was invented. A planimeter is an instrument specially designed for measuring the area of a planar figure regardless of the shape of its outline. A brief description of the planimeter and directions for its use follow if you wish to introduce it to your students.

A simple hatchet planimeter is a metal rod bent at right angles at the ends (Figure KK). One end is shaped like the blade of a hatchet and the other is formed into a point. Obtain a metal rod approximately 32 cm in length. Use a vise to bend this rod so that the length of R is exactly 20 cm and the two legs are 6 cm each. Use a file to taper one leg to a smooth tracing point, P. Use a hammer to flatten the other end into a small hatchet blade. Make certain the blade and tracer point are aligned (in the same plane).

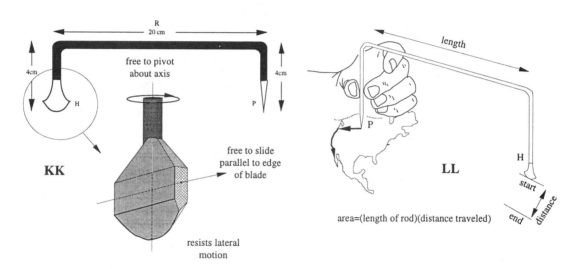

area=(length of rod)(distance traveled)

(1) Cover a smooth flat table with a large sheet of paper secured to the table with tape or other adhesive and place the figure to be measured on the paper in a convenient location and secure it with tape or other adhesive. (2) Locate the approximate center of area of the shape. (3) Use a ruler to draw a straight line from the center of area to one edge of the object being measured as shown in Figure LL. (4) Place the tracer point of the planimeter on the center of area. Hold the planimeter so the legs are vertical (perpendicular to the surface) and the hatchet blade is at some convenient position. Mark the initial position of the blade by pressing the blade into the paper so the indentation mark can easily be seen. Label this mark. (5) Hold the tracer leg of the planimeter lightly but steadily between thumb and first two fingers, using tip of little finger as glider support. The rod must rotate freely between your fingers as you move the planimeter. (6) Follow the line and pull the tracer leg from the center of area to the perimeter of the shape. Carefully trace the perimeter of the shape clockwise back to the starting point on the perimeter and then trace from this point back to the center of area. Mark the new position of the hatchet blade by pressing the blade firmly into the paper. Measure the distance, d, between the initial and final marks of the hatchet blade to the nearest millimeter. (7) Repeat the steps listed in 4, 5 and 6. But this time trace the figure in a counterclockwise direction. (8) Average the two distances between the initial and final marks of the hatchet blade. Multiply this distance by the length of the arm, 20 cm, to find the area.

Answers: (1) The square counting method is less accurate because it involves more estimations. (2) The same absolute error produces a greater relative error for light weight paper than for heavy cardboard. For example, a one gram error represents a 50% error when weighing a 2 gram piece of paper, but only a 5% error when weighing a 20 gram piece of cardboard. (3) The cut and weigh technique will generally be more accurate because it involves less estimations. The cut and weigh technique is an analog (continuous) measurement technique, while the box-counting is a digital (discrete) technique.

1.3.3 VOLUME: ESTIMATING AND MEASURING

Discussion: The water from the bottle should fill the box, illustrating that one liter (L) is equal to 1000 cubic centimeters. $1\ L = 1\ dm^3 = 1000\ mL = 1000\ cm^3$. The liter is defined in SI as exactly 1000 cubic centimeters.

Table 14: Apparent Volumes of Illusions

	Volume (cm³)	*Volume (mL)*	*Volume (L)*
(a) Cube	12,200	12,200	12.2
(b) Stairs (6)	405,000	67,500	67.5
(c) Cylinder	256	256	0.256
(d) Blocks (6)	11.7	11.7	0.0117
(d2) Blocks (7)	13.7	13.7	0.0137

Remind students that the volume of a regularly shaped object may be found directly by using a formula or indirectly by methods such as displacement. Observe them reading the volume of liquid in a graduated cylinder to ensure they are reading the meniscus correctly as shown in Figure L. The volume of an irregularly shaped object is most easily determined using indirect methods.

The instructor may elect to substitute acetone if he or she performs this activity as a demonstration. *Acetone is a volatile, toxic solvent and should be handled in a fume hood or outdoors.* It is available through scientific supply companies, and is the principal component of some brands of fingernail polish remover. The reduction in volume accompanying the mixing of acetone and water or isopropyl alcohol and water is about 4%. The reduction in volume can be felt if you plug the end of the buret with your thumb. As the liquids mix, a partial vacuum will develop and your thumb will stick to the tube. The reduction in volume accompanying the mixing of two different liquids may be understood as a packing phenomenon. Fill a graduate cylinder to the 50 mL mark with dry peas. Fill another graduated cylinder to 50 mL mark with copper B-B shot. Now mix the two in a beaker and then pour them into a 100 mL cylinder and note that the total volume is less than 100 mL due to the fact that some of the B-Bs settled between the larger peas. (Figure MM)

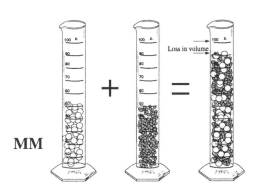

MM

Answers: (1) (a) 1 dm³ = 1000 cm³   (b) 1 mL = 1 cm³   (c) 100,000 mL = 100 L   (d) 1 m³ = 1,000,000 cm³   2 km³ = 2 × 10¹⁸ mm³. (2) Use a dropper and count the number of drops required to fill a 10 mL graduated cylinder to the 1-mL mark, being careful to observe the meniscus correctly. To find the volume of one drop, divide 1 mL by the number of drops. For example, if 20 drops are required, the volume of a drop is 1 mL/20 = 0.05 mL. (3) (a) volume of beaker = 283 mL; (b) 1.083 × 10¹² km³; (c) 76.4 cm³; (d) 0.67m³. (4) The final volume of the water/alcohol mixture is less than 200 mL because the smaller water molecules fill some of the spaces among the larger alcohol molecules. Ask students to make a drawing of the water and alcohol molecules in the cylinder.

1.3.4 MEASURING MASS

Discussion: Although students can measure mass more accurately using a professional balance than a home-made one, the process of constructing this measurement tool demystifies the measurement process and gives them a deeper understanding of the concepts involved. We encourage you to analyze class data whenever possible. This helps students understand that scientific inquiry is based on repeated investigation rather than single observations, and gives them a better understanding of data analysis.

Answers: (1) Leonid Taraneko lifted 475.0 kg, which was 1046 pounds (4655 N) on Earth and only 174.4 pounds (775.8 N) on the Moon, and approximately 0 pounds (0 N) in deep space. (2) A spring balance responds to force. The greater the force (in this case gravity), the greater the deformation of the spring and the higher the resulting measurement of weight. When using a double pan balance, both pans are subject to the same gravitational field and so the objects will balance only when their weights are identical. (3) The double pan balance would accurately measure mass on Mars, but not in deep space because of the absence of force on either pan.

Table 15: Mass and Weight

	Earth	*Deep Space*	*Moon*
Mass	475.0 kg	475.0 kg	475.0 kg
Weight (pounds)	1047 lb	0 lb	174.3 lb
Weight (newtons)	4655 N	0 N	775.8 N

1.3.5 DENSITY OF SOLIDS

Discussion: You may wish to introduce the concept of density by holding a piece of pumice (a low density volcanic rock) and a piece of ebony (a dark brown or black wood used to make black piano keys) above an aquarium or other water-filled container. When questioned, students will generally predict that the rock will sink and the wood will float. Pumice, however, is filled with air chambers and has a density lower than water and thus floats. By contrast, the density of ebony is greater than water and thus it sinks. These simple demonstrations may help pique student interest in the concept of density.

Part 1: Originally, U.S. pennies were made of approximately 95% copper and 5% zinc. Because of the soaring cost of copper, Congress authorized a change in the composition of the penny to 99.2% zinc and 0.8% copper. Thus, pre-1982 pennies have a mass of approximately 3.1 grams and a density close to that of copper, while post-1982 pennies have a mass of 2.5 grams and a density close to that of zinc. Post-1982 pennies are electroplated with copper to appear the same as before. If you take a metal file and score the surface of a post-1982 penny, you will note the silvery color of zinc beneath the surface. If you were to place such scored pennies in hydrochloric acid, the acid will erode the zinc core leaving a very thin copper shell.

$$Zn + 2HCl \longrightarrow ZnCl_2 + H_2$$

Hydrogen bubbles can be observed wherever the hydrochloric acid contacts the zinc. By soaking the penny with water after such a treatment, you would avoid contacting the acid with your skin.

Part 2: Students generally enjoy trying to determine the identity of unknown substances because of the element of mystery. Many metals are available as "shot" (small spheres) and such form serves well for density determinations. For unknown metals, you may choose coins (U.S. and foreign), sections of metal pipe, nails, tacks, ball bearings, etc.

Answers (1) Intrinsic properties such as density remain constant, regardless of the quantity of substance analyzed. The intrinsic properties of a gram of substance are the same as they are for a kilogram. Extrinsic properties, however, are dependent upon the extent (amount) present. Thus, a gram of a substance would have very different properties (mass, energy content, etc.) than a kilogram of the same substance. (2) Density increases with increasing atomic number within a given family of the periodic table. (3) Post-1982 pennies are considerably denser than pre-1982 pennies, suggesting that the U.S. Mint substituted a less dense metal (zinc) for copper in the center of the coin.

1.3.6 DENSITY OF LIQUIDS

Discussion: You may wish to introduce this section with the following two discrepant events.

Teacher Demonstration 1: Floating and sinking ice: Fill one beaker with water (1.00 g/mL), and another with isopropyl alcohol (0.79 g/mL) and place them on the desk without telling students their contents. Place an ice cube in each. The ice cube (0.92 g/mL) will sink in the alcohol, but will float in the water (Figure NN). Since both liquids are colorless, students may initially assume that they are both water and may be surprised to see the difference between the two beakers. You may then ask them to hypothesize about what could have caused the difference in behavior of the cubes. Water is unusual in that its solid phase (ice) is less dense than its liquid phase. You may contrast the behavior of solid and liquid water with solid and liquid paraffin (Figure OO). Heat paraffin until it melts, and then place a chunk of solid paraffin in the solution and students will observe it sink, indicating that paraffin is indeed denser as a solid than as a liquid.

Teacher Demonstration 2: A dynamic density gradient: Fill a beaker one fourth full with Karo® Syrup or other similar corn syrup. Slowly add vegetable oil on top until the beaker is three quarters full of liquid. Be careful not to mix the corn syrup and vegetable oil! Place a colored ice cube (add food coloring before freezing) on top of the oil. Ice is less dense than vegetable oil, so it floats. Liquid water, however, is denser than vegetable oil, but not as dense

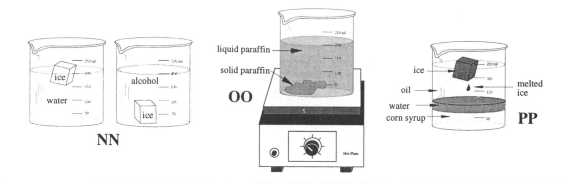

as corn syrup. As the ice cube melts, colored droplets of water fall through the oil layer and land on the syrup layer, creating yet another layer in the density gradient (Figure PP)!

Part 1: Density gradient: The densities of the six liquids are as follows:

isopropyl alcohol (colorless) (0.79 g/mL)   detergent (green) (1.04 g/mL)

vegetable oil (yellow) (0.90 g/mL)   glycerol (colorless) (1.26 g/mL)

water (colorless) (1.00 g/mL)   corn syrup (brown) (1.37 g/mL)

These liquids were selected because they are relatively safe household products that the students can relate to. Many older texts suggest a density gradient of mercury, dichloroether, water and oil. Although such a gradient is more dramatic and more stable (the fluids are mutually immiscible), we believe that the hazard of mercury and dichloroether is too great and should be avoided in the secondary school classroom.

Part 2: The effect of temperature on density: Although it is relatively easy to balance two similar flasks on top of one another as required in this lab, you may wish to do this as a teacher demonstration rather than a student activity due to the potential for spilling. At higher temperatures, molecules move faster, collide harder, move farther apart, and therefore occupy more space for the same amount of mass. Thus, the density (mass to volume ratio) of a fluid is generally inversely related to its temperature. Warm water is less dense than cool water (except at temperatures between 0°C and 4°C where the warmer water is denser), and will remain on top if placed there initially. The thermocline (plane between the warm and cool water) will be visible from the back of the class if you have used different food coloring as suggested. If the cool water is placed on top, it will descend rapidly as the warm water ascends. A purple color will rapidly develop indicating a mixing of the warm red water and cold blue water.

Answers: (1) Mercury is the densest and would occupy the bottom of the column. Water is the least dense and would rest upon the syrup which would be in the middle. The pine block (0.8 g/mL) would float on top of the water phase (1.0 g/mL), while the ebony wood (1.2 g/mL) would sink to the top of the syrup phase (1.4 g/mL). The copper coin (8.9 g/mL) and lead fishing weight (11.4 g/mL) would sink through the syrup and rest on the mercury (13.6 g/mL) while the gold ring (19.3 g/mL) would sink all the way to the bottom. (2) The purple color was of intermediate temperature because it formed from a mixing of the warm red water and the cool blue water. (3) Cold water is denser than warm water. The sun heats the surface of a lake or the ocean, and as the water warms, it becomes less dense and continues to float on the top. As you dive down, you cross a thermocline into colder, denser water that has received less of the sun's warming rays. (4) During cold weather, the surface waters cool more than the deeper waters. The cooler, denser surface waters sink and are replaced by warmer waters from the deep that bring nutrients back to the surface as they rise. (5) The radiator with a specific gravity of 0.976 has more anti-freeze than the one with a specific gravity of 0.976, and thus will freeze at a lower temperature.

1.3.7 DENSITY OF SOLUTIONS

Discussion: Archimedes' principle states that an object will float if the buoyant force (the weight of the fluid displaced) exceeds the force of gravity upon it (the weight of the object). A can of regular soft drink contains approximately 40 grams of sugar, which increases the density of the fluid contents by approximately 10%. Since the weight of the can and fluid exceeds the weight of water it displaces, the can sinks. Most diet soft drinks contain an artificial sweetener known as aspartame, a substance that is about 200 times as sweet as sugar. Since aspartamine is extremely sweet, only tiny amounts are added to diet soft drinks, and the resulting increase in density is negligible. Students may wonder how the diet drink can float since it must be slightly denser than water because it has some dissolved solutes (sodium, asmpartamine), and the aluminum is surely denser than water. It can float because soft drinks are always packed with a little extra space to prevent them from spilling when opened. Since this space is filled with air and carbon dioxide, the density of the closed container is sufficiently reduced so that it will float in water. Ask your students if it is possible to raise the can of soft drink to the surface without touching it. After some discussion of possible techniques, add salt or sugar to the water and stir to dissolve. When sufficient salt or sugar has been added, the can will rise to the surface because the weight of the salt solution it displaces now is greater than its own weight.

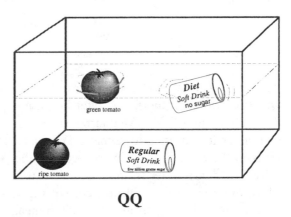

QQ

Answers: (1) Sugars are produced when a fruit ripens, increasing the density of the fruit. Therefore, the ripe tomatoes sink, while the green tomatoes float (Figure QQ). (2) A variety of machines may be proposed, but the simplest will probably be one that places tomatoes in a vat of water and then "drains off" the denser, ripe tomatoes, or "scoops off" the less dense, green tomatoes. (3) Regular soft drinks have greater density due the presence of dissolved sugar. Far less aspartamine (artificial sweetener) is added in diet drinks than sugar in regular drinks because aspartamine is approximately 200 times as sweet. (4) Most regular soft drinks will list total carbohydrates (basically sugar) and sodium. Sugar is the solute that explains the higher density of regular soft drinks. (5) Student values will vary depending upon the soft drinks used. Diet soft drinks may have a density of approximately 1.05 g/mL, while regular soft drinks a density of 1.08 g/mL. Students may be surprised to see that the diet soft drink floats even though it has a density greater than that of water. Remind them that the density of the entire can of diet soft drink (can, soft drink and trapped gasses) will be less than 1.00 g/mL (the density of water) due to undisolved gaseous carbon dioxide trapped inside the can. In other words, the can is not completely full of soft drink, but rather contains a small amount of gas that decreases the density of the system.

1.3.8 DENSITY OF SOLUTIONS: THE MYSTERY OF THE STRAIT OF GIBRALTAR

Discussion: An interesting discrepant event is to "suspend" an egg in the middle of a beaker as shown in Figure RR. Although it is possible to produce a solution which has a density identical to the egg, this is very difficult. It is easier to make two layers of solution by placing a very concentrated solution at the bottom of a beaker and fresh water at the top. (Add the fresh water as slowly as possible so as to not disturb the salty layer). If you slowly release the egg in the beaker, it will sink through the fresh water layer and come to rest on the dense, saline layer. The egg will stay suspended this way for hours. Don't tell your students how you were able to suspend the egg, and challenge them to suspend an egg as you have done. You may wish to challenge your students to calculate the density of each solution used.

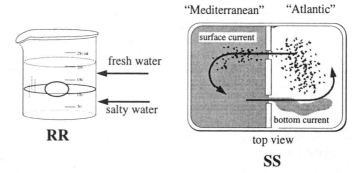

Answers: (1) Salt water is denser than fresh water because of the dissolved salt. (2) Boats will float lower in the fresh water because it provides less buoyant force (it is less dense) than salt water. (3) The Mediterranean Sea is saltier than the Atlantic due to large evaporative water loss in its arid climate. This water is denser than the water of the Atlantic, so it sinks to the bottom when in contact with the Atlantic waters at the Strait of Gibraltar. Less salty, less dense water from the Atlantic rushes in to replace the saltier water that is exiting. Thus, there is a strong surface current flowing into the Mediterranean, and another strong deep current flowing from the Mediterranean to the Atlantic. Figure SS illustrates the current that is generated in this activity to simulate what happens at the Straight of Gibraltar. Early travelers were unaware of the deep current and were therefore perplexed by this constant current into the Mediterranean. (4) Halophytes tend to live deeper in the water because the fresh water from the river is less dense and tends to float on top of the denser, saltier water. (5) The salt water is denser than the oil, and it sinks to the bottom, buoying the oil to the surface.

1.3.9 DENSITY OF GASES

Discussion: Teacher demonstration 1: Methane bubbles. *Note: This demonstration should be performed only in a very well ventilated environment where there is no potential for methane build-up. Wear protective eyeware and clothing and make sure that students are at least 10 feet from the demonstration table. Make sure that there is nothing flammable near the methane bubbles.*

Methane (natural gas, CH_4) has a lower molecular weight (16 g/mole) than either nitrogen (N_2, 28 g/mole) or oxygen (O_2, 32 g/mole), the two principal components in air. Since it has a lower molecular weight, it will have a lower density and consequently will rise in air. It is easy to show that methane is less dense than air by making methane bubbles and watching them rise.

Make a bubble solution by mixing dishwashing liquid (Dawn® works well) with water and a small amount of glycerin. We recommend the following ratio, but optimal ratios may vary from detergent to detergent: one liter of water; 50 milliliters of dishwashing liquid (Dawn®); 3 milliliters of glycerin. Let the bubble solution age for a day or more.

Use tape to attach a candle to the end of a long stick. Attach one end of the gas hose to a gas jet, and the other to a small funnel. Place the funnel in the soap solution and regulate the gas jet so methane bubbles form. Hold the funnel in a horizontal position as shown in Figure TT. Gas bubbles will form, automatically release from the funnel and drift upwards toward the ceiling. Light the bubbles before they hit the ceiling (Figure UU). There will be a brief flame (no explosion) as the methane burns. This demonstration is very dramatic when done in a darkened room.

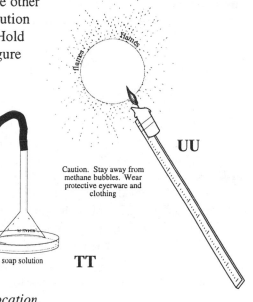

Caution. Stay away from methane bubbles. Wear protective eyerware and clothing

UU

soap solution   **TT**

Teacher demonstration 2: Hydrogen and carbon dioxide balloons. *Caution: Concentrated sulfuric acid should be handled with extreme caution. Wear protective eyeware and clothing, and perform in a fume hood or other well-ventilated location.*

Clamp an Erlenmeyer flask in place as illustrated in Figure VV and place approximately 25 grams of zinc in the flask and stopper it securely. Carefully add 150 mL of dilute sulfuric acid. You may wish to add a few drops of copper(II) sulfate solution to the generator if the gas is evolved slowly. Place a balloon over the lip of the flask. Hydrogen gas will be produced according to the following equation:

$$Zn + H_2SO_4 \longrightarrow ZnSO_4 + H_2(g)$$

Hydrogen has a molecular weight of 2 grams/mole (density of 0.09 g/mL), and is much less dense than either

H_2

VV

$$Zn + H_2SO_4 \longrightarrow ZnSO_4 + H_2(g)$$

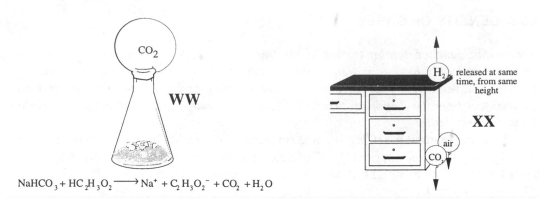

$$NaHCO_3 + HC_2H_3O_2 \longrightarrow Na^+ + C_2H_3O_2^- + CO_2 + H_2O$$

nitrogen (28 g/mole; 1.25 g/mL) or oxygen (32 g/mole; 1.43 g/mL), the two main components of air. The balloon will fill with hydrogen as well as the air displaced from the flask by the hydrogen that is being produced. Because of the presence of hydrogen, the density of the balloon will be significantly less than air, and it will rise toward the ceiling. You may wish to tie the balloon to a string and then ignite it with a candle taped to a meter stick (*Use Caution!*). The balloon will explode with a loud report because the balloon contains both hydrogen and oxygen:

$$2H_2 + O_2 \longrightarrow H_2O$$

You may wish to compare the explosion of this balloon with the flame of the methane bubble. The methane bubble contains virtually no oxygen, and thus can burn only at the interface between the methane and the air, whereas the hydrogen can burn throughout because it contains a mixture of hydrogen and oxygen. You may use this demonstration to introduce the principle of carburetion in an internal combustion engine, or the Hindenburg disaster of 1937, when the world's largest hydrogen-filled dirigible burst into flames apparently following a leak and a mixing of hydrogen and oxygen.

While hydrogen has a density lower than air, carbon dioxide (*MW* 44 g/mole) has a higher density. You may fill a balloon with carbon dioxide by placing it over a flask in which you have mixed baking soda (sodium hydrogen carbonate) and vinegar (acetic acid). The resulting reaction produces carbon dioxide and will fill the balloon (Figure WW).

$$NaHCO_3 + HC_2H_3O_2 \longrightarrow Na^+ + C_2H_3O_2^- + CO_2 + H_2O$$

Fill one balloon with air (by exhaling), another with hydrogen, and a third with carbon dioxide. Label each clearly and then let them go from the same height at the same time (Figure XX). The hydrogen-filled balloon will rise to the ceiling, the air balloon will drop slowly to the ground (because of the added weight of the balloon), and carbon dioxide balloon will drop rapidly to the ground.

Teacher Demonstration 3: Determining the density of a gas. You may wish to show your class how to determine the density of air. Evacuate a round-bottom vacuum flask using a vacuum pump. *Caution: Do not use other flasks that are not designed for this purpose!* Place the evacuated flask on a balance and determine its mass. Let air into the flask and determine the mass again. The mass of the air is the difference between the two masses. The volume of the flask can be determined by filling it with water to the level of the stopper, and then pouring the water into a graduated cylinder and measuring it. The approximate (vacuum pumps will not remove all of the air) density of air may then be calculated by dividing mass by volume.

Answers: (1) Lake Nyos is in a crater, and carbon dioxide, being denser than air, collected in the crater where the inhabitants lived. The atmosphere normally contains 0.03% carbon dioxide, and when levels of carbon dioxide exceed 10%, humans can no longer survive. Because carbon dioxide is denser than air, it collected in the crater. (2) Nitrogen (N_2, $MW =$ 28 g/mole) and oxygen (O_2, $MW = 32$ g/mole) both have lower molecular weights than carbon dioxide (CO_2, $MW = 44$ g/mole). Unlike liquids and solids, most of a gas is empty space. Thus, the critical factor determining the space occupied by a gaseous molecules is not their size, but rather their speed. At the same temperature, all gaseous molecules occupy roughly the same space. This is why we can say that all gases have essentially the same molar volume at STP. Since the molecular weight of carbon dioxide exceeds that of the two principal components of air, we would expect it to have a greater density than air, since there is more mass (which is a function of molecular weight) per unit volume (which is independent of the type of gas). (3) Always make certain there is adequate ventilation to drain off the carbon dioxide. Neither humans nor animals should rest at the bottom of an enclosed area containing carbon dioxide. (4) Carbon dioxide is denser than air and sinks to the ground, smothering ground fires. Unfortunately, it has little effect on ceiling fires. (5) Halon is denser than air. Halon 1301 (bromotrifluoromethane, $CBrF_3$) has a molecular weight of 147 g/mole, and thus it must have a density much greater than air.

Applications to Everyday Life

Why measure?: You make measurements on a daily basis to determine such things as the distance traveled during a vacation, the amount of grass seed required to plant a lawn, the volume of milk required for a recipe, the temperature necessary to bake bread, the amount of carpet required to cover a floor, the time required to complete a task or the weight lost on a diet. Without measurement, people could not build houses, design clothes that fit, follow favorite recipes, design automobiles, judge sporting competitions or build spacecraft to explore our solar system.

Cooking: The *Boston Cooking School Cook Book,* written by Fannie Farmer in 1896, had a profound influence on the development of cooking in the English speaking world. Farmer's book was the first major publication to provide recipes with precise measurements of ingredients using standardized utensils such as the teaspoon and cup. Her inclusion of specific measurements of ingredients enabled even novice cooks to follow recipes and prepare excellent meals. Today, many cooking utensils are graduated in metric and Customary units to facilitate accurate measurement of ingredients.

Medicine/pharmacy: Given the appropriate dosage, aspirin may help relieve minor aches and pains associated with headaches, colds and the flu. Too small a dosage is ineffective, while too large a dosage may cause gastrointestinal problems, internal bleeding, and even death. Pharmaceutical researchers must make careful measurements to determine recommended dosages for all medications, and physicians, pharmacists and consumers must make careful measurements to implement these recommendations and achieve optimal results.

Anesthesiology: A general anesthetic affects the brain and renders the patient unconscious and insensible to pain and stimulation by surgical procedures. Unfortunately, all anesthetics are poisonous in excessive dosages, and on occasion, certain anesthesiologists have made inaccurate measurements and administered harmful or fatal dosages.

Separation of metal ore by density: Miners and metallurgists use density differences to separate ore from rock. The density of coal varies from about 1.1–1.5 grams/milliliter, while most of the rock in which it is found has a density greater than 1.5. Coal is extracted from the rock by crushing the ore and then placing it in a high-density liquid so that the coal floats while the crushed rock sinks.

Winds and ocean currents: Currents occur in liquids or gases where there are horizontal or vertical differences in density. Denser fluids move down under the force of gravity, buoying up less dense materials. Differences in density may arise from differences in salinity, temperature or turbidity (sediments). Density differences are responsible for currents in the ocean and winds in the atmosphere.

Structure of the Earth: The Earth has a series of continents and ocean basins. Geologists believe that the continents are higher (above water) because they are composed of lower density rock that floats higher on the mantle than does the higher density rock that underlies the oceanic basins.

UNIT TWO

Matter

2.1 ATOMIC STRUCTURE

A massive iron girder and a lead fishing sinker are mostly empty space! There is so much empty space in even such "dense" objects that under the extreme pressures that exist at the center of our Sun, a girder would be compressed to the size of a small wire and a fishing sinker to a ball with a diameter smaller than the period at the end of this sentence. How can something as dense as iron or lead contain so much empty space?

Iron and lead are forms of matter. Matter is anything that has mass and occupies space, but how is it composed? The Greek philosopher Aristotle believed that matter was continuous and could be divided indefinitely without changing its intrinsic properties, while another 4th century BC philosopher, Democritus, believed that matter was ultimately composed of tiny, discrete, indivisible particles (atoms; coming from the Greek word meaning indivisible). Whose model of matter was correct?

Approximately 2000 years later, an English school teacher named John Dalton developed a model of the nature of matter that explained a wide variety of experimental findings, such as the previously discovered laws of mass conservation and definite proportions. Dalton's atomic theory was based on Democritus' ideas, but went much further. Dalton stated that: (1) all matter is composed of extremely small particles called atoms; (2) atoms of one element are identical in size, mass, and chemical properties; (3) the atoms of a given element are different from the atoms of all other elements; (4) atoms cannot be subdivided or destroyed; (5) in chemical reactions, atoms are combined, separated, or rearranged and (6) atoms of different elements can combine to form compounds in which the ratio of the number of atoms of any two of the elements is an integer or simple fraction. It is important to understand that Dalton never saw an atom! He had no idea that an atom has a nucleus composed of protons and neutrons, and that electrons orbit the nucleus. Dalton proposed his atomic theory based solely on macroscopic observations (phenomena large enough to be observed by the human eye)!

Today we understand that Dalton was correct in his belief that elements are composed of atoms that enter into chemical combination with each other, but was incorrect in his assumption that atoms are indivisible. We now know that an atom is made up of nuclei containing protons and neutrons that are surrounded by much empty space in which tiny electrons exist. The electrons may be separated from their nuclei, and nuclei split or fused. To understand chemistry, it is essential to understand the structure of the atom.

In 1897, the English physicist Joseph John Thomson confirmed the existence of the electron, a fundamental particle that has a negative charge. Thomson believed that an atom was a uniform, sphere of positive matter in which the negative electrons were embedded, somewhat like raisins in a bowl of pudding (Figure A). Later, Ernest Rutherford showed that Thomson's model was incorrect. Rutherford bombarded thin foils of gold with positively charged alpha (α) particles (helium nuclei). If the "pudding model" were correct, all the al-

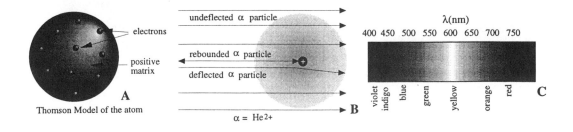

Table 1: Characteristics of the Fundamental Particles

Particle	Mass (g)	Charge (C)	Electric Charge
Proton	1.673×10^{-24}	$+1.602 \times 10^{-19}$	$+1$
Neutron	1.675×10^{-24}	0	0
Electron	9.109×10^{-28}	-1.602×10^{-19}	-1

pha particles should have passed through the pudding with little interference because the negative and positive charges in the pudding would have been diffuse and evenly distributed. However, some of the alpha particles were deflected at a large angle and some even rebounded in the direction from which they had come. Clearly, the "pudding model" could not account for these findings. Rutherford proposed a model suggesting that an atom is mostly empty space with a proton-containing nucleus at its center. Positively charged protons concentrated in this nucleus can account for the wide scattering of the incoming positively charged alpha particles in Rutherford's experiments (like charges repel; Figure B). Rutherford's careful measurements of the scattering of α particles indicated that only about half of the atomic mass of the nucleus could be accounted for by protons. He suggested that there must be another particle in the nucleus, electrically neutral, with a mass nearly equal to that of a proton. His conjecture was verified by J. Chadwick who bombarded beryllium with α particles and found that highly energetic, uncharged particles were emitted. These particles, which are called neutrons, have a mass only slightly larger than that of a proton. Some properties of the three major subatomic particles are shown in the Table 1.

When solids, liquids, and gases under high pressure are heated, they release a continuous spectrum of light as shown in Figure C. The visible region (visible to the human eye) ranges from wavelengths of 400 nm (violet) to 700 nm (red). In contrast, fluorescent, or electrically excited gases under low pressure produce bright line spectra as shown in Figure D, indicating that energy is emitted only at specific wavelengths. Each line in the spectrum corresponds to a particular frequency of light emitted by the atoms. It is now known that each element has a unique emission spectrum. Compare the positions of the bright lines for each element, and you can see that every element produces a unique spectrum that can be used to identify that element, much as a fingerprint may be used to identify a person.

On the basis of this data, the German physicist Max Planck proposed that atoms and

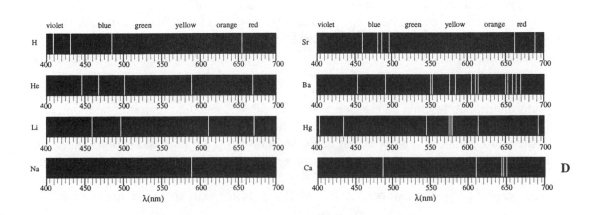

molecules cannot absorb or emit any arbitrary amount of radiant energy, but instead can absorb or emit radiant energy only in discrete (specific) quantities. The name quantum was given to the smallest quantity (bundle) of energy that can be absorbed or emitted as electromagnetic radiation. Albert Einstein explained the photoelectric effect, in which light striking metals eject electrons, using Planck's ideas. If the frequency of the impinging light is below what is called the threshold frequency, no electrons are ejected no matter how intense the light. A very intense light with too low a frequency could shine on a metal forever without causing the photoelectric effect. While wave theory could not account for the photoelectric effect, particle theory could. In explaining the photoelectric effect, Einstein suggested that light was a stream of particles which he called photons. He conjectured that each photon possesses energy E as indicated by the following equation: $E = h\nu$, where E is energy, ν is the frequency of the light, and h is Planck's constant. If the frequency of photons is such that $h\nu$ is equal to the binding energy of the electrons in the metal, then the light will have just enough energy to knock the electrons loose. Light of a higher energy will knock the electrons loose and will impart to them some kinetic energy.

In 1913 Niels Bohr (1885–1962) was able to explain the hydrogen-atom line spectrum (Figure D) by hypothesizing that the single electron of the hydrogen atom can circle the nucleus only in allowed paths (orbits). An electron in any of these orbits has a definite (fixed) amount of energy. The energy is said to be quantized. Thus a line spectrum is produced when an electron drops from a higher-energy orbit to a lower-energy orbit because as the electron drops, a photon is emitted that has an energy equal to the difference in energy between the initial higher energy orbit and the final lower energy orbit. Likewise, to move an electron from a lower energy orbit to one of higher energy requires that the electron absorb a fixed amount of energy. Bohr thought that electrons orbit the nucleus in definite paths, and thus it should be possible to determine the exact velocity and position of the electron at any given time.

To further explain the emerging quantum model of the atom, French chemist Louis de Broglie proposed that, like light, electrons also exhibit a wave-particle nature. Bohr's quantized electron orbits were consistent with known wave behavior. Standing waves have only certain frequencies. Consequently, if electrons are considered as waves confined in a given space around a nucleus, this would explain why only certain frequencies and energies are possible.

The Swiss physicist Erwin Schrödinger was intrigued by the work of de Broglie, and in 1926 formulated the now famous Schrödinger wave equation to describe the nature of electron waves. Whereas Bohr's model described definite orbits occupied by electrons, Schrödinger's model describes general orbital clouds in which electrons may be found. Schrödinger's idea that the location of an electron cannot be "pinpointed" in a specific orbit but only approximated in a general orbital cloud was consistent with the uncertainty principle (some properties of atoms and their particles can be determined simultaneously only to within a certain degree of accuracy) developed by Werner Heisenberg in 1927. An electron orbital describes a region of space around the nucleus in which an electron is most likely to be found, and can be considered as the wave function of an electron in an atom. Electron density gives the probability that an electron will be found in a specified region of an atom.

Schrödinger's equation suggests that an atomic orbital can be described by a series of three "quantum numbers": the principal quantum number *(n)*, angular momentum quantum number *(l),* and the magnetic quantum number *(m_l)*. These numbers indicate the region occupied by a given orbital in terms of distance from the nucleus, orbital shape, and orbital position with respect to the three-dimensional x, y, z axes. In addition, there is a fourth quantum number called the spin quantum number (m_s). The spin quantum number reflects the fact that each electron spins either "clockwise" or "counter-clockwise," creating a tiny magnetic field akin to that of a bar magnet.

Each electron in an atom can be assigned a set of values for its four quantum numbers, n, l, m_l, and m_s, that determine the orbital in which the electron will be found (n, l, m_l) and the direction in which the electron will be spinning (m_s)—that is, these four quantum numbers provide the "address" and direction of spin for any electron in an atom. Just as no two telephones, homes or Internet servers may have the same address, so no two electrons in an atom may have the exact same quantum address. The Austrian theoretical physicist Wolfgang Pauli expressed this principle in his famous Pauli exclusion principle, which states that no two electrons in an atom can have the same four quantum numbers. Knowledge of the four quantum numbers will help you decide the electronic configuration (arrangement of electrons) in a given atom.

The *principal quantum number (n)* indicates the main energy levels surrounding the nucleus of an atom. These levels are often referred to as *shells* (a shell is a collection of orbitals) and are roughly equivalent to the Bohr orbits. Values of n can have only integral values such as 1,2,3,4, etc. The larger the value of n, the greater the average distance of an electron in an orbital from the nucleus and, consequently, the larger and less stable the orbital. Orbitals of the same principal quantum number belong to the same shell. In the past, shells were often referred to by the following capital letters: K = 1, L = 2, M = 3, and N = 4.

The *angular momentum quantum number (l)* indicates the shape of an orbital. Within each main energy level beyond the first, orbitals with different shapes occupy different regions in space. These regions are referred to as *sublevels* or *subshells*. The number of subshells (possible orbital shapes) in each main energy level is equal to the principal quantum number n. Although the energy of an orbital is mainly determined by the n quantum number, the energy also depends somewhat on the l quantum number. Orbitals with the same n but different l belong to different subshells and are denoted by the letters s, p, d, and f. These letters

Table 2: Quantum Number Relationships

Shell Principal Quantum Number (n)	Sublevels (Orbital Shapes)	Orbitals per Sublevel	Orbitals per Principal Quantum Number = n^2	Electrons per Sublevel	Electrons per Principal Quantum Number = $2n^2$
1	s	1	1	2	2
2	s	1	4	2	8
	p	3		6	
3	s	1	9	2	18
	p	3		6	
	d	5		10	
4	s	1	16	2	32
	p	3		6	
	d	5		10	
	f	7		14	

were derived from earlier studies in spectroscopy terminology describing the lines in a spectrum with which they are associated: s stands for sharp, p for principal, d for diffuse, and f for fundamental.

The *magnetic quantum number (m_l)* describes the orientation of an orbital in space about the nucleus. The number of orientations for any given magnetic quantum number is two times the angular quantum number plus one. Table 2 shows the relationship between principal quantum number, angular momentum quantum number, and magnetic quantum number.

If you play the sleuth and examine this table carefully, noting that *n* stands for the number of the principal quantum number, you can discover some important relationships. Notice that the number of sublevels (orbital shapes) for each principal quantum number is equal to the principal quantum number. The total number of orbitals for a principal quantum number is equal to the square of the principal quantum number.

The wave-particle model is certainly not intuitive, but it has withstood many experimental tests. Discoveries concerning the nature of light (one kind of electromagnetic radiation) have led to a revolutionary view of nature and the atom. You will learn that light and electrons in atoms have some properties in common. To understand the wave-particle model, you must understand the nature of waves.

How can we know about things we can't see such as atoms and electrons? You will have an opportunity to perform activities in this chapter that will allow you to determine what something might look like without your actually seeing it. We can often determine the makeup of something based on its interaction with, or effect on, something else. Such indirect analysis is a very important method of scientific investigation.

2.1.1 ATOMS ARE MOSTLY EMPTY SPACE

Concepts to Investigate: Atom, nucleus, electron, indirect analysis, Rutherford experiment.

Materials: Pegboard (at least 25 holes spaced in a square grid, approximately 3 cm apart), 3 or more pegs to fit holes, board to cover pegboard so pegs cannot be seen, marbles with a diameter less than the height of the pegs and less than the distance between the pegs in the board.

Principles and Procedures: Thomson's model of the atom, sometimes noted as the "plum pudding" model (Figure A in 2.1), depicted electrons embedded in a uniform, positively charged sphere. In this model, the positive and negative charges were evenly distributed in space. Consequently, a particle with positive charge traveling through the space occupied by the negative and positive charges would be traveling through a "neutral zone" because the effects of the positive and negative charges would cancel and the particle would experience no unbalanced force to move it one way or another. In other words, a positive particle should move straight through the "plum pudding" model, experiencing no deflection.

Ernest Rutherford investigated the structure of the atom by shooting alpha particles (positively charged helium ions; helium nuclei) through very thin foils of gold and other metals. Most of the incoming alpha particles passed through the foil either undeflected or with only a slight deflection, as would be predicted by the Thomson model. However, there were some startling occurrences in which the alpha particles were deflected at large angles and, at times, right back in the direction from which they had come! (Figure B). Rutherford explained these results by proposing that the atom is: (a) mostly empty space (which explains why most of the alpha particles pass through undeflected) with (b) positive charges concentrated in a dense central core (which explains why positively charged alpha particles are occasionally deflected or reflected).

Rutherford never saw an atom. He inferred the structure of an atom by the interaction of the atom with incoming charged particles. This is a case of indirect measurement. You can gain a sound understanding of the idea of indirect measurement by carefully performing the following activity.

Work in pairs. Obtain three pegs and a pegboard that has at least five holes on a side (minimum of 25 holes per board, approximately 3 cm apart). Wooden pegs may be made by cutting and sanding dowels that have a diameter similar to the holes in the pegboard. The pegs should be long enough that the marbles can freely move under the apparatus when set up as shown in Figure F. While one of the pair is not observing, the other places three pegs randomly in pegboard holes (Figure E). Turn the board over and place it on a flat surface so it rests on the pegs with one partner holding the board so it remains level (Figure F). Place a sheet of graph paper, the coordinates of which match the position of holes in the pegboard, on top of the board (Figure G). One partner rolls marbles under the pegboard at selected intervals and records the original path of the marble and any resulting deflections on the graph paper. To ensure that marbles travel straight, launch them between two straight edges (Figure G). Repeat this for each side of the pegboard. If the ball is deflected, then it indicates that there is a peg in that row or column. Analyze the results and use these to identify the positions of the pegs. Repeat the procedure until you can accurately determine the positions of all three pegs. This activity is analogous to Rutherford's experiment. What do the marbles represent? What do the pegs represent?

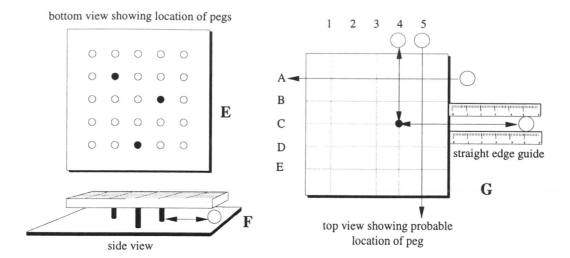

bottom view showing location of pegs

E

side view

F

straight edge guide

G

top view showing probable location of peg

Questions

(1) How does this activity use the concept of "indirect measurement?"

(2) Explain how you were able to locate the pegs by rolling the marble under the board. Relate this to Rutherford's use of alpha particles and gold foil.

(3) Would an increase in the number of pegs make it more difficult to determine the position of each of these pegs? Explain.

2.1.2 ATOMIC SPECTRA

Concepts to Investigate: Atoms, electrons, protons, continuous spectra, emission spectra, line spectra, spectroscope, flame test, element identification.

Materials: Part 1: small ball, staircase; Part 2: spectroscope, gas tubes, spectrum tubes of various gases, spectrum power supply, prism; Part 3: nichrome or platinum wire, burner, distilled water, barium chloride, calcium chloride, potassium chloride, lithium chloride, sodium chloride, strontium chloride (you may substitute nitrate salts of these metals); cobalt glass.

Safety: Carefully follow manufacturer's safety recommendations when using the high voltage spectrum tube power supply in part 2. Wear goggles and laboratory apron when performing the flame tests in part 3.

Principles and Procedures: If you shine a bright beam of light from the Sun or an incandescent light through a prism or diffraction grating, the incoming white light will be separated into a continuous spectrum of bright colors ranging from red to violet, with no gaps between any of the colors (Figure C). Likewise if you point a spectroscope at the blue sky (not directly at the Sun) or at an incandescent bulb, you will see a continuous spectrum of colors from red to violet. However, if you point your spectroscope at a fluorescent lamp, you may see a noncontinuous "line" spectra—bright lines of colored light with gaps in between (Figure D). The existence of such line spectra can not be explained by classical physics, which assumes that energy can be absorbed or emitted by an electron in any arbitrary quantity. Bright line emission spectra clearly indicate that electrons can absorb or emit energy only in specific quantities. This quantization of energy was difficult for scientists to understand and accept, but as experiments progressed and the evidence for the "quantum theory" mounted, the era of modern physics was eventually ushered in.

Every element has a unique line spectrum which can be used to identify that element (Figure D) much as a fingerprint or DNA sequence can be use to identify an individual. The lines in the spectrum indicate the energy of the light emitted. A simple spectroscope can be used to view the spectrum of any source of light. Some simple spectroscopes have a scale which indicates the wavelength of the light emitted. A source such as the Sun (never look directly at the Sun!) or an incandescent light will show a continuous spectrum. However, a source such as a fluorescent light commonly found in the home, mercury and sodium lamps commonly used to illuminate streets or neon signs that you see in store windows will show line spectra (Figure D). In this activity you will play detective to determine the luminous gases in various lamps.

Part I: Line spectra—Staircase analogy for the quantization of energy: You can visualize quantization of energy by observing the action of a ball as it ascends or descends a flight of stairs or a ramp. Find a flight of stairs that is not occupied. Place a ball at the top of the stairs and roll it gently toward the flight of stairs (Figure H). Observe the motion and intermittent resting points of the ball as it moves down the stairs. As it rolls, the ball may stop and remain on a given stair (energy level), but it never rests at any point between one stair and another. The potential energy of the ball will be converted to discreet values of kinetic energy proportional to the height of a given step. This is analogous to what happens as an electron falls from an excited state to a lower state (Figure I). Energy can be released only in discrete amounts as it moves from a higher-energy orbit to a lower-energy orbit.

Toss a small ball toward the top of the stairs with as little spin as possible. The ball may come to rest on top stair or some stair in between, but never at a point between one stair and an-

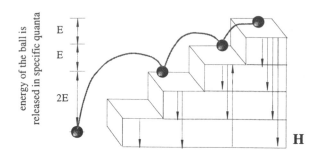

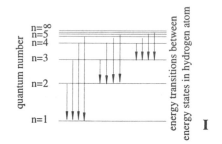

other. To throw the ball to the higher steps in the staircase, you must throw it harder, meaning that you must give it more energy. The ball may bounce from one stair down to the stair directly below, or it may bounce down to a stair located more than one step below. Whatever the case, only a discrete amount of energy will be required to throw the ball to any given step, and only a discrete amount of energy will be emitted (potential energy changed to kinetic energy) when the ball moves from any given step down to another step. The energy change (kinetic to potential) required to move the ball from one step to the next higher step is the same as the energy change (potential to kinetic) when the ball moves from the higher step to the lower.

Part 2: Line spectra of fluorescent tubes: *Caution: Only the instructor should change tubes in the high voltage spectrum tube power supply.*

Obtain a simple spectroscope from your teacher, preferably one that has a scale to show the magnitudes of the wavelengths of light. Point the spectroscope at an incandescent light bulb. Do you see a continuous spectrum with no gaps? Now point the spectroscope at a fluorescent lamp. You should see a distinct line spectra. (You will probably need to practice looking at slightly different angles until the bright lines are clearly visible). Compare the spectra you see with the those shown in Figure D and determine the contents of the lamp.

At night use your spectroscope to analyze the light emitted from those yellowish and bluish lamps often used to light streets, yards around homes, and businesses. Match up the main lines of the spectra emitted by these lamps with the emission spectra illustrated in Figure D. What vapor is used in the street lamps on your street?

Tubes filled with hydrogen, helium, argon, oxygen, mercury, neon and other gases emit distinctive colors when exposed to high voltage. Your instructor will cover up the names of the gases and place the tubes one at a time in a spectrum tube power supply (Figure J). Record the colors of these gases and try to match their bright line spectra with those in Figure D. List those gases that you were able to correctly identify on the basis of their bright line spectra.

Part 3: Flame tests: It is rather easy to excite the electrons of the group 1 and 2 elements (first and second column of the periodic table) by heating solutions containing these elements. Prepare approximately 0.5 M solutions (the concentrations are not critical) of barium chloride, calcium chloride, potassium chloride, lithium chloride, sodium chloride, and strontium chloride. Prepare an equal mixture of 0.5 M sodium chloride and 0.5 M potassium chloride. You may substitute nitrates of each of these metals if necessary. After *putting on goggles and a lab coat,* light a burner or propane torch and adjust for a non-luminous flame with a double cone. Fold the end of a nichrome or platinum wire into a ball and then tape the straight end to a wooden stick. Dip the end of the wire into dilute hydrochloric acid and then hold it in the burner until the wire imparts no color to the flame. If the wire imparts any color to the flame, it may mask the colors of the group 1 and 2 elements.

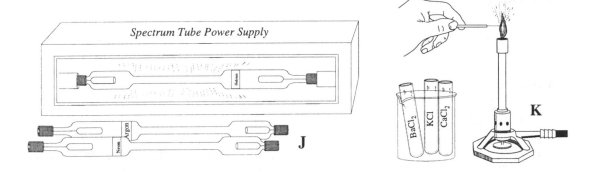

Place the end of the wire into a test tube containing a solution of one of the metal salts. Hold the wire just above the inner cone of the laboratory burner as shown in Figure K and note the color imparted to the flame: Record this color in Table 3. Repeat for all solutions. Perform those involving sodium chloride last.

When two group 1 or 2 elements are present, as in the solution of sodium chloride and potassium chloride, one bright color (yellow for sodium) may obscure another color (violet for potassium). View the flame for the sodium chloride-potassium chloride solution through a piece of cobalt glass (which will not transmit the yellow color of sodium) to observe the violet color of potassium.

Table 3: Flame Tests

Salt Solution	Ion	Flame Color
barium chloride ($BaCl_2$)	Ba^{2+}	
calcium chloride ($CaCl_2$)	Ca^{2+}	
potassium chloride (KCl)	K^+	
lithium chloride (LiCl)	Li^+	
strontium chloride ($SrCl_2$)	Sr^{2+}	
sodium chloride (NaCl)	Na^+	
sodium chloride (NaCl) and potassium chloride (KCl)	Na^+ and K^+	

Questions

(1) Compare and contrast continuous and line spectra.

(2) On the basis of your observations, which element is primarily used in standard fluorescent tubes? In the yellowish street lamps? In the bluish street lamps?

(3) Compare the flame color of sodium to the color you saw using the spectroscope when viewing a sodium vapor lamp.

(4) Line spectra may be used as "fingerprints" to identify the elements. Explain.

(5) If your spectroscope has a scale, give the wavelengths in nanometers of the lines you observed when you viewed a standard (room) fluorescent lamp.

(6) What colors are associated with barium, calcium, potassium, lithium, sodium, and strontium?

2.1.3 WAVE CHARACTERISITICS

Concepts to Investigate: Wavelength, amplitude, frequency, period, standing wave, nodes, antinodes, wave nature of electrons, de Broglie's equation.

Materials: Part 1: Small plastic or paper cup, string, sand or paint, nail, burner, tongs, tape, rolls of white paper about 30 cm wide; Part 2: wooden dowel (or rolling pin), rectangular pan; Part 3: wave demonstration spring or rope. Part 4: balloon.

Principles and Procedures: In the early 1900s, Albert Einstein showed that in certain situations light "waves" behave as particles. Although it is difficult to conceive how light can simultaneously be a wave and a particle (photon), much research suggests that this is the case! In the 1920s, the French physicist Louis de Broglie suggested that if waves had the properties of particles, then perhaps particles may have the properties of waves. De Broglie postulated that a particle of mass m and speed v has an associated wavelength according to the following equation:

$$\lambda = h/mv$$

where λ is the wavelength associated with the particle and h is Planck's constant (6.626×10^{-34} J·s). This equation shows that the wavelength of a particle is inversely related to its mass. According to this equation, if the mass of the particle is much greater than an atom, then the wavelength is too small to ever be detected. De Broglie's equation does suggest, however, that extremely small particles, such as electrons, will display significant wave characteristics. It is now widely accepted that electrons, like photons, have a dual wave-particle nature. In some experiments we see their wave characteristics, and in others, we see their particle characteristics. Although we can obviously not investigate the wave nature of electrons in a simple laboratory experiment, we can understand certain aspects of waves by examining some macroscopic examples.

Part 1: Picturing transverse waves: *Caution: Wear goggles whenever using an open flame.* Hold a nail with pliers in the flame of a burner, and then use the heated nail to melt one hole in the bottom of a plastic cup as well as two holes on opposite sides near the rim. Tie a string through the upper holes as shown in Figure L and cover the bottom hole with a piece of tape. Fill the cup with fine dark sand or dilute paint. Place a sheet of white paper under the cup. Uncover the hole, and swing the cup in a small arc. If the sand or paint does not leak fast enough to make an easily observable straight track on the sheet, increase the diameter of the hole until it does. The swinging cup is a pendulum, and if its arc (amplitude) is small, it will demonstrate simple harmonic motion.

Tie the cup to a support, unroll about one meter of paper, and position one end of the sheet perpendicular to the direction of the cup's swing. The middle of the sheet should be positioned directly under the resting cup. Pull the cup back to the edge of the paper, remove the tape from the hole, and allow the cup to swing as your partner slowly pulls the paper at constant speed in a direction perpendicular to the cup's swing as illustrated in Figure L.

The trace left by the paint or sand will be a sine wave such as shown in Figure M. The amplitude of the sine wave represents the maximum displacement of the pendulum (cup) from its rest position. The distance from crest (high point) to crest or from trough (low point) to trough is called the wavelength, λ. How can you obtain a wave pattern with the same wavelength but with different amplitude? How can you obtain a wave pattern with the same am-

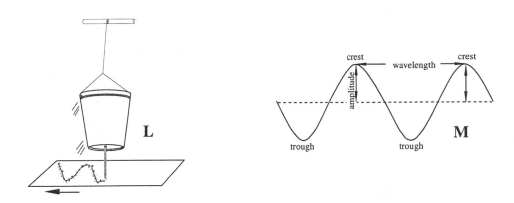

plitude but with a shorter wavelength? Experiment with the length of the pendulum, its arc, and the speed at which the paper is moved until you obtain wave patterns that answer these questions.

Frequency is a measure of the number of waves per unit time, and in this activity it is determined by how rapidly the pendulum swings. If the pendulum makes one complete swing in a second, the frequency is one vibration/s, also known as one cycle per second or one Hertz (1 Hz). The period is the time required to make one vibration. Since frequency is the number of crests or troughs passing a given point in unit time, and period is the time between the passage of two successive crests or troughs, the relationship between frequency f and period T is reciprocal: $f = 1/T$ or $T = 1/f$. How can you obtain a wave with a longer period? How can you obtain a wave with a higher frequency? Experiment with the length of the pendulum, its arc, and the speed at which the paper is moved until you obtain wave patterns that answer these questions

Part 2: Transverse waves in water: Fill a rectangular pan with water to a depth of about 1.5 cm. Place the pan on a level surface. Cut a wooden dowel (2 cm diameter or thicker) to a length slightly less than the width of the pan and place the dowel in the water at one end. Touch a finger to the dowel (or rolling pin) and roll it back and forth once and observe the transverse wave that moves across the water's surface. Roll the dowel back and forth repeatedly and observe the train of waves moving across the water's surface (Figure N).

The speed of a wave through a given medium is constant. Roll the dowel back and forth at a slow rate and note the length of the wave. Roll the dowel back and forth faster (increased frequency) and note that the wavelength is shorter. Roll the dowel even faster and note that the wavelength is shorter yet. These activities show that there is an important rela-

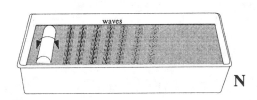

tionship between the frequency, length, and speed of a wave: wave speed is the product of the frequency and wavelength (wave speed = frequency × wavelength). If v is speed, f is frequency, and λ is wavelength, we have: $v = f\lambda$. Thus, in a given media, frequency and wavelength are inversely related. If the frequency increases, the wavelength decreases and vise versa. This fundamental relationship is true for waves of any type, including electromagnetic waves and electron waves.

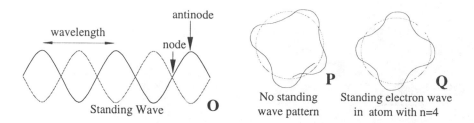

Part 3: Standing waves in a spring: Obtain a wave demonstration spring (coiled spring about 3/4 inch in diameter and about 6 feet in length) or a rope. Place the spring (or rope) on a smooth, flat floor. One student should hold one end of the spring tightly against the floor so it cannot move. The other student should grip the other end of the spring and send a pulse down the spring by moving the end of the spring quickly to the left or right and then back to the original position. Observe the pulse as it travels down the spring, and observe the reflected pulse. Is the reflected pulse on the same or opposite side of the sent pulse?

Send one pulse down the spring and, when the reflected pulse moves toward you, send another pulse of the same magnitude down the spring. Note the results when the two waves meet. Do the pulses reinforce or cancel each other?

Rapidly move one end of the spring from side to side, sending waves down the spring, and observe the returning waves. Increase the rate of movement of the end of the spring and observe the results. Finally, adjust the rate of movement of the end of the spring so a standing wave is established. You will know that a standing wave has been established when the spring seems to barely undulate from side to side (moving back and forth from one side to another) with no apparent waves moving either up or down the length of the spring. Figure O shows a standing wave in a rope with six nodes, including the two at the ends.

De Broglie suggested that electrons act as standing waves that just fit the circumference of the orbit. Figure Q shows the conditions that must be met to establish a standing electron wave. In some regions there are nodes, indicating that the probability of finding an electron there at any time is zero. In other regions there are antinodes, indicating that the probability of an electron being in that region at any time is significant.

Part 4: Three-dimensional waves: The standing waves you have produced in the springs or ropes are two dimensional. An atom, however, is three dimensional, and consequently a standing wave of an electron has three dimensions. To illustrate this three-dimensional aspect, inflate a balloon and then repeatedly squeeze and release one side so the opposite side alternately expands and contracts. This is analogous to a three-dimensional electron wave.

Questions

(1) What is the relationship among the frequency, wavelength, and velocity of a wave?

(2) Describe the location (same or opposite side as the sent pulse) of the returning wave after you sent a pulse down the spring. Describe the result when you sent a pulse down the spring toward a returning pulse.

(3) What is a standing wave? What is a node?

(4) For a given length of spring, only certain wavelengths are possible if a standing wave is to exist. Explain.

2.1.4 QUANTUM NUMBERS
AND ELECTRON ORBITALS

Concepts to Investigate: Atoms, electrons, electron "addresses," principal quantum number, angular quantum number, magnetic quantum number, spin quantum number, subshell, electron orbital, Aufbau principle, Hund's rule, Pauli exclusion principle, orbital shapes, electron density.

Materials: None.

Principles and Procedures: According to the principles of quantum mechanics, each electron in an atom is described by four different quantum numbers, the combination of three of which gives the probability of finding an electron in a given region of space (atomic orbital) and the fourth which specifies the spin of the electron on its axis ("clockwise" or "counterclockwise") in an orbital. Atomic orbitals have definite shapes, indicating those spaces of high probability of finding an electron. Orbitals do not end abruptly at a particular distance from the nucleus, so atoms actually have indefinite sizes.

Each electron in an atom has a unique energy address, just as each house or building has a unique address. For example, the Empire State Building is located in the *country* of the United States, in the *state* of New York, in the *city* of New York, at the *street address* of 350 5th Avenue. Just as no two buildings can occupy the same address, so no two electrons can have the same quantum numbers in a given atom. When locating a building we specify the country, state, city and street address. When identifying a specific electron we specify the (1) principal quantum number n indicating distance from the nucleus, the (2) angular momentum quantum number l indicating shape of the orbital, the (3) magnetic quantum number m_l indicating orientation of the orbital, and the (4) spin quantum number m_S indicating whether the spin of an electron is "clockwise" or "counterclockwise" (these terms have meaning only as opposites to each other in the same atom).

The *principal quantum number (n)* indicates the distance from the nucleus and thus the size of an orbital, and is the main factor determining its energy. The principal quantum number has a positive integer value: 1,2,3,4,5,6,7, etc. Orbitals that have the same principal quantum number form a "shell."

The *angular momentum quantum number (l)* indicates the shape of the orbital and can have any integer value from 0 to $n-1$. For example, if $n = 4$, l can be either 0, 1, 2 or 3. If $n = 1$, l can be only one value, 0, and consequently there can be only one orbital shape, the sphere (s-orbital) shown in Figure R. If $n = 2$, then 1 may have two values, 0 or 1, and consequently two shapes, the spherical (s-orbital) or polar (p-orbitals) shown in Figures R and S. If $n = 3$, then l may have three values, 0, 1 or 2, and consequently three shapes: the spherical (s-orbital), polar (p-orbitals), or dual-polar (d-orbital) shapes shown in Figures R, S and T. Orbitals within a shell that have the same angular momentum number are said to be in the same subshell (indicated as s,p,d,f, ...). Chemists refer to the shell/subshell with a two-character code. For example, the configuration 2p identifies electrons in the p subshell of the 2nd shell.

The *magnetic quantum number (m_l)* describes the orientation of the orbital about the nucleus. The magnetic quantum number (m_l) can be any integer between $-l$ and $+l$. If, for example, $l = 2$, m_l can be either -2, -1, 0, $+1$ or $+2$. If $n = 1$, then l must equal 0, and there can be only one value for m_l which is 0. This makes sense since there is only one way to orient a sphere (Figure R). If, however, $n = 2$, l may have values of 0 or 1, indicating two shapes (Figures R and S). If $l = 1$, then m_l can have values of -1, 0, 1, indicating the three primary

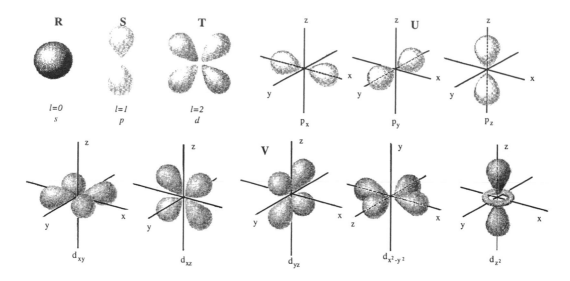

orientations of the orbital (Figure U). These are commonly referred to as the x, y, and z orientations, as described by their axes. Thus, the configurations may be p_x, p_y, and p_z. If $n = 3$, then l can have values of 0, 1 or 2. If l has a value of 2, then m_l may have values of -2, -1, 0, $+1$ or $+2$, indicating five distinctive orientations (Figure V).

The *spin quantum number (m_s)* refers to the two possible orientations of the spin axis of an electron which are $+1/2$ and $-1/2$.

An electron, spinning on its axis, behaves like a tiny magnet and has polarity that we may indicate by $+1/2$ or $\uparrow$. An electron spinning on its axis in the opposite direction has the opposite polarity that we may indicate by $-1/2$ or $\downarrow$. Since like poles repel each other, two similarly spinning electrons can never occupy the same orbital. However, since opposite poles attract, two oppositely spinning electrons can occupy the same orbital: $\uparrow\downarrow$.

Table 4 lists the permissible quantum numbers for all orbitals through the 4th (N) shell. Since each orbital can hold two electrons (with opposite spins) the total number of electrons in a subshell will be twice the number of orbitals.

Figure W represents the information from Table 4 in graphic form. Each small rectan-

Table 4: Quantum Numbers

n	l	m_l	Number of Orbitals in Subshell	Subshell Designations	Possible Electrons
1	0	0	1	1s	2
2	0	0	1	2s	2
2	1	$-1,0,+1$	3	2p	6
3	0	0	1	3s	2
3	1	$-1,0,+1$	3	3p	6
3	2	$-2,-1,0,+1,+2$	5	3d	10
4	0	0	1	4s	2
4	1	$-1,0,+1$	3	4p	6
4	2	$-2,-1,0,+1,+2$	5	4d	10
4	3	$-3,-2,-1,0,+1,+2,+3$	7	4f	14

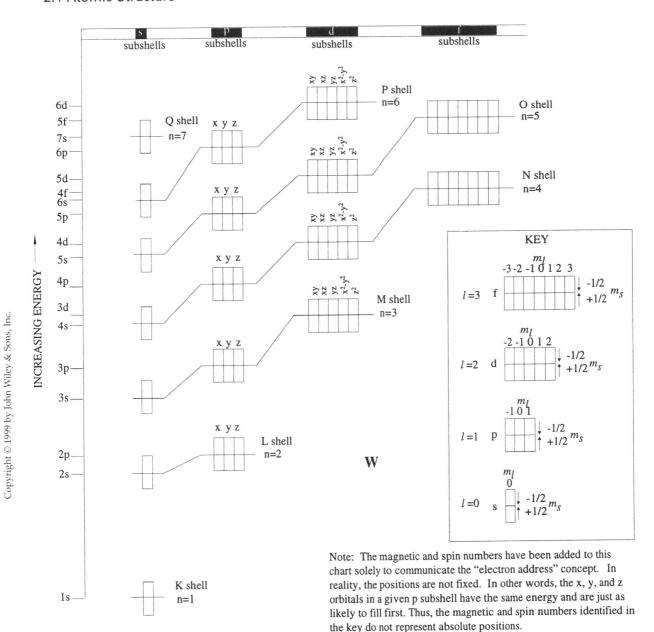

Note: The magnetic and spin numbers have been added to this chart solely to communicate the "electron address" concept. In reality, the positions are not fixed. In other words, the x, y, and z orbitals in a given p subshell have the same energy and are just as likely to fill first. Thus, the magnetic and spin numbers identified in the key do not represent absolute positions.

gle indicates an orbital capable of holding two electrons, one in the box above the line, and one in the box below the line. The Pauli exclusion principle specifies that no two electrons in the same atom can have the same set of quantum numbers, just as no two homes can have the same address or no two phones exactly the same telephone number. Therefore, on our chart, no two electrons can occupy the same box.

The Aufbau principle states that an electron occupies the lowest-energy orbital that can receive it. Thus, if an atom has only one electron, it will be in the 1s orbital, and if an atom has three electrons, it will have two in the 1s orbital, and one in the 2s (written $1s^2 2s^1$).

Hund's Rule states that orbitals of equal energy (for example all of the three 2p orbitals) are occupied by single electrons of the same spin before any are filled with second electrons with opposite spins. Two electrons occupying the same orbital are known as an electron pair or an orbital pair ($\uparrow\downarrow$).

The structure of an electron cloud is analogous to an apartment building where each floor represents an energy level (principal quantum number, n), each wing represents a sublevel (orbital quantum number, l), and each apartment represents an orbital (magnetic quantum number, m_l) that is occupied by one or two people, husband or wife (spin quantum number, m_s). Each person in the apartment complex can be specified given four pieces of data. For example, [6th floor, wing 2, apartment 1, husband] gives the address for one and only one individual. In a similar manner, you can specify a unique address for any electron in the electron cloud surrounding an atom, however there are a variety of addressing systems! Use your knowledge of quantum numbers to identify the elements represented by items 1–20, and place the corresponding numbers in the appropriate boxes ("energy addresses") on Figure W.

(1) H; hydrogen, 1 electron

(2) He; helium, 2 electrons

(3) Be; beryllium, 4 electrons

(4) B; boron, 5 electrons

(5) $n = 3$, $l = 0$, $m_l = 0$, $m_s = -1/2$

(6) $n = 3$, $l = 1$, $m_l = 1$, $m_s = +1/2$

(7) $n = 5$, $l = 0$, $m_l = 0$, $m_s = -1/2$

(8) $n = 3$, $l = 1$, $m_l = -1$, $m_s = +1/2$

(9) $4d_{xz}$; $m_s = +1/2$

(10) $6d_{xy}$; $m_s = +1/2$

(11) $5p_x$; $m_s = +1/2$

(12) $6p_z$; $m_s = -1/2$

(13) Ge; [Ar] $4s^2\ 3d^{10}\ 4p^2$

(14) Br; [Ar] $4s^2\ 3d^{10}\ 4p^5$

(15) C; $1s^2 2s^2 2p^2$

(16) S; [Ne] $3s^2\ 3p^4$

(17) n = 4; 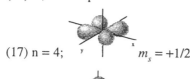 $m_s = +1/2$

(18) n = 3 , $\uparrow$

(19) M shell; ; $\downarrow$

(20) n = 4; 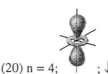 ; $\downarrow$

<u>Important note:</u> The magnetic and spin numbers have been added to Figure W solely to communicate the "electron energy address" concept. In reality, all orbitals within a subshell have the same energy and are equally as likely to fill first. In other words, the x, y, and z orbitals in a given p subshell have the same energy so the p orbital sequence shown in Figure W does not have to read in the x,y,z sequence. Thus, the magnetic and spin numbers identified in the key do not represent absolute positions.

Questions

(1) Describe in your own words the meaning of principal quantum number, angular momentum quantum number, magnetic quantum number, and spin quantum number.

(2) No electron in an atom may have the same four quantum numbers. Use the analogy of your address: country, state, city, and street to explain this important concept.

(3) You may live at 1000 First Street in the city of Portland, Oregon, and your friend may live at 1000 First Street in the city of Portland, Maine. Is it legal to have two identical street addresses in two towns of the same name in the same country? Explain.

(4) Consider the rules for quantum numbers and decide which of the following sets of quantum numbers is permissible for an electron in an atom and explain:

(a) $n = 1, l = 1, m_l = 0, m_s = -1/2$

(b) $n = 2, l = 1, m_l = 0, m_s = -1/2$

(c) $n = 3, l = 2, m_l = +3, m_s = +1/2$

(5) What is an atomic orbital?

(6) Does an atom have a definite or indefinite size? Explain

(7) The shapes and energies of all p orbitals in the same subshell are the same but differ in one important respect. Explain.

(8) The shape of an orbital determines the space in which an electron will be found with high probability. Explain.

2.1.5 ELECTRON CONFIGURATION

Concepts to Investigate: Orbitals, orbital notation, Hund's rule, Pauli exclusion principle, paramagnetic, diamagnetic, Aufbau principle, electron configuration.

Materials: None.

Principles and Procedures: An electron configuration shows the distribution of electrons among available subshells in an atom. To indicate this configuration, we list the subshell symbols, one after the other, using superscripts to indicate the number of electrons in the subshells. For example, a configuration of the Be atom (atomic number 4) is written $1s^2 2s^2$, indicating there are two electrons in the 1s subshell and two electrons in the 2s subshell.

The notation just described gives the number of electrons in each subshell but does not indicate the spins of electrons. To do this, we use orbital notation in which vertical arrows represent the spin orientation of individual electrons in each orbital. The Pauli exclusion principal states that no two electrons in an atom may have the same four quantum numbers, so no two electrons in an orbital will ever have the same spin:

illegal ↑↑   legal ↑↓

What determines the arrangement of electrons in the subshells of an element (for example carbon) in which there is more than one possible arrangement that does not violate the Pauli exclusion principal as shown here?

Which one is correct? Fortunately the German chemist Friedrich Hund discovered that the lowest energy configuration of electrons is obtained by placing electrons in separate orbitals of the subshell with the same spin before pairing electrons. This means that the most stable arrangement of electrons in subshells is the one with the greatest number of parallel spins (not opposite spins which cancel each other). Of the three possible arrangements above, only "3" meets the criteria. By remaining unpaired in separate orbitals, the two 2p electrons of carbon are in a lower energy state than if they were paired in the same p orbital because in separate p orbitals the electron-electron electrostatic repulsion is minimized.

The Aufbau principle ("Aufbau" is a German word meaning "building up") states that we can mentally "build up" the electron configurations of any atom by placing electrons in the lowest available orbitals until the total number of electrons added equals the number of protons in the nucleus (Z, the atomic number of the element). According to this principle, the electron configuration of an atom is determined by filling subshells shown on the vertical axes of Figure W in 2.1.4 or shown in the following sequence:

1s, 2s, 2p, 3s, 3p, 4s, 3d, 4p, 5s, 4d, 5p, 6s, 4f, 5d, 6p, 7s, 5f

With a few exceptions, this order reproduces the experimentally determined electron configurations. Using the Aufbau principle, "build up" the missing electron configurations and orbital notations in the following table.

Table 5: Orbital Notation

Z	Symbol	Configuration	Orbital Notation		
			1s	*2s*	*2p*
1	H	$1s^1$	—— ——	—— —— ——
2	He		—— ——	—— —— ——
3	Li	$1s^22s^1$	—— ——	—— —— ——
4	Be		—— ——	—— —— ——
5	B		—— ——	—— —— ——
6	C		—— ——	—— —— ——
7	N		—— ——	—— —— ——
8	O		—— ——	—— —— ——
9	F		—— ——	—— —— ——
10	Ne	$1s^22s^2\,2p^6 = [Ne]$	—— ——	—— —— ——

Questions

(1) Identify the following atoms by their electron configurations: (a) $1s^22s^22p^5$, (b) $1s^22s^22p^63s^23p^2$, (c) $1s^22s^22p^63s^23p^6$.

(2) How does Hund's rule help you determine the electron configuration of an atom?

(3) Write the orbital diagram for the element chlorine.

(4) Use Figure W to determine the electron configuration of aluminum.

(5) Is there anything unusual about the electron configuration of chromium (Z = 24) $[Ar]3d^54s^1$? Explain.

FOR THE TEACHER

It is very important to know the atomic structure of an element because it determines the chemical and physical properties of that element. In order to understand chemistry, one must understand atomic structure.

The size of an atom is on the order of 1×10^{-10} m. Nearly all the mass of an atom is concentrated in the nucleus as protons and neutrons, with the surrounding electrons constituting most of the atomic volume. Examination of line spectra fostered the determination of the electron structure of atoms. Bohr's interpretation of line spectra was in terms of an atom in which the electrons are located in orbits of different energy and radii. According to Bohr, electron transitions between orbits occur with the absorption or emission of discrete quanta (amounts) of energy, and he thus established the theory of quantized energy levels. Bohr's theory could not explain the emission spectra of atoms containing more than one electron.

De Broglie suggested that moving matter possesses an associated wavelength, too small to be measured for macroscopic particles but measurable for minute particles such as the electron, proton, and neutron. Schrödinger developed a wave model of the hydrogen atom in which the positions of the electrons are determined by probability considerations with the electron energy states, called orbitals, defined in terms of four quantum numbers: n, l, m_l, and m_s. These quantum numbers uniquely specify the quantized energy state of the electron in the hydrogen atom: n indicates orbital size, l indicates orbital shape, m_l indicates orbital orientation, and m_s indicates electron spin. We can use this hydrogen model to build up the electron structures of multi-electron atoms.

A description of molecular orbitals is beyond the scope of this book. However, it should be noted that the valence bond theory, which pictures a bond as forming when atomic orbitals overlap when individual atoms come together, does not explain certain observed phenomena such at the paramagnetism of oxygen. Oxygen contains an even number of electrons and, according to simple valence bond theory, the O_2 molecule should be diamagnetic. Actually the oxygen molecule is paramagnetic. Molecular orbital theory easily explains this paramagnetism. The molecular orbital model considers a molecule to consist of a collection of atomic nuclei surrounded by a set of molecular orbitals. These molecular orbitals are spread over several atoms or the entire molecule. An atomic orbital is associated with only one atom, whereas a molecular orbital is associated with the entire molecule.

2.1.1 ATOMS ARE MOSTLY EMPTY SPACE

Discussion: It is important that you stress the importance of indirect measurement in science. Before Rutherford's work, it was generally believed that the electrons and protons were distributed throughout the entire volume of an atom. Scientists are able to infer the structure of one entity by probing it with another entity and examining the results, much as Rutherford probed the atom using alpha particles as the probes and examined the resulting deflections. Students actually accomplished an analogous task as Rutherford in using the marbles to locate the pegs. If there are too many pegs, students will quickly find out that the marble may bounce back and forth among pegs and never emerge from under the board.

You should explain that there are many occasions in science and in their everyday lives in which direct measurement is not possible or feasible. For example, no one has ever been on the Sun, but we are able to determine that the Sun is composed primarily of hydrogen and helium by examining the Sun's spectra. In fact helium was identified, using absorption spectra, as an element on the Sun long before it was identified on Earth.

Compare and contrast direct and indirect measurement for your students by giving an example of each. Placing a ruler directly over the cover of a book to determine the length of the cover is an example of direct measurement. In contrast, using the ruler to measure the width of the pages (cover not included) of a book and then dividing by the number of pages to find the thickness of a page is an example of indirect measurement.

Answers: (1) The position of the pegs is determined not by direct examination, but by the initial and final paths of the marble probes. (2) Locating the pegs ("nuclei") was accomplished by observing the path of the marbles ("alpha particles") as they exited from under the board as shown in Figure G. (3) Yes, because the marble will tend to bounce around between the pegs. As the number of pegs is increased, the diameter of the marble must be decreased to provide more precise measurement.

2.1.2 ATOMIC SPECTRA

Discussion: The staircase activity provides an analogy by which students may understand electron transitions among orbitals in atoms. Make certain students realize that the energy they put into throwing the ball is emitted in steps as the ball falls down the stairs.

Students are sometimes perplexed when asked to explain why certain objects emit continuous spectra while others emit line spectra. Continuous spectra are emitted by objects such as the Sun in which electrons in an uncountable number of atoms are moving up and down between innumerable orbitals, absorbing energy and emitting light of all visible wavelengths. The bands of wavelengths merge with one another creating a continuous spectrum. However, a low-pressure fluorescent bulb has fewer atoms, all of the same substance, and so we are therefore able to view their individual spectra more easily. Line spectra are also referred to as atomic spectra because they are unique to each element.

When a spectroscope is pointed at an incandescent lamp, we see a continuous spectrum because electrons are falling from innumerable orbitals down to a wide variety of lower orbitals producing the entire range of visible light. When the spectroscope is pointed at a low-pressure, mercury-vapor lamp such as some street lamps, only the line spectra associated with mercury is visible. By contrast, when a spectroscope is pointed at a high-pressure, sodium-vapor lamp, a dim continuous spectrum is observed with the bright line sodium spectrum superimposed on top.

The flame tests produce the same colors (line spectra) as produced by other means of excitation. For example, the flame test for sodium produces a bright yellow light of the same color observed when a sodium-vapor lamp is viewed through a spectroscope.

Answers: (1) A continuous spectrum contains light of all wavelengths like that of a rainbow or incandescent light (Figure C). In contrast a line spectrum shows only specific wavelengths (Figure D). (2) Fluorescent tubes and bluish street lamps generally contain mercury vapor, while yellow street lamps contain sodium vapor. (3) They are both brilliant yellow. (4) Each element has a unique line spectra just as each person has a unique fingerprint. (5) If the spectroscope has no scale, students should observe the following colors: purple, blue, green, yellow, red. If the spectroscope has a scale the wavelengths in nanometers of these lines are approximately: 405, purple; 436, blue; 546, green; 577, yellow; 579, yellow; 610, red. (6) The colors that we see when these metal ions are excited are as follows: barium (green), calcium (red-orange), potassium (violet), lithium (red), sodium (yellow), strontium (scarlet-red). When sodium and potassium are together the bright yellow of sodium masks (obscures) the violet light of potassium.

2.1.3 WAVE CHARACTERISTICS

Discussion: Louis de Broglie reasoned that if light (a wave-phenomenon) exhibits characteristics of particles as in the case of the photoelectric effect, then perhaps particles of matter may show characteristics of waves under the appropriate circumstances. He postulated that a particle of mass m and speed v has an associated wavelength according to the following equation:

$$\lambda = h/mv$$

where λ is the wavelength associated with the particle, h is Planck's constant (6.626×10^{-34} J·s), m its mass, and v its velocity. This equation shows that the wavelength of a particle is inversely related to its mass. The wavelength associated with a macroscopic object such as a tennis ball moving at serving speed is about 10^{-34} m and cannot be detected by any existing measuring device, whereas the wavelength associated with an electron is about 10^{-10} m, a distance that is large relative to the dimensions of an electron, and measurable using appropriate equipment.

The concept of "standing waves" is of fundamental importance in understanding quantum mechanics. The standing waves that students induced in water or the spring (rope) were two dimensional. Make certain your students observed that, for a given length of spring, only certain wavelengths are possible for standing waves to be established (Figures O and Q).

In the case of an electron revolving about a nucleus in a path of fixed circumference, a standing wave can exist only if the circumference is equal to a whole (integral) number of wavelengths. An electron bound to a nucleus behaves like a standing wave which means that the length of the wave must fit the circumference of the orbit exactly. Figure Q shows a case in which the circumference of the orbit is equal to an integral number of wavelengths and a standing wave is produced. Figure P shows a case in which the circumference is not equal to an integral number of wavelengths, resulting in interference that collapses the wave.

Answers: (1) $v = f\lambda$. (2) When a pulse is sent down the spring and strikes the end which is held stationary, it reflects back on the opposite side of the spring. When a pulse is sent toward a returning pulse of the same magnitude, the two pulses interfere destructively. They cancel each other so the spring is straight in that area for a moment until the two pulses pass each other when again they are seen traveling the length of the spring in opposite directions. (3) If waves traveling in opposite directions in a spring have the same wavelength and velocity, the spring becomes divided into a series of vibrating segments of equal length, separated by stationary points of zero amplitude called nodes. Such a single frequency mode of vibration (the spring seems to undulate back and forth with no apparent movement of waves down its length) is called a standing wave. (4) For a standing wave to exist, the length of the spring must be equal to an integral number of half-wave lengths.

2.1.4 QUANTUM NUMBERS AND ELECTRON ORBITALS

Discussion: Figure X identifies the "energy addresses" of the 20 elements referenced in this activity. Because an atom is three dimensional, we must consider an electron wave to be three dimensional in terms of the x, y, and z axes. Consequently, three quantum numbers (n, l, and m_l) are required to describe the wave function of each electron in an atom. That is, three quantum numbers are required to specify the probable location of an electron in three-dimensional space.

To show students why two electrons with the same spin cannot occupy the same orbital, place the north ends of two magnets towards each other on the overhead and note how they

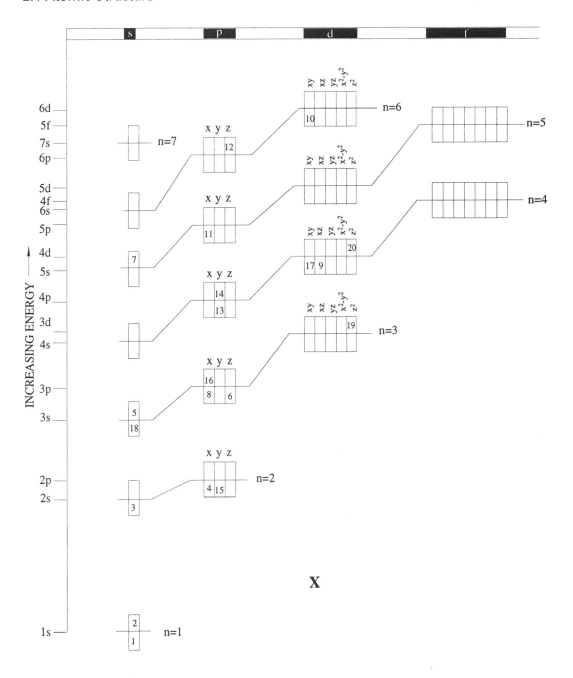

repel each other. To show that two electrons with opposite spins can occupy the same orbital, point the north end of one magnet to the south end of another.

Atomic orbitals do not end abruptly as is often shown in diagrams. An atom has an indefinite extension or size. The probability of finding an electron in an atom is greatest in a small volume near the nucleus and decreases exponentially with increasing distance in any direction from the nucleus, meaning that the probability becomes quite small at larger distances, but never becomes zero. Consequently, there is no fixed boundary to the size of an atom. Think of an atom as an electron cloud, densest near the nucleus, but without a sharp surface boundary. A contour is defined as a region in which a given percent of the probability will lie. For example, the 90% boundary contour is a sphere enclosing 90% of the probable electron density.

You may use balloons to illustrate orbital shapes. A normal spherical balloon may be used to represent a spherical orbital. To illustrate a p orbital, obtain an oblong balloon (the kind used at carnivals to make balloon animals) and twist it in the middle. You may place three of these on separate axes to illustrate the p_x, p_y and p_z orbitals. Use your creativity to illustrate the d and f orbitals using twisted and taped balloons. Make sure students realize that the balloons represent clouds with indefinite boundaries.

Answers: (1) These four quantum numbers indicate the address in an atom of an electron. No electron in the same atom can have the same four quantum numbers. The energy of an electron depends *principally* on the principal quantum number (hence the name). The angular momentum quantum number distinguishes the shapes of orbitals having the same *n*. The magnetic quantum number indicates the orientation of orbitals having the same *n* and *l*. The spin quantum number indicates the two possible orientations of the spin axis of an electron. (2) Within a given country such as the United States, the street address of a home within a given state and city is unique just as the address of an electron in a given atom. (3) Yes, because the series of four "quantum" numbers for each home are different. While the "quantum numbers" for the country, city, and street are identical, the "quantum numbers" for the state are different. (4) The first set is not permissible because the *l* quantum number is equal to *n:* when it must be less than *n*. The second set is permissible. The third set is not permissible because m_l must be between $-l$ and l. (5) An atomic orbital is the wave function of an electron in an atom. An atomic orbital is pictured qualitatively by describing the region of space where there is a high probability of finding the electron. Within each shell of quantum number *n* there are *n* different types of orbitals, including the s, p, d, and f. The shapes of these orbitals indicate the regions in which there is a high probability of finding an electron. (6) An atom does not have a definite size because the distribution of electrons does not end abruptly but simply decreases to very small values as the distance from the nucleus increases. Normally we consider the size of an atom as that volume that contains 90% of the total electron density around the nucleus. (7) The shapes differ in orientation. (8) An electron in an s orbital has the greatest probability of being found in the confines of the sphere defining this orbital. An electron in a p orbital has the greatest probability of being found in the dumbbell shape along the axis (x,y,z) with which the dumbbell is aligned. See Figure U.

2.1.5 ELECTRON CONFIGURATION

Discussion: Students should produce a table such as Table 6.

To simplify the writing of electron configurations for the larger atoms, we abbreviate using the noble gas core. The electron configuration of helium [He] is $1s^2$, of neon [Ne] is $1s^2 2s^2 2p^6$, and of argon [Ar] is $1s^2 2s^2 2p^6 3s^2 3p^6$. Examine the following to see how these noble cores are used to simplify writing electron configurations:

Li	$[1s^2]2s^1$	$[He]2s^1$
Na	$[1s^2 2s^2 2p^6]3s^1$	$[Ne]3s^1$
Cr	$[1s^2 2s^2 2p63s^2 3p^6]4s^1 3d^5$	$[Ar]4s^1 3d^5$

Students who examine the periodic table will note that there are minor irregularities in the Aufbau principle. These irregularities are attributed to the extra stability associated with half-filled and completely filled sublevels. The elements from scandium ($Z = 21$) to copper ($Z = 29$) are known as the transition elements which have incompletely filled d subshells. Exceptions occur in the building up of this series as a consequence of the overlap of the 3d and

Table 6: Orbital Notation

Z	Symbol	Configuration	Orbital Diagram 1s	2s	2p
1	H	$1s^1$	↑	—	— — —
2	He	$1s^2$ = [He]	↑↓	—	— — —
3	Li	$1s^2 2s^1$	↑↓	↑	— — —
4	Be	$1s^2 2s^2$	↑↓	↑↓	— — —
5	B	$1s^2 2s^2\, 2p^1$	↑↓	↑↓	↑ — —
6	C	$1s^2 2s^2\, 2p^2$	↑↓	↑↓	↑ ↑ —
7	N	$1s^2 2s^2\, 2p^3$	↑↓	↑↓	↑ ↑ ↑
8	O	$1s^2 2s^2\, 2p^4$	↑↓	↑↓	↑↓ ↑ ↑
9	F	$1s^2 2s^2\, 2p^5$	↑↓	↑↓	↑↓ ↑↓ ↑
10	Ne	$1s^2 2s^2\, 2p^6$ = [Ne]	↑↓	↑↓	↑↓ ↑↓ ↑↓

4s orbital energies (see Figure W). For example the "building up" principle predicts the configuration $1s^2 2s^2 2p^6 3s^2 3p^6 3d^4 4s^2$ for chromium but the experimentally observed configuration is $1s^2 2s^2 2p^6 3s^2 3p^6 3d^5 4s^1$. Likewise, the building up principle predicts the following configuration for copper: $1s^2 2s^2 2p^6 3s^2 3p^6 3d^9 4s^2$, but empirical evidence suggests this configuration: $1s^2 2s^2 2p^6 3s^2 3p^6 3d^{10} 4s^1$.

Measurements of magnetic properties provide the most direct and conclusive evidence to support specific electron configurations of atoms. Sophisticated instruments can determine if atoms are paramagnetic (attracted by a magnetic field) or diamagnetic (slightly repelled by a magnetic field). A paramagnetic substance is weakly attracted to a magnetic field, a property that results from unpaired electrons. The magnetic fields of paired electrons are oriented in opposite directions and cancel each other. A diamagnetic substance is not attracted to a magnetic field or is slightly repelled, indicating that the substance has only paired electrons. An atom with an odd number of electrons should be paramagnetic while an atom with an even number of electrons may be paramagnetic or diamagnetic. That is, if one or more electrons are unpaired, as in hydrogen and lithium, the magnetic fields of the unpaired electrons will be attracted by an external magnetic field. Consequently, measuring the degree of paramagnetism makes it possible to determine the number of unpaired electrons in a substance.

Answers: (1) Fluorine, silicon, argon. (2) Hund's Rule states that the most stable arrangement of electrons in subshells is the one with the greatest number of parallel spins. In other words, electrons within a subshell have parallel spins to the extent possible. (3) [Ne]$3s^2 3p^5$. (4) [Ne]$3s^2 3p^1$. (5) The electron configuration of chromium is [Ar]$3d^5 4s^1$ and not [Ar]$3d^4 4s^2$ as predicted by the Aufbau principle. These two configurations are actually very close in total energy because of the closeness of the 3d and 4s orbital energies. At the beginning of the series, the 4s level has a lower energy than the 3d level because it is more penetrating. But as the nuclear charge increases, the argon core of electrons is pulled closer toward the nucleus and the penetration effect decreases making the 3d level increasingly more stable compared to the 4s level. A chromium atom has six orbitals that each contain only one electron, all of which have the same spin, thereby producing a very stable condition as predicted by Hund's Rule. The 3d and 4s are exactly half-filled, and special stability is associated with half-filled and completely filled sublevels.

Applications to Everyday Life

Lasers: Because of its unique properties, laser light is used in many applications including telecommunications, eye surgery, laser printers, videodiscs, compact discs and the reading of bar codes on packaging. Laser is an acronym for Light Amplification by Stimulated Emission of Radiation, and is a phenomenon that depends upon the emission of light as excited electrons fall to lower energy levels. The first laser was the ruby laser (ruby is aluminum oxide containing a small concentration of chromium (III) ions). A ruby laser consists of a ruby rod encircled by a flash lamp. The ruby rod is silvered at one end to provide a completely reflective surface, while the other end has a partially reflective surface. When the flash lamp is discharged, a bright green light of 545 nm wavelength is absorbed by the ruby. This light excites electrons in the chromium ions to a higher energy level. These ions are unstable, and at a given instant, some will return to the ground state by emitting a photon in the red region of the spectrum. This photon bounces back and forth many times between the mirrors and can stimulate other excited chromium ions to emit photons of exactly the same wavelength. As the photons are reflected back and forth between the reflective surfaces, more and more ions are stimulated to emit, and the light quickly builds in intensity, producing the laser beam that emerges from the semi-reflective end of the ruby.

Electron microscope: A microscope is an instrument that produces enlarged images of small objects. The most familiar type of microscope is the optical (light) microscope. Compound optical microscopes may have magnifying powers only up to 1000 times. According to the laws of optics, it is impossible to form an image of an object that is smaller than half the wavelength of the light used for the observation. Since the range of visible light wavelengths starts at approximately 400 nm, we cannot see an object smaller than 200 nm using an optical microscope. In 1924 Louis de Broglie showed that an electron has an associated wavelength very much shorter than that of visible light. Based on this idea, the electron microscope was developed in 1930. Because electrons are charged particles, they can be focused in the same way the image on a TV screen can be focused by applying an electric or magnetic field to the beam. Hence, electron lenses are appropriately shaped magnetic or electrostatic fields. According to the de Broglie Relation ($\lambda = h/mv$), the wavelength of a body such as an electron is inversely proportional to its velocity. Consequently, by accelerating electrons to very high velocities, it is possible to obtain wavelengths as short as 0.004 nm. This allows modern electron microscopes to provide detailed images at magnifications of more than 250,000 times!

Sodium- and mercury-vapor lamps: An electric discharge lamp is a lighting device consisting of a transparent container, within which a gas is energized by application of a high voltage, and thereby made to glow. Two lamps now popular for lighting streets and other outside areas are the yellowish sodium vapor and the bluish mercury-vapor lamps. A low-pressure, sodium-vapor lamp consists of a glass shell with metal electrodes, filled with neon gas and a little sodium. When current passes between the electrodes, it ionizes the neon, producing a red glow, until the hot gas vaporizes the sodium to produce a nearly monochrome yellow. High-pressure sodium-vapor lamps commonly used in the United States contain both small amounts of sodium and mercury to produce a whiter light.

Fluorescent lamps: A fluorescent lamp produces light mainly by converting ultraviolet energy from a low-pressure mercury arc to visible light. A fluorescent lamp consists of a glass tube containing two electrodes, a coating of powdered phosphor, and small amounts of mercury. In operation, the mercury is vaporized and emits ultraviolet light. The inside of the lamp is coated with a mixture of powders called phosphors, chemicals that absorb ultraviolet light and re-radiate at longer wavelengths. The composition of the phosphors determines the color of the light produced. Since fluorescent light involves only the transfer of radiant energy, very little heat is produced so the lamp is cool to the touch, unlike the common incandescent bulb. Two great advantages of a fluorescent lamp light are its high light output per watt and its long life. The new compact fluorescent lamps, which screw into light sockets like conventional incandescent bulbs, consume 75 to 85% less electricity, and last up to 13 times longer!

Advertising signs: The colors of light produced by various advertising signs are the result of spectra produced when electrons emit only certain amounts of energy as they fall from one orbital to a lower orbital in an atom. The noble gases absorb and emit electromagnetic radiation in a much less complex manner than do other substances, and this behavior is exploited in the use of these gases (with the exception of the highly radioactive radon) in colorful fluorescent lighting devices and discharge lamps. Helium, neon, argon, and krypton, and mixtures of these gases, are used in familiar advertising signs. First electrodes are sealed into the ends of the tubes that are bent to the desired shape. The air is pumped out of the tube. Then an inert noble gas under low pressure is introduced into the tube. The inert gas vapor conducts the electric current through the tube. Neon gas has long been used in advertising signs (often as tubes that spell out words) and produces the highly visible orange-red light characteristic of these signs. Helium is used to produce a pink glow. Argon and mercury vapor, or a mixture of these, produces various shades of green and blue. Krypton and xenon produce shades of blue. Creative sign makers are learning to use various combinations of the noble gases in their signs, together with various combinations of phosphors on the inner walls of the glass, to produce a wide variety of colors.

Nebulae: A nebula consists of a hot cloud of interstellar gas. Nebula emit line spectra in the same manner that a gas filled tube excited by high voltage emits line spectra. Their main energy source, which ionizes and heats interstellar gas and causes it to glow, is ultraviolet radiation emitted by very hot stars. We can determine the nature of the gases in a nebula by the line spectra we receive.

Fireworks: When a skyrocket explodes, the contents are heated to extreme temperatures. Electrons are excited to higher energy levels and emit light as they return to their ground states. If you analyzed the light emitted from a skyrocket, you would be able to identify the material that is emitting the light. In the flame tests we showed that when heated, barium releases green light, calcium a red-orange light, potassium a violet light, sodium a yellow light, lithium a red light, and strontium a scarlet-red light. These elements produce similar colors in skyrocket explosions.

2.2 PERIODIC LAW

Many things in life occur over and over again in a repetitive or "periodic" manner. The Sun rises and sets at predictable times, ocean tides come and go on schedule and hopefully your school bus arrives and departs on time each day! Many other phenomena, such as the swinging of the pendulum of a grandfather clock, your circadian rhythm (daily waking and sleeping schedule), the seasons of the year, and the daily opening and closing of many flowers are periodic, and thus predictable. It so happens that there is periodicity and predictability among the elements as well.

An element is a substance composed of only one kind of atom: the element iron is composed of iron atoms, the element oxygen is composed of oxygen atoms, and the element gold is composed of gold atoms. There are presently 112 known elements, some naturally occurring, and some man-made. Element 112 was recently made by bombarding lead with zinc until atoms of these elements fused to form the new element. Although 83 elements are found in nature, they are not equally distributed. While the Sun is primarily hydrogen (95% hydrogen, 5% helium and other elements), the Earth's crust is primarily oxygen and silicon, the Earth's core is primarily iron, and our bodies are primarily hydrogen and oxygen: (63% hydrogen, 25.5% oxygen, 9.5% carbon, 1.4% nitrogen, 0.31% calcium, 0.22% phosphorous, 0.03 chlorine, 0.06% potassium, 0.05% sulfur, 0.03% sodium, 0.01% magnesium). How does one keep track of, and make sense of, all these elements?

In the 19th century, chemists did not know much about atoms and molecules, and they knew nothing about electrons and protons. However, they did realize that some groups of elements shared common properties, and they thought these properties might be related to atomic mass. Dimitri Mendeleev (1834–1907), a Russian chemist and teacher, was writing a chemistry book and wished to include new values for the atomic masses of the elements that had been recently determined. He was hoping to use this information, and the known chemical and physical properties of the elements, to arrange them according to their properties. Mendeleev approached the task in an organized manner. On separate cards, he listed the names of each element, together with their atomic masses and known properties. He organized the cards according to various properties and then searched for trends and patterns. Mendeleev noticed that when elements were arranged in order of increasing atomic mass, similar properties appeared at regular (periodic) intervals. He also noticed that when he did this, three gaps remained—spaces where there were no known elements with the appropriate masses and properties. Mendeleev boldly suggested that these spaces represented elements that were yet undiscovered, and within 15 years of his prediction, all three were found.

The following is a simplified example of how Mendeleev came upon his discovery. Suppose we have nine elements: A_1 (gas), A_2 (liquid), A_3 (solid), A_4 (gas), A_5 (liquid), A_6 (solid), A_7 (gas), A_8 (liquid), and A_9 (solid) with the subscript representing the atomic mass. Construct your own periodic table of these nine elements, sequencing them by atomic number, and grouping them by "families" with similar properties. Suppose someone discovers a new element that is a liquid with atomic weight between 9 and 13. Place this element in your periodic table and predict its atomic weight.

Does your table resemble Table 1? Were you able to place the newly discovered element in an appropriate row (period, series) and column (group, family)? Notice that in your table, the properties (gas, liquid, solid) of elements in any period change as you move through the period. At the end of one period, another period begins in which the properties again change in a predictable manner. Also notice that, within any group, the properties are the same: all elements in Group α are gases, all elements in Group β are liquids, and all elements in Group

PERIODIC TABLE OF THE ELEMENTS

A

Key:

1 (atomic number)
H (symbol)
Hydrogen (name)
1.008 (atomic mass)

Main table (by group):

Group	1	2	3	4	5	6	7	8	9	10	11	12	13	14	15	16	17	18
1	1 H Hydrogen 1.008																	2 He Helium 4.003
2	3 Li Lithium 6.941	4 Be Beryllium 9.012											5 B Boron 10.81	6 C Carbon 12.011	7 N Nitrogen 14.007	8 O Oxygen 15.999	9 F Fluorine 18.998	10 Ne Neon 20.179
3	11 Na Sodium 22.990	12 Mg Magnesium 24.305											13 Al Aluminum 26.981	14 Si Silicon 28.086	15 P Phosphorus 30.974	16 S Sulfur 32.06	17 Cl Chlorine 35.453	18 Ar Argon 39.948
4	19 K Potassium 39.098	20 Ca Calcium 40.08	21 Sc Scandium 44.956	22 Ti Titanium 47.88	23 V Vanadium 50.942	24 Cr Chromium 51.996	25 Mn Manganese 54.938	26 Fe Iron 55.847	27 Co Cobalt 58.93	28 Ni Nickel 58.69	29 Cu Copper 63.546	30 Zn Zinc 65.39	31 Ga Gallium 69.72	32 Ge Germanium 72.59	33 As Arsenic 74.92	34 Se Selenium 78.96	35 Br Bromine 79.904	36 Kr Krypton 83.80
5	37 Rb Rubidium 85.468	38 Sr Strontium 87.62	39 Y Yttrium 88.906	40 Zr Zirconium 91.224	41 Nb Niobium 92.906	42 Mo Molybdenum 95.94	43 Tc Technetium (98)	44 Ru Ruthenium 101.07	45 Rh Rhodium 102.906	46 Pd Palladium 106.42	47 Ag Silver 107.868	48 Cd Cadmium 112.41	49 In Indium 114.82	50 Sn Tin 118.71	51 Sb Antimony 121.75	52 Te Tellurium 127.60	53 I Iodine 126.905	54 Xe Xenon 131.29
6	55 Cs Cesium 132.905	56 Ba Barium 137.33	57 La Lanthanum 138.906	72 Hf Hafnium 178.49	73 Ta Tantalum 180.948	74 W Tungsten 183.85	75 Re Rhenium 186.207	76 Os Osmium 190.2	77 Ir Iridium 192.22	78 Pt Platinum 195.08	79 Au Gold 196.967	80 Hg Mercury 200.59	81 Tl Thallium 204.383	82 Pb Lead 207.2	83 Bi Bismuth 208.980	84 Po Polonium (209)	85 At Astatine (210)	86 Rn Radon (222)
7	87 Fr Francium (223)	88 Ra Radium 226.025	89 Ac Actinium 227.028	104 Rf Rutherfordium (261)	105 Db Dubnium (262)	106 Sg Seaborgium (263)	107 Bh Bohrium (262)	108 Hs Hassium (265)	109 Mt Meitnerium (266)	110 Uun Ununnilium (269)	111 Uuu Unununium (272)	112 Uub Unununbium (277)						

Also shown (group 18 column, separated): 71 Lu Lutetium 174.967 and 103 Lr Lawrencium (260)

Lanthanide Series:

58 Ce Cerium 140.12	59 Pr Praseodymium 140.908	60 Nd Neodymium 144.24	61 Pm Promethium (145)	62 Sm Samarium 150.36	63 Eu Europium 151.96	64 Gd Gadolinium 157.25	65 Tb Terbium 158.925	66 Dy Dysprosium 162.50	67 Ho Holmium 164.930	68 Er Erbium 167.26	69 Tm Thulium 168.934	70 Yb Ytterbium 173.04	71 Lu Lutetium 174.967

Actinide Series:

90 Th Thorium 232.038	91 Pa Protactinium 231.036	92 U Uranium 238.029	93 Np Neptunium 237.048	94 Pu Plutonium (244)	95 Am Americium (243)	96 Cm Curium (247)	97 Bk Berkelium (247)	98 Cf Californium (251)	99 Es Einsteinium (252)	100 Fm Fermium (257)	101 Md Mendelevium (258)	102 No Nobelium (259)	103 Lr Lawrencium (260)

Table 1: Hypothetical "Periodic Table"

Your Periodic Table	Group α (gas)	Group β (liquid)	Group χ (solid)
Period α	A_1	A_2	A_3
Period β	A_4	A_5	A_6
Period χ	A_7	A_8	A_9
Period δ		A_{11}	

χ are solids. Although your table is greatly simplified, it helps explain what is meant by periodicity and illustrates how properties change as one moves from left to right across a period.

The success of Mendeleev's predictions led to the acceptance of his periodic table. However, although Mendeleev's table was good, it was not perfect. For example, to get properties to match, Mendeleev placed argon (atomic mass 39.95) before potassium (atomic mass 39.10) even though this was inconsistent with his principle of arranging the elements in order of increasing mass. Although such discrepancies may seem minor, they indicated that atomic mass was not a perfect predictor of periodicity. This problem was resolved in 1911

Table 2: Atomic Numbers, Masses and Electron Configuration

Element	Symbol	Atomic Number	Atomic Mass	Electrons			
				$n = 1$	$n = 2$	$n = 3$	$n = 4$
hydrogen	H	1	1	1			
helium	He	2	4	2			
lithium	Li	3	7	2	1		
beryllium	Be	4	9	2	2		
boron	B	5	11	2	3		
carbon	C	6	12	2	4		
nitrogen	N	7	14	2	5		
oxygen	O	8	16	2	6		
fluorine	F	9	19	2	7		
neon	Ne	10	20	2	8		
sodium	Na	11	23	2	8	1	
magnesium	Mg	12	24	2	8	2	
aluminum	Al	13	27	2	8	3	
silicon	Si	14	28	2	8	4	
phosphorous	P	15	31	2	8	5	
sulfur	S	16	32	2	8	6	
chlorine	Cl	17	35	2	8	7	
argon	Ar	18	40	2	8	8	
potassium	K	19	39	2	8	8	1
calcium	Ca	20	40	2	8	8	2

when the English chemist Henry Moseley determined the atomic number (nuclear charge—the number of protons in the nucleus) of elements and discovered that discrepancies disappeared when the elements were arranged by atomic number rather than by atomic mass. Moseley's work led to the conclusion that the chemical and physical properties of the elements are periodic functions of their atomic numbers. This principle is now known as the periodic law and is one of the major principles in chemistry.

The modern periodic table (Figure A) arranges elements by atomic number. Hydrogen (atomic number 1), because of its many unique properties, is placed at the top of the table in a cell by itself. Helium (atomic number 2) is placed at the top of the right-hand column above the other noble gases. Hydrogen and helium form the first series or period (row). The number at the top of each cell represents the atomic number of the element. The number at the bottom represents the average atomic mass. Examine the periodic table to find adjacent elements in which the mass of the first is greater than the mass of the second. These pairs represent the discrepancies that accompanied Mendeleev's table.

Table 2 lists the first 20 elements, arranged in order of increasing atomic number. The series are separated by bold lines. Can you see any patterns (periodicity) among the electrons of each series when the elements are arranged in this manner? Look carefully, because periodicity of electron configuration underlies periodicity in chemical and physical properties.

As you prepare to investigate the periodicity of the elements, keep in mind these general principles:

(1) An element has the same number of protons as electrons. The number of protons is the atomic number of the element.

(2) The electrons exist outside the nucleus of an atom in orbitals.

(3) The outer electrons of an atom, which are those involved in chemical reactions (bonding), are referred to as valence electrons.

(4) Electron configurations of elements help explain the recurrence of physical and chemical properties.

(5) An element with eight electrons in its outer shell is stable and does not normally enter into chemical reactions. If the outer shell has less than four electrons, the element normally gives up electrons in chemical reactions. If the outer shell has more than four electrons, the element normally accepts electrons in chemical reactions.

In this chapter you will investigate the periodic table, the reasons for chemical and physical periodicity, and how the periodic law can be used to predict physical and chemical properties of elements. In addition, you will have an opportunity to develop your own periodic table in the same manner as Mendeleev.

2.2.1 FINDING THE "MISSING ELEMENTS"

Concepts to Investigate: Periodicity, predicting properties, Periodic Table of the Elements, groups, families, series, periods.

Materials: Paint color samples (available at paint stores).

Principles and Procedures: Mendeleev's original periodic table arranged elements according to observed properties. You will go through the same process as you attempt to arrange paint color "chips" in a logical fashion. Your instructor will provide you with an envelope containing paint chips in a variety of colors and intensities. The basic color of a paint chip represents its "chemical" properties. For example, all blue paint chips can be considered to have similar properties which are different from those of all red paint chips. The shade of a paint chip represents its "atomic mass." Thus, a light blue paint chip represents an element of low atomic mass while a dark blue paint chip represents an element that has similar properties but more mass. Arrange all chips with similar colors in the same column (family), and all colors with similar intensity (shade) in the same row (series). In the real Periodic Table of the Elements, properties gradually change from metallic to nonmetallic as you proceed through a series from the left to the right across the table. You may illustrate this concept by arranging your columns in a logical manner such as the sequence of colors in the visible spectrum: red-orange-yellow-green-blue-violet. Place the reddest colors on the left of your table, and the most violet colors on the right (Figure B).

After Mendeleev arranged the known elements in a table he noted that there were holes (vacancies) and he predicted that new elements would be found to fill these. Within 15 years of his prediction, all holes were filled with elements that had properties similar to those Mendeleev predicted. Examine your "Periodic Table of Paint Chips." Are any paint chips missing? Describe the properties of those missing paint chips. When you have completed your table, ask your instructor for the envelope containing the missing elements for your set. Were your predictions correct? Can you see how the Periodic Table is useful in predicting properties of unknown elements?

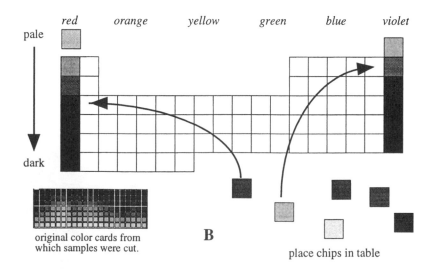

original color cards from
which samples were cut.

B

place chips in table

Questions

(1) Were you able to form a periodic table with rows (periods) and columns (groups)? Explain how you arranged your table.

(2) Were you able to predict the properties (color and shade) of the three elements not yet discovered? Where did you place these elements in your table?

(3) Explain the value of your periodic table in predicting properties of paint chips, and explain how chemists used the Periodic Table to predict the existence of unknown elements.

2.2.2 DESIGNING YOUR OWN PERIODIC TABLE

Concepts to Investigate: Periodicity, properties, atomic mass, period, group (family), family, series, predicting characteristics.

Materials: Figure C.

Principles and Procedures: In the previous activity we used a rather simple idea, color and shade, to arrange elements in a logical order. Mendeleev's original periodic table was arranged according to chemical and physical properties. He placed the name of an element, its atomic mass, and a list of the element's properties on a card. He then arranged these cards according to atomic mass and then grouped them according to observed properties and searched for patterns and trends. In this activity you will repeat Mendeleev's procedure. Figure C lists the first 20 elements of the periodic table and gives the type of information that Mendeleev had available when he set out to organize the elements. Photocopy Figure C and cut out all 20 cards. A member of another lab team should select two of the cards to represent "undiscovered elements," and should place them in a separate location where you will not see them. Shuffle the cards, place them on a desk or table, and then organize them in a logical pattern (tabular form) as Mendeleev might have done. Remember that you will need to leave two blanks for the "undiscovered elements." What is the best way to sequence the elements? At what points do properties appear to repeat themselves?

Questions

(1) Explain the importance of periodicity in the historical development of chemistry.
(2) Were you able to form a periodic table with rows (periods) and columns (groups)? Was the task more difficult than in the previous activity where one color represented a variety of properties?
(3) Which of the properties on the element cards is most appropriate for sequencing the elements?
(4) Which properties are periodic? Explain.
(5) Compare your table with Figure A to identify the elements. What properties are common to elements on the left side of the periodic table? The right side?

C

	Λ
average atomic mass:	**39.95**
density at 293K:	1.784 Kg/m^3
melting point:	83.78 K
boiling point:	87.29 K
thermal conductivity:	0.0177 Wm^{-1}K^{-1}
properties: nonmetal, colorless, odorless gas; inert	

	θ
average atomic mass:	**4.00**
density at 293K:	0.1785 Kg/m^3
melting point:	0.95 K
boiling point:	4.216 K
thermal conductivity:	0.152 Wm^{-1}K^{-1}
properties: colorless, odorless gas, inert	

	Ω
average atomic mass:	**6.94**
density at 293K:	534 Kg/m^3
melting point:	453.69 K
boiling point:	1620 K
thermal conductivity:	84.7 Wm^{-1}K^{-1}
properties: soft, white, silvery metal, reacts slowly with oxygen and water	

	Ψ
average atomic mass:	**20.20**
density at 293K:	0.900 Kg/m^3
melting point:	24.48 K
boiling point:	27.10 K
thermal conductivity:	0.0493 Wm^{-1}K^{-1}
properties: nonmetal, colorless, odorless gas, chemically inert	

	ζ
average atomic mass:	**35.45**
density at 293K:	3.24 Kg/m^3
melting point:	172.17 K
boiling point:	239.18 K
thermal conductivity:	0.0089 Wm^{-1}K^{-1}
properties: nonmetal, yellow-green, dense gas	

	ϕ
average atomic mass:	**19.00**
density at 293K:	1.696 Kg/m^3
melting point:	53.53 K
boiling point:	85.01 K
thermal conductivity:	0.0248 Wm^{-1}K^{-1}
properties: nonmetal, pale, yellow gas, most reactive of all elements	

	ω
average atomic mass:	**10.81**
density at 293K:	2340 Kg/m^3
melting point:	2573 K
boiling point:	3931 K
thermal conductivity:	27 Wm^{-1}K^{-1}
properties: metalloid, dark powder, unreactive with water and acids.	

	ψ
average atomic mass:	**16.00**
density at 293K:	1.429 Kg/m^3
melting point:	54.8 K
boiling point:	90.188 K
thermal conductivity:	8.2674 Wm^{-1}K^{-1}
properties: nonmetal, colorless gas, very reactive with all elements except nobel gases	

	ε
average atomic mass:	**32.07**
density at 293K:	1957 Kg/m^3
melting point:	386 K
boiling point:	717.8 K
thermal conductivity:	0.269 Wm^{-1}K^{-1}
properties: nonmetal, stable in water and air, but burns if heated	

	π
average atomic mass:	**9.01**
density at 293K:	1847.7 Kg/m^3
melting point:	1551 K
boiling point:	3243 K
thermal conductivity:	200 Wm^{-1}K^{-1}
properties: silvery-white, relatively soft metal, does not react with water oxygen	

C

δ	**Σ**
average atomic mass: **1.00**	average atomic mass: **39.10**
density at 293K: 0.08988 Kg/m^3	density at 293K: 862 Kg/m^3
melting point: 14.01 K	melting point: 336.80 K
boiling point: 20.28 K	boiling point: 1047 K
thermal conductivity: 0.1815 Wm^{-1}K^{-1}	thermal conductivity: 102.4 Wm^{-1}K^{-1}
properties: colorless, odorless gas, burns in air	properties: soft, silvery metal, reacts with oxygen and vigorously with water
Φ	**ϑ**
average atomic mass: **28.09**	average atomic mass: **40.08**
density at 293K: 2329 Kg/m^3	density at 293K: 1550 Kg/m^3
melting point: 1683 K	melting point: 1112 K
boiling point: 2628 K	boiling point: 1757 K
thermal conductivity: 148 Wm^{-1}K^{-1}	thermal conductivity: 200 Wm^{-1}K^{-1}
properties: metalloid, semi-conductor; unreactive toward oxygen and water	properties: silvery white, soft metal; reacts with oxygen and water
Π	**Δ**
average atomic mass: **14.01**	average atomic mass: **22.99**
density at 293K: 1.25 Kg/m^3	density at 293K: 971 Kg/m^3
melting point: 63.29 K	melting point: 370.96 K
boiling point: 77.4 K	boiling point: 1156.1 K
thermal conductivity: 0.0260 Wm^{-1}K^{-1}	thermal conductivity: 141 Wm^{-1}K^{-1}
properties: colorless, odorless gas; unreactive at room temperatures	properties: soft, silvery metal, oxidizes rapidly, reacts vigorously with water
Ξ	**α**
average atomic mass: **26.98**	average atomic mass: **12.01**
density at 293K: 2698 Kg/m^3	density at 293K: 3513 Kg/m^3
melting point: 933.52 K	melting point: 3820 K
boiling point: 2740 K	boiling point: 5100 K
thermal conductivity: 237 Wm^{-1}K^{-1}	thermal conductivity: 990-2320 Wm^{-1}K^{-1}
properties: hard, strong, silvery-white metal, forms oxides	properties: nonmetal
Γ	**ς**
average atomic mass: **30.97**	average atomic mass: **24.30**
density at 293K: 1820-2690 Kg/m^3	density at 293K: 1738 Kg/m^3
melting point: 317.3 K	melting point: 922 K
boiling point: 553 K	boiling point: 1363 K
thermal conductivity: 0.235-12.1 Wm^{-1}K^{-1}	thermal conductivity: 156 Wm^{-1}K^{-1}
properties: nonmetal, flammable, does not react with water	properties: silvery white, lustrous, relatively soft metal, burns in air and reacts with hot water

2.2.3 FAMILY CHARACTERISTICS

Concepts to Investigate: Atomic radius, ionization energy, electron affinity, periodic table, family characteristics.

Materials: None.

Principles and Procedures: Elements in the same family show "family characteristics" just as animals or plants in taxonomic families share many similar characteristics. All species of the pine family (Pinaceae) have needle-like leaves and produce seeds in cones. By contrast, all species in the palm family (Palmaceae) have broad frond-like leaves and produce seeds in fruits. Although pines and palms have many things in common, their family characteristics distinguish them from each other. The same is true among elements.

Part 1: Atomic radius: The atomic radius is defined as half the distance between the nuclei of two atoms of the same element that are bonded together. The atomic radius helps us predict many other characteristics about an element including how it will react with other elements. In general, it is more difficult to remove electrons from atoms with small atomic radii because those electrons are held more tightly by the nearby positive charge of the nucleus. By contrast, elements with large atomic radii are generally more prone to lose electrons because their valence (outermost) electrons are far from the attractive force of the nuclei. Although there are many other factors to consider, atomic radius is of primary importance in helping us predict properties of elements.

Is there any periodicity of atomic radii? Figure D plots atomic radii vs. atomic number for the first half of the periodic table. Connect the circles from atomic number 1 (hydrogen) to atomic number 54 (xenon) on Figure D using black pen or pencil. Use different colors to identify the circles that represent the members of the following families: group 1 (alkali metals), group 2 (calcium family), group 13 (boron family), group 14 (carbon family), group 17 (halogens), and group 18 (noble gases). For example, color all circles representing elements in the first family red, all circles representing elements of the second family orange, and so on. Now draw lines between circles of the same color (elements in the same family). Do the

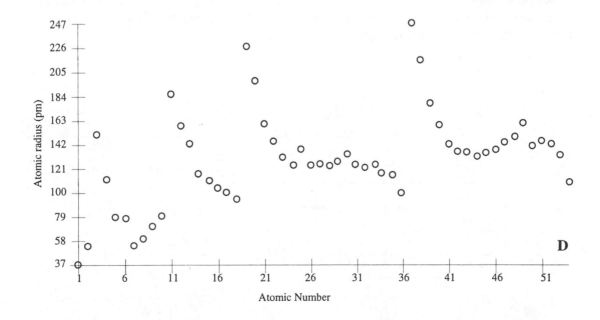

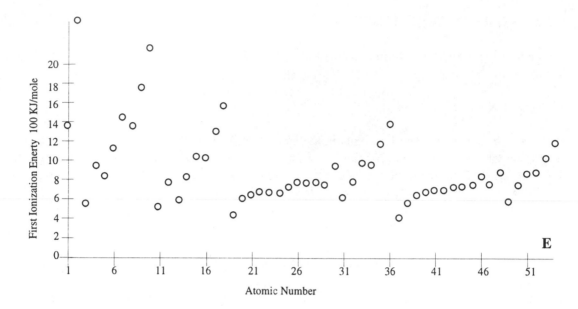

lines representing the different families cross each other? Are there strong similarities between elements within the same family? Does atomic radius appear to be a periodic property?

Part 2: First ionization energy: The first ionization energy is the energy required to remove one valence electron from an atom of an element. If the first ionization energy is low, it indicates that the element will readily surrender an electron in a chemical reaction, and will often exist in the cationic (positive) form. If, however, the first ionization is very high, then we know that it is unlikely that the element will lose electrons. Connect the circles from atomic number 1 (hydrogen) to atomic number 54 (xenon) on Figure E using a black pen or pencil. Use different colors to identify the circles that represent the members of the following families: group 1 (alkali metals), group 13 (boron family), group 15 (nitrogen family), group 17 (halogens), and group 18 (noble gases). Now draw lines between circles of the same color (elements in the same family). Do the lines representing the different families cross each other? Are there strong similarities between elements within the same family? Does first ionization energy appear to be a periodic property?

F

Electron Affinities (kJ/mol)

-77																	21
-58	241											-23	-123	0	-141	-322	29
-53	230											-44	-120	-74	-200	-349	35
-48	154											-36	-116	-77	-195	-325	39
-47	120											-34	-121	-101	-190	-295	41
-45	52											-50	-101	-101	-170	-270	41
-44																	

Questions

(1) Does atomic radius appear to be a periodic property? Explain.

(2) Does first ionization energy appear to be a periodic property? Explain.

(3) Which family has the largest atomic radii within any given period?

(4) In general, what happens to atomic radius as you proceed through a period (row) from the alkali metals to the noble gases? Explain why this might be so in terms of the attractive force between the nucleus and electrons.

(5) Which family has the smallest radius? Explain.

(6) Does the family with the lowest first ionization energy have relatively large or small radii? Explain this relationship.

(7) Which families have the highest first ionization energies? Is there any relationship between their ionization energies and their radii? Explain.

(8) Electron affinity (Figure F) represents the pull nuclei have for additional electrons. A large negative value indicates a strong attraction. Do you think that electron affinity is also a periodic property? Examine Figure E and identify as many periodic trends as you can find, providing they exist!

2.2.4 TRENDS WITHIN FAMILIES

Concepts to Investigate: Reactivity, periodicity, predicting properties, electron shielding, nuclear attraction, periodic table, electron affinity.

Materials: Part 1: Lithium, sodium, potassium, Petri dish, overhead, copper (pre-1982 U.S. penny), silver (U.S. Mercury dime), gold (ring or other jewelry), projector, phenolphthalein; Part 2: 0.2 M solutions of the following: KCl, KBr, KI; test tubes, chlorine water (or bleach and hydrochloric acid), bromine water (or potassium bromate and hydrochloric acid), iodine water (or potassium iodate, potassium iodide and hydrochloric acid), test tube rack.

Safety: This should be performed as a teacher demonstration only. Use protective eyewear and clothing. Lithium, sodium, and potassium react violently with water to produce hydrogen. The heat from the reaction may ignite the hydrogen causing a small explosion and splattering material. The resulting solution is strongly basic and should be handled with appropriate precautions. The halogen gases produced in part 2 are toxic, and should be handled only in a fume hood.

Principles and Procedures:

Part 1: Reactivity trends in the first family: Although the elements in groups 1 (Li, Na, K, Rb, Cs, Fr) and 11 (Cu, Ag, Au) are metals and therefore share many properties in common, they possess many family distinctives that set them apart from each other. While elements in both groups (families) are malleable, ductile, good conductors of heat, and good conductors of electricity, they differ widely with respect to their reactivity.

It is obvious that group 11 members do not react readily with water. A copper penny looks the same after sitting for a week in a "wishing well"; silverware looks the same after being washed in the sink; and a gold wedding band still appears gold even at a 50th wedding anniversary. By contrast, elements in the first family react vigorously with water to form metal hydroxides and hydrogen gas:

$$2X + 2H_2O \longrightarrow 2X^+OH^- + H_2$$

Examine the label on a container of lithium, sodium, or potassium and note the firm warning to keep away from water. It is clear that the metals in group 1 share many "family characteristics" with each other that are distinct from those of group 11.

Although all members of the first family react with water, not all react with the same intensity. Just as there are differences within a taxonomic family (not all pine trees have the same length needles or same size cones), so not all elements in a family share exactly the same properties. Which element do you think—lithium (period 2), sodium (period 3), or potassium (period 4)—will react most violently with water? Although all three of these elements have only one valence electron, the valence electron of potassium is farther away from the nucleus than is the valence electron of sodium, which itself is farther away than the valence electron of lithium. In addition to being farther away from the nucleus, the valence electron in potassium is shielded from the attractive pull of the nucleus by the repulsive force of one more shell of electrons than is the valence electron in sodium. Similarly, the valence electron in sodium is shielded from the pull of the nucleus by the repulsive force of one more shell of electrons than is the valence electron in lithium. Based on this knowledge, which do you think will react most violently with water—lithium, sodium, or potassium? Make your prediction before your instructor continues with the demonstration.

Having considered these issues, and made your predictions, you are now ready to investigate the relative reactivity of these elements in water. Reactivity will be qualitatively assessed by the apparent rate and vigor of the reaction, and by the rapidity with which the phenolphthalein turns pink (indicating the rate of hydroxide formation). Place three beakers away from students in a location where nothing will be damaged should splattering occur. Fill the beakers half full with water and add a couple of drops of phenolphthalein. In the first beaker place a "pea"-sized chunk of lithium. When the reaction is complete, repeat the process with sodium and then potassium using different beakers. Which of these first family elements is the most reactive? Does the reactivity of alkali metals increase or decrease as you proceed from top to bottom in the periodic table?

Part 2: Reactivity trends in halogens: The halogens, like the alkali metals, have many distinctive family characteristics. All have seven valence electrons and a high electron affinity. In other words, all have a tendency to remove electrons from other atoms to become negative ions. The high electron affinity makes the halogens reactive, but does reactivity increase or decrease within the halogen family?

Iodine is a large atom with four inner shells of electrons that shield its valence electrons from the pull of the nucleus. Bromine is smaller than iodine, with only three inner shells, and chlorine is smaller yet, with only two inner shells. Knowing this, which do you think has the greatest electron affinity? In other words, which has the greatest pull for the electrons of another element and is consequently the most reactive? To find out, perform the following activity.

Important: Carry out these activities in a fume hood. Prepare 0.2 M solutions of KCl, KBr, and KI by placing 1.5 g of KCl, 2.4 g of KBr or 3.4 g of KI into one of three labeled containers, and adding 100 mL of distilled water to each. If you do not have chlorine water, you may prepare it by combining 60 mL of household bleach (NaClO solution) and 40 mL of 2.0 M HCl. Chlorine from the hypochlorite ion (ClO^-) and the hydrochloric acid combine to form molecular chlorine gas (Cl_2).

$$ClO^-(aq) + Cl^-(aq) + 2H^+(aq) \longrightarrow Cl_2(g) + H_2O(l)$$

Prepare bromine water by mixing 90 mL of 0.2 M KBr solution, 0.1 g of potassium bromate ($KBrO_3$), and 10 mL of 2.0 M HCl. The chlorine from hydrochloric acid replaces bromine; the bromine atoms then combine to form dissolved bromine gas (Br_2). Iodine water may be prepared by combining 80 mL water, approximately 0.1 g of potassium iodate (KIO_3), 5 mL of 0.2 M potassium iodide solution, and 15 mL of 2.0 M HCl. All halogen water solutions should be capped to prevent the escape of these gases. Add 10 mL of each potassium salt solution to 10 mL of each halogen solution, stopper, shake, and record the resulting colors in Table 3.

Table 3: Reactivity Trends within the Halogen Family

	Chlorine Water (10 mL)	*Bromine Water (10 mL)*	*Iodine Water (10 mL)*
0.2 M KCl solution (10 mL)			
0.2 M KBr solution (10 mL)			
0.2 M KI solution (10 mL)			

The color of the final solution indicates which gas is present. Water containing molecular chlorine (Cl_2) is relatively colorless, while water with bromine (Br_2) is straw-yellow and water with iodine (I_2) is brownish. Identify which halogen gases are present after each mixing.

All of the halogens have significant electron affinity (tendency to gain and retain electrons):

$$Cl_2(aq) + 2e^- \longrightarrow 2Cl^-(aq)$$

$$Br_2(aq) + 2e^- \longrightarrow 2Br^-(aq)$$

$$I_2(aq) + 2e^- \longrightarrow 2I^-(aq)$$

This activity allows you to determine whether electron affinity increases or decreases within the halogens by pitting molecular halogens (Cl_2, Br_2, I_2) against different halogen salts (KI, KBr, KCl). The halogen with the greater electron affinity will emerge in ionic form (Cl^-, Br^-, I^-) while the halogen with lesser electron affinity will emerge as a molecular halogen gas (Cl_2, Br_2, I_2). Thus, in the "battle for electrons," the "winner" will appear in ionic form, and the "loser" will emerge as a diatomic gas. The color of the solution indicates the "loser," or the halogen with less electron affinity. If the resulting solution is colorless, then chlorine is the "loser"; if it is yellow, bromine is the "loser"; and if it is brown, iodine is the "loser." Let's begin the competition for electrons by mixing solutions according to the specifications of Table 3.

From the color changes reported in Table 3, determine which halogen has the greatest electron affinity. Does electron affinity (reactivity) increase or decrease with the increased shielding that occurs as you descend within the halogens?

Questions

(1) What characteristics can be used to distinguish metals in the first family from those in Group 11?

(2) Phenolphthalein turns pink in the presence of base. Which elements reacted with water to produce bases? What are the names of the bases that were produced?

(3) Which element reacted most strongly with the water? Explain why this is the case. Does reactivity increase or decrease within the first family as you proceed to higher periods?

(4) Was there any evidence of a chemical reaction between the 11th family elements and water? Between the 1st family elements and water? Explain.

(5) Members of the 11th family may be found in elemental form in nature, while those in the first family are never found except in compounds. Explain.

(6) Was there a color change when chlorine water was added to the solution of KCl?

(7) Was there a color change when chlorine water was added to the solution of KBr? Explain what this means about the comparative electron affinities of chlorine and bromine.

(8) Was there a color change when bromine water was added to the solution of KI? Explain what this means about the comparative electron affinities of bromine and iodine.

(9) Does electron affinity increase or decrease within the halogens? In other words, is electron affinity higher at the top or bottom of the family?

(10) Summarize trends in reactivity for the alkali metals and the halogens.

FOR THE TEACHER

2.2.1 FINDING THE "MISSING ELEMENTS"

Discussion: Most stores that sell house paints offer free color matching cards that contain various shades (intensities) of a given color of paint. Customers take these cards home to determine which colors and shades will look best in their own homes. Select at least eight basic colors (to represent groups 1,2,13,14,15,16,17 and 18), excluding white or black, and cut the paint cards into pieces so that each portion has one and only one shade of a given color. It is recommended that you select chips that match up well with the periodic table. For example, you may wish to have only two very pale chips, representing the two elements in the first series, while you have eight slightly darker chips representing the slightly heavier elements of the second series. We recommend that you use at least 18 different chips to represent the first three series, although you may wish to use enough paint chips to represent the entire periodic table. Remove three chips from each set (to represent "undiscovered elements") and place these in one envelope while you place the rest in a second envelope that you mark with the same code number. Repeat the process for as many lab teams as you have in your class.

Since three chips have been set aside from each set, there will be vacancies in the students' tables just as there were in Mendeleev's table. Make sure students see the value of their tables in predicting the properties of these yet unknown elements (colors) and in determining where these fit in their tables. At the end of the activity, give each student the matching envelope that contains the "missing elements" to see if their predictions were correct.

You may perform a variation of this activity using nuts, bolts, and assorted fasteners. Families (groups) may be represented by the type of fastener (e.g., square-headed bolt, hex-headed bolt, wood screw, sheet metal screw, washer, hex nut, square nut, cotter pin, etc.), and series (period) by relative size. For example, group 1 may be represented by square-headed bolts, with the smallest bolt at the top of the table, and the largest at the bottom. Group 2 (e.g., hex-headed bolts) should resemble group 1 (square-headed bolts), but should be distinct, just as the group 2 elements share properties in common with group 1, but also have their own distinctive characteristics. You may wish to select square nuts for group 17, and hex-nuts for group 16, to indicate that these groups have properties that are opposite and complementary to those of the first two families. Just as nuts and bolts may combine, so the members of the groups 1 (the alkali metals) and 2 (the calcium family) may react with the elements of groups 16 (the oxygen family) and 17 (the halogens). You may wish to represent group 18 (the noble gases) with a fastener unlike the rest (e.g., a cotter pin) to indicate that the noble gases are distinct and relatively inert. Make certain your students understand the limitations of these analogies.

Answers: (1) Yes. The rows represent elements with similar atomic mass as identified by similar color shades (intensities). The columns represent elements with similar chemical properties as identified by similar basic colors. (2) Student answers will vary. (3) When the paint chips were arranged it was clear that certain shades of certain colors were missing. In a similar manner, chemists noticed that certain elements were missing when the elements were arranged by atomic mass or number (shades) in groups with similar properties (colors). These "missing" elements were simply ones not yet discovered.

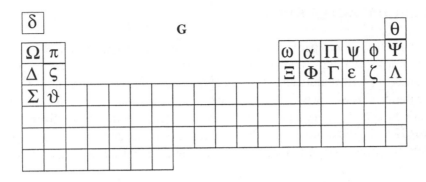

2.2.2 DESIGN YOUR OWN PERIODIC TABLE

Discussion: In this activity the student is faced with a task similar to Mendeleev's. Although the number of elements is less than what confronted Mendeleev, the outcome and concomitant understanding is the same. Figure G shows how the cards should be arranged to correspond to the periodic table.

Answers: (1) The periodicity of the elements enabled chemists to predict the existence of yet unknown elements, and more importantly stimulated research to understand the physical reasons for the periodicity that is observed. (2) Student answer. (3) Atomic mass. Atomic number would be better, but Mendeleev did not have this information. (4) All of the properties listed are periodic except atomic mass. (5) The left side of the periodic table is characterized by elements that are metallic, often silvery, and good conductors of heat (high thermal conductivity). They have high melting and boiling points and exist as solids at room temperature. The elements on the right side tend to have properties that are opposite of these.

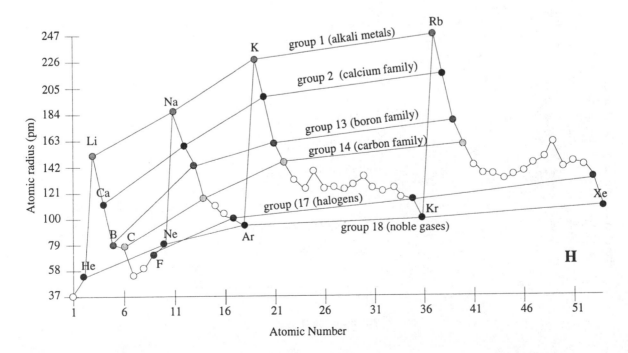

2.2.3 FAMILY CHARACTERISTICS

Discussion: This "paper and pencil" exercise is designed to encourage analysis of empirical data. By examining such data, students can discover numerous examples of periodicity. We believe that students will understand the concepts better and remember them longer if they can discover them on their own. These activities help build inductive reasoning as students look for trends in specific data and try to develop reasons for the generalizations they discover. Figures H and I illustrate the results students should have produced. You may wish to introduce data to show the periodicity of other phenomena such as ionic radii and electronegativity.

Answers: (1) Yes. Although the graph of atomic radius drops within a period, it increases with each increasing shell. With each repeating period (return to the alkali metals) the graph of atomic radius jumps up again. This repetitious behavior within each new period is known as periodicity. (2) Yes. As with radius, the graph of first ionization energy goes through cycles. The first family (alkali metals) has very small ionization energies, while the noble gases have very high ionization energies. (3) The alkali metals have the greatest radius within any period. (4) The atomic radius decreases across a period. The alkali metals have a single electron in their outermost (valence) shell. With each successive element in this shell, there is an additional electron and an additional proton. The attractive force of the nucleus therefore increases as you proceed through a series, and this collapses the orbitals so they are closer to the nucleus. (5) The noble gases. The noble gases have complete outer shells, the smallest radii, and consequently exhibit the greatest pull for valence electrons. (6) Large. In large atoms, the valence electrons are quite distant from the attractive forces of the nucleus. As a result, valence electrons in large atoms are lost more easily. (7) The noble gases have the highest ionization energies. Noble gases have the smallest radii, and therefore their electrons are closest to the attractive forces of the nuclei and consequently are most difficult

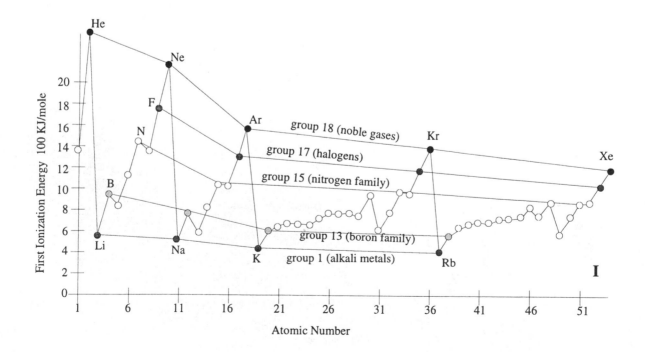

to remove. (8) Yes. Students should note that the halogens have the strongest electron affinity and the second family has the weakest. They may also see other more subtle trends.

2.2.4 TRENDS WITHIN FAMILIES

Discussion: The results from part 2 should appear as follows:

	Chlorine Water (10 mL)	*Bromine Water (10 mL)*	*Iodine Water (10 mL)*
0.2 M KCl solution (10 mL)	colorless Cl_2	straw yellow Br_2	brown I_2
0.2 M KBr solution (10 mL)	straw yellow Br_2	straw yellow Br_2	brown I_2
0.2 M KI solution (10 mL)	brown I_2	brown I_2	brown I_2

The reactivity series for the halogens is nicely demonstrated in these reactions showing that reactivity (electron affinity) decreases with increasing atomic number. Although each halogen has seven valence electrons, shielding occurs as shells are added. Hence, molecular chlorine replaces the bromide ion and molecular bromine replaces the iodide ion. The reactions are as follows:

$$Cl_2 + 2KBr \longrightarrow 2KCl + Br_2 \text{ [straw yellow]}$$

$$Br_2 + 2KI \longrightarrow 2KBr + I_2 \text{ [brown]}$$

Notice that we did not include fluorine in this activity. Molecular fluorine can replace chloride, bromide, and iodide ions in solution. However, molecular fluorine is so reactive that it even reacts with water. Consequently, the reactions we have described for chlorine, bromine, and iodine in aqueous solutions cannot occur with fluorine. The halogens as a group are the most reactive of the nonmetallic elements and are strong oxidizing agents.

The colors of halogen gases in water are different than they are in air. In air, chlorine is yellow-green, but in water it is nearly colorless. As a gas, bromine is reddish brown, but in water it is straw yellow. As a gas, iodine is violet, but in water it is brown. You may wish to tell your students this to avoid confusion if they have previously studied the nature of these halogen gases.

Answers: (1) Elements in the first family react readily with water to form metal hydroxides, while those in the 11th family do not. (2) The elements in the first family react with water to form hydroxides according to the following equation.

$$2X + 2H_2O \longrightarrow 2X^+OH^- + H_2$$

Lithium hydroxide, sodium hydroxide and potassium hydroxide will be formed depending upon which alkali metal is added to the water. (3) Potassium reacts the most violently with water because its valence electron is at the highest energy level (the 4th shell), and is shielded by three inner shells. This electron is more easily lost than the valence electron of sodium, which is lost more easily than the valence electron of lithium. Reactivity increases with increasing period number within elements of the first family. (4) There is no visible reaction between the 11th family metals and water. Chemical reactions between first family elements and water are evidenced by the production of light, heat, and the color change of the base indicator, phenolphthalein. (5) The 11th family metals are relatively unreactive, and so it is possible that they may exist in elemental form. The alkali metals react vigorously with water and other materials to form various compounds, and as a result, are never found in elemental form. (6) No. Chlorine water is colorless, and so there is no color change. (7) Yes. Chlorine has a greater affinity for electrons than bromine and thus molecular bromine forms, turning the solution straw yellow. (8) Yes. Bromine has a greater affinity for electrons than iodine and thus molecular iodine forms, turning the solution brown. (9) Decrease. Electron affinity is greatest at the top of the halogen family, and decreases with increasing size. (10) As atomic number increases, the reactivity of alkali metals increases (ionization energy becomes lower), while the reactivity of halogens decreases (electron affinity becomes lower).

Applications to Everyday Life

Predicting the properties of unknown elements: Just as Mendeleev predicted the properties of unknown elements on the basis of their positions in the periodic table, so chemists today have predicted the properties of elements that have yet to be discovered or synthesized.

Selecting materials: The Periodic Table can be helpful when selecting materials for use in various products. For example, we know that gold is malleable, conductive, and unreactive and therefore useful in coinage and electrical circuits. When looking for less expensive substitutes, one only needs to look for other members of the same family that are found in greater abundance, namely copper and silver. When looking for semi-conducting materials for use in transistors, chemists looked for elements similar to silicon, a known semiconductor. Germanium, the element directly below silicon in the 14th group, was examined and found to meet the criteria, and is now used extensively in computer chips and similar applications.

Hazards: Elements that are in the same family tend to share similar properties. Many chemistry students have witnessed the dramatic reaction between sodium and water and may correctly infer from the periodic table that other members of the 1st family, namely lithium, sodium, potassium, rubidium, cesium and francium, share similar properties and must be handled with caution.

Periodicity in nature: The periodicity within the Periodic Table is but one example of the periodicity in the natural world. Electrons spin about their axes and orbit around nuclei in known orbitals, quartz crystals vibrate at predictable frequencies, the Moon orbits the Earth in predictable periods, the planets orbit the Sun with known frequencies, etc. Ask your students to list as many natural phenomena as they can think of that exhibit an element of periodicity.

2.3 DIFFUSION AND OSMOSIS

How many of the following items do you think you can identify simply on the basis of smell? Freshly baked bread, roofing tar, pine trees, perfume, the interior of a new car, garlic, gasoline, smoke, ammonia, ocean air, dirty socks, a rose, a rotten egg, natural gas, freshly brewed coffee, vanilla? Our sense of smell provides us with important information about our environment and helps us identify useful and harmful substances. You may have noticed a gas leak in your home or lab by the distinctive odor accompanying natural gas, or perhaps your stomach has started to rumble when you detected the smell of freshly baked bread. Although smell is important to humans, it is far more important to many insects and animals. Dogs, for example, rely heavily on smell to identify their masters and to locate food, other animals, and their mates. Bloodhounds have an extremely sensitive sense of smell and use their noses to track down fugitives or missing persons and locate smuggled stashes of illegal drugs in airports and at border crossings.

You smell something when airborne molecules of that substance settle on receptors located high in the nasal cavity, stimulating a signal to your brain. When you smell a rose, it is because molecules of phenylethyl alcohol (the fragrant molecules in roses) have landed on the receptor cells in the nose, stimulating a specific signal that is sent to the brain. However, when you smell a rotten egg, it is because molecules of hydrogen sulfide (rotten egg gas) have landed in the same region but have stimulated a different signal. How do molecules of phenylethyl alcohol get from a rose to your nose, or molecules of hydrogen sulfide get from a rotten egg to your nose?

The kinetic theory of matter suggests that all atoms and molecules are in constant motion. The hotter a substance is, the faster its molecules or atoms move. The movement of atoms or molecules is random, and as a result the number of molecules exiting a given volume of higher concentration will be greater than the movement of molecules into this region from an area of lower concentration. This process, in which there is a net flow of matter from a region of high concentration to a region of low concentration due to the random motion of molecules, is known as diffusion.

When an onion is cut, molecules of 1-propenylsulfenic acid (the chemical that makes your eyes tear) are released. The molecules are in very high concentration on the cut surface, but in low concentration throughout the room. As a result, the 1-propenylsulfenic acid diffuses away from the onion and within a few seconds reaches the eyes of the one who cut the onion, making them tear. As time proceeds, people farther and farther from the onion will feel the effect of the lacrimator (a lacrimator is any chemical that makes your eyes water) as the molecules of 1-propenylsulfenic acid continue to diffuse from regions of higher concentration in the vicinity of the onion, to regions of lower concentration throughout the room. In this chapter you will investigate diffusion and its applications in everyday life.

2.3.1 BROWNIAN MOTION

Concepts to Investigate: Brownian motion, kinetic theory, diffusion.

Materials: Whole (regular) milk (or India ink), 1000X microscope, microscope slide, coverslip.

Principles and Procedures: In 1827, British botanist Robert Brown was observing pollen grains under his microscope when he noticed that the grains were moving in an erratic, zigzag fashion (Figure A). When he observed similar movement with pollen grains that had been dead for more than 100 years, he concluded that this motion was not a form of propulsion such as seen in micro-organisms, but rather a response to some inanimate (non-living) force in the environment. Later in the 19th century, scientists used Brownian motion to support the newly developed kinetic theory of matter that stated that atoms or molecules are in a constant state of motion. They suggested that the movement of the tiny pollen grains resulted from collisions with rapidly moving molecules in the surrounding fluid.

You can observe Brownian motion in the laboratory by looking at the fat droplets suspended in homogenized whole milk. Place a drop of homogenized whole (regular) milk on a microscope slide and place a cover slip over it. Focus on the drop first under low power, and then rotate the lens turret to view the milk under medium and high power. By modifying the intensity of the light source or the diameter of the substage aperture, it is possible to observe fat droplets that will appear as tiny dots. Describe the motion that you observe. While watching through the microscope, gently heat the specimen by directing air from a hair drier onto the slide (Figure B). Does the movement of the droplets appear to be influenced by a temperature change?

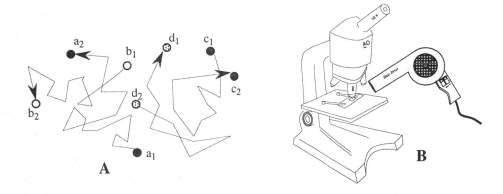

Questions

(1) Describe the motion of the particles in solution. Is the motion random?
(2) What influence does temperature appear to have on the motion of the fat droplets?

2.3.2 DIFFUSION OF GASES

Concepts to Investigate: Diffusion, odors.

Materials: Measuring tape or meter stick, liquid with a strong but safe odor (e.g., air freshner, vinegar, perfume, onion juice, cologne).

Principles and Procedures: Note: this activity works best when the air is very calm. Soak a rag in a jar of perfume, vinegar, cologne, or onion juice (a solution of onion juice can be made by puréeing an onion in a blender and then soaking the product in a small amount of water). Remove the rag and suspend it from a ring-stand or place it on a table in the middle of the room (Figure C). Reseal the jar immediately. (Alternatively, you may wish to spray short bursts of air freshener.) Each student in the class should raise his or her hand the moment they first detect the odor (Figure D). Record the time when each student raises his or her hand and the distance from the student to the source of the odor. Calculate the rate of diffusion to each individual in the class by dividing the distance from the object by the time required for the student to detect the odor. Do you predict that odors will be detected sooner on a warm day or a cool day? If possible, repeat this activity when the air temperature is considerably different. Do the molecules diffuse faster when the temperature is warmer or cooler?

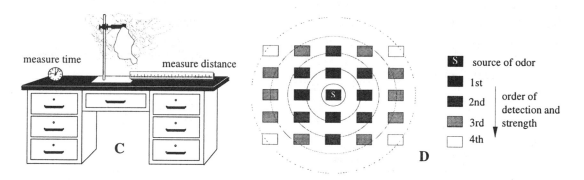

Questions

(1) Which students detected the odor first? Which detected it to be strongest? Explain.

(2) The fragrance of flowers is stronger on warm days than on cool days. Explain.

(3) Party balloons filled with hydrogen (atomic number 1) or helium (atomic number 2) collapse in a short time. Explain.

2.3.3 THE EFFECT
OF TEMPERATURE ON DIFFUSION

Concepts to Investigate: Diffusion rates, kinetic theory, molecular motion.

Materials: Part 1: Beakers (or clear drinking glasses), pipets (or medicine dropper), food coloring, time pieces; Part 2: Perfume, vinegar, cologne or onion juice; rag, ice.

Principles and Procedures:

Part 1: The effect of temperature on diffusion in liquids: Obtain three beakers or clear drinking glasses. Fill one with ice water, one with room temperature tap water, and one with hot tap water. Place white paper underneath and behind the containers to highlight diffusion of the dye. Use a pipet or medicine dropper to place a single drop of concentrated food coloring on the surface of the liquid in each beaker as shown in Figure E. Record your observations regarding the rate of diffusion of the dye in each beaker. Record the time required for the color to become uniform throughout the container (Figure F).

Part 2: The effect of temperature on the rate of diffusion in gases: Place a rag in a container of perfume, vinegar, cologne or onion juice. Place the container in an ice water bath until the temperatures have equilibrated. Open the jar, place the rag on a desk in the center of the room (Figure C in 2.3.2), and reseal the container. Each student in the class should raise his or her hand the moment they first detect the odor (Figure D in 2.3.2). Record the time each student raises his or her hand and the student's distance from the source of the odor. On day 2 repeat the process after soaking the container in a water bath at room temperature. On day 3, repeat the process after soaking the container in a hot water bath (approximately 60°C).

E   room temperature   hot water   ice water   F

Questions

(1) According to your observations, describe the change in the diffusion rate of the dye as the temperature is increased in part 1.

(2) How does the diffusion rate of odorous material change as the temperature is increased in part 2?

(3) Are the odors associated with horse stables, gasoline stations, and soiled socks more noticeable on hot days or cool days? Explain.

2.3.4 THE EFFECT OF MOLECULAR SIZE
ON DIFFUSION RATE

Concepts to Investigate: Diffusion rate, molecular weight, Graham's Law of Diffusion, kinetic theory, density.

Materials: Part 1: Petri dishes, agar, potassium permanganate crystal, methylene blue powder, mm ruler; Part 2: cotton swabs, hydrochloric acid, ammonia solution (cleaning ammonia), graduated cylinders (preferably 100 mL or greater).

Safety: *Part 1: Wear goggles, laboratory apron. Part 2: Instructor demonstration only. See precautions below.*

Principles and Procedures: You may have noticed that small children can move through crowds more easily than adults. While children can squeeze through small openings in the crowd, adults are often blocked because of their size. Molecules behave in much the same way, with larger molecules moving more slowly through gases, liquids and solids than smaller molecules (Figure G). Thus, it is possible to infer relative molecular weights simply by the rate at which a molecule diffuses if all other factors are kept constant.

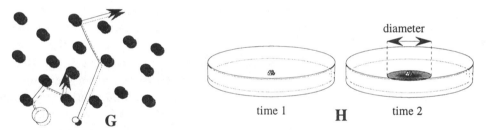

Part 1: The influence of molecular size on diffusion rate in liquids and gels: In this activity your goal is to determine the relative sizes of molecules of two dyes: potassium permanganate and methylene blue. Measure an equivalent mass of potassium permanganate and methylene blue (1 g is sufficient.) Place the potassium permanganate in the middle of a Petri dish filled with agar, and the methylene blue in the middle of an identically prepared dish (Figure H). As molecules in the dyes diffuse through the agar they will leave a stain. The faster they diffuse, the faster the stains will grow. Construct a data table and record the diameter of each stain at fixed time intervals.

Part 2: Graham's Law of Diffusion: *Teacher demonstration only. Wear goggles, face shield, and lab coat whenever working with concentrated hydrochloric acid.*

Graham's Law of Diffusion states that the relative rates of diffusion *(r)* of two gases are inversely proportional to the square root of their molar masses *(m):*

$$\frac{r_a}{r_b} = \sqrt{\frac{m_b}{m_a}}$$

This means that as molar mass (molecular size) increases, the rate of diffusion decreases. For example, if the molar mass of gas *a* (m_a) is 4 times greater than the molar mass of gas *b* (m_b), then the rate of diffusion of *b* (r_b) will be twice as great as the rate of diffusion of *a* (r_a). Since the molar mass of a gas is directly proportional to its molecular weight (assuming constant pressure), we can extend the relationship:

$$\frac{r_a}{r_b} = \sqrt{\frac{m_b}{m_a}} = \sqrt{\frac{MW_b}{MW_a}}$$

Thus, if you know the relative diffusion rates of two gases (r_a, r_b), you can determine their relative molecular weights (MW_a, MW_b).

If you have ever opened a bottle of cleaning ammonia or pool acid, you have probably noticed strong odors. You detect an odor after molecules have diffused from the container to receptors in your nose. According to Graham's Law of Diffusion, which gas would you predict diffuses faster, the ammonia (NH_3) gas or hydrogen chloride (HCl) gas? Test your prediction by performing the following activity.

<u>Part 2a:</u> Moisten a piece of blue litmus paper or Hydrion paper. Use a glass rod to carefully transfer this paper to the bottom of the tallest graduated cylinder available. Place the cylinder on its side and insert a cotton ball saturated with concentrated hydrochloric acid at the mouth of the cylinder, and start your stopwatch (Figure I). Immediately seal the cylinder with a rubber stopper and record the distance between the cotton ball and the litmus paper. Watch the litmus paper and record the time at which it <u>begins</u> to change color. Since blue litmus paper turns red in the presence of acid, the color change marks the time when the first molecules have diffused from the cotton ball to the litmus paper. Determine the diffusion rate of hydrogen chloride gas (r_{HCl}) by dividing the distance by the time. Repeat the process using red litmus paper and a cotton ball soaked in ammonium solution (household ammonia glass cleaner). Red litmus paper turns blue in the presence of a base like ammonium hydroxide, so the first color change indicates the time at which ammonia molecules have diffused into the water on the litmus paper, forming ammonium hydroxide. Determine the diffusion rate of ammonia (r_{NH_3}) by dividing the distance between the ammonia-soaked cotton ball and the red litmus paper by the time required for the litmus paper to begin to turn color. Which molecule diffused more rapidly? Is this what you expected?

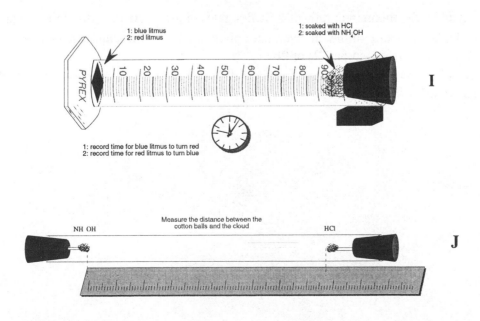

Part 2b: Obtain a piece of glass or Plexiglas tubing with an inner diameter greater than 1 cm and a length greater than 50 cm. Shorten and fasten cotton swabs to the inner surfaces of two one-holed stoppers as shown in Figure J. Apply concentrated HCl to one swab using a dropper, and ammonia solution to the other. Insert the two stoppers in the tube at the same time and support the tubing on a ring stand or place on an overhead projector so all can observe (Figure J). The ammonia and hydrogen chloride molecules will diffuse at different rates depending upon their molecular weights. When ammonia molecules contact hydrogen chloride molecules, the white salt ammonium chloride forms:

$$HCl(g) + NH_3(g) \longrightarrow NH_4Cl(s)$$

Carefully observe the tube for the formation of a white ring. Record the distance between this ring and both the ammonia and hydrogen chloride sources. The substance that traveled farther must have traveled faster and must have been the smaller molecule. Which molecule is smaller?

Questions

(1) Which molecule diffused faster in part 1, methylene blue or potassium permanganate?

(2) On the basis of your data, which substance do you think is composed of larger molecules, methylene blue or potassium permanganate? Explain.

(3) On the basis of data from part 2a or 2b, which molecule is smaller, ammonia or hydrochloric acid? Explain.

(4) Using Graham's Law of Diffusion,

$$\frac{r_a}{r_b} = \sqrt{\frac{m_b}{m_a}} = \sqrt{\frac{MW_b}{MW_a}}$$

calculate the theoretical ratio of diffusion rates of ammonia to hydrochloric acid.

(5) Calculate the ratio of the diffusion rates of ammonia to hydrochloric acid based on the data you collected in part 2a or 2b.

(6) What is the relative error of the ratio of diffusion rates you computed to the theoretical value?

2.3.5 OSMOSIS

Concepts to Investigate: Semi-permeability, osmosis, diffusion, solute, solvent, food preservation.

Materials: Part 1: potatoes, knife, balance, salt, beakers.

Principles and Procedures: Before the refrigerator and freezer were invented, people from many cultures relied on salt to preserve meat and other perishable foods. By packing foods in salt, the growth of bacteria and other micro-organisms was slowed, thereby lengthening the "shelf-life" of the food. This ancient process of food preservation relies on a form of diffusion know as osmosis—the movement of a fluid across a semi-permeable membrane from a region of higher concentration to a region of lower concentration. A semi-permeable membrane is one that allows certain materials to pass, while restricting the passage of others.

Biological membranes are semi-permeable, allowing water to pass more readily than solutes such as sodium and chloride ions. Thus, if a bacterium is placed in a highly saline solution, such as the salt brine used to preserve meat, water will flow from inside the bacterium (where the concentration of water is relatively high) towards the outside, where the concentration of water is relatively low. If sufficient water leaves the bacterium by osmosis, it dies due to dehydration. Thus, salt preserves food by dehydrating bacteria, fungi or other pathogens that might otherwise multiply and spoil the food. Although refrigeration and pasteurization have greatly decreased the need for preservatives like salt, many food companies still place substantial amounts of salt and sugar into their canned foods to increase shelf-life in non-refrigerated environments.

Part 1: Osmosis in plant tissues: Prepare a saturated salt solution by slowly mixing salt into a container of water. Continue to add salt until the bottom of the beaker is covered with undissolved salt. Fill one beaker with tap water and another with concentrated salt solution.

Using a sharp knife (use caution!), prepare 10 sections of potato that are 1 cm wide, by 1 cm deep, by 5 cm long. Separate these pieces into two groups of 5 and determine the average weight and length of each group. Place one group of potato pieces into the beaker of tap water and one into the beaker of salt water (Figure K). At the end of the period remove the slices from beaker 1, blot them dry with a towel, and again determine their average length and weight. Repeat the process with the potato slices in group 2. Repeat the measurements on the following day. Are there differences between the potatoes in salt water and those in tap water?

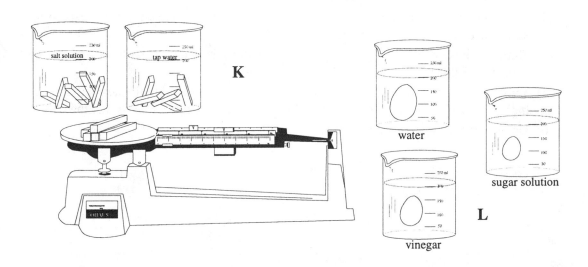

Table 1: Osmosis in plant tissues

	Group 1 (tap water)		Group 2 (salt solution)	
	Average Weight (g)	*Average Length (mm)*	*Average Weight (g)*	*Average Length (mm)*
(1) Before soaking				
(2) At end of period				
(3) Next day				

Part 2: Osmosis in animal tissues: The membrane of a chicken egg is semi-permeable, allowing the free movement of water, but restricting ions and larger molecules. Although the membrane around the chicken egg is hidden beneath the shell, it can be exposed if the egg is soaked for a sufficient length of time in vinegar (dilute acetic acid). The acid dissolves the calcium carbonate in the egg shell, exposing the membrane. Once the membrane is exposed it can be used to study osmosis.

Place three eggs in vinegar. Replace the vinegar as necessary until the shell has completely dissolved, leaving the egg surrounded only by its membrane. The shell can generally be dissolved in a period of about four hours. Once the shells have dissolved, carefully remove the eggs from the vinegar, blot them dry and weigh them. Place one egg in fresh water, one in a solution of saturated sugar (Karo® syrup works well), and one in vinegar (Figure L). Predict what will happen to the mass and volume of each egg, and then check your predictions by making measurements at the end of the period and again on the next day. The volume of the eggs can be determined by displacement (Figure M).

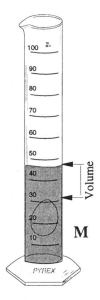

Questions

(1) Did any of the potato sections lose weight? Explain.

(2) Did any of the potato sections gain weight? Explain.

(3) Most vegetables become limp as they age. Describe how you can use osmosis to restore the crispness of such vegetables.

(4) Tanners (those who prepare leather) soak leather in salt water when they are preparing it for use. Explain.

(5) Which of the eggs in part 2 is hypertonic to its solution? (Hypertonic means that it has higher osmotic pressure, evidenced in this case by expansion). Why is this the case?

(6) Do any of the eggs shrink? Explain.

2.3.6 OSMOTIC PRESSURE

Concepts to Investigate: Osmosis, semi-permeable membranes, solute, solvent, diffusion, root pressure, osmotic pressure.

Materials: Large carrots (you may substitute potatoes), apple corer, syrup, beaker, glass tubing, one-holed rubber stopper, glycerin.

Principles and Procedures: For centuries people have pondered the mechanisms by which water rises in plants from roots to leaves. We now know that one of the processes involved is osmosis. Since there are generally more solutes (salts, sugars, dissolved organic products) in the epidermal cells of a root than there are in the surrounding water in the soil, water will flow by osmosis from the soil (region of high water concentration) to the root (region of lower water concentration). This increases the pressure of water in the cells of the root, forcing water to rise up the conductive tissue (xylem) of the roots (Figure N).

Using an apple corer, remove a cylinder (approximately 4 or 5 cm section) of carrot tissue from the top of a carrot as shown in Figure O. Fill the well with a concentrated sugar solution (Karo® syrup works well). Place a long section of glass tube fitted with a stopper into the well as shown. Record the initial height of the sugar solution. Immerse the carrot in water as shown and re-measure the height of the solution in the tube at three or four intervals during the next two days. Repeat the procedure with a second carrot, but this time fill the well with water.

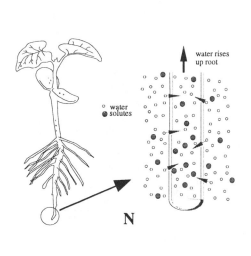

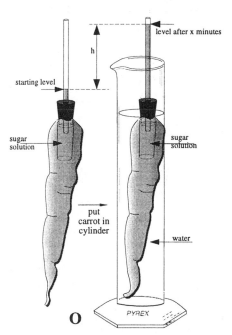

Questions

(1) Does "the sap" rise more noticeably when the well is filled with fresh water or with sugar water? Explain.

(2) Pressure is often measured in mm of mercury, but can also be measured in mm of water or mm of syrup. What was the highest osmotic pressure recorded in your experiment?

(3) Suppose the wells of three carrots were filled with increasingly more concentrated sugar solutions. Predict the results.

2.3.7 DIALYSIS

Concepts to Investigate: Dialysis, diffusion, molecular size, semi-permeability, membranes.

Materials: Dialysis tubing, glucose, starch, string, beakers, iodine-potassium iodide solution (starch indicator I_2-KI), glucose test tape.

Principles and Procedures: Your kidneys work continually to filter out toxic wastes from your blood and maintain a proper pH and salt balance. Patients who suffer from kidney failure are generally placed on dialysis machines that imitate the work done by the kidneys. The term dialysis refers to a special form of diffusion in which smaller molecules are separated from larger molecules by selective movement through a semi-permeable membrane. In this experiment, you will use the process of dialysis to determine the relative molecular size of starch and glucose molecules.

Cut a length of dialysis tubing approximately 12 cm in length. Wet the tubing with water until it becomes pliable, then rub it with your fingers until it opens. Tie one end of the tubing tightly with a string and fill it with a solution of glucose and starch (Figure P). Tie the other end of the tubing and place it in a beaker of tap water in which 10 drops of iodine solution have been mixed (Figure Q). It is essential that there be no leaks, so if you are unable to close the ends of the tube securely with string, then cut longer sections of tubing and tie knots in the ends of the tubing itself. Allow the tubing to stand for at least 20 minutes. A blue-black color appears wherever iodine comes in contact with starch. Test for the presence of glucose in the beaker by using glucose test tape. Evaluate your results by comparing the tape with the color key on the container.

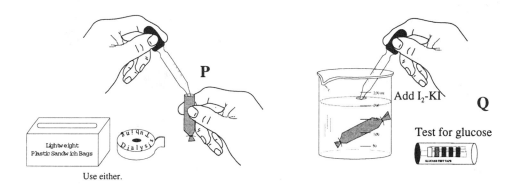

Questions

(1) Did iodine diffuse into the "cell"? How do you know?
(2) Did starch diffuse out of the "cell"? How do you know?
(3) Did glucose diffuse out of the "cell"? How do you know?
(4) Which of the three molecules—starch, iodine or glucose—appears to be the largest? Explain.
(5) How might dialysis be used to filter blood?

FOR THE TEACHER

The rate of diffusion (*j;* the amount of substance passing per unit area per unit time) is proportional to the ratio of the change in concentration (*dc*) per unit distance (*dx*): $j = -D(dc/dx)$ where *D* is a constant of proportionality. In other words, the rate of flow of diffusion is directly proportional to the concentration gradient. If the concentration gradient is great, the rate of diffusion will be great. The rate of diffusion slows as the concentration gradient (*dc/dx*) decreases, and eventually stops when the concentration of the substance is equal throughout the system (*dc/dx* = 0)

In gases diffusion is rapid and is proportional to the square root of temperature and inversely proportional to the square root of molecular weight. For example, a quadrupling of the absolute temperature will cause a doubling of the diffusion rate, while a quadrupling of particle size will result in a 50% reduction in diffusion rate. In liquids, diffusion is dependent upon the viscosity of the medium as well as the size and shape of molecules. Diffusion can also occur in solids, though much more slowly than in liquids. Diffusion is important in living systems, because the movement of substances into and out of cells usually involves diffusion through a cell membrane.

2.3.1 BROWNIAN MOTION

Discussion: Brownian motion can be observed in a variety of colloidal suspensions when particle size is very small. The process of homogenization used in the preparation of "whole" milk fractures globules of the fat into droplets approximately 1/100th their original size. Because the droplets of fat are so small, they move in response to molecular collisions, but most movement will look merely like vibration to the student. India ink works well for this activity, and students can observe Brownian motion when focusing on the carbon particles suspended in solution.

Answers: (1) The particles appear to vibrate. They move relatively short distances before they shift directions. The motion appears to be random. (2) Students should note that the droplets vibrate more rapidly when heated by the hair drier. This is consistent with the kinetic theory which states that the velocity of molecules is a function of the temperature of the system. As the temperature increases, the molecules move more rapidly and the resulting collisions produce a more dramatic movement of the fat droplets.

2.3.2 DIFFUSION OF GASES

Discussion: This activity allows students to visualize the invisible diffusion process. Although students cannot see individual molecules of the volatile fragrance, they can observe how it slowly diffuses from its source to the walls of the classroom by watching students respond to the odor. The pattern of diffusion may be irregular if you have drafts due to air conditioning or open windows. Use this as an opportunity to show how small, invisible air currents can be detected.

Answers: (1) Diffusion is the random movement of molecules from a region of higher concentration to a region of lower concentration. The concentration of the odoriferous molecules is greatest at the center of the room on the surface of the cloth. The net movement of molecules out of the cloth is similar to the radial movement of sound or light from a point source. Students closest to the rag will detect the odor first and strongest in the same way that those closest to thunder will hear it first and loudest. (2) Molecular motion is a function of temperature. On warm days, molecules move more rapidly and thus diffuse more rapidly, so they are detected more readily and in greater quantity. (3) The hydrogen molecule (H_2) and the helium atom (He) are extremely small and diffuse through the tiny pores in the walls of the balloon.

2.3.3 THE EFFECT OF TEMPERATURE ON DIFFUSION

Discussion: Temperature is a measure of the average kinetic energy of particles in a sample of matter. The higher the temperature, the higher the average kinetic energy of the molecules. Since the kinetic energy of a molecule is a function of its velocity *($E_k = 1/2\ mv^2$)*, we can assume that more energetic molecules (those at higher temperature) travel faster, and therefore diffuse faster.

Answers: (1) The diffusion rate increases as a function of temperature. The higher the temperature, the more rapid the diffusion. (2) As with liquids, diffusion in gases is temperature dependent. The higher the temperature, the more rapid the diffusion. (3) The vapor pressure and diffusion rate of molecules increases with increasing temperature. Odors are more noticeable on warm days than on cool days because more odor molecules are in the air, and they reach you faster.

2.3.4 THE EFFECT OF MOLECULAR SIZE ON DIFFUSION RATE

Discussion: Methylene blue ($C_{16}H_{18}ClN_3S$) is a common bacteriological stain and is often used as an oxidation-reduction indicator. It has a molecular weight of 320 g/mole, while the weight of potassium permanganate ($KMnO_4$) is only 158. Most of the diffusion equations found in textbooks deal only with the diffusion of ideal gases. It is commonly stated that the average speed of molecules is inversely proportional to the square root of their molecular weight. Although we are not dealing with ideal gases, a similar but more complex relationship holds.

Answers: (1) Potassium permanganate (*MW* = 158) diffuses more rapidly than methylene blue (*MW* = 320). (2) The methylene blue is a larger molecule as evidenced by the fact that it diffuses more slowly than the potassium permanganate. (3) Ammonia, with a molecular weight of 17.0 is smaller and travels faster than hydrogen chloride with a molecular weight of 36.5.

$$(4) \quad \sqrt{\frac{MW_{HCl}}{MW_{NH_3}}} = \sqrt{\frac{36.5\,g/mole}{17.0\,g/mole}} = 1.46 = \frac{r_{NH_3}}{r_{HCl}}$$

(5) The theoretical value is 1.46. Results will vary depending on how carefully the stoppers are inserted. Inserting them too quickly sets up air currents which change the apparent diffusion rate. Inserting the stoppers at different times makes the data uninterpretable because the material inserted first gets a "head start." (6) Relative error is calculated as follows:

$$\frac{(\text{Ratio}_{\text{theoretical}} - \text{Ratio}_{\text{experimental}})}{\text{Ratio}_{\text{theoretical}}} \times 100\%$$

2.3.5 OSMOSIS

Discussion: The principle of osmosis can be easily demonstrated by soaking one piece of celery in salt water, and another in fresh water. The celery soaked in fresh water is very crisp while the celery soaked in salt water is flaccid. Students are often confused with the terms hypotonic, hypertonic and isotonic because they do not realize that these are relative terms rather than absolute terms. For example, the contents of a cell may be hypertonic when compared to freshwater, but hypotonic when compared to salt water. Remember that *hypo-* means below (e.g., a hypodermic needle goes below the dermis or skin), *hyper-* means above (e.g., a hyperactive person is overly active), and *iso-* means the same (e.g., an isosceles triangle has three sides of equal length).

The cells in the potato have a greater concentration of dissolved solutes than the fresh water in which they are placed. The concentration of water outside the potato is greater than it is inside, and water flows into potato cells. Tissue swelling is evidence that the cells are hypertonic (have higher osmotic pressure) to the surrounding medium. If these same cells are placed in a saturated solution, water will exit and the tissue will shrink, indicating that the potato is now hypotonic to the solution.

Part 2: Osmosis in animal tissues: Calcium carbonate is the most abundant component of egg shells. Acetic acid dissolves calcium carbonate as shown by the following equation:

$$CaCO_3(s) + 2CH_3COOH(aq) \longrightarrow Ca^{++}(aq) + 2CH_3COO^-(aq) + H_2CO_3(aq)$$

Students will notice the formation of bubbles on the surface of the egg shell. These bubbles are carbon dioxide, resulting from the dissociation of the carbonic acid:

$$H_2CO_3 \longrightarrow H_2O + CO_2$$

Answers (1) The potatoes should lose weight in salt water as water leaves them through osmosis. (2) The potatoes should gain weight in fresh water as water enters them through osmosis. (3) The turgor of vegetables can be restored by soaking them in fresh water. (4) Tanners soak leather in salt water to prevent bacterial decay. The salt solution kills the bacteria by dehydration, thereby preserving the leather from decay. (5) The egg in the fresh water is hypertonic to the water. There are more dissolved solutes in the egg than in the water, and therefore the water is purer outside than inside. Water moves from a region of higher water concentration (outside) to a region of lower water concentration (inside) causing the egg to swell. The swelling is evidence that it is hypertonic. (6) The egg in the sugar solution shrinks because it is hypotonic (has lower osmotic pressure) to the solution. The water was in greater concentration (less dissolved solutes) inside the egg than in the outside medium, thus water left the egg through osmosis, leaving it shriveled.

2.3.6 OSMOTIC PRESSURE

Discussion: In this activity students were introduced to the concept of root pressure and were shown how it is created by osmosis. Osmosis is also important in drawing water into leaves at the top of a plant. As water transpires (evaporates through the stomatal pores) from leaves, the solute concentration in the leaves increases (water concentration decreases), and water flows in from surrounding cells in the conductive xylem tissue).

Answers: (1) Water will rise in the carrot whose well is filled with sugar solution because water flows from a region of higher water concentration (lower solute concentration) in the cells of the carrot to a region of lower water concentration (higher solute concentration) in the well of the carrot. As water flows into the well, pressure rises and the water level in the glass tubing rises. (2) Student answers will vary, but the syrup frequently rises more than a meter before it starts to fall as the carrot tissue dies. One could express such pressure as "100 mm of syrup." To convert to millimeters of mercury, it would be necessary to divide this number by the ratio of the density of mercury to the density of the solution in the tube. This ratio is 13.6 for water, but will be less than this for the syrup used. (3) Within limits, the higher the concentration of sugars, the higher the osmotic pressure, and the higher the water will rise.

2.3.7 DIALYSIS

Discussion: Most dialysis tubing is made from regenerated cellulose. This material blocks the diffusion of substances with a molecular weight in excess of 10,000 (most proteins and nucleic acids), while permitting the diffusion of smaller molecular substances such as salts and amino acids. Hemodialysis is a process used for removing toxic wastes from the blood when an individual has suffered kidney failure. Surgical tubing is connected to a patient's vein, allowing blood to pass into the dialysis machine where toxic wastes are removed before the blood returns to the patient's body.

Answers: (1) Yes. The inside of the cell turns purple, indicating that iodine has diffused across the membrane. (2) No. There is no purple coloration in the water outside the "cell," indicating that starch did not diffuse across the membrane. (3) Yes. Glucose test tape indicates the presence of glucose in the solution outside the cell, showing that it must have diffused across the membrane. (4) Starch appears to be the largest molecule because it was the only one of the three that did not diffuse across the membrane. (5) Blood flows on one side of the membrane, and the dialysis solution flows on the other. Small molecular weight toxins diffuse out of the blood and are washed away, but larger molecular weight proteins remain in the blood.

Applications to Everyday Life

Flames: As a fire burns, oxygen is consumed and the concentration of oxygen near the flame decreases, creating an oxygen gradient. Oxygen from the surrounding atmosphere diffuses down the oxygen concentration gradient into the region of the flame, keeping the flame alive. Diffusion is a relatively slow process, and this prevents such flames from getting as hot as flames in a Bunsen burner or blowtorch where oxygen is premixed with the fuel.

Respiration: In the lungs oxygen diffuses from oxygen-rich air into deoxygenated blood. As this newly-oxygenated blood moves into muscle tissue, oxygen diffuses to muscle cells where it is continually consumed. Carbon dioxide diffuses out of muscle cells (where it is relatively concentrated due to respiration) into the blood. Carbon dioxide is carried in the blood until it arrives at the lungs where concentrations are still lower, causing it diffuse out and be exhaled.

Animal communication: Many animals communicate by chemicals known as pheromones. These chemicals diffuse from a region of high concentration near their source to a region of low concentration in the surrounding environment. For example, female silk moths secrete a pheromone as they fly. When male silk moths detect the presence of the pheromone in the air they fly towards regions where the concentration of the pheromone is greater. If they continue to follow the concentration gradient toward higher levels of the pheromone, they will eventually find the female.

Taste and smell: The taste buds of the tongue detect four primary taste sensations (sweet, bitter, salty, and sour), but all other flavor characteristics are determined by smell. Molecules from the food being eaten diffuse to the receptors in the nasal cavity where they are detected. When mucous blocks the diffusion of the flavor-inducing molecules, as during a cold, foods may taste bland.

The atomic bomb: During World War II the United States government began a top secret research program to develop a weapon that utilized self-sustaining nuclear fission. Researchers found that uranium-235 would support such fission, but uranium-238 would not. Naturally occurring uranium ore is only 0.7% U-235 (99.3% U-238). To construct a bomb, it was necessary to use uranium that was enriched in U-235, but because U-235 and U-238 are isotopes of the same element, they could not be separated by standard chemical means. The problem was solved using uranium hexaflouride (UF_6), a compound with a high vapor pressure at room temperature. Because $^{235}UF_6(MW = 349)$ is slightly less dense than $^{238}UF_6(MW = 352)$ it diffuses slightly faster through porous barriers. Each time a mixture of the two gases diffuse through such a barrier, the diffused material becomes slightly richer in $^{235}UF_6$ because it diffuses faster. After thousands of diffusion processes it is possible to obtain highly enriched uranium.

Desalination by reverse osmosis: Much of the Middle East (Egypt, Israel, Saudi Arabia, Jordan, Syria, Iraq, Iran, Kuwait, etc.) is very dry and in need of new ways to provide water for their growing populations. Some have developed desalination plants (factories that remove salt from sea water) by a process known as reverse osmosis. If a semi-permeable membrane is placed between fresh and salt water, water will flow from the fresh water to the salt water creating osmotic pressure on the salty side. If, however, pressure is applied to the salty side, this process can be reversed (LeChatelier's principle) and water will actually move from the salty side to the pure side. By applying constant pressure on the salty side of special membranes, salts and minerals can be removed from the water, creating water of high purity for drinking and other purposes.

Determination of molecular weight: Osmosis is employed to determine the molecular weights of large molecules. A known mass of the substance in question is dissolved on one side of a semi-permeable membrane. Water will flow from the pure side of the membrane into this chamber, creating osmotic pressure which can be measured. Since osmotic pressure depends only on the number of dissolved molecules, it is possible to calculate the number of molecules dissolved. By dividing the measured mass of the substance by the quantity of molecules, the molecular weight can be determined.

Preserving food: For centuries people have preserved food by storing it in salt brine or sugar solution. Salt brine and sugar solution kill the micro-organisms that can destroy food. Water flows by osmosis out of bacteria into the surrounding brine solution, leaving the bacteria dehydrated. This dehydration kills the bacteria responsible for food spoilage.

Artificial kidney: In 1943, the Dutch medical researcher Dr. Willem Kolff developed the first dialysis machine to assist patients with kidney failure. Today, kidney dialysis machines are in use around the world, prolonging the lives of thousands of patients. Dialysis machines rely upon the diffusion of molecules across a semi-permeable membrane. The blood from a patient moves across one side of a membrane, while a sterile solution moves across the other side. Waste particles such as urea diffuse down a concentration gradient into the urea-free sterile solution and are thus removed from the blood. The sterile dialysis solution contains vital sugars, amino acids and salts. Thus, although these substances are lost by diffusion into the sterile solution, they are replaced by the diffusion of similar molecules into the blood.

2.4 CHANGES OF STATE

Terms are added continually to the English language to describe new inventions, technologies and discoveries. One term introduced in recent years is "desertification," a term that describes the gradual expansion of deserts. Although the term is new, the process is not. Scientists estimate that during the past several thousand years, the Sahara desert in Africa has gradually advanced 1000 km (600 miles) southward! The expansion of this massive desert has accelerated during the 20th century, with devastating impact upon the people of the Sahel (the vast semi-arid region south of the Sahara). Fields that once supported crops and livestock are now barren and unusable.

The peoples of the Sahel continue to move south to escape the growing desert, but unfortunately bring the desert with them. Soil is destabilized as the native vegetation is removed to make room for crops and pastures. Winds may remove the top soil, leaving the ground barren and desolate. Rain once absorbed by the plants now percolates through the soil or runs off in muddy streams. Plants release water into the atmosphere through a process known as transpiration, but with fewer plants in such regions there is less returned into the atmosphere. Some scientists now believe that a reduction in transpiration results in lower humidity and less rainfall. If true, this loss of moisture would accelerate the spread of deserts.

Today, hydrologists (scientists who study water and the water cycle) and meteorologists (scientists who study weather) are trying to determine the influence human activities have on weather patterns. To understand processes such as desertification, it is essential to understand the nature of water and its movement in the environment (the hydrologic cycle). Water exists in three states (phases): solid (ice or snow), liquid and gas (water vapor or steam). Although you can't see it, water exists as vapor in the air you are now breathing. Meteorologists describe the concentration of water vapor in the atmosphere as "absolute humidity," and the percentage of water vapor in the air relative to the maximum that air may hold as "relative humidity." A relative humidity of 50% means that the air holds 50% of the maximum moisture it can hold at that temperature. Cool air can hold less water vapor than warm air. As warm air rises and cools, water vapor condenses as liquid water droplets or freezes as tiny ice crystals. Clouds appear when many such droplets and/or crystals occur in the same region. When water droplets grow to sufficient size they fall to the Earth as rain, and when ice crystals attain sufficient mass they fall as snow. The hydrologic cycle is completed when water returns to the atmosphere from lakes, rivers, and soil by evaporation; from plants by transpiration (loss of water from leaves); or from the surface of snow or ice by sublimation (the transition of a solid directly to its vapor state).

Although you may be familiar with water in its solid, liquid, and gaseous states, are you aware that all substances may exist in these three states given appropriate temperatures and pressures? The oxygen we breathe is a gas, yet it will condense to a liquid if the temperature drops below −183°C, and will freeze if decreased to −218°C. By contrast, the iron used to make our cars and bridges melts when its temperature is increased to 1538°C, and boils when raised to 2861°C!

Solids: At lower temperatures, molecules move slower and intermolecular forces (attractive forces between similar molecules) cause molecules to cohere (stick together). When such coherence is strong, a material exhibits a high viscosity and a rigid shape. In other words, it has a definite shape (it won't flow) and a definite volume (it does not expand or contract very much). This is known as the solid state.

Liquids: As temperature is raised, molecules move faster and disperse, reducing the influence of attractive intermolecular forces, and allowing the substance to flow while maintaining a constant volume. This liquid state is characterized by indefinite shape (it can flow), but a definite volume (it does not expand or contract very much.) For example, when you pour a quantity of water from a tall, narrow glass into a flat pan, the volume remains the same, but the shape changes.

Gases: As the temperature is raised further, nearly all restraining intermolecular forces are overcome and the substance is free to flow and expand. This gaseous state is characterized by an indefinite shape (it can flow) and an indefinite volume (it will expand to fill the available space).

In this section you will have the opportunity to study the various phases (states) of matter and the transitions between them known as phase changes. The knowledge you gain from the following experiments and activities will help you understand a variety of important phenomena, from the water cycle to freeze-dried foods.

2.4.1 RELATIVE VOLUMES OF SOLID, LIQUID, AND GAS PHASE

Concepts to Investigate: Phase changes; states (phases) of matter; liquids, solids, gases; volume.

Materials: Part 1: Balloon, milk carton, plaster of Paris; Part 2: ring stand, support ring, round-bottom or heavy duty Erlenmeyer flask, one-hole stopper, glass tubing, heat source, food coloring; Part 3: tongs, soda can, burner or hot plate; Part 4: balloon, liquid nitrogen.

Safety: Wear protective goggles and clothing for __all__ activities. Parts 2 and 4 should be performed only by the instructor. The flask in part 2 gets very hot and should be handled with insulated gloves.

Principles and Procedures: According to the kinetic theory, atoms and molecules are always in motion, and the magnitude of this motion is proportional to the temperature. In solids, intermolecular forces restrict motion, so particles move back and forth in fixed positions. As the temperature is increased this vibrational motion becomes more pronounced, until, at the melting point, intermolecular forces are overcome and molecules flow freely as a liquid. As the temperature continues to rise, molecules move more rapidly until they eventually separate from each other at the boiling point. Molecules in the gas phase have high energy and move nearly independently of each other. The molecules in a gas are so widely dispersed that it occupies a volume approximately 1000 times as great as it would in the liquid or solid state.

Part 1: Relative volumes of solid and liquid water (weathering of rock): In most substances, the solid phase is denser than the liquid phase which in turn is denser than the gas phase. In water, however, the solid phase is less dense than the liquid phase. As a solid, ice forms a hexagonal crystal latticework that has a lower density than liquid water. Thus, water expands as it freezes. The following activity will demonstrate the force of this expansion.

Attach a balloon to a faucet and fill with water until the balloon is approximately 10 cm in diameter. Remove all air and tie the end of the balloon. Pour a layer of plaster of Paris in the bottom of an old milk container and once the plaster has nearly dried, place the water-filled balloon in the middle and fill around it with fresh plaster of Paris. When the balloon dries it will be encased in the plaster of Paris. Now place the entombed balloon in a freezer and leave it for at least 24 hours (Figure A). What happens to the plaster of Paris cast as the water freezes?

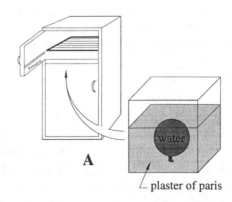

A

plaster of paris

Part 2: The air pressure fountain—relative volumes of liquids and gases: *Caution: This demonstration should be performed by the teacher only.* Fill a 1000 mL beaker with water and add a few drops of food coloring to improve visibility. Place approximately 20 mL of uncolored water in a 500 mL flask and heat uncovered (Figure B). *NEVER HEAT A SEALED CONTAINER!* The flask fills with water vapor as the water boils.

Allow the water to boil until almost all is gone. This will ensure that the environment inside the flask is almost entirely composed of water vapor. Using heat-resistant gloves, remove the flask from the heat source and immediately place a one-hole stopper, fitted with a hollow glass tube as shown in Figure C, in the mouth of the flask. Quickly invert the flask and support it on a ring stand as illustrated. The glass tubing should extend nearly to the bottom of the 1000 mL beaker. As the flask cools, the water vapor inside condenses and the pressure drops. While the pressure inside (internal pressure) the flask drops, the pressure outside of the flask (atmospheric pressure) remains constant, creating a pressure differential. As a result, water is slowly pushed up the tube into the flask (Figure C). As water enters the partially evacuated flask it absorbs heat

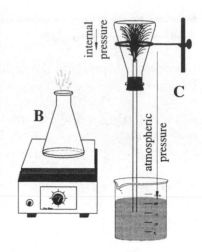

and further cools the internal atmosphere. The remaining vapor condenses rapidly, resulting in a dramatic drop in pressure, and a strong jet of water is pushed into the flask to fill the void. Once it has cooled and the water level has stabilized, remove the flask assembly and set it on a table. Mark the height of the base of the stopper on the side of the flask using a grease pencil or tape. Remove the stopper assembly, pour the water into a graduated cylinder, and determine its volume (V_1). Now fill the flask to the line previously marked and measure this volume as before. This second volume (V_2) represents the volume originally occupied by water vapor. What percent of the original water vapor volume (V_2) was lost as gaseous water condensed: (V_1/V_2) × 100%? This provides a <u>rough</u> estimate of the reduction in volume that accompanies the condensation of gases to liquids.

Part 3: The collapsing can—relative volumes of liquids and gases: Fill a large beaker or bucket with water. Pour water into an empty aluminum soft drink can to a depth of approximately 1 cm and place it on a hot plate until the water boils. Do not allow the can to boil dry! As soon as the water begins to boil, remove the can from the heat source and hold it in

an upright position with its base in the water bucket or beaker. Is there any change in the can? Repeat the process, only this time invert the can and submerge the opening in the water as illustrated in Figure D. Is there any change in the can? When one milliliter of water boils (vaporizes) it changes into approximately 1000 milliliters of steam. As water in the can boils, it displaces air which was originally in the can. When the can is sealed and cooled, the steam condenses to liquid water, but now occupies only 1/1000th the volume it occupied as steam! In other words,

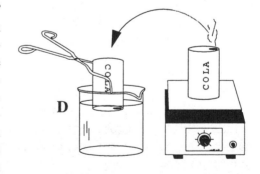

for every milliliter of water that condenses inside the can, approximately one thousand milliliters of vacuum are left behind. The air pressure outside the can remains the same while the pressure inside drops, creating a difference in pressure that collapses the can.

Part 4: Liquid and gaseous air: *Caution: Teacher demonstration only. Liquid nitrogen is extremely cold. Wear insulated gloves, face shield and a lab coat.* Inflate a balloon with your breath and place it on top of a liquid nitrogen bath (Figure E). Why does the volume of the balloon decrease so dramatically? Is there liquid in the balloon? If so, where did it come from? What happens if the balloon is allowed to warm at room temperature?

E

Dewar Flask

— liquid nitrogen

Questions

(1) With a few exceptions (e.g., water, bismuth and antimony), the solid phase of a substance is denser than the liquid phase. What do you think might happen to aquatic life in far northern latitudes if this were not the case? Explain.

(2) Geologists believe that freezing is one of the major forces contributing to the breakdown of rocks. Explain.

(3) Under normal circumstances, a given amount of gas will occupy 1000 times the volume of an equal mass in liquid form. What might account for the variation between this value and the value you obtained?

(4) The density of a gas is generally about 1/1000 the density of the same substance in liquid state. Explain.

(5) What caused the can to collapse in part 3?

(6) Explain why the balloon of air in part 4 shrinks dramatically when placed on a liquid nitrogen bath.

2.4.2 HEATS OF FUSION AND VAPORIZATION

Concepts to Investigate: Heat of fusion, heat of vaporization, phase changes, melting, boiling.

Materials: Beaker, ice, thermometer, heat source, clock with second hand.

Safety: Wear goggles and lab coat.

Principles and Procedures: In 490 BC the Greeks battled the Persians at Marathon, Greece. According to legend, a Greek soldier named Phidippides ran 22.5 miles (36.2 km) from Marathon to Athens to announce a Greek victory, but died shortly after his announcement. When the modern Olympic Games began in 1896, the marathon was introduced as the main long-distance running event to commemorate Phidippides' run. The marathon (now 26 miles; 42.19 km long) is still the king of running events, and severely tests the physical endurance of runners. Although it is not known how Phidippides died, it is possible that he could have died of heatstroke, a condition that occurs when body temperatures soar above 105°F (40.5°C). It is unlikely that Phidippides had much water to drink along his run, probably became quite dehydrated, and no longer was able to sweat. Sweating is essential for temperature regulation, and without it body temperatures can rise dangerously. What is it about the evaporation of water that helps cool the body so effectively? Perform the following experiment and find out.

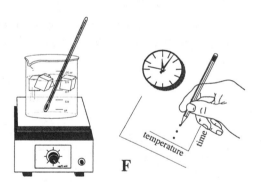

Fill a beaker with ice and water. Place a thermometer in the water and measure water temperature (Figure F). Heat the beaker, recording the temperature at equal intervals (every 30 seconds, or every minute). Record the time at which the ice is completely melted. Continue to record the temperature until the water has boiled for a couple of minutes. Remove the heat before all of the water has boiled off. Construct a graph with temperature on the vertical axis, and the time heated on the horizontal axis.

In this experiment time serves as a reasonable substitute for the heat energy input if the flame or heat source is constant. The amount of energy required to melt a given quantity of water at its melting point is known as the heat of fusion (80 cal/g), and the amount required to boil at its boiling point is known as the heat of vaporization (540 cal/g).

Questions

(1) Draw a chart with water temperature on the vertical axis, and time of heating on the horizontal axis.
(2) Does the temperature rise when the ice is melting? Explain.
(3) Does the temperature rise after the ice has melted? Explain.
(4) Does the temperature rise when the water is boiling? Explain.

(5) Chemists use the melting point and boiling point to identify substances because these are fixed points and are relatively easy to measure. Explain why they are relatively easy to measure.

(6) Was much energy required to vaporize water? If so, how can this explain why sweating is an important means of temperature regulation, and how the first marathon runner may have died because of heatstroke after suffering dehydration?

2.4.3 BOILING: THE INFLUENCE OF PRESSURE

Concepts to Investigate: Barometric pressure, boiling, vacuum, vapor pressure.

Materials: Flask, one-hole stopper, thermometer, hot plate or burner, ring stand, clamp, ice (optional).

Safety: Wear goggles, insulated gloves and a lab coat. Part 1 should be performed only by the instructor.

Principles and Procedures: Imagine living on a planet where cooling a liquid caused it to boil. How would life be different? Would life as we know it be possible? Surprisingly, you live on a planet where this occurs. You don't believe it? Well, perform the following investigation and see for yourself.

A liquid will boil if its vapor pressure is equal to or greater than the pressure of the atmosphere (Figure G). At sea level, the vapor pressure must equal 101.3 kPa for the liquid to boil. If the atmospheric pressure is increased the liquid will not boil until heated to the point where its vapor pressure equals the new atmospheric pressure. If the barometric pressure is decreased using a vacuum pump, liquid will boil at much lower temperatures.

atmospheric pressure

G

vapor pressure

Part 1 Boiling by reduction of pressure ("boiling by cooling"): *Caution: Instructor demonstration only! Boiling water is dangerous and should be handled with great caution. Make certain that your lab coat and clothing covers and protects all of your skin in the event of a spill.*

Apply glycerol or another suitable lubricant to the end of a thermometer and gently push it through a rubber stopper with a slow twisting motion applied at its base. Fill a flask to approximately 25% of its capacity with tap water and heat without the stopper until the water begins to boil (Figure H). *NEVER HEAT A SEALED CONTAINER!* Using hot mitts or tongs, remove the flask from the hot plate and then quickly place the thermometer-stopper assembly in the mouth of the flask. Using hot mitts, position the flask in a ring support as illustrated in Figure H. Place a container under the flask to collect water that will be poured over the flask. Using a beaker or cup, pour tap water over the flask and watch the water inside the flask boil! When tap water no longer causes the water to boil, use ice water and see if it will start boiling again. Why does water boil when it is cooled?

Record the lowest temperature at which the water will boil, and record the pressure that must be present in the flask using the information in the accompanying table. To express pressure in kilopascals or millibars, multiply by 0.133 or 1.33 respectively. What percentage of standard atmospheric pressure remains in the flask at this temperature? (The percentage of atmospheric pressure remaining in the flask can be calcu-

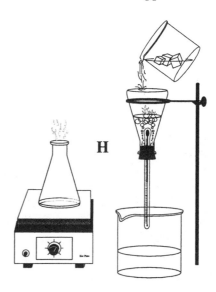

H

lated by dividing by standard atmospheric pressure (760 mm Hg) and then multiplying by 100%.)

Temperature of Water (from thermometer)	Barometric Pressure (from table)	% Atmospheric Pressure (calculated)
°C	mm Hg	%

Table 1: Vapor Pressure of Water

Temperature °C	−5	0	5	10	15	20	25	30	35	40	45	50
Pressure (mm Hg)	3	5	7	9	13	18	24	32	42	55	72	93

Temperature °C	55	60	65	70	75	80	85	90	95	100	105
Pressure (mm Hg)	118	149	188	234	289	355	434	526	634	760	906

Part 2: Boiling by reduction of pressure (syringe technique): *Wear goggles, lab coat and insulated gloves.* Heat water to boiling using a burner or hot plate. Turn off the heat and allow the water to stop boiling. Fill a syringe approximately half-full with the hot water but no air (Figure I). Clamp the end of the syringe with pliers so no air can enter the syringe and wait until the boiling stops (Figure J). To obtain a good seal, it may be necessary to bend back the tip of the syringe before clamping. Retract the plunger in the syringe and notice how the water boils once again (Figure K). If you let go of the plunger it will return to its original position and the boiling will stop. Repeat the procedure and determine the lowest temperature at which the water will boil in the syringe.

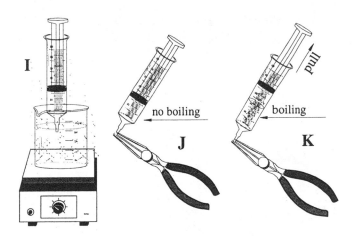

Part 3: Boiling by reduction of pressure (vacuum pump technique): Water boils when its vapor pressure equals atmospheric pressure. This occurs at 100°C under normal atmospheric conditions (pressure of 760 mm Hg = 101.3 kPa = 1 atm). But at what temperature will it

boil at lower atmospheric pressures? Fill 4 beakers with water at 0°C (ice water); 20°C (room temperature); 50°C and 99°C (just under boiling). Place the beakers, one at a time, in a bell jar that is attached to a vacuum pump as illustrated in Figure L. Turn the vacuum pump on and record the pressure at which the water first starts to boil. Turn the vacuum pump off as soon as boiling begins to prevent the flow of water into the pump. Plot pressure on the *x*-axis and temperature on the *y*-axis. How is the boiling point related to atmospheric pressure?

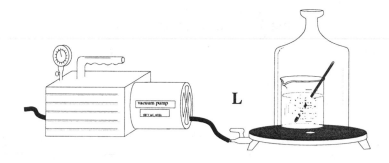

L

Questions

(1) Why did the water in this activity boil when cooled? Would the water have boiled if the cooling flask were open to the atmosphere? Explain.

(2) You observed that water will boil at temperatures far below 100°C if the pressure on the water's surface is reduced sufficiently. Given this information, explain why many recipes recommend increased cooking time at high altitudes.

(3) Unlike normal pots, pressure cookers have lids which lock securely to their pots and allow for a significant increase in pressure. Explain the advantage of using such cookware.

(4) Why does the water boil in the syringe when the plunger is retracted?

(5) Why does water boil at lower temperatures when at lower pressure?

2.4.4 DISTILLATION

Concepts to Investigate: Distillation, boiling point, condensation.

Materials: <u>Part 1</u>: Erlenmeyer flask, one-hole stopper, glass tubing, laboratory burner, flame spreader, food coloring, salt; <u>Part 2</u>: conductivity meter, salt, apparatus in Figure M; <u>Part 3</u>: apparatus in Figure M; <u>Part 4</u>: pulse glass (Figure P); <u>Part 5</u>: funnel, flask, plastic tarp.

Safety: Wear goggles, lab coat, and insulated gloves when performing distillation activities.

Principles and Procedures: Kuwait is a tiny country at the head of the Persian Gulf. Although it has some of the richest oil wells in the world, it has virtually no fresh water. The population of Kuwait has grown rapidly in recent years as people from all over the world have flocked to this desert kingdom to work in its oil fields. To support the growing population, Kuwait developed massive water desalination plants. In these plants, sea water from the Persian Gulf is heated to boiling. Steam rises from the surface of the water, leaving salt and pollutants behind. The steam is then cooled and condensed to pure liquid water that can be used for drinking, irrigation or normal household uses. In this activity you will construct a simple distillation apparatus to see if you can purify colored water, salt water, and acidic or basic water.

Part 1: Distillation of colored water: Assemble the apparatus shown in Figure M using standard safety procedures for glass bending and stopper assembly. Fill an Erlenmeyer or round-bottom flask one-third full of water. Add a couple of drops of food coloring and then heat the flask to boiling. As the water boils, steam is produced. The steam rises and condenses in the tubing and then the liquid water drains into the collection beaker. Is it possible to obtain pure water by distilling it from the food coloring?

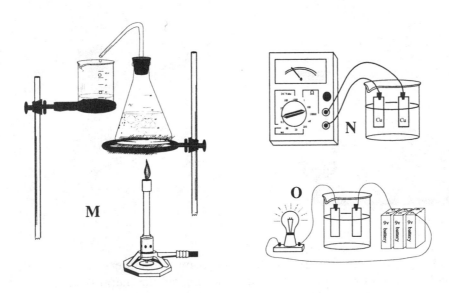

Part 2: Distillation of salt water: Fill a flask one-third full with water. Slowly mix sodium chloride (table salt) into the flask until no more will dissolve as evidenced by an accumulation of a layer of salt on the bottom of the flask. Test for the presence of salt using a conduc-

tivity meter. Heat the apparatus as shown in Figure M and collect the water that is distilled off. Using the conductivity meter, test for the presence of salts in the distillate. The higher the concentration of salts, the higher the conductivity. If you do not have a conductivity meter, you may analyze the resistance of the solution using a multimeter (Figure N). The higher the salt concentration, the lower the resistance. Alternatively, you may test the conductivity by placing a low wattage bulb in series with a set of batteries as shown in Figure O. The higher the salt concentration, the more brightly the bulb will glow. Is the distillate (the water that vaporized and condensed) fresh or salty? Was your still effective in preparing pure water?

Part 3: Distillation of dirty water: Many areas of the world have abundant fresh water, but it is too polluted for home use. Run-off from agricultural fields and pollution from factories and cities are but a few of the sources that pollute many of the major rivers of the world. Is it possible to purify such water using the process of distillation? Fill a flask one-third full with water. Slowly mix in soil until the mixture is muddy in appearance. Heat the still as shown in Figure M and collect the water that is distilled off. Is the distillate (the water that vaporized and condensed) pure or muddy?

Part 4: Pulse glass: The pulse glass (Figure P) is partially evacuated and contains a volatile liquid such as methylene chloride, ether or alcohol. Empty all of the liquid into one of the glass bulbs and hold as illustrated in Figure P. The liquid will evaporate from the bulb in your hand and the vapor will gradually condense in the cooler bulb. Record the time at which all of the liquid is in the cooler bulb and compare your time versus that of other students. Why might the process occur more rapidly with some students than with others? Now hold the pulse glass as shown in Figure Q. The fluid moves to the other bulb, but is the process the same?

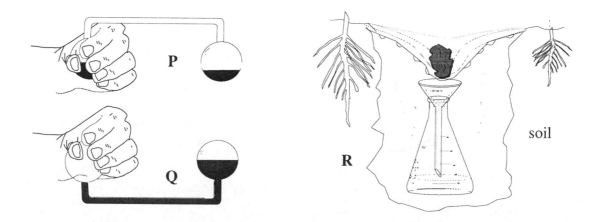

Part 5: Getting water in the desert: In 1849 many adventurers came to California in search of gold. Some of the gold-seekers decided to avoid the Sierra Nevada mountains by venturing south through a large desert basin in southeastern California. Unfortunately, many died of dehydration as they crossed the hot dry valley. The region became known as Death Valley, and now is a National Park. Although there are few sources of running water in desert regions, it may be possible to get water from the soil using an apparatus such as the one shown in Figure R. Dig a hole in soil approximately 1/2 meter wide and 1/2 meter deep.

Place a flask or jug with funnel in the center of the hole, and cover the hole with a clear plastic tarp. Place a rock in the center of the tarp immediately above the funnel. As the sunlight hits the tarp, water evaporates from the soil, condenses on the tarp, runs down to the tip and drops into the container. How much water can you collect in a 24-hour period? How could you collect more water? This technique works best in warm weather after soil has recently been soaked by rain.

Questions

(1) Why is the water in the collection containers of parts 1–3 pure?

(2) Why do you think desalination is rarely employed to provide water for agriculture?

(3) How can the rate of distillation be increased?

(4) Why does the liquid in the pulse glass move more rapidly for some students than for others?

(5) Describe and contrast the processes that drive the fluid to the opposite bulb in Figures P and Q.

(6) What factors affect the success of your effort to collect water from the soil? Under what conditions could you collect the most water?

2.4.5 SUBLIMATION OF CARBON DIOXIDE

Concepts to Investigate: Sublimation, phase change, carbon dioxide.

Safety: This activity uses dry ice which is extremely cold! (The sublimation temperature of dry ice is −78°C; (−108°F). Always wear protective goggles, gloves and lab coats when handling dry ice.)

Materials: Dry ice (solid carbon dioxide), coins.

Principles and Procedures: California has a "Mediterranean" climate, receiving most of its precipitation in the winter and very little in the summer. Those who manage the water resources in California carefully monitor the mountain snowfall each year in an effort to predict how much water will be available for the people of the state when the snows melt. On the average, ten inches of snowfall yield one inch of water, but snow surveyors can't simply divide by 10 to determine the amount of liquid water that will be produced upon melting because some of the snow turns to vapor without ever melting. The process whereby solids change directly to gases, bypassing the liquid state, is known as sublimation. Although the conversion of solid to liquid (melting) and liquid to gas (boiling) are commonly observed, few people ever notice sublimation unless they make very careful observations like California's water resource specialists. Although the sublimation rates of most substances are extremely low, the sublimation of solid carbon dioxide (dry ice) is rapid enough to observe in a few minutes.

Part 1: Observing sublimation: Obtain a block of dry ice from a refrigeration, ice cream or party supply store. Always use gloves when handling dry ice because it is so cold that it will harm your skin on contact. Using a screwdriver and a hammer, break off a section of the dry ice and place it on an overhead projector. Turn off the room lights and observe the screen to see the vapor trails leaving the dry ice. Crush the dry ice into finer particles and repeat the process. Do you see any liquid carbon dioxide?

Part 2: "Shivering coins": Press a large coin (U.S. quarter size or larger) into a block of dry ice as show in Figure S. In a short time the coin should start to shake back and forth (vibrate) vigorously, almost as if the coin were shivering! Why does the coin "shiver"? How long does it take before the coin stops "shivering"? Do you see any liquid carbon dioxide in the process?

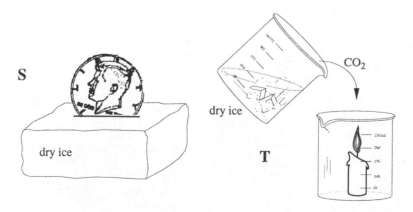

Part 3: Rapid sublimation of carbon dioxide: Dry ice sublimes at $-78°C$ ($-108°F$). When dry ice placed in water at room temperature at approximately $20°C$ ($68°F$) the sublimation process is greatly accelerated as observed by a vigorous bubbling that may be confused with boiling. Place a small (approximately 50 g) chunk of dry ice in a half-filled glass of water. The carbon dioxide will rapidly sublime, but since it is denser than air much of it will remain in the beaker. Place a candle in a second beaker as illustrated in Figure T. Light the candle, then slowly pour the gaseous carbon dioxide from the beaker onto the candle, without pouring any water. The candle will be extinguished when the carbon dioxide level rises above the wick, displacing the oxygen necessary for combustion.

Questions

(1) Did you ever observe any liquid carbon dioxide when observing the crushed dry ice? Explain.

(2) Why does the coin in part 2 appear to shiver when inserted into a block of dry ice? Why does it eventually stop vibrating?

(3) In many cold climates, people hang their laundry on the line in the winter. Their clothes eventually dry even though the temperature never exceeds $0°C$, the melting point of water. Explain.

(4) Why does solid carbon dioxide (dry ice) sublime more rapidly when placed in water at room temperature than in air at room temperature?

(5) Moth balls (material that is hung in closets to ward of wool-eating moths) are often made of solid para-dichlorobenzene. After a long time in the closet, moth balls may disappear. Explain.

2.4.6 TRIPLE POINT: PHASE DIAGRAM
OF CARBON DIOXIDE

Concepts to Investigate: Phase diagrams, carbon dioxide, triple point, phase changes.

Materials: Disposable transfer pipet (flexible plastic "Beral" pipet), beaker or clear plastic cup, pliers, scoopula or small spatula.

Safety: Wear goggles and lab coat.

Principles and Procedures: You may have seen ice cream trucks driving up and down the street during the warm months of summer. Ice melts rather rapidly, and most ice cream trucks are not equipped with expensive refrigeration units, so how do the ice cream vendors keep their products from melting on long trips through the city? The answer is that most mobile ice cream vendors pack their ice cream in dry ice (solid carbon dioxide) at temperatures lower than $-78°C$ ($-108°F$; 195 K). Dry ice keeps things very cold, and instead of melting, it sublimes (converts directly to vapor), so there are no soggy ice cream containers to deal with. Movie makers frequently allow dry ice to sublime when they want to give the appearance of fog or smoke. Perhaps you have seen dry ice (solid carbon dioxide) or the fog it produces (gaseous carbon dioxide), but you have probably never seen liquid carbon dioxide. In this activity you will have the opportunity to see all three phases of carbon dioxide and to observe sublimation, melting, boiling, freezing, and solidification in a short period of time.

Figure U illustrates the phase diagram for carbon dioxide. A phase diagram indicates the temperature and pressure conditions necessary for the various states of matter (liquid, solid, gas) to coexist. At atmospheric pressure (approximately 1 bar), solid carbon dioxide will sublime (convert from solid to gas) at $-78°C$ ($-108°F$; 195 K). The phase diagram shows that carbon dioxide cannot exist as a liquid at pressures less than 5 bars (approximately 5 times atmospheric pressure). In other words, solid carbon dioxide does not melt under standard atmospheric conditions, but will melt if both the temperature and pressure are great enough.

Obtain some flexible plastic disposable Beral style pipets. Note: Do not use pipets made of glass, or hard plastic! Use scissors to remove the narrow tip of the pipet so you will be able to fill the bulb with powdered dry ice (Figure V). Crush some dry ice with a hammer and transfer the powder to the pipet using a scoopula or small spatula (Figure W). Fill approximately one-third of the bulb with dry ice, and then bend over the end of the tip of the pipet and clamp it with a pair of pliers (Figure X). Submerge the bulb in a beaker or clear cup that is half filled with water at room temperature. Water is a better conductor of heat than air, and as a result the carbon dioxide will warm rapidly. As the carbon dioxide sublimes, the pressure increases. Eventually the pressure increases above 5 bars and the carbon dioxide begins to melt rather than sublime.

For a brief moment you may notice solid, liquid, and gaseous (as evidenced by the swelling of the bulb) carbon dioxide all present at the same time. This point is known as the triple point, where the temperature and pressure are such that all three states coexist. Unfortunately, it is very difficult to maintain these conditions as the liquid starts to boil with a slight increase in temperature. As the liquid boils, the pressure increases dramatically. If you release pressure on the pliers at this point, the internal pressure will be reduced and the gaseous carbon dioxide will immediately solidify, producing a white carbon dioxide "snow" in the bulb. If you do not release the pressure in time, the bulb will burst and you will get soaked as water is pushed out of the beaker! Bursting is very common with this experiment, but it is not

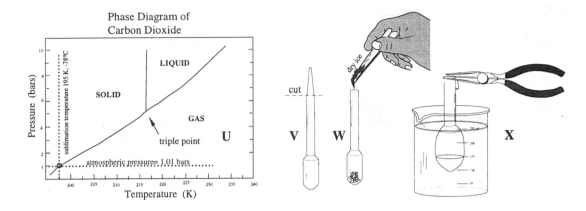

dangerous if you use only soft plastic Beral style pipets, keep the bulb in the water, and *wear goggles*. See how many times you can repeat the melting/freezing cycle without bursting the bulb.

Questions

(1) Why is liquid carbon dioxide not normally observed at room temperature?

(2) What is the snow-like material that appears in the bulb of the Beral pipet when you release the pressure immediately after the carbon dioxide boils? Explain how it is formed.

(3) Explain why emergency rafts aboard cruise ships are equipped with canisters of liquid carbon dioxide.

(4) Some fire extinguishers contain liquid carbon dioxide. You can recognize them by the hard horn and the lack of a pressure gauge. When the pin is released, small bits of solid carbon dioxide (dry ice) and much gaseous carbon dioxide are released. Explain.

2.4.7 REGELATION: PHASE DIAGRAM OF WATER

Concepts to Investigate: Regelation, phase diagrams, phase changes, melting, and freezing.

Materials: Block of ice, high test fishing line, weights.

Principles and Procedures: Ice skating is thought to have developed in Scandinavia over a thousand years ago as a means of transportation across the frozen lakes and rivers of what is now Norway, Finland and Sweden. Today ice skating is a popular form of recreation and a

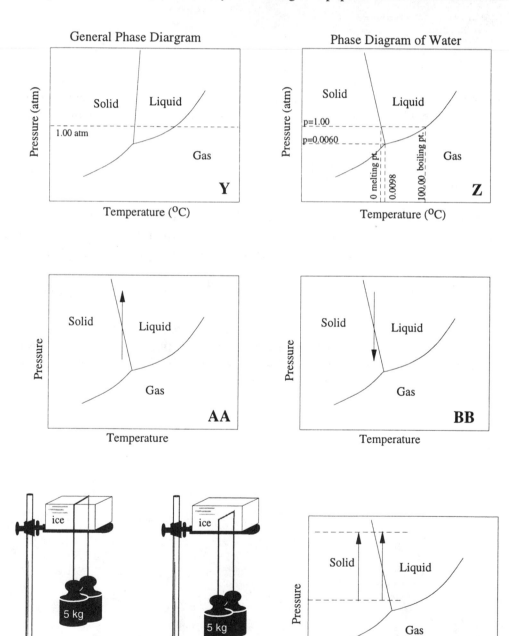

serious sport. Few know, however, that ice skaters really aren't skating on ice—they are skating on liquid water! In this activity you will study regelation, the process that accounts for the nearly effortless glide of an ice skater across the rink.

The solid/liquid phase boundary of most substances has a positive slope (Figure Y). This means that the melting point increases as the pressure increases. By contrast, the solid/liquid phase boundary of water is negative (Figure Z) indicating that the melting point of water decreases as the pressure increases. Thus, if sufficient pressure is placed on ice at temperatures just below freezing, the ice will melt (Figure AA). This process is known as regelation, and allows ice skaters to glide across the surface of the ice with minimal effort. The blades of the skates are very narrow, and thus the pressure on the ice very great, melting the ice under the skates. Once the skater has passed, the pressure returns to normal and the ice freezes again (Figure BB).

To observe regelation, first freeze water in a half-gallon cardboard milk container. As the water freezes, it expands, and the sides of the container will swell or burst. Remove the ice from the container and place it on a ring stand or other support so that weights can hang off each side as illustrated in Figure CC. Suspend two 5 kg objects from a heavy duty (50-pound test or greater) fishing line as shown. You may use bags of sand or other objects for the weights. Let the weights hang for at least an hour, and record the depth of the line as a function of time (Figure DD). Compare the results using 5 kg masses with those using 1 kg masses or 10 kg masses. Is the rate of regelation dependent on the pressure applied to the ice?

Questions

(1) Does the water refreeze after the line has passed? Explain.

(2) Draw a phase diagram for water. Use an arrow to indicate the process of regelation.

(3) Do you think that regelation will occur if 10-gram weights are suspended from the lines illustrated in Figure CC? Explain.

(4) In many parts of North America and northern Europe people skate on frozen ponds or lakes. These skaters notice that it is more difficult to skate when the weather is extremely cold (−30°C or colder) than when it is close to the melting temperature of water (approximately 5°C). Explain, using the principle of regelation and Figure EE.

FOR THE TEACHER

In this chapter we have introduced the three most common phases of matter <u>on Earth</u> (solid, liquid and gas), but have not discussed the fourth major phase, known as plasma, which is the most common in the visible universe. Plasma may be defined as an electrically neutral gas composed of ions, electrons, and electrical particies, such as is found in stars, solar wind, the ionosphere, auroras, lightning, welding arcs and fluorescent tubes. You may wish to illustrate plasma using a "plasma ball" (Figure FF) which may be purchased from novelty stores or scientific supply companies. In this unit we focus on solids, liquids and gases.

2.4.1 RELATIVE VOLUMES OF SOLID, LIQUID AND GAS PHASE

Discussion: Part 1: Relative volumes of solid and liquid water: For most materials, the solid phase is denser than the liquid phase. This can be illustrated by dropping solid candle wax into a container of molten wax. As mentioned in the student section, water (like antimony and bismuth) is unusual in that it is denser as a liquid than as a solid. As a result, water expands when it freezes. In this activity, the plaster of Paris should rupture as the water freezes. Plaster of Paris is made of calcium sulfate dihydrate ($CaSO_4 \cdot 2H_2O$), the primary component in gypsum (wall board) and artificial marble, and can be obtained from craft supply or home improvement stores.

Another simple activity to illustrate the relative densities of water and ice is as follows: Place an unopened soft drink can in a freezer. Soft drinks are primarily water and will freeze if temperatures are sufficiently low. Record the volume measurement that is on the outside of the can. After freezing the can, measure its volume by seeing how much water it displaces.

Part 2: Air Pressure Fountain: Before heating, the pressures inside and outside the soft drink can in part 2 are the same. Since the can does not deform while being heated, one can assume pressures on both sides remain the same. The air that escapes from the can is gradually replaced by water vapor until the internal atmosphere is composed almost entirely of water vapor. The vapor pressure of water drops dramatically when it is allowed to cool. The vapor pressure decreases from 101.3 kPa at 100°C to about 5 kPa at room temperature. Thus, as the temperature drops to room temperature, the pressure inside the can drops 95%. If the can is open to the atmosphere, air will flow back into the can as the water condenses. If the opening to the can is submerged, the vapor in the can will not equilibrate with the atmosphere. Water rapidly removes heat from the surroundings, and thus lowers the temperature of the atmosphere inside the can. The water vapor quickly condenses, creating a pressure differential of nearly 96 kPa (13.9 lb/in²). Water is forced in to fill this partial vacuum, but before it does, air pressure on the walls implodes the can. Note that the collapsed can contains water, indicating water entered at the same time the walls collapsed.

Part 3: The collapsing can: A nice follow-up to this activity uses a re-sealable metal can such as those used to package ditto fluid or paint solvents. *The instructor should make certain the can is completely clean prior to the demonstration or dangerous fumes might enter the atmosphere.* Seal the can and ask a student to try crushing the can with his or her hands. It will be very difficult for the student to do much more than slightly dent the can. Now add

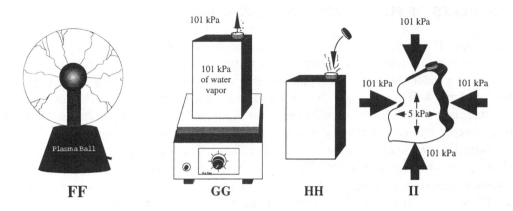

water to a depth of 1 centimeter and heat <u>without the lid</u> until it boils (Figure GG). *NEVER HEAT A SEALED CONTAINER!* Using pot holders, remove the can from the heat and seal it with its lid (Figure HH). *Do not reseal the can while it is being heated or an explosion may occur!* As the can is allowed to cool on a bench top, it will gradually collapse as the water vapor condenses and the internal pressure drops to approximately 5% of atmospheric pressure (Figure II). Cooling the outside of the can with water or a damp cloth will speed this process. Students can calculate the force upon the outside of the can by first calculating the surface area and then solving the equation $F = PA$ where $P = 101$ N/m^2.

Part 4: Liquid and gaseous air: The temperature of liquid nitrogen at atmospheric pressure is −196°C (its boiling point) or less, and as a result it must be handled with great care. Liquid nitrogen is used in surgery to destroy tissues as a "cryogenic scalpel," and it can kill skin tissue if you spill it on you. A nice follow-up to this activity it to demonstrate the properties of liquid and gaseous nitrogen. *Put on gloves, face shield and a lab coat.* Students should stand back from the demonstration table. Slowly pour liquid nitrogen into a metal coffee can or similar strong metal container and seal it with the flexible soft-plastic lid. As the coffee can warms, liquid nitrogen will turn to vapor. Eventually the pressure inside the can will cause the plastic lid to pop off.

Answers: (1) If ice were denser than liquid water it would sink and a sheet of ice would develop along the bottoms of lakes and streams. This layer would get thicker each year since it would be shielded from the warmth of the sunlight. Eventually, lakes and streams would freeze solid, and fish and other organisms that require liquid water would die. (2) Water seeps into cracks in rocks. When it freezes, it expands, cracking the rocks further. (3) The flask is an open system when heated. As a result, much water vapor may be lost to the atmosphere. Unfortunately, students only measure the volume of vapor that still is in the flask at the time it is sealed following its removal from the heat source. As a result, students will underestimate the volume difference between liquid and gaseous phases. (4) Intermolecular forces are minimal in the gaseous phase. As a result, gaseous molecules are not attracted to each other as are molecules in the liquid or solid states, but rather move independently of each other, occupying a much larger volume in the process. (5) The gas (steam) occupied approximately 1000 times as much volume as the condensate (liquid water). As a result, a vacuum was created when the steam condensed. The can was then subjected to a substantial pressure differential and was crushed by atmospheric pressure. (6) The balloon shrinks according to Charles' Law $(V_1T_1 = V_2T_2)$, and also because oxygen and carbon dioxide in the air are liquefied in liquid nitrogen.

2.4.2 HEATS OF FUSION AND VAPORIZATION

Discussion: If possible perform this experiment using a temperature probe (thermistor or thermocouple) and probeware (computer software that automatically records data). Place the probe in the water and track the temperature as a function of time using a "strip chart" display. Students will see a graph that looks very similar to Figure JJ. A dramatic follow-up demonstration is to boil water and/or make tea in a paper cup on an open flame (Figure KK). Place a paper cup (not plastic or Styrofoam!) on a clay triangle or wire mesh, fill the cup with water, add a tea bag, and heat on an open flame. The water in the cup will warm to the boiling point (approximately 100°C), but will not go higher, because at this temperature all additional energy is used to vaporize water (heat of vaporization), not to increase temperature (Figure JJ). Since 100° is considerably below the kindling temperature of paper, the paper cup will not burn.

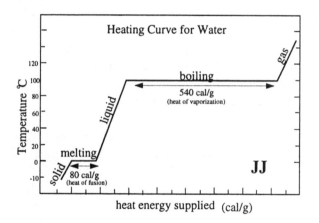

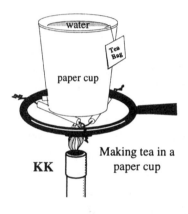

KK   Making tea in a paper cup

Heat of fusion is the energy given off as water changes from liquid to solid. The heat of fusion of water is 6.01 kJ/mole or 80 cal/g. The heat of vaporization is the energy consumed as water changes form from liquid to gas. The heat of vaporization of water is 40.66 kJ/mol or 540 cal/g. Students often get confused when values are expressed in different units, so if you use different units, show how to convert between the two values to indicate that they are indeed the same. Given that water has a molecular weight of 18 g/mole, and there are 4.18 joules/cal, it can be shown that the values are equivalent. The following equation shows the equivalency of 40.66 kJ/mole and 540 cal/g:

$$\frac{40.66kJ}{mole} \cdot \frac{mole}{18g} \cdot \frac{cal}{4.18J} \cdot \frac{1000J}{kJ} = \frac{540cal}{g}$$

Answers: (1) Figure JJ shows the relationship between heat input and temperature. If the heating is constant, this graph will strongly resemble the graph of temperature vs. time. (2) The temperature of the ice-water remains constant until all of the ice has melted, at which point it rises. (3) After the ice has melted, the temperature rises continually until the boiling point. (4) The temperature of boiling water is constant, because all additional energy is used to vaporize water, not to increase the temperature. (5) The temperature of a substance rises continually when heat is applied, except during the process of melting or boiling. At the melting point, energy is used to change the phase from solid to liquid, and thus the temperature remains constant until all solid is melted. Similarly, temperature will remain constant at the boiling point until all water has evaporated. Because the temperature plateaus while the substance is melting or boiling, it is easy to measure. It should be noted that the reverse is true upon cooling: 540 calories of heat are released for every gram of water vapor that condenses, and 80 calories are released for every gram of water that freezes. (6) The temperature vs. time plot remains constant at 100°C as water boils because a significant amount of energy is required to vaporize water (540 cal/g). In this experiment the heat of vaporization has been provided by the burner, but when humans sweat it is provided primarily by body heat. For every gram of water that humans sweat, 540 cal of heat are removed from the body and surrounding air. This removal of energy cools the body and keeps its temperature within appropriate parameters.

2.4.3 BOILING: THE INFLUENCE OF PRESSURE

Discussion: Everyday experience indicates that removal of heat inhibits boiling, and yet in this activity it causes it! The counter-intuitive results of this activity will pique student curiosity. Although heat is essential to produce the phase change, its effect is masked by the influence of the reduction in air pressure that occurs as the flask is cooled. At sea level, the pressure exerted by the atmosphere is 101.3 kPa (760 mm Hg, or 14.7 PSI). The vapor pressure of water does not reach 101.3 kPa until the water is heated to a temperature of 100°C, which is why 100°C is the boiling temperature of water at standard pressure. As pressure is reduced, the boiling point of water drops.

Prior to heating, the air inside the flask is in equilibrium with the external atmosphere with respect to pressure and composition. When heated, air expands and exits, and is replaced by water vapor. The pressure remains constant because the flask is open to the atmosphere. After the flask is removed from the heat source and sealed, it is no longer an open system. When the flask is cooled, its temperature drops and water condenses. As condensation continues, the pressure drops because there are fewer molecules in the gaseous state. As the pressure drops, the boiling point of water decreases.

Answers: (1) See discussion. (2) At high altitudes, water boils at a lower temperature and foods don't get as hot. To ensure that foods get fully cooked, it is necessary to heat them for a longer period of time at this lower temperature. (3) Under normal atmospheric conditions, water will not get hotter than 100°C because it turns into vapor at this temperature. In a pressure cooker the boiling point of water is substantially higher (see Figure Z), and foods cook faster. In open cookware, the energy from the burners goes into vaporizing the water, while in a pressure cooker, a larger percentage of the energy is used to cook the food. Table 2 shows how the boiling point of water increases as a function of pressure.

Table 2: Boiling Point as a Function of Pressure

Pressure (mm Hg)	760	788	816	845	875	906	937	970	1004	1039	1075
Temperature °C	100	101	102	103	104	105	106	107	108	109	110

(4) Water boils when its vapor pressure equals atmospheric pressure. When the plunger was retracted, the pressure dropped, thereby allowing the water to boil. (5) Molecules are in con-

stant motion. This motion is restricted by intermolecular forces in a liquid, but not in a gas. Atmospheric pressure acts to prevent molecules from leaving a liquid, but when this pressure is reduced it is easier for molecules to leave the liquid and enter the gas phase.

2.4.4 DISTILLATION

Discussion: The simple still is an excellent way to introduce the practical significance of phase changes. Distillation will produce pure water regardless of whether the source is colored, salty or muddy. Because water has a lower boiling point than either the food coloring, salt or soil particles, it vaporizes first, leaving the less volatile substances behind. Distillation is the principal method of purifying liquids from nonvolatile substances.

If you do not have a conductivity meter, you may use an inexpensive "conductivity of solutions apparatus." Using such a device you can determine relative conductivity by observing how bright a light bulb glows when the electrodes are placed in the different solutions.

Answers: (1) The boiling point of water (100°C) is very low compared to that of sodium chloride (1465°C) or silicon dioxide (2950°C). Thus, at 100°C water will vaporize, but salt (sodium chloride) or mud (silicon dioxide and other materials) will remain as solids. When water condenses it will be pure because only the water was vaporized. (2) Desalination is effective, but very expensive because of the amount of fuel that must be consumed. (3) The distillation rate may be increased by increasing the heat and cooling the collection arm and flask. (4) The rate of evaporation depends on the temperature of the person's hands. Circulation to the hands increases when a person must dissipate heat. Thus, hand temperatures will be warmer if a person has exercised or is in a warm environment. In addition, circulation rates vary dramatically between individuals. Approximately 5% of the population suffers from Raynaud's disease, also known as cold hands syndrome, in which circulation to the hands is greatly reduced at certain times. (5) When held as shown in Figure P, the fluid vaporizes and condenses in the opposite bulb. When held as shown in Figure Q, the liquid vaporizes, and the increased pressure forces the liquid to the opposite bulb. (6) Water is most easily collected when (a) the soil is saturated with water; and (b) the temperatures are warm during the day (to maximize evaporation), and cool at night (to promote condensation).

2.4.5 SUBLIMATION OF CARBON DIOXIDE

Discussion: All solids consisting of discrete molecules sublime, but generally at rates that are so low that they are hardly detectable. Under normal conditions most solids exhibit a vapor pressure that is less than one thousandth the prevailing atmospheric pressure, and as a result, very little sublimation is observed. Certain solids, such as iodine and carbon dioxide (dry ice), have very high vapor pressures and exhibit high sublimation rates, which is why they were selected for these activities.

Sublimation is the process in which a solid transitions to a gas. The reverse process is known as condensation sublimation and can be illustrated if you have carbon dioxide gas and liquid nitrogen. Fill a balloon with carbon dioxide gas, or place sufficient crushed dry ice into a balloon so that it fills the balloon upon sublimation. Place the balloon on top of a liquid nitrogen bath. The volume of the balloon will decrease dramatically due to Charles Law (see chapter on gas laws), but also due to the condensation of carbon dioxide and the formation of dry ice powder. If the balloon is made of a light color, students should be able to see chunks of frozen carbon dioxide (dry ice) in the balloon.

Answers: (1) No. The phase diagram for carbon dioxide (Figure U) shows that carbon dioxide cannot exist as a liquid at atmospheric pressure. (2) Dry ice sublimes at −78°C (−108°F). The coin is a conductor of heat, and because it is initially at room temperature (approximately 20°C or 68°F) it causes the carbon dioxide to sublime. As it sublimes, gas is produced and the pressure from this gas pushes against the coin, moving it toward the other side of the slot. The coin now warms this side of the carbon dioxide and the process is repeated. The coin will stop "shivering" when it has cooled to a point that no longer stimulates rapid sublimation of the carbon dioxide. (3) Water slowly sublimes from the ice on the surface of the clothes. (4) Water is a better conductor of heat than air, and is more effective in raising the carbon dioxide above the sublimation temperature. (5) Para-dichlorobenzene sublimes slowly, releasing vapors into the closet that ward off moths. Eventually, all of the para-dichlorobenzene is in vapor form.

2.4.6 TRIPLE POINT: PHASE DIAGRAM OF CARBON DIOXIDE

Discussion: In this activity we have introduced the unit of pressure known as the bar (100,000 N/m^2). This may confuse students who are accustomed to using other units of pressure. Table 3 lists the common units for measuring pressure, and a quick glance will make it obvious why there is so much confusion regarding pressure. It may be helpful to show your students this table so they can see that pressure is measured in different units just as temperature is measured in Celsius, Fahrenheit, and Kelvin.

The triple point is a set of physical conditions at which all three phases of a substance (solid, liquid, and gas) coexist in equilibrium. Students may see these three phases at once, but their observations will be short lived because it is difficult to maintain the precise temperature and pressure necessary (216K, 518 kPa; −57°C, 5.18 bars). Triple points are invariant and therefore serve as excellent calibration points for temperature and pressure. The triple point of water is 273.16K; 616.66 kPa.

Answers: (1) Most of the time we observe things that are under atmospheric pressure. The phase diagram of carbon dioxide (Figure U) shows that carbon dioxide is a gas at room temperature under normal atmospheric pressure. (2) It is dry ice, solid carbon dioxide. When pressure is released the carbon dioxide boils, and as it boils heat is lost and it cools. At a lower temperature and pressure, carbon dioxide solidifies, producing the white snow-like material (see Figure U). (3) When triggered, the canisters will discharge carbon dioxide into the chambers of the raft. The pressure in these chambers is relatively low (less than 6 bars) so the carbon dioxide immediately boils, and the resulting gas inflates the raft. (4) The fire extinguishers are charged using compressed carbon dioxide. Under sufficient pressure, carbon dioxide liquefies (see Figure U). When carbon dioxide is released into the air at normal atmospheric pressure, it immediately vaporizes. Occasionally, some solid carbon dioxide will also form. Carbon dioxide is denser than air and it therefore covers the flame and smothers it.

Table 3: Units of Pressure and Their Equivalents in Pascals

Unit	Definition	Pascal Equivalents	Where It Is Used
pascal (Pa)	N/m^2	1	Standard SI Unit. Used when mass is measured in kg and area in meters.
kilopascal (kPa)	$1000 \ N/m^2$	1000	Practical metric unit of measuring gaseous, fluid or mechanical pressure (Pa is generally too small).
bar	$100,000 \ N/m^2$	100,000	Practical metric unit of measuring atmospheric pressure. One bar is very close to 1 atmosphere.
millibar (mb)	$100 \ N/m^2$	100	Weather reports. Note: Many weather maps drop the first two digits (e.g., 1013.3 mb may be reported as 13.3)
barye (dyne/cm²)	$0.1 \ N/m^2$	0.1	Standard CGS unit. Used when measurements are made in centimeters and grams.
torr	1/760 of standard atmospheric pressure	133.3	Used when pressure is measured using a mercury manometer or barometer.
mm Hg	pressure able to support a column of Hg 1 mm in height	133.3	Blood Pressure measurements. Normal blood pressure is 120/80 (systolic/diastolic)
cm H_2O	pressure able to support a column of water 1 cm in height	98.1	Used when pressure is measured using simple water barometer or manometer.
atmosphere (atm)	atmospheric pressure at sea level	101,325	Used when a comparison to standard atmospheric pressure is desired.
PSI	lb/in^2	6894	Common measurement in mechanical and structural engineering. Tire pressures are rated in PSI.

2.4.7 REGELATION: PHASE DIAGRAM OF WATER

Discussion: There is some disagreement among scientists as to what melts the water under the skates of an ice skater. While most books mention regelation, many state that frictional heating is more important. Regelation is thought to be an important process in the movement of glaciers. The high pressure under glaciers may cause regelation, allowing the glacier to move slowly on a thin film of water.

Answers: (1) The ice melts under the pressure of the line (regelation), but once the pressure is removed, it will refreeze (see Figures AA & BB). (2) As pressure increases, ice will melt (see Figure AA). (3) Regelation will occur only when pressure is sufficiently great. Ten-gram weights do not generate sufficient pressure to cause regelation to occur. (4) Under very cold conditions, skaters complain that their skates do not glide well. The colder it is, the higher the pressure required to melt ice by regelation (Figure EE). Under extremely cold conditions, it may not be possible to melt ice by regelation to provide the water on which the skater glides.

Applications to Everyday Life

Fire fighting (heat of vaporization): To vaporize one gram of water requires 540 cal of heat. When water is sprayed on a fire, much of it is converted to steam. For every gram of water that is vaporized, 540 cal of heat are removed from the system. As heat is removed, the temperature may drop below the kindling temperature, and the fire will be extinguished.

Cooling systems (heat of vaporization): Many industrial activities generate excessive amounts of heat and must be cooled by spraying water. A diamond tip concrete saw blade, a jackhammer, a dentist's drill, and an oil drilling bit generate significant amounts of heat by friction. Equipment operators spray water on the blades or bits to prevent them from getting too hot and being ruined. For every gram of water vaporized by the hot tool, 540 calories of heat are removed, allowing the tool to stay within proper operating temperatures.

Frost protection of crops (heat of fusion): When threatened with the loss of crops due to frost, some farmers turn on the sprinklers! As the water freezes on the crops, heat of fusion is released and this may warm the crop enough to keep plant tissues from freezing.

Calibrating thermometers (latent heats of fusion and vaporization): When thermometers are manufactured, they must be calibrated to known temperatures. The freezing temperature and boiling temperature of water are convenient temperatures because water has high latent heats of fusion and vaporization. For example, the temperature of an ice water bath at standard atmospheric pressure will remain 0°C until the last bit of ice has melted because all of the energy goes into melting the ice before the temperature rises. In a similar manner, the temperature of boiling water remains constant at 100°C until the last drop has evaporated because all heat goes into changing the state of water before increasing the temperature.

Freeze-dried foods (sublimation): To reduce weight, some backpackers carry "freeze-dried" foods rather than the traditional foods found in the market. Freeze-dried foods are very light because the water content has been removed through the freeze-drying process. Foods are first frozen, and then warmed in a vacuum so that the ice sublimes. Freeze-dried foods lose at least 90% of their water, but they gain it back when soaked in water.

Driving at high altitudes (influence of pressure on boiling): Cars may fail to run at high altitudes due to the formation of vapor locks. The boiling point of gasoline is reduced as pressures are dropped. At high altitudes it may boil in the fuel lines, preventing delivery of gasoline to the engine.

Cooking at high elevations (influence of pressure on boiling): It is necessary to cook food longer at higher elevations because water does not get as hot as it does at lower elevations. While water boils at 100°C at sea level, it may boil at only 95°C in the mountains. Cooking for longer periods of time helps compensate for lower water temperature.

Pressure cookers (influence of pressure on boiling): When cooking with an uncovered pot, temperatures will not rise above 100°C because at that temperature all additional energy goes into vaporizing the liquid rather than raising its temperature. If the system is closed, the pressure will continue to build. Increased pressure prevents the water from boiling and will allow the temperature of the water to increase substantially, thereby cooking food faster.

Liquefied natural gas (phase diagrams): Gases can be liquefied given sufficient pressure (observe the phase diagrams for carbon dioxide, Figure U, and water, Figure Z). Liquid natural gas (primarily methane) occupies only about 1/600 the space of gaseous natural gas. To facilitate transport, natural gas is first pressurized and liquefied. Liquefied natural gas (LNG) is produced by cooling it below its boiling point −162°C (−259°F) and storing it in double-wall cryogenic containers. Special tankers carry LNG from where it is produced to the major markets in Europe, Japan and the United States. Liquefied butane is used in backpacking stoves, and liquefied propane in welding torches and backyard barbecues.

Aerosol propellants (phase diagrams): For years chlorofluorocarbons (CFCs) were used as propellants for spray cans because they have a high vapor pressure and will instantly vaporize when the pressure is released, propelling paint or other substances forward. Unfortunately CFCs have been shown to damage the stratospheric ozone layer that protects us from harmful ultraviolet radiation. Chemists have substituted other materials such as hydrochlorofluorocarbons (HCFCs), hydrocarbons, and various compressed gases, such as carbon dioxide dissolved in acetone that have similar phase diagrams.

Glacial movement (regelation): Glaciers are huge bodies of ice that move slowly under their own weight. It is thought that glacial movement is partially responsible for carving broad "U" shaped valleys like those in Yosemite National Park. Some believe that glaciers can move over rocks because of regelation. The pressure on the uphill side of a rock will be so great that the water melts, but on the downhill side the pressure is less and the water refreezes.

Preparation of fuels (distillation): Many products, such as gasoline, kerosene, methane, paraffin, and asphalt, are derived from crude oil. These materials can be separated from each other by fractional distillation because they have different boiling points. Fractional distillation involves continuous condensation and re-evaporation and causes the composition of the vapor to change. Each component (fraction) is distilled off at a different temperature. Those with the lowest boiling points vaporize first and are collected at the top of the distillation column (often 60 meters tall) while those with the lowest boiling points are collected near the bottom.

2.5 CLASSIFICATION OF MATTER

Archeologists gather information about past cultures through material evidence such as bones, buildings and artwork. Much of what archeologists have learned about ancient civilizations has been gained from artifacts made of calcium carbonate ($CaCO_3$), one of the main components in bone. Because calcium carbonate is resistant to decay, skeletal remains from past civilizations may be found in crypts, graves, burial mounds or embedded in ice. Archeologists study such remains to determine when and how people in ancient cultures lived.

Calcium carbonate is also the main component in seashells. Over long periods of time, such shells collect on the ocean floor and are compacted and transformed into a sedimentary rock known as limestone. Limestone has been a popular building material for thousands of years. White limestone was used to cover the great pyramids of Egypt built approximately 4,500 years ago. Limestone continues to be a popular building material and has been used in many famous modern structures, such as the Empire State Building in New York City, which at 448.7 m high (1,472 ft), held the world height record for buildings for four decades (1930–1970).

It is thought that limestone gradually turns into a metamorphic rock known as marble, given sufficient heat, pressure, and time. Marble has been the rock of choice for sculptors throughout the ages. The columns of the Acropolis in Athens, the Pieta of Michelangelo, and the statue of Abraham Lincoln in the Lincoln Memorial (as seen on the back of a penny or five dollar bill) are made of marble. Marble, like limestone and bone, is composed primarily of calcium carbonate.

Chemists can identify calcium carbonate by its unique physical properties. The *Handbook of Chemistry and Physics* reports that calcium carbonate has a molecular weight of 100.09, a density of 2.710 g/mL, a melting point of 1339°C and a solubility of 0.0014 g/100 mL in cold water. If an unknown material has these specific properties, it is probably calcium carbonate. Physical properties can be observed or measured without changing the identity of the material. For example, determining the density of calcium carbonate does not change its identity—it is still calcium carbonate with all of its distinct physical properties. By contrast, there are other properties that cannot be determined without changing the identity of a substance. These are known as chemical properties. One of calcium carbonate's chemical properties is that it reacts with acids to produce a salt, water and carbon dioxide. Calcium carbonate reacts with hydrochloric acid as shown below:

$$CaCO_3(s) + 2HCl(aq) \rightarrow CaCl_2(aq) + CO_2(g) + H_2O(l)$$

This reaction can be observed by placing a piece of chalk, an old dry bone or a chunk of marble or limestone in a container of concentrated hydrochloric acid. All of these substances are composed primarily of calcium carbonate, and will react with hydrochloric acid. The products of this reaction (calcium chloride, carbon dioxide, and water) have different physical and chemical properties from the reactants (calcium carbonate and hydrochloric acid). It is this chemical property of calcium carbonate (reactivity with acids) that has archeologists and preservationists concerned. Air pollution frequently contains large concentrations of nitrogen dioxide and sulfur dioxide that react with moisture in the air to form nitric and sulfuric acids that make rain acidic. Acid rain slowly erodes the calcium carbonate in bones, limestone, and marble. In severely polluted regions, architectural and artistic works are being seriously eroded.

Chemists use chemical and physical properties to classify matter (Figure A). If matter can be separated by physical means (separated by color, density, solubility, melting point, etc.) it is known as a mixture, but if it cannot be separated by physical means, then it is known as a pure substance. If the composition of the mixture is uniform, then it is classified as a homogenous mixture, and if not, it is known as a heterogeneous mixture. If a pure substance can be separated by ordinary chemical means (reactivity with acids, combustibility, etc.) then it is a compound, and if not, then it is an element. Figure A is a flowchart that may be used for classifying all matter into four basic categories.

2.5.1 PHYSICAL AND CHEMICAL CHANGES

Concepts to Investigate: Physical properties, chemical properties, physical change, chemical change, mixtures, pure substances.

Materials: Iron filings (40–60 mesh), sulfur (powdered), magnet, test tube, burner.

Safety: Wear goggles and a lab coat. Perform in a fume hood or well-ventilated environment.

Principles and Procedures: Chemists classify matter as shown in Figure A. If a substance can be separated by normal physical means such as evaporation or filtration, it is known as a mixture, but if it cannot, then it is known as a pure substance. In this activity you will mix iron and sulfur at room temperature and at an elevated temperature, and will examine the product(s) to see if they are mixtures or pure substances.

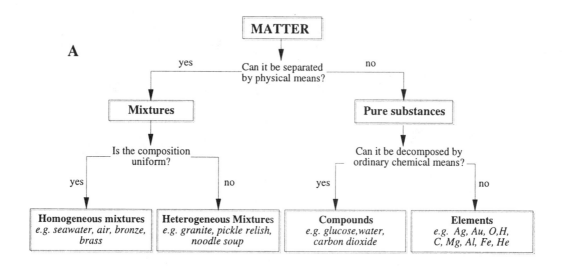

Iron is the second most abundant metal in the earth's crust and has been used for centuries in the construction of tools, machines and structures. It is ferromagnetic and is the main element in most common magnets. Sulfur is another important element and is used in the manufacture of sulfuric acid, paints, cements, dyes, pesticides, matches and gunpowder. Unlike iron, sulfur is not magnetic. Will iron and sulfur keep their unique physical properties when mixed together at room temperature? Thoroughly mix approximately 2.9 grams of sulfur powder with 5.0 grams of iron filings (1:1 mole ratio). Drag a magnet through the mixture (Figure B). If it is possible to sepa-

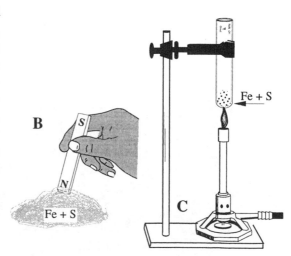

rate iron from sulfur, then we can assume that no chemical changes have occurred and that the test tube contains a mixture. On the basis of your observations, does it appear as though a chemical change has occurred?

Do sulfur and iron coexist at elevated temperatures? Place the iron/sulfur mix in a Pyrex test tube. Heat the tube over a flame until the sulfur and iron have fully reacted (Figure C). The hottest portion of a burner flame is the internal light-blue flame. Allow the test tube to cool. Wrap the tube in several layers of paper, break it with a hammer, and use forceps to separate the contents from the glass. Is it possible to separate iron from sulfur on the basis of different magnetic properties (Figure B)? If not, then a chemical reaction must have occurred and changed the identity of the material in the test tube. Does the product of this reaction yield a pure substance or a mixture?

Questions

(1) Did a physical or chemical change occur when iron and sulfur were mixed together at room temperature? What evidence do you have for your conclusion?

(2) Is the mixture of iron and sulfur a homogeneous mixture (same throughout) or a heterogeneous mixture (composition and properties not uniform)?

(3) Do the physical properties of iron and sulfur change when mixed together at room temperature? Explain.

(4) Did a physical or chemical change occur when iron and sulfur were heated together in the test tube?

(5) Is it possible to separate the iron and the sulfur with a magnet after heating the tube? Explain.

(6) Is the product of the heating of iron and sulfur a mixture or a pure substance?

2.5.2 SEPARATION OF PURE SUBSTANCES AND MIXTURES: CHROMATOGRAPHY

Concepts to Investigate: Classification of matter, mixtures, pure substances, homogeneous mixtures, heterogeneous mixtures, compounds, elements, chromatography.

Materials: Part 1: Water-soluble markers (overhead pens work well), filter paper, paper clips, test tubes; Part 2: Same as part 1, optional: pen ink and isopropyl alcohol (rubbing alcohol).

Principles and Procedures: Nothing satisfies your thirst on a hot day like cold pure water—but how pure is "pure" water? Environmental scientists have identified four categories of contaminants that may exist in municipal water supplies: Microbial pathogens that cause diseases such as dysentery, giardiasis and salmonella; organic pollutants like pesticides and fuel additives that may cause damage to the liver, kidney, central nervous system and reproductive system; inorganics like chromium, lead and mercury that can cause cancer and acute poisoning; and radioactive elements like uranium and radon that may cause cancer. Fortunately, public health officials are aware of the myriad of contaminants in water and attempt to reduce them to safe levels before sending water to the consumer. To make their water even purer, many people install water purifiers that remove contaminants that get past the municipal water treatment plants. Purists may even buy distilled water to ensure a very high level of purity.

All matter can be classified as either a pure substance or a mixture. Distilled water is a pure substance because it contains nothing except H_2O. River water, however, is a mixture because it may contain pathogens, organics, inorganics and radioactive elements. A pure substance is homogeneous (the same throughout). Every sample of a pure substance has exactly the same composition and properties, and cannot be separated into other substances without changing its identity and properties. This is true of distilled water, but not true of river water.

Before public health officials can effectively remove contaminants from our water supplies, they must first know what is in the water. One technique for separating components from a mixture is known as chromatography. Although most technical analysis is done using gas or liquid chromatography, you will use a very inexpensive and effective technique known as paper chromatography to determine if pen inks are pure substances or mixtures.

Part 1: Basic chromatography: Arrange a series of test tubes in a rack. Measure the internal diameter of the tubes and cut strips of filter paper that are 5 mm narrower than the tube and at least 1 cm longer. Feed one end of each paper strip through a paper clip and adjust it so that paper reaches to within about 1 cm of the bottom of the tube. Remove the papers from the tubes and draw pencil lines across them two centimeters from the bottom. The graphite from the pencil will not move with the solvent and thereby serves as a fixed reference line. Using water soluble marking pens (overhead pens work well), draw straight lines across the strips on top of the pencil lines. Fill each of the tubes to a depth of 2 cm with water, and then suspend each of the strips in the tubes such that the bottom 5 mm of the strip is submerged (Figure D). The pen lines should be 1.5 cm above the level of the water.

Water is absorbed by paper and gradually moves up the paper strip. When the water hits the pen line it dissolves water soluble pigments which then move upward as well (Figure E). The rate at which a pigment moves is dependent on the attraction it has for water, and the attraction it has for the cellulose in the paper. It moves rapidly if its attraction for the solvent is much greater than its attraction for the paper, and it flows slowly if its attraction for the paper is greater than its attraction for the solvent. When the water reaches the paper clip, remove the strips from the test tubes and allow them to air dry. Which of the inks appear to be mixtures (two or more colored bands)? Which (if any) of the inks might be pure substances (only one color band)? Record the color compositions for each of the inks used.

The pigments in ball point pens can be separated in a similar fashion, although it is necessary to use solvents composed of 50%/50% isopropyl alcohol/water or 50%/50% ethyl alcohol/water.

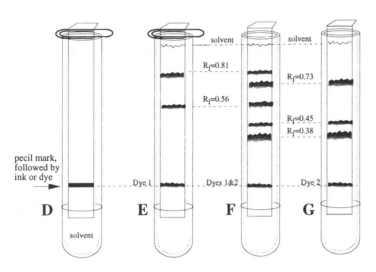

Part 2: Detective work: Most major police departments have crime labs where forensic scientists analyze evidence in an effort to help solve cases. For example, forensic chemists might analyze the composition of a paint chip from a hit and run accident to identify the make and model of the car that fled the scene, or they might study the composition of a bullet at the scene of a homicide in an effort to identify the stores where the bullets may have been purchased.

In this case you will be given unknown substances (mixtures of two food colors), and your goal is to determine the composition of each mixture by comparing their chromatograms with those of known dyes. Repeat the set-up used in part 1, but use a paper clip or toothpick to make lines of each of the basic food coloring dyes (red, yellow, green and blue). Suspend the strips as shown in Figure D, and remove them when the water reaches the paper clip. Record the distance each pigment front (the leading edge) traveled. Calculate an R_f value for each pigment by dividing the distance the pigment front traveled by the distance the water front traveled in the same time.

Once you have identified the R_f values for each pigment, repeat the process using the unknown mixtures. Compare the R_f values and colors of the chromatograms of the unknowns with those of the known food colorings. Identify which colors were mixed to make each of the unknowns. The sample in Figure F is a mixture of the dye 1 (Figure E) and dye 2 (Figure G). Note that the R_f values of the individual pigments in Figure F match those from dyes used in Figures E and G.

Questions

(1) Which of the inks are pure substances, and which are mixtures?

(2) Were the pigments in the inks separated by physical means or chemical means? Explain.

(3) How many bands of color would result if a pure substance is analyzed using paper chromatography? Explain.

(4) A police officer finds a red paint chip at the scene of a hit-and run traffic fatality. The paint looks exactly like red paint used on a late-model Chevrolet and a late-model Ford. How might a forensic chemist identify whether the paint came from a Chevy or Ford?

(5) Chromatography separates components in a mixture on the basis of different R_f values. What other physical properties could be used to separate components in a mixture?

2.5.3 IDENTIFICATION OF PHYSICAL AND CHEMICAL CHANGES

Concepts to Investigate: Physical changes, chemical changes, indicators of chemical change.

Materials: Match, chalk, mortar, pestle, vinegar, silver nitrate, light sticks (Cyalume®), baking soda, sugar, overhead pens.

Principles and Procedures: While a physical property can be observed without altering the identity of a material, a chemical property cannot. Chemical properties are observed when substances are converted to different substances with different properties. Flammability, for example, is a chemical property that can only be observed when a substance reacts with oxygen. If a chemical change has occurred, the products will differ from reactants. Although one must perform chemical analyses to show that a chemical reaction has taken place, there are certain easily observed changes that generally indicate a chemical reaction has occurred: (a) the simultaneous production of light and heat; (b) the production of a gas when two or more substances are mixed; and (c) the formation of a precipitate when two or more solutes are dissolved in a solution.

Make careful observations of the following actions. On the basis of your observations, indicate whether a physical or chemical change has occurred.

Table 1: Physical and Chemical Changes

Activity	Chemical or Physical	Evidence
Lighting a match.		
Crushing chalk with a mortar and pestle.		
Mixing vinegar with crushed chalk.		
Mixing 1 mL of $AgNO_3$ solution with 5 mL of NaCl solution.		
Bending a Cyalume® light stick.		
Boiling water.		
Crumpling a sheet of paper.		
Adding vinegar to baking soda.		
Crushing a large crystal of rock candy.		
Dissolving/re-crystallizing sugar.		
Separating pigments by chromatography (see 2.5.3).		

Questions

(1) Which of the activities involved chemical reactions? Which involved physical changes? Give evidence for your conclusions in Table 1.

2.5.4 ELEMENTS AND COMPOUNDS

Concepts to Investigate: Pure substances, compounds, elements, electrolysis, law of definite composition (law of definite proportions).

Materials: 9-volt battery, sodium sulfate, beaker, test tubes, pencil leads from mechanical pencils (or other carbon rod), test leads (insulated copper wire).

Principles and Procedures: On January 24, 1848, James Marshall noticed a shiny substance in a stream near Coloma California. Thinking that he may have discovered gold, Marshall took the substance back to his boss, John Sutter. Fearing that others might hear their discussion, the two locked themselves in a room, closed the shutters and performed various chemical tests to see if it was indeed gold. The substance was pure (they couldn't separate it into different components by physical means), and it was elemental (it couldn't be broken down into other substances by chemical means). These and other tests convinced them that they had indeed discovered gold. Although they tried to keep their discovery a secret, word soon got out and the great California Gold Rush was on. In four years the population of California grew from 14,000 (1848) to 250,000 (1852), with gold hunters from the Eastern United States, Europe, China, Australia and Latin America.

For thousands of years people have known that gold cannot be broken down into other substances. We say that gold is an element because it is elementary, and cannot be reduced into simpler chemicals. Today, chemists recognize 112 elements and have organized them in the Periodic Table of the Elements (Appendix 5). All known substances are composed of these 112 elements, just as all words in the English language are composed of the 26 different letters of the alphabet.

An element is a pure substance that cannot be reduced to simpler substances by normal chemical means. A compound is also a pure substance, but consists of two or more elements. A compound cannot be separated by physical means, but can be broken down by chemical means. Water is a pure substance, but is it an element or a compound? Although water cannot be broken down into simpler substances by physical means, can it be decomposed by chemical means? Perform the following activity to determine if water is a compound or an element.

Construct an apparatus like that shown in Figure H. Prepare a 0.1 M solution of sodium sulfate (Na_2SO_4; 142 g/mole) by dissolving 14.2 g of sodium sulfate in a small amount of water and diluting to a final volume of one liter. Fill two test tubes and a beaker with the sodium sulfate solution. Connect a pencil lead (carbon, graphite) to one end of each of two wires using alligator clips or tape. Place these carbon electrodes in the tubes, seal the tubes with your thumb, invert the tubes and submerge the open ends in the beaker as shown, making sure that no air enters. Connect the free ends of the wires to the

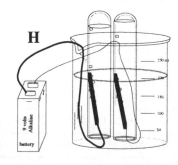

electrodes of a 9-volt battery and observe the gas produced at the electrodes. Does it appear as though water is a compound and can be decomposed into simpler substances?

The law of definite composition states that chemical compounds contain the same elements in the same proportions regardless of sample size. Measure the relative volumes of the gases produced at the cathode and anode at one minute, five minutes, and ten minutes. Does the ratio of the volume of gas collected at the two electrodes remain constant as would be predicted by the law of definite composition? Does water appear to be an element or a compound?

Questions

(1) Is water a homogeneous pure substance?

(2) How much gas collects at the cathode (negative terminal) compared to the anode (positive terminal)?

(3) Does water appear to be an element, or a compound? Explain.

(4) Knowing that the formula for water is H_2O, determine which gas collects at the anode, and which collects at the cathode.

(5) The law of definite composition states that a chemical compound contains the same elements in the same proportions of mass, regardless of the size of the sample. Did the ratio of the gases remain constant throughout your experiment? Does this support the notion that water is a compound?

2.5.5 EXTENSIVE AND INTENSIVE
PHYSICAL PROPERTIES

Concepts to Investigate: Extensive physical properties, intensive physical properties, density.

Materials: Copper shot, small lead fishing weights, aluminum shot or turnings, graduated cylinder, balance.

Principles and Procedures: An extensive physical property is one that depends on the amount (extent) of matter present. Length, volume and mass are extensive physical properties. The greater the amount of a substance, the greater its mass, volume and dimensions. Intensive physical properties do not depend on the amount of material. Color, malleability, ductility, refractive index, crystal shape, boiling point and melting point are examples of intensive physical properties. Increasing the amount of a substance does not change its color, boiling point or any other intensive property.

Density is defined as the ratio of mass to volume *(m/V)*. Is density an extensive or intensive physical property? Fill a graduated cylinder one-third with water. Carefully record the volume and the total mass of the cylinder and water (Figures I, J). Pour enough copper shot into the cylinder so the water level rises to approximately two thirds the height of the cylinder (Figure K). Tap the cylinder until all air bubbles are released. Carefully record the volume and the mass of the cylinder, water and shot. The mass of the copper is the difference between the final and initial masses. The volume of the copper is the difference between the final and initial volumes. Calculate the density by dividing the mass of the copper by its volume. Add additional copper shot until the water level rises nearly to the top of the graduations (measurement markings on the cylinder). Determine the density of all of the copper shot using the same procedure as before. The mass and volume of copper changes as more is added, indicating that mass and volume are extensive physical properties. Does the density of copper change as the amount of copper changes?

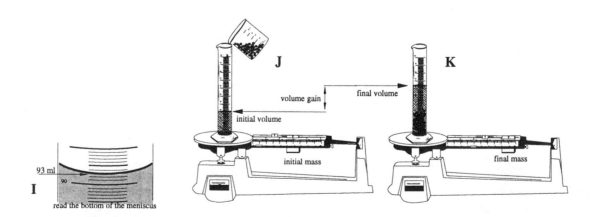

Repeat the procedure with aluminum turnings and with lead fishing weights. Is density an intensive property, totally independent of the amount of material present?

Questions

(1) What was your first determination of density for copper?

(2) What was your second determination of density for copper?

(3) Is density an extensive or intensive property?

(4) According to your calculations, what are the densities of lead and aluminum?

2.5.6 IDENTIFYING UNKNOWNS BY PHYSICAL AND CHEMICAL PROPERTIES

Concepts to Investigate: Intensive physical properties, chemical properties, density, activity series.

Materials: Balance, 100 mL graduated cylinder, pennies (20 or more pre-1982, and 20 or more post-1982).

Principles and Procedures:

Part 1: Using density to identify unknowns. In ancient times, people used shells, chunks of metal and other objects as currency to trade for products they desired. In approximately 700 BC, the Greeks invented the first mint to stamp uniform coins for use in trade, and the idea gradually spread throughout Europe, Africa and Asia. Shortly after gaining independence from Britain, the United States established a mint in Philadelphia to produce coins for the new nation. Today, American coins continue to be minted in Philadelphia and Denver (indicated by a "D" on the coin). The chemical content of U.S. coins has varied greatly with time. Gold was used in certain coins until 1933 when the price of gold became so high that the metal in the coins cost more than their face value. Silver was used to mint dimes, quarters, half dollars and silver dollars until 1965 when it was replaced by other metals. Pennies were made of copper until 1982 when the rising price of copper forced Congress to change the composition of these as well. Post-1982 pennies appear to be made of copper due to a thin electroplating of copper on the surface, but the core is made of another metal. In this investigation you will attempt to discover what this metal is.

Collect 20 or more pre-1982 pennies and 20 or more post-1982 pennies. (Do not use 1982 pennies because this was the year in which the transition took place). Fill a graduated cylinder (50 mL or 100 mL) one-third full of water. Record the volume of the water by measuring the level of the meniscus (Figure I in 2.5.5). Determine the mass of the cylinder and water, and then add 20 or more pre-1982 pennies. Measure the final mass and the final volume, and then subtract the initial mass and volume measurements to determine the mass and volume of the coins you added. Calculate the density of the pre-1982 pennies by dividing their mass by their volume. Repeat this procedure with post-1982 pennies. Examine the table of metal densities (Table 2) and generate a hypothesis regarding the composition of the core of the post-1982 pennies.

Table 2: Densities of Various Metals

Density (g/mL)	*Metal*
2.7	aluminum
5.7	tin
7.1	zinc
7.9	iron
8.9	copper
8.9	nickel
10.5	silver
11.3	lead
19.3	gold
21.5	platinum

Part 2: Using chemical activity to identify unknowns: *Teacher demonstration only: Wear goggles, lab coat, and gloves.* In Part 1 you generated a hypothesis about the content of post-1982 pennies using an intensive physical characteristic, density. Table 3 is a listing of the chemical activities of various metals. The higher the position in the table, the more reactive the metal. This data indicates that zinc will react with acids, while copper will not. If it were not for legislation protecting coinage from defacing, you could show that the center of a new penny is made of zinc by scoring its edges with a file and placing it in concentrated hydrochloric acid. The 2% of the coin that is copper (the surface) would not react, while the 98% that is zinc (the core) would. If left in acid for a prolonged period, only the copper shell would remain. Although we can't use pennies for this purpose, we can still illustrate the difference in reactivity between copper and zinc. Place copper (copper wire or shot) and mossy zinc in the same container of 6 M hydrochloric acid. Leave the container in a fume hood or other safe, ventilated area overnight. Decant the hydrochloric acid, flushing it down the sink with plenty of water. Fill the beaker with water and decant. Repeat twice to ensure that the acid has been removed. How much copper remains? How much zinc remains?

Table 3: Chemical Activity of Various Metals

Metal	Reactivity	Chemical Activity
aluminum zinc iron	high ↑	reacts with steam and acids, replacing hydrogen
nickel tin lead	medium	can react with acids, replacing hydrogen
copper		reacts with oxygen to form oxides
silver platinum gold	↑ low	fairly unreactive

Questions

(1) What are the densities of the pre-1982 pennies and the post-1982 pennies?

(2) On the basis of density, what does the core of a post-1982 penny appear to be made of?

(3) Is the zinc core of a post-1982 penny more or less reactive than copper?

FOR THE TEACHER

2.5.1 PHYSICAL AND CHEMICAL CHANGES

Discussion: Stirring iron and sulfur together at room temperature produces a heterogeneous mixture. No change in identity occurs as evidenced by the fact that iron remains ferromagnetic while sulfur remains non-ferromagnetic. The separation of iron from the sulfur with a magnet shows that the contents of the test tube represents a mixture. It is also possible to separate iron from sulfur on the basis of differing solubilities in carbon disulfide. Sulfur is highly soluble in carbon disulfide, while iron is not. The instructor may add carbon disulfide, decant the liquid, and then evaporate the solvent to obtain pure sulfur. Although this is an instructive exercise, *it should only be carried out in a fume hood and by an experienced teacher wearing protective gloves, lab coat, and goggles.* Carbon disulfide is very poisonous and explosive and should be treated with great caution.

At high temperatures, sulfur and iron react as follows:

$$Fe + S \rightarrow FeS \qquad \Delta H_f^0 = -100 \text{ kJ / mole}$$

This is classified as a chemical reaction because a new substance (iron sulfide) forms at the expense of two reactants (iron and sulfur). Students will find that iron sulfide is attracted to the magnet, but that it is not possible to separate the iron from the sulfur by physical means.

Answers: (1) A physical change has occurred as evidenced by the fact that iron can be separated from the sulfur on the basis of a physical difference (magnetism). (2) The iron/sulfur mixture at room temperature is heterogeneous. Small chunks of iron and sulfur coexist side by side. (3) No. The appearance of iron and sulfur remain unchanged, and it is possible to separate them from each other because iron is attracted by a magnet while sulfur is not. (4) Chemical change. The iron reacted with the sulfur to form a new compound, iron sulfide. (5) No. A chemical change has occurred and the product, iron sulfide, is a new compound whose components cannot be separated by physical means. (6) The product, iron sulfide, is a pure substance. If sulfur and iron were not mixed in 1:1 mole ratio, there would be excess of one of the reactants and the tube will contain a mixture of the remaining reactant and the new product (iron sulfide).

2.5.2 SEPARATION OF PURE SUBSTANCES AND MIXTURES: CHROMATOGRAPHY

Discussion: Chromatography is a very powerful method for separating mixtures. It makes use of the relative rates at which components of a mixture are absorbed from a moving stream of liquid or gas onto a stationary substance. Liquid chromatography uses a mobile liquid phase, and gas chromatography uses a mobile gas phase.

The instructor must prepare the unknowns for part 2 prior to the laboratory. Prepare an unknown by mixing equal quantities of each of two dyes together. Label the unknowns as "Unknown A" and "Unknown B." Many pigments have the same color, but are chemically different. It is therefore important to use R_f values as an additional physical characteristic when identifying pigments. For example, two pigments may appear the same color of red, but one travels close behind the water front and has an R_f of 0.85, while the other travels much farther behind and has an R_f of 0.40. Although the two pigments appear the same to the eye, they must be different chemicals as evidenced by differing attraction for the paper.

It should be noted that different brands of food coloring have different chromatographic behavior. If laboratory filter paper is not available, you may substitute coffee filter paper or even unprinted newspaper.

Answers: (1) Most inks are mixtures of pigments. For example, green inks are generally made from a mixture of blue and yellow pigments. (2) The pigments separate because they have different physical properties (different attraction for water and paper). No chemical reactions were necessary to separate the pigments. (3) Pure substances will yield only one band. A pure substance is one that has the same properties and composition throughout, and cannot be separated into other substances by physical means. (4) The forensic chemist could perform some type of chromatography to separate the pigments in the paint chip and then compare the results with similar tests performed on paint supplied by the two car manufacturers. (5) Boiling point (e.g., fractional distillation), melting point (e.g., separating metal ore from a rock), density (e.g., cream separates from raw milk), etc.

2.5.3 IDENTIFICATION OF PHYSICAL AND CHEMICAL CHANGES

Discussion: It should be noted that the indicators of chemical change do not prove that a chemical reaction has occurred. It is necessary to perform chemical analyses of the reactants and products to confirm that a chemical reaction has taken place.

If you have a fume hood or outdoor demonstration table you may wish to perform the following activity to illustrate a dramatic chemical change. *Put on goggles, gloves, and lab coat when preparing*

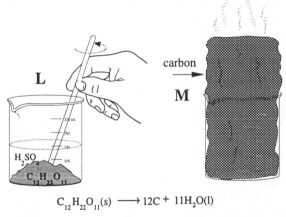

$$C_{12}H_{22}O_{11}(s) \longrightarrow 12C + 11H_2O(l)$$

$$H_2SO_4 \cdot nH_2O + mH_2O \longrightarrow H_2SO_4 \cdot (n+m)H_2O$$

this demonstration or whenever dealing with concentrated acids. Fill a beaker one-quarter full of concentrated sulfuric acid. Add an equivalent mass of granulated sugar and stir until the sugar and acid are evenly distributed (Figure L). The contents will gradually turn golden brown, and then black as a solid column of carbon begins to rise out of the beaker (Figure M). Students will be amazed to see how mixing a liquid and a solid will cause the formation of such a large column of carbon. This is a clear example of a chemical reaction in which the products are dramatically different from the reactants. Sulfuric acid dehydrates the sugar (removes hydrogen and oxygen as water), leaving only carbon behind. The reaction is very exothermic and must be handled with care. Rinse the mass of carbon thoroughly with water before discarding to remove the hydrated sulfuric acid.

$$C_{12}H_{22}O_{11}(s) \longrightarrow 12C(s) + 11H_2O(l)$$

$$H_2SO_4 \cdot nH_2O + mH_2O \longrightarrow H_2SO_4 \cdot (n+m)H_2O$$

You may illustrate the effect that acid has upon clothing by dripping concentrated sulfuric acid onto an old cotton rag or a paper towel. Black spots will appear where the sulfuric acid reacts with the cellulose fibers to produce carbon. When the cloth or towel is rinsed in water, the unattached carbon is washed away, leaving holes where the sulfuric acid once was. This demonstration should convince students of the necessity of wearing laboratory aprons!

Table 4: Physical and Chemical Changes

	Chemical or Physical	*Evidence and Explanation*
lighting a match	chemical	Light and heat are produced. This occurs when a sesquisulfide of phosphorous is oxidized by the oxygen released when potassium chlorate in the match head decomposes. Also, the wood or paper chars, showing that carbon is produced.
crushing chalk with a mortar and pestle	physical	Chalk (primarily calcium carbonate) is broken into smaller pieces, but retains its chemical identity.
mixing vinegar and crushed chalk	chemical	A gas is produced. Acetic acid reacts with the calcium $$CaCO_3(s) + 2HC_2H_3O_2(aq) \rightarrow Ca(C_2H_3O_2)_2(aq) + CO_2(g) + H_2O(l)$$
mixing 1 mL of silver nitrate solution with 5 mL of sodium chloride solution	chemical	A precipitate (silver chloride) is formed: $$AgNO_3 + NaCl \rightarrow NaNO_3 + AgCl(s)$$
bending a Cyalume® light stick (contents)	chemical	Light and a slight amount of heat are produced. A phenyl oxalate ester decomposes in the presence of hydrogen peroxide, transferring energy to a dye molecule which glows as it returns to its ground state.
boiling water	physical	Water vapor will condense to form liquid vapor with exactly the same properties as it had before boiling.
crumple a sheet of	physical	Crumpled paper has the same physical characteristics as paper regular paper.
mixing vinegar and baking soda	chemical	Gas (carbon dioxide) is produced. $$NaHCO_3 + HC_2H_3O_2 \rightarrow Na^+ + C_2H_3O_2^- + CO_2 + H_2O$$
crush a large crystal of rock candy	physical	The resulting pieces have the same properties (color, taste, etc.) as the original.
dissolving/re-crystallizing sugar	physical	As water evaporates, crystalline sugar will reappear, with the physical properties it had before.
separation of pigments by chromatography	physical	Chromatography separates chemicals, but doesn't change them.

2.5.4 ELEMENTS AND COMPOUNDS

Discussion: Electrolysis decomposes a compound (H_2O) into elements (H_2 and O_2). The overall reaction is:

$$2H_2O(l) + 571.8kJ \rightarrow 2H_2(g) + O_2(g)$$

Hydrogen collects at the cathode (negative electrode) as a result of the following reduction reaction:

$$2H_2O(l) + 2e^- \rightarrow 2OH^-(aq) + H_2(g)$$

Oxygen collects at the anode (positive electrode) as a result of the following oxidation reaction:

$$6H_2O(l) \rightarrow 4H_3O^+(aq) + O_2(g) + 4e^-$$

An indicator such as phenolphthalein can be used to indicate that the water surrounding the cathode becomes basic (becomes pink; basic due to the production of hydroxide ions; OH^-), while the water around the anode becomes acidic (remains colorless; acidic due to the production of hydronium ions; H_3O^+)

Without an electrolyte, no current will flow through the liquid from the cathode to the anode. Although other substances like sulfuric acid and sodium chloride can be used as an electrolyte source, sodium sulfate is preferred because it is safer than using sodium chloride, which releases chlorine gas and sulfuric acid which can cause burns.

Answers: (1) Water is the same throughout, and therefore can be classified as a homogeneous, pure substance. (2) Twice as much gas collects at the cathode than at the anode. (3) The data from this experiment suggest that water is a compound that can be split into two gases. (4) Twice as much gas collects at the cathode. This gas must be hydrogen because the formula (H_2O) indicates that water is composed of twice as much hydrogen as oxygen. (5) The ratio of gas volumes remains 2:1 (cathode:anode) throughout the reaction. Assuming that the quantity of a gas is proportional to its volume (at constant temperature and pressure), this constant 2:1 ratio supports the assertion that water is a compound composed of a two parts hydrogen and one part oxygen.

2.5.5 EXTENSIVE AND INTENSIVE
PHYSICAL PROPERTIES

Discussion: You may wish to have your students calculate the relative error of their measurements. Relative error is calculated as the difference between the observed value and the accepted value, divided by the accepted value, multiplied by 100%. For example, if students calculate the density of copper to 8.7 g/mL, then the relative error would be calculated as follows:

$$\text{Relative error} = \frac{(\text{accepted} - \text{measured})}{\text{accepted}} \times 100\%$$

$$\text{Relative error} = \frac{(8.9 - 8.7)}{8.9} \times 100\%$$

$$\text{Relative error} = 2.2\%$$

Answers: (1) 8.9 g/mL. (2) 8.9 g/mL. (3) Density is an intensive property. The density of a metal remains constant regardless of how much is present. (4) The density of aluminum is 2.70 g/mL; the density of lead is 11.34 g/mL.

2.5.6 IDENTIFYING UNKNOWNS BY PHYSICAL AND CHEMICAL PROPERTIES

Discussion: Prior to 1982, pennies were made of copper. In 1982, the United States mint started producing coins with a core made of an alloy composed of 99.2% zinc and 0.8% copper. Post-1982 pennies have been electroplated with copper to give a final composition of 97.5% zinc and 2.5% copper.

Answers: (1) Pre-1982 pennies are composed of copper, with a density of 8.9 g/mL. Post-1982, made primarily of zinc, have a density of approximately 7.1 g/mL. (2) Zinc. (3) The zinc core is much more reactive. Bubbles of hydrogen stream from the mossy zinc as the following reaction takes place:

$$Zn + 2HCl \rightarrow ZnCl_2 + H_2$$

Applications to Everyday Life

Cooking: The preparation of food involves physical changes (e.g. boiling water, freezing ice cream, preparation of a tossed green salad) and chemical changes (e.g. denaturing albumin in an egg when frying, the destruction of toxic oxalic acid in rhubarb leaves with cooking, the denaturing of proteins when pickling.)

Body physiology: Body physiology involves physical changes (e.g. dissolving gases in the blood, evaporation of water from the skin, diffusion of nutrients into the bloodstream in the intestines) and chemical changes (conversion of ATP to ADP in cell processes, metabolism of sugars to produce carbon dioxide and water, construction of proteins from amino acids).

Jewelry: Pure gold is too soft and malleable to be of use in jewelry. As a result, jewelers prefer an alloy or amalgam (a homogeneous mixture or solid solution of two or more metals) of gold. "White gold" is an alloy of nickel and gold, "red gold" is an alloy of gold, silver, and copper. The purity of gold is measured in karats (known as carats outside the U.S.), not to be confused with carats used to measure the weight of gemstones. A gold karat represents 1/24th part (4.167 %) of the whole. Thus, an object that is 16 karat gold contains 16/24 (2/3) gold, and 8/24 (1/3) alloying metal.

Metallurgy and building materials: Mixtures of metals (alloys) often have desirable characteristics that pure metals do not. Brass, an alloy of copper and zinc, is widely used in decorative furnishings in the home. Steel, an alloy of iron and carbon, is the most important building material in the construction of vehicles and high rise buildings. Each alloy has its unique chemical and physical properties (e.g. hardness, toughness, corrosion resistance, magnetizability, color, and ductility) that suits it for specific applications.

Chemicals for the consumer market: Chemists have identified 112 elements. By understanding the unique properties of these elements, chemists can design new compounds. Approximately one million compounds have been identified, and more are being discovered each day.

Patents: To encourage the development of new inventions, a government may grant an inventor a patent which guarantees him or her the exclusive right to make, use or sell an invention for a limited period of time. The chemical industry is one of the largest industries in the world, and companies carefully guard their patented chemical compounds. Before a compound may be patented, chemists must accurately describe its unique physical and chemical properties so that lawyers will be able to defend the company against infringement of the patent by other manufacturers.

UNIT THREE

Chemical and Nuclear Reactions

3.1 CHEMICAL BONDING

The English alphabet is composed of only 26 letters, yet from these letters are made nearly a half million words. Each day new words are made to describe new products, discoveries, and ideas. In recent years we have seen the addition of words like scuba (**s**elf **c**ontained **u**nder-water **b**reathing **a**pparatus), laser (**l**ight **a**mplification by **s**timulated **e**mission of **r**adiation), email (electronic mail), fax (facsimile) and snowboard ("surfboard" for the snow).

Chemists have identified 112 elements ("the letters of chemistry") from which more than a million compounds ("the words of chemistry") are made. Each day new compounds are being discovered or synthesized—compounds such as acetaminophen (the active pain relieving ingredient in products such as Tylenol®, Nyquil®, and Excedrin®), Kevlar, poly(p-phenyleneterephthalamide; a synthetic material that is stronger than steel and used to make bullet-proof vests, trampolines, tennis rackets and wind-surfing sails), and melatonin (N-acetyl-5-methoxytryptamine, a natural hormone that researchers believe may help regulate sleep and help combat cancer).

Just as not all combinations of letters make real words, not all combinations of elements make compounds. There are chemical rules guiding the bonding of elements, just as there are phonetic rules governing the combination of letters to compose words. For example, just as all words require a vowel, so all chemical bonds require electrons. Without electrons, no chemical bonding will form. Chemical bonding involves the transfer or sharing of electrons between two or more atoms. Bonds form because the product is more energetically stable (lower energy) than its components.

Ionic Bonding: The simplest type of bond is the ionic or electrovalent bond. In ionic bonds (Figure A), one or more electrons are transferred from one neutral atom or group of atoms to another, resulting in a cation (positively charged particle resulting from the loss of electrons) and an anion (negatively charged particle resulting from the gain of electrons). Because opposite charges attract, the cation and anion bind together. Ionic bonds are strong, and the resulting crystals are relatively hard. Ionic compounds are poor conductors of electricity as solids, but good conductors as liquids or when dissociated in a solvent. They have moderate to high melting points and are soluble in polar solvents, but insoluble in nonpolar solvents. Most minerals, including common table salt ($NaCl$), are ionic compounds.

Covalent Bonding: Compounds held together by mutual attraction for a pair of electrons are known as covalent compounds. If the electron pair is evenly distributed between the two bonding atoms, the bond is nonpolar covalent (Figure B). If, however, the electrons are held more closely by one atom than another, the bond develops a polarity (Figure C), with the end nearest the electron pair being more negative and the other end more positive. Covalent (electron shared) bonds are generally very strong, and covalent compounds are relatively insoluble in most solvents and unable to conduct electricity in the solid or liquid state. Covalent compounds have low melting points, and at room temperature are frequently liquid or gas. In their solid state, covalent compounds are very hard and brittle.

Metallic Bonding: Metallic bonding represents the third major type of chemical bonding. Metal atoms are closely packed, and in most cases the outermost electron shell of one metal atom overlaps with a large number of neighboring atoms, and as a result, the valence electrons move freely from one atom to another. Valence electrons are not associated with any specific atom or pair of atoms, but wander freely among adjacent metal atoms. Rather than being attracted to a specific pair of electrons, each positive metal ion is attracted to all of the

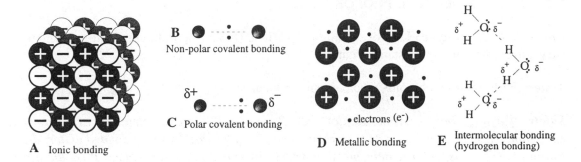

A Ionic bonding

B Non-polar covalent bonding

C Polar covalent bonding

D Metallic bonding • electrons (e⁻)

E Intermolecular bonding (hydrogen bonding)

electrons in its vicinity (Figure D). Metals may be described as positive ions in a sea of electrons. The free-electron character of metals explains why they are excellent conductors of electricity and heat. Since the binding forces in metals are nondirectional, metals can be re-shaped easily and do not fracture when stretched or hammered.

Intermolecular Bonds: Intermolecular bonds are generally much weaker than the covalent bonds that join atoms together in molecules, the ionic bonds that join ions together in ionic compounds, and the metallic bonds found in solid metals. Intermolecular forces act between the positive region of one polar molecule and the negative region of another (Figure E). Crystals held together by such intermolecular forces generally do not conduct electricity, have a low melting point, and are soluble in most organic solvents. Most organic compounds are held together by intermolecular forces.

Table 1 summarizes the different properties that are conferred on a compound as a result of the chemical bonds it possesses. It should be noted that these are broad generalizations and do not hold for all substances.

Table 1: Comparison of the Properties of Substances with Ionic, Covalent, Metallic or Intermolecular Bonds
Note: These are broad generalizations and do not apply for all substances.

	Ionic	*Covalent*	*Metallic*	*Intermolecular*
bond strength	strong	very strong	variable strength, generally moderate	weak
hardness	moderate to high	very hard, brittle	low to moderate; ductile, malleable	crystals soft and somewhat plastic
electrical conductivity	conducts by ion transport, but only when liquid or dissociated	insulators in solid and liquid states	good conductors; conducts by electron transport	insulators in both solid and liquid states
melting point	moderate to high	low	generally high	low
solubility	soluble in polar solvents	very low solubilities	insoluble except in acids or alkalis by chemical reaction	soluble in organic solvents
examples	most minerals	diamond, oxygen, hydrogen, organic molecules	Cu, Ag, Au, other metals	organic compounds

3.1.1 LAW OF DEFINITE PROPORTIONS

Concepts to Investigate: Law of definite proportions (law of definite composition), chemistry, atoms, heating to constant weight.

Materials: Potassium chlorate, crucible, burner, balance.

Safety: <u>Warning:</u> *Teacher demonstration only. Potassium chlorate is potentially explosive if contaminated with ammonium salts, carbon, combustible materials, finely divided materials, sulfur, phosphorous, sulfuric acid, metal powders, sugar and other substances. It should not come in contact with paper, rubber or other flammable substances. Wear a face mask and lab coat.*

Principles and Procedures: Chemistry is the science that studies the properties, reactions, composition and structure of matter. Our ancient ancestors had a working knowledge of some basic chemical reactions, but did not understand how or why substances behaved the way they did. For example, they used fire (an oxidation reaction) to prepare food, cure bricks, and refine gold ore, but they did not understand what fire was, nor how it produced these important transformations.

During the fourth and third centuries BC, Greek philosophers began to ponder the nature of matter. Democritus (460–370 BC) suggested that all matter was made of infinitesimally small, indivisible particles called "atoms." By contrast, Aristotle (384–322 BC) argued that no fundamental particles exist, and that material could be divided *ad infinitum*. Aristotle had a profound influence on scientific thought, and for more than 2000 years his concept of the continuity of matter was accepted by most scientists.

The development of sensitive balances in the late 1700s gave scientists a tool for studying the composition of matter in a quantitative manner. In 1799, the French chemist Joseph Louis Proust presented experimental evidence indicating that chemical compounds are composed of elements in exactly the same proportions by mass, regardless of sample size. Proust decomposed many samples of copper carbonate ($CuCO_3$) and found that it was always composed of 51.4% Copper, 9.7% Carbon, and 38.9% oxygen. Proust's work led to the law of definite proportions (also known as the law of definite or constant composition) which states that a chemical compound is composed of elements in exactly the same proportions by mass, regardless of the sample size.

Scientists realized that Aristotle's theory could not explain Proust's findings. Five years after Proust's discovery, an English schoolteacher named John Dalton proposed a theory of matter to explain the law of definite proportions and other newly discovered principles such as the law of the conservation of mass. Like Democritus, Dalton suggested that all elements are composed of extremely small particles (atoms). Dalton's atomic theory stated that the atoms of a given element are identical in mass, size and other properties, but differ from the properties of other elements. Dalton stated that these "atoms" cannot be created, destroyed or broken into pieces, and that compounds can be formed by the combination of atoms in simple, whole-number ratios. Dalton said that chemical reactions occur when atoms separate, combine or rearrange. Although modern atomic theory realizes that there are slight variations in the atomic mass of elements (isotopes and ions) and that atoms can be broken into smaller pieces (fission), the basics of Dalton's theory paved the way for the development of the new science of chemistry.

In this investigation you will gather data on the composition of matter in much the same way that Joseph Proust did prior to formulating the law of definite proportions. However, rather than computing the percentage of oxygen in copper carbonate ($CuCO_3$), you will compute the percentage oxygen in potassium chlorate. Like Proust, your goal is to determine if percentage composition is independent of sample size.

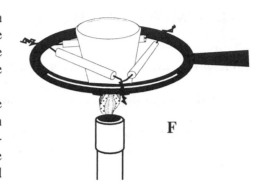

F

Weigh an empty crucible with cover to the nearest hundredth of a gram (a) and record in Table 2. Place approximately 1.5 grams of potassium chlorate in the crucible and re-weigh to the nearest hundredth of a gram (b). Determine and record the weight of the potassium chlorate by subtracting the first weight from the second (c). Place the covered crucible on a clay triangle and heat very gently for two minutes. Remove the cover and gently increase the heat every two minutes for the next eight minutes (Figure F). Potassium chlorate decomposes upon heating, releasing oxygen. Allow the crucible to cool to room temperature and re-weigh it with the cover (d). Determine the mass of oxygen driven off (e) and the percentage of the weight of potassium chlorate that is oxygen (f). Repeat the experiment with another sample of approximately 3.0 g of potassium chlorate. Compare your data with the data of other class members. Does the percentage of oxygen in potassium chlorate remain constant or vary?

Table 2: Determination of the Percentage of Oxygen in Potassium Chlorate

	1st Trial	*2nd Trial*
(a) mass of empty crucible and cover	g	g
(b) mass of crucible, cover, and contents before heating	g	g
(c) mass of potassium chlorate (c = b − a)	g	g
(d) mass of crucible, contents, and cover after heating to constant weight	g	g
(e) mass of oxygen driven off (e = c − d)	g	g
(f) percentage oxygen (f = e/c · 100%)	%	%

Questions

(1) What is the average percentage of oxygen in potassium chlorate based on a 1.5-gram sample? A 3.0-gram sample?

(2) Is your data and the class data consistent with the law of definite proportions? Explain.

(3) What is the theoretical percentage of oxygen in potassium chlorate ($KClO_3$)? Determine the average for all of the class data and determine the percentage error.

3.1.2 BOND FORMATION

Concepts to Investigate: Bond formation, exothermic reactions, covalent bonds, ionic bonds.

Materials: Magnesium ribbon, coffee can, long forceps, burner, deflagrating spoon, sulfur.

Safety: The activities in this section should be performed only by the instructor. Pay particular attention to the individual warnings associated with each part. Always wear goggles and lab coat.

Principles and Procedures: Atoms differ in their ability to attract electrons. Fluorine has the greatest attractive force, and francium, in the opposite corner of the periodic table, has the least. American chemist Linus Pauling developed a concept known as electronegativity to describe the ability of an atom in a compound to attract electrons. He arbitrarily assigned fluorine a value of 4.0, and calculated the electronegativities of other elements with reference to it (Figure G). A bond is totally ionic if the difference in electronegativities between the bonded atoms is 100% (this is the theoretical maximum and never actually occurs), and totally covalent if both atoms have identical electronegativities (as occurs in a molecule formed by the bonding of two identical atoms). Just as the colors of the rainbow are not distinct, but rather blend into one another, so the ionic nature of bonds represents a continuum. If the electronegativity difference between two atoms is 1.7 or greater (50–100% ionic character), then we categorize the bond as an ionic bond. If the electronegativity difference is between 0.3 and 1.7 (5–50% ionic character), then it is classified as polar covalent. Finally, if the difference is less than 0.3, (less than 5% ionic character), then it is considered nonpolar covalent.

Your teacher will perform a series of reactions in which elements combine to form compounds. Describe the appearance and stoichiometry (the quantitative relationship between reactants and products in a chemical reaction) of these reactions and determine if the bonds in the new compounds are ionic, polar covalent or nonpolar covalent by determining the difference in electronegativities of the atoms involved, and comparing this data with (Figure H).

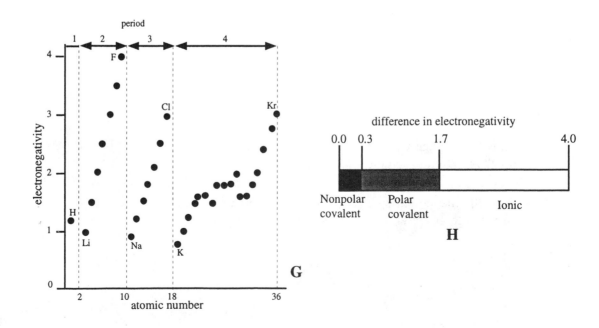

Part 1: Formation of magnesium oxide from magnesium and oxygen: *Warning: Do not look directly at the flame produced by burning magnesium.* Cut a 5 cm section of magnesium ribbon. Darken the room. Hold the ribbon with forceps, ignite it in the flame of a burner (Figure I), and hold it inside an empty tin can (Figure J). Magnesium will react with the oxygen in the atmosphere to form magnesium oxide. In addition, some magnesium will react with nitrogen to form magnesium nitride. Write balanced equations for these reactions and determine if the resulting compound has ionic, polar covalent or nonpolar covalent bonds.

Part 2: Formation of sulfur dioxide from sulfur and oxygen: *Warning! This demonstration should be performed in a fume hood.* Place approximately 10 grams of sulfur in a deflagrating spoon and ignite (Figure K). The sulfur reacts with oxygen to form sulfur dioxide. Write a balanced equation for this reaction and determine if the resulting compound has ionic, polar covalent or nonpolar covalent bonds.

Part 3: Formation of sodium chloride from sodium and chlorine: *Warning! This demonstration should be performed in a fume hood. Sodium is dangerous when exposed to moisture and should be stored under kerosene. Chlorine gas is a strong oxidizing agent and irritant. Keep chlorine gas away from flammable vapors.* Cut a small piece of sodium (approximately 5 mm in diameter) and place it on a bed of sand in the bottom of an Erlenmeyer flask. Place the flask in the fume hood and fill with chlorine gas. Add a few drops of water on top of the sodium (Figure L). An extremely exothermic reaction will occur and sodium chloride (table salt) will form. Write a balanced equation to show how two dangerous substances, chlorine and sodium, bond together to produce common table salt. Determine if the resulting compound has ionic, polar covalent or nonpolar covalent bonds.

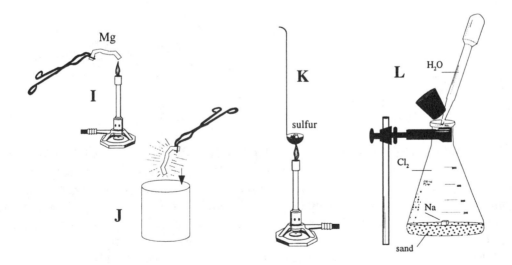

Part 4: Formation of water from hydrogen and oxygen: *Teacher demonstration only. Wear goggles and lab coat.* Fill the reservoir of a Hoffman apparatus (Figure M) or similar electrolysis device with 2% sulfuric acid. Open the stopcocks until both arms completely fill with the dilute acid solution. Connect the wire leads to the power supply. Hydrogen will collect at the cathode (connected to the negative terminal of your power supply):

$$2H_2O(l) + 2e^- \longrightarrow 2OH^-(aq) + H_2(g)$$

Oxygen will collect at the anode (connected to the positive terminal of your power supply):

$$6H_2O(l) \longrightarrow 4H_3O^+(aq) + O_2(g) + 4e^-$$

Disconnect the power supply when an entire tube of hydrogen and a half tube of oxygen have been collected. The ratio of hydrogen to oxygen will always be 2:1 since water is made of two parts hydrogen and one part oxygen (H_2O). Connect tubes to both arms and collect oxygen and hydrogen in an Erlenmeyer flask (Figure M). Seal the flask immediately after collecting the gas. Observe that the flask is clear and dry. Open the flask and insert a glowing splint or match. A loud "pop" will occur and water will be produced (look for condensation on the sides of the flask). Write a balanced equation to show how two gasses, hydrogen and oxygen, bond together to produce water. Determine if the resulting compound has ionic, polar covalent or nonpolar covalent bonds.

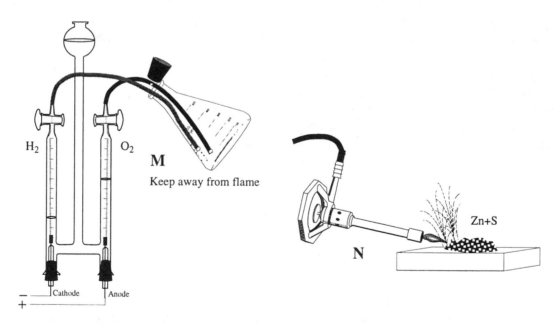

Part 5: Formation of zinc sulfide from zinc and sulfur: *Warning: Teacher demonstration only. This demonstration should be performed in a fume hood behind a protective panel.* Weigh out 20 grams of zinc and 10 grams of sulfur. Mix them together thoroughly on a heat resistant tile. Ignite with a burner (Figure N), and remove the flame once the reaction has started. Zinc sulfide is formed in a dramatic, exothermic reaction. Write a balanced equation to show how two elemental solids combine to form the compound zinc sulfide. Determine if the resulting compound has ionic, polar covalent or nonpolar covalent bonds.

Questions

(1) Write the equation for the reactions of parts 1–5. Are the products ionic, polar covalent or nonpolar covalent?

3.1.3 NONPOLAR AND POLAR COVALENT BONDS

Concepts to Investigate: Covalent bonds, nonpolar covalent molecules, polar covalent molecules, polarity, electrostatic attraction.

Materials: Rubber rod (or hard plastic comb), wool or fur, buret, water, cyclohexane, isopropyl alcohol (2-propanol, rubbing alcohol), plastic pipet.

Safety: Wear goggles and a lab coat. Isopropyl alcohol and cyclohexane are volatile and flammable and should be handled in a fume hood. As with all chemicals, avoid contact with cyclohexane.

Principles and Procedures: If you have emptied clothes from a warm clothes drier, you have probably observed clothes sticking to each other. This phenomenon, commonly known as "static cling," occurs when electrons accumulate on one material at the expense of another, so that one material obtains a net negative charge, and the other a net positive charge. The electrostatic attraction between these two materials causes them to cling together. When you comb your hair, the plastic in the comb pulls electrons from your hair, and acquires a negative charge. Plastic also acquires a negative charge when rubbed with fur or wool which, like human hair, are made primarily of a protein known as keratin. In this activity, you will use a charged plastic comb or rod to determine the degree of polarity of three different liquids. If a molecule is polar it will rotate so that its positive pole points toward the negatively charged comb. When oriented in this manner, the attraction between opposite charges (the negative comb and the positive pole of the molecule) will be greater than the repulsion between like charges (the negative comb and the negative end of the molecule), causing the molecule to be attracted toward the comb. If a molecule is nonpolar, it will not be affected by the presence of a charged object.

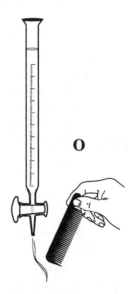

Water, isopropyl alcohol (2-propanol, rubbing alcohol) and cyclohexane are all covalent molecules. Which of them has the most polar bonds? Fill burets with water, isopropyl alcohol, and cyclohexane. Rub a hard rubber rod or hard plastic comb repeatedly with wool or fur. Open the stopcock of the buret containing water. Move the comb or rod close to the stream of water and observe carefully to see if it is attracted by the electrostatic field of the comb (Figure O). Repeat the process with cyclohexane and isopropyl alcohol. The more polar a molecule is, the more it will be deflected by the electrostatically charged comb. Which liquid is the most polar? Which is the least polar?

Questions

(1) Which of these molecules is the most polar? Explain.

(2) In this investigation you have used a positively charged rod. Do you think that a negatively charged rod would produce the same effects? Explain.

3.1.4 COVALENT AND IONIC BONDS

Concepts to Investigate: Covalent bonds, ionic bonds, solubility, conductivity, polarity, electrolyte.

Materials: Conductivity apparatus (or conductivity meter or multimeter), table salt (sodium chloride), table sugar (sucrose), rubbing alcohol (isopropyl alcohol, 2-propanol), vinegar (acetic acid), bleach (sodium hypochlorite).

Principles and Procedures: An electric current results whenever there is a net movement of electric charge. The movement of electrons (carrying a negative charge) in metal wires supplies the electric power used in our homes and businesses. The movement of positively charged ions (cations) and negatively charged ions (anions) in batteries provides the electric current necessary to start our cars and power a variety of cordless electric devices.

Ionic materials are good conductors of electricity if they are in their liquid state or are dissolved in a polar solvent (like water). When an electrical field is applied, the cations (positive ions) migrate toward the cathode (negative electrode), and the anions (negative ions) migrate toward the anode (positive electrode). The strength of the electric current is dependent on the quantity of ions moving per unit time. By contrast, nonpolar covalent materials are good insulators because there are no separate charged particles to move. If there is no movement of electrical charge, then there will be no current.

The greater the ionic character of a bond, the better conductor the substance will be in its liquid state or when dissolved in a polar solvent. By measuring the potential of dissolved substances to conduct electricity, it is possible to gather information on the type of bonding. The greater the ionic character, the greater the current.

A conductivity apparatus may be purchased from a scientific supply company or constructed as follows. Obtain a clear glass tumbler or beaker to hold the solution. Mount a flashlight bulb in a miniature receptacle and attach the receptacle in the center of a small piece of cardboard or wood as illustrated in Figure P. Punch two holes on opposite sides of the cardboard. Place two straight bare copper wires through the holes to serve as electrodes, and use patch cables to make the connections illustrated. Connect two 9-volt batteries in series (total potential of 18 volts) to the apparatus as shown.

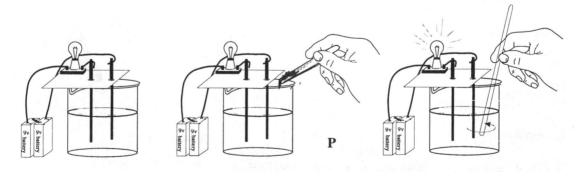

P

Fill the container with water. Does the light glow? Slowly add salt to the container, mixing it with a glass stirring rod to help it dissolve more rapidly. Does the light glow? The light will glow if the solute is an ionic substance because the dissociated ions carry electrical charge and will migrate in the electrical field. The light will not glow if the solute is a nonpolar covalent substance because such substances do not carry charge.

Is sodium chloride (table salt) an ionic substance? Wash the container and repeat with table sugar. Is sucrose (table sugar) an ionic or covalent substance? Empty the water, and clean the electrodes with water.

Test equal quantities of the following liquids: rubbing alcohol (isopropyl alcohol, 2-propanol), vinegar (acetic acid), bleach (sodium hypochlorite). Which of these substances appear to have ionic character (conduct an electrical current), and which do not?

Questions

(1) Which of the substances conduct electricity? What does this indicate about the bonding in these substances?

(2) Pure water is a poor conductor of electricity. Why?

(3) Salt appears to be a good conductor of electricity when dissolved in water, but will not conduct electricity in the solid form. Place the two dry electrodes of your conductivity apparatus into a pile of salt and note that the light does not glow. Explain.

3.1.5 METALLIC BONDING

Concepts to Investigate: Metals, metallic bonding, ionic bonding, electrical resistance.

Materials: Multimeter, copper, copper sulfate, aluminum, aluminum sulfate, iron, iron sulfate.

Safety: Use gloves when working with copper sulfate because it is a skin irritant.

Principles and Procedures: Metals have more shine (luster), are better conductors of heat and electricity, and are more malleable (easily reshaped) and ductile (easily drawn into wires) than either ionic or covalent compounds. The properties of metals are substantially different from the properties of ionic or covalent compounds, indicating that bonding in metals is quite different.

Metal atoms have relatively low ionization energies and electronegativities. Metal atoms readily surrender electrons, and do not attract electrons as strongly as nonmetals. The electrons in a metal do not belong to any one ion, but are free to move throughout the metal. Thus, metals can be visualized as positive nuclei in a sea of mobile electrons. Metallic bonds result from the attraction between the nuclei and the mobile electrons that surround them. Figure S shows an electric current in a metal.

In the previous investigation it was learned that covalent compounds do not conduct electricity, while dissolved ionic compounds do because the dissociated ions are free to move. Ionic compounds may conduct electricity when liquid because their ions are free to move (Figure Q), however they do not conduct electricity in the solid state because their ions are bound to each other in an immobile lattice (Figure R). Metals are the only materials that are good conductors when in the solid state because their electrons are free to move (Figure S). You will use this property of metals to distinguish metals from nonmetals.

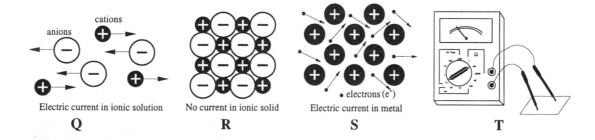

Electric current in ionic solution	No current in ionic solid	Electric current in metal	
Q	R	S	T

Solid covalent and ionic compounds have extremely high resistance to the flow of electrons, while metals have very low resistance. Thus, electricity flows readily through a copper (metal) wire, but not through its plastic (covalent material) insulation. Resistance to the flow of electrons is measured in ohms.

Multimeters are able to measure electrical resistance and can be used to determine if a substance is made primarily of metallic or nonmetallic material. Determine which of the materials provided (copper, copper sulfate, aluminum, aluminum sulfate, iron, iron sulfate) has metallic character by measuring the resistance when the probes are placed two centimeters apart (Figure T).

Questions

(1) On the basis of electrical resistance, which of the materials provided appear to be metals?

(2) What other characteristics do the materials you identified as metals have in common besides their low electrical resistance?

(3) Give examples of products that take advantage of the following properties of metals: malleability, electrical conductivity, thermal conductivity, reflectivity, ductility.

3.1.6 INTERMOLECULAR FORCES

Concepts to Investigate: Intermolecular forces, dipole-dipole interactions, van der Waals forces, hydrogen bonding, surface tension.

Materials: Water, isopropyl alcohol (rubbing alcohol), pennies, soap, paper clips, flask, jar, eyedropper, wax paper.

Principles and Procedures: Although the concepts of covalent, ionic, and metallic bonding help explain a wide variety of properties such as electrical conductivity, hardness, melting point, solubility and structure (Table 1), there are other properties that they cannot explain. Why, for example, does water boil at 100°C while methane boils at −164°C although they are both covalent molecules with very similar molecular weights?

The boiling point is the highest temperature at which a substance can exist as a liquid. Above the boiling point, the attraction between particles is not strong enough to overcome their kinetic energy. Table 3 shows that metallic and ionic materials typically have much higher boiling points than polar or nonpolar molecular compounds. It is difficult to separate metal atoms from each other because each atom is attracted to the sea of electrons around it. It is difficult to separate an ion from an ionic substance because the oppositely charged surrounding ions attract it. In contrast, covalent molecular compounds have relatively low boiling points because bonding is internal to the molecule, not external to other molecules or atoms. As discrete, separate molecules, without covalent bonding to each other, they separate relatively easily one from another.

The fact that the covalent compound water (H_2O, *MW* = 18) has a boiling point of 100°C while the similarly sized covalent compound methane (CH_4, *MW* = 16) has a boiling point of −164°C suggests that forces exist between molecules in covalent compounds. These intermolecular forces (van der Waals forces), like the forces in metallic, covalent, and ionic

Table 3: Boiling Points of Various Materials (°C)

noble gas	helium	He	−269
	neon	Ne	−246
	argon	Ar	−186
nonpolar covalent	hydrogen	H_2	−253
	oxygen	O_2	−183
	methane	CH_4	−164
	chlorine	Cl_2	−34
polar covalent	ammonia	NH_3	−33
	hydrogen fluoride	HF	19.5
	water	H_2O	100
ionic	potassium chloride	KCl	771
	sodium chloride	NaCl	1413
	magnesium oxide	MgO	2826
metallic	copper	Cu	2567
	iron	Fe	2750
	tungsten	W	5660

bonds, are due to the attraction between oppositely charged particles. Some molecules do not have an even distribution of charge, but rather have a positive end and a negative end so that they are dipolar. The positive pole of one molecule is attracted to the negative pole of an adjacent molecule. Such dipole-dipole forces explain why polar molecules tend to have higher boiling points than nonpolar molecules (Figure E).

When hydrogen (electronegativity of 2.1) combines with a very electronegative element such as nitrogen (3.0), oxygen (3.5) or fluorine (4.0) a polar covalent bond is formed (Figure E). The hydrogen electron is attracted strongly by the other member of the bond, exposing the proton of the nucleus and giving the hydrogen a partial positive charge. By contrast, the more electronegative partner in the bond assumes a partial negative charge due to the presence of the electron it has attracted from hydrogen. The partial positive charge on the hydrogen (indicated as $\delta+$) of one molecule is attracted to the partial negative charge (indicated as $\delta-$) on the electronegative end of an adjacent molecule. This intermolecular force, known as hydrogen bonding (indicated by a dotted line in Figure E), increases the viscosity, boiling point, and surface tension of molecular liquids.

Surface tension is the force that pulls adjacent molecules on the surface of a liquid together. The greater the surface tension, the more difficult it is to penetrate the surface of a liquid. Hydrogen bonding, a strong intermolecular force, increases surface tension by bonding surface molecules to each other. In this activity you will compare the surface tension of two liquids (water and isopropyl alcohol) to compare the strength of intermolecular forces in both.

Part 1: Surface tension and vortex: When a liquid is swirled, a vortex is developed in which the surface level of the center of the liquid is substantially below the surface level of the perimeter. The greater the surface tension, the longer the vortex will remain after you have stopped swirling the container. Fill one flask half-full with isopropyl alcohol and the other half-full with water. *Stopper the flask to prevent vapors from polluting the room.* Swirl each flask (Figure U) and record the time until the vortex can no longer be seen. Which liquid appears to have greater surface tension and greater intermolecular forces? You may wish to float a few tiny pieces of finely ground pepper on the fluids so movement can be seen more easily.

Part 2: Surface tension and droplet shape: Using an eyedropper or pipet, transfer one drop of each fluid (water, isopropyl alcohol, and other fluids of your choosing) to a sheet of wax paper. The liquid with greater surface tension will maintain a higher profile and will not spread out as much as the one with lower surface tension (Figure V). Which liquid appears to have the greater surface tension and greater intermolecular forces?

Part 3: Surface tension and impenetrability: Liquids with strong intermolecular bonding will be less penetrable than those with weaker intermolecular bonding. Try to float a paper clip on both water and isopropyl alcohol by gradually lowering a dry paper clip into each liquid on a cradle fashioned from another paper clip (Figure W). Which liquid appears to have the greater surface tension and greater intermolecular forces?

  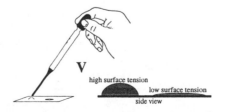 

U

vortex

V

high surface tension

low surface tension

side view

W

Part 4: Visualization of surface tension: The surface of a liquid with strong hydrogen bonding will exhibit great tension much like the head of a drum that has been pulled tight. If a drumstick ruptures the head of a drum, the sides recoil under the tension. In a similar manner, if a chemical ruptures the surface tension of a fluid, the "skin" of the liquid will recoil away from the point where the chemical was applied. Fill one Petri dish with water and the other with isopropyl alcohol. Sprinkle crushed pepper on the surface of both. The pepper will be more likely to float on the fluid with greater surface tension (Figure X). Cover the tip of a paper clip with liquid dish soap and hold over the center of each Petri dish until a drop of soap falls into the liquid. If the surface of the liquid is under tension, the pepper will recoil towards the sides immediately (Figure Y). Which liquid appears to have the greater surface tension and greater intermolecular forces?

Part 5: Comparing surface tension of liquids: Obtain two cups or jars that have a continuous flat rim (no pouring spouts). Fill one to the brim with isopropyl alcohol and the other with water. Examine the containers from side view. Which exhibits greater surface tension? Carefully add pennies to each jar, edge first, one at a time until additional fluid overflows (Figure Z). How many pennies can be added to each liquid before it overflows? Which liquid appears to have the greater surface tension and greater intermolecular forces? (If you wish, you may substitute paper clips, nails or other similar objects for the pennies in this investigation.)

X
before soap

Y
after soap

water
Z

Questions

(1) Which of the two liquids, isopropyl alcohol or water, displays greater surface tension (greater intermolecular forces)?

(2) Which liquid, isopropyl alcohol or water, do you think will boil more easily? Why? If you have a fume hood and an electric hot plate you may determine the boiling point of each to test your hypothesis.

(3) You may have noticed mosquitoes, water striders, and other insects walking on the surface of a pond. Why don't they sink?

FOR THE TEACHER

3.1.1 LAW OF DEFINITE PROPORTIONS

Discussion: Potassium chlorate melts at approximately 384°C, and decomposes at 400°C. As the potassium chlorate is decomposed, potassium chloride and oxygen are produced:

$$2KClO_3 \rightarrow 2KCl + 3O_2$$

A dramatic demonstration of the oxidizing power of potassium chlorate can be performed by placing a wood splint in potassium chlorate and then heating slowly with a burner. Although wood may reach its kindling temperature prior to the decomposition of potassium chlorate, the stick will not burst into flame until the oxygen is released. At this point, a violent flame erupts, often reaching a half meter in height and accompanied by a rocket-like sound (Figure AA). *This instructor demonstration should be performed outside and behind a safety shield. Wear protective face mask and lab coat, and keep students far away from the reaction.*

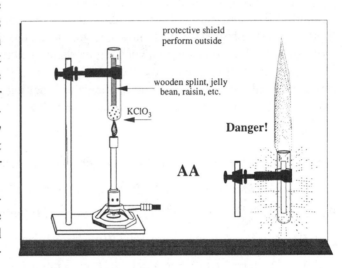

    The law of definite proportions (composition) can also be studied by examining the removal of water from copper sulfate pentahydrate:

$$CuSO_4 \cdot 5H_2O \rightarrow CuSO_4 + 5H_2O$$

Weigh out a sample of copper sulfate pentahydrate in a crucible, and then heat it. As it is heated, water is given off and the crystal turns from blue to white. Students may be assigned different masses of copper sulfate pentahydrate, but in all situations they should determine that the crystal is composed of approximately 32.0% water.

    You may also use the electrolysis of water to show that water is composed of twice as much hydrogen (by volume) as oxygen, regardless of the sample size.

Answers: (1) The percentage of oxygen in potassium chlorate should be approximately 39.2% regardless of the sample size.

> K: 39.09
> Cl: 35.45
> O: $16.00 \times 3 = 48.00$
> _____
> $KClO_3 = 122.54$ $(48.0/122.54) \times 100\% = 39.2\%$

(2) All student data should show that potassium chlorate is approximately 39% by weight, regardless of sample size. Such data are consistent with the law of definite proportions.
(3) Theoretical percentage: 39.2%.

Percentage error can be calculated as:

$$\left(\frac{\text{observed} - \text{theoretical}}{\text{theoretical}} \right) \times 100\%$$

3.1.2 BOND FORMATION

Discussion: This investigation introduces students to a series of composition reactions in which a compound is made from two elemental substances. Some of the bonds that form are ionic and others are covalent. Students determine the nature of the bonds by determining the difference in electronegativity of the atoms involved. These reactions are dramatic and should be performed only as teacher demonstrations, and not as student investigations.

The burning of magnesium is a very dramatic reaction because of the tremendous amount of light produced. Approximately 10% of the energy from this reaction is released as light, one of the highest values known. If you have an old-style flash bulb, you can illustrate a practical application of the magnesium oxidation reaction. Flash bulbs contain a fine mesh of magnesium that is quickly oxidized when a current flows through it. Clamp the bulb to a ringstand, and while you and your students are looking away from the bulb, connect wires from a 3V battery to the terminals of the flash bulb.

Answers:

<u>Part 1</u>: $2Mg(s) + O_2(g) \rightarrow 2MgO(s)$; Mg-O bond: 2.3 (ionic)

$\qquad 3Mg(s) + N_2(s) \rightarrow Mg_3N_2(s)$; Mg-N bond: 1.8 (ionic)

<u>Part 2</u>: $S(g) + O_2(g) \longrightarrow SO_2(g)$; S-O bond: 1.0 (polar covalent)

<u>Part 3</u>: $2Na(s) + Cl_2(g) \longrightarrow 2NaCl(s)$; Na-Cl bond 2.1 (ionic)

<u>Part 4</u>: $2H_2(g) + O_2(g) \longrightarrow 2H_2O(l)$; H-O bond 1.4 (polar covalent)

<u>Part 5</u>: $Zn(s) + S(s) \longrightarrow ZnS(s)$; Zn-S bond 0.9 (polar covalent)

3.1.3 NONPOLAR AND POLAR COVALENT BONDS

Discussion: A plastic object acquires a negative charge when rubbed with wool, fur or hair. A glass rod acquires a positive charge when rubbed with silk. Students will note that the positive glass rod produces the same effect as a negatively charged rubber rod. This seemingly strange phenomenon is due to the fact that polar molecules in a fluid are free to rotate when exposed to an electric field. Their positive ends will orient closer to a negatively charged object, and their negative ends will orient closer to a positively charged object. Because electrostatic forces decrease with distance, the repulsive forces will always be less than the attractive forces. Figure BB illustrates this principle with water and a negatively

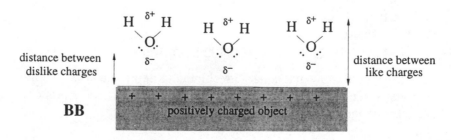

charged object. Thus, the attractive forces on polar molecules will always exceed the repulsive forces, explaining why polar fluids bend towards both positive and negative objects.

Answers: (1) Water is the most polar. The stream of water is deflected significantly in the presence of an electrostatically charged object. Cyclohexane, a nonpolar material, is not deflected at all. (2) Yes. Polar molecules would rotate so their negative poles were pointing toward the positive rod. The attraction between opposite charges (positive rod and negative pole of molecule) would be greater than the repulsive force of like charges (positive rod and positive pole of molecule) because the opposite charges are closer to each other.

3.1.4 COVALENT AND IONIC BONDS

Discussion: You may choose to use a commercial conductivity device that plugs into a standard 110V AC wall socket. This apparatus works very well for teacher demonstrations because the bulb is larger and more easily seen by the class. For individual student use it is not advisable to use such devices because of the high voltage required. If you have multimeters, you can measure electrical resistance instead of lamp brightness. Low resistance is indicative of strong ionic character.

Students may be surprised to find that water is a poor conductor of electricity. They have heard that it is dangerous to stand in water when working with electrical devices because of the possibility of electrocution. It is indeed very dangerous to work with electricity in a wet environment, but not because water is a good conductor of electricity. Rather, water is an excellent solvent, and ionic materials dissociate readily in water. These ions conduct electricity, raising the risk of electrocution.

Answers: (1) Sodium chloride and bleach (sodium hypochlorite solution) conduct electricity because they have bonds with high ionic character. Vinegar (acetic acid) conducts electricity because it has a highly polar covalent bond which ionizes water. (2) Water is a very poor conductor of electricity because it is a polar covalent molecule that only slightly ionizes. The concentration of hydroxide or hydronium ions in pure water is a mere 10^{-7} moles per liter. (3) Electrical currents occur when charged particles (electrons or ions) move. When an ionic material exists as a solid, the ions are tightly bound in position by attraction to oppositely charged ions around them. There will be no current unless the crystal melts or is dissolved and the ions are free to move.

3.1.5 METALLIC BONDING

Discussion: Metals can be described as positive nuclei (cations) immersed in a sea of electrons. This nondirectional metallic bonding can be used to explain all five of the basic properties of metals. You may wish to contrast the malleability of metals with the fragility of ionic materials by hammering on samples of each. Ionic materials fracture as bonds between ions are broken. By contrast, metals bend as one plane of metal ions flows past another without breakage of bonds.

Answers: (1) Copper, aluminum, iron. (2) Student answers will vary depending on the nature of the samples provided. The classic answers are: ductility, malleability, luster, and heat conductivity, although students may not be able to conclude all of these from the samples provided without doing further tests. (3) Student answers will vary. Some sample answers are:

Malleability: Metals are stamped in a variety of forms to create a variety of objects such as coins, automobile fenders, and pie tins.

Electrical conductivity: Copper wires are used to conduct currents in electronic devices. Electrical circuit boards frequently use gold and silver to conduct signals between various components.

Thermal conductivity: Cookware (pots, pans, griddles, etc.) are made of metals (primarily copper, aluminum, and iron) to conduct heat to the food being cooked.

Reflectivity: Mirrors are made by placing a protective glass sheet over a surface of highly polished silver.

Ductility: Steel (iron/carbon alloy) is drawn into long strands that are woven together to make strong yet flexible cables.

3.1.6 INTERMOLECULAR FORCES

Discussion: In 1873 the Dutch scientist Johannes van der Waals postulated the existence of intermolecular forces to help explain the behavior of real liquids and gases. Dipole-dipole and London dispersion forces are often referred to as van der Waals forces. The hydrogen bond is a special case of dipole-dipole interaction. A hydrogen bond is the intermolecular attraction between a hydrogen atom bonded to a strongly electronegative atom and an unshared pair of electrons on a strongly electronegative atom. Hydrogen has just one electron, and once this electron is pulled toward a highly electronegative atom such as fluorine, oxygen or nitrogen, the nucleus of the hydrogen atom (a single proton) is exposed. With hydrogen's electron pulled aside, the unshared electrons of another atom may approach quite close. Since the force between two charged objects is proportional to the inverse square of the distance between them, halving the distance between two charges will result in a four-fold increase in attractive force. Hydrogen bonds are therefore particularly strong examples of dipole-dipole forces.

Answers: (1) All of the experiments should indicate that water has substantially higher surface tension than isopropyl alcohol. (2) Isopropyl alcohol has weaker intermolecular bonding than water and boils at 82.5°C, while water boils at 100°C. (3) The hydrogen bonding in water creates sufficient surface tension to support small objects.

Applications to Everyday Life

Metal ores (ionic compounds): With the exception of some unreactive metals like gold, most metals are not found in their pure form in nature, but rather as ionic compounds. The following is a list of some common metal ores and the metal that is extracted from them:

Table 4: Common Metal Ores

Mineral	Ionic Compound	Metal
cuprite	(copper oxide)	copper
galena	(lead sulfide)	lead
dolomite	(magnesium carbonate)	magnesium
bauxite	(aluminum oxide)	aluminum
hematite	(iron oxide)	iron

Lithosphere: the Earth's crust (ionic and polar covalent compounds): The lithosphere (crust) is the hard outer layer of the Earth and is the source of all mineral wealth. The thickness of the crust varies from about 6 km (4 miles) under some ocean basins to approximately 35 km (22 miles) beneath continents. It is composed of inorganic compounds such as polar covalent quartz (63%), and ionic compounds such as pyroxene and olivine (14%), hydrated silicates (15%), and carbonates (2%).

Atmosphere: the air around us (nonpolar covalent bonds): Substances with covalent bonds tend to have low boiling points, and therefore often exist as gases under normal environmental conditions. Nitrogen (N_2, a nonpolar covalent molecule) comprises 78% of the atmosphere, while oxygen (O_2, another nonpolar covalent molecule) comprises 21%.

Hydrosphere: the oceans (hydrogen bonding): As a result of strong hydrogen bonding, water (H_2O; $MW = 18$; b.p. 100°C) has a much higher boiling point than other compounds with similar molecular weight such as methane (CH_4; $MW = 16$; b.p. −164°C) or ammonia (NH_3, $MW = 18$; b.p. −33°C). Hydrogen bonding prevents water molecules in the liquid phase from easily escaping to the gaseous phase and allows water to exist in the liquid phase under the environmental conditions that prevail on Earth. Without hydrogen bonding, there would be little or no liquid water on Earth, and consequently no oceans, no lakes, and no life.

Centrosphere: the core of the Earth (metallic bonds): Many geologists think that the core of the Earth is composed of iron—but how can they ever make such a prediction if the deepest bore-hole ever made extends only about 10 km (6 miles) into the crust, thousands of kilometers short of the core? Geologists reason that the core is made of metal because chemical data indicate that only materials with metallic bonds are capable of generating a magnetic field of the magnitude observed. One model suggests that the Earth has an electrically conductive molten core that moves slowly through a stationary magnetic field, generating its own current and magnetic field by a dynamo-like action. Only metallic substances are capable of conducting a current of the magnitude necessary to create a magnetic field in this manner, and seismic data indicate that the Earth's core has a density similar to iron. Consequently, geologists have proposed that the core of the Earth is composed primarily of iron.

Biochemistry (covalent bonds): Biochemistry is the study of the chemical substances and vital processes occurring in living organisms. The vast majority of biological chemicals (proteins, carbohydrates, lipids, nucleic acids, vitamins, and hormones) and biological reactions involve covalent bonds.

Organic chemistry (covalent bonds): Organic chemistry is the branch of chemistry that studies carbon-based compounds. Most of the raw materials used in organic chemistry came originally from organisms (hence the name organic) in the form of fossil fuels like oil, natural gas, and coal. From these materials, organic chemists have extracted or developed an abundant array of compounds useful to modern society such as fuels (methane, propane, butane, kerosene, octane, acetylene), pharmaceuticals (tetracycline, acetaminophen), synthetic materials (nylon, rayon, polyester, Kevlar, Teflon), and plastics (PETE [polyethylene terephthalate], HDPE [high density polyethylene], PVC [polyvinyl chloride]) to name a few. Carbon's ability to establish four covalent bonds makes this wide range of molecules possible.

3.2 TYPES OF CHEMICAL REACTIONS

In 1886 workmen completed assembly of French sculptor Frédéric-Auguste Bartholdi's classic work, the *Statue of Liberty*. For more than a century Bartholdi's bold statue (Figure A) has greeted millions of immigrants who have entered New York Harbor en route to a new life in the United States. Although this icon of American freedom initially gleamed with the brilliance of polished copper, it quickly faded to the pale green color we see today. While *Liberty's* color change came as a surprise to many of her admirers, it was fully expected by the sculptor himself. Bartholdi knew that his copper masterpiece would react with atmospheric oxygen to form a green, protective copper oxide skin that would ultimately protect the statue from further weathering.

A

$$2Cu + O_2 \rightarrow 2CuO$$

The oxidation of copper, the rusting of a nail or the tarnishing of a silver spoon are evidences of chemical change. Not all chemical changes are slow, however. For example, gasoline in an automobile engine burns rapidly (Figure B) to push steel pistons and thus propel a car, while dynamite explodes violently to demolish a building or clear boulders for a new highway. Chemical changes also occur when you fry an egg, digest your breakfast, or take a breath of fresh air! Life itself cannot exist without chemical change.

$$2C_8H_{18} + 25O_2 \longrightarrow 16CO_2 + 18H_2O + energy$$

B

When chemical changes occur, they are always accompanied by energy changes such as the emission or absorption of heat, the emission of light or the production of electricity. Any change in which one or more substances are converted into different substances with different properties is called a chemical change. Substances that undergo change are called reactants while the substances formed are known as products. For example, when the reactants hydrogen and oxygen combine, a new product, water, is formed; or when the reactants sodium metal and chlorine gas combine, the product sodium chloride (table salt) is formed. In this chapter you will investigate some of the most common and important types of chemical reactions.

A composition (synthesis, combination) reaction occurs when two or more substances combine to form a new compound, as when A reacts with X to form AX according to the equation, $A + X \rightarrow AX$. While A and X may be elements or compounds, AX is a compound. An example of a composition reaction is the formation of water from hydrogen gas and oxygen gas according to the equation: $2H_2 + O_2 \rightarrow 2H_2O$. Another example is the reaction of calcium oxide with water to form calcium hydroxide according to the equation: $CaO + H_2O \rightarrow Ca(OH)_2$. Most composition reactions are exothermic (they release energy).

A decomposition reaction occurs when a compound is broken apart by heat, light or electricity into elements or simpler compounds. The compound AX decomposes to A and X according to the equation $AX \rightarrow A + X$. An example of a decomposition reaction is the heating of calcium carbonate to produce calcium oxide and carbon dioxide gas according to the equation $CaCO_3 \rightarrow CaO + CO_2$. Electrolysis (decomposition of a substance by electric current) may be used to decompose water: $2H_2O \rightarrow 2H_2 + O_2$.

Single replacement reactions occur when one element replaces another element in a compound: $A + BX \rightarrow AX + B$ or $Y + BX \rightarrow BY + X$. For example, in the reaction of zinc with hydrochloric acid, hydrogen-chlorine bonds are broken and zinc-chlorine bonds are formed: $Zn + 2HCl \rightarrow ZnCl_2 + H_2$.

Double replacement reactions are those in which two compounds exchange ions to produce two new compounds according to the equation: $AX + BY \rightarrow AY + BX$, in which A and B represent positive ions and X and Y represent negative ions. An example of a double replacement reaction occurs when a solution of sodium chloride is mixed with a solution of silver nitrate, and a precipitate of silver chloride is produced: $NaCl + AgNO_3 \rightarrow AgCl(s) + NaNO_3$. Double replacement reactions are also known as ionic reactions. Shown in ion form the equation is: $Na^+ + Cl^- + Ag^+ + NO_3^- \rightarrow AgCl + Na^+ + NO_3^-$.

Combustion reactions are those in which a substance rapidly combines with oxygen, releasing a large amount of energy in the form of heat and light. Organic compounds usually burn in oxygen to produce carbon dioxide. If the organic compound contains hydrogen, as most do, then water is also a product. For example, the combustion of propane gas, such as used in gas barbecues, produces heat and light with the formation of carbon dioxide and water:

$$C_3H_8(g) + 5O_2(g) \rightarrow 3CO_2(g) + 4H_2O(g) + light + heat$$

In an addition reaction, parts of a reactant are added to each carbon atom of a carbon-carbon double or triple bond, thereby reducing the bond to a double or single bond. An example of an addition reaction is the addition of bromine to ethyne:

$$Br_2 + CH \equiv CH \longrightarrow Br - CH_2 = CH_2 - Br$$

$$Br_2 + Br - CH_2 = CH_2 - Br \longrightarrow Br_2HC - CHBr_2$$

How may we determine if a chemical reaction has occurred? To be certain, it is necessary to see if the final materials (products) differ from the initial materials (reactants). If such analyses are impractical, it may be possible to make inferences by looking at circumstantial evidence, such as the formation of a precipitate, the release of light or heat or the production of a gas. For example, when solutions of sodium chloride and silver nitrate are mixed, a precipitate of silver chloride forms. Unlike the reactants, the product is insoluble (which is why it precipitates), indicating that it is chemically different from either of the reactants. Similarly, the release of heat and light is strong evidence that a chemical reaction has occurred. Methane gas burns in oxygen, producing light and heat according to the equation: $CH_4 + O_2 \rightarrow 2H_2O + CO_2$. Finally, the production of a gas is evidence of a chemical reaction. For example, when zinc is placed in a solution of hydrochloric acid, bubbles rise to the surface, indicating that a substance (in this case hydrogen gas) with properties different from the reactants has formed.

It is important to recognize that the release of heat and light, the formation of a precipitate and the formation of a gas are evidence, but not proof, of chemical change. For example, the appearance of gas with the opening of a bottle of carbonated soda is not the result of a chemical reaction, but simply the result of depressurization (carbon dioxide gas comes out of solution). Similarly, when hydrogen chloride gas is added to a saturated solution of sodium chloride, a precipitate of sodium chloride forms as a result of the common ion effect, not because a new product has been formed. To be certain a chemical reaction has occurred, one must examine the products and confirm that they are different from the reactants.

3.2.1 COMPOSITION (SYNTHESIS, COMBINATION) REACTIONS

Concepts to Investigate: Composition (synthesis, combination) reactions, oxidation, chemical reactions, exothermic reactions.

Materials: <u>Part 1</u>: Magnesium ribbon, tongs, burner; <u>Part 2</u>: Liquid soap, glycerin (to strengthen bubbles), container to hold soap-water solution, hydrogen gas generator (zinc, hydrochloric acid, flask with side arm, tubing), match or lighter.

Safety: These activities should be performed by the instructor only! Wear protective goggles and clothing. The light produced by burning magnesium is extremely bright. Students should not look directly at the flame! Keep all flames far away from the hydrogen gas generator. Leave approximately one meter of tubing between the generator flask and the container with the soap solution.

Principles and Procedures: In a composition reaction, two or more substances combine to form a new compound according to the general equation: $A + X \rightarrow AX$. A and X may be compounds or elements, but AX is always a compound. For example, acid rain starts with a composition reaction when gaseous sulfur dioxide (emitted from coal-burning power plants and other sources) combines with water vapor to form sulfurous acid: $SO_2 + H_2O \rightarrow H_2SO_3$.

Part 1: Burning of magnesium: *Teacher demonstration only!* Adjust the flame of a burner to blue. Holding a magnesium strip with tongs, insert the strip into the hottest part of the flame. Remove when ignited, and hold over a metal or glass tray filled with sand (Figure C). The magnesium burns rapidly and releases intense light (never look directly at the flame!). Examine the solid product. Is it still magnesium metal? Has a chemical reaction occurred? Can the powder be changed back into magnesium? What evidence suggests that a chemical reaction took place?

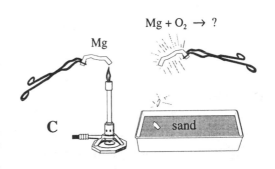

Part 2: Hydrogen reacts with oxygen: *Teacher demonstration only!* Fill a beaker or similar container approximately three-quarters full with water. Add some liquid soap and a couple of drops of glycerin and mix completely by stirring. Make a hydrogen gas generator by attaching tubing (1 meter or longer) to the side arm of a flask or to a one-holed stopper fitted with a short glass tube. Place approximately 10 grams of mossy zinc in the base of the flask, add 1 *M* hydrochloric acid, and seal the container so that gases can escape only through the tubing. *Make certain that there are no leaks in the generator or tubing!*

Place the free end of the tubing from the hydrogen generator under the surface of the soapy water in the container that has been placed at least one meter from the generator (Figure D). Initially, the stream of gas will be primarily air, but within approximately one minute the stream of gas will be mostly hydrogen. Tape a match to a meter stick as shown, light the match with another match and bring it to the bubbles until explosions are readily seen. These explosions are not dangerous because the hydrogen gas within the bubbles is under low pressure. Darken the room to observe the explosions more easily. What evidence is there that a chemical reaction has taken place? What is the product of the explosion?

Now collect hydrogen gas in a dry test tube by simply clamping a test tube upside down and allowing it to fill with hydrogen (Figure E). Since hydrogen is less dense than air, it will displace air until the tube is eventually filled with hydrogen. Hold the test tube with a clamp and move it mouth down to a lighted candle or burner and observe the small flame or explosion. Pure hydrogen will burn quietly at the mouth of the tube, while a mixture of hydrogen and oxygen will cause a small explosion. Do you have pure hydrogen or a mixture of hydrogen and oxygen? Carefully examine the tube. What evidence do you have that a chemical reaction took place? What evidence is there of the new product? What is the new product?

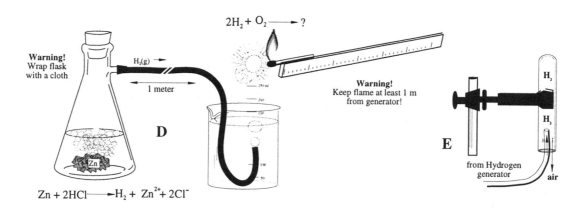

Questions

(1) What is a composition reaction? Give a specific example.

(2) In the general equation for composition reactions, $A + X \rightarrow AX$, AX is a compound but A and X may be elements or compounds. Explain with examples.

(3) Write the equation for the burning of magnesium. Exothermic reactions give off heat while endothermic reactions absorb heat. Was this an endothermic or exothermic reaction?

(4) Write the equation for the burning of hydrogen. Is this an endothermic or exothermic reaction?

(5) What evidence is there of a new product when igniting the hydrogen collected in a dry test tube? Explain.

3.2.2 DECOMPOSITION REACTIONS

Concepts to Investigate: Decomposition reactions, exothermic reactions, dehydration reactions, electrolysis.

Materials: Part 1: Sulfuric acid, Hoffman electrolysis device (Figure F) or test tubes, copper wire and a beaker, 12-volt rectangular lantern battery or DC power supply; Part 2: Table sugar (sucrose), concentrated sulfuric acid, beaker; Part 3: Baking soda (sodium hydrogen carbonate), burner, test tube, test tube clamps, matches or wooden splints.

Safety: Wear protective goggles and clothing. The decomposition of sugar (part 2) should be performed by the instructor in a fume hood or outdoors. Wear gloves when handling concentrated sulfuric acid! Do not allow students to use concentrated sulfuric acid since it is a very strong acid and a powerful dehydrating agent.

Principles and Procedures: Decomposition is the reverse of composition. In decomposition reactions, a single compound produces two or more simpler substances according to the general equation: $AX \rightarrow A + X$. AX is always a compound and A and X may be elements or compounds. For example, the compound mercuric oxide decomposes upon heating into the elements mercury and oxygen, $2HgO \rightarrow 2Hg + O_2$, while the compound potassium chlorate decomposes to form a compound and an element according to the equation: $2KClO_3 \rightarrow 2KCl + 3O_2$.

Part 1: Decomposition of water: Water can be decomposed into hydrogen and oxygen by a process known as electrolysis. We can investigate the process of electrolysis using either a Hoffman apparatus (Figure F) or a simple test tube set up (Figure G). If using the Hoffman apparatus, fill the reservoir with 2% sulfuric acid. Open the stopcocks until both arms completely fill with the dilute acid solution. Connect the wire leads to the DC power supply (battery). If using the simple test tube apparatus, fill the beaker and test tubes with 2% sulfuric acid. While wearing protective gloves, seal the ends of the test tubes, in-

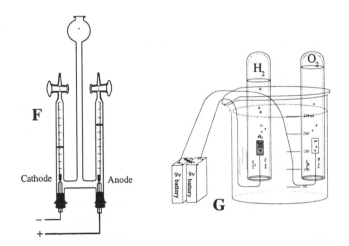

vert them in the conducting medium, and release the seals, allowing no air to enter. Connect the leads to the 12-volt battery or similar source of low voltage direct current. If necessary, connect batteries in series (positive terminal of one to the negative terminal of the next) until you get significant bubbling. Electrolysis involves the breakdown of water into oxygen and hydrogen:

$$2H_2O(l) \longrightarrow 2H_2(g) + O_2(g)$$

Hydrogen will collect at the cathode (connected to the negative terminal of your power supply):

$$2H_2O(l) + 2e^- \longrightarrow 2OH^-(aq) + H_2(g)$$

Oxygen will collect at the anode (connected to the positive terminal of your power supply):

$$6H_2O(l) \longrightarrow 4H_3O^+(aq) + O_2(g) + 4e^-$$

Are equal quantities of hydrogen and oxygen produced? Why is the electrolysis of water considered a decomposition reaction?

Part 2: Decomposition of sugar: *Teacher demonstration only! This activity should be performed outdoors or in a fume hood.* In the early part of the 19th century, chemists determined that the most common plant products, cellulose (wood), sugars and starch, are composed of carbon, hydrogen and water. With further research, it was determined that all of these substances had approximately twice as much hydrogen as carbon or oxygen. The general formula for these substances could therefore be expressed as $C_n(H_2O)_n$, where n represents a whole number. These substances became known as "carbohydrates," meaning "watered carbon" because of their chemical composition.

Glucose ($C_6H_{12}O_6$), the most important sugar in animals, is an example of a carbohydrate that fits the $C_n(H_2O)_n$ ratio. Table sugar, sucrose ($C_{12}H_{22}O_{11}$), has a very similar ratio. In the process of photosynthesis, plants combine water and carbon dioxide to form carbohydrates:

$$6CO_2 + 6H_2O \longrightarrow C_6H_{12}O_6 + 6O_2$$

Is it possible to decompose carbohydrates into simpler atoms or molecules? In this activity we will expose sucrose ($C_{12}H_{22}O_{11}$), a common carbohydrate, to the dehydrating influence of concentrated sulfuric acid. A dramatic decomposition reaction will ensue as water is removed from the sucrose, leaving only carbon behind:

$$C_{12}H_{22}O_{11}(s) \longrightarrow 12C + 11H_2O(l)$$

Add approximately 50 g of granulated table sugar ($C_{12}H_{22}O_{11}$) to a 250 mL beaker. Slowly add approximately 50 mL of concentrated sulfuric acid (18 *M*) and stir with a glass rod. As you slowly stir the solution it will turn yellow, then golden brown. The heat of dilution of concentrated sulfuric acid (–41 kJ/mole) and the heat of reaction are so great that steam forms. Eventually black carbon begins to form as a carbon "snake" that eventually climbs out of the beaker (Figure H). How tall does the carbon column grow? Why is this considered a decomposition reaction?

Part 3: Decomposition of sodium hydrogen carbonate: In cooking or baking, sodium bicarbonate (baking soda, $NaHCO_3$) is added to acidic batters (containing acidic substances such as lemon juice, yogurt, vinegar or sour cream) to produce carbon dioxide.

$$NaHCO_3(s) + HC_2H_3O_2(aq) \rightarrow NaC_2H_3O_2(aq) + CO_2(g) + H_2O(l)$$

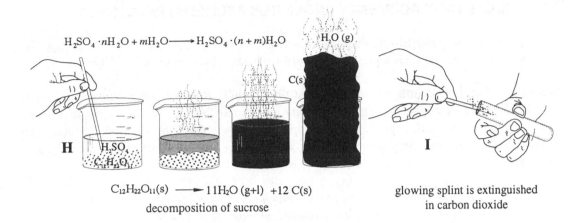

The carbon dioxide gas forms bubbles in the batter, causing the batter to "rise" during baking. Will any carbon dioxide be produced simply by heating baking soda in the absence of acids? In other words, is there any value to baking soda in a neutral or basic batter?

Place approximately 5 grams of sodium bicarbonate in a test tube and heat. If baking soda decomposes into sodium carbonate, water, and carbon dioxide, as indicated in the equation below, then you should be able to see evidence of these new products.

$$2NaHCO_3(s) \longrightarrow Na_2CO_3(s) + H_2O(g) + CO_2(g)$$

Is there any evidence of water? Test for the presence of carbon dioxide by putting a flaming or glowing splint into the mouth of the test tube. If the environment is filled with carbon dioxide, the flame will be extinguished (Figure I). On the basis of your observations, does it appear as though sodium hydrogen carbonate is decomposed by heating?

Questions

(1) What is a decomposition reaction? Give a specific example.

(2) In decomposition reactions, compound AX decomposes to A and X according to the equation AX → A + X. AX is a compound, but A and X may be elements or compounds. Explain with examples.

(3) The term electrolysis comes from the roots for "electricity" *(electr-)* and "break" or "loosen" *(-lysis).* Explain why this is an appropriate name for the process it specifies.

(4) When sulfuric acid was added to sugar, a black "snake" was formed and heat was released. What caused the snake to grow? Explain.

(5) What evidence exists to suggest that baking soda decomposes upon heating? Will baking soda help non-acidic batters rise? Explain.

3.2.3 SINGLE DISPLACEMENT (SINGLE REPLACEMENT) REACTIONS

Concepts to Investigate: Single displacement reaction, (single replacement reaction), activity series, metallurgical techniques, tarnish, electrochemical reactions.

Materials: Part 1: Calcium, mossy zinc, test tube, match, tub or similar container, copper (pre-1982 penny or copper wire); Part 2: Large and small beakers, mossy zinc, test tubes, match, hydrochloric acid, copper; Part 3: Copper sulfate pentahydrate, zinc strip, beaker; Part 4: Silverware (make certain you are not using stainless steel!), eggs, beaker, baking soda, aluminum pan, aluminum foil, hot plate.

Safety: Wear goggles and a lab coat. Do not touch copper sulfate or other chemicals. Concentrated hydrochloric acid should be dispensed only by the instructor.

Principles and Procedures: In a single displacement reaction (also called a single replacement reaction), one element replaces another element in a compound as indicated by the general equations, $A + BX \rightarrow AX + B$ or $Y + BX \rightarrow BY + X$. In the first, A replaces B and B is liberated. In the second, Y replaces X and X is liberated. In single displacement reactions, an element reacts with a compound, displacing an element from that compound. An example of the first type of single replacement is the reaction of zinc with hydrochloric acid in which Zn replaces hydrogen, liberating hydrogen gas: $Zn + 2HCl \rightarrow ZnCl_2 + H_2$. An example of the second case is the replacement of bromine in potassium bromide by chlorine: $Cl_2 + 2KBr \rightarrow 2KCl + Br_2$. Most single replacement reactions occur in aqueous solution.

Table 1 shows the activity series of common metals. An activity series is a list of elements organized according to the ease with which they undergo certain chemical reactions (generally single replacement reactions). The metals in Table 1 are arranged according to their ability to displace hydrogen from an acid or water.

Part 1: Activity series; reactions of metals with water: The activity series (Table 1) lists elements in order of their ability to replace other elements. Any element listed can replace all elements below it, but none above it. The most active element, which is placed at the top of the series, can replace every element below it. Let's investigate the activity series by comparing the reactivity of two metals, calcium and zinc, with water.

Fill a large container with water to a depth of about 10 cm. Immerse a test tube in the water in a horizontal position until it is completely filled with water (Figure J). Grasp the tube by its base and hold it vertically, open end down, with the opening below the surface so the water cannot escape (Figure K). (Your fingers should not touch the surface of the water.) Drop a fresh piece of calcium (about 0.2 g) in the large container, and hold the test tube in place over the calcium so gas produced by the reaction enters and displaces the water in the test tube. If calcium is more reactive than hydrogen, we would expect the following reaction:

$$Ca(s) + 2H_2O(l) \longrightarrow Ca(OH)_2(aq) + H_2(g)$$

To see if this reaction has taken place, examine for the presence of hydrogen (a flammable gas) and calcium hydroxide (a base).

When the tube has filled with gas, remove it and continue to hold it upside down with a test tube clamp so the gas cannot escape. Take the test tube to a lighted candle or burner. A small "pop" indicates the presence of hydrogen. Is hydrogen present? Test the solution in the

Table 1: Activity Series of Common Metals

Metal	Displace Hydrogen from Acids?	Displace Hydrogen from Steam?	Displace Hydrogen from Liquid Water?	Summary
Li K Ba Ca Na	yes (vigorously)	yes (vigorously)	yes (vigorously)	Can react with cold water and acids, replacing hydrogen
Mg Al Zn Cr Fe Cd	yes	yes (readily)	no	Can react with steam and acids, replacing hydrogen
Co Ni Sn Pb	yes	no	no	Can react with acids, replacing hydrogen
H Cu	— no	— no	— no	Forms oxides
Hg Ag Pt Au	no	no	no	Relatively unreactive

pan with pH paper or red litmus paper (red litmus paper turns blue in base). Does a base appear to be present? Is calcium more reactive than hydrogen?

Repeat the activity described in part 1, but use a piece of mossy zinc (about 0.5 g) and then copper (copper wire or pre-1982 U.S. penny). Does zinc or copper react with water in the same manner as calcium? Is your data consistent with the activity series (Table 1)?

Part 2: Activity series; reaction of metals with acids: The data from part 1 showed that calcium is more reactive than either zinc or copper, but it did not allow us to differentiate between the reactivity of copper and zinc. To determine relative activities of less reactive metals, it is often necessary to use a more reactive substance such as hydrochloric acid.

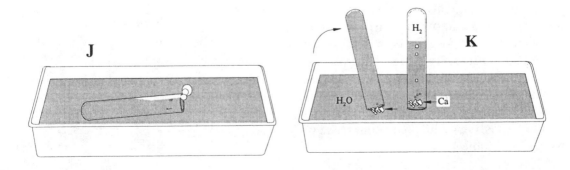

Fill a small (250 mL) beaker with water to a depth of about 3 cm. Fill a small test tube with water, place your finger over the opening, invert the tube holding it vertically, and place the opening under the surface of the water in the beaker so the water remains in the tube when you remove your finger. Grasp the tube by the bottom as in part 1, and hold it vertically with the opening under the surface. (Your fingers should not touch the surface of the water.) Drop some pieces of mossy zinc into your beaker and ask your instructor to slowly add 2 *M* hydrochloric acid, while stirring, until bubbling occurs. Hold the test tube so the rising gas displaces the water. Holding the test tube with a clamp, move it to a lit candle or burner. A small "pop" indicates the presence of hydrogen gas, which is a product that we would expect if indeed zinc reacts with hydrochloric acid in a single replacement reaction:

$$Zn(s) + 2HCl(aq) \longrightarrow ZnCl_2(aq) + H_2(g)$$

Repeat the same procedure using a pre-1982 penny or piece of wire, adding only as much acid as before. If copper is as reactive as zinc, then we should expect the formation of hydrogen gas at approximately the same rate. Which is more reactive, copper or zinc? Is your data consistent with the activity series (Table 1)?

Part 3: Replacement of ions in solution by metals: Metallurgy is the art and science of extracting metals from their ores and modifying the metals for use. One of the many techniques available to metallurgists is to react crushed mineral ore with solutions containing reactive metals. Chalcanthite (copper sulfate pentahydrate, $CuSO_4 \cdot 5H_2O$) is a water-soluble copper-based ore. Is it possible to extract metallic copper from chalcanthite merely by reacting it with a more reactive metal such as zinc (see Table 1)? Perform the following activity to determine if you can extract copper in this manner. Pour 5 mL of 1 *M* copper sulfate solution into a small test tube. Immerse a short strip of zinc metal in the copper sulfate solution. Allow the solution to stand for at least 10 minutes. If zinc is more reactive, as Table 1 suggests, then we should expect the following single replacement reaction:

$$CuSO_4(chalcanthite) + Zn \longrightarrow ZnSO_4 + Cu$$

Is there any evidence (red or copper colored deposits) of the release of copper? Does it appear as though zinc displaces copper in this reaction?

The activity series suggests that copper, while being less reactive than zinc, is more reactive than silver. Thus, we might expect copper to replace silver when copper is immersed in silver nitrate solution:

$$Cu + 2AgNO_3 \longrightarrow 2Ag + Cu(NO_3)_2$$

To test this, pour 5 mL of 1 *M* silver nitrate solution into a small test tube. Immerse a piece of copper wire in the silver nitrate solution. Observe carefully and record the results. Use a magnifying lens, microscope or videomicroscope to check for the presence of beautiful silver crystals that will deposit on the copper wire if indeed copper is more reactive than silver (Figure L). Are your findings consistent with predictions made with the activity series? (Table 1).

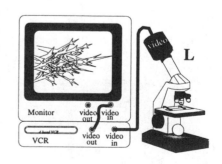

Part 4: Cleaning silverware: The activities in part 3 illustrated that it was possible to obtain copper from copper sulfate, and silver from silver nitrate. Is it possible to obtain metallic silver from tarnished silver (silver sulfide) by a similar replacement reaction?

Although silverware is beautiful, it tarnishes with time. Tarnish results from a chemical reaction in which silver reacts with hydrogen sulfide and oxygen in the air to form silver sulfide:

$$4Ag(s) + 2H_2S(g) + O_2(g) \longrightarrow 2Ag_2S(s) + 2H_2O(l)$$

Silver will also react with various sulfides found in rubber, egg yolks, and other substances, including some vegetables. There are always traces of hydrogen sulfide in the atmosphere. Thus, it is important you protect silver items by wrapping them in protective cloth or placing them in an environment containing substances that will absorb the hydrogen sulfide. If silverware does become tarnished, however, how can it be restored?

Fill an aluminum pie pan (any aluminum container will do) with hot water. Add several teaspoons of sodium bicarbonate (baking soda, $NaHCO_3$). Place 3 or 4 pieces of tarnished silverware in the solution. (To create a tarnished piece of silverware, dip it in egg yolk and allow to remain until next day, Figure M). To completely clean the silverware, it is necessary to totally immerse it in the solution. The silverware must touch the aluminum pan. One to five hours may be required to clean the silverware, depending on the amount of tarnish (Figure N). To accelerate the cleaning process, loosely wrap each piece of silverware in a piece of aluminum foil and make certain foil and silverware are completely submerged. Place the pan on a hot plate to ensure the solution remains hot (not boiling) throughout the cleaning process. Remove the silverware and polish with a soft cloth.

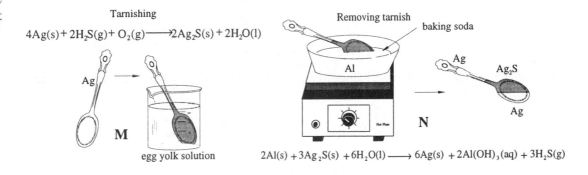

The silverware is cleaned by an electrochemical process in which electrons are transferred from aluminum to the silver in the silver sulfide, thus producing elemental silver according to the following equation:

$$2Al(s) + 3Ag_2S(s) + 6H_2O(l) \longrightarrow 6Ag(s) + 2Al(OH)_3(aq) + 3H_2S(g)$$

In the electrochemical process, the silver, surrounded by the electrolyte (sodium hydrogen carbonate, baking soda), forms one plate of an electric cell and the aluminum forms the other. The equation suggests that hydrogen sulfide gas (the gas produced in rotting eggs) is evolved in small quantities. If this reaction occurs, then you may be able to detect the odor of rotten eggs (rotten eggs produce hydrogen sulfide gas) by removing part of the aluminum foil from a piece of silver as the reaction is proceeding. The equation also predicts that the solution will become basic due to the production of aluminum hydroxide. Test the pH of the solution using red litmus paper or pH paper. Does the solution become basic? Why is this reaction considered to be a replacement reaction?

Questions

(1) What is a single displacement reaction? Give an example.

(2) What element in water was replaced by the calcium (part 1)? What results confirmed your answer?

(3) Did zinc replace hydrogen from water? From acid? Which metal is more reactive, calcium or zinc?

(4) What observations did you make when the zinc strip was immersed in the copper sulfate solution? What do these observations indicate has occurred?

(5) What observations did you make when the copper wire was immersed in the silver nitrate solution? What do these observations indicate has occurred?

(6) According to your observations from part 2, is copper or zinc more reactive? Explain.

(7) On the basis of your observations in part 3, is silver or copper more reactive? Explain.

(8) The chemical cleaning of silver is an electrochemical process in which electrons move from aluminum to silver in the tarnish, thereby restoring the silver. Explain.

(9) Consult the activity series for metals (Table 1) and use it to predict which of the following three reactions would actually occur:

$$Zn(s) + CuSO_4(aq) \longrightarrow ZnSO_4(aq) + Cu(s)$$

$$Co(s) + 2NaCl(aq) \longrightarrow 2Na(s) + CoCl_2(aq)$$

$$2K(s) + 2H_2O(aq) \longrightarrow 2KOH(aq) + H_2(g)$$

(10) The activity series for the halogens is: $F_2 > Cl_2 > Br_2 > I_2$. Would the following reaction occur?

$$Cl_2(aq) + 2KBr(aq) \longrightarrow 2KCl(aq) + Br_2(aq)$$

3.2.4 DOUBLE REPLACEMENT (ION-COMBINING) REACTIONS

Concepts to Investigate: Double replacement (ion-combining reactions), neutralization, acids, bases, precipitates, solubility rules, predicting unknowns.

Materials: <u>Part 1</u>: 0.2 *M* silver nitrate solution, 0.5 *M* sodium chloride solution, dilute ammonia-water solution (1:4), 1.0 *M* aluminum chloride solution, 1.0 *M* sodium iodide solution, 1.0 *M* lead nitrate solution; <u>Part 2</u>: 0.10 *M* hydrochloric acid, 0.10 *M* sodium hydroxide, pipet, test tubes, pH meter or pH paper, evaporating dish or crucible, burner, ringstand and support, magnifying lens, buret or pipet, phenolphthalein; <u>Part 3</u>: 1.0 *M* hydrochloric acid, 1.0 *M* sodium sulfite, test tubes.

Safety: Wear goggles, lab coat and gloves. Observe warnings on chemical containers.

Principles and Procedures: Double replacement reactions have the form: AX + BY → AY + BX, where the reactants (AX and BY) usually are soluble salts, acids or bases. When a solution of AX is mixed with a solution of BY, the mixture begins with all four ions in solution: AX + BY → A^+ + X^- + B^+ + Y^-. The cation of one of the compounds may combine with the anion of the other, forming a compound that is not a soluble salt.

$$AX + BY \rightarrow B^+ + X^- + AY \quad \text{or} \quad AX + BY \rightarrow A^+ + Y^- + BX$$

where AY and BX are insoluble products. Because one of the products is insoluble, the reaction proceeds in the forward direction until one of the reactants is completely consumed. The formation of an insoluble product, whether it is a precipitate, gas or a molecular compound, "drives" the forward reaction by removing those species that might engage in the reverse reaction.

Double replacement reactions are also called ionic reactions because ions combine to form new products. For example, mixing solutions containing silver ions with those containing chloride ions results in the formation of a precipitate of silver chloride. We can write an equation for such a reaction:

$$AgNO_3(aq) + NaCl(aq) \longrightarrow AgCl(s) + NaNO_3(aq)$$

Expressed in ionic form we have:

$$Ag^+(aq) + NO_3^-(aq) + Na^+(aq) + Cl^-(aq) \longrightarrow AgCl(s) + Na^+(aq) + NO_3^-(aq)$$

Notice that in the ionic equation, sodium ions and nitrate ions show up on both sides but don't actually take part in the reaction. We call these "spectator ions" because they "watch" while the "real players" react. Omitting the spectator ions from the equation, we can write:

$$Ag^+(aq) + Cl^-(aq) \longrightarrow AgCl(s)$$

This equation shows only those ions that combine to form a new compound and is called the net ionic equation. The formation of insoluble AgCl "drives" the reaction to completion, removing silver and chloride ions from solution. The precipitate AgCl can be separated from solution by filtration. If we evaporate the remaining solution, the residue will contain only $NaNO_3$. Such ion-combining reactions are often used to form new compounds.

In double-replacement reactions, one of the compounds formed is usually a precipitate, an insoluble gas or a molecular compound such as water. The formation of these products "drives" double-replacement reactions by removing species from solution that might participate in reverse reactions. In this activity you will examine double-replacement reactions that are "driven" by the formation of a precipitate, insoluble gas or molecular compound.

Part 1: Formation of a precipitate (identifying unknown products): A precipitate is an insoluble solid compound formed during a chemical reaction in solution. Precipitates are first recognizable by the cloudy appearance they impart to a solution. With time, the tiny particles of precipitate sink to the bottom of the container, although the time required for such settling varies widely between precipitates. To determine if a precipitate might form when solutions are mixed, you must determine if any of the possible products are insoluble (Table 2).

Add 1 mL of 0.2 M silver nitrate solution to 5 mL of 0.5 M sodium chloride solution. Examine the solubility rules (Table 2), determine the name of the precipitate, and write a balanced equation.

Add 1 mL of dilute ammonia-water ($NH_4^+OH^-$) solution to 5 mL of aluminum chloride solution. Examine the solubility rules (Table 2), determine the name of the precipitate, and write a balanced equation.

Add 5 mL of 1.0 M sodium iodide solution to 5 mL of 1.0 M lead nitrate solution. Examine the solubility rules (Table 2), determine the name of the precipitate, and write a balanced equation.

Part 2: Formation of water; acid-base neutralization: Another common type of double replacement (ion-combining) reaction is acid-base neutralization. The classic definition of an acid was provided by Arrhenius when he defined an acid as a substance that donates hydrogen ions (H^+) when dissolved in water. (Later in this resource you will be introduced to other more general definitions of acids and bases.) Since the hydrogen atom is composed of only one proton and one electron, the hydrogen ion is simply a proton. Protons do not exist independently in solution, but are associated with water molecules: $H^+ + H_2O \rightarrow H_3O^+$.

Table 2: General Solubility Rules

1. All common compounds of Group I and ammonium ions are soluble.

2. All nitrates, acetates, and chlorates are soluble.

3. All binary compounds of the halogens (other than F) with metals are soluble, except those of Ag, Hg(I), and Pb. Pb halides are soluble in hot water.

4. All sulfates are soluble, except those of barium, strontium, calcium, lead, and mercury (I). The latter three are slightly soluble.

5. Except for rule 1, carbonates, hydroxides, oxides, silicates, and phosphates are insoluble.

6. Sulfides are insoluble except for calcium, barium, strontium, magnesium, sodium, potassium, and ammonium.

H_3O^+ is known as the hydronium ion. For simplicity, chemists often write equations showing H^+ ions, but we must remember that these are really hydronium ions, H_3O^+. When hydrogen chloride gas (HCl) is dissolved in water, it dissociates (splits apart) into ions: $HCl (aq) \rightarrow H^+ (aq) + Cl^-(aq)$. Thus, HCl (aq) is an acid.

According to Arrhenius, a base is a substance that produces hydroxide ions (OH^-) when dissolved in water. When sodium hydroxide, an ionic solid, is dissolved in water, sodium ions and hydroxide ions are produced: $NaOH(s) \rightarrow Na^+(aq) + OH^-(aq)$. Thus, sodium hydroxide is a base. What occurs if we mix an acid such as HCl with a base such as NaOH?

Place 30.0 mL of 0.10 *M* sodium hydroxide in a flask and add a couple of drops of phenolphthalein. Using a buret or pipet add exactly 29.0 mL of 0.10 *M* hydrochloric acid (Figure O). Swirl the flask and measure the pH (Figure P). Then add more acid or base drop by drop until the solution is neutralized (pH 7). Neutralization is a double replacement reaction that results in the formation of water and a salt. Is there evidence of the production of a salt?

Place the contents in an evaporating dish or crucible (Figure Q) and carefully boil off the water until the dish is dry. Scrape the crystals from the evaporating dish and examine them using a magnifying lens. Sodium chloride crystallizes as cubes. Does it appear as though sodium chloride is produced in this neutralization reaction? Do not taste the product! Although the "taste test" may confirm your hypotheses, it should never be done in a laboratory setting for safety reasons!

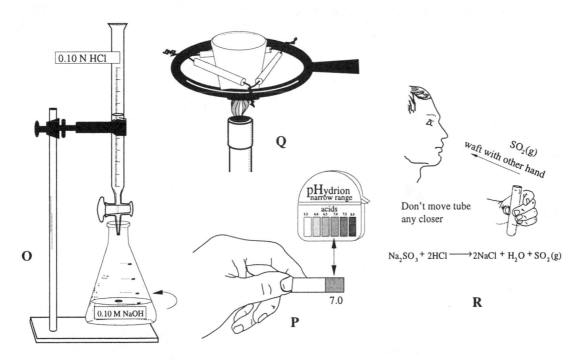

Part 3: Formation of a gas: Have you ever opened a box of golden raisins and smelled a slight choking odor? That odor is caused by sulfur dioxide, a gas used to preserve the golden color of dried raisins, apricots and pears. Sulfur dioxide is produced in a double replacement reaction between sodium sulfite and hydrochloric acid.

$$Na_2SO_3(s) + 2HCl(aq) \longrightarrow 2NaCl(aq) + H_2O(l) + SO_2(g)$$

The reaction proceeds to the right as sulfur dioxide gas escapes from solution.

Add 5 mL of 1.0 *M* hydrochloric acid to 5 mL of 1.0 *M* sodium sulfite solution. Do you see the formation of a gas? While holding the tube at least 50 centimeters from your face, gently waft the vapors towards you with the other hand until you can detect the odor (Figure R). (Never "sniff" any chemical!) Does the odor resemble that of golden raisins or golden dried apricots?

Questions

(1) What is a double replacement reaction? Give a specific example.

(2) What criteria are necessary for a double replacement reaction to proceed?

(3) Write balanced equations for the double replacement reactions in part 1.

(4) When a solution of sodium chloride is mixed with a solution of potassium bromide, no precipitate forms. Explain, using information from Table 2.

(5) If we mix equivalent amounts of solutions of slightly soluble silver sulfate (Ag_2SO_4) and barium chloride ($BaCl_2$), two insoluble products are formed: AgCl and $BaSO_4$. The remaining liquid, after filtration, is almost pure water. Explain.

(6) Salt is produced by the neutralization of sodium hydroxide and hydrochloric acid in part 2. Why should you not use the taste-test to test for the presence of salt? Why should you never use the taste-test in a laboratory?

3.2.5 COMBUSTION REACTIONS

Concepts to Investigate: Combustion reactions, destructive distillation, fuels, acetylene, natural gas.

Materials: Part 1: Natural gas jet, liquid detergent, glycerin, funnel, tubing to fit funnel and gas jet, long stick, tape, candle, matches; Part 2: Calcium carbide, balloon, pipet or dropper, burner, long stick, tape; Part 3: Wood splints, Pyrex® or Kimax® test tubes, matches, one-hole rubber stopper, glass or plastic tubing to fit stopper, burner, ring stand, test tube clamp.

Safety: Parts 1 and 2 are designed as teacher demonstrations and should not be attempted by students! Students should be kept a safe distance from the explosions. As always, wear goggles and a lab coat. Do not ignite the balloons or bubbles of methane or acetylene gas at close distance! Do not have any other flammable substances in the vicinity when performing these demonstrations. The combustion of acetylene produces a very bright light and may produce a loud sound that may startle students. Warn your students accordingly.

Principles and Procedures: What is fire? How important is fire to civilization? How would civilization be different without the use of fire? Would civilization even exist without fire?

In pre-historic times, people discovered how to use fire for warmth and cooking. About 5000 years ago they discovered how to use fire to fuse copper and tin together into the hard, durable alloy known as bronze. News of this discovery gradually spread throughout Europe, the Middle East, and beyond, ushering in the Bronze Age. Much of what we know about civilizations from this period has been learned from bronze tools and artwork that have survived to this day.

In the first century AD, the Egyptian inventor, Hero of Alexandria, developed the first successful fire-powered steam engine. Hero's engine used fire to boil water in a metal container. When steam was produced, it exited through nozzles positioned so as to cause the container to rotate on its shaft. Figure S shows how the principle of Hero's engine can be illustrated in the laboratory. Although Hero's invention was interesting, it did not serve any practical use and was soon forgotten. In the 18th century Hero's ideas were revived by numerous inventors, including James Watt, a Scottish inventor who developed the first practical fire-powered steam engine. Watt's invention was a huge success, and within a very short time fire-powered steam engines were doing the labor once performed by horses, mill-wheels and humans. The steam engine powered the Industrial Revolution that eventually swept around the world, transforming rural, agricultural communities into urban, manufacturing societies.

More recently, fire has been used to power the internal combustion engines in our automobiles, as well as the rocket engines that have taken space probes to the outer reaches of our solar system. Fire is one of the most important chemical processes known, and is used daily in natural gas water heaters, stoves, and furnaces, gasoline powered automobiles, and oil and coal-burning electrical power plants.

Fire is a combustion reaction—a reaction in which a substance combines with oxygen to release a substantial amount of energy in the form of heat and light. The burning of wood, coal, gasoline, butane, methane, propane and other hydrocarbons are examples of combustion reactions. The combustion of hydrocarbons releases heat, light, carbon dioxide (CO_2), and water (H_2O). For example, when methane (CH_4, natural gas used in water heaters, stoves, and household furnaces) or propane (C_3H_8, used in camping stoves, portable heating equipment, and some cars and buses) are burned, the products are carbon dioxide, water vapor, heat and light:

$$CH_4 + 2O_2 \longrightarrow CO_2 + 2H_2O + \text{heat} + \text{light}$$

$$C_3H_8 + 5O_2 \longrightarrow 3CO_2 + 4H_2O + \text{heat} + \text{light}$$

In this section you will investigate a few of the many interesting and useful combustion reactions.

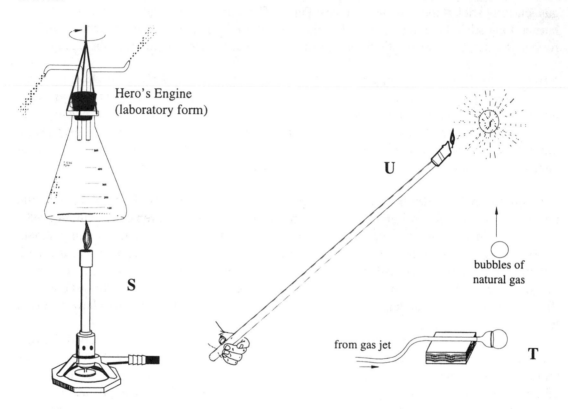

Part 1: Combustion of natural gas, methane: *Teacher demonstration only! There should be no flammable materials around or above this setup! Students should be kept a safe distance away.*

Natural gas is a highly flammable mixture of gases composed primarily of methane (CH_4) and ethane (C_2H_6). Prepare a soap solution consisting of one part liquid dish detergent, seven parts water, and a few milliliters of glycerin (to strengthen the bubbles). Because of the differences between liquid soaps, it may be necessary to vary the ratio of soap to water to obtain the optimal mixture for bubble formation. Attach the end of a plastic delivery funnel, or reasonable substitute, to the end of a section of flexible tubing. Attach the tubing to a gas jet, and place the mouth of the funnel in the soap solution. Rest the funnel horizontally above the table top as shown in Figure T. Slowly turn on the gas until a bubble releases and rises toward the ceiling. While the bubble is ascending, ignite it with a candle attached to the end of long pole (Figure U). What color is the flame? Compare this flame with the flame produced by acetylene in part 2.

Part 2: Production and burning of acetylene: *Teacher demonstration only! There should be no flammable materials around or above this setup! Students should be kept a safe distance away.*

Have you ever seen a construction worker welding or cutting steel with an extremely bright torch? Welders mix acetylene and oxygen gas to produce an oxyacetylene flame that can easily melt steel. At about 6000°F (3300°C), the oxyacetylene flame is hotter than any other known mixture of combustible gases!

Acetylene, C_2H_2, burns with a very bright flame because it has a higher percentage of carbon than other hydrocarbons. The brightness of the flame is actually the result of tiny carbon particles glowing to incandescence in the heat of the flame. Prior to the advent of battery powered lamps, acetylene lamps were used widely on cars, bicycles and miner's helmets. Portable acetylene generators mixed water with calcium carbide (CaC_2) to produce acetylene (ethyne) gas:

$$CaC_2 + 2H_2O \longrightarrow C_2H_2 + Ca^{2+} + 2OH^-$$

The gas (C_2H_2) was then burned to produce light.

Using a pipet or dropper, add approximately 3 mL of water to a balloon. Weigh out approximately 1 gram of calcium carbide, place in the balloon and seal immediately! Acetylene gas is produced the moment water contacts the calcium carbide, so the longer it takes to seal the balloon, the more acetylene is lost!

Feel the balloon. Is the reaction of calcium carbide and water an exothermic (heat producing) or endothermic (heat consuming) reaction? Shake the balloon to mix the water and calcium carbide. Tie the balloon to the end of a long stick or pole after the expansion has ceased. Bring the balloon close to a flame (Figure V). Be prepared for a rather loud explosion and/or a very bright flame!

$$2C_2H_2 + 5O_2 \longrightarrow 4CO_2 + 2H_2O + light + heat$$

To fill the balloon to normal size with acetylene gas, it may be necessary to react approximately 5 grams of calcium carbide with approximately 15 mL of water.

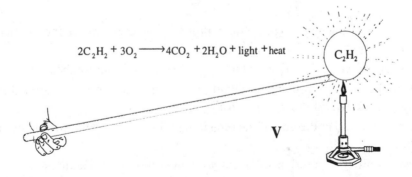

Compare the flame produced by acetylene with the flame produced by methane in part 1. Which gas appears to contain more energy?

Part 3: Destructive distillation of wood: Many American homes are equipped with natural gas appliances such as stoves, water heaters, clothes dryers, and furnaces. Although we take natural gas for granted, its use in homes dates back only to the 1930s when improved pipeline technology made it feasible to deliver natural gas to homes and businesses. Prior to the 1930s, people relied on coal, and gas distilled from coal, to fuel their home appliances. When heated, coal is broken down and releases flammable gases which can be collected for later use. By the late 18th century, "coal gas" was being manufactured in England for use in street lights and household appliances. Coal gas remained the fuel of choice for such applications until the advent of electricity in the late nineteenth and early twentieth centuries. How is "coal gas" produced from coal? Perform this investigation and find out!

Coal was formed primarily from plant material deposited in ancient swamps and wetlands. Buried by thick sediments, this organic material was exposed to tremendous pressures and temperatures which caused metamorphosis to the coal we see today. Just as it is possible to produce gas by heating coal, so it is possible to produce gas by heating wood, one of the materials from which coal was made. This process is known as destructive distillation, because the gases are distilled from the wood which is destroyed in the process. The destructive distillation of wood is similar to the destructive distillation of coal.

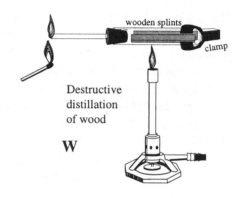

Destructive distillation of wood

W

Place several wood splints in a large Pyrex test tube. Fit a 10-centimeter piece of glass tubing into a one-hole stopper that fits the test tube. Place the stopper assembly in the test tube. Light the Bunsen burner and adjust for the hottest flame. Hold the test tube with a clamp and slowly move the burner along the length of the test tube. After the wood has begun to turn black, hold a lighted match to the end of the tubing extending from the stopper and observe the results (Figure W). Is the gas emanating from the tube flammable? What is happening to the wood? To produce "coal gas," simply substitute coal for the wood, and heat in a fume hood.

Questions

(1) Which flame appears brighter (and probably hotter), the flame produced by the methane bubble or the balloon containing acetylene?

(2) Why is acetylene, rather than natural gas, used in welding torches?

(3) What is the black substance remaining in the test tube in part 3 after the wood was strongly heated? Did the wood "burn"?

(4) A flame occurred at the end of the tube in part 3 when a lighted match was introduced. Explain.

(5) Describe how life would be different without combustion reactions.

3.2.6 ADDITION REACTIONS

Concepts to Investigate: Addition reactions, substitution reactions, saturation, hydrogenation, fats, polyunsaturated fats, saturated fats, mono-unsaturated fats.

Materials: Part 1: None; Part 2: Colorless or lightly colored vegetable oil and shortening, bromine water (or potassium bromate, potassium bromide, and hydrochloric acid), beaker or test tube.

Safety: *Part 2: Wear goggles and lab coat. Bromine gas may be released when making bromine water. Since bromine is toxic, this investigation should be performed by the teacher in a fume hood.*

Principles and Procedures: Have you ever stopped to examine the nutrition facts panel on a package of food (Figure X)? This panel gives important information regarding the chemistry of the food, addressing those factors with implications for your health. Note that nutrition facts panels list the number of grams of saturated fat per serving size.

An unsaturated fat (Figure Y) is one that contains at least one fatty acid group with double bonds, while a saturated fat contains only single (saturated) bonds (Figure Z). Many natural plant oils, like those in liquid vegetable oil (corn oil, safflower oil, etc.) are unsaturated. They contain double bonds in their carbon chains, have low melting points, and flow relatively freely at room temperature. When such free flowing oils are treated with hydrogen in the presence of catalysts, hydrogen adds to the carbons that are connected by double bonds. Since carbon can only form four bonds at a time, a double bond must be broken in order to bond with the hydrogen. As a result, double bonds are reduced to single bonds (Figures Y and Z). We say that such hydrogenated fats are saturated when no more hydrogen may add because all double bonds have been reduced to single bonds. Saturated fats are less fluid than unsaturated fats. Hydrogenated (saturated) oils, such as shortening and margarine, are solid or semi-solid, and are less susceptible to oxidation. Although saturated fats may have a desirable consistency and stability, excessive consumption of these is correlated with heart disease. As a result, nutritionists recommend that we minimize our intake of saturated fats, and food producers are required by law to list the amount of saturated fats in their products.

Table 3: Saturated and Unsaturated Fats in the Household

Fats	% Poly-unsat.	% Mono-unsat.	% Sat.	Unsaturated to Saturated Fat ratio	Ranking 1(best), 12(worst)
canola	32	62	6		
coconut	2	6	87		
corn	59	24	13		
cottonseed	52	18	26		
olive	9	72	14		
palm kernel	2	11	82		
palm oil	37	9	49		
peanut	32	46	17		
safflower	75	12	9		
sesame seed	40	40	18		
soybean	59	23	14		
sunflower	66	20	10		

Part 1: Saturated and unsaturated fats in the household: Overall, it is believed that the higher the ratio of unsaturated fat to saturated fat, the healthier the oil. You should not increase this ratio by adding more unsaturated fats to your diet, but by reducing saturated fats. Table 3 lists the common oils used in food preparation. Which ones are the lowest in saturated fats and which are highest? Determine the ratio of unsaturated (polyunsaturated +

Table 4: Ranking by Best (Highest) Unsaturated to Saturated Fat Ratio

Fats	% Poly-unsat.	% Mono-unsat.	% Sat.	Ratio of Unsat. to Sat. Fat	Comment
					Best fatty acid ratio.
					Highest in polyunsaturates.
					Blander than olive oil.
					Often used for deep frying.
					Most commonly used oil.
					Highest in monounsaturates.
					Very distinct flavor.
					Used in Asian & Middle Eastern cooking.
					Used in processed foods.
					Almost equal unsaturated and saturated fat.
					High in saturated fat.
					Highest in saturated fat.

monounsaturated) fats to saturated fats, and rank the oils from highest (best) to lowest (worst) in Table 4. Which oil has the best (highest) fatty acid ratio? Which is highest in saturated fat?

Part 2: Addition of bromine to vegetable oil: *(Teacher demonstration only. Perform in a fume hood).* Vegetable shortening and margarine are made by hydrogenating vegetable oils. Hydrogen is mixed with vegetable oil in the presence of a catalyst to convert freely flowing unsaturated oil into a semi-solid saturated oil. It is also possible to saturate fatty acids using halogens such as bromine, chlorine or iodine. These reactive gases bind to the carbons at both ends of the double bonds (Figure AA) without any need of a catalyst.

AA

Bromine is a reddish-brown, easily vaporized liquid which dissolves to a limited extent in water. At low concentrations, bromine water appears straw yellow. If you do not have access to bromine water, you can make it by mixing 90 mL of 0.2 M KBr solution, 0.1 g of potassium bromate ($KBrO_3$), and 10 mL of 2.0 M HCl. The characteristic yellow or reddish-brown color of bromine water is lost when bromine binds to a hydrocarbon chain (Figure AA). Thus, we can determine if the bonds in an oil are saturated by observing the impact of the oil on the color of bromine water. If bromine water is mixed with vegetable oil and the bromine color persists, then we can assume that the oil was already saturated because bromine did not react with it. If, however, the bromine color is lost, then we can assume that bromine has bonded to double bonds, indicating that the oil was not initially saturated.

Which has a higher percentage of saturated bonds, vegetable shortening or vegetable oil? Pour 10 mL of melted, uncolored vegetable shortening (e.g. Crisco®) into a beaker. Add a few drops of bromine water and stir vigorously with a glass rod. Does the color of bromine persist? Pour 10 mL of pure clear vegetable oil into a beaker. Add a few drops of bromine water and stir vigorously again. Does the color of bromine persist or disappear? Test a variety of oils available in your local supermarket to determine whether they are saturated or unsaturated.

Once you have found an oil that is unsaturated (the bromine color disappears), continue to add more bromine water until the bromine color persists. At this point you have saturated all of the double bonds. Is it possible to remove the bromine color by adding more oil? Try it! What happens to the oil when it has been saturated by the bromine? Does it become more or less fluid?

Questions

(1) Which oil has the highest unsaturated/saturated ratio? Which has the lowest?

(2) Why do food manufacturers often advertise that their products contain no tropical oils?

(3) Which of the oils is often used in deep frying?

(4) Is the saturated (brominated) vegetable oil from part 2 more or less fluid than the original vegetable oil?

(5) Food producers saturate (hydrogenate) vegetable oil to prevent it from oxidizing and becoming rancid. (Double bonds are susceptible to oxidation as well as saturation by hydrogen and other substances.) Is there any evidence that the saturated (brominated) vegetable oil in part 2 is less reactive (more stable) than the unsaturated oil? Explain.

(6) Suppose one molecule of bromine (Br_2) were added to one molecule of acetylene (C_2H_2) according to the following reaction: $H_2C_2(g) + Br_2(aq) \rightarrow C_2H_2Br_2(aq)$. What are the possible product(s)? Hint: The double bond between two carbon atoms prohibits the rotation of the carbon atoms in space.

(7) There is a higher incidence of cardiovascular disease in countries where people consume large amounts of meat and dairy products than in countries where these are not part of the normal diet. Explain.

FOR THE TEACHER

There are different ways to classify reactions, and this may lead to some confusion. For example, in the next chapter we introduce redox (oxidation-reduction) reactions. Students may have the impression that redox is another category that is mutually exclusive with those introduced here. Clarify for your students that this is not the case. After studying redox reactions in the next chapter, review the various types of reactions introduced in this chapter and show by equations that many may also be classified as oxidation-reduction reactions. Make certain students understand, that in oxidation-reduction reactions, an element may be oxidized in one reaction while reduced in another. For example, when copper wire is placed in a silver nitrate solution, silver metal deposits on the copper wire (copper is oxidized while silver is reduced): $Cu(s) + 2Ag^+(aq) \rightarrow Cu^{2+}(aq) + 2Ag(s)$. However, when an iron nail is placed in a solution of copper sulfate, iron is oxidized while copper is reduced: $Fe(s) + Cu^{2+}(aq) \rightarrow Fe^{2+}(aq) + Cu(s)$. In the first reaction, electrons are transferred from copper to silver, while in the second reaction, electrons are transferred from iron to copper. Relate this to the activity series of metals introduced in this chapter.

Two of the most important types of reactions in organic chemistry are addition and substitution reactions. Unfortunately, most substitution and addition reactions require the use of organic solvents that are too dangerous to use in most secondary school classrooms. For this reason, we introduce only one addition reaction, and no substitution reactions. Substitution reactions are extremely important in organic chemistry, and we therefore suggest that the teacher introduce these concepts through lectures and readings.

A substitution reaction is one in which a part of the reagent molecule is substituted for an H atom on a hydrocarbon or hydrocarbon group. For example, when the alkanes react with a halogen like chlorine, a chlorine atom substitutes for an atom of hydrogen:

$$CH_4 + Cl_2 \longrightarrow CH_3Cl + HCl$$

Substitution reactions are important in converting compounds such as benzene, toluene, and xylene into a myriad of useful and important derivatives.

3.2.1 COMPOSITION (SYNTHESIS, COMBINATION) REACTIONS

Discussion: Composition reactions are commonly called combination or synthesis reactions because two or more substances combine to synthesize a new compound. There are a variety of composition reactions, including reactions of metals with oxygen ($2Al + 3O_2 \rightarrow 2Al_2O_3$), reaction of two nonmetals ($S + O_2 \rightarrow SO_2$), reaction of metals with nonmetals other than oxygen ($2Na + Cl_2 \rightarrow 2NaCl$), and reactions of oxides ($CO_2 + H_2O \rightarrow H_2CO_3$).

Answers: (1) A composition reaction is a reaction in which two substances combine to form a third substance, such as $Fe + S \rightarrow FeS$ or $CaO + CO_2 \rightarrow CaCO_3$. (2) In the following composition reaction, A and X are elements: $4Li + O_2 \rightarrow 2Li_2O$. In the following composition reaction, A and X are compounds: $SO_2 + H_2O \rightarrow H_2SO_3$. (3) $2Mg(s) + O_2(g) \rightarrow 2MgO(s)$. The reaction gives off much heat and light, indicating that it is exothermic. Because of the high temperature achieved in this reaction, a small portion of the magnesium reacts with nitrogen in the air to form magnesium nitride: $3Mg(s) + N_2(g) \rightarrow Mg_3N_2(s)$.

(4) $2H_2(g) + O_2(g) \rightarrow 2H_2O(g)$. This reaction gives off much heat and is therefore classified as exothermic. (5) Moisture condenses on the inside walls of the test tube, indicating that water is a product of this composition reaction.

3.2.2 DECOMPOSITION REACTIONS

Discussion: In a decomposition reaction, a compound breaks down into two or more simpler substances as indicated by the general equation $AX \rightarrow A + X$, where AX is a compound and A and X may be elements or compounds. Note that decomposition reactions are the opposite of composition reactions. For example, hydrogen gas burns in oxygen (composition reaction) to form water. In contrast, electrolysis can be used to decompose water into hydrogen gas and oxygen gas. Make certain students understand the fundamental relationship between composition and decomposition. When a given amount of hydrogen burns in a given amount of oxygen, energy in the form of light and heat is produced. When the same amounts of hydrogen and oxygen are produced through the electrolysis of water, an equal amount of energy, in the form of an electric current, must be supplied.

Answers: (1) A decomposition reaction is a reaction in which a single compound reacts to produce two or more substances. For example: $2KClO_3(s) \rightarrow 2KCl + 3O_2$, or $2KNO_3 \rightarrow 2KNO_2 + O_2$. (2) In the decomposition reaction, $2HgO(s) \rightarrow 2Hg(s) + O_2(g)$, A and X are elements. In the reaction, $CaCO_3(s) \rightarrow CaO(s) + CO_2(g)$, A and X are compounds. (3) Electricity is used to break water into hydrogen and oxygen. (4) The chemical formula for sugar (sucrose) is $C_{12}H_{22}O_{11}$. Notice that the ratio of hydrogen to oxygen is the same as in water. Sulfuric acid is a strong acid and a powerful dehydrating agent (it has a strong affinity for water). Sulfuric acid can remove the elements of H_2O from many organic materials including your skin! When sulfuric acid is mixed with sugar, an exothermic reaction occurs in which the hydrogen and oxygen in sugar are removed as water. This heat, plus the heat released by the dilution of acid, transforms water into steam. The steam pushes the growing mass of carbon up in the form of a black "snake"! (5) As baking soda is heated, water condenses in the mouth of the tube, indicating that water is a product of heating. Carbon dioxide, another decomposition product, is evidenced as a flame is extinguished when placed in the mouth of a tube. These data suggest that baking soda will be of some value in helping batters rise, regardless of their pH.

3.2.3 SINGLE DISPLACEMENT (SINGLE REPLACEMENT) REACTIONS

Discussion: Single replacement reactions of metals occur when the atoms of one metal give up electrons (atoms give up electrons and are oxidized) to the positive ions of another metal in solution (ions gain electrons and are reduced). The positive ions gaining electrons become metal atoms, and the atoms giving up electrons become positive ions.

    Suppose we place a strip of copper in a solution of silver nitrate. The molecular, ionic, and net ionic equations for the reaction are as follows:

$$Cu(s) + 2AgNO_3(aq) \longrightarrow Cu(NO_3)_2(aq) + 2Ag(s)$$

$$Cu(s) + 2Ag^+(aq) + 2NO_3^-(aq) \longrightarrow Cu^{2+}(aq) + 2NO_3^-(aq) + 2Ag(s)$$

$$Cu(s) + 2Ag^+(aq) \longrightarrow Cu^{2+}(aq) + 2Ag(s)$$

The net ionic equation indicates that NO_3^- is simply a spectator ion and does not enter into any reaction. The actual reaction is an oxidation-reduction reaction in which there is a transfer of electrons from copper metal to silver ions.

The activity series of metals (Table 1) is useful in predicting whether single displacement reactions of metals with metal ions and of metals with water and acids will occur. Help your students learn to make informed generalizations by providing them with a table showing the activity series for metals and asking questions such as: (a) Above which metal will substances replace hydrogen from liquid water? (b) Above which metal will substances replace hydrogen from steam? (c) Will all metals in the series above hydrogen replace hydrogen from acids?

An analogous activity series exists for the halogens: F_2, Cl_2, Br_2, and I_2. Molecular fluorine can replace chloride, bromide, and iodide ions, however it is so reactive that it attacks water, and so such reactions cannot be carried out in aqueous solutions. Molecular chlorine can replace bromide and chloride ions in aqueous solutions, and molecular bromine can replace iodide ions. For example: $Cl_2 + 2KBr \rightarrow 2KCl + Br_2$.

When students placed the strip of zinc metal in the blue copper sulfate solution, Zn atoms entered the solution as Zn^{2+} ions. Cu^{2+} ions were converted to Cu which could be seen covering the zinc strip. As the reaction proceeded, the blue color of the copper sulfate solution disappeared. When the copper wire was placed in the silver nitrate solution, Cu atoms entered the solution as Cu^{2+} ions and Ag^+ ions were converted to Ag which could be seen covering the copper wire. The solution gradually acquired the characteristic blue color associated with hydrated Cu^{2+} ions. From the equations,

$$Zn(s) + CuSO_4(aq) \longrightarrow ZnSO_4(aq) + Cu(s)$$

$$Cu(s) + 2AgNO_3(aq) \longrightarrow Cu(NO_3)_2(aq) + 2Ag(s)$$

it appears that zinc displaces copper in copper sulfate and copper displaces silver in silver nitrate. The net ionic equations show that the reactions involve the transfer of electrons from zinc metal to copper ion and from copper metal to silver ion. That is, the zinc metal displaces Cu^{2+} ions from the solution and copper metal displaces Ag^+ ions from the solution according to the following ionic reactions:

$$Zn(s) + Cu^{2+}(aq) \longrightarrow Zn^{2+}(aq) + Cu(s)$$

$$Cu(s) + 2Ag^+(aq) \longrightarrow Cu^{2+}(aq) + 2Ag(s)$$

In part 4 students were exposed to a practical application of replacement reactions, namely the removal of tarnish from silverware. Students might have seen ads describing "magic plates" that clean silverware without the use of abrasive compounds. These plates are nothing more than aluminum plates and are much more expensive than the aluminum pie plates used in this investigation.

Answers: (1) A single displacement reaction is a reaction of an element with a compound in which the element replaces one of the elements in the compound while combining with the other element: $A + BX \rightarrow AX + B$ or $Y + BX \rightarrow BY + X$. Examples: $Ba + ZnSO_4 \rightarrow BaSO_4 + Zn$; $Cl_2(aq) + 2KBr(aq) \rightarrow 2KCl(aq) + Br_2(g)$. (2) Hydrogen was replaced by calcium: $Ca(s) + 2H_2O(aq) \rightarrow Ca(OH)_2(aq) + H_2(g)$. This result was confirmed by the presence of hydrogen, as evidenced by the "pop." (3) Zinc replaced hydrogen from acid but not water.

Since calcium replaced hydrogen from water it is the more reactive metal. (4) Copper metal covers the zinc. The blue color of the copper sulfate solution disappears, indicating that Cu^{2+} ions were converted to Cu. (5) Silver metal covers the copper. Copper atoms enter the solution as Cu^{2+} ions as indicated by the change in color of the solution to blue. (6) Zinc is more reactive because it displaces the hydrogen in hydrochloric acid, while the copper does not. (7) Copper is more reactive because it displaces the silver in silver nitrate so that silver is free to crystallize. (8) This reaction, like the others in this section, is an oxidation-reduction reaction. The chemical cleaning of silver is an electrochemical process in which electrons move from aluminum to the silver atoms in the tarnish. The silver, touching the aluminum pan and surrounded by the electrolyte, forms one plate of an electric cell. By the action of this cell, the tarnish (silver sulfide) is first dissolved, then the sulfur is separated and the silver redeposited. As a result, less silver is removed by this type of cleaning than by ordinary rubbing with mild abrasives. The sodium bicarbonate helps remove the coating of aluminum oxide from the aluminum to provide pure aluminum for the reaction, and it provides a conductive solution in which the electrochemical process can occur. The odor of rotten eggs (hydrogen sulfide gas, H_2S) is evident in the reaction. Electrons are transferred from the aluminum to the silver. The reaction is:

$$2\underset{0}{Al}(s) + 3\underset{+1}{Ag_2}S(s) + 6H_2O(aq) \longrightarrow 6\underset{0}{Ag}(s) + 2\underset{+3}{Al}(OH)_3(aq) + 3H_2S(g)$$

Make certain students note that a total of 6 electrons are transferred from aluminum to silver. (9) The first and third reactions will occur because zinc is more reactive than copper, and potassium is more reactive than hydrogen. The second reaction will not occur because cobalt is less reactive than sodium. (10) Yes, this reaction will occur because chlorine is more reactive than bromine.

3.2.4 DOUBLE REPLACEMENT (ION-COMBINING) REACTIONS

Discussion: In double replacement reactions, two water-soluble compounds react to form new compounds, one or more of which is either water or an insoluble gas or solid. For example, when soluble barium chloride is mixed with soluble sodium sulfate, the insoluble barium sulfate precipitate is formed. When a slution of silver sulfate is mixed with a solution of barium chloride, insoluble silver chloride and insoluble barium sulfate are formed, leaving almost pure water.

Table 2 gives the general solubility rules for many common laboratory chemicals. Students should be able to use this data to predict that silver chloride, aluminum hydroxide, and lead(II) iodide will be insoluble precipitates as shown in the following series of equations:

$$AgNO_3(aq) + NaCl(aq) \longrightarrow NaNO_3(aq) + AgCl(s)$$

$$AlCl_3(aq) + 3NH_4OH(aq) \longrightarrow 3NH_4Cl(aq) + Al(OH)_3(s)$$

$$2NaI(aq) + Pb(NO_3)_2(aq) \longrightarrow 2NaNO_3(aq) + PbI_2(s)$$

Answers: (1) In a double displacement reaction, the positive and negative ions of the two compounds simply exchange partners. For example, two compounds which are soluble in water react to form new compounds, one of which is insoluble in water. The other may be recovered by evaporating the water. Some examples are listed in the answer to question 2. (2) A double displacement reaction occurs if one of three criteria is satisfied: formation of a gas, formation of a precipitate, or formation of a molecular compound. Examples: (a) $BaCl_2(aq) + Na_2SO_4(aq) \rightarrow BaSO_4(s) + 2NaCl(aq)$, the production of barium sulfate precipitate acts as the driving force for the reaction; (b) $FeS(s) + 2HCl(aq) \rightarrow H_2S(g) + FeCl_2(aq)$, the production of a hydrogen sulfide gas acts as the driving force for this reaction; (c) $HCl(aq) + NaOH(aq) \rightarrow NaCl(aq) + H_2O(l)$, the formation of water (a molecular substance and weak electrolyte) acts as the driving force for this reaction. The formation of a weak electrolyte acts in the same manner as the formation of a precipitate or gas by removing ions from solution. In this case, H^+ and OH^- ions are removed from solution as water forms. (3) See equations in the discussion section. (4) The resulting solution contains Na^+, Cl^-, K^+ and Br^-. No combination of these ions will form a precipitate, gas or weak electrolyte (see Table 2). The ions simply remain in solution and no reaction occurs. (5) The reaction is: $Ag_2SO_4(aq) + BaCl_2(aq) \rightarrow 2AgCl(s) + BaSO_4(s)$. If the two solutions contain equivalent amounts of Ag_2SO_4 and $BaCl_2$, this means that the number of Ag^+, SO_4^{2-}, Ba^{2+} and Cl^- in the resulting solution are equal. Hence, all the Ag^+ combine with all the Cl^- to form the precipitate $AgCl$, and all the Ba^{2+} ions combine with all the SO_4^{2-} ions to form the precipitate $BaSO_4$. Other than the precipitates, all that remains is water. (6) Taste tests should never be performed in a laboratory because of the dangers of chemical contamination, incomplete neutralization, etc.

3.2.5 COMBUSTION REACTIONS

Discussion: A combustion reaction is one in which a substance reacts with oxygen with the rapid release of heat to produce a flame. All combustion reactions that involve elemental oxygen are redox reactions because the products include one or more oxides, indicating that oxygen has changed oxidation number from 0 to -2. Organic compounds usually burn in oxygen (air is approximately 20% oxygen) to produce carbon dioxide, water and substantial amounts of heat.

The combustion of the natural gas bubbles in part 1 and the acetylene balloon in part 2 are very dramatic and are sure to be "crowd-pleasers." Students should notice that the flame from the natural gas bubble is relatively yellow, while that from acetylene is bright white. Acetylene burns substantially hotter than methane or ethane (the two major components in natural gas), and its carbon atoms are heated to the point where they glow, creating the white color seen in the flame.

The reaction by which acetylene (ethyne) is made is very significant because it shows how an organic compound, acetylene, can be made from inorganic reactants:

$$CaC_2 + 2H_2O \longrightarrow C_2H_2 + Ca^{2+} + 2OH^-$$

Note that calcium carbide is an *inorganic compound* while acetylene is an *organic compound*. Calcium carbide is readily obtainable from coke (the residue left after the destructive distillation of coal is rich in carbon) and limestone (limestone is rich in calcium oxide, CaO) by the reaction: $5C + 2CaO \rightarrow 2CaC_2 + CO_2$. These reactions make possible the conversion of coal and limestone into an organic compound (acetylene), which may then be converted to many other organic compounds.

Answers: (1) The white flame of acetylene appears to be much brighter (and we may infer hotter) than the yellow flame of the methane. (2) The extremely high temperatures required to melt steel may be obtained by burning acetylene, but not by burning methane. (3) The black substance is carbon. If you remove the carbon from the tube, it will burn slowly with an invisible flame and leave almost no ash. The wood did not burn while in the tube. It decomposed in the absence of air to form gases which burned at the mouth of the tube. (4) Wood is mainly cellulose, which decomposes in the absence of air to form liquids and gases including methanol, methane gas, and turpentine. These flammable gases burned as they escaped from the end of the tube. (5) Student answers will vary.

3.2.6 ADDITION REACTIONS

Discussion: Addition reactions are very important in the syntheses of organic compounds. Hydrogenation is the process of adding hydrogen to compounds containing multiple bonds in the presence of a catalyst such as platinum or nickel. The catalyst weakens the H-H bond in molecular hydrogen to facilitate the reaction. Hydrogenation is widely used in the food industry to change liquid vegetable oils to solid fat. Oils containing many multiple bonds (polyunsaturated) can quickly become rancid upon exposure to the air as they undergo oxidation, and yield unpleasant-tasting products. Hydrogenation removes multiple bonds, thus retarding oxidation. Cooking oils and margarine are prepared by hydrogenation from vegetable oils.

   Hydrocarbons may be classified as saturated or unsaturated. A saturated hydrocarbon is one in which all carbon atoms are bonded to the maximum number of hydrogen atoms. Examples of saturated hydrocarbons called alkanes are: methane (CH_4), ethane (C_2H_6), propane (C_3H_8), and butane (C_4H_{10}). The general formula is: C_nH_{2n+2}. Figure BB shows the structural formulas of the four simplest alkanes.

Table 5: Ranking of Oils by Unsaturated to Saturated Fat Ratio

Oils	% Poly- unsat.	% Mono- unsat.	Sat.	Unsat. to Sat. Fat	Comments
canola	32	62	6	15.7:1	Best fatty acid ratio.
safflower	75	12	9	9.7:1	Highest in polyunsaturates.
sunflower	66	20	10	8.6:1	Blander than olive oil.
corn	59	24	13	6.4:1	Often used for deep frying.
soybean	59	23	14	5.9:1	Most commonly used oil.
olive	9	72	14	5.8:1	Highest in monounsaturates.
peanut	32	46	17	4.6:1	Very distinct flavor.
sesame seed	40	40	18	4.4:1	Used in Asian and Middle Eastern cooking.
cottonseed	52	18	26	2.7:1	Used in processed foods.
palm oil	37	9	49	0.9:1	Almost equal unsaturated and saturated fat.
palm kernel	2	11	82	0.2:1	High in saturated fat.
coconut	2	6	87	0.1:1	Highest in saturated fat.

Alkenes are unsaturated hydrocarbons that contain a carbon-carbon double bond. Ethylene (ethene) is the simplest alkene (C_2H_4) and has the structural formula shown in Figure BB. The general formula for alkenes is: C_nH_{2n}.

Alkynes are unsaturated hydrocarbons that contain a carbon-carbon triple bond. The simplest alkyne is acetylene (ethyne) with the structural formula shown in Figure BB. The general formula for the alkynes is: C_nH_{2n-2}.

Saturated hydrocarbons contain only single bonds between carbon atoms. Unsaturated hydrocarbons contain double or triple bonds between carbon atoms. In general, animals produce fats (mostly saturated lipids), while plants produce oils (mostly unsaturated lipids).

Answers: (1) Canola; coconut. (2) Palm trees and coconut palms grow in the tropics, and therefore palm and coconut oils are considered to be tropical oils. Table 5 illustrates that these oils have a large amount of saturated fats, and are therefore to be consumed in limited amounts. (3) Corn oil. (4) Less. (5) Yes. The unsaturated vegetable oil is reactive as evidenced by the rapid loss of bromine's color. Once it is fully saturated, it does not react with bromine, and this suggests that it will also be relatively stable in the presence of oxygen. (6) Two products are possible. This is most easily shown using some structural formulas:

$$Br_2 + H-C\equiv C-H \longrightarrow \begin{array}{c} Br \\ \diagdown \\ H \end{array} C=C \begin{array}{c} Br \\ \diagup \\ \diagdown H \end{array} \quad or \quad \begin{array}{c} H \\ \diagdown \\ Br \end{array} C=C \begin{array}{c} Br \\ \diagup \\ \diagdown H \end{array}$$

Rotation is prohibited by the double bond between the carbons, so these two compounds are structurally different. Does structural difference mean chemical difference? The two possible products are called structural isomers because they have the same formula, but different structures. When the two bromines are on the same side we call it a *cis* isomer, and when they are on opposite sides, a *trans* isomer. The bromines will not add to the same carbon. (7) These foods are traditionally high in saturated fats and cholesterol, substances that have been linked with heart disease.

Applications to Everyday Life

Note: Examples of everyday applications of chemical reactions are so numerous that they have been integrated throughout the book rather than listed here.

3.3 OXIDATION-REDUCTION (REDOX) REACTIONS

The Golden Gate Bridge across the entrance to California's San Francisco Bay is one of the longest (central span of 1280 m) and most famous suspension bridges in the world. Painters are employed year-round to keep the towers, cable housings and bridge supports coated with paint to preserve its appearance, and more importantly, its structural integrity. The Golden Gate Bridge is located on the Pacific coast where it is exposed to marine air laden with salt and moisture. If not protected with paint, the iron and steel in the bridge would rapidly oxidize (rust) and weaken. Oxidation is a serious threat to man-made structures, for no building material will last indefinitely if subjected to an environment in which it undergoes chemical change, and the Earth is such an environment!

Approximately one-fifth of our atmosphere is oxygen, a highly reactive gas responsible for the rusting of iron, the burning of wood, and the slow degradation of rubber and plastic. Oxidation causes caulking to crack, homes to burn, cars to rust and paint to peel. Oxidation is involved in the weathering of rocks, the combustion of gasoline, the bleaching of clothes and the spoiling of foods. Although oxidation is often destructive, it is essential for life as both plants and animals oxidize sugars and other compounds to derive the energy necessary to live.

Originally, oxidation was defined as that process by which oxygen combines with some other substance, such as when oxygen combines with iron to form rust:

$$4Fe(s) + 3O_2(g) \longrightarrow 2Fe_2O_3(s)$$
$$\text{rust}$$

When the oxidation process occurs rapidly with the release of light and heat, we say that a substance is burning. Burning of wood, coal and propane are examples of combustion in which substantial amounts of light and heat are evolved. A simple example of combustion (burning) is the oxidation of hydrogen gas to form water according to the equation:

$$2H_2(g) + O_2(g) \longrightarrow 2H_2O(g) + \text{heat} + \text{light}$$

The oxygen oxidizes the hydrogen to produce water, heat and light. The energy release from such an oxidation reaction is what destroyed the German airship *Hindenburg* in May of 1937, bringing a swift end to the use of hydrogen as a buoyant gas for airships.

The opposite of oxidation is reduction, a process in which oxygen is removed from a substance. For example, if a stream of hydrogen gas is passed over heated copper (II) oxide ore (cuprite), the hydrogen reduces copper oxide to useful metallic copper by removing oxygen.

$$CuO(s) + H_2(g) \longrightarrow Cu(s) + H_2O(g)$$

Although the terms oxidation and reduction originally referred only to the addition or subtraction of oxygen from a compound, their meanings have expanded to include reactions not involving oxygen. Oxidation and reduction are now understood to refer to the loss or gain of electrons, whether through a reaction with oxygen or with another substance. For example, when the halogens react with metal, they gain electrons (they are reduced) while the metal loses electrons (it is oxidized). When sodium metal reacts with chlorine, sodium is oxidized (it loses an electron to go from metallic to ionic form, Na^+), while chlorine is reduced (it gains an electron to become chloride, Cl^-).

$$2Na(s) + Cl_2(g) \longrightarrow 2Na^+Cl^-(s)$$

To keep track of electrons, chemists assign oxidation numbers that show the general distribution of electrons in bonded atoms. Negative oxidation numbers are assigned to those atoms that possess more electrons than in their neutral state (remember that electrons are negative), while positive oxidation states are assigned to those that possess fewer than their neutral state (the loss of a negative charge results in the establishment of a positive charge). For example, when zinc reacts with oxygen, each zinc atom loses two electrons, while each oxygen gains two:

$$2\underset{0}{Z}n(s) + \underset{0}{O}_2(g) \longrightarrow 2\underset{+2}{Zn}\underset{-2}{O}(s)$$

The numbers below the elements are the oxidation numbers. In this reaction, the oxidation number of zinc goes from 0 (the oxidation number of an element in the free state is 0) to +2, indicating the loss of two electrons to oxygen. By contrast, the oxidation number of oxygen goes from 0 to −2, indicating the acquisition of the two electrons lost by zinc. We say that zinc has been oxidized, and oxygen reduced. Oxygen is not the only substance that can remove electrons from zinc as the following reaction illustrates:

$$\underset{0}{Zn}(s) + \underset{0}{Cl}_2(g) \longrightarrow \underset{+2}{Zn}\underset{-1}{Cl}_2(s)$$

Note that chlorine, rather than oxygen, is responsible for removing electrons from zinc. Zinc loses electrons and is oxidized (its oxidation number goes from 0 to +2) while chlorine gains electrons and is reduced (its oxidation number goes from 0 to −1).

Note that the common feature of the two preceding reactions is a loss of electrons from zinc to an element with higher electron affinity (oxygen or chlorine). Chlorine is playing the same role as oxygen in that it is accepting electrons from a substance. Since the oxygen and chlorine cause the oxidation of Zn to Zn^{2+}, they are called oxidizing agents. Since zinc causes the reduction of oxygen to O^{2-} and chlorine to Cl^-, zinc is called a reducing agent. In nature, oxidation cannot occur without reduction, so we use the term oxidation-reduction (redox) to refer to reactions in which electrons are transferred between species or in which atoms change oxidation numbers. If one species in a reaction loses electrons, other species in the same reaction must gain the same number of electrons in order to maintain neutrality of charge. Oxidation is thus the part of an oxidation-reduction reaction in which there is a loss of electrons by a species or an increase in the oxidation number of an atom, and reduction is the part in which there is a gain of electrons or a reduction in the oxidation number.

Consider the following two reactions: (a) the formation of an ionic bond when sodium reacts with chlorine and, (b) the formation of a covalent bond when hydrogen reacts with chlorine:

$$2Na(s) + Cl_2(g) \longrightarrow 2NaCl(s)$$

$$H_2(g) + Cl_2(g) \longrightarrow 2HCl(g)$$

In the reaction of sodium and chlorine, an electron is transferred from Na to Cl to produce Na^+ and Cl^- ions. Thus, sodium has a +1 oxidation number, and chlorine a −1. In the reaction of hydrogen gas and chlorine gas, a polar covalent bond is formed in which an electron is only partially transferred (shared) from hydrogen to chlorine. In hydrogen chloride gas, the hydrogen and chlorine share the hydrogen's electron, but the electron pair (one electron from hydrogen and one from chlorine) resides closer to the chlorine nucleus because chlorine is more electronegative than hydrogen. Since the pair of electrons is closer to the chlorine nucleus, we say there is an apparent transfer of electrons to chlorine. In an apparent transfer of electrons we assign the electrons to the more electronegative element, giving an oxidation number of −1 to chlorine, and +1 to hydrogen.

Bookkeeping methods using oxidation numbers (also called oxidation states) have been devised to help keep track of electrons during chemical reactions. An oxidation number may be defined as the charge that an atom would have if both of the electrons in each bond were assigned to the more electronegative element. The oxidation number reflects the extent to

Table 1: Rules for Oxidation Numbers

	Classification	*Rule*
(1)	free elements	In free (uncombined) elements, each atom has an oxidation number of zero (0).
(2)	monatomic ions	For ions composed of only one atom, the oxidation number is equal to the charge on the ion. The ions Na^+, Ba^{2+}, I^-, S^{2-}, Al^{3+} have oxidation numbers of +1, +2, −1, −2, and +3, respectively.
(3)	fluorine	Fluorine is the most electronegative element and therefore always has an oxidation number of −1 in compounds. Each of the other halogens has an oxidation number of −1 in binary compounds (those that contain only two elements), except when the other element is another halogen above it in the Periodic Table, or when the other element is oxygen.
(4)	oxygen	The oxidation number of oxygen in most compounds is −2. In peroxides the oxidation number of oxygen is −1.
(5)	hydrogen	The oxidation number of hydrogen is +1 in all compounds except metallic compounds (hydrides) in which the oxidation state is −1.
(6)	neutral compounds	The sum of all the oxidation numbers of all the atoms in a neutral compound is zero.
(7)	polyatomic ions	For a polyatomic ion, the algebraic sum of the oxidation numbers must be equal to the ion's charge. For example, consider the ammonium ion, NH_4^+. The oxidation number of N is −3 and the oxidation number of H is +1. The sum of the oxidation numbers is: −3 + 4 = +1, which is equal to the net charge of the ammonium ion as required.
(8)	position	Since oxidation states are related to the electron structure of the parent element, the position of an element in the Periodic Table is related to the possible oxidation state(s) for the element. Group IA elements (alkali metals) have an oxidation number of +1 in compounds, while Group IIA elements (alkaline earth metals) have an oxidation number of +2. For groups IIIA–VIIA the group number represents the highest possible oxidation state, although others may exist.

which an element has been oxidized or reduced. Each element in a reaction must be assigned an oxidation number.

In the case of monatomic ions that have undergone a complete exchange of electrons, the oxidation state is obvious. For example, Na^+ and Cl^- ions have oxidation states equivalent to their charges, +1 and −1. In other types of reactions, such as those in which electrons are shared, the assignment of oxidation numbers may not be so clear. Hence, guidelines have been established for assigning oxidation numbers. Note that for oxidation numbers, we write the sign before the number (e.g. +1) to distinguish oxidation numbers from actual electric charges, for which we write the number before the algebraic sign (e.g. 1+). For example, in the following equation, the 0 below Fe, the +2 below Cu, the +2 below Fe and the 0 below Cu indicate oxidation numbers. The 2+ after Cu and the 2+ after Fe indicate the actual charges on these ions.

$$\underset{0}{Fe(s)} + \underset{+2}{Cu^{2+}(aq)} \longrightarrow \underset{+2}{Fe^{2+}(aq)} + \underset{0}{Cu(s)}$$

Oxidation numbers can be associated with the electron structure of the elements, but it is important not to think of an oxidation number as a charge on an atom. The oxidation number is simply an imaginary, albeit convenient, number assigned to indicate the extent of oxidation or reduction relative to the element. The following examples show how the rules in Table 1 are applied to determine oxidation numbers.

What are the oxidation numbers of all the atoms in the SO_2 molecule? The oxidation number of O by rule 4 is −2. There are two oxygen atoms in the molecule, so by rule 4 the sum of their oxidation numbers is: $2 \times (-2) = -4$. Since by rule 7 the sum of all the oxidation numbers in a neutral compound is zero, the oxidation number of S in SO_2 is +4.

What are the oxidation numbers of the atoms in KNO_3? There are three atoms of O: $3 \times (-2) = -6$ (rule 4). By rule 8 the oxidation number of K is +1. Since rule 6 states that the sum of all the oxidation numbers of all the atoms in a neutral compound is zero, the oxidation number of N must be +5 ($-6 + 1 = +5$).

What are the oxidation numbers of the atoms in the ion, $Cr_2O_7^{2-}$? Oxygen: $7 \times (-2) = -14$. Since the charge on the ion is 2−, we must account for a charge of +12 (rule 7). There are two chromium atoms. Hence the oxidation number of each chromium atom is +6.

Appendix 5.1 lists the common oxidation states for the elements most frequently used in the laboratory.

3.3.1 OXIDATION STATES

Concepts to Investigate: Oxidation states, oxidation-reduction reactions, disproportionation.

Materials: <u>Part 1</u>: Test tubes, 0.01 M KMnO$_4$ (potassium permanganate), 1.0 M H$_2$SO$_4$, 1 M NaOH, 0.01 M NaHSO$_3$ (sodium bisulfite); <u>Part 2</u>: White paper towel or filter paper; <u>Part 3</u>: Photocopies of Figure A, scissors. Make a photocopy of Figure A on overhead transparency film to aid in discussion.

Safety: Wear goggles, lab coat and gloves.

Principles and Procedures: A blood bank is a storage facility where human blood is "banked" to be "withdrawn" for those patients who are in need of transfusions to replace blood lost due to accidents or operations. Churches, colleges, and businesses often sponsor blood drives in which volunteers may donate blood to replenish blood bank supplies. When giving blood, donors frequently comment that it is much darker in color than the bright red associated with open wounds. This difference in color is due to the different oxidation states of iron, the element at the center of the blood's oxygen-transporting hemoglobin molecule. The reduced state of iron (ferrous, Fe^{2+}, iron (II)) found in deoxygenated hemoglobin (Fe^{2+}–hemoglobin) is dark red, while the oxidized state (ferric, Fe^{3+}, iron (III)) found in oxygen-rich hemoglobin (Fe^{3+}–hemoglobin) is bright red. Phlebotomists (technicians who extract blood) remove blood from deoxygenated veins and store it in air-free bags. Such blood appears dark red because its iron exists as Fe^{2+}. However, if those same veins are cut in an accident, oxygen from the atmosphere immediately oxidizes the hemoglobin, turning it bright red. Many biology texts include pictures of the circulatory system in which oxygenated blood is identified with red ink, and deoxygenated blood with blue. Such conventions are used only to help identify blood flow patterns, and it should be realized that deoxygenated blood is actually dark red, not blue!

Many elements are like iron, displaying different colors depending on their oxidation state. Manganese, for example, may exist in a variety of oxidation states and corresponding colors including: MnO$_4^-$ (+7, purple), MnO$_4^{2-}$ (+6, green), MnO$_2$ (+4, orange/brown), Mn$_2$O$_3$ (+3, violet), Mn^{2+} (+2, light pink to colorless). Use this information to determine the products of the following oxidation-reduction reactions involving the manganese ion.

Part 1: Oxidation states of manganese: A stock solution of 0.01 M potassium permanganate solution may be made by dissolving 1.58 g of KMnO$_4$ per liter of water. A stock solution of 1.0 M NaOH may be made by dissolving 40 g of sodium hydroxide per liter of solution. A stock solution of 0.01 M NaHSO$_3$ may be made by dissolving 1.04 grams of sodium bisulfite (sodium hydrogen sulfite) in 1 liter of solution.

Number four test tubes. Place white paper underneath and behind the test tubes so that it will be easier to notice color changes. Add 0.01 M potassium permanganate (KMnO$_4$), 1.0 M sulfuric acid (H$_2$SO$_4$), and 1.0 M sodium hydroxide (NaOH) to the numbered test tubes as described in Table 2. What is the color of the permanganate (MnO$_4^-$) ion in test tube 1? What is the oxidation state of manganese in this tube?

While stirring, slowly add 0.01 M sodium bisulfite to test tube 2 until the there is no further color change. What colors did you notice in this process? What is the color of the final solution? Repeat with test tubes 3 and 4.

Table 2: Observing Colors of Various Oxidation States of Manganese

	0.01 M KMnO$_4$	1.0 M H$_2$SO$_4$	1.0 M NaOH	0.01 M NaHSO$_3$	Color	Ion
1	5 mL	—	—	—	purple	MnO$_4^-$
2	5 mL	3 mL	—	stir in slowly	pink-colorless	Mn^{2+}
3	5 mL	—	4 mL	to see color	green	MnO$_4^{2-}$
4	5 mL	—	—	changes	brown	MnO$_2$

The equations for the reactions that occur in test tubes 2, 3 and 4 are as follows:

$$2MnO_4^-(aq) + H^+(aq) + 5HSO_3^-(aq) \longleftrightarrow 2Mn^{2+}(aq) + 5SO_4^{2-}(aq) + 3H_2O(l)$$

$$2MnO_4^-(aq) + 3OH^-(aq) + HSO_3^-(aq) \longleftrightarrow 2MnO_4^{2-}(aq) + SO_4^{2-}(aq) + 2H_2O(l)$$

$$OH^-(aq) + 2MnO_4^-(aq) + 3HSO_3^-(aq) \longleftrightarrow 2MnO_2(s) + 3SO_4^{2-}(aq) + 2H_2O(l)$$

What is the final oxidation state of manganese in each reaction?

Part 2: Reaction of manganese (VII) ion with cellulose: Add approximately 2 mL of 1.0 M NaOH solution to 10 mL of 0.01 M potassium permanganate solution and mix. The solution should appear purple, indicating the presence of the manganese (VII) ion. Place two or three layers of white filter paper (folded white paper towel will suffice) in a Petri dish. Dampen the paper with the solution. Any color changes are due to changes in the oxidation state of manganese. The colors associated with the oxidation states of manganese are purple (+7), green (+6), orange/brown (+4), violet (+3), and light pink to colorless (+2). What state(s) do you observe?

Part 3: Oxidation numbers in compounds: The sum of all of the oxidation states in a neutral compound is zero. Knowing this, and the oxidation states of the component elements, it is possible to derive the empirical formula for a compound. Conversely, if one knows the empirical formula, it is possible to derive the oxidation states of the component atoms. Figure A illustrates some common oxidation states for various elements. Photocopy Figure A

A

Table 6: Oxidation Numbers in Compounds

	H	*S*	*O*	*N*	*Mn*	*Ca*	*Cl*	*K*	*Li*
LiH									
CaH$_2$									
H$_2$S									
H$_2$SO$_3$									
H$_2$SO$_4$									
H$_2$O									
H$_2$O$_2$									
NH$_3$									
HNO$_3$									
NO									
NO$_2$									
Ca$_3$N$_2$									
Li$_3$N									
KMnO$_4$									
MnO$_2$									
MnCl$_2$									

and use scissors to separate all of the circles from each other. Select the discs with appropriate oxidation states and "form" compounds by moving appropriate discs adjacent to each other. Using the discs, construct the following compounds: LiH, CaH$_2$, H$_2$S, H$_2$SO$_3$, H$_2$SO$_4$, H$_2$O, H$_2$O$_2$, NH$_3$, HNO$_3$, NO, NO$_2$, Ca$_3$N$_2$, Li$_3$N, KMnO$_4$, MnO$_2$, MnCl$_2$. Remember that all of the oxidation numbers in a neutral compound must add up to zero. Examine the oxidation states in your compounds and transcribe their oxidation states into Table 3:

Questions

(1) What are the final oxidation states in test tubes 1, 2, 3 and 4?

(2) Was the manganese ion in permanganate oxidized or reduced by cellulose in part 2?

(3) Explain, in terms of the transmission and absorption of light by solutions, the variety of colors associated with the different oxidation states of manganese.

(4) Determine the oxidation numbers of the atoms in the following: NH$_3$, NO$_3^-$, K$_2$Cr$_2$O$_7$, MnO$_4^-$, H$_2$O$_2$.

(5) Use the discs from part 3, and some that you construct yourself, to form some combinations of elements of your choice (making certain the charges sum to zero). Consult chemical reference books to see if the combinations you made are real compounds.

(6) The bonding electron pair is closer to chlorine in HCl than to bromine in HBr, yet the oxidation number of hydrogen in both compounds is +1, while the oxidation number of the halogens is −1. Explain.

3.3.2 OXIDATION AND REDUCTION

Concepts to Investigate: Oxidation states, oxidation-reduction reactions, reversible processes.

Materials: <u>Part 1</u>: Copper (wire, sheet, or pre-1982 US penny), burner, tongs, test tube, mossy zinc, sulfuric acid, generator apparatus, (see Figure E), calcium chloride; <u>Part 2</u>: Glucose (dextrose), methylene blue (solution or powder), potassium hydroxide, flask.

Safety: Wear goggles, lab coat and gloves. Part 1 is a teacher demonstration only. Caution: Hydrogen is explosive in the presence of oxygen, so it must be kept away from all flames.

Principles and Procedures: In 1801 Sir Humphrey Davy demonstrated that platinum strips would glow when heated by electricity. Although Davy's electric incandescent lamp was an interesting invention, it was not very useful because it would last for only brief periods before the platinum strip would oxidize and break. You can perform a corollary to Humphrey's experiment by holding threads of steel wool across the terminals of a battery with a pair of pliers (Figure B; *Wear goggles!*). Notice that the iron threads immediately glow, but when combustion starts the circuit is broken and the light ceases.

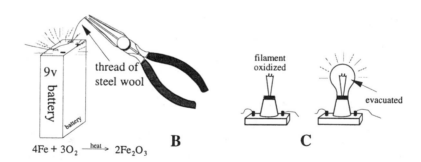

$$4Fe + 3O_2 \xrightarrow{\text{heat}} 2Fe_2O_3 \qquad \textbf{B}$$

Although Davy's "electric lamp" was invented at the turn of the 19th century, it was 78 years before American inventor Thomas Edison introduced a practical, long-life electric lamp. Edison realized that the reason Davy's filament failed was that it was rapidly oxidized in air. Thomas Edison used the recently invented vacuum pump to remove air from glass bulbs that he placed around the filament. With only trace quantities of oxygen remaining, oxidation was minimized and the filament glowed for many hours (Figure C). We still use evacuated bulbs to protect filaments in incandescent light bulbs today. The slightest leak in a light bulb permits oxidation and shortens the life of the bulb.

Platinum, iron, copper, tungsten, and other metals react with oxygen in the atmosphere to form oxides. Although this process is accelerated at the high temperatures found in light bulbs or the mantle of the Earth, it also occurs at temperatures commonly found on the Earth's surface. Fortunately, oxidation is a reversible process, allowing us to recycle oxidized metals as well as purify them from oxide ores such as cuprite (Cu_2O), magnetite (Fe_3O_4), hematite (Fe_2O_3), and periclase (MgO). By exposing an oxidized metal to a reducing environment, it is possible to remove oxygen and return the metal to its pure state.

In part 1, which follows, copper is oxidized at high temperatures in an oxygen rich environment, and then reduced in a hydrogen rich environment, showing that oxidation and reduction are reversible processes. In part 2 you will oxidize and reduce an organic substance (methylene blue), illustrating that oxidation and reduction processes occur in organic materials as well as inorganic ones.

Part 1: Oxidation and reduction of copper: *Teacher demonstration only. Work in a fume hood and wear goggles, gloves, and lab coat. Remove all flammable materials from the fume hood.*

Copper, like all other metals, may be oxidized by heating in the presence of oxygen. Heat a copper wire, small sheet of copper, or pre-1982 copper U.S. penny in a hot flame for approximately 3 to 4 minutes (Figure D):

$$\text{heat} + 2Cu(s) + O_2(g) \longrightarrow 2CuO(s)$$

In this reaction copper is oxidized from a state of 0 to a state of +2. Copper can now be reduced from the +2 state back to 0 by exposing it to reducing agent such as hydrogen.

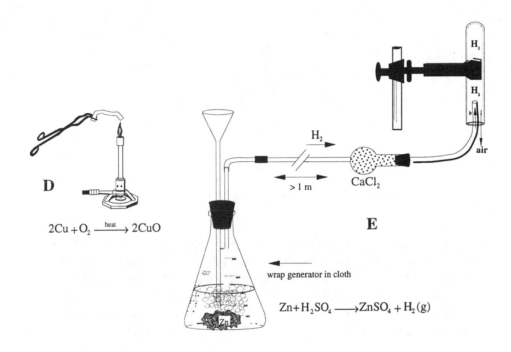

Set up a hydrogen generator as shown in Figure E. Keep all flames at least one meter away form the generator. Place 10 to 15 grams of mossy zinc in the bottom of the generator flask. Seal the flask with the stopper-funnel assembly, making certain the funnel tube extends to within 0.5 cm of the bottom of the flask. Wrap the generator in a heavy towel to contain glass in the unlikely event of a hydrogen explosion. Add sufficient 3 *M* sulfuric acid through the funnel to cover the base of the funnel tube. Hydrogen is produced according to the following reaction:

$$Zn(s) + H_2SO_4(aq) \longrightarrow ZnSO_4(aq) + H_2(g)$$

If bubbling is too slow, add a few drops of the catalyst copper (II) sulfate solution to increase hydrogen production. Collect a series of tubes of hydrogen by the downward displacement of air as shown in Figure E. Remove each tube far from the generator assembly and test with a glowing splint. If it "barks," oxygen is still present. If it burns slowly at the mouth, the tube contains relatively pure hydrogen. Once the generator is producing pure hydrogen you may continue. It is not safe to continue if oxygen is present in the stream because fire may spread through the tube and into the generator!

Place the sheet of copper that you just oxidized in the base of a test tube. Heat the oxidized copper in the test tube for at least two minutes (Figure F). Rotate the tube in the clamp until it is horizontal, and position the tube so the hot copper (II) oxide is exposed to the stream of hydrogen as shown in Figure G. The copper oxide should be reduced, yielding a bright copper metal.

$$\text{heat} + CuO(s) + H_2(g) \longrightarrow H_2O(g) + Cu(s)$$

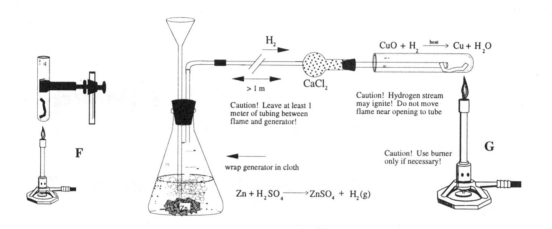

You may also perform this experiment by heating the copper oxide in position as shown in Figure G. Although this technique works better, it should only be done if you are certain there is no more oxygen mixed with the hydrogen coming from the generator! Is there any indication of the reduction of copper (II) to copper or of the production of water? Once the copper color has returned allow the metal to cool in the presence of the hydrogen stream. Can the copper be re-oxidized by heating it in the flame once more (Figure D)? Try it!

Part 2: Oxidation and reduction of methylene blue: Add the following to an Erlenmeyer flask: 200 mL of 0.5 *M* KOH (5.7 grams KOH in 200 mL water; allow to cool before adding other substances), 7 grams of dextrose (glucose), and a few drops of methylene blue indicator solution (or approximately 0.5 grams of methylene blue powder). Under basic conditions methylene blue is reduced to its colorless state:

$$\overset{oxidized}{\underset{\text{(blue)}}{\text{methylene blue}}} \xrightarrow{\text{reducing environment}} \overset{reduced}{\underset{\text{(colorless)}}{\text{methylene blue}}}$$

Methylene blue may be subsequently oxidized by shaking the flask vigorously. Atmospheric oxygen dissolves into the solution, oxidizing methylene blue to the blue state.

$$\underset{\text{(colorless)}}{\underset{reduced}{\text{methylene blue}}} \xrightarrow{\text{oxidizing environment}} \underset{\text{(blue)}}{\underset{oxidized}{\text{methylene blue}}}$$

After shaking, allow the flask to stand undisturbed. What happens to the blue color? Is the methylene blue once again reduced? If so, can it be oxidized again? How many times will the methylene blue in your flask undergo oxidation and reduction by shaking and allowing the flask to stand?

Questions

(1) Platinum is found in nature as platinum (II) oxide and platinum (IV) oxide. How might it be purified using a reduction process?

(2) One of the principal industrial uses of hydrogen is as a reducing agent in the extraction of metals from mineral ores. Explain.

(3) Is it possible to oxidize the copper that was produced by reduction in part 1? Explain. Can you repeatedly oxidize and reduce the same copper sample?

3.3.3 DRAMATIC OXIDATION REACTIONS

Concepts to Investigate: Spontaneous combustion, oxidation, reduction, oxidation-reduction (redox) reactions, oxidizing agent, reducing agent, exothermic reactions.

Materials: Part 1: Potassium permanganate, spatula, glycerin, evaporating dish; Part 2: Sodium metal, Petri dish, overhead projector, phenolphthalein solution; Part 3: Sodium metal, cylinder of chlorine gas (if you do not have a chlorine cylinder you can generate chlorine gas in a fume hood using the following technique. Place 4 teaspoons of calcium hypochlorite, $Ca(OCl)_2$, in a sidearm flask. Add sufficient water to form a slurry. Attach a piece of rubber tubing to the sidearm flask and place the other end in the bottom of the collection flask. Add approximately 30 mL of 6 *M* HCl to the sidearm flask and stopper it. Collect the chlorine gas by the upward displacement of air in the collection flask. Part 4: Ammonium chloride, ammonium nitrate, zinc dust, Beral pipet or eye dropper, evaporating dish or crucible; Part 5: Dry ice, deflagrating spoon, propane torch, magnesium powder.

Safety: Wear face mask, lab coat and gloves. Observe all additional precautions. All demonstrations in this section are to be performed by instructor only!

Principles and Procedures: On January 14, 1996, a massive earthquake struck Northridge (Los Angeles), California, causing greater financial damage than any other natural disaster in American history. On the first anniversary of the Northridge quake, an even more massive quake hit Kobe, Japan, causing substantially greater damage. Industrial and educational laboratories were particularly hard hit by these earthquakes due to accompanying chemical fires and explosions. In many instances, oxidizers mixed with flammable materials, causing spontaneous combustion and dangerous chemical fires.

Much of the damage in these and other quakes could have been avoided if people had followed appropriate safety precautions. For example, one should never store oxidizers in the

NFPA Safety Diamond

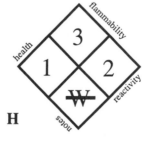

NFPA Hazard Codes
4 = extreme hazard
3 = severe hazard
2 = moderate hazard
1 = slight hazard
0 = no known hazard

H

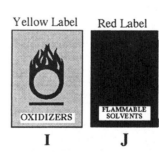

Yellow Label   Red Label

I   J

same location as flammable chemicals. Oxidizers are highly reactive and may release oxygen to cause flammable substances to burn. Figure H illustrates the NFPA (National Fire Protection Association) label manufacturers place on containers to warn consumers of chemical hazards. A strong oxidizer is considered very reactive, and must be given a reactivity rating of 3 or 4. In addition, chemical manufacturers and shipping companies must identify cartons containing chemicals with appropriate warning labels such as the yellow oxidizer label (Figure I) or the red flammable liquids label (Figure J). The following activities will be performed by your instructor to illustrate the potential hazards associated with strong oxidizers.

Part 1: Spontaneous combustion by mixing an oxidizer and hydrocarbon: *Teacher demonstration only. Work in a fume hood and wear face shield, gloves, and lab coat. Remove all flammable materials from the fume hood.* Place approximately 10 grams of potassium permanganate in an evaporating dish. Using a spoon or spatula, create a small crater in the middle of the pile. Add approximately 3 mL of glycerin to the crater and step back. Within approximately 20 seconds, smoke should rise from the pile, and then an intense violet flame will erupt as glycerin is oxidized.

$$14KMnO_4(s) + 4C_3H_5(OH)_3(l) \longrightarrow$$
$$7K_2CO_3(s) + 7Mn_2O_3(s) + 5CO_2(g) + 16H_2O + \text{ light} + \text{heat}$$

Why should oxidizers, such as potassium permanganate, be stored in different cabinets from flammable substances? Dissolve the solid waste in water and filter it. Discard the filtrate down the drain and the solid material in a solid waste container.

Part 2: Spontaneous combustion by mixing a strong reducing agent with water: *Teacher demonstration only. Wear face shield, gloves and lab coat.* Strong reducers (reducing agents), like strong oxidizers, are highly reactive and potentially dangerous. Metallic sodium is a strong reducing agent (it is easily oxidized), and reacts vigorously with water. Place the bottom (smaller) half of a Petri dish on the stage of an overhead projector. Pour water into the dish until it is half-full. Add a drop of phenolphthalein and stir. Phenolphthalein is an acid-base indicator, and turns bright pink in basic conditions, and colorless in acidic conditions. Turn off the lights in the classroom. Use tweezers to add a very small piece (no larger than one quarter of a very small pea—about 0.5 cm^3) of freshly cut sodium to the water in the dish. Quickly place the cover on the dish. The small piece of sodium metal dances rapidly over the surface of the water as sodium (the reducing agent) is oxidized from Na to Na^+ (Figure K).

$$Na(s) \longrightarrow Na^+(aq) + e^-$$

The electrons donated by sodium are used to reduce the hydrogen in water to molecular form, H_2:

$$2H_2O(l) + 2e^- \longrightarrow H_2(g) + 2OH^-(aq)$$

Phenolphthalein turns pink in basic conditions, and the pink trail that follows the chunk of sodium is due to hydroxide ions. Hydrogen produced in this reaction mixes with oxygen in the atmosphere to form a flammable and perhaps explosive mixture. The heat released in this exothermic reaction may be sufficient to ignite the hydrogen, causing a flame or small explosion. Do not be surprised if you hear a loud pop or bang!

$$2H_2(g) + O_2(g) \longrightarrow 2H_2O(l) + \text{ light} + \text{heat}$$

Part 3: Reaction between a strong oxidizer and strong reducer: *Teacher demonstration only. Perform in a fume hood. Wear face shield, lab coat, and gloves.* What happens when a strong oxidizing agent meets a strong reducing agent? Chlorine is a toxic gas and a strong oxidizing agent, while sodium is a reactive metal and a strong reducing agent. When sodium and chlorine react, table salt, the most common food additive known, is formed. Pour

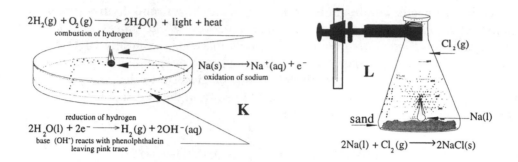

$$2H_2(g) + O_2(g) \longrightarrow 2H_2O(l) + light + heat$$
combustion of hydrogen

$$Na(s) \longrightarrow Na^+(aq) + e^-$$
oxidation of sodium

K

reduction of hydrogen
$$2H_2O(l) + 2e^- \longrightarrow H_2(g) + 2OH^-(aq)$$
base (OH⁻) reacts with phenolphthalein
leaving pink trace

$Cl_2(g)$

L

sand ———— Na(l)

$$2Na(l) + Cl_2(g) \longrightarrow 2NaCl(s)$$

enough sand in a 1-liter Florence or Erlenmeyer flask to cover the bottom to a depth of about 1.5 cm. Using long forceps, place a very small piece of freshly cut sodium (about 0.5 cm³) in a small depression in the center of the pile of sand. Fill the flask with chlorine gas (see materials section). Place a stopper in the flask and attach the flask to a ring stand as shown in Figure L. Remove the cork and use a dropper to add 3 drops of water, making certain the water contacts the sodium. Leave the flask unstoppered in the fume hood with the exhaust fan on. The sodium reacts with the water to produce hydrogen gas, which ignites and melts the remaining sodium. The molten sodium reacts vigorously with the chlorine gas to produce a bright yellow flame and white fumes of sodium chloride powder.

$$2Na(l) + Cl_2(g) \longrightarrow 2NaCl(s)$$

What is oxidized? What is reduced?

Part 4: Oxidation of zinc: *Teacher demonstration only: Perform in fume hood. Wear face shield, lab coat, and gloves. This demonstration involves a violent reaction that may splatter reactants and products. All students should remain at least 2 meters from the reaction.* Federal laws require identification of dangerous chemicals with labels such as: "explosive," "corrosive material," "flammable liquid," "flammable gas," "flammable solid," "poison," "radioactive material" or "oxidizer." Although most people understand the dangers associated with flammable, poisonous, corrosive, explosive or radioactive materials, many do not understand the dangers associated with oxidizers.

In common language, an oxidizer is defined as a substance that readily yields oxygen to stimulate combustion. Ammonium nitrate, a common lawn and garden fertilizer, is such a substance, and must therefore be transported and stored with caution. In the following activity, ammonium nitrate provides oxygen to oxidize zinc in a dramatic reaction that produces a brilliant flame and substantial smoke.

Mix 4 grams of ammonium chloride with 1 gram of ammonium nitrate in a crucible or evaporating dish. Cover the surface with a thin layer of powdered zinc. Using a pipet, add a couple of drops of water to the inner surface of the reaction vessel so that it will run down into the chemicals. When the water contacts the ammonium chloride, chloride ions are formed:

$$NH_4Cl(s) \xrightarrow{H_2O} NH_4^+(aq) + Cl^-(aq)$$

The chloride ions serve as a catalyst for the subsequent decomposition of ammonium nitrate:

$$NH_4NO_3(s) \xrightarrow{Cl^-} N_2O(g) + 2H_2O(aq)$$

The water produced stimulates the further decomposition of ammonium nitrate. The decomposition of ammonium nitrate is so exothermic that the reaction vessel heats up, creating an environment in which zinc is oxidized by the oxygen released from decomposing ammonium nitrate:

$$Zn(s) + NH_4NO_3(s) \longrightarrow N_2(g) + ZnO(s) + 2H_2O(g) + light + heat$$

In this reaction, is zinc oxidized or reduced? Is this an exothermic or endothermic reaction?

Part 5: Carbon dioxide as an oxidizing agent: *Teacher demonstration only! Wear face shield, lab coat, and insulating gloves. This demonstration involves a violent reaction that may splatter reactants and products. Protect the lab bench around the dry ice with ceramic tiles. All students should remain at least two meters from the reaction. No one should look directly at the magnesium flame because it is so bright that it may harm vision. Rather than lighting the magnesium with a torch, you may wish to use a magnesium ribbon as a fuse and seal the slabs before lighting. This is safer than using the propane torch, but does not always ignite the powdered magnesium.*

Carbon dioxide is used in some chemical fire extinguishers to stop oxidation reactions. Place a chunk of carbon dioxide in a beaker half-filled with tap water. The space above the water in the beaker will rapidly become filled with carbon dioxide gas. Pour the carbon dioxide gas (not the water) over a lighted flame and note how quickly the flame is extinguished (Figure M). Some may assume that carbon dioxide extinguishes flames because it is inert, but this is not the case. Although carbon dioxide extinguishes rapid oxidation reactions accompanying wood or paper fires, under special circumstances it may also serve as an oxidizing agent to promote combustion!

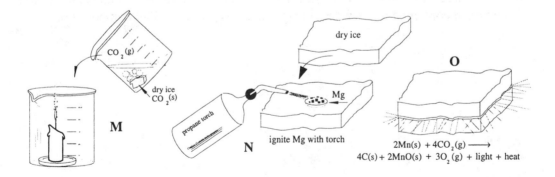

Using a heated deflagrating spoon or similar utensil, melt a crater in one slab of dry ice. Fill the hole with powdered magnesium. Heat the magnesium with a burner until it ignites (Figure N; *Do not look directly at the flames!*), then cover it quickly with another slab of dry ice, step back and darken the room (Figure O). The dry ice will begin to glow brightly, indicating that the reaction inside is not extinguished. Eventually sparks of hot magnesium oxide may spatter from the seam between the two slabs. In this reaction, magnesium reacts with carbon dioxide as follows:

$$2Mn(s) + 4CO_2(g) \longrightarrow 4C(s) + 2MnO(s) + 3O_2(g) + light + heat$$

Under normal circumstances carbon dioxide extinguishes flames, but the magnesium fire is so hot that carbon dioxide actually reacts with the hot magnesium! After the reaction has ceased and cooled, remove the top slab and extract the ball using tongs. What is the ball made of? What is the oxidizing agent in this reaction?

Questions

(1) What is the oxidizer in part 1?

(2) Trucks shipping materials such as potassium permanganate carry large yellow diamond-shaped signs reading "Oxidizer!" What is the danger associated with transporting an oxidizer such as potassium permanganate?

(3) Distinguish between the processes of oxidation and reduction.

(4) What two quantities must be conserved in redox reactions?

(5) Oxidation is accompanied by reduction. Explain.

(6) Write the full balanced equation for the reaction of sodium metal with water. Which element is reduced and which is oxidized? Explain the change in the color of the solution to pink.

(7) Compare and contrast the following two reactions: (a) A solution of HCl (a strong acid) is mixed with a solution of NaOH (a strong base) forming salt and water. On evaporation of the water, $NaCl(s)$ remains. (b) Sodium metal reacts with chlorine gas to form $NaCl(s)$. Are these reactions both oxidation-reduction reactions? Explain.

(8) Explain the connection among oxidation, oxidizing agent, reduction and reducing agent.

(9) In the reaction between zinc and ammonium nitrate (part 4), what is oxidized and what is reduced?

(10) After the reaction of carbon dioxide and zinc, a black solid mass remains in the well that once contained the powdered magnesium. What is this ball composed of?

3.3.4 BALANCING OXIDATION-REDUCTION REACTIONS

Concepts to Investigate: Oxidation, reduction, oxidation-reduction reactions, half-reactions, balancing equations, metallurgical reduction.

Materials: <u>Part 1</u>: Copper (II) oxide, carbon (charcoal powder), test tube, burner; <u>Part 2</u>: 0.1 *M* copper sulfate solution, powdered zinc; <u>Part 3</u>: 1.0 *M* silver nitrate solution, copper wire; <u>Part 4</u>: None.

Safety: Wear goggles and lab coat.

Principles and Procedures: The redox reactions in Part 1 and Part 2 may be balanced by inspection (appendix 2.4). In part 3 we introduce the half-reaction technique for balancing redox reactions, and in part 4 we introduce steps for balancing redox reactions in acidic or basic solutions.

Part 1: Obtaining metallic copper by reduction with carbon: Perhaps by accident, ancient peoples learned that if copper oxide ore is heated in the presence of charcoal (carbon), metallic copper is formed. Today, the process of heating metal oxide ores in the presence of coke (carbon) is one of the most important means of reducing oxidized copper to metallic form. Mix approximately 2 grams of copper (II) oxide powder together with 4 grams of powdered charcoal. Pour the mixture into a Pyrex® or Kimax® test tube. Heat the test tube gently at first, tapping the tube with a glass rod to free trapped gas from the mixture. Once all the gas has escaped, heat the test tube vigorously in the hottest part of the flame for at least five minutes. *Always point the mouth of a heated test tube away from people.* Remove the test tube and allow it to cool in the air before pouring out the powdered mixture. Notice that metallic copper (a reddish-brown deposit) remains on the surface of the test tube. By inspection, formulate a balanced reaction for the reduction of copper.

Part 2: Obtaining metallic copper by reduction with zinc: Fill a large test tube two-thirds full with 0.1 *M* copper sulfate solution, noting the blue color characteristic of the Cu^{2+} ion. Add approximately 3 grams of zinc powder to the test tube. Firmly stopper the test tube and shake it vigorously for about 20 seconds. Is there any sign of the formation of metallic copper (appearance of a red-brown or copper-colored precipitate) or of the loss of the copper (II) ion from solution (disappearance of the blue color)? By inspection, formulate a balanced reaction for the reduction of copper.

Part 3: Obtaining silver by reduction: Pour 5 mL of 1 *M* silver nitrate into a small test tube. Immerse a piece of copper wire in the silver nitrate solution. Use a magnifying lens or microscope to observe the beautiful silver crystals that form on the copper wire. (If performed as a teacher demonstration, this should be displayed using a videomicroscope). The skeleton equation (unbalanced equation showing reactants and products) for the reaction is:

$$Cu(s) + AgNO_3(aq) \rightarrow Cu(NO_3)_2(aq) + Ag(s)$$

To illustrate balancing of this simple equation using the half-reaction method, we separate each reaction into two half-reactions, showing electrons gained or lost in each:

$$Cu(s) \rightarrow Cu^{2+}(aq) + 2e^- \quad \text{(half-reaction in which copper is oxidized)}$$

$$Ag^+(aq) + 1e^- \rightarrow Ag(s) \quad \text{(half-reaction in which silver is reduced)}$$

Since electrons gained must equal electrons lost, we multiply the half-reaction involving silver by two.

$$2Ag^+(aq) + 2(1e^-) \rightarrow 2Ag(s)$$

$$Cu(s) \rightarrow Cu^{2+}(aq) + 2e^-$$

Adding these two half reactions we have:

$$Cu(s) + 2Ag^+(aq) + 2e^- \rightarrow Cu^{2+}(aq) + 2Ag(s) + 2e^-$$

The number of electrons on each side cancels, leaving the final balanced equation:

$$Cu(s) + 2Ag^+(aq) \rightarrow Cu^{2+}(aq) + 2Ag(s)$$

Part 4: Balancing redox reactions in acidic or basic solutions: Many redox reactions occur in acidic or basic solutions. These reactions are more difficult to balance because there are often several reactants and several products. We present in Table 4 a list of general steps to follow to help balance equations for such reactions.

Table 4: Steps for Balancing Redox Reactions in Acidic or Basic Solutions

For Acidic Solutions

(1) Write separate equations for the oxidation and reduction half-reactions.
(2) For each half-reaction, balance all atoms except hydrogen and oxygen.
(3) Balance oxygen using H_2O.
(4) Balance hydrogen using H^+.
(5) Balance the charge using electrons.
(6) If necessary, multiply one or both half-reactions by an integer to equalize the number of electrons transferred in the two half-reactions.
(7) Add the half-reactions and cancel identical species that occur on both sides. Reduce the coefficients to smallest integers.

For Basic Solutions

If the solution is basic, use steps 1 through 7 to balance the equation as if the reaction occurred in an acidic solution (containing H^+ ions), then add these steps:

(8) Note the number of H^+ ions in the equation.
(9) Add this number of OH^- ions to <u>both</u> sides of the equation (to eliminate H^+ ions by forming H_2O).
(10) Cancel any H_2O molecules that occur on both sides of the equation and reduce the equation to simplest terms.

Consider the oxidation of iodide ion (I^-) by permanganate ion (MnO_4^-) in basic solution to produce molecular iodine (I_2) and manganese oxide (MnO_2). The skeleton equation is: $I^- + MnO_4^- \rightarrow MnO_2 + I_2$. Table 5 shows how to apply the steps introduced in Table 4 to balance the equation.

Table 5: Balancing an Equation Using Half-Reactions (Sample)

Step	Equation
$1_{(red)}$	$MnO_4^- \rightarrow MnO_2$
$1_{(ox)}$	$I^- \rightarrow I_2$
$2_{(ox)}$	$2I^- \rightarrow I_2$
$3_{(red)}$	$MnO_4^- \rightarrow MnO_2 + 2H_2O$
$4_{(red)}$	$MnO_4^- + 4H^+ \rightarrow MnO_2 + 2H_2O$
$5_{(red)}$	$MnO_4^- + 4H^+ + 3e^- \rightarrow MnO_2 + 2H_2O$
$5_{(ox)}$	$2I^- \rightarrow I_2 + 2e^-$
$6_{(red)}$	$2(MnO_4^- + 4H^+ + 3e^- \rightarrow MnO_2 + 2H_2O)$
$6_{(ox)}$	$3(2I^- \rightarrow I_2 + 2e^-)$
7	$2MnO_4^- + 8H^+ + 6I^- + 6e^- \rightarrow 2MnO_2 + 4H_2O + 3I_2 + 6e^-$
7	$2MnO_4^- + 8H^+ + 6I^- \rightarrow 2MnO_2 + 4H_2O + 3I_2$
9	$2MnO_4^- + 8H^+ + 6I^- + 8OH^- \rightarrow 2MnO_2 + 4H_2O + 3I_2 + 8OH^-$
9	$2MnO_4^- + 6I^- + 8H_2O \rightarrow 2MnO_2 + 4H_2O + 3I_2 + 8OH^-$
10	$2MnO_4^- + 6I^- + 4H_2O \rightarrow 2MnO_2 + 3I_2 + 8OH^-$

Perform the activities described in part 1 of 3.3.1 to produce products with the various oxidation states of manganese. Balance these reactions using the half-reaction methods described in Table 4.

Questions

(1) Write a balanced reaction for the reduction of copper (II) oxide to copper in the presence of carbon as performed in part 1.

(2) Write a balanced reaction for the reduction of copper (II) sulfate to copper in the presence of zinc as performed in part 2.

(3) What is a half-reaction?

(4) Write the two half-reactions for the following reaction: $Ce^{4+}(aq) + Sn^{2+}(aq) \rightarrow Ce^{3+}(aq) + Sn^{4+}(aq)$. Which element is oxidized and which is reduced? Which is the oxidizing agent and which is the reducing agent?

(5) Use half-reactions to balance the following reaction in <u>acidic</u> solution as performed in part 4:

$$MnO_4^- + HSO_3^- \rightarrow Mn^{2+} + SO_4^{2-}$$

(6) Use half-reactions to balance the following reaction in <u>basic</u> solution as performed in part 4:

$$MnO_4^- + HSO_3^- \rightarrow MnO_4^{2-} + SO_4^{2-}$$

FOR THE TEACHER

Redox reactions and acid-base reactions are analogous in that they involve the transfer of charge. Acid-base reactions involve the transfer of protons while redox reactions involve the transfer of electrons. Acid-base reactions are easily recognizable, but some redox reactions are not. To be certain that a reaction is a redox reaction, compare the oxidation numbers of the reactants and products. If there is a change in oxidation numbers, it is a redox reaction. Combination, decomposition, single displacement and combustion are examples of oxidation-reduction reactions.

The oxidizing or reducing ability of a substance depends on the magnitude of its attraction for electrons. Elements with high electronegativities (high attraction for electrons) such as oxygen and chlorine are good oxidizing agents. Elements with low electronegativities such as hydrogen, sodium, magnesium, and aluminum are good reducing agents.

We use the term "skeleton equation" in this resource to indicate a chemical equation that is not balanced. Technically, the term "equation" should only be used to indicate a balanced equation because "equation" means balanced or equal.

3.3.1 OXIDATION STATES

Discussion: The experiment in part 1 with manganese clearly illustrates the influence that oxidation state may have on physical properties such as color. It is possible to produce colors in the manganese series by disproportionation, a special type of redox reaction in which an element in one oxidation state is simultaneously oxidized and reduced. One reactant in a disproportionation reaction always contains an element that can have at least three oxidation states. Since manganese is such an element, it can undergo disproportionation. (Chromium and vanadium are two other elements that have many oxidation states and show a variety of colors.) Oxidation and reduction can be shown to occur for MnO_4^{2-} simply by changing the pH of the solution. You can demonstrate disproportionation using the green MnO_4^{2-} solution from test tube 3. By slowly adding drops of 6 M HCl to a test tube half-filled with green MnO_4^{2-} solution, it is possible to observe the simultaneous formation of soluble purple MnO_4^- and the insoluble orange precipitate MnO_2:

$$3\overset{green}{\underset{+6}{Mn}}O_4^{2-} + 4H^+ \longrightarrow 2\overset{purple}{\underset{+7}{Mn}}O_4^- + \overset{orange}{\underset{+4}{M}}nO_2(s) + 2H_2O$$

The disks in part 3 should be photocopied onto an overhead transparency so the instructor may illustrate the technique to the class before they proceed with the exercise. Students should understand that although the sizes of the disks in this exercise are identical, the sizes of the atoms they represent are not. You may wish to have your students make a new set of discs whose radii are proportional to true ionic radii. The ionic radii for the elements illustrated in part A (expressed in angstroms) are: hydride 1.40, sulfide 1.84, sulfur (IV) 0.37, sulfur (VI) 0.12, peroxide 0.93, oxide 1.21, potassium 1.33, lithium 0.59, nitrogen (II) 0.15, nitrogen (V) 0.12, lithium 0.59, manganese (VII) 0.26, manganese (IV) 0.54, manganese (II) 0.65, nitride 1.48, calcium 1.97, and chloride 1.81.

Make certain students understand that oxidation numbers merely indicate the extent to which an element has been oxidized or reduced. For a free element, the oxidation number is zero. Since any compound can be considered as having been formed from the neutral elements, the sum of the oxidation numbers in any compound is zero. The numerical value of an oxidation number is obtained by assuming that all bonds between unlike atoms are ionic (electrovalent). For example, when determining the oxidation numbers of sulfur and oxygen in SO_2, we consider the sulfur to have an oxidation number of +4 and each oxygen to have an oxidation number of −2, which would be the case if the compound were formed by ionic bonds. The oxidation number of an element in an oxidized state is greater than it is in a reduced state. For example, the oxidation number of N in NO is +2, while the oxidation number of N in NO_2 is +4. The oxidation number of O in H_2O is −2 while the oxidation number of O in H_2O_2 is −1. Part 3 in this activity is designed to show students that elements may possess various oxidation numbers depending on the compounds of which they are a part. Student answers should resemble those in Table 6.

Table 6: Oxidation Numbers in Compounds

	H	*S*	*O*	*N*	*Mn*	*Ca*	*Cl*	*K*	*Li*
LiH	−1								+1
CaH_2	−1					+2			
H_2S	+1	−2							
H_2SO_3	+1	+4	−2						
H_2SO_4	+1	+6	−2						
H_2O	+1		−2						
H_2O_2	+1		−1						
NH_3	+1			+3					
HNO_3	+1		−2	+5					
NO			−2	+2					
NO_2			−2	+4					
Ca_3N_2				−3		+2			
Li_3N				−3					+1
$KMnO_4$			−2		+7			+1	
MnO_2			−2		+4				
$MnCl_2$					+2		−1		

Answers: (1) +7, +2, +6, +4, respectively. (2) Reduced. The initial color was purple, indicating the presence of the +7 manganese in the MnO_4^- ion. It was reduced to green, indicative of the +6 manganese in MnO_4^{2-}. Eventually, a further reduction can occur, indicated by the presence +4 manganese in brown MnO_2. (3) Natural sunlight is composed of a spectrum of colors which combine to form white light. The color of a liquid is determined by the light transmitted by that liquid. For example, a green liquid transmits green while absorbing all other colors. (4) In NH_3 the oxidation numbers are: N, −3; H +1. In NO_3^- the oxidation numbers are: N, +5, O, −2. In $K_2Cr_2O_7$ the oxidation numbers are: K, +1; Cr, +6; O, −2. In MnO_4^- the oxidation numbers are: Mn, +7; O, −2. In H_2O_2 the oxidation numbers are: H, +1; O, −1. (5) Student answers will differ. Make certain the charges on their creations sum to zero and that they check appropriate references such as the *Merck Index, CRC Handbook* *of Chemistry and Physics* or the Internet-based *NIST Chemistry Web Book*. (6) Oxidation numbers indicate that a bond is polar, but do not indicate the magnitude of the polarity.

3.3.2 OXIDATION AND REDUCTION

Discussion: Part 2 may be performed as a "magic trick." A teacher shakes a colorless flask until it turns blue, and then lets the flask stand still until the blue color disappears. This procedure can be repeated many times. If you choose to introduce this activity as a "magic trick," challenge your students to list the variables that may be responsible for the color change.

Answers: (1) Heat platinum oxide in an atmosphere of hydrogen. (2) Hydrogen is used to reduce the metal in ores. Oxygen is eliminated as water, leaving the metal in its elemental state. (3) Yes. You can repeat the oxidation and reduction of copper numerous times by heating it alternately in the presence of oxygen and hydrogen.

3.3.3 DRAMATIC OXIDATION REACTIONS

Discussion: Redox reactions require the actual or apparent transfer of electrons. Since not all reactions involve a movement of electrons, not all reactions are redox reactions. In ionic reactions, for example, no exchange of electrons takes place. When a solution of Na^+Cl^- is mixed with a solution of $Ag^+NO_3^-$, the Ag^+ ions combine with the Cl^- ions to form a precipitate of Ag^+Cl^-. Since there is no transfer of electrons in this reaction, but merely a movement of ions, it is not an oxidation-reduction reaction. By contrast, when sodium metal reacts with chlorine gas to form sodium chloride (table salt) there is a direct transfer of electrons from sodium to chlorine. This is clearly an oxidation-reduction reaction because an electron actually migrates from one atom to another. When hydrogen and chlorine gases react to form hydrogen chloride gas, electrons become shared in the resulting covalent H-Cl bond. Although there is only a sharing of electrons, and no direct transfer, this is also considered to be an oxidation-reduction reaction because the shared electrons are held more closely to the chlorine atom. Through their study of chemistry, students should realize that most chemical reactions are redox reactions. There are many, many chemical reactions occurring in the human body, and most of these are redox reactions.

Answers: (1) Potassium permanganate. (2) Oxidizers are very reactive and may cause spontaneous combustion when mixed with flammable materials such as gasoline. As a result of this danger, Haz-mat (hazardous materials) teams must be called to the scenes of accidents involving trucks carrying oxidizers. (3) Oxidation is the loss or apparent loss of electrons by a substance. Reduction is the gain or apparent gain of electrons by a substance. The substance that supplies the electrons is the reducing agent and the substance that gains the electrons is the oxidizing agent. Consequently, the substance that is oxidized is the reducing agent and the substance that is reduced is the oxidizing agent. (4) Atoms and charge must be conserved. There must be the same number of atoms and the same charge on each side of the equation. (5) Whenever one substance loses electrons, another substance must gain these electrons. Consequently, oxidation cannot occur without reduction. (6) Sodium metal reacts with water: $2Na(s) + 2H_2O(l) \rightarrow 2NaOH(aq) + H_2(g)$. Hydrogen is reduced (gains electrons) and sodium is oxidized (loses electrons). In the reaction, sodium hydroxide, a strong base, is formed. Phenolphthalein turns from colorless, in a neutral or acidic environment, to bright pink in a basic environment such as is formed here by the hydroxide ions. (7) The acid contains H^+ ions and Cl^- ions. The base contains Na^+ ions and OH^- ions. When mixed, the H^+ ions combine with the OH^- ions to form water. Na^+ ions and Cl^- ions remain in solution. When the liquid is evaporated, the Na^+ ions and Cl^- ions combine (associate) to form solid ionic salt. This is not an oxidation-reduction reaction, because there is no transfer of electrons from one substance to another. When sodium metal reacts with chlorine to form sodium chloride ($2Na(s) + Cl_2(g) \rightarrow 2NaCl$), there is an actual transfer of electrons (sodium loses electrons to chlorine). This is an oxidation-reduction reaction in which sodium is oxidized and chlorine is reduced. (8) In a reaction, the substance oxidized (the one losing electrons) is the reducing agent (it provides electrons to reduce the oxidizing agent) and the substance reduced (the one gaining electrons) is the oxidizing agent (it accepts electrons from the reducing agent). (9) Zinc is oxidized. Some of the nitrogen is oxidized, and some is reduced. (10) Carbon (graphite) and magnesium oxide. Like pencil lead (graphite) or charcoal, it leaves a gray-black trace on paper.

3.3.4 BALANCING OXIDATION-REDUCTION REACTIONS

Discussion: Although many redox reactions may be balanced by inspection (appendix 3.4), others, particularly those occurring involving numerous species in acidic or basic solutions, require an alternative method, such as the half-reaction technique or oxidation number technique (not explained here).

Answers: (1) $2CuO(s) + C(s) \rightarrow 2Cu(s) + CO_2(g)$ (2) $Cu^{2+}(aq) + SO_4^{2-}(aq) + Zn(s) \rightarrow Zn^{2+}(aq) + SO_4^{2-}(aq) + Cu(s)$. (3) A half-reaction is one of the two parts of an oxidation-reduction reaction. One half-reaction involves a loss of electrons or an increase in oxidation number (oxidation) and the other half-reaction involves a gain of electrons or a decrease in oxidation number (reduction). (4) $Sn^{2+}(aq) \rightarrow Sn^{4+}(aq) + 2e^-$. Tin is oxidized (loses electrons) and is therefore the reducing agent. $1e^- + Ce^{4+}(aq) \rightarrow Ce^{3+}(aq)$. Cerium is reduced (gains electrons) and is therefore the oxidizing agent. (5) The reaction is:

$$MnO_4^- + HSO_3^- \rightarrow Mn^{2+} + SO_4^{2-}$$

The skeleton half-reactions are:

$$MnO_4^- \rightarrow Mn^{2+} \quad \text{and} \quad HSO_3^- \rightarrow SO_4^{2-}$$

We add H_2O to balance oxygen and H^+ to balance hydrogen in the first half reaction:

$$MnO_4^- + 8H^+ \rightarrow Mn^{2+} + 4H_2O$$

We add electrons to balance charge:

$$MnO_4^- + 8H^+ + 5e^- \rightarrow Mn^{2+} + 4H_2O$$

In the second half-reaction, we add H_2O to balance oxygen and H^+ to balance hydrogen:

$$HSO_3^- + H_2O \rightarrow SO_4^{2-} + 3H^+$$

We add electrons to balance charge:

$$HSO_3^- + H_2O \rightarrow SO_4^{2-} + 3H^+ + 2e^-$$

We now multiply half-reactions by appropriate factors to equate the transfer of electrons:

$$2(MnO_4^- + 8H^+ + 5e^- \rightarrow Mn^{2+} + 4H_2O)$$
$$5(HSO_3^- + H_2O \rightarrow SO_4^{2-} + 3H^+ + 2e^-)$$

We now add half-reactions:

$$2MnO_4^- + 16H^+ + 5HSO_3^- + 5H_2O \rightarrow 2Mn^{2+} + 8H_2O + 5SO_4^{2-} + 15H^+$$

and cancel H_2O and H^+ ions that appear on each side to get the final balanced equation:

$$2MnO_4^- + H^+ + 5HSO_3^- \rightarrow 2Mn^{2+} + 3H_2O + 5SO_4^{2-}$$

(6) The reaction is:

$$MnO_4^- + HSO_3^- \rightarrow MnO_4^{2-} + SO_4^{2-}$$

The half-reactions are:

$$MnO_4^- \rightarrow MnO_4^{2-} \quad \text{and} \quad HSO_3^- \rightarrow SO_4^{2-}$$

Add electrons to equalize charge:

$$MnO_4^- + 1e^- \rightarrow MnO_4^{2-}$$
(balanced reduction half-reaction)

To the other half-reaction, add H_2O and H^+ to balance oxygen and hydrogen:

$$HSO_3^- + H_2O \rightarrow SO_4^{2-} + 3H^+$$

Add electrons to equalize charge:

$$HSO_3^- + H_2O \rightarrow SO_4^{2-} + 3H^+ + 2e^-$$
(balanced oxidation half-reaction)

Multiply the balanced reduction half-reaction by 2 to equate transfer of electrons to the balanced oxidation half-reaction:

$$2(MnO_4^- + 1e^- \rightarrow MnO_4^{2-})$$

Add half-reactions:

$$2MnO_4^- + HSO_3^- + H_2O \rightarrow 2MnO_4^{2-} + SO_4^{2-} + 3H^+$$

Since the reaction occurs in basic solution, we add $3OH^-$ ions to each side and combine the OH^- ions and H^+ ions to form 3 molecules of H_2O. Canceling H_2O that occurs on each side we have:

$$2MnO_4^- + HSO_3^- + 3OH^- \rightarrow 2MnO_4^{2-} + SO_4^{2-} + 2H_2O$$

Applications to Everyday Life

Photographic film: Black and white film contains a dispersion of silver bromide in a layer of emulsion. Light-activated silver bromide grains are more susceptible to chemical reduction by mild reducing agents (developers) than nonactivated grains. Hydroquinone, a common developer, reduces the Ag^+ ion in the excited silver bromide to metallic silver, and is itself oxidized to quinone. When the exposed emulsion is developed, black metallic silver forms where the film was struck by light. By shining light through this photographic "negative" (in a photographic negative, light regions appear as dark images, and dark regions appear as light images) onto another emulsion, a positive print (light regions appear light, and dark regions appear dark) is produced. In color film there are three emulsion layers, each of which is sensitive to one of the primary colors, red, green or blue.

Deriving metals from ores: Most metals do not occur in the free state in the Earth's crust and must be obtained from mineral ores. Metals in their combined forms always have positive oxidation states. Consequently, the production of a free metal is always a reduction process. In such processes, the combined metal in the ore gains electrons to form the free metal. If such reduction reactions did not exist, we would not have metals to build bridges, buildings, cars, trains, bikes or many other things we take for granted.

The least expensive and most frequently used reducing agent is carbon in the form of coke or charcoal. Metal ores such as FeO, ZnO, and Al_2O_3 are heated with carbon or carbon monoxide to yield pure metals:

$$ZnO(s) \; + \; C(s) \rightarrow Zn(l) \; + \; CO(g)$$

$$FeO(s) \; + \; CO(g) \rightarrow Fe(l) \; + \; CO_2(g)$$

$$2Al_2O_3(s) \; + \; 3C(s) \rightarrow 4Al(l) \; + \; 3CO_2(g)$$

Hydrogen is a good reducing agent and is used to retrieve many metals including tungsten, the metal of which light bulb filaments are made:

$$WO_3(g) \; + \; 3H_2(g) \rightarrow W(s) \; + \; 3H_2O(g)$$

Fire refining: Iron, copper and lead ores are fire-refined by selective oxidation to remove impurities. Oxygen is added to impure liquid metals to oxidize the impurities. The impurities may then be removed as an oxide slag or a volatile oxide gas as shown in the reaction below:

$$Cu_2S(l) \; + \; O_2(g) \rightarrow 2Cu(l) \; + \; SO_2(g)$$

Corrosion: It requires substantial energy to reduce metal ore to pure metal. The reverse process, corrosion, happens spontaneously as metals return to their oxidized state. The rusting of iron, the tarnishing of silver, and the formation of patina on copper and brass are some common examples of corrosion. Only the very unreactive metals, such as gold and platinum, do not corrode.

Rusting: Rusting is the greatest corrosion problem because it occurs rapidly and because so many objects are made of iron and steel. A great deal of the annual production of iron goes simply to replace that lost by rusting. Iron will not rust in dry air or in water that is completely free of air. Oxygen gas and water must be present for iron to rust. Rust has the general formula $Fe_2O_3 \cdot nH_2O$, where n indicates that the water content may vary. Inspection of a rusted tool will often show that in one location a buildup of rust has occurred, while in another location, possibly covered by dirt or otherwise shielded from the atmosphere, pitting of the iron has occurred. This suggests two concurrent reactions in the rusting process. An anode (oxidation electrode) is established at a site on the tool covered by water. Here iron is oxidized, causing pits to form according to the half-reaction:

$$Fe(s) \rightarrow Fe^{2+}(aq) + 2e^-$$

Where the iron is exposed to the atmosphere (oxygen), a cathode reaction occurs in which the electrons given up by iron reduce atmospheric oxygen to hydroxide:

$$O_2 + 2H_2O + 4e^- \rightarrow 4OH^-$$

Slightly soluble iron(II) hydroxide is formed: $Fe^{2+}(aq) + 2OH^-(aq) \rightarrow Fe(OH)_2(s)$. $Fe(OH)_2(s)$ is rapidly oxidized by oxygen to rust (we assume n is 1 here for clarity): $4Fe(OH)_2(s) + O_2(g) \rightarrow 2Fe_2O_3 \cdot H_2O(s) + 2H_2O(l)$. Corrosion is accelerated by salt water because this electrolyte solution improves electrical conduction. Thus, cars rust more rapidly near the beach or in cold climates where salt is used to de-ice the roads.

Corrosion resistance: A thin oxidized coating develops on the surface of many metals, protecting them from further oxidation. For example, a layer of aluminum oxide (Al_2O_3) forms on aluminum, a layer of silver sulfide (Ag_2S) on silver, and copper carbonate ($CuCO_3$, patina) on copper. Unlike iron oxides, aluminum, silver, and copper oxides adhere tightly to the metal and do not flake.

Protecting steel structures from oxidation: Many iron and steel objects such as ships, pipes, underground storage containers, and drilling platforms are subjected to strongly oxidizing environments. The rusting of iron can be prevented by galvanization (coating steel with zinc to seal it off from atmospheric oxygen) or by supplying a "sacrificial anode" made of zinc, magnesium or other reactive metal. Zinc or magnesium oxidizes faster than iron and supplies electrons to the iron to keep it in the reduced (metallic) state.

Fuels for transportation, heating and power: Combustion is an oxidation-reduction process. We depend on the combustion of wood, natural gas, oil, coal, gasoline and other fuels to heat our homes, cook our food, generate our electricity, and power our boats, cars, trains, buses and airplanes.

Rocket motors: Methylhydrazine ($N_2H_3(CH_3)$) is a powerful reducing agent and reacts upon contact with dinitrogen tetroxide (N_2O_4), a strong oxidizing agent:

$$5N_2O_4(g) + 4N_2H_3(CH_3)(g) \rightarrow 12H_2O(g) + 9N_2(g) + 4CO_2(g) + heat$$

This redox reaction is very exothermic and is used in rocket motors because it generates a large quantity of gaseous molecules, and consequently a tremendous thrust.

Biological protection mechanisms: The bombardier beetle is an insect that uses a violent redox reaction to defend itself from predators. The beetle stores two chemicals, hydrogen peroxide (H_2O_2) and hydroquinone ($C_6H_6O_2$), in an abdominal sac. The sac also contains an inhibitor which prevents these two chemicals from reacting and blowing the beetle to pieces. When approached by a predator, enzymes are released and a redox reaction occurs between the hydrogen peroxide and hydroquinone, generating sufficient heat to boil the liquid. The boiling mixture is expelled from the insect, warding off approaching predators.

Water treatment: Water may contain taste or odor substances, such as dissolved iron, manganese and volatile oils, which make it undesirable for consumption. These substances may be transformed to unobjectionable compounds by oxidation with atmospheric oxygen. For this reason, water companies aerate river and well water by running it through cascades, spray aerators or mechanical agitators.

Metabolism: History has shown that humans survive only a few minutes without oxygen. Oxygen is used in every cell of your body to oxidize sugars and other food molecules to produce ATP (adenosine triphosphate), a substance that can then be used to power a myriad of cellular functions.

Pottery: Under normal firing conditions, the iron in clay is oxidized to produce the reddish color commonly observed in Spanish tile roofs, red bricks or terra-cotta pots. If, however, clay is fired in a reducing atmosphere, the iron turns gray or black. By exposing clay to oxidizing and reducing environments, ancient potters achieved the beautiful red and black patterns seen in native American and classical Greek and Egyptian pottery.

Bleaches: Bleaches (hydrogen peroxide, chlorine gas, sodium hypochlorite) remove colored stains by oxidizing them to noncolored states.

3.4 ELECTROCHEMISTRY

Many are familiar with the fact that metal wires, notably copper, can be used to conduct electricity. Our homes, schools and businesses are wired with metal cables to conduct electricity for power and communication. Can pure water or aqueous solutions of salt or sugar conduct an electric current? Pour some distilled water into each of three beakers. Test for conductivity by placing copper wire electrodes, batteries, and a flashlight bulb or light-emitting diode in series as shown in Figure A. Note that the lamp will not light in distilled water (Figure A), nor in a sugar solution (Figure B), but will light in a salt solution (Figure C). It is clear from this activity that the salt water conducts electricity, but how is current conducted in the absence of wires? By carrying out the electrochemical investigations in this chapter, you will find out.

Electrochemistry is the study of the interchange of chemical and electric energy. There are primarily two processes in electrochemistry, both involving oxidation-reduction (redox) reactions. One process is the generation of an electric current from a chemical reaction, and the other is the use of an electric current to produce a chemical reaction. An example of the first is the production of a current from a battery to light a lamp. An example of the second is the use of an electric current to separate water into hydrogen and oxygen gas in the process known as electrolysis.

Under normal conditions a redox reaction occurs when an oxidizing agent contacts a reducing agent, such as when a strip of zinc is placed in a solution of copper sulfate. Zinc atoms lose electrons and enter solution while copper ions gain electrons and are deposited as metallic copper on the zinc strip. In such a redox reaction there is a direct transfer of electrons from one species to another. However, if the oxidizing agent (copper in this case) is physically separated from the reducing agent (zinc in this case) the transfer of electrons can be forced to take place through an external conducting medium such as copper wire, and the resulting electric current can be used to perform useful work.

Work *(W)* is defined as the product of the force *(F)* required to move an object and the distance *(d)* the object is moved *(W = Fd)*. Work is required when you lift a box from a lower step to a higher step since the box at the higher step is at a higher energy level (possesses more gravitational potential energy). The difference in potential energy between the box on the higher step and the box on the lower step can be referred to as the "potential difference." Analogously, work is needed to move electrons in a wire or to move ions through a solution to an electrode. An electric charge moves from a point of higher electric potential (higher "electric pressure") to a point of lower electric potential (lower "electric pressure") just as a box can fall off a higher step to a lower step. Electric potential difference determines the movement of charge just as air pressure determines the movement of weather fronts and water pressure determines the movement of water in the pipes in your home or city. Electric potential difference is the difference in electric potential between two points, and is measured in volts. To determine the electrical work expended in moving a charge through a conductor, you must multiply the charge by potential difference:

Electrical work (joules) = *charge* (coulombs) × *potential difference* (volts)

A joule (J) is the amount of energy required to move a coulomb (C) of electric charge through a potential difference of one volt (V): $J = CV$. In this chapter you will learn how to separate oxidation and reduction reactions in order to make cells and batteries that can be used to perform useful work such as the lighting of a lamp or the separation of compounds into their elements.

3.4.1 ELECTRODE POTENTIALS

Concepts to Investigate: Electrode potentials, oxidation-reduction, electrochemical cells (voltaic cells, galvanic cells), wet cells, batteries, electrolytes, electrodes, cathodes, anodes, reduction potential, voltage.

Materials: Lemon (or other citrus fruit), tomato (or apple, potato or pineapple), strips of magnesium, aluminum, zinc, iron, nickel, tin, and copper (see appendix 4.1 for inexpensive sources of various substances used in this resource), multimeter (an inexpensive analog multimeter will suffice, although a digital multimeter is more accurate because it draws less current).

Safety: Do not eat the food used in this or any other experiment. Discard the fruits after completion of the activity.

Principles and Procedures: In 1780, Italian anatomy professor Luigi Galvani was probing dissected frog legs when one of them spontaneously twitched. Needless to say, Galvani was quite surprised to see the leg of a frog move hours after the frog had died! Galvani was fascinated by this event and tried to create conditions in which it could be repeated. After careful study, he noted that the leg would contract whenever it simultaneously touched two different metals (such as an iron probe and a copper pan) that were themselves in contact with each other. In his study of anatomy, Galvani had inadvertently discovered the basics of an electrochemical (galvanic) cell, varieties of which we now use to provide electricity to start our cars, light our flashlights, run our watches, and power numerous portable electronic devices.

In oxidation-reduction reactions (see chapter 3.3) electrons are transferred from reducing agents to oxidizing agents as the reactants collide. The energy of the electrons exchanged in an oxidation-reduction reaction can be tapped to perform work if the oxidizing and reducing agents are physically separated, yet connected by a conducting material. Electrons released from the reducing agent travel through the conductor to reduce the oxidizing agent. As these electrons move through the conductor, their energy may be transformed into light in a flashlight filament, heat in an electric hand warmer, sound in the buzzer of a car alarm or motion in a frog's leg! Oxidation occurs at one end of the conductor called the anode, while reduction occurs at the other, known as the cathode. Since the reactions that take place at the electrodes are physically separated but interdependent, we can refer to them as half-reactions (see chapter 3.3), and the locations at which they occur as half-cells.

Suppose we make two deep slits several centimeters apart in a lemon and place a strip of zinc in one slit and a strip of copper in the other. The strip of zinc and the lemon solution in which it is immersed constitute one half-cell, while the strip of copper and the lemon solution in which it is immersed constitute the other half-cell. Membranes in the lemon keep the two half-cells separate, while the citric acid of the lemon allows for current to flow between the electrodes. If the two metal strips are connected with an external copper wire, electrons flow through the wire from zinc (the reducing agent) to copper (the oxidizing agent). The combination is an electrochemical cell (also known as a galvanic or voltaic cell), and the metal strips at which the transfer of electrons occur are called the electrodes. The zinc electrode at which oxidation occurs (electrons are lost) is called the anode, while the copper electrode at which reduction occurs (electrons are gained) is called the cathode. The potential difference of a galvanic cell (expressed in volts) is a measure of how readily electrons flow from one electrode to the other, and can be thought of as the force which pushes the electrons through the wire. Do different combinations of metals produce different voltages? Perform the following activities to find out!

Obtain similar sized strips of a variety of metals, such as copper, iron, magnesium, tin, lead, nickel, aluminum, magnesium, carbon, and zinc. If strips are not available, you may use wire or rods, but this introduces more variables. Appendix 4.1 indicates common sources for numerous materials used in this and other activities, but it should be realized that these may not be as pure as those acquired from a chemical supply house. Rub the metal strips with steel wool to remove oils and oxide coats. Make two slits in the lemon (any citrus fruit will suffice) a few centimeters apart (far enough apart so that the two strips of metal do not touch when inserted in the lemon). Place a piece of copper in one slit and a piece of iron in

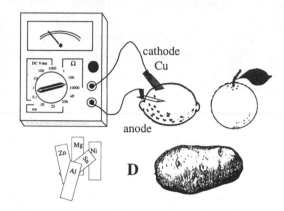

the other slit. Connect the leads of a voltmeter (multimeter) to both strips as shown in Figure D. Reverse the leads if necessary to obtain a positive voltage reading. Record the voltage in Table 1. Leave the copper strip in the lemon. Remove the iron strip and test the potential difference between copper and each of the following: magnesium, tin, nickel, aluminum, zinc. Use the voltages to rank the metals in terms of the ease with which electrons are lost to copper. The more easily electrons are transferred to copper, the higher the voltage of the galvanic cell. Repeat the procedure using tomatoes, oranges, potatoes or apples for the wet cell. Does the type of fruit used for the wet cell affect the ranking of potential differences? Do you think silver loses electrons more easily than copper? How could you find out?

Table 1: Voltages for Cells with Copper Cathodes

Anode ↓	Fruit		Anode ↓	Fruit	
iron	V	V	tin	V	V
zinc	V	V	nickel	V	V
magnesium	V	V	aluminum	V	V

Questions

(1) Rank the cell voltage of the anodes tested (iron, magnesium, tin, nickel, aluminum, zinc) when using copper as the cathode (reference electrode).

(2) Why was copper a good choice for the cathode in this activity?

(3) Compare the voltages of the following combinations of metals: magnesium-copper, zinc-copper, tin-copper. What might this suggest about the ability of magnesium, zinc and tin to give up electrons? Consult the table of standard reduction potentials (appendix 5.3; Table 2) to check your answer.

(4) Does the type of fruit affect the rank-order of electrode potential?

3.4.2 ENERGY TRANSFORMATION

Concepts to Investigate: Conservation of energy, energy transformation, oxidation-reduction, cathodes, anodes, electrochemical cells (voltaic cells, galvanic cells), potential difference.

Materials: Parts 1 and 2: Flashlight bulb or light-emitting diode (1.5-volt or less), patch cables with alligator clips, galvanometer or sensitive ammeter, 2 *M* hydrochloric acid, beakers; Part 1: Magnesium ribbon, bare copper wire; Part 2: Zinc strip, carbon rod (if necessary, you may bundle 5 soft mechanical pencil leads together).

Safety: Wear goggles, laboratory coat and gloves. Hydrochloric acid irritates all tissues, including the lungs. Work only in a well-ventilated area and avoid contact with the skin.

Principles and Procedures: The law of conservation of energy states that energy can be neither created nor destroyed, but only transformed from one form to another. In this activity you will observe the transformation of chemical energy from a simple voltaic cell, through electromagnetic energy in a copper wire, into heat and light.

Part 1: Lighting a light bulb with a copper/magnesium cell: *Put on goggles, lab coat and gloves.* Fill a small beaker two-thirds full of 2 *M* hydrochloric acid (see appendix 4.3). Create a coil of bare copper wire by wrapping a wire around a pencil. Remove the wire from the pencil and attach to a patch cable. Attach a second patch cable to a strip of magnesium ribbon. Connect the free ends of both patch cables to the terminals of a small flashlight bulb (1.5-volt or less), place the copper and magnesium electrodes on opposite sides of the beaker containing the acid, and watch the light bulb filament glow (Figure E)!

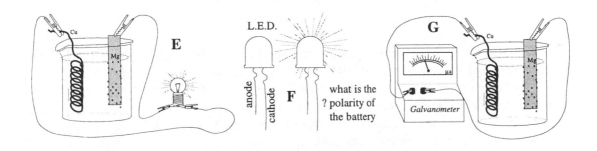

Replace the light bulb with a light-emitting diode (LED). LEDs are polar devices and will glow only if their leads are attached in the appropriate fashion. The longer lead of an LED serves as the cathode and the shorter as the anode (Figure F). Switch the leads to determine the polarity of the oxidation-reduction reaction occurring in the beaker. Measure the current using a galvanometer (Figure G), starting with the highest (least sensitive) setting and working down to the lowest (most sensitive) setting at which the meter still reads on scale. This strategy insures that you will not overload the meter and damage its circuitry. As electrons flow through the external wire from magnesium (the site of oxidation) to copper (a site of reduction), their energy is used to light the flashlight filament or the light-emitting diode.

Part 2: Lighting a light bulb with a series of carbon/zinc cells: *Wear goggles, lab coat and gloves.* Zinc (reduction potential of -0.76 volts) is a reactive metal, but not as reactive as magnesium (reduction potential of -2.37). Zinc is easily oxidized in acids:

$$Zn(s) \rightarrow Zn^{2+}(aq) + 2e^- \quad (E_0 = 0.76 \text{ V})$$

The electrons released from this oxidation process reduce hydrogen ions in the acid:

$$2H^+(aq) + 2e^- \rightarrow H_2(g)$$

The reaction rate of zinc with hydrochloric acid is limited by the rate at which zinc ions diffuse away from the zinc strip and hydrogen ions flow toward it. If we connect the zinc strip to a carbon rod by an external wire, then excess electrons will travel through the wire and reduce hydrogen on the surface of the carbon rod as well. Since the voltage generated by the zinc/carbon battery is less than that generated by the magnesium/copper battery, it is necessary to place two or more cells in series (Figure H) to provide sufficient voltage to light a flashlight lamp or LED.

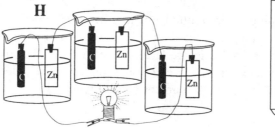
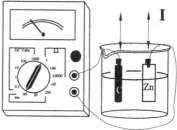

Note that the presence of the carbon electrode affects the formation of hydrogen at both the carbon and zinc electrodes. Although the voltage generated by a cell is a function of the difference in reduction potentials of the electrodes used, the current is a function of their surface area. Connect a galvanometer or ammeter in series with the cells and slowly lower the zinc electrode into the acid (Figure I). Plot the amperage as a function of the depth of the electrode. If the read-out is negative, reverse the leads of the meter. Interpret the findings of your graph.

Questions

(1) What forms of energy were used in this activity? Explain.

(2) What causes a battery to die? How could you design a zinc/carbon or magnesium/copper cell that would last longer than the one developed here?

(3) Why does the amperage of a cell increase as the electrode is lowered farther into the acid?

(4) Why does reversing the leads affect the direction the needle swings in an analog galvanometer or ammeter?

3.4.3 VOLTAIC CELL

Concepts to Investigate: Voltaic (galvanic, electrochemical) cell, salt bridge, half-reactions, half-cells, reduction potentials, cell potentials, oxidation-reduction.

Materials: Flexible plastic tube, 250-mL beakers or small jars, 1 *M* copper sulfate solution, 1 *M* zinc sulfate solution, clean zinc strip or rod, clean copper strip or rod, cotton ball, multimeter (voltmeter), steel wool (to polish zinc and copper).

Safety: Wear goggles, lab coat and gloves.

Principles and Procedures: If you place a strip of zinc in a solution of copper sulfate, an oxidation-reduction reaction occurs in which electrons are transferred directly from the zinc to the copper according to the equation:

$$Zn(s) + Cu^{2+}(aq) \rightarrow Zn^{2+}(aq) + Cu(s)$$

This electron transfer occurs because the zinc has less attraction (is less electronegative) than copper and tends to give up electrons more easily. Overall, two electrons are transferred from a zinc atom to a copper ion. The zinc atom becomes a zinc ion and the copper ion becomes copper metal. We can write the reaction as two half-reactions:

$Zn(s) \rightarrow Zn^{2+}(aq) + 2e^-$ Zinc loses electrons and is oxidized, and is therefore the reducing agent.

$Cu^{2+}(aq) + 2e^- \rightarrow Cu(s)$ Copper gains electrons and is reduced, and is therefore the oxidizing agent.

If these two half-reactions occur in the same vessel, no current is generated. If, however, these two half-reactions take place in two different vessels but are connected by a "salt bridge" and a conducting wire (see Figure J), electrons will flow, and their energy can be tapped to perform useful work. In the first half-reaction, a zinc metal atom loses two electrons and moves into solution as a Zn^{2+} ion. The two electrons flow through the zinc electrode and copper wire to the copper electrode in the other half-cell, causing the electrode to develop a negative charge which attracts the positively charged copper ions (opposite charges attract). A Cu^{2+} ion then gains two electrons and becomes a copper atom which plates on the copper electrode. A salt bridge permits the flow of charged ions between the two half-cells to occur, maintaining a balance of charge, and providing a current.

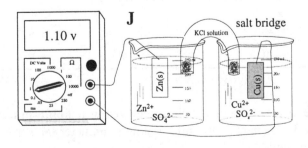

Part 1: Copper-zinc voltaic cell: Zinc and copper react in a single replacement reaction. Place a zinc strip in a 1 M solution of copper sulfate and note that after a couple of hours copper forms on the zinc strip, indicating that the following reaction has taken place:

$$Zn + CuSO_4 \rightarrow Cu + ZnSO_4$$

Zinc has been oxidized, and copper reduced. However, we cannot use the energy from this reaction unless we separate the oxidation half-reaction from the reduction half-reaction and tap the energy of the electrons as they flow through the wire from the anode in one half-cell to the cathode in the other.

Fill a beaker three-fifths full of a 1 M solution of zinc sulfate ($ZnSO_4$) and another three-fifths full of 1 M solution of copper sulfate ($CuSO_4$) solution. Clean strips of copper and zinc with steel wool. Place a clean zinc strip in the beaker containing the zinc sulfate solution and a clean copper strip in the beaker containing the copper sulfate solution. Using copper wires and alligator clips, attach a multimeter (voltmeter) to the zinc and copper strips. Note the reading of the voltmeter at the instant the last clip is attached, and observe it for a period of one minute after the connection is made.

Fill a plastic tube with a 1 M solution of potassium chloride so that there are no air bubbles. *While wearing gloves,* place a piece of cotton in each end of the tube. Avoid getting any chemicals on your hands. Place the tube in the beakers as shown in Figure J, making certain that no bubbles form in the tube. This tube will act as a "salt bridge" to connect the two half-cells. The salt bridge allows the flow of ions between half-cells but prevents a mixing of the copper sulfate and zinc sulfate solutions. Put the salt bridge in place, making certain not to get any of the copper sulfate solution or zinc sulfate solution on your hands. What is the voltage now?

The voltmeter connected across the Zn-Cu voltaic cell measures the cell potential, which should be approximately 1.1 V. What part of the cell potential comes from the zinc half-reaction and what part comes from the copper half-reaction? To determine this, we need a standard by which to measure the voltage of each half-reaction. It would be convenient to assign a potential to each half-reaction so we could obtain the cell potential simply be adding the half-cell potentials. Fortunately this has been accomplished using a standard hydrogen electrode which provides a measure of the tendency of one half-reaction to occur when compared to a hydrogen half-cell (Table 2).

Inspection of Table 2 indicates that the standard reduction potential for zinc is −0.76 V while the standard reduction potential for copper is +0.34 V. A positive reduction potential indicates that reduction occurs spontaneously, while a negative reduction potential indicates that oxidation occurs spontaneously, and the reaction should be written in reverse. Thus, to find the total cell potential, we add the oxidation of zinc (0.76 V) with the reduction of copper (+0.34 V) and obtain a cell potential of 1.10 V.

$Zn(s) \rightarrow Zn^{2+}(aq) + 2e^-$	+0.76 V
$Cu^{2+}(aq) + 2e^- \rightarrow Cu(s)$	+0.34 V
$Zn(s) + Cu^{2+}(aq) \rightarrow Zn^{2+}(aq) + Cu(s)$	+1.10 V

Part 2: Detecting the current from a voltaic cell using a home-made meter: Use the technique described in 3.4.4 (part 3) to build a simple ammeter, and use this to detect the current from your voltaic cell.

Table 2: Standard Reduction Potentials at 25°C
For all half-reactions the concentration is 1 *M* for dissolved
species and the pressure is 1 atm for gases.

Half-Reaction	$E°$ (V)
$Li^+(aq) + e^- \rightarrow Li(s)$	−3.05
$K^+(aq) + e^- \rightarrow K(s)$	−2.92
$Ba^{2+}(aq) + 2e^- \rightarrow Ba(s)$	−2.90
$Ca^{2+}(aq) + 2e^- \rightarrow Ca(s)$	−2.87
$Na^+(aq) + e^- \rightarrow Na(s)$	−2.71
$Mg^{2+}(aq) + 2e^- \rightarrow Mg(s)$	−2.37
$Al^{3+}(aq) + 3e^- \rightarrow Al(s)$	−1.66
$2H_2O(l) + 2e^- \rightarrow H_2(g) + 2OH^-(aq)$	−0.83
$Zn^{2+}(aq) + 2e^- \rightarrow Zn(s)$	−0.76
$Cr^{3+}(aq) + 3e^- \rightarrow Cr(s)$	−0.73
$Fe^{2+}(aq) + 2e^- \rightarrow Fe(s)$	−0.44
$Cd^{2+}(aq) + 2e^- \rightarrow Cd(s)$	−0.40
$Co^{2+}(aq) + 2e^- \rightarrow Co(s)$	−0.28
$Ni^{2+}(aq) + 2e^- \rightarrow Ni(s)$	−0.25
$Sn^{2+}(aq) + 2e^- \rightarrow Sn(s)$	−0.14
$Pb^{2+}(aq) + 2e^- \rightarrow Pb(s)$	−0.13
$\mathbf{2H^+(aq) + 2e^- \rightarrow H_2(g)}$	**0.00**
$Cu^{2+}(aq) + e^- \rightarrow Cu^+(aq)$	+0.16
$Cu^{2+}(aq) + 2e^- \rightarrow Cu(s)$	+0.34
$O_2(g) + 2H_2O(l) + 4e^- \rightarrow 4OH^-(aq)$	+0.40
$I_2(s) + 2e^- \rightarrow 2I^-(aq)$	+0.54
$O_2(g) + 2H^+(aq) + 2e^- \rightarrow H_2O_2(aq)$	+0.68
$Fe^{3+}(aq) + e^- \rightarrow Fe^{2+}(aq)$	+0.77
$Hg_2^{2+}(aq) + 2e^- \rightarrow 2Hg(l)$	+0.80
$Ag^+(aq) + e^- \rightarrow Ag(s)$	+0.80
$Hg^{2+}(aq) + 2e^- \rightarrow Hg(l)$	+0.85
$NO_3^-(aq) + 4H^+(aq) + 3e^- \rightarrow NO(g) + 2H_2O(l)$	+0.96
$Br_2(l) + 2e^- \rightarrow 2Br^-(aq)$	+1.07
$O_2(g) + 4H^+(aq) + 4e^- \rightarrow 2H_2O(l)$	+1.23
$Cl_2(g) + 2e^- \rightarrow 2Cl^-(aq)$	+1.36
$MnO_4^-(aq) + 8H^+(aq) + 5e^- \rightarrow Mn^{2+}(aq) + 4H_2O(l)$	+1.51
$Au^{3+}(aq) + 3e^- \rightarrow Au(s)$	+1.50
$H_2O_2(aq) + 2H^+(aq) + 2e^- \rightarrow 2H_2O(l)$	+1.78
$F_2(g) + 2e^- \rightarrow 2F^-(aq)$	+2.87

Questions

(1) Where do oxidation and reduction occur in Figure J? Which strip is the anode and which strip is the cathode?

(2) When a strip of zinc is placed in a solution of copper sulfate, atoms of zinc lose electrons and move into solution as Zn^{2+} ions, and copper ions gain the electrons to form copper atoms that adhere to the zinc strip. No work can be done with such a system. However, when a zinc strip is placed in a solution of zinc sulfate and a copper strip is placed in a solution of copper sulfate, and if the strips are connected by a copper wire with the half-cells connected by a salt bridge, work can be done by the electrons. Explain.

(3) What is the purpose of the salt bridge?

(4) If you place a strip of zinc metal in an aqueous solution of copper sulfate, copper plates out on the zinc strip. But if you place a strip of copper metal in a solution of zinc sulfate, zinc does not plate out on the copper strip. Explain.

(5) Calculate the voltage for the magnesium/copper cell (activity 3.4.2) using electrode potentials from Table 2:

$$Mg(s) + Cu^{2+}(aq) \rightarrow Mg^{2+}(aq) + Cu(s)$$

(6) Use the data in Table 2 to determine if the following oxidation-reduction reaction would occur spontaneously:

$$Sn(s) + Ni^{2+} \rightarrow Sn^{2+} + Ni(s)$$

3.4.4 BATTERIES

Concepts to Investigate: Batteries, oxidation-reduction, electrochemical cells (voltaic cells, galvanic cells), potential, parallel circuits, series circuits, instrumentation, current detection, magnetism.

Materials: Part 1: Lemons or other citrus fruit, copper and zinc sheeting or other pair of metals with very different reduction potentials (see Table 2), galvanometer, multimeter, steel wool; Part 2: Salt, compass, fine insulated copper wire, absorbent paper towel or filter paper, steel wool, and sheets of iron and copper, or U.S. copper pennies (pre-1982) and silver dimes, quarters or half-dollars (pre-1964).

Safety: Do not eat the food used in this or any other experiment. Discard the fruits after completion of the activity.

Principles and Procedures: In the early years of the automobile it was necessary to turn the crank of a magneto (an alternator with permanent magnets) to generate current necessary to start the automobile engine. In response to consumer demand for an easier system, the automotive industry introduced the lead-acid storage battery, a form of which is still in use today. In a car battery, lead serves as the anode, and lead oxide as the cathode. Both electrodes are immersed in a solution of sulfuric acid, which serves as the electrolyte. The balanced redox reaction is:

$$Pb(s) + PbO_2(s) + 2H^+(aq) + 2HSO_4^-(aq) \longrightarrow 2PbSO_4(s) + 2H_2O(l) \quad E^0_{cell} = 2V$$

Note that the potential of this reaction is merely 2 volts, too low to be of use in starting an automobile. To remedy this situation, developers placed six lead-acid cells in series to produce a 12-volt battery. A battery is a voltaic cell or series of cells. When cells are connected in series, a battery with higher voltage is produced. Can you create a battery from the fruit wet-cells developed in activity 3.4.1?

Part 1: Batteries; wet cells in series: Prepare three fruit wet-cells using copper as the cathode and zinc (or other reactive metal) as the anode (Figure D in 3.4.1). Place two cells in series by connecting the cathode of one to the anode of the next (Figure K). Record this voltage and then connect additional cells in series and record these voltages in Table 3. Is voltage additive when cells are added in series? With enough cells you should be able to produce a 12-volt battery, but don't expect it to start your car! Although your battery may have sufficient voltage, it does not generate sufficient amperage (current) to start a car, or much else for that matter. The current a battery generates is inversely related to the internal resistance (which for your cells is quite high). The resistance is reduced and the current in-

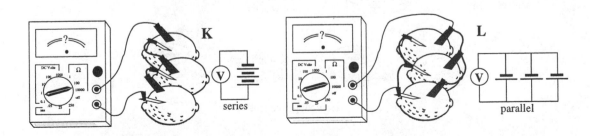

creased by improving the electrolyte solution and by increasing the surface area of the electrodes. The greater the surface area, the greater the capacity for oxidation and reduction, and the greater the number of electrons transferred. The electrodes in automobile batteries are made of layered grills, providing a large surface area on which oxidation and reduction may take place.

What is the advantage of placing batteries in parallel as shown in Figure L? Using a multimeter and galvanometer, measure the resistance and current across parallel and series cells as indicated in Table 3. What effect does arrangement have upon resistance and current?

Table 3: Series vs. Parallel Circuits

	Potential *Volts, V*	*Current* *Milliamps, mA*	*Resistance* *Ohms, Ω*
single cell			
2 cells in series			
3 cells in series			
2 cells in parallel			
3 cells in parallel			

Part 2: Voltaic pile: In 1800, Italian physicist Alessandro Volta introduced the world's first operational battery. Volta's battery consisted of a stack of alternating zinc and silver disks separated by layers of cloth soaked in a solution of either sodium hydroxide or brine. By combining zinc/silver cells in series, Volta produce a battery with appreciable voltage and power. It is possible to make a make a simple "voltaic pile" battery using any two metals with significantly different potentials. Construct a simple cell by inserting a piece of saltwater-soaked paper towel between sheets of polished copper (use steel wool to polish the copper, or a pre-1982 penny will suffice) and iron (an iron washer will work) as shown in Figures M, N and O. Measure the voltage using a multimeter. Now connect a second and third cell in series as shown in Figure P. Is the voltage additive?

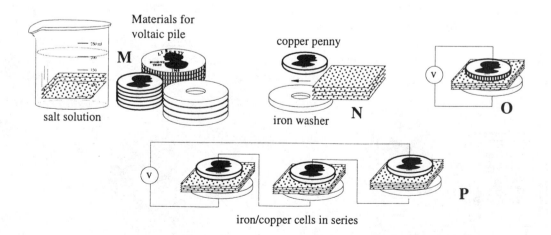

iron/copper cells in series

A battery is a set of cells connected in series. A 12-volt car battery is composed of six lead/lead oxide cells, each with a voltage of approximately 2 volts. On the basis of your voltage measurements, how many of your home-made copper/iron cells would you need to generate 12 volts? Try it! Although you may be able to generate high voltage with your copper/iron battery, you will notice that it has insufficient power to start a car or even a light a small light bulb. The voltage of a battery is determined by the chemical energy available when an electron is transferred from one electrode to the other, and thus is a function of the type of electrodes, not their size. However, the current from a cell or battery is a function of the resistance of the total circuit, including the battery itself. While the car battery has a very low internal resistance and is able to deliver a strong current, your simple battery has a very high internal resistance and is therefore unable to deliver as much current. The resistance of a cell can be decreased by increasing the surface area of the electrodes. Use large sheets of copper and iron or other metal and compare the amperage of batteries with these larger electrodes with those that have small electrodes.

When Volta constructed his battery (voltaic pile), he did so by stacking two different metals in series, each separated from the others by a felt pad soaked with an electrolyte. You can make a voltaic pile, and eliminate the need for patch cables, by stacking cells as shown in Figure Q. Make wads of filter paper or paper towel by folding them back and forth on each other four or five times. Soak the wads in salt solution, and then gently squeeze excess salt solution out of the wads before placing them between the alternating metals as shown. You can also make a voltaic pile out of coins (Figure R) by alternating copper (pre-1982 U.S. pen-

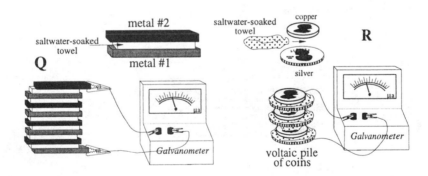

nies) and silver coins (pre-1964 U.S. dimes, quarters, or half-dollars). Whenever making a voltaic pile, make certain that the coins do not touch each other, that the towel wads do not touch, and that the electrolyte solution (saltwater) does not run between one wad and another. We do not recommend using iron washers because the towel wads may touch in the center of the washer.

The energy content of a voltaic cell is determined by the quantity of electrons that can be transferred from the anode to the cathode. When the electrodes have been consumed, the voltage of the cell falls to zero and will not recover. Since the current produced by your copper/zinc battery is small, it will maintain its potential for a significant amount of time.

Part 3: Detecting small currents: We have previously used meters to measure voltage and current. What are these meters actually measuring? Meters, such as an inexpensive analog multimeter, do not actually count (measure) the number of electrons moving through a wire, but rather measure the effect of these moving electrons. An electric current (moving electrons) in a wire generates (induces) a magnetic field around the wire. It is this magnetic field that is detected by a meter. The greater the movement of electrons through the wire, the greater the magnetic field generated and the greater the deflection of the meter. Hence the meter is measuring the current indirectly. Indirect measurements are very important and are often the only methods of measurement available (see chapter 1.3).

We can use a simple device that employs indirect measurement to determine if a copper-iron cell or battery produces an electric current. Wind approximately 50 turns of fine insulated copper wire around a compass, leaving a few centimeters of uninsulated wire on each end. Polish large sheets of copper and iron with steel wool. Place the copper sheet on the table, then place 5 or 6 paper towels that have been soaked in salt solution on the copper sheet and place the iron sheet on top so that it contacts only the saltwater-soaked paper. Do not allow the two metals to touch.

Position the compass on a table so the needle is parallel (aligned with) the coils of wire. Connect one end of the wire from the coil to the copper sheet and the other end to the iron sheet. Any deflection of the needle indicates that a magnetic field has been induced by a current in the wire. The magnitude of the needle deflection is related to the magnitude of the current. You can change the sensitivity of your meter by increasing or decreasing the number of coils. Is your meter more or less sensitive if you increase the number of coils? If you have difficulty observing the deflection of the compass needle using these two metals, try using a magnesium/copper cell such as is discussed in 3.4.2. You may also try making a voltaic pile using larger sheets of metal as shown in Figure S. If so, make certain that metal sheets do not touch each other, that the paper spacers do not touch, and that the electrolyte solution does not run between the paper spacers.

Questions

(1) Compare the voltages of the cells connected in series with those connected in parallel.

(2) Compare the resistance and current of the cells connected in series with those connected in parallel.

(3) When an automobile battery fails, it can be "jump-started" by another battery placed in parallel. Why?

(4) What voltage did you obtain for the copper/iron battery? In what direction did electrons flow in this battery?

(5) Explain how a compass is used to determine if an electric current exists.

3.4.5 ELECTROLYSIS

Concepts to Investigate: Electrolysis, cathodes, anodes, electrodes, oxidation, reduction, acids, bases, properties of hydrogen and oxygen.

Materials: Part 1: 6 or 12 V lantern battery, insulated copper wire, alligator clips, litmus paper or pH paper, small test tubes, sodium sulfate, soft pencil leads (or small strips of platinum or small carbon rods), dish about six inches in diameter and about two inches deep, wooden splints, matches; Part 2: Sulfuric acid, 12 V lantern battery or DC power supply, and a Hoffman electrolysis device (Figure U) or test tubes, copper wire and a beaker.

Principles and Procedures: In previous activities you observed the generation of electric current from spontaneous chemical reactions. The reverse process is also possible, using electric current to produce chemical change. In this activity you will decompose water into its constituent elements, hydrogen and oxygen, using an electric current:

$$2H_2O(l) \longrightarrow 2H_2(g) + O_2(g)$$

Part 1: Electrolysis of water: Fill a dish with distilled water (alternatively, you may use the Hoffman apparatus described in 3.2.2). Submerge two small test tubes in the container until they fill with water, invert and position as shown in Figure T so no water escapes. Using alligator clips, connect one end of a copper patch cable to the negative terminal (cathode) of a 6-volt lantern battery and the other end to a carbon rod (soft pencil lead will suffice). Connect a second wire to another carbon rod and the positive terminal (anode) of the battery. You may substitute copper wire for the electrodes if necessary. Immerse the electrodes on opposite sides of the container under the water-filled tubes as shown in Figure T and observe the areas surrounding them. Do you see any bubbles? Now place a few grams of sodium sulfate in the water and observe again as you slowly stir the solution with a glass rod. Do bubbles form more rapidly as the sodium sulfate dissolves? Sodium sulfate is an electrolyte, and when dissolved completes the circuit allowing current to flow. As water is broken down, hydrogen will collect in one tube, and oxygen in the other.

Test the gases collected in the tubes with a glowing splint. If oxygen is present, the glowing splint will burst into flames. If hydrogen is present, it will burn as it mixes with oxygen at the mouth of the tube. Can you identify the gases produced at each electrode? Which gas is found in greater abundance? Why?

Place a piece of litmus or wide-range pH paper in the solution adjacent to each electrode and note the color. At which electrodes are acids or bases formed?

Part 2: Electrolysis and pH: Electrolysis is an oxidation-reduction reaction. As oxidation of oxygen occurs at the anode, hydronium ions are formed, causing the surrounding solution to become acidic (see chapter 3.3).

$$6H_2O(l) \longrightarrow 4H_3O^+(aq) + O_2(g) + 4e^-$$

As reduction of hydrogen occurs at the cathode, hydroxide ions are formed, causing the surrounding solution to become basic:

$$2H_2O(l) + 2e^- \longrightarrow 2OH^-(aq) + H_2(g)$$

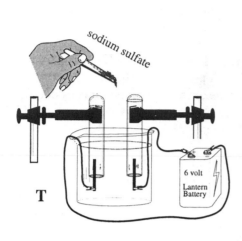

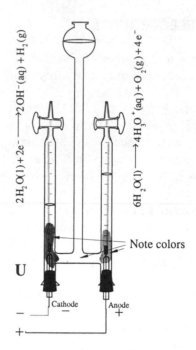

As the hydronium ions and the hydroxide ions diffuse they eventually reach each other and react to form water:

$$H_3O^+(aq) + OH^-(aq) \longrightarrow 2H_2O(l)$$

You can determine the acidic, basic and neutral colors of various indicators by mixing them in an electrolyte solution in which electrolysis is occuring. Add a couple of drops of bromthymol blue indicator to a 1 M solution of sodium sulfate (Na_2SO_4) and use this solution to fill a Hoffman (Figure U) or test-tube (Figure T) electrolysis apparatus. Note the color of the solution and then connect the apparatus to a 6- or 12-volt power supply. Allow electrolysis to continue for at least ten minutes or until you see definite color differences between the cathode and anode. Repeat the process using litmus, phenolphthalein, and other indicators of your choice and record your results in Table 4. Finally, test anthocyanin, the red/purple plant pigment found in such things as purple grapes, red cabbage and blue flowers. Chop up some red cabbage, place in a beaker and cover with water. Heat the mixture until the water turns dark purple. Turn the burner off and allow the beaker to cool to room temperature. Mix the purple extract 50:50 with 1 M sodium sulfate and fill your electrolysis device. Connect the battery until a definite color difference exists between the electrodes. What color is anthocyanin under acidic conditions? What color is it under basic conditions? Do you think pH can explain the color differences cabbage displays in different foods?

Table 4: Colors of Indicators as Determined by Electrolysis

Indicator	Acid Color	Neutral Color	Base Color
phenolphthalein			
bromthymol blue			
litmus			
anthocyanin			
other: _____			

Questions

(1) In electrolysis, the electrodes should be inert so they do not react with any chemical species. However, "pencil lead" was used for the electrodes and lead is not inert. Explain.

(2) What is the purpose of the sodium sulfate? Why was it selected rather than other common electrolytes such as sulfuric acid or sodium chloride?

(3) Identify the gases produced at the anode and cathode and give the half-reactions. Write the net reaction for the electrolysis of water.

(4) At which electrode is acid formed. Why? At which electrode is base formed. Why?

(5) For a given current, twice as much hydrogen as oxygen is produced. Explain.

3.4.6 ELECTROPLATING

Concepts to Investigate: Electroplating, oxidation, reduction, anodes, cathodes.

Materials: Parts 1 and 2: 6, 9 or 12 V lantern battery, beaker, patch cables, and steel knife, fork or spoon; Part 1: Copper sulfate, copper sheet; Part 2: Silver nitrate, silver sheet or pre-1964 U.S. dime or quarter.

Safety: Wear goggles, lab coat and gloves. Dispose of solutions appropriately (see appendix 3.3).

Principles and Procedures: Electroplated coatings are applied for decorative purposes and to improve resistance to corrosion and abrasion. For example, electroplating chrome on steel wheels or hub caps improves their appearance while preventing rusting. The following activities introduce the concept of electroplating, but do not produce the high quality results that are produced in industry.

Part 1: Electroplating a spoon with silver: To electroplate an object, you must connect the object to be plated to the negative terminal of a source of direct current, and another metal to the positive terminal, and then immerse both in a solution containing ions of the metal to be plated. For example, we may wish to plate silver on an object such as a steel spoon. The spoon is connected to the negative terminal of the battery and becomes the cathode, while a polished silver U.S. dime or quarter (pre-1964) or other silver object is connected to the positive terminal to serve as an anode, and both are placed in a solution of 1 M silver nitrate. Silver atoms in the anode lose electrons and move into solution as silver cations (Ag^+). These silver cations, as well as those from the electrolyte solution, gain electrons (are reduced) at the cathode and are deposited on the spoon as a thin metallic coat. The formation of silver ions at the anode replenishes those lost from the solution at the cathode. In effect, silver atoms are transferred from the silver anode to the steel cathode (spoon).

Part 2: Electroplating a spoon with copper: Fill a beaker with 1 M copper sulfate solution. Attach one end of a patch cable to the handle of a steel spoon and the other end to the negative terminal of a 6- or 12-volt lantern battery. Connect one end of a second patch cable to the positive terminal of the battery and the other end to a bare strip of clean, polished copper. Immerse the spoon and the copper strip on opposite sides of the beaker containing copper sulfate solution (Figure V). When do you first notice the deposition of copper on the spoon? How long does it take until the entire surface is coated with copper?

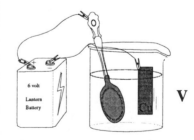

Questions

(1) What is the purpose of electroplating?

(2) An object can be plated by making it the cathode in a tank containing ions of the plating metal. Explain.

(3) How can you increase the thickness of an electroplated coat?

FOR THE TEACHER

3.4.1 ELECTRODE POTENTIALS

Discussion: The citrus-cell is a simple example of an electrochemical cell, but unfortunately, many students make the same mistake Galvani did, believing that the source of electricity is the fruit, rather than the difference in potentials of the two electrodes. The fruit is simply a source of electrolyte. By measuring the voltage of cells made with the same types of electrodes, but different fruits, students will see that the voltage is relatively independent of the electrolyte.

The potential difference (voltage) of an electrochemical cell is dependent upon the difference in affinity the two electrodes have for electrons. In the case of the zinc/copper cell, copper has a stronger affinity for electrons. Consequently, electrons flow from the zinc electrode through the wire to the copper electrode, creating current. The voltage of a cell can be predicted by adding the standard electrode potentials (Table 2):

$$Zn \rightarrow Zn^{++} + 2e^- + 0.76 \text{ V} \qquad\qquad E° = 0.76V$$

$$Cu^{++} + 2e^- \rightarrow Cu + 0.34 \text{ V} \qquad\qquad E° = 0.34V$$

$$\overline{Zn + Cu^{++} \rightarrow Zn^{++} + Cu + 1.10 \text{ V}} \qquad\qquad E° = 1.10V$$

It should be noted that many common substances you may select for electrodes are actually alloys, and thus will show different reduction potentials from those listed in the table. For example, U.S. "nickels" are made of an alloy of nickel and copper (see appendix 4.1).

Citrus fruits such as lemons and limes contain citric acid, a weak organic acid with the formula, $C_6H_8O_7$, which is responsible for the relatively sour taste of many fruits (acids activate the "sour" taste buds). Citric acid is present in almost all natural foods, including tomatoes. Citric acid is the electrolyte in a lemon which allows ions to migrate from one electrode to the other and, consequently, electrons to flow through the external circuit (wire). The citrate ions migrate to the positive electrode (anode) and hydrogen ions migrate to the negative electrode (cathode). Membranes in the lemon serve to partially separate the cathodes into compartments, but this separation is not complete and, consequently, the voltage developed for each pair of metals may be lower than that calculated from the Table of Standard Electrode Reduction Potentials (Table 2). However, qualitative results give the following ranking of highest to lowest voltage: Mg‖Cu, Al‖Cu, Zn‖Cu, Fe‖Cu, Ni‖Cu, Sn‖Cu. This series shows that magnesium is more readily oxidized than aluminum (aluminum loses electrons more easily than zinc), aluminum is more easily oxidized than zinc, etc.

Standard electrode potentials are expressed in terms of reduction reactions and are often referred to as standard reduction potentials. Make certain your students understand that, in older science textbooks, standard electrode potentials were often expressed as oxidation potentials. Hence, the + and − signs will be reversed in these tables for any given half-reaction.

Answers: (1) Mg > Al > Zn > Fe > Ni > Sn > Cu. (2) Since copper has the highest reduction potential (it is the most difficult to oxidize), all other electrodes in the series will be anodes and generate positive voltages, making comparisons between cells simple and direct. (3) The voltage of the magnesium-copper combination is highest, followed by zinc-copper and tin-copper. Magnesium gives up electrons more readily than zinc, and zinc gives up electrons more readily than copper. In Table 2, those elements above others have a greater tendency to give up electrons. You can see that magnesium is above zinc, and zinc is above copper. (4) No. The voltages of the metal combinations in the lemon and tomato were the same in rank-order.

3.4.2 ENERGY TRANSFORMATION

Discussion: In most voltaic cells, the oxidation and reduction processes are physically separated. This forces electrons to travel through an external wire where their energy can be tapped to perform useful work. In this activity, however, both the cathode and anode are immersed in the same solution with no intervening barrier. You may use the following information to explain to your students how this works.

Magnesium is a very reactive metal (reduction potential of −2.37 volts) and oxidizes readily in hydrochloric acid:

$$Mg(s) \rightarrow Mg^{2+}(aq) + 2e^-$$

The electrons released from this oxidation process are used not only to reduce hydrogen ions at the magnesium electrode, but at the copper cathode as well:

$$2H^+(aq) + 2e^- \rightarrow H_2(g)$$

The reaction rate of magnesium with hydrochloric acid is limited by the rates at which hydrogen ions diffuse toward the electrode, and magnesium ions flow away from it. By connecting to a copper cathode, you provide a second electrode at which the reduction of hydrogen may occur. The energy of electrons is tapped as they flow through the wire from the magnesium cathode/anode to the copper cathode. It should be noted that the copper electrode serves as a cathode while the magnesium electrode serves as both a cathode and anode. Encourage students to examine both electrodes and note the hydrogen bubbles forming at each.

Many books suggest activities similar to this one, but often students are frustrated to find that the light bulb does not light. This problem may be due to any of the following: (a) The copper wire looked bare, but actually wasn't. The reddish "bell wire" often used in such experiments is coated with an insulating shellac that must be scraped off with a knife or similar tool in order to provide a connection with the electrode. (b) The electrodes chosen were not very reactive. We selected magnesium in part 1 because it has a very large reduction potential and therefore provides the voltage necessary to light the bulb. (c) Sometimes people try to light bulbs that have too high of a voltage requirement. Select bulbs with as low a voltage requirement as possible. (d) The glow of the light bulb is faint, and it may be necessary to dim the lights in order to see it. (e) It may be necessary to connect two or three cells together in series to generate sufficient voltage to light the bulb used.

Answers: (1) Chemical potential energy was transformed to electrical energy which was transformed into heat and light in the light bulb filament. (2) A battery functions only as long as oxidation occurs at its anode and reduction at its cathode. A battery dies when the anode is fully oxidized. The life of a battery or cell can be extended by increasing the amount of material in its electrodes. (3) Amperage is a measure of the amount of charge moving through the circuit. As electrodes are lowered into solution, the surface area where oxidation and reduction occurs increases, thereby increasing the flow of electrons through the circuit. (4) Current traveling through a wire produces a magnetic field that deflects the needle of the meter in a given direction. When the leads are reversed, the current is in the opposite direction, creating a magnetic field with opposite polarity that causes the needle to move in the opposite direction.

3.4.3 VOLTAIC CELL

Discussion: The salt bridge is required to maintain charge balance. It allows the flow of ions but prevents the mixing of the different solutions. When a zinc atom gives up two electrons that flow through the external wire, ions carrying a total of two negative charges must move into the zinc half-cell to maintain charge balance. Likewise, when the two electrons from the zinc atom have moved through the external circuit to the copper electrode, ions carrying a total charge of +2 must move through the bridge to the copper half-cell to neutralize this charge.

Observant students may ask why it is necessary to separate the half-cells in the copper-zinc cell while it was not necessary to separate the magnesium and copper half-cells in activity 3.4.2. Review the discussion in the teachers' section of activity 3.4.2 to explain this phenomenon.

Answers: (1) Oxidation occurs at the zinc electrode (anode) while reduction occurs at the copper electrode (cathode). (2) When a strip of zinc is placed in a solution of copper sulfate there is no connection to channel electrons lost by the zinc to force them to do work on their way to the copper. When each electrode is in a separate half-cell, the zinc ion and copper ion solutions cannot mix and no direct transfer of electrons from zinc to copper is possible. However, when there is an external circuit, the electrons lost by the zinc atoms can flow through this circuit on their way to the copper strip and perform useful work during the trip. (3) The two half-cells must be connected internally to allow ions to flow between them while at the same time keeping the two solutions from mixing. Without a salt bridge, as zinc ions continue to be produced, the zinc ion solution would build up a positive charge (more zinc ions than sulfate ions) and as copper ions plated out as copper, the copper ion solution would build up a negative charge (more sulfate ions than copper ions). Consequently, the half-reactions would stop if there were not a salt bridge which allows the positive potassium ions to move into the copper ion solution and the negative chloride ions to move into the zinc ion solution to maintain charge balance. (4) Zinc has a greater tendency than copper to give up electrons. Consequently, when the zinc strip is placed in a solution of copper sulfate, zinc gives up electrons to copper ions which plate out on the zinc strip. However, when a copper strip is placed in a solution of zinc sulfate, zinc does not plate out on the copper strip because copper does not give up electrons to the zinc ions. (5) The half-reactions are:

$Mg(s) \rightarrow Mg^{2+}(aq) + 2e^-$	+2.37 V
$Cu^{2+}(aq) + 2e^- \rightarrow Cu(s)$	+0.34 V
$Mg(s) + Cu^{2+}(aq) \rightarrow Mg^{2+}(aq) + Cu(s)$	+2.71 V

(6) The half reactions are:

$Sn(s) \rightarrow Sn^{2+}(aq) + 2e^-$	+0.14 V
$Ni^{2+}(aq) + 2e^- \rightarrow Ni(s)$	−0.23 V
$Sn(s) + Ni^{2+} \rightarrow Sn^{2+} + Ni(s)$	−0.09 V

Since the cell potential is negative (−0.23 V + 0.14 V = −0.09 V), the reaction in this direction is nonspontaneous.

3.4.4 BATTERIES

Discussion: Make certain students understand the concept of indirect measurement by giving some examples. We can determine the thickness of a page in a book by measuring the thickness of the book (not including covers) and dividing by the number of pages. Likewise, we can determine the volume of a drop of water by counting the number of drops required to fill a graduated cylinder to the 1-mL mark and dividing by the number of drops. In this activity, students were able to rank the magnitudes of small currents produced by their copper-iron batteries because compass needle movement is directly related to the magnitude of the magnetic fields generated by these electric currents. Thus, needle movement is an indirect means of measuring current. Although it is simpler and more accurate to use a commercial meter, students gain a deeper understanding of the underlying principles when they design and/or build their own.

Answers: (1) Voltage is additive for cells connected in series, but is unaffected by cells added in parallel. (2) The cells connected in parallel have lower resistance, greater amperage, and thus a greater capacity for delivering power. (3) Batteries in parallel deliver more amperage, which is what is required to start the motor. (4) Approximately 0.78 volts. The electrons flowed from the iron to the copper.

$Fe(s) \rightarrow Fe^{2+}(aq) + 2e^-$	+0.44 V
$Cu^{2+}(aq) + 2e^- \rightarrow Cu(s)$	+0.34 V
$Fe(s) + Cu^{2+}(aq) \rightarrow Fe^{2+}(aq) + Cu(s)$	+0.78 V

(5) A magnetic compass needle aligns with the magnetic field created around a wire in which there is a current.

3.4.5 ELECTROLYSIS

Discussion: Given a spark, $H_2(g)$ and $O_2(g)$ will spontaneously combine to form water to produce $H_2O(l)$, plus heat and light energy. However, $H_2O(l)$ will not spontaneously decompose to form $H_2(g)$ and $O_2(g)$ because $H_2O(l)$ contains less energy and is therefore more stable than $H_2(g)$ and $O_2(g)$. However, the reverse process can be forced to occur by electrolysis. When inert electrodes such as platinum are immersed in pure water and connected to a battery, practically no reaction occurs because there are not enough ions in pure water to carry an electric current. However, if an acid or soluble salt is added, a reaction occurs immediately with the evolution of hydrogen gas at the cathode and oxygen gas at the anode. If the anode and cathode compartments are physically separated, the $H^+(aq)$ ions and $OH^-(aq)$ ions cannot come into contact to form water. Blue litmus will turn red in the anode compartment and red litmus will turn blue in the cathode compartment. If the solutions from the two compartments are mixed, neutralization will occur.

Electrode potentials are measured under standard conditions in which the half-reactions are at or close to equilibrium. It is important to remember that the potential of a cell depends on the concentrations of the species being oxidized and reduced. Temperature also has an effect. In electrolysis, half-reactions can be far from equilibrium, and a voltage larger than predicted from electrode potentials may be required. This additional voltage, called overvoltage, may be quite substantial, especially in the formation of a gas.

Answers: (1) The "lead" in a pencil is not lead metal. Rather pencil "lead" is made by powdering graphite and mixing it with clay. The hardness of a pencil depends upon the relative amount of clay used. Graphite is relatively inert, making it useful for electrodes. Graphite is a nonmetal but is a fairly good conductor of electricity and does not dissolve in common solvents. (2) Pure water contains so few ions as to conduct only a negligible amount of electricity. Addition of a soluble salt such as sodium sulfate or an acid such as sulfuric acid increases the number of ions and, hence, provides for a greater current. Sodium sulfate was selected because it is an inexpensive substance and does not change the pH (as sulfuric acid would) nor produce chlorine gas (as sodium chloride would). (3) Hydrogen gas is produced at the cathode and oxygen gas is produced at the anode. The half-reactions and net reactions are:

Anode	$2H_2O(l) \rightarrow O_2(g) + 4H^+ + 4e^-$	-1.23 V
Cathode	$4H_2O(l) + 4e^- \rightarrow 2H_2(g) + 4OH^-(aq)$	-0.83 V
Net	$2H_2O(l) \rightarrow 2H_2(g) + O_2(g)$	-2.06 V

The -2.06 V means that the reaction is not spontaneous and must be forced to occur using an external voltage greater than this. (4) Acid is formed at the anode as water is decomposed into oxygen gas and hydrogen ions (acid), turning blue litmus paper red. Base is formed at the cathode as water is decomposed into hydrogen gas and hydroxide ions (acid), turning red litmus paper blue. (5) Inspection of the net equation for the electrolysis of water shows that two molecules of hydrogen and one molecule of oxygen are formed from two molecules of water. Hence, the volume of hydrogen is twice that of oxygen.

3.4.6 ELECTROPLATING

Discussion: Electroplating is a process in which a thin layer of the corrosion-resistant metal is deposited on an object through the use of an electric current. Metals that readily corrode can be protected by plating them with other metals resistant to corrosion. For example, "tin" cans are actually made of steel with a thin coating of tin. Other examples include the protection of steel with a coating of zinc (galvanization) or the protection of steel car parts with a coating of chromium. Because they add beauty to an object, silver, chromium, and copper are frequently plated on items made of less expensive and stronger metals such as steel.

Some of your students may correctly surmise that there is a quantitative relationship between the amounts of substances released or plated at the electrodes during electrolysis and the total electric current. It was Michael Faraday who showed that the amounts of substances released or plated at the electrodes during electrolysis are related to the total charge that has flowed in the electric circuit. That is, the amount of chemical reaction occurring in an electrolytic cell depends on the number of electrons passing through the cell. Michael Faraday discovered that the weight of substance produced at an electrode is proportional to the amount of electricity transferred at the electrode and to the gram-equivalent weight of the substance. The faraday (F) is defined as the amount of electricity represented by one mole of electrons: 1 faraday is one mole of electrons. In electrical units, one faraday is equal to 96,500 coulombs of charge. One coulomb (C), the SI unit of electric charge, is the amount of charge that moves past any given point in a circuit when a current of 1 ampere is supplied for 1 second (s). In summary: 1 F = 96,500 C = 1 mole of electrons.

If you know the current and time of electrolysis (duration of current), you can calculate the amount of substance produced at an electrode. Conversely, if you know the amount of substance produced at an electrode and the time of electrolysis, you can determine the current, and if you know the amount of substance and the current, you can determine the time.

The amount of electricity required to electroplate a given quantity of metal is dependent upon the charge on the metal ion. The reduction of silver ion (Ag^+) to metallic silver requires the addition of one electron, whereas the reduction of copper ion (Cu^{2+}) to metallic copper requires the addition of two electrons. Consequently, one mole of electrons (1 F) is required to reduce one mole of Ag^+ to metallic silver, while two moles of electrons (2 F) are required to reduce 1 mole of Cu^{2+} ions to metallic copper.

Answers: (1) To protect metal objects from corrosion. (2) The positive ions of the plating metal migrate to the negative cathode where they give up electrons and plate out. (3) Keep it connected for a longer period.

Applications to Everyday Life

Common dry-cell (Leclanche) battery: The common "dry-cell" battery (i.e. 1.5-volt A, AA, AAA, C, and D batteries) is used in many everyday applications including flashlights, portable radios, toys, and tape players. The "dry-cell" battery is really not dry, but contains a moist paste of ammonium chloride. Inside is a zinc anode, and a graphite cathode. The voltage produced by a dry cell is approximately 1.5 V. Dry-cells cannot be recharged.

Alkaline battery: The alkaline battery is similar to the Leclanche battery but contains potassium hydroxide or sodium hydroxide. The alkaline battery lasts longer than the Leclanche battery because the zinc anode corrodes less rapidly in base than acid. In addition, an alkaline battery performs better under current drain and in cold weather.

Lead-acid storage battery: The lead-acid storage battery commonly found in automobiles can function for many years under a wide range of temperatures, is quite resilient to the vibrations accompanying road travel, and can be recharged by forcing current through it in the opposite direction.

Nickel-cadmium battery (nicad): The nickel-cadmium battery has enjoyed widespread use in recent years in calculators, portable power tools, shavers and electric toothbrushes because it has a long life and can be recharged an indefinite number of times. In addition, the battery can be manufactured as a sealed unit. Recharging is possible in nickel-cadmium batteries (as it is in lead storage batteries) because the products adhere to the electrodes. The anode is cadmium and the cathode is NiO_2. The reactions for the nickel-cadmium battery are:

Anode $\quad\quad\quad Cd + 2OH^-(aq) \rightarrow Cd(OH)_2 + 2e^-$

Cathode $\quad\quad NiO_2(s) + 2H_2O(l) + 2e^- \rightarrow Ni(OH)_2 + 2OH^-$

Lithium battery: The solid-state lithium battery is a rechargeable battery that consists of a lithium anode and a metal oxide cathode. Lithium batteries are characterized by high energy density and long life, and are often used to control computer clocks, pacemakers, and other devices in which battery decay or death can cause serious problems.

Environmental issues: Battery disposal is becoming a serious environmental problem because unrechargable batteries, such as the common dry-cell and alkaline battery, are being discarded in landfills. Disposal of nickel-cadmium and lead-acid batteries raises additional concern because of the toxicity of nickel, cadmium, and lead. When these batteries are placed in landfills, toxic substances may contaminate ground water. For these reasons, rechargeable batteries, such as the lithium battery, may be destined to become the batteries of the future.

Electric vehicles: Electric vehicles are believed by many to offer the best hope for cleaner air in the near future. In 1900, 38 percent of new American automobiles ran on batteries, but gasoline won the race because batteries could not store and release sufficient energy to power an automobile for long periods, and because they required recharging which put the automobile out of use for a significant length of time. Environmental concerns have renewed interest in electric-powered vehicles, and the development of new effective and efficient batteries such as the zinc-air battery will undoubtedly foster competition in the development of electric-powered automobiles. It is incorrect, however, to state that electric vehicles will be "pollution-free." The vehicle itself may not directly pollute, but the fossil-fuel power plant from which the electric vehicle will be charged via electric power lines will definitely add more pollution to the environment surrounding the power plant. In essence, pollution is transferred from the vehicle to the power plant!

Element production by electrolysis: Many elements of commercial importance, such as sodium, chlorine, and aluminum, are produced by electrolysis. For example, sodium metal and chlorine gas are produced by the electrolysis of molten sodium chloride. Aluminum, the most abundant metal in the Earth's crust, is purified by electrolysis, and today, nearly 5% of all the electricity used in the United States is consumed in the production of this metal! Therefore, when you recycle an aluminum can, you are conserving energy as well as aluminum.

Purification of metals by electrolysis: Many metals are purified by electrolysis. Impure copper sheets produced by the reduction of copper ore serve as the anode, and ultrapure copper sheets serve as the cathode. These sheets are immersed in an aqueous solution of copper sulfate. During electrolysis, copper ions leave the impure anode and plate out on the ultrapure cathode, creating a mass of copper of sufficient purity for demanding "high-tech" applications.

Painful fillings: Dentists often fill cavities with gold or silver. A simple wet cell is created when a steel spoon contacts the filling. The spoon acts as one electrode, the filling as the other electrode, and the saliva as the electrolyte solution. The minor current may cause pain by stimulating nerves in the tooth.

3.5 POLYMERS

On his second voyage to the New World in 1493–1496, Christopher Columbus saw natives playing a game with balls made from the gum of a *Hevea* tree. Archaeologists suggest the use of such balls was common in the cultures of the Caribbean and Central and Southern America long before the arrival of European explorers. The native Americans gathered the milky exudate from cuts they made in a variety of trees. As it dried they fashioned it into balls, footwear and even bottles. In 1736 French explorers collected some of the condensed juice of the *Hevea* tree and sent it to Europe where it was analyzed by Joseph Priestly and other scientists. Priestly noted that the gum could "rub" pencil marks off paper, and thus the term "rubber" was coined. Although most 18th century scientists initially thought that rubber was just an interesting curiosity, its many valuable properties were later discovered, and inventors eventually incorporated it in a wide variety of materials including tires, waterproofing and sporting goods.

Rubber is one of many naturally occurring polymers—high molecular weight compounds consisting of up to millions of repeated low molecular weight units. The term "polymer" is derived from the Greek words "polys" meaning many and "meros" meaning parts, a term that aptly describes the structural nature of these substances. The most abundant organic molecules in the world are polymers. Cellulose and lignin (the main fibers in wood), starch (a natural storage form of sugar in plants), chitin (a key fiber in the cell walls of algae, fungi and arthropods), collagen (the fiber that holds soft tissues together in our bodies), DNA, RNA and proteins (key biological informational and structural molecules), and even cotton, wool, silk and flax (natural fibers used in clothing) are all polymeric.

Many polymers like starch, cellulose and chitin are homopolymers, chains consisting of only one repeating sub-unit, or monomer (Figure A illustrates the beginning of the starch polymer.) Others, like DNA and protein, are known as copolymers because they contain two or more different monomers. Copolymers are described as "random," "block" or "alternating" depending on the arrangement of their constituent monomers. You can visualize these by putting differently colored pop-beads, gum drops or other substances together in chains like those shown in Figure B.

In 1856 Andrew Parkes combined cellulose nitrate and camphor to invent the first man-made plastic (a plastic is a moldable high molecular weight organic polymer) known as celluloid. A variety of uses for celluloid were soon found, including billiard balls, piano keys, and photographic and motion picture film stock. Although the development of new plastics was initially very slow (it took more than fifty years for the development of the next synthetic polymer), the pace accelerated during the first half of the twentieth century as the German chemist Herman Staudinger (subsequently a Nobel prize winner in chemistry) and others provided a theoretical understanding of polymer chemistry. Armed with this new knowledge,

Starch: a homopolymer made of
alpha-D-glucopyranose monomers

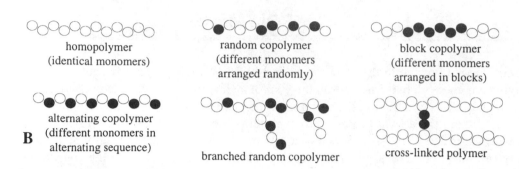

B

homopolymer
(identical monomers)

random copolymer
(different monomers
arranged randomly)

block copolymer
(different monomers
arranged in blocks)

alternating copolymer
(different monomers in
alternating sequence)

branched random copolymer

cross-linked polymer

chemists were able to develop a wide variety of useful polymers that have found their way into virtually every aspect of life.

Some polymers are linear, while others are branched or cross-linked (Figure B). Cellophane tape is an example of a product made of linear polymers, most of which lie parallel to each other the way strands of spaghetti lie in a pack. Just as it is easier to separate the pieces of spaghetti (between noodles) into two bunches than it is to break them into shorter pieces (across noodles), so it is easier to tear cellophane tape lengthwise (between chains) than crosswise (across chains).

Although there is no theoretical limit to the length of a polymer chain, most are composed of 1000 to 10,000 monomers and have molecular weights that vary from approximately 15,000 to 500,000 grams/mole. Most linear polymers such as polyethylene can be repeatedly softened or melted by heating and are known as thermoplastics.

Many polymers have branches or are cross-linked (Figure B). The strength and rigidity of a polymer generally increases with the number of cross-links. If all of the polymers in a substance are connected by cross-links, then that substance can be considered to be a single molecule. A bowling ball or a tire is essentially one molecule because all of the polymer chains are cross-linked with each other. Most extensively cross-linked polymers do not soften when heated because the polymer strands are not free to move. Such polymers are known as thermosets.

Polymers are made by step reactions and chain reactions. Figure A shows the formation of a starch molecule by a step reaction known as condensation because water is released each time a monomer binds. Wool, silk, cellulose, nylon, Dacron® and Kevlar® are formed by condensation reactions. Chain, or addition reactions, involve the opening of double (or triple) bonds by the action of an initiator. The most common type of initiator is a free radical which contains an unbonded electron such as occurs in a split-peroxide (indicated as R* in our equations). A free radical is a highly reactive species that contains an unpaired electron. Free radicals bind to a carbon in a double bond (or triple bond), breaking the extra bond and leaving an unpaired electron (active site) at the adjoining carbon. The process is repeated as this new unpaired electron breaks a double bond and creates another active site in yet another monomer. Monomers only react with the active site and not with other monomers. Figure C

$$R^* + CH_2{=}CH_2 \longrightarrow R{-}CH_2{-}CH_2^*$$
initiator ethylene

C

$$R{-}CH_2{-}CH_2^* + CH_2{=}CH_2 \longrightarrow R{-}CH_2{-}CH_2{-}CH_2{-}CH_2^*$$
beginning of polyethylene chain

shows how polyethylene is made by a chain (addition) reaction. The chain reaction is terminated when another free radical reacts with the growing end of the chain to cap its growth.

Polymers are now an integral part of life in industrialized countries, and are widely used as adhesives, coatings, textiles, packagings, foams, elastomers, optic elements, electronic components, structural composites, engineering plastics and in many other applications. In this chapter you will investigate this extremely important class of chemicals.

3.5.1 POLYMERIZATION

Concepts to Investigate: Polymers, monomers, polymerization, elastomers, allotropes.

Materials: Part 1: Sodium silicate (water glass; avoid contact with skin), 95% ethyl alcohol (flammable: extinguish all flames), small paper cups, popsicle sticks or stirring rods, paper towels; Part 2: Sulfur, beaker, test tube, test tube clamp, ring stand.

Safety: Wear goggles, lab coat and gloves. Part 2 must be performed as a teacher demonstration only.

Principles and Procedures: The Mayans of Central America were one of the first to use natural latex polymers from the rubber tree to produce elastic, bouncing balls. Archaeologists believe that the neighboring Aztecs used rubber balls in ceremonial games. In this activity, you, like the ancient Mayans and Aztecs, will make a rubbery ball, but rather than making it from organic latex, you will make it from the inorganic liquid sodium silicate.

Part 1: Silicone rubber: *Put on a pair of disposable gloves.* Place 20 mL of sodium silicate solution in one paper cup. Slowly add 5 mL of 95% ethyl alcohol while stirring with a wooden stick. Continue stirring with a circular motion until the material polymerizes. Moisten your gloves with water and roll the polymerized material into a ball. Gently squeeze excess alcohol from the ball and wet it occasionally until its surface glistens. Sometimes the silicone tends to dry out and crumble. If this occurs, moisten your gloves and try to reform the ball as before. The product of this reaction is a silicone polymer (Figure D). The group in brackets in Figure D is the monomer that is repeated numerous times to produce a long chain. The "R"s represent ethyl groups ($CH_3CH_2^-$) contributed by ethyl alcohol. Try bouncing the ball. How high will it bounce when dropped from 1.0 or 0.5 meters? Calculate the rebound ratio by dividing the height of the rebound by the height from which it is dropped (Figure E). Compare the rebound ratios of this ball at a given height with those formed by others in the class. Is there any similarity between those that exhibit the highest rebound ratios?

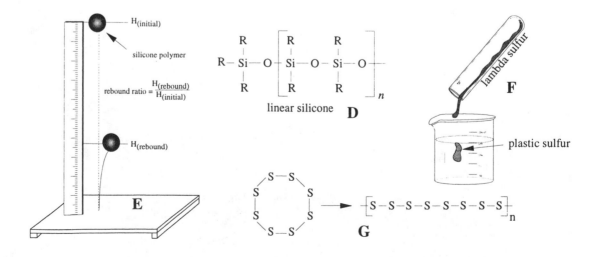

Elastomers ("elastic polymers") are rubbery polymers. They are composed of long chains that recover their shape after being stretched or deformed. Is the silicone material that you made an elastomer?

Part 2: Polymeric sulfur: *Note: Teacher demonstration only!* An allotrope is a different form of the same element. Sulfur has four allotropes: The normal, yellow sulfur that is found in large deposits in the Earth is known as rhombic sulfur. When heated, rhombic sulfur melts to form liquid lambda sulfur. If lambda sulfur is allowed to cool slowly it crystallizes into monoclinic sulfur, but if it is cooled rapidly it forms polymeric (plastic) sulfur.

Fill a beaker about three-fourths full of water and place in a fume hood. Fill a test tube two-thirds full with sulfur. Support this test tube with a metal clamp, place in a fume hood, and heat the sulfur gently until it melts. *Avoid igniting the sulfur vapors that emanate from the mouth of the tube.* Continue heating and notice that the color of the sulfur changes from yellow through orange, red and brown to black. After the sulfur boils, pour it in a narrow stream into the center of the cold water (Figure F). A brown strand of plastic polymerized sulfur will form. Once it is cooled, remove the sulfur with tongs and examine its properties. What properties suggest that this form of sulfur is polymeric? Allow the polymeric sulfur to stand for a week or more. Does it appear to be as flexible as it was initially? At room temperature the only stable form of sulfur is rhombic, and so the plastic polymeric sulfur will eventually revert to the rhombic form. As the S-S bonds in the chain are broken, the monomer units S_8 re-form.

Questions

(1) What was the rebound ratio of the silicone ball that you made?

(2) What characteristics are shared by those balls demonstrating the highest rebound ratios?

(3) Most commercial polymers are carbon-based. What similar properties do carbon and silicon share that may contribute to their abilities to polymerize?

(4) Plastics are made of organic (carbon-based) polymers. What similar properties does the silicone polymer in part 1 share with plastics?

(5) Perform some library research to identify practical applications of silicone polymers.

(6) Is polymeric sulfur a stable form of sulfur at room temperature? Explain, based on your observations from part 2.

(7) What is the monomer unit in the sulfur polymeric chain in Figure G?

3.5.2 CROSS-LINKING POLYMERS

Concepts to Investigate: Cross-linking, polymers, cross-linking agents, viscosity, elastomers, thermoplastic polymers, thermoset polymers.

Materials: <u>Part 1</u>: Polyvinyl alcohol; sodium borate decahydrate (e.g. Twenty Mule Team Borax® Laundry Booster), Styrofoam cups, wooden stirring stick, plastic sandwich bags; <u>Part 2</u>: Substitute white glue for polyvinyl chloride.

Safety: Wear goggles, lab coat and gloves.

Principles and Procedures: In 1839, American chemist Charles Goodyear discovered that rubber could be made much stronger by heating it in the presence of sulfur. Figure H shows how sulfur can cross-link hydrocarbon polymer chains to form a stronger interlocking mass.

Goodyear recognized the potential industrial applications of his "vulcanization" process and applied for numerous patents. Although Goodyear's discovery was indeed revolutionary, he was unable to make money on the process and died in substantial debt. By the end of the 19th century technological and economic conditions improved, and the need for vulcanized rubber increased with the growing popularity of the bicycle. An Ohio entrepreneur by the name of Frank Seiberling borrowed a few thousand dollars to develop a plant to make bicycle tires made of vulcanized rubber. Seiberling named his company in honor of the man who discovered the vulcanization process. The booming bicycle industry created huge sales and catapulted the Seiberling's Goodyear Tire and Rubber Company into international prominence. The rapid growth of the automotive industry in the twentieth century fostered Goodyear's sales, and by 1996 sales exceeded thirteen billion dollars a year! Polymer-cross-linking has proved to be a very lucrative business.

In the following activities, you will be investigating the influence that cross-linking has on the nature of two polymers. Can you think of any possible practical applications for these cross-linked polymers?

Copyright © 1999 by John Wiley & Sons, Inc.

H
Cross-linking of polymers by sulfur

Cross-linked polymer

polyvinyl alcohol

I

$$\text{H}-\underset{\underset{\text{OH}}{|}}{\overset{\overset{\text{H}}{|}}{\text{C}}}-\underset{\underset{\text{H}}{|}}{\overset{\overset{\text{H}}{|}}{\text{C}}}-\underset{\underset{\text{OH}}{|}}{\overset{\overset{\text{H}}{|}}{\text{C}}}-\underset{\underset{\text{H}}{|}}{\overset{\overset{\text{H}}{|}}{\text{C}}}-\underset{\underset{\text{OH}}{|}}{\overset{\overset{\text{H}}{|}}{\text{C}}}-\underset{\underset{\text{H}}{|}}{\overset{\overset{\text{H}}{|}}{\text{C}}}-\underset{\underset{\text{OH}}{|}}{\overset{\overset{\text{H}}{|}}{\text{C}}}-\underset{\underset{\text{H}}{|}}{\overset{\overset{\text{H}}{|}}{\text{C}}}-\underset{\underset{\text{OH}}{|}}{\overset{\overset{\text{H}}{|}}{\text{C}}}-\underset{\underset{\text{H}}{|}}{\overset{\overset{\text{H}}{|}}{\text{C}}}-\underset{\underset{\text{OH}}{|}}{\overset{\overset{\text{H}}{|}}{\text{C}}}-\underset{\underset{\text{H}}{|}}{\overset{\overset{\text{H}}{|}}{\text{C}}}-\text{H}$$

Part 1: "Slime" (cross-linked polyvinyl alcohol): Polyvinyl alcohol (Figure I) is a polymer used extensively in the plastics industry in molding compounds, surface coatings, and chemical-resistant films. Sodium borate ($Na_2B_4O_7 \cdot 10H_2O$) is a mineral used in cleaning compounds such as Twenty Mule Team Borax® Laundry Booster. Both polyvinyl alcohol and sodium borate are water soluble, but when mixed, form a cross-linked polymer. Sodium borate acts as a cross-linking agent to bind polyvinyl alcohol chains together. This solidifies the polyvinyl alcohol and traps water, forming a slimy mass.

Sodium borate dissolves in water to form boric acid, H_3BO_3, which then accepts a hydroxide from water to become $B(OH)_4^-$.

$$H_3BO_3 + 2H_2O \longrightarrow B(OH)_4^- + H_3O^+$$

It is thought that $B(OH)_4^-$ then reacts in a condensation reaction with polyvinyl alcohol as indicated in Figure J. The water from this condensation reaction as well as the excess water from the two solutions gets trapped in the cross-linked polymer, producing the slimy, flexible properties.

Make a 4% polyvinyl alcohol solution by slowly stirring in 4 grams of polyvinyl alcohol powder into 96 mL of hot (approximately 80°C; not boiling!) distilled water (use a magnetic stirrer if possible). Do not add the polyvinyl alcohol rapidly or it may clump and form a sticky mass. Allow the solution to stand in a covered container. Make a 4% solution of sodium borate by dissolving 0.4 gram of sodium borate decahydrate (borax) in 9.6 mL of distilled water. Pour the polyvinyl alcohol solution into a Styrofoam or plastic cup and stir in the sodium borate solution.

Although the "slime" that develops is nontoxic and can be handled, stretched, and formed into various shapes (Figure K), you may wish to wear gloves to reduce the possibility of skin irritation. Be sure to wash your hands thoroughly after handling the polymerized slime. Repeat the procedure using twice as much sodium borate solution. What effect does the amount of sodium borate solution have on the viscosity (thickness) of the slime? Describe the characteristics of the slime. You can keep the slime sealed in a plastic bag.

J

$+ B(OH)_4^-$ $\longrightarrow$

cross-linking of
polyvinyl alcohol

$+ 4 H_2O$

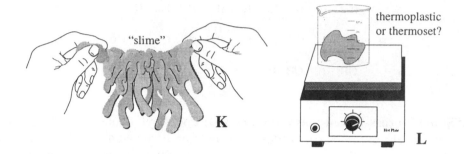

Part 2: "Silly Putty": In 1943 a team of chemists developed a new putty-like polymer that could be repeatedly shaped, twisted, tied, stretched, flattened and rolled. The chemists were sure that the highly unusual properties of this polymer would make it useful for some new product, and distributed samples to thousands of engineers. Surprisingly, none of the engineers could find a practical use for this odd material until someone realized that it would make a great toy. Entrepreneurs soon packaged and sold the polymer as "Silly Putty®" which came to be one of the best-loved toys of the second half of the twentieth century. Although the real Silly Putty® is made from a relatively expensive siloxane polymer, we can make a cross-linked polymer that has many of the same properties using simple household materials.

Prepare a glue solution by adding equal quantities of water and white glue (Elmer's® glue works well) to a plastic or paper cup. Prepare a borax (sodium borate decahydrate) solution by dissolving 10 grams of borax in 90 mL of water. If you wish to make colored putty, add a couple of drops of food coloring to the glue solution. Mix equal volumes of the glue and borax solutions and stir for a couple of minutes. Roll the lump around in your hands until it ceases to be sticky.

White glue is a solution consisting of many small hydrocarbon globules suspended in water. It is viscous (thick) because all of the long molecular chains are tangled together just like a pot of stirred spaghetti. Sodium tetraborate acts as a cross-linker and ties the hydrocarbon chains together, resulting in an extremely viscous substance that exhibits properties of both a liquid and a solid. An elastomer has elastic properties and returns to its original shape after being twisted, pulled and compressed. Is the cross-linked glue-based polymer you made an elastomer? Does it bounce? Drop the ball from a height of 50 cm and measure its rebound ratio (Figure E). Compare the rebound ratio with those found by the other students in your class. Did everyone get the same rebound ratio? If your polymer ball cracks when dropped from this height, try measuring the rebound ratio when dropped from 25 cm. Place the ball in a refrigerator for 15 minutes and try bouncing it again. How does temperature affect the elasticity of this substance?

If the rigidity of a polymer decreases as the temperature is raised past a critical temperature, it is said to be a thermoplastic polymer. If, however, the polymer chemically decomposes before it softens, it is known as a thermoset plastic. Place the polymer clump in a beaker and heat gently and slowly on a hot plate (Figure L). Does this appear to be a thermoset or a thermoplastic polymer?

Questions

(1) Describe the unusual properties of the cross-linked polyvinyl alcohol.

(2) Describe the characteristics of the slime once it has been allowed to dry.

(3) A polymer is a string of repeating monomers. What is the monomer in polyvinyl alcohol?

(4) Is the rebound ratio for the polymer ball in part 2 the same for everyone in the class? If it is significantly different, what variables might explain this difference?

(5) Does the glue-based polymer in part 2 appear to be a thermoplastic or thermoset polymer? Explain.

(6) How would your polymer be different if more sodium tetraborate were added? Try it!

(7) Why will a car tire sometimes "bump" in cold weather but roll smoothly after the car has been driven for a short distance?

3.5.3 USES OF POLYMERS

Concepts to Investigate: Uses of polymers, commercial polymers, neoprene, polyacrylonitrile, polychlorotrifluoroethylene (Teflon®), polyester, high-density polyethylene (HDPE), low-density polyethylene (LDPE), polyethylene terephthalate (PET, PETE), polyolefin, polystyrene, polysulfone, polytetrafluoroethylene, polyurethane, polyvinyl alcohol, polyvinyl chloride, polyvinyl fluoride, polyvinylacetate.

Materials: None required.

Principles and Procedures: Historians and anthropologists have described the stages of civilization in terms of the most important and advanced building materials employed. The

Table 1: Uses of Polymers

Polymer	Properties	Applications
neoprene	very chemical-resistant, rubbery	shoe soles, hoses, radiator hoses, wetsuits
polyamide (nylon)	fibrous, strong, durable, moisture-resistant	parachutes, carpet, ropes, form-fitting skiwear, hosiery, swimwear, boat sails
polyacrylonitrile	resinous, fibrous or rubbery, combines with butadiene and styrene to form hard, tough ABS copolymer	ABS plumbing pipe, structural panels, kettle handles, housewares; Orlon® fabric
polychloro-trifluoroethylene	can be molded by extrusion, chemically resistant	gaskets, linings for containers, parts for valves and pumps
polyester	fibers recover quickly after extension and absorb very little moisture	filters, conveyor belts, sleeping bag insulation, coat insulation, tire cords; brand name polyesters include Dacron®, Fortrel®, Terylene®, Mylar® & Lexan®
polyethylene (high-density) HDPE	can be easily formed into light-weight containers	milk, water, and juice containers; toys, liquid detergent bottles
polyethylene (low-density) LDPE	can be stretched into fine, tough films	bread bags, frozen food bags, grocery bags
polyethylene terephthalate (PET, PETE)	strong, easily moldable, chemically resistant, light-weight	soft drink bottles, peanut butter jars, salad dressing bottles, nonbreakable bottles
polyolefin	fiber composed of at least 85% polyethylene or polypropylene	hosiery, sportswear, under-garments, pile fabrics, upholstery, outdoor furniture, indoor carpeting, indoor-outdoor rugs and carpets, filters, marine cordage, automobile seat covers, electrical insulation, carpet backing

(continued)

Table 1: *(continued)*

Polymer	Properties	Applications
polystyrene	thermoplastic; resists attack by acids, alkalis, and many solvents; does not absorb water; excellent electrical insulator	Styrofoam® cups, grocery store meat trays, fast-food sandwich containers, video cassette cases, compact disk jackets, cafeteria trays, refrigerator insulation
polysulfone	tough, strong, stiff, chemically and thermally resistant	household and plumbing items, various automotive parts, wire coatings
polytetrafluoro-ethylene (PFTE)	strong, tough, waxy, nonflammable, chemically resistant, slippery surface, thermally stable	Viton®: gaskets, bearings, linings for containers and pipes Teflon®: nonstick cookware, cooking utensils, pump valves, plumbing tape
polyurethane	flexible foams, highly elastic quick-drying fibers, or hard-drying films	flexible foams: upholstery material, mattresses rigid foams: cores for airplane wings fibers: spandex clothing fiber, support hosiery; Lycra®, Numa®, Spandelle®, and Vyrene® hard films: polyurethane varnishes
polyvinyl alcohol	colorless, water-soluble, flammable resin	component in: adhesives, emulsifiers, lacquers, coatings and films
polyvinyl chloride	rigid when unplasticized; flexible when plasticized	unplasticized form: water pipe, plumbing fittings, phonograph records, synthetic floor tiles, credit cards plasticized form: raincoats, shower curtains, and packaging films
polyvinyl fluoride	resistant to attack by chemicals or by weathering	protective films for: building sidings, pipes, corrosive chemical containers
polyvinylacetate	water-insoluble resin	carpet backings; film-forming ingredient of water-based (latex) paints, adhesives, lacquers, and cements

Stone Age was first and was followed by the Bronze, Iron, and Steel Ages, and now we are in the Age of Polymers, a time in which synthetic polymers are the material of choice for a large variety of industrial and domestic applications.

In 1907 Leo Bakeland patented Bakelite®, the first fully synthetic polymer. This hard plastic was used as an electrical insulator and paved the way for the more than 60,000 different synthetic plastics on the market today. Each year companies manufacture more than 30 million tons of plastics that are used in myriad applications. We wear clothes containing polyester and nylon fibers, eat food packaged in polyethylene containers, drink water delivered through polyvinyl chloride pipes, walk on carpets made of polyolefin fibers, and sleep on mattresses made of polyurethane foam. The variety of applications of synthetic polymers is mind-boggling. Table 1 lists some of the major classes of polymers and describes some of their useful properties and uses. Examine the list of applications and <u>circle each item you have used in the last week.</u> For example, if you have been a passenger in a car, then you would circle the word "radiator hose" under "neoprene" because automobiles use radiator hoses (unless it was an old air-cooled automobile such as the original Volkswagen Beetle).

Questions

(1) Which categories of polymers do you use most often on a weekly basis?

(2) The price of most polymers is tied to the price of petroleum. Explain.

(3) Nylon, polyester, olefin and other synthetic fibers have replaced many natural polymers for use in clothing, carpets and similar applications. Which natural fibers have they replaced?

(4) Name ten applications of synthetic polymers that are not already listed in the table.

3.5.4 RECYCLING PLASTIC POLYMERS

Concepts to Investigate: Recycling, polymers, solid waste, polymer characteristics.

Materials: Part 1: Variety of empty plastic household containers such as detergent containers, ketchup bottles, peanut butter jars, etc; Part 2: 400-mL beaker, acetone, stirring rod, Styrofoam® cup, Styrofoam® packing material.

Safety: Part 2 must be performed as a teacher demonstration only. Wear goggles, lab coat, and gloves.

Principles and Procedures: In the 40 years between 1960 and 2000, the total annual solid waste in the United States doubled from approximately 80 million tons to 160 million tons. Many communities have run out of suitable locations to bury their trash and must pay to ship it out of the area. Currently approximately 20% of the volume of trash (approximately 10% of the mass) that is dumped into landfills is composed of plastics. Plastic trash is not only a serious problem for landfills, but it is also an eyesore. Unlike paper and garden debris, plastics are not biodegradable and thus persist in the environment indefinitely unless someone picks them up. The persistence of plastic trash in the environment, the looming shortage of petroleum reserves, and the shortage of landfill space have increased the urgency to recycle plastics. By 1990 Americans were recycling approximately one-third of waste aluminum and one-quarter of waste paper, but only 2% of waste plastic. Today more and more communities are adopting mandatory recycling programs in which citizens must separate recyclable plastic trash so it can be reprocessed into new products.

Environmentalists both within and outside the plastics industry have become very concerned about the waste problems caused by synthetic polymers. In an effort to recycle these polymers more effectively, the plastics industry adopted a coding system to identify the type of plastic so that they could be categorized for recycling purposes. Plastic containers are now labeled with a letter code that appears inside the recycling symbol.

Part 1: Identifying classes of polymers: Examine as many disposable plastic items as available and look for the recycling figure. Classify each product (i.e., shampoo bottle, grocery bag, etc.) under one of the seven recycling codes. After examining three or more samples of a polymer, try to describe its characteristics. For example, does it float (make sure you fill the container) in water? Is it crinkly? Does it appear glossy? Is it flexible or rigid? Complete Table 2 on page 318.

Part 2: Recycling: When you turn plastics in for recycling they are reprocessed and made into new products. Synthetic polymers can be recycled by burning (to produce energy in a incineration-generator), by melting (to reform a similar polymer), by shredding (to produce fibrous filling) or by treatment with chemicals. The following summarizes the principal recycled products:

(1) Polyethylene terephthalate (PET or PETE): Most of the recycled PET is from beverage containers. Recyclers are able to make 99% pure, granulated PET that sells at approximately half the cost of new PET. Approximately 50% is used as fiberfill for jackets and for strapping. The remainder is used to make such things as liquid soap bottles, surfboards, paint brushes, fuzz on tennis balls and more soft drink bottles.

(2) High-density polyethylene (HDPE): The process for recycling HDPE is well-developed. Recycled HDPE finds its way into drainage pipes, flower pots, plastic lumber,

Table 2: Recycling Codes

Recycling Code	Polymer Resin	Description	Sample Products
1 PETE	polyethylene terephthalate (PET or PETE)		
2 HDPE	high-density polyethylene (HDPE)		
3 PVC	polyvinyl chloride or vinyl (PVC-V)		
4 LDPE	low-density polyethylene (LDPE)		
5 PP	polypropylene (PP)		
6 PS	polystyrene (PS)		
7 OTHER	multi-layer plastics		

trash cans, automotive mud flaps, kitchen drain boards, beverage bottle crates, pallets, signs, stadium seats, recycling bins, traffic barrier cones, golf bag liners and toys.

(3) Polyvinyl chloride or vinyl (PVC-V): Recycled PVC has been used in drainage pipes, pipe fittings, floor tiles, bottles, door mats, hoses and mud flaps. It is generally not burned in incinerators because it releases hazardous fumes such as dioxins and furans.

(4) Low-density polyethylene (LDPE): LDPE is burned in incinerator-powered generators to produce electrical energy. It is also recycled into items in which color is not critical such as garbage can liners, grocery bags, paint buckets, fast food trays, lawn mower wheels and automobile battery parts.

(5) Polypropylene (PP): Recycled polypropylene is used in license plate holders, desk top accessories, hanging files, food service trays, flower pots and trash cans.

(6) Polystyrene (PS): One of the most challenging polymers to recycle is polystyrene, the material from which Styrofoam® cups and Styrofoam® packing material are made. Although some methods for recycling are in place, chemists are still looking for more effective ways to recycle the huge amounts of waste polystyrene.

Teacher demonstration only: Wear goggles, lab coat and gloves. One of the techniques that may be used in recycling Styrofoam® is to first "melt" it using acetone. Place a Styrofoam® cup in a 400-mL beaker and place in a fume hood or other well-ventilated location. Add 30 mL of acetone to the Styrofoam® cup. What happens to the Styrofoam®? What happens if you stir the acetone? Place 30 mL of acetone in a second beaker and add a Styrofoam® packing kernel. How many kernels can you add before they no longer melt? Using a glass stirring rod pick up the styrene clump and place it on a paper towel and flush the acetone down the drain with excess water. What new properties does this styrene clump have compared to the original Styrofoam? Can you think of any potential uses for this form of styrene?

Questions

(1) Describe the properties of each polymer.

(2) List the types of containers commonly made from each class of polymer.

(3) Which plastics are accepted for recycling in your community? Call the waste disposal service if you are not certain.

(4) Why do waste disposal or recycling companies want you to crush all waste plastic containers?

FOR THE TEACHER

3.5.1 POLYMERIZATION

Discussion: Challenge the students to determine how to make the most elastic polymer balls. In this process, students will begin to understand some of the mechanical and chemical variables involved in the making of practical polymers. If ethyl alcohol is not available, you may substitute 2-propanol (rubbing alcohol is approximately 70% 2-propanol, also known as isopropyl alcohol) but it may not work as well.

A dramatic demonstration of polymerization may be performed using a two-component (A:isocyanate, B:polyol) polyurethane foam kit available from many plastic supply companies (e.g. TC-300 hard coat polyurethane foam from BJB Plastics). *This should be performed only as a teacher demonstration. Read product warnings and directions carefully before proceeding. Perform in a fume hood and wear goggles, lab coat and gloves.* Add components A and B in the specified quantities and mix as directed. The polymerization reaction is quite exothermic and produces carbon dioxide and water vapor which are trapped in the polyurethane as it forms, creating many tiny bubbles. Heat from the reaction causes the bubbles to expand and the foam to grow to perhaps ten times its original volume. Within a few minutes the foam cools and hardens, and can then be cut and shaped with a knife. Hard coat polyurethane foams are used extensively for insulation and cushioning. They are also used in the entertainment industry to make light-weight stage props that can be easily carried from set to set.

Answers: (1) Student responses. (2) Student responses. (3) Carbon and silicon are in the same family in the Periodic Table, and both form four bonds which allow them to form long chains with cross branches. (4) Most plastics and this silicone polymer are flexible, elastic, water-repellent, electrical insulators and thermal insulators. (5) Silicones are relatively unreactive and thermally stable and are therefore useful in applications where there are extreme variations in temperature. They are used as lubricants, hydraulic fluids, and electrical insulators, and also to treat fabrics to make them waterproof. (6) As the plastic sulfur is allowed to stand at room temperature, it slowly reverts back to the crystalline rhombic form, indicating that the plastic form of sulfur is unstable at room temperature. (7) The monomer unit is an 8-sulfur atom chain. Some students might think that the monomer is simply single sulfur atoms, but when allowed to stand, plastic sulfur reverts to rhombic sulfur (S_8), indicating that the monomer is actually S_8.

3.5.2 CROSS-LINKING POLYMERS

Discussion: To make this activity more colorful, you may wish to add food coloring to the polyvinyl alcohol prior to the addition of the sodium borate solution. If you allow the polyvinyl alcohol solution to stand uncovered, a thin film will develop on the surface as the water evaporates. You may wish to show your students this polymerized film. If time is limited, it is recommended that the instructor make stock solutions of the polyvinyl alcohol and sodium borate. Results seem to be best if the polyvinyl alcohol solution has been allowed to stand for one or two days. Both solutions will keep for more than a year if hermetically sealed.

Table 3: Examples of Products Made of Recyclable Polymers

Recycling Code	Polymer Resin	Description	Sample Products
1 PETE	polyethylene terephthalate (PET or PETE)	usually clear or green; sinks in water; rigid	peanut butter jars, salad dressing bottles, soft drink bottles
2 HDPE	high-density polyethylene (HDPE)	semi-glossy, crinkly; may be hard when thick	toys, liquid detergent bottles, motor oil containers, toys, plastic bags; milk, water, and juice containers
3 PVC	polyvinyl chloride or vinyl (PVC-V)	semi-rigid, glossy, sinks in water	clear food packaging, shampoo bottles, vegetable oil bottles, blister packages
4 LDPE	low-density polyethylene (LDPE)	flexible, not crinkly	frozen-food bags, grocery bags, shrink-wrap, garment bags, bread bags
5 PP	polypropylene (PP)	semi-rigid, low gloss	yogurt containers, margarine tubs, medicine bottles, refrigerated containers, most bottle tops
6 PS	polystyrene (PS)	often brittle, glossy	coffee cups, throw-away utensils, cafeteria trays, grocery store meat trays, fast-food sandwich containers, video cassette cases, compact disk jackets
7 OTHER	multi-layer plastics	squeezable	"squeezable" containers, ketchup bottles, syrup containers

You will find the polymer in part 2 described as "Silly Putty®" in many books and on many web pages. It should be realized that the white glue-based polymer shares some of the properties of the commercial Silly Putty® (Dow Corning 3179 Dilatant Compound) which is a complex mixture made primarily of hydroxy-terminated polymers of dimethyl siloxane.

If you do not have access to the materials listed in these activities, you may wish to make a "Gak®"-like starch-based polymer by mixing two parts Elmer's® glue with one part liquid Sta-Flo® starch. Put on gloves, add a couple of drops of food coloring, and kneed with your hands for 5 to 10 minutes. If it is too sticky, add a little starch. If it is too runny, add some glue.

Answers: (1) A gel develops almost immediately. It can be rolled into an elastic ball and stretched into long strands. (2) The linked polyvinyl alcohol returns to a solid phase. It is relatively rigid and somewhat transparent. (3) $(-CH_2CH(OH)-)$. (4) Student responses. (5) Thermoplastic. It softens with gentle heating. (6) Increasing the number of cross-links increases the rigidity of the polymer. (7) The artificial rubber in the tires is a thermoplastic polymer and softens upon frictional heating.

3.5.3 USES OF POLYMERS

Discussion: The market for polymers has grown rapidly since Bakeland's discovery. Today, chemists are examining the potential for new applications of polymers, including molecular information storage and the conduction and storage of light and electricity. More than half of American chemists and chemical engineers are employed by polymer-related industries. The polymer industry in the United States employs more than three million and contributes more than one hundred billion dollars to the U.S. gross national product. Students should be aware of the vast economic significance of the polymer industry.

Answers: (1) Student answers will vary. (2) The vast majority of synthetic fibers are by-products of petroleum. Thus, when the price of crude petroleum increases, the cost of making polymers increases and this cost is generally passed on to the consumer. (3) Cotton, hemp, sisal and flax. (4) Student answers will vary.

3.5.4 RECYCLING PLASTIC POLYMERS

Discussion: Students are impressed with the way Styrofoam melts in acetone. You may wish to compare the apparent "solubility" of Styrofoam packing material with newer environmentally safe cornstarch packing material. The cornstarch material dissolves easily in water, but not in acetone while the Styrofoam material does not dissolve in water, but "melts" rapidly in acetone. Students should recognize that the starch packing material is more environmentally friendly because it will dissolve with the first rainstorm while the Styrofoam® material will persist in the environment until heavily oxidized and mechanically broken down. Table 3 lists some examples of the most commonly recycled plastics.

Answers: (1) See chart. (2) See chart. (3) Student answers may vary. The most commonly recycled plastics are polyethylene terephthalate (PETE) and high-density polyethylene (HDPE). (4) Plastics occupy approximately 20% of the trash volume in many communities. Crushing containers produces significantly less volume and simplifies transport.

Applications to Everyday Life

Household plastics: All of the plastics in your home are made of polymers. Refer to section 3.5.3 for examples.

Thermoplastics: Thermoplastics are easily moldable at high temperatures and may be heated and shaped into a wide variety of forms. Thermoplastics are used in a wide variety of molded products and applications, such as soft drink containers, electrician's tape, food packaging, and insulation.

Thermoset plastics: Thermoset plastics are extensively cross-linked and do not deform or soften upon heating. As a result, thermoset plastics are used extensively in machinery where they must retain their shape even under conditions of high temperature. They are also used in kettle handles, epoxies, and plywood adhesives.

Toys: All plastic toys are made of polymers. Some polymers, such as those in Slime®, Silly Putty®, and Silly String®, are sold as toys simply because of their fascinating (slimy, bouncy, stringy) properties. Sodium polyacrylate is a super-absorbent polymer used in many "disappearing water" tricks (as well as disposable diapers) because of its ability to absorb 500 to 1000 times its own weight of water. Polyacrylamide is used in Grow Beasts® and other toys that expand dramatically when placed in water.

Employment: Polymer chemistry dominates today's material industry. More than half of the nation's chemists and chemical engineers work in polymer-related industries. It is estimated that the polymer field contributes in excess of one hundred billion dollars to the gross national product each year.

Politics: Polymers are used in products necessary to virtually every conceivable industry in today's world, yet almost all polymers and plastics are derived from petroleum and other fossil fuels. A petroleum shortage not only affects the price we pay for gasoline and other fuels, but also the price we pay for all petroleum-based products. Because of the significance of petroleum to the fuel and polymer industries, the governments of industrialized countries are particularly concerned about maintaining political stability in petroleum producing regions of the world so as to prevent a petroleum crisis and a "polymer crisis."

Agriculture: Polymeric materials are added to agricultural soils to improve aeration (air circulation in soils).

Medical plastics: A variety of high-tech plastics are being developed for specific surgical applications. Dacron®, Teflon®, and polyurethane-based plastics are already being used for such things as heart valve replacements, blood vessel repair, and hernia support meshes.

Sporting goods: Virtually every sport uses equipment made of synthetic polymers: football helmets, tennis rackets, hockey pucks, uniforms, balls, motorcycle windshields, skis, bicycle tires, and backpacks are but a few of the many sporting goods composed partially or completely of synthetic polymers.

Substitute building materials: Synthetic polymers are used in place of traditional building materials: Corian® countertops replace ceramic ones, fiberglass shower stalls replace tiles, elastomers replace inorganic grout, fiberboard replaces wood, PVC and ABS replace copper and steel for plumbing pipes, nylon and olefin replace wool in carpets, and Plexiglas® and Lucite® replace glass for windows.

Clothing: Read the manufacturer's labels on the clothing you are wearing and you may find that many are made of polymers. Nylon, olefin, polyester, rayon and polyurethane are a few of the artificial polymers commonly used in clothing. Cotton, wool, flax and silk are the most common natural polymeric substances used.

3.6 NUCLEAR CHEMISTRY

The combustion of one kilogram of coal in a power plant produces enough energy to propel a small electric automobile for a distance of approximately four kilometers. By contrast, the fission of an equivalent mass of uranium in a nuclear reactor yields enough energy to propel that same car approximately 12 million kilometers! In other words, the nuclear reactions involved in the fission of uranium yield approximately 3 million times as much energy as the chemical reactions involved in the combustion of an equivalent mass of coal! How is it possible for two items of the same mass to produce such great differences in energy? Chemical reactions, such as those occurring in the combustion of coal, involve the interaction of electrons. By contrast, nuclear reactions, such as those occurring in the fission of uranium, involve the interaction of nuclear particles. Since the energies that bind nuclear particles together are orders of magnitude greater than those that bind electrons to nuclei, reactions that change the structure of nuclei must involve much more energy than those that simply reposition electrons. Table 1 contrasts chemical reactions with nuclear reactions.

The stability of an isotope (i.e., its resistance to nuclear change) is determined by the ratio of neutrons to protons in its nucleus. Figure A plots stable isotopes as a function of their atomic number (Z) and neutron number (N). For stable isotopes of elements of low atomic number, the neutron-to-proton ratio is about one. As atomic numbers increase, the number of neutrons in the nucleus begins to exceed the number of protons. The neutron to proton ratio of bismuth-209, the largest stable isotope, is greater than 1.5.

Figure A indicates that isotopes with a neutron/proton ratio less than that exhibited by the band of stability tend to decay by electron capture, while those with a higher ratio tend to decay by beta emission. All isotopes with an atomic number greater than bismuth (Z > 83) are radioactive and generally decay by alpha emission. Note that some particles involved in nuclear reactions have more than one symbol (Table 2). The superscript denotes the mass

Table 1: Comparison of Chemical and Nuclear Reactions

	Chemical Reactions	*Nuclear Reactions*
nature of reaction	Chemical reactions involve the interactions between and among the outermost electrons of two or more atoms.	Nuclear reactions involve changes in the nuclei of atoms or isotopes.
nature of bonds	Chemical bonds involve electrons in atomic orbitals.	Nuclear bonds involve protons, neutrons, electrons and other elementary particles.
energy involved	Reactions are accompanied by absorption or release of relatively small amounts of energy.	Reactions are accompanied by absorption or release of tremendous amounts of energy.
outside influences	Rates of reaction are influenced by temperature, pressure, concentration and catalysts.	Rates of reaction normally are not affected by temperature, pressure and catalysts.

number (neutrons plus protons) and the subscript denotes the atomic number (number of protons). An alpha ($_2^4\alpha$) particle is actually a helium nucleus ($_2^4$He). Note that the symbol $_{-1}^{0}$e represents an electron in or from an atomic orbital while the symbol $_{-1}^{0}\beta$ represents an electron which is physically identical to the former but which comes from the nucleus. The positron has the same mass as an electron but possesses a positive charge.

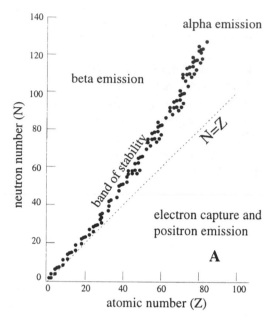

Each unstable element decays with the emission of radiation to become a different element. If this product is itself radioactive, then the decay process continues until a stable nucleus is formed. For example, $_{92}^{238}$U decays through a series of 13 intermediate radioactive nuclides until the stable isotope $_{82}^{206}$Pb is formed. Alpha particle production is a very common mode of decay for heavy radioactive nuclides. For example, $_{92}^{238}$U decays according to the following equation:

$$_{92}^{238}\text{U} \longrightarrow {}_{90}^{234}\text{Th} + {}_2^4\text{He}$$

Emission of an α particle reduces the atomic number by two units and the atomic mass by four units. Notice that in the nuclear equation, both the mass and nuclear charge are conserved. Conservation of mass is indicated by summing the masses on both sides of the equation (238 = 234 + 4), while conservation of charge is indicated by summing the charges on both sides (92 = 90 + 2).

The thorium-234 nuclide undergoes disintegration when a β particle is emitted:

$$_{90}^{234}\text{Th} \longrightarrow {}_{91}^{234}\text{Pa} + {}_{-1}^{0}\text{e}$$

Note that the emission of a β particle increases the atomic number by one but does not change the atomic mass. In other words, the number of protons is increased while the number or neutrons is decreased.

Since the nucleus occupies a very small part of the total volume of an atom but contains nearly all of the mass, its density is extremely great (2×10^{14} g/cm^3). If, for example, it were possible to create a ping-pong ball-sized sphere of nuclear material, it would have a mass of 2.5 billion tons, much greater than the total mass of all of the automobiles in the world. What holds the nucleons (neutrons and protons) so closely together? Since like charges repel, one

Table 2: Comparison of Elementary Particles

Alpha Particle	Electron	Neutron	Positron	Proton
$_2^4\alpha$	$_{-1}^{0}\beta$	$_0^1$n	$_{+1}^{0}\beta$	$_1^1$p
$_2^4$He	$_{-1}^{0}$e		$_{+1}^{0}$e	$_1^1$H

would think that the protons in the nucleus would fly away from each other rather than stick to one another. Overcoming this electrostatic repulsion is nuclear force, a force that acts only at very short distances (approximately 10^{-15} m). If the repulsion between protons is greater than the nuclear force, the nuclide disintegrates emitting nuclear particles and/or radiation. If, however, the nuclear force is greater than the electrostatic repulsion, the nucleus is stable.

The following are some general rules that will help you determine the stability of a nucleus. (1) All nuclides with 84 or more protons are unstable and will experience radioactive decay. (2) Light nuclides (atomic number <20) are stable when the ratio of neutrons to protons is one (n/p = 1). (3) Nuclides with even numbers of both protons and neutrons are generally more stable than those with odd (uneven) numbers of neutrons and protons (only five stable nuclides have an odd number of both protons and neutrons). (4) Particular stability occurs in the case of nuclides that have a number of protons or neutrons equal to 2, 8, 20, 28, 50, 82, and 126. To summarize, the following emissions will often occur under the conditions indicated:

Alpha emission:	Z > 83
Beta emission:	N/Z too large
Positron emission:	N/Z too small
Electron capture:	N/Z too small
Gamma emission:	Excited nucleus

In the following activities you will investigate nuclear reactions and their implications for our modern world.

3.6.1 DETECTING RADIATION
WITH A CLOUD CHAMBER

Concepts to Investigate: Alpha particles, condensation, condensation tracks, nuclear decay, magnetic field.

Materials: Commercial cloud chamber kit, dry ice, ethanol (or isopropyl alcohol), magnet. (Such kits contain a simple cloud chamber and an alpha source that generally contains less than 0.1 picocuries of lead-210. Although you may build your own cloud chamber from a clear sandwich box or Petri dish, we suggest the kit because it provides the alpha source, which you need anyway.)

Safety: This should be performed as a teacher demonstration only. Wear goggles, lab coat and gloves. Handle dry ice with tongs as it can freeze to the skin and cause tissue damage. Obey specific warnings as printed on the kit. Return radioactive source to the manufacturer for waste disposal. Alpha particles can be dangerous if ingested or inhaled, so use in a ventilated area, well away from any sources of food.

Principles and Procedures: A variety of devices have been developed to detect and observe ionizing radiation. The Geiger counter counts the number of high energy particles emitted by a source, but does not provide information regarding the charge or motion of such particles. Other detectors, including photographic emulsions, bubble chambers and cloud chambers detect the trails left by high energy particles. The cloud chamber employs a gas vapor that is cooled to just below its condensation temperature. As high energy particles pass through the gas, ions are created and condensation occurs on these ions. The condensation track can be easily seen with the naked eye, however you may need patience and practice to get the conditions just right to see the condensation trails.

Part 1: Observing vapor (condensation) trails caused by alpha particles: Place a black cardboard base in the chamber or use black paint to paint the outside of the bottom of the chamber. Cut blotter paper to fit inside the chamber as shown in Figure B. Wet this paper with ethanol, and place inside the chamber as indicated. Place the chamber on a block of dry ice *(do not touch the dry ice as it may freeze the skin).* Position an alpha particle source in the middle of the chamber and replace the lid. Dim the room lights and shine a bright light through the side as shown in Figure C. Look straight down on top of the chamber to view the momentary trails of condensed alcohol vapor. Look for thin white lines of condensation that originate near the tip of the radioactive source and travel out in all directions.

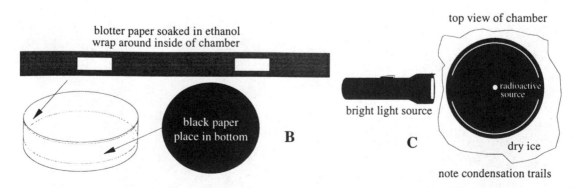

Part 2: Altering the tracks of alpha particles using magnets: Alpha particles ($^4_2$He) carry a positive charge. Magnetic fields interact with charged particles and cause them to deviate from their straight-line course. Place a strong magnet near the cloud chamber and observe the condensation tracks. Position the magnet in various locations and describe the effect of the magnetic field on the trajectory of these particles.

Questions

(1) Describe the purpose and use of a cloud chamber.

(2) The alpha particles that cause alcohol vapor to condense are approximately 0.0012 picometer in diameter. Express their diameter in meters.

(3) A magnetic field causes alpha particles to curve in a specific direction. Suppose alpha particles carried a negative charge. Would they curve in the same direction? Explain.

3.6.2 DETECTING RADIATION WITH AN ELECTROSCOPE

Concepts to Investigate: Radioactivity, electroscopes, charges, electrostatic repulsion.

Materials: Electroscope (alternatively you may make your own using an Erlenmeyer flask, one-holed stopper, copper wire, and gold leaf [available from art-supply stores]), piece of fur or wool cloth, hard rubber rod or a hard rubber or plastic comb, tongs, alpha source.

Safety: This should be performed as a teacher demonstration only. Wear goggles, lab coat and gloves. Obey specific warnings as printed on the kit. Return radioactive source to the manufacturer for waste disposal. Alpha particles can be dangerous to ingest or inhale, so use in a ventilated area, well away from any food source.

Principles and Procedures: Electricity is invisible, so to study it we must develop instruments that allow us to observe its effects. One such instrument, an electroscope, can be easily constructed in the science classroom or at home. Obtain a flask or jar which can be fitted with a one-holed rubber stopper. Place a heavy gauge copper wire through the stopper as shown in Figure D, and seal it in place with paraffin (candle wax) or other nonconducting material. Place the round end of a hollow metal curtain rod over the exposed end of the wire. If such a ball is not available, you can solder a circular piece of copper sheet metal to the end of the wire, or fashion a ball from aluminum foil. Bend the other end of the copper wire and carefully fold a rectangular piece of gold leaf or other very thin metal foil over the end as shown, keeping the surfaces from touching. Gold leaf works best because it is very thin and very conductive. If you must use another metal for the vanes, use as thin a foil as possible.

After placing the stopper assembly in the flask, the metal vanes should hang straight down because they are uncharged and affected only by gravity. Rub a plastic rod or hard-rubber comb vigorously with a wool or flannel cloth. As you rub, the rod removes electrons from the fabric, and develops a net negative charge. Touch the negatively charged rubber rod to the ball of the electroscope (Figure E). Electrons flow from the rod to the vanes. Since both vanes have the same charge (negative), they repel and stay separated even after the rod has been removed (Figure F). You have charged the electroscope by conduction.

Using tongs, bring a packaged radioactive alpha source close to the ball of the electroscope (not touching) and observe the gold leaves (Figure G). Is there any motion? Do they start to collapse? Clamp the alpha source in place and determine the length of time before the

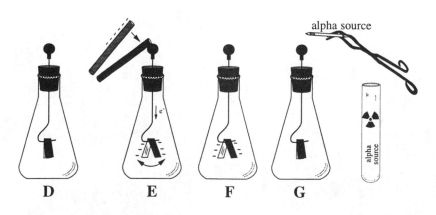

D   E   F   G

vanes collapse and contrast this with the time required for an identical electroscope to collapse where no radioactive source is present.

Questions

(1) What charged particles were transferred from the fur (wool) to the rubber rod?

(2) What charges were transferred from the rod to the electroscope and why did the gold leaves separate (move apart)?

(3) Why did the leaves remain apart after you removed the rod?

(4) When the radioactive source was moved close to the electroscope, the gold leaves collapsed (moved back together). Explain.

3.6.3 DETECTING RADIATION
WITH A GEIGER COUNTER

Concepts to Investigate: Ionizing radiation, Geiger counter, inverse square law, shielding.

Safety: This should be performed as a teacher demonstration only. Wear goggles, lab coat and gloves. Obey specific warnings as printed on the kit. Return radioactive source to the manufacturer for waste disposal. Alpha particles can be dangerous to ingest or inhale, so use only in a ventilated area, well away from any food source.

Materials: Geiger counter (hand-held Geiger counters are available from most scientific supply companies); alpha source, ruler. As many of the following as possible: smoke detectors, camping lantern mantels, old radium (glow-in-the-dark timepieces), static eliminators, cloisonné jewelry, old "fiestaware" (brightly colored glazed pottery).

Principles and Procedures: A Geiger counter can detect very small amounts of radioactivity. When an alpha particle or other form of radiation passes through the gas-filled chamber of the device, ions are produced. These ions complete a circuit that registers on the counter as a "click," flash of light, or meter movement. Geiger counters are widely used to indicate the presence and intensity of nuclear radiation.

Part 1: Shielding of radiation: Place the sensor of the Geiger counter 5 cm from the radioactive source and record the meter reading (Figure H). You will probably need to be on the most sensitive scale (1× scale). Test the effectiveness of various materials in their ability to block radiation from the alpha source by placing them sequentially at the same location in front of the sensor. To make a valid comparison you should use materials of the same thickness. Compare such things as cloth, aluminum foil and paper. It may be necessary to use a couple of sheets of a particular material to match the thickness of the other materials. X-ray radiation is capable of penetrating all three of these materials. Does alpha radiation have the same penetrating capacity as X-rays? Which material provides the best shielding against alpha rays, or are they all equally effective?

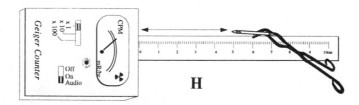

H

Part 2: Radiation and the inverse square law: Place the Geiger counter tube at one end of a ruler. Grasp the radioactive alpha source with tongs and place it one centimeter from the sensor and record the meter reading. Move the source to the two-centimeter mark and record the reading of the meter. Repeat the procedure at every centimeter for five to ten centimeters and plot the results in cpm (counts per minute) versus distance. Is there a relation between the distance from the source and the amount of radiation received by the counter? By what factor is the detectable radiation reduced if the distance between the source and the detector is doubled? Tripled?

Part 3: Common sources of radiation: When people think of radioactivity, they often think of a major disaster like the Chernobyl nuclear power plant failure in the former Soviet Union. Most do not realize, however, that there are many sources of radioactivity in our daily environments, some of which are used to actually improve the quality of life. Things like smoke detectors, camping lantern mantles, and old luminescent dial clocks are often radioactive. Just how radioactive are such common household items? To find out, it is necessary to compare these items against background radiation, the naturally occurring radiation that is always present. High energy gamma rays from the sun and other stars enter our environment from outer space, while alpha, beta, and gamma radiation is released by radioactive elements in the earth. Set a Geiger counter on the ground outside of your room, and record the counts (clicks) per minute. Move the Geiger counter and repeat twice and calculate the average. Compare the radioactivity of the following items by positioning each a distance of one centimeter from the Geiger counter sensor window. Which is the most radioactive?

Camping lantern mantles: Some of the mantles used in camping lanterns contain radioactive thorium. Do not breathe or ingest any of the fine powder that forms after the mantle has been used.

Smoke detectors: Most models of smoke detectors installed in U.S. homes are "ion chamber" detectors which contain a small amount of americium-241 ($^{241}_{95}$Am).

Old luminescent dial time clocks and watches: Most of the original "glow-in-the-dark" timepieces were painted with a radium-containing paint. Tritium is now commonly used to give the same effect, but the energy it emits is so low that it does not penetrate the lens of the time piece and therefore is generally not detectable.

Static eliminators: Static eliminators were developed to reduce the static on photographic film and old musical records. Many of these devices used polonium, a strong alpha emitter, to help eliminate the static.

Jewelry: Some brightly colored cloisonné jewelry has glazing that contains uranium oxide.

Pottery: Some of the older (pre-1960) brightly colored glazed pottery contains uranium oxide. Old "Fiestaware" plates and bowls may contain a significant amount of uranium oxide. In recent years uranium oxide has been removed from glazing materials, but much of this pottery is still in circulation.

Questions

   (1) Compare a cloud chamber to a Geiger counter.

   (2) Which of the shielding materials provided the greatest amount of shielding, or are they all the same?

   (3) What happens to the radiation level as the distance from the source increases?

   (4) Which of the household items tested proved to be radioactive? How could you tell?

3.6.4 MODELING NUCLEAR REACTIONS

Concepts to Investigate: Half-life, radioactive decay, rate constant, nuclear reactions, protons, neutrons, electrons, alpha particles, beta particles, electron capture, chain reactions, critical mass, fission, fusion.

Materials: <u>Part 1</u>: Large and small marshmallows, toothpicks; <u>Part 2</u>: Two 100 mL graduated cylinders, three eye-droppers or Beral pipets of various sizes (must be long enough to reach the 50 mL mark in cylinder); <u>Part 3</u>: 100 coins, 100 small wooden cubes (cut from square wood molding) or 100 sugar cubes; marking pen; bag; box; <u>Part 4</u>: Ringstand, metal rod, books of matches, clamp.

Principles and Procedures: Although we cannot see nuclear particles, we can design models that help explain various aspects of their behavior. In the activities that follow you will model radioactive decay, half-life, fusion, fission, and chain reactions using simple household and laboratory materials. Although our models adequately describe certain aspects of nuclear behavior, they are inadequate in other important ways. As you proceed, think about the strengths and limitations of each model or analogy.

Part 1: Radioactive decay: In the following activity you will model the nuclei of a hypothetical element called "mysterium" (My). Mysterium is intended to represent a variety of unstable radioactive isotopes, even though we have assigned it the atomic number associated with boron.

Obtain large and small marshmallows. The large marshmallows will represent protons while the small ones will represent electrons (in reality, protons are approximately seventeen hundred times more massive than electrons ($m_{proton} = 1.6 \times 10^{-27}$ kg; $m_{electron} = 9.31 \times 10^{-31}$ kg). A neutron will be represented by the combination of a large marshmallow and a small marshmallow. Using marshmallows, form the nucleus of $^{15}_{5}$My. Break toothpicks into several short sections and use these to attach 10 large marshmallows ("protons") to 10 small marshmallows ("electrons"), thereby producing 10 "neutrons." A neutron is represented by one large marshmallow combined with one small marshmallow. Place 10 "neutrons" in a pile with five "protons." This now represents the nucleus of a heavy isotope of mysterium: $^{15}_{5}$My. Now use the marshmallows to indicate the emission of an alpha particle. Remove two "neutrons" and two "protons" and place these in another pile that represents an alpha particle (Figure I). The remaining isotope (X) is composed of the 8 neutrons and 3 protons that are left.

(10 neutrons + 5 protons) → (8 neutrons + 3 protons) + (2 neutrons + 2 protons)

$$^{15}_{5}\text{My} \rightarrow ^{11}_{3}\text{X} + ^{4}_{2}\text{He}$$

X represents the element created by this radioactive disintegration (which in this case is a nonexistent isotope of lithium). Now simulate a beta emission by removing a small marshmallow and placing it in a location by itself (Figure J). What element results?

$$^{11}_{3}\text{X} \longrightarrow ^{11}_{4}\text{Y} + ^{0}_{-1}\beta$$

Using marshmallows, model the following nuclear reactions:

$$^{14}_{6}\text{C} \longrightarrow ^{14}_{7}\text{N} + ^{0}_{-1}\beta \quad \text{(beta decay)}$$

$$^{14}_{7}\text{N} + ^{4}_{2}\text{He} \longrightarrow ^{17}_{8}\text{O} + ^{1}_{1}\text{H} \quad \text{(transmutation)}$$

$$^{9}_{4}\text{Be} + ^{4}_{2}\text{He} \longrightarrow ^{12}_{6}\text{C} + ^{1}_{0}\text{n} \quad \text{(neutron emission)}$$

$$^{2}_{1}\text{H} + ^{3}_{1}\text{H} \longrightarrow ^{4}_{2}\text{He} + ^{1}_{0}\text{n} \quad \text{(nuclear fusion)}$$

The following diagram illustrates the decay series of uranium-238. Determine whether each transition is due to an alpha decay (α) or a beta decay (β), and place the appropriate symbols above the arrows.

$$^{238}_{92}\text{U} \longrightarrow ^{234}_{90}\text{Th} \longrightarrow ^{234}_{91}\text{Pa} \longrightarrow ^{234}_{92}\text{U} \longrightarrow ^{230}_{90}\text{Th} \longrightarrow ^{226}_{88}\text{Ra} \longrightarrow ^{222}_{86}\text{Rn} \longrightarrow$$

$$^{218}_{84}\text{Po} \longrightarrow ^{214}_{82}\text{Pb} \longrightarrow ^{214}_{83}\text{Bi} \longrightarrow ^{214}_{84}\text{Po} \longrightarrow ^{210}_{82}\text{Pb} \longrightarrow ^{210}_{83}\text{Bi} \longrightarrow ^{210}_{84}\text{Po} \longrightarrow ^{206}_{82}\text{Pb}$$

When balancing chemical equations, the symbols for each element must be indicated and the number of atoms and charges on each side must be identical. When balancing nuclear equations we must also explicitly indicate the number of protons, neutrons and electrons. The sum of the masses and nuclear charges must be the same on each side. For example, in the alpha decay of polonium-218 there is an equivalency of mass (218 = 214 + 4) and charge (84 = 82 + 2) on both sides of the equation:

$$^{218}_{84}\text{Po} \longrightarrow ^{214}_{82}\text{Pb} + ^{4}_{2}\text{He}$$

Balancing nuclear equations is a simple matter if you remember two important rules: (1) there must be conservation of mass number (the total number of protons plus neutrons in the reactants and products must be the same), and (2) there must be conservation of charge (the total number of nuclear charges in the reactants and products must be the same). Given this knowledge, balance the following nuclear reactions that occur in the synthesis of americium-241, the isotope used to ionize air in common battery-operated smoke detectors.

$$^{239}_{94}\text{Pu} + \longrightarrow ^{240}_{94}\text{Pu}$$

$$^{240}_{94}\text{Pu} + ^{1}_{0}\text{n} \longrightarrow$$

$$^{241}_{94}\text{Pu} \longrightarrow + ^{0}_{-1}\beta$$

Part 2: An analogy to demonstrate half-life: *Teacher demonstration.* The half-life of a radioactive isotope is the time required for half of that isotope to decay into some other

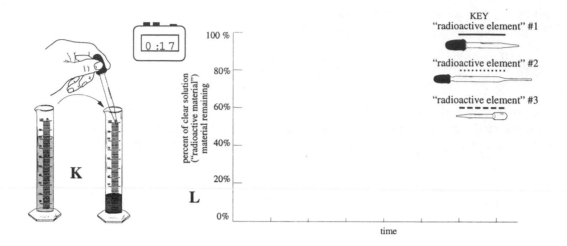

element. The half-life is independent of the amount of sample. For example, 1.000 g of iodine-131 decays to 0.5000 g in 8.07 days. Consequently, the half-life is 8.07 days. In an additional 8.07 days, half of the remaining 0.5000 g of iodine will decay so that only 0.2500 g will remain. The following activity illustrates the concept of half-life.

Fill a 100 mL graduated cylinder to the 100-mL mark with 0.01 *M* sodium hydroxide solution (any dilute base solution will work well). Place one drop of phenolphthalein solution in a second, empty graduated cylinder of the same size. When solution is transferred from the first to the second cylinder it will turn pink (phenolphthalein is pink in basic solutions). In this analogy, the clear solution represents a radioactive material while the pink represents its decay product. The time required to go from 100% (100 mL) to 50% (50 mL) represents the half-life of the radioactive material. Transfer material from the first cylinder to the second at a steady, even rate, recording the volume remaining in the first cylinder at even time intervals (Figure K). Plot your data on Figure L and determine the "half-life" (the time at which only 50% of the original solution remains in the first cylinder). Repeat the procedure using two other pipets of different sizes. Just as each pipet displays a standard transfer rate and "half-life," so each radioactive element has a natural decay rate and half-life. Compare the "half-lives" of the three "radioactive elements" in Figure L. Table 3 shows the half-lives of a few real isotopes.

Part 3: Comparing decay rates: In this activity you will determine the half-lives of two mythical isotopes that we will call "coinium (Cn)" (represented by a penny or other coin) and "cubium (Cb)" represented by a sugar cube or small wooden cube. Shake 100 pennies in a bag and then dump them out into a cardboard box. A "heads" represents the original isotope of coinium, while a "tails" represents its decay product. Remove all of the "tails" so that only the "original nuclides" remain. Put the "heads" back in the bag, shake, dump, and record the number of "heads" again. Once again remove all of the "tails," put the "heads"

Table 3: Half-Lives for Selected Isotopes

tritium	12.3 y	potassium-40	1.28×10^9 y	cesium-137	30 y
carbon-14	5730 y	calcium-45	165 d	radium-226	1.62×10^3 y
fluorine-20	11.4 s	cobalt-60	5.26 y	uranium-235	7.1×10^8 y
sodium-24	15.0 h	strontium-90	28 y	uranium-238	4.51×10^9 y
phosphorous-32	14.3 d	iodine-131	8.1 d	plutonium-239	2.44×10^4 y

back in the bag, and repeat until coinium has fully decayed and no heads are thrown. Graph the number of "heads" (original isotope) as a function of the number of trials. What is the "half-life" of coinium, expressed in number of trials? How long does it take before coinium has completely decayed?

Repeat the process for "cubium." Obtain a rod of square wood molding, and cut it into 100 cubes with a miter box saw. Using a permanent marker, mark one face on each cube. The marked face represents the decay product of cubium. Shake the 100 cubes in a bag and dump them out into a box. Remove those whose marked face is up. Graph the number of unmarked faces (original cubium isotope) as a function of the number of trials. Repeat the process until cubium has fully decayed and no unmarked faces remain. What is the half-life of cubium? How long did it take before cubium completely decayed? Which decays more rapidly, cubium or coinium?

Part 4: Model of a chain reaction: *(Teacher demonstration only. Perform outside or in a fume hood. Wear goggles and lab coat):* Nuclear fission is a reaction in which a heavy nucleus splits into lighter nuclei with the release of a large quantity of energy. The first human-initiated nuclear fission reaction resulted from the bombardment of uranium-235 by neutrons. The nucleus of a uranium-235 atom absorbs a neutron and the resulting activated intermediate uranium-236 can then split in a variety of ways (fissions of uranium nuclei produce approximately 30 different elements). One such reaction is:

$$\ce{^{235}_{92}U} + \ce{^{1}_{0}n} \longrightarrow \ce{^{141}_{56}Ba} + \ce{^{92}_{36}Kr} + 3\ce{^{1}_{0}n} + \text{energy}$$

Since the products are more stable than the uranium-235 nucleus (the binding energies of the products are greater) the reaction must be exothermic, as indicated. The energy released in a nuclear reaction is much greater than that released in a chemical reaction. For example, 1 mole of uranium-235 produces 2.0×10^{13} J of energy in a nuclear reaction (fission) while an equivalent mass of coal produces only about 5×10^5 J of energy in a chemical reaction (oxidation to carbon dioxide). The three neutrons that are released in this reaction may be used to stimulate similar reactions in the surrounding uranium, starting what is known as a chain reaction.

In order for the fission process to be self-sustaining, at least one neutron from each fission must impact and split another nucleus, and so on. If the sample of fissionable material

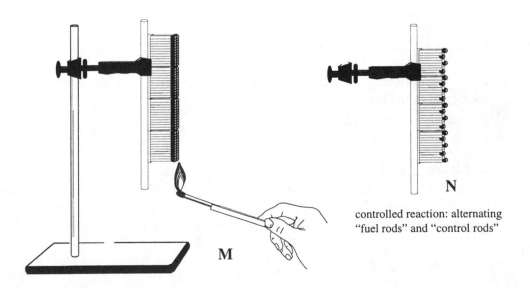

N

controlled reaction: alternating "fuel rods" and "control rods"

M

is too small, too many neutrons leave the sample without striking nuclei, and the reaction slows down and is said to be subcritical. At critical mass, one neutron from each fission reaction splits another nucleus, thereby sustaining a chain reaction. Such reactions represent the controlled, self-sustaining fission processes used in commercial nuclear power plants. If the mass is greater than the critical mass (supercritical), more than one neutron from each fission causes another fission, and the number of splitting nuclei multiplies rapidly, producing a violent explosion such as occurs in the atomic bomb.

You can simulate a chain reaction using ordinary book matches. *Perform the following demonstration outdoors or in a fume hood.* Tape books of paper matches to a metal rod as shown in Figure M. Light the lowest match, remove your hand quickly and observe. The reaction that takes place is analogous to an uncontrolled nuclear reaction. In other words, the heat from one match is sufficient to light more than one additional match, and so the process accelerates. To control nuclear reactions, engineers position control rods (rods that absorb neutrons) around the fuel rods (those containing the fissionable material). By regulating the spacing of fuel and control rods, it is possible to regulate the rate of nuclear fission.

You can simulate the influence of control rods by cutting the tips off of match heads so that intact matches are widely spaced (see Figure N). The intact matches act like fuel rods, and the cut match sticks act like control rods by absorbing some of the heat. Experiment with different configurations until you obtain a slow, controlled chain reaction. It may be necessary to cover the "control rods" with tiny pieces of clay to slow the reaction to the desired rate.

Questions

(1) In your own words, describe what is meant by "half-life."

(2) Does a radioactive substance remains radioactive forever?

(3) The "fallout" from a nuclear explosion is radioactive, containing such isotopes as cesium-137, strontium-90, and plutonium-239. Examine Table 3 and determine which isotopes decay the fastest and which decay the slowest.

(4) Find the missing particle (M) by analyzing the reactants and products in the following nuclear reactions:

$$^{14}_{6}C \longrightarrow ^{14}_{7}N + M$$

$$^{219}_{86}Ra \longrightarrow ^{215}_{84}Po + M$$

(5) Identify the following nuclide symbols and indicate which ones are synonyms (i.e., which refer to the same nuclides):

$$^{1}_{1}H, \ ^{1}_{1}p, \ ^{1}_{0}n, \ ^{0}_{-1}e, \ ^{0}_{-1}\beta, \ ^{0}_{1}e, \ ^{0}_{0}\gamma$$

(6) The nuclide $^{234}_{90}Th$ decays by emitting a beta particle. Write the nuclear equation.

(7) If each trial in part 3 represents 1000 years, what are the half-lives of coinium and cubium? How long are the second and third half-lives of coinium and cubium?

(8) Explain a nuclear chain reaction in terms of the books of matches.

FOR THE TEACHER

Within the nucleus the protons and neutrons are bound together by very strong forces, so a large amount of energy is required to overcome these forces to separate a nucleus into its component protons and neutrons. Likewise, if the same nucleus were formed from the individual protons and neutrons, this same large amount of energy would be released and the nucleus would be more stable than the protons and neutrons from which it was formed. The binding energy of a nucleus is the energy needed to break it into its individual protons and neutrons. One would suppose if we added up the mass of all the nucleons (protons and neutrons) needed to form a nucleus, that the mass of the nucleus would equal the combined masses of the protons and neutrons. Actually the mass of the nucleus is always somewhat less than the total mass of the individual protons and neutrons. This difference between the mass of the nucleus and the sum of the masses of its protons and neutrons is called the mass defect. Where does this mass go? It is converted into energy according to Einstein's equation, $E = mc^2$, where E is energy, m is mass and c is the speed of light. This equation indicates that a very small change in mass creates a very large amount of energy.

Let's consider a specific example to see what happens to the disappearing mass. The $_2^4He$ nucleus consists of two protons and two neutrons. The mass of two protons is: 2×1.00728 amu $= 2.01456$. The mass of two neutrons is: $2 \times 1.00867 = 2.01734$ amu. The total mass of nucleons is 4.03190 amu. However, the actual mass of the $_2^4He$ nucleus (as determined by mass spectrometer) is only 4.00150 amu. The difference in mass between the calculated and observed values (mass defect) is 4.03190 amu $-$ 4.00150 amu $= 0.03040$ amu. Thus when a helium nucleus is formed from two protons and two neutrons, 0.03040 amu of mass is converted to energy. If one mole of helium atoms is formed, the total mass will be 0.03040 g (3.040×10^{-5} kg). Using Einstein's equation ($E = mc^2$), and knowing the speed of light ($c = 2.998 \times 10^8$ m/s), we have: $E = (3.040 \times 10^{-5}$ kg$) \times (2.998 \times 10^8$ m/s$)^2 = 2.7 \times 10^{12}$ kg·m^2/s$^2 = 2.7 \times 10^9$ kJ/mol. By comparison, the combination of 1 mole of methane (natural gas, CH_4) liberates only about 8.9×10^2 kJ. This shows that binding energy represents a tremendous amount of energy.

Be certain students understand the difference between nuclear fission and nuclear fusion. In nuclear fission, a heavy nucleus splits into lighter nuclei and energy is released. In nuclear fusion, light nuclei combine to produce a stable, heavier nucleus, and neutrons and energy are released. In both fission and fusion, there is a loss of mass which is converted into energy, but the loss of mass is greater in the fusion process, and hence the energy liberated is greater.

3.6.1 DETECTING RADIATION WITH A CLOUD CHAMBER

Discussion: A cloud chamber is a particle detector in which the path of a rapidly moving charged particle is made visible by the formation of liquid droplets on the ions left as a particle passes through the gas of the chamber. Cloud chambers are used in atomic research to provide detailed information on nuclear particles. Some kits suggest setting the chamber in a dish containing liquid nitrogen. Although this produces a wider temperature gradient, liquid nitrogen is more difficult to obtain and more dangerous to handle, and thus we suggest using dry ice. The vapor trails produced in a cloud chamber are analogous to the ice-crystal condensation trails left in the atmosphere by high-flying jets.

Answers: (1) A cloud chamber shows a visible path of ionizing radiation in the form of fog trails. When placed in a strong magnetic field, a cloud chamber can provide information about the charge, mass, and momentum of the charged particles. (2) 1.2×10^{-15} m. (3) No, they would curve in the opposite direction.

3.6.2 DETECTING RADIATION WITH AN ELECTROSCOPE

Discussion: An electroscope is an instrument for detecting the presence and sign of an electric charge. An electroscope can be charged by conduction or induction. If a rubber rod bearing a negative charge touches the metal knob, electrons flow from the rod to the leaves and the electroscope is charged by conduction. Since the leaves contain like charges (each leaf has a negative charge) the leaves separate. The amount of separation indicates the magnitude of the charge. When an alpha source is brought close to the electroscope the vanes collapse as the positively charged alpha particles remove electrons from the air surrounding the electroscope and consequently drain electrons from the vanes.

If a rubber rod bearing a negative charge is held near the knob, but not touching it, negative charges are repelled to the leaves. If you touch the knob with your finger while the charged rod is close, the electrons move through your body to the ground. When you remove the rod from the proximity of the knob, the leaves again separate, but this time the charge on the leaves is positive. You may wish to show students that the vanes do not collapse in this instance because the charge on the vanes is the same as the charge on the alpha particles.

It should be noted that the electroscope was originally used by both Becquerel and Curie to detect radioactivity. The motion of the vanes may be rather difficult to detect if your alpha source is very weak.

Answers: (1) Electrons were transferred from the wool (fur) to the rubber rod. (2) Electrons were transferred from the rod to the electroscope. The leaves separated because like charges repel. (3) There was no pathway for the electrons to move from the electroscope to the ground. If you had touched the ball of the electroscope with your finger, providing a pathway for the electrons to the ground, the leaves would collapse. (4) The positively charged alpha particles remove electrons from the vanes. If charge is removed, the vanes no longer repel each other, and collapse under the force of gravity.

3.6.3 DETECTING RADIATION WITH A GEIGER COUNTER

Discussion: Common hand-held Geiger counters are able to monitor alpha, beta, gamma and X-ray radiation. Gamma and X-rays are measured in milli-Roentgens per hour (mR/hr) while alpha and beta particles are measured in counts per minute (cpm). To avoid contamination, the meter should never touch the suspected radioactive source. Alpha radiation is recommended for most investigations dealing with radioactivity because it does not penetrate well.

Answers: (1) Cloud chambers allow you to visualize particle movement, while Geiger counters allow you to count individual particles. (2) Lead produces the greatest shielding, but this may not be seen because even a sheet of paper is sufficient to stop an alpha particle.

(3) The radiation level falls rapidly, indicating that the relationship is not linear. It is an inverse square relation: $E = 1/d^2$. (4) Student answers will vary depending upon the type of material used. Something is radioactive if the detection rate (counts per minute) is greater than the background radiation.

3.6.4 MODELING NUCLEAR REACTIONS

Discussion: Ask students to identify the strengths and limitations of the marshmallow-nucleus model and other models or analogies that you incorporate in your teaching.

In part 1, students were required to balance nuclear reactions involved in the synthesis of americium-241. The answers to these equations are:

$$^{239}_{94}\text{Pu} + ^{1}_{0}\text{n} \longrightarrow ^{240}_{94}\text{Pu}$$

$$^{240}_{94}\text{Pu} + ^{1}_{0}\text{n} \longrightarrow ^{241}_{94}\text{Pu}$$

$$^{241}_{94}\text{Pu} \longrightarrow ^{241}_{95}\text{Am} + ^{0}_{-1}\beta$$

Students were asked to identify the form of radiation accompanying each of the steps in the decay uranium-238. Using the formulas for alpha ($^{4}_{2}\text{He}$) and ($^{0}_{-1}\beta$) radiation, show how mass and charge are conserved at each step.

$$^{238}_{92}\text{U} \xrightarrow{\alpha} ^{234}_{90}\text{Th} \xrightarrow{\beta} ^{234}_{91}\text{Pa} \xrightarrow{\beta} ^{234}_{92}\text{U} \xrightarrow{\alpha} ^{230}_{90}\text{Th} \xrightarrow{\alpha} ^{226}_{88}\text{Ra} \xrightarrow{\alpha} ^{222}_{86}\text{Rn} \xrightarrow{\alpha}$$

$$^{218}_{84}\text{Po} \xrightarrow{\alpha} ^{214}_{82}\text{Pb} \xrightarrow{\beta} ^{214}_{83}\text{Bi} \xrightarrow{\beta} ^{214}_{84}\text{Po} \xrightarrow{\alpha} ^{210}_{82}\text{Pb} \xrightarrow{\beta} ^{210}_{83}\text{Bi} \xrightarrow{\beta} ^{210}_{84}\text{Po} \xrightarrow{\alpha} ^{206}_{82}\text{Pb}$$

In part 2, students were asked to model the concept of half-life. The following information may be useful in explaining how it is possible to determine the half-lives of isotopes which decay very slowly. It has been shown that the half-life of any substance is inversely proportional to the rate constant for its decay. This rate constant is characteristic of each radioactive nuclide, and can be calculated by counting the nuclear disintegrations over a period of time. The relationship between half-life ($t_{1/2}$) and decay constant (k) is:

$$t_{1/2} = 0.693/k$$

From this equation, we can see that if the decay constant is large, the half-life will be small and vice versa. For example, the rate constant for the decay of radon-222 is 0.181 day^{-1} and the half-life is therefore:

$$t_{1/2} = 0.693/0.181 \text{ day}^{-1} = 3.83 \text{ days}$$

At an isotope's "half-life," half of the initial material remains. Since there is always something remaining, is there ever an end to the radioactive decay process for a given amount of an isotope? It's like the proverbial problem of standing in front of a wall and walking half the distance to the wall, then walking half of the remaining distance, then walking half of the remaining distance and so on. Does one ever reach the wall? Although it is possible to divide distances in half ad infinitum, the same logic does not pertain to the decay of isotopes. Eventually the last radioactive atom will decay and the process will end.

Answers: (1) The half-life of a radioactive element is the time required for half of the atoms in a sample to disintegrate. If the half-life of an element is 30 days, only half will remain unchanged after 30 days. After another 30 days, only half of the remaining atoms will remain unchanged. (2) The activity of a substance is proportional to the number of radioactive atoms present. Thus the fraction of the initial activity remaining is 50% at one half-life, 25% at two half-lives, 12.5% at three half-lives, etc. However, at a certain point the last radioactive atom will disintegrate and the remaining substance will not be radioactive provided the products are stable. (3) Of these three, strontium-90 decays the fastest, and plutonium-239 the slowest. (4) Beta, alpha. (5) Proton, proton, neutron, electron, electron, positron, gamma photon. $_{-1}^{0}e$ and $_{-1}^{0}\beta$ both refer to electrons, while $_{1}^{1}H$ and $_{1}^{1}p$ both refer to protons. (6) $_{90}^{234}Th \longrightarrow _{-1}^{0}e + _{91}^{234}Pa$. (7) The half-life of coinium is 1000 years. The half-life of cubium is substantially longer because it decays at only one third the rate of coinium. There should be no difference in the lengths of successive half-lives. (8) Each match represents one atom that splits. The heat from one match ignites one or more matches, thereby sustaining a "chain reaction."

Applications to Everyday Life

Radiation and our environment: Contrary to popular belief, the nuclear industry produces less than 1 percent of the radiation to which we are exposed. Common sources of radiation exposure are:

Natural radon	55%
Radiation inside the body	11%
Medical X-rays	11%
Rocks and soil	8%
Cosmic radiation	8%
Nuclear medicine	4%
Consumer products	3%
Nuclear industry	0.05%
Other (fallout etc.)	<1%

Nuclear pollution: In 1986, the Chernobyl nuclear power plant in the Soviet Union (now Russia) experienced an explosion that blew the 1000-ton concrete lid off the reactor, spewing deadly radioactive material into the environment. Thirty-one persons died. It is estimated that 24,000 people among the 116,000 people evacuated received quite serious radiation doses of approximately 45 rem. Five rem is considered acceptable for a nuclear-plant employee, with 25 rem considered an acceptable once-in-a-lifetime dose. Engineers are continuing to develop new safeguards to prevent similar accidents from occurring in the future.

Biological damage of radiation: The effectiveness of radiation in causing biological damage depends on its: (1) energy, (2) penetrating ability, (3) ionizing ability, and (4) the chemical properties of the source of the radiation. Alpha (α) particles, although they do not penetrate deeply, cause a great deal of ionization and disrupt atoms and molecules. Gamma (γ) rays, although they penetrate deeply, cause little ionization. If an ingested radioactive nuclide remains in the body for only a short time its ability to cause damage is limited. If, however, it remains in the body for a prolonged period, the damage can be substantial. Such is the case with strontium-90. Strontium is in the same family as calcium, and like calcium, is readily incorporated into bones. Not surprisingly, strontium-90 has been linked to bone cancer and leukemia.

Smoke detectors: Most models of smoke detectors installed in the U.S. employ "ion chambers" which contain a very small amount of americium-241. This nuclide emits alpha radiation which ionizes the air in a gap between two electrodes, allowing a very small current to travel between them. When smoke enters the space between the electrodes, it absorbs the alpha particles, reducing the current and thereby triggering the alarm. The radiation exposure from a smoke detector is essentially zero because alpha particles are readily absorbed within a few inches of air.

Nuclear bombs: The first application of nuclear fission was in the development of the atomic bomb, first detonated on July 16, 1945, near Los Alamos, New Mexico. The atomic bomb was subsequently used twice at the end of World War II, causing unimaginable death and destruction. The development of nuclear warheads expanded dramatically during the Cold War, but in recent years many countries have been taking steps to reduce the spread of this technology. In 1995, 174 countries of the United Nations agreed to extend the Nuclear Non-Proliferation Treaty of 1968 indefinitely, thereby promising not to assist other nations in the development of nuclear arms.

Smoking tobacco: Polonium-210 and lead-210 are found in tobacco leaves. These nuclides emit alpha particles that may cause cellular mutations. Many years of exposure to low-level alpha particle radiation may increase the probability of cancer among smokers. Although the radiation hazard associated with smoking is real, it is not nearly as great as the hazard associated with the chemical carcinogens in smoke, such as tar.

Disposal of hazardous wastes: Radioactive wastes emit ionizing energy that can harm living organisms. What do we do with particularly troublesome wastes such as plutonium-239, which has a half-life of 24,400 years? It has been suggested that we store such wastes underground, but if there is leakage of radioactive material into the ground water, entire communities could be endangered. Some have suggested that we send radioactive wastes out into space, but if only one of the many spacecraft used for this purpose exploded on lift-off—what then?

Cancer treatment: Rapidly dividing cells, such as those in cancerous tumors, are more sensitive to radiation than normal cells. Cancer patients may be given dosages of radiation in an effort to selectively damage these cells and stop the proliferation of cancerous tissue.

Medical diagnosis: Isotope scanning is a process in which a radioisotope is introduced into the body by intravenous injection. Distribution and concentration of the isotope in various organs makes it possible to recognize the presence, size, and shape of various abnormalities in body organs. A form of X-ray imaging called computerized axial tomography (CAT scanning) measures the attenuation of X-rays entering the body from many different angles. From these measurements the computer reconstructs the organ as a series of cross sections, allowing soft tissues such as the heart to be seen. Positron emission tomography (PET) involves the emission of positrons by substances injected into the body. When positrons collide with electrons in the tissue, annihilation occurs, accompanied by the production of gamma radiation. The gamma photons easily pass through human tissue and are recorded by external detectors. Computers are programmed to interpret this information and generate digital images that physicians may interpret.

Nuclear reactors: In a nuclear fission reactor, fission reactions occur at a controlled rate: slow enough to avoid an explosion but rapid enough to produce usable heat. Stated succinctly, a nuclear fission reactor is a device that permits a controlled chain reaction of nuclear fissions. The heat removed from the reactor is used to convert water to steam and drive turbines to generate electricity. Scientists are hoping to develop nuclear fusion reactors to meet our growing need for energy. Although there are many obstacles, nuclear fusion is attractive because the fuel supply is abundant (deuterium found in water) and the energy produced is very great.

Radioactive dating: The dating of objects that were once living can be accomplished by studying the ratio of carbon-14 to carbon-12. Radioactive carbon-14 is incorporated by all plants in the photosynthetic process. Once the plant dies, however, no more carbon-14 is added. Thus, a high carbon-14/carbon-12 ratio is associated with more recent artifacts, while a low ratio is associated with older artifacts. Radioactive carbon dating is valid over a range from about 900 to 15,000 years, which is the period of greatest interest to most historians and archeologists.

The universe: Our Sun is a fusion reactor producing copious amounts of energy. It would require a conversion of only one percent of the Sun's mass from hydrogen to helium to keep the Sun shining at its present rate for another billion years. Nuclear reactions occur in the billions of other stars that are spread across the universe.

Food preservation: Food scientists are always looking for ways to improve the preservation of food, and one promising technique involves treatment with gamma radiation. Food is sealed within an airtight container and then bombarded with gamma rays to kill any bacteria or other pathogens. Although irradiated food can be stored for years at a time, some consumers don't like the idea that their food has been "nuked," even though it is not radioactive.

UNIT FOUR

Thermodynamics and Kinetics

4.1 Thermochemistry

4.2 Heat Transfer

4.3 Chemical Kinetics

4.4 Chemical Equilibrium

4.1 THERMOCHEMISTRY

In 1497 the Portuguese explorer Vasco da Gama discovered that it was possible to reach the Orient by sailing around the southern tip of Africa. Soon Portuguese merchants were bringing back spices and other prized goods by way of this long and dangerous route. As trade increased, explorers began searching the Arctic waters for a more direct route to the Orient. In the 16th century, Richard Chancellor, Willem Barents, Henry Hudson and others sailed north of Norway in search of a Northeast passage, but ultimately were blocked by ice. During the same period, Martin Frobisher, John Davis, Henry Hudson and others searched for a Northwest passage in the icy waters between Greenland and the Canadian islands, but met with similar problems. Many of these Arctic explorers lost their fingers or toes to frostbite as a result of prolonged exposure to sub-freezing temperatures.

Today, there are still those who dare to explore the frigid Arctic and alpine regions of the world. Although these hearty explorers encounter the same treacherous conditions that confronted early explorers, they have modern protection against the cold that their predecessors did not. Among the items that today's explorers carry are "heat packs" that can be applied to the skin to prevent frostbite in dangerously cold conditions.

If you go to a sporting goods store, you may find heat packs on the same shelf as "cold packs." While heat packs are often purchased by skiers, backpackers and other adventurers, cold packs are more frequently purchased by participants of contact sports such as football, rugby and the martial arts. In such sports, players often receive bruises, a condition resulting from the breaking of minor blood vessels in the soft tissues beneath the skin. Blood leaks into surrounding tissues and may cause swelling and pain. To reduce swelling, athletes crush the contents of the cold pack and apply it to the inflamed region.

Chemical processes or reactions that produce heat, like those occurring in heat packs, are termed exothermic (*exo-* out; *therm-* heat). The reactions that take place in your fireplace, the cylinders of your automobile engine or the furnace in your home are exothermic. Processes or reactions like those in cold packs that remove heat and cool the surrounding environment are termed endothermic (*endo-* within; *therm-* heat). The dissolving of salt in the drum of an ice cream maker or the expansion of freon or other refrigerant gases in an air conditioning unit are endothermic processes.

One brand of hot pack contains a mixture of powdered iron, activated carbon, sodium chloride, cellulose (sawdust), zeolite and water in an air-permeable package. Although all of these components are important to the proper functioning of the heat pack, the heat-producing reaction is simply the oxidation (rusting) of iron:

$$4Fe(s) \ + \ 3O_2(g) \longrightarrow 2Fe_2O_3(s) + heat$$

One brand of cold pack contains ammonium nitrate crystals and water in two separate packages. When crushed, the ingredients mix and the ammonium nitrate dissolves according to the following endothermic reaction:

$$water + \ heat + NH_4NO_3(s) \longrightarrow NH_4^+(aq) + NO_3^-(aq)$$

Notice that in exothermic reactions, heat is a product, while in endothermic reactions it is a reactant. When standardizing heats of reaction for purposes of comparison, chemists express these on the reactant side. Thus, a negative heat indicates an exothermic reaction, while a positive heat indicates an endothermic reaction. For example, the rusting reaction described above has a total energy change (the sum of the internal energy of a system is known as enthalpy, ΔH^0) of -1652 kJ, meaning that 1652 kJ of energy are released for every mole of iron oxide Fe_2O_3 produced. In a heat pack, this energy may be released slowly over a six-hour period, allowing the user to keep his or her hands warm through periods of emergency.

Energy is required to break a chemical bond between two atoms, and energy is released when a chemical bond between two atoms is formed. Thus, bond-breaking is an endothermic process while bond-making is an exothermic process. A reaction is exothermic (as in hand warmers) if the sum of the energy released from bond formations exceeds the sum of the energy required by bond formations. By contrast, a reaction is endothermic (as in cold packs) if the sum of the energy required to break bonds exceeds the energy released by bond formation. In this chapter you will be investigating various aspects of thermochemistry, the branch of chemistry that examines heat changes accompanying chemical processes.

4.1.1 ENDOTHERMIC REACTIONS

Concepts to Investigate: Dissolution, endothermic reactions, thermochemistry.

Materials: Ammonium nitrate-based cold pack (Kwik Kold® or similar brand), ammonium nitrate (a common garden fertilizer), beaker, scoop, water, thermometer, sodium chloride (table salt), calcium chloride.

Safety: Ammonium nitrate is a strong oxidizer. Wear goggles and lab coat when performing part 2.

Principles and Procedures: Many chemicals have a variety of uses. Ammonium nitrate, for example, is used as an explosive in fireworks, a source of nitrogen in fertilizers, and as the key ingredient in cold packs. When decomposed in fireworks it releases significant amounts of heat in a vigorous, exothermic reaction. However, when dissolved in water it consumes heat in a quiet, endothermic reaction:

$$\text{water} + \text{ heat} + NH_4NO_3(s) \longrightarrow NH_4^+(aq) + NO_3^-(aq)$$

Part 1: Cold packs: Cold packs are often made of an outer pouch that contains solid ammonium nitrate, and an inner pouch that contains water (Figure A). Squeeze the pack as shown in Figure B. When the inner pouch breaks, water is released and ammonium nitrate is dissolved in an endothermic reaction.

Part 2: Cold pack reaction: *Put on safety goggles and lab coat.* Pour 100 mL of tap water into a beaker or test tube and record the temperature. Weigh out 50 grams of ammonium nitrate, pour it into the beaker and stir with a glass rod (Figure C). Record the coldest temperature reached. Repeat the procedure using 50 grams of table salt (NaCl) and 50 grams of calcium chloride. Are all reactions in which a solid dissolves endothermic? You may conserve chemicals by using a test tube and reducing portions to 5 g of solute and 10 mL water.

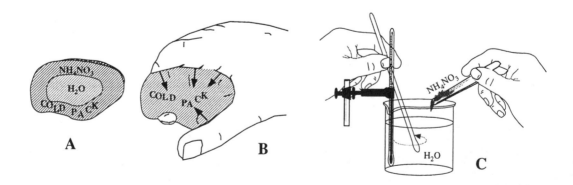

Questions

(1) Approximately 326 joules of heat are consumed per gram of ammonium nitrate in this reaction. Where does this heat come from since there are no burners or heaters involved? Explain.

(2) What change in temperature occurs when ammonium nitrate is dissolved? When sodium chloride is dissolved? When calcium chloride is dissolved?

(3) Are all dissolution reactions (the process of dissolving) endothermic? Explain.

(4) Would any of the chemicals used in part 2 serve well for a "hot pack"? Explain.

4.1.2 HEATS OF DILUTION AND SOLUTION

Concepts to Investigate: Exothermic reactions, heat of solution, heat of dilution, thermochemistry.

Materials: Calcium chloride, lithium chloride, sodium chloride, concentrated sulfuric acid, Styrofoam® cups, beakers.

Safety: Only the instructor should dispense concentrated sulfuric acid. Sulfuric acid is severely corrosive to eyes, skin and other tissue, and even dilute solutions are harmful. Sulfuric acid has a high heat of dilution, and therefore containers in which it is diluted may get very hot. Wear goggles, lab coat and gloves when working with sulfuric acid.

Principles and Procedures: More sulfuric acid is produced than any other inorganic chemical in the world. The United States manufactures more than 40 million tons each year, much of which is used in the production of fertilizers, paints, synthetic fibers, detergents, explosives and pharmaceuticals. Although sulfuric acid is a familiar chemical, it is also quite dangerous because it is a strong acid and has a high heat of dilution. Like all acids, it should be diluted by slowly adding it to water and not vice versa. In this activity you will investigate the heat associated with the dilution of sulfuric acid (heat of dilution) as well as the heat associated with the dissolution of various mineral salts (heat of solution).

Part 1: Heat of dilution: *This activity requires concentrated sulfuric acid which should be poured only by the instructor. Everyone should wear goggles and a lab coat.* Place a Styrofoam® cup inside each of three beakers. The beakers improve the stability of the cups and minimize the danger of spillage. Add 50 mL of water to each cup and record the temperature. The instructor should slowly add 5 mL of concentrated sulfuric acid (18 M H_2SO_4) to the first cup and then students should stir with glass rods and record the highest temperature reached. When measurements are concluded, the instructor should neutralize the solution with baking soda ($NaHCO_3$), and flush it down the drain with much water. Repeat the process using 10 mL and 15 mL of concentrated sulfuric acid. Is the amount of heat produced related to the amount of sulfuric acid diluted?

Part 2: Heat of solution: Place a Styrofoam® cup inside each of three beakers. The beakers improve the stability of the cups and minimize the danger of spillage. Add 50 mL of water to each cup. Record the temperature of the water and then place 5 g of calcium chloride ($CaCl_2$) into the first cup and stir with a glass rod until completely dissolved. Record the highest temperature reached (Figure D).

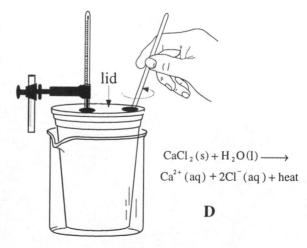

lid

$$CaCl_2(s) + H_2O(l) \longrightarrow$$
$$Ca^{2+}(aq) + 2Cl^-(aq) + heat$$

D

$$CaCl_2(s) + H_2O(l) \longrightarrow Ca^{2+}(aq) + 2Cl^-(aq) + heat$$

Determine the heat of solution by multiplying the rise in temperature (measured in degrees Celsius) by the mass of water (measured in grams). The product will represent the number of calories of heat released as the calcium chloride dissolved. A calorie is the amount of heat required to raise one gram of water one degree Celsius. To convert to joules, multiply this value by 4.2 (1 calorie = 4.184 joules). Repeat the procedure in the second cup using 5 grams of table salt (NaCl), and in the third cup using 5 grams of lithium chloride. Are all solubility reactions exothermic? Which of the three compounds released the most heat per mole when dissolved?

Questions

(1) Is the amount of heat produced in the dilution of sulfuric acid related to the amount of sulfuric acid diluted? Explain.

(2) A reaction is exothermic if the energy released by bond formations exceeds the energy required to break bonds. Explain.

(3) Which of the chemicals tested released heat upon dissolving (was exothermic)? Which consumed heat (endothermic)?

(4) Write the reaction for the dissolving of lithium chloride in water.

4.1.3 CHEMICAL HAND-WARMER

Concepts to Investigate: Exothermic reactions, rusting, corrosion, oxidation.

Materials: 100 mesh iron powder (unoxidized electrolytic powder, 100 mesh or finer), vermiculite (from garden store), salt, plastic bag, twist-tie.

Safety: Wear goggles and lab coat.

Principles and Procedures: Frostbite is a condition that results from the formation of ice crystals in body tissues. Circulation is reduced drastically, and tissues become numb and turn a grayish blue. Gangrene, the death of tissues due to lack of oxygen, will set in if blood flow ceases. Those who work outdoors in cold climates often carry chemical hand-warmers to prevent frostbite in emergency situations. In this activity you will make your own hand-warmer.

Mix 25 g of unoxidized iron powder (iron powder must be gray or black, not red or brown), 1 g of table salt (sodium chloride) and 5 g of vermiculite together in a small plastic bag that is supported by a beaker (Figure E). When all the materials are evenly distributed, add approximately 5 mL of water, remove all the air and seal the bag. To activate your hand-warmer, open the bag and allow oxygen to enter. Gently knead the bag to mix the contents and note any changes in temperature (Figure F). Unoxidized iron rusts rapidly when exposed to salt water and oxygen, generating a substantial amount of heat:

$$4Fe(s) + 3O_2(g) \longrightarrow 2Fe_2O_3(s) \qquad \Delta H = -1652 \text{ kJ/mole}$$

Is it possible to "turn off" your hand-warmer by removing the air from the bag and re-sealing it? Try it and monitor the temperature of the bag for 10 to 15 minutes. What happens if you once again open the bag and allow air to re-enter?

What is the role of sodium chloride in this reaction? Repeat the procedure described above, but without the salt. Compare this reaction to the previous one. Does sodium chloride facilitate the oxidation of iron?

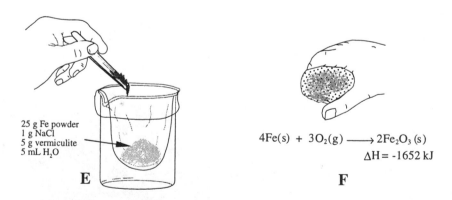

25 g Fe powder
1 g NaCl
5 g vermiculite
5 mL H₂O

E

$$4Fe(s) + 3O_2(g) \longrightarrow 2Fe_2O_3(s)$$
$$\Delta H = -1652 \text{ kJ}$$

F

Questions

(1) Is this an exothermic reaction? How do you know?

(2) Why is it necessary to open the hand-warmer bag to start the reaction?

(3) What effect does removing the air and sealing the bag have upon the temperature of the hand-warmer?

(4) Does sodium chloride facilitate this reaction? Explain.

(5) Salt is often added to melt ice on streets. Drivers complain that this salt causes their cars to rust. Is this a valid complaint? Explain.

4.1.4 HEAT OF REACTION

Concepts to Investigate: Exothermic reactions, chemical bond energy, heat of reaction.

Materials: Styrofoam® cup, calcium oxide, scoop, thermometer.

Safety: Wear goggles, lab coat, and gloves. Lime (calcium oxide) is quite caustic, irritates skin and mucous membranes, and should therefore be used with caution.

Principles and Procedures: Chemical reactions involve the breakage and formation of chemical bonds. Energy is required to break existing bonds, and energy is released when new bonds form. A reaction is exothermic if the energy released by the formation of new bonds exceeds the energy consumed in the breaking of existing bonds.

We use exothermic reactions to power our homes and industries. The energy released from the burning of coal, natural gas and oil is used to heat homes, power automobiles, and drive the generators that provide electricity to our homes and businesses. Exothermic chemical reactions are essential to civilization.

The stronger a bond, the more energy is required to break it, and the more energy is released when the bond is formed. In this activity you will investigate reactions that release energy because the bonds of the products are stronger than the bonds of the reactants. The quantity of heat liberated or absorbed during a reaction is called the heat of reaction. The change in heat is defined as negative if the reaction liberates energy (exothermic reaction) and positive if the reaction absorbs energy (endothermic reaction).

Lime (calcium oxide, CaO) has been used in construction for thousands of years. The Roman official Cato (234–149 BC) described how lime was prepared and used in the mortar between bricks in some of the famous buildings of ancient Rome. Throughout the ages, construction workers have realized that lime expands and heats when it combines with water. As a result, building contractors must keep their supplies of lime dry. In this activity you will determine the average amount of heat per mole released when calcium oxide reacts with water to form calcium hydroxide:

$$CaO(s) + H_2O(l) \longrightarrow Ca(OH)_2(s) + heat$$

Place 50 mL of water in a Styrofoam® cup and record the temperature. Use a scoop to place 20 grams of fresh calcium oxide in the cup and step back from the container. As the reaction slows, carefully approach the container, record the highest temperature reached and note changes in volume (Figure G). As water evaporates, calcium hydroxide is exposed to carbon dioxide and forms calcium carbonate. Allow your mixture to stand until it forms a hard plaster. Archeologists have found such plasters in the ruins of Mesopotamian structures built more than four thousand years ago.

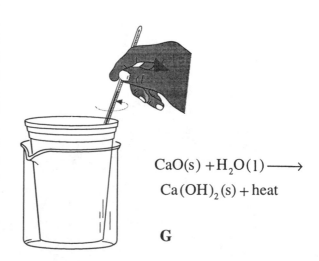

$$CaO(s) + H_2O(l) \longrightarrow$$
$$Ca(OH)_2(s) + heat$$

G

Determine the number of moles of CaO used by dividing its mass by its formula weight (56 g/mole). Determine the heat released by multiplying the increase in water temperature by the number of grams of water. (The number of grams of water is the same as the number of milliliters since water has a density of 1 g/mL). Determine the molar heat of reaction by dividing the heat released by the number of moles of calcium oxide consumed.

Questions

(1) What is the molar heat (kcal/mole) of reaction of calcium oxide in water? Convert your answer from kcal/mole to kJ/mole by multiplying by 4.2 kJ/kcal.

(2) What is the chemical explanation for the increase in temperature associated with this reaction?

(3) In the 7th century AD, the Greeks developed incendiary devices that burst into flames when they became wet, and used these to set fire to invading ships. Although the formula remained a secret, many chemists believe that it was a mixture of lime, sulfur, and pitch. Explain the role that lime may have played in this mixture.

4.1.5 CALORIC CONTENT OF FOODS

Concepts to Investigate: Calorie (kilocalorie), calorie, food energy, heat.

Materials: Aluminum soft drink can, ring stand, paper clip or twist-tie, test tube clamp, modeling clay (or large eraser), straight pin, peanut, marshmallow, match.

Safety: Never eat any food materials used in experiments!

Principles and Procedures: Exothermic chemical reactions are essential for life. As you digest food, glucose and other molecules are absorbed into the bloodstream and taken to cells to be metabolized. In the process of metabolism, energy is released and then stored in molecules of adenosine tri-phosphate (ATP). ATP molecules subsequently undergo an exothermic decomposition, and the energy released is used to power endothermic processes necessary for growth.

We measure the energy that foods give us in terms of Calories. A Calorie (written with a large "C") is actually a kilocalorie or 1000 calories (written with a small "c"). Since a calorie is the amount of energy required to raise one gram of water one degree Celsius, a kilocalorie or Calorie is the amount of energy required to raise 1000 grams (1 kg) of water one degree Celsius. Teenagers generally consume between 1500 and 3000 Calories (kilocalories) of food energy each day. Those foods which release a large amount of chemical energy when metabolized are frequently referred to as "fattening" foods because people store excess energy as fat. In this activity you will investigate the energy content of some simple foods.

In order to measure the caloric content of foods, it is necessary to construct a simple calorimeter such as illustrated in Figure H. Place 100 mL (100g) of water in an empty aluminum soft drink can, record the water temperature, and suspend the can from a ring stand using a twist-tie or paper clip as shown. Weigh a shelled peanut to the nearest tenth of a gram. Carefully skewer the peanut with a straight pin and embed the other end of the pin in a lump of clay to make a stand as shown. Light the peanut on fire and lower the can so that it is immediately above the flame. The calorimeter will be accurate only if the heat from the burning food is used to heat the water in the can. To reduce heat loss to the surrounding environment, reflect it back to the can by surrounding the flame with a shield made of perforated aluminum foil. (It is necessary to make holes in the foil to allow oxygen in to sustain the flame.) When the peanut has been consumed by the flame, determine the increase in temper-

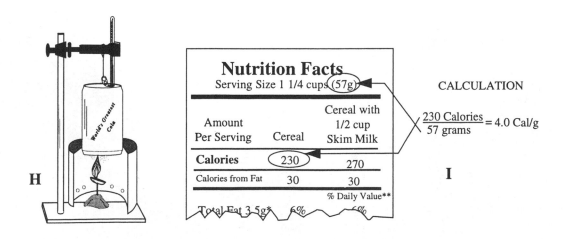

ature of the water in the can and calculate the amount of energy transferred to the can in terms of calories by multiplying:

$$100 \text{ g water} \times \underline{\hspace{1cm}}°C = \underline{\hspace{1cm}} \text{ calories}$$

Convert this value to Calories (kilocalories) by dividing by 1000:

$$\underline{\hspace{1cm}} \text{ calories} \times 1 \text{ Cal}/1000 \text{ calories} = \underline{\hspace{1cm}} \text{ Cal}$$

Determine the number of calories per gram by dividing by the mass of the peanut:

$$\underline{\hspace{1cm}} \text{ Cal}/\underline{\hspace{1cm}} \text{ g}_{(peanut)} = \underline{\hspace{1cm}} \text{ Cal/g}$$

Repeat the procedure using a miniature marshmallow, a cashew, or other food of your choice. Which food has the greatest amount of energy per gram?

Questions

(1) Calculate the energy released per gram of food. Which of the foods tested contains the most energy per gram?

(2) A 150-pound person will burn approximately 750 Calories per hour playing a full court game of basketball. How many peanuts would they need to eat to give them enough energy to play a one-hour game?

(3) Energy from the combustion of the peanut was used to heat the water in the can. How is energy from the metabolism of a peanut used in a human body?

(4) Read the nutrition labels of three cereals and determine the Caloric content per gram of each. (A sample calculation is shown in Figure I.) Which one would you recommend for a person on a weight loss diet? Why?

(5) Do you think that this activity will yield a value that is higher or lower than the true caloric content of the food tested? Explain.

4.1.6 ENTROPY

Concepts to Investigate: Entropy, second law of thermodynamics, spontaneity.

Materials: Part 1: Photocopy machine; Part 2: Erlenmeyer flasks, note card or overhead transparency, food coloring, thermometer.

Principles and Procedures: One of the toughest and most lawless gold-mining camps in the West was the town of Bodie, located high in the mountains of eastern California. As the ore was gradually exhausted, the 10,000 residents abandoned their homes and businesses and left behind only a "ghost town." Today, when visitors peer through windows into rooms left vacant for more than a century, they see faded fabric, dusty furniture, warping floorboards and peeling paint. The town of Bodie, like your room, the authors' desks, or anything else in life, is subject to the second law of thermodynamics (the law of entropy), which drives it toward a more disordered state.

Entropy is a measure of the randomness or disorder in processes or systems. The more disordered a system, the greater its entropy. According to the second law of thermodynamics, the total entropy, or randomness, of a system and its surroundings always increases during spontaneous processes. So while we are not surprised to find that the rooms in a ghost town have become more disorderly (run down) with time, we would never expect them to appear in a more orderly condition today than they were when abandoned.

When a cube of sugar is placed in a cup of coffee, it gradually dissolves, and the sugar molecules become evenly distributed throughout. The sugar molecules move from an orderly state (cube), to a disorderly state (dissolved). While such a process is a common occurrence, you would never see the dissolved sugar spontaneously forming a cube again. Similarly, if a bottle of perfume is left open, the molecules spontaneously diffuse into the air, but will never return to fill the bottle. The law of entropy (second law of thermodynamics) is commonly observed.

Place three drops of blue food coloring in each of two flasks, and an equivalent amount of yellow food coloring in two more identical flasks. Fill one blue and one yellow flask to the brim with cold water and record the temperature. Cover the top of the blue flask with a 3″ × 5″ card, or a small square cut from an overhead transparency. With the card held tightly against the mouth of the flask, invert the blue flask and place it carefully on top of the yellow flask as shown in Figure J. Pull the card out, and secure the flask with a clamp as illustrated

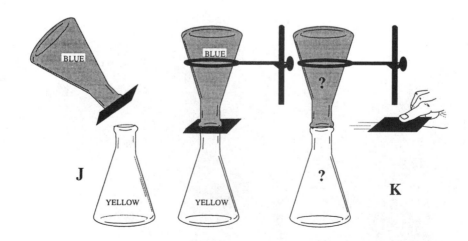

J   K

YELLOW   YELLOW

(Figure K). Allow the flasks to stand, and record the time necessary for both flasks to become the same shade of green. Repeat the procedure using warm water, and then once again with ice water. Does temperature influence the rate of this process? If possible, perform both activities at the same time, as this will allow for direct comparisons and minimize the time necessary for the complete investigation. *Do not use hot water because of the danger of spills and burns.*

Questions

(1) Is the entropy greatest when the colors of the flasks in part 2 are different or the same? Explain.

(2) Explain the relationship between diffusion and entropy.

(3) What influence does an increase in temperature have on the diffusion observed in part 2?

4.1.7 ENTROPY-DRIVEN REACTIONS

Concepts to Investigate: Gibbs free energy, spontaneity, entropy, enthalpy, second law of thermodynamics.

Materials: Ammonium thiocyanate (NH_4SCN), barium hydroxide octahydrate ($Ba(OH)_2 \cdot 8H_2O$), mortar and pestle, small block of wood.

Safety: Because of cost and safety issues this activity should be performed only as a teacher demonstration. Wear goggles, lab coat and gloves.

Principles and Procedures: Although it is not surprising to see a cone fall from a pine tree, it would be startling to see it rise spontaneously from the ground. Scientists have long recognized the tendency of processes to occur that lead to lower (more stable) energy states. The potential energy of a pine cone on the ground is less than in the tree, so cones can fall spontaneously, but cannot rise spontaneously. Such observations led many 19th-century scientists to believe that spontaneous reactions are always exothermic and result in a decrease in heat energy (enthalpy, H). If this were true, then all spontaneous reactions would be exothermic, but, as we shall see in this activity, this is not the case. There are many reactions that are endothermic, and yet occur spontaneously.

We now know that two factors influence the drive to spontaneous change—the tendency toward lowest heat energy (enthalpy, H), and the tendency toward greatest disorder (entropy, S). The enthalpy/entropy function of a system is the energy available to do useful work (Gibbs free energy, G). At constant temperature and pressure, the free-energy change (the chemical reaction potential, ΔG) of a system can be expressed as the difference between the change in enthalpy (ΔH), and the product of the Kelvin temperature and the entropy change ($T\Delta S$):

$$\Delta G = \Delta H - T\Delta S$$

Whenever the change in free energy is negative (free energy is lost from the system) the reaction is spontaneous. Losses in heat energy (negative ΔH as in exothermic reactions) and increases in randomness (positive ΔS) increase the driving force of the reaction (move ΔG in the negative direction), while gains in heat energy (a positive ΔH, as in endothermic reactions) and decreases in randomness (negative ΔS) reduce the driving force of the reaction (move ΔG in the positive direction). Thus, while the majority of spontaneous reactions (reactions with a negative ΔG) are exothermic (negative ΔH), endothermic reactions (positive ΔH) may be spontaneous if the increases in temperature/entropy term ($T\Delta S$) outweigh the gain in enthalpy. In this activity we shall investigate such a reaction.

Carefully grind approximately 20 grams of barium hydroxide octahydrate ($Ba(OH)_2 \cdot 8H_2O$) to a fine powder with a mortar and pestle. Mix the powdered barium hydroxide with approximately 10 grams of ammonium thiocyanate (NH_4SCN) in a 250 mL Erlenmeyer flask. Seal the flask with a stopper fitted with a thermometer as shown in Figure L. Swirl the flask and record the temperature at five second intervals. As a liquid starts to appear in the flask, set the flask on a small block of wood whose surface has been thoroughly wetted. As the reaction proceeds, heat will be removed from the water on the board, causing the water to freeze and the flask to stick to the board. Carefully lift the flask (Figure M).

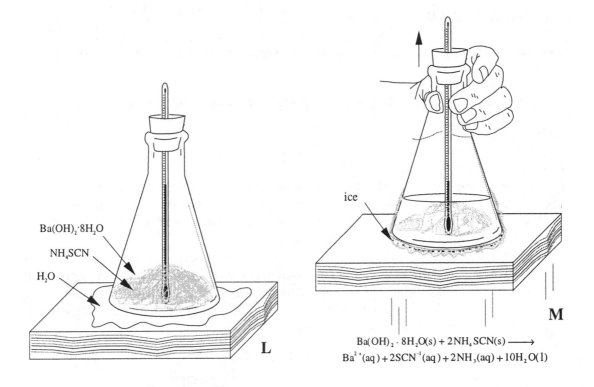

Ba(OH)$_2$·8H$_2$O

NH$_4$SCN

H$_2$O

ice

L

M

$$Ba(OH)_2 \cdot 8H_2O(s) + 2NH_4SCN(s) \longrightarrow$$
$$Ba^{2+}(aq) + 2SCN^{-1}(aq) + 2NH_3(aq) + 10H_2O(l)$$

Does the block come with it? What is the coldest temperature reached by the liquid in the flask? The following equation describes the reaction:

$$Ba(OH)_2 \cdot 8H_2O(s) + 2NH_4SCN(s) \longrightarrow Ba^{2+}(aq) + 2SCN^{-1}(aq) + 2NH_3(aq) + 10H_2O(l)$$

Open the flask and carefully waft the fumes toward you, keeping your face at least a half a meter from the flask. Never sniff any chemical! Can you detect an ammonia odor?

Questions

(1) Of the three states of matter (solid, liquid, gas), which has the highest entropy (most random state)? Explain.

(2) For this highly endothermic reaction to proceed spontaneously, there must be a significant increase in entropy. Examine the reaction and explain the reason for this increased entropy.

(3) How cold did the liquid in the flask get?

(4) This combination of chemicals is never used in medical cold packs. Explain.

4.1.8 ENTROPY AND ENTHALPY

Concepts to Investigate: Entropy, enthalpy, free energy, Gibbs free energy equation, spontaneous processes.

Materials: Wide rubber bands, goggles, ring stand, paper clips, weights, hair dryer.

Safety: Wear goggles.

Principles and Procedures:

Part 1: *Put on goggles!* Hold a strong, wide rubber band tightly across your forehead. Quickly stretch the rubber band while keeping it pressed to your skin. Does the temperature of the rubber band increase or decrease? After approximately 20 seconds, relax the rubber band. Does the temperature rise or fall when the rubber band is relaxed?

The stretching of the band is not a spontaneous process because it will not occur without energy from the outside. We know that stretching the band is exothermic (negative ΔH) since heat is released and felt by thermoreceptors in the skin. An analysis of the Gibbs free energy equation indicates that if ΔG is positive, and ΔH is negative, then the change in entropy (ΔS) must be negative if the equation is to be balanced:

$$\Delta G = \Delta H - T\Delta S$$

Thus, the arrangement of molecules in a stretched rubber band must be less random (lower entropy) than when relaxed.

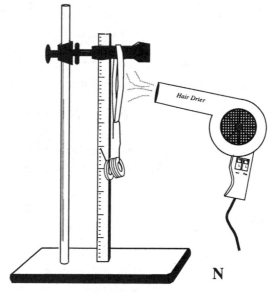

N

Part 2: Place a wide rubber band over a lateral post on a ringstand. Using a paper clip, hang weights (fishing weights, washers, balance weights, etc.) from the rubber band until it is fully stretched as shown in Figure N. Measure the length of the rubber band, and then heat it with a hair drier. Does the rubber band shorten or lengthen? Is this what you expected? Record the percentage change in length.

Questions

(1) Is the relaxation of the rubber band a spontaneous process? Explain. Is the ΔG value of the rubber band relaxation process positive or negative? Explain.

(2) Is stretching the band exothermic or endothermic? Is the contraction of the band exothermic or endothermic? Explain.

(3) Did the rubber band shrink or expand when heated?

(4) Is the arrangement of molecules more orderly when stretched or relaxed? Is the entropy of the band greater when stretched or relaxed? Explain.

(5) What is the driving force that causes a stretched band to contract (relax)?

(6) Why does heating the stretched rubber band cause it to contract?

FOR THE TEACHER

Thermodynamics is the branch of science that deals with the transfer and interconversion of heat and work in physical and chemical processes. Thermochemistry focuses on heat changes accompanying chemical processes and is dependent upon the principles of thermodynamics. You may wish to introduce or review all three fundamental laws of thermodynamics before discussing issues of thermochemistry. The first law of thermodynamics states that energy can be converted from one form to another, but can never be created or destroyed. The second law of thermodynamics states that for any process, the total entropy of a system and its surroundings always increases. The third law of thermodynamics states that the entropy of a perfect crystal is zero only at absolute zero ($-273°C$, 0K).

This chapter also deals with the concept of spontaneity. A spontaneous process is one that will occur by itself under the prevailing conditions once it has been initiated. A reaction is said to be spontaneous if the quantity of the products increases while the quantity of the reactants decreases under the specified conditions. Chemical reactions always occur in the direction that results in a decrease in the free energy of the system. Spontaneous chemical reactions continue until the minimum free energy is reached so that the ΔG value is zero. At this point a dynamic equilibrium is reached. From a thermodynamic perspective, equilibrium is defined as that situation in which ΔG is zero.

A reaction is spontaneous when ΔG is negative (i.e. when there is a loss in free energy).

$$\Delta G = \Delta H - T\Delta S$$

Whether a reaction occurs under specific conditions depends on the tendency to reach a lower energy level *(ΔH)* and the tendency to reach greater disorder *(ΔS)*. If the entropy change *(ΔS)* is positive (i.e. disorder is increasing), the quantity $T\Delta S$ makes a negative contribution to ΔG, thereby increasing the tendency for a spontaneous change.

4.1.1 ENDOTHERMIC REACTIONS

Discussion: You may wish to pass around a beaker of water that has been saturated with ammonium nitrate so students will see how cold the contents will get. Glass beakers are recommended for part 2 because they conduct heat and allow students to feel the temperature changes. If, however, you desire to make accurate measurements of changes in temperature, use Styrofoam cups because Styrofoam® is a much better insulator than glass and will minimize heat exchange with the room.

Answers: (1) Heat is removed from the solution, explaining why the temperature drops. (2) The temperature drops approximately 6–9°C when ten grams of ammonium nitrate are dissolved in 100 mL water. By contrast, the temperature rises approximately 12°C when calcium chloride is dissolved, and drops one or two degrees when sodium chloride is dissolved. (3) No. The dissolution of calcium chloride and many other substances is exothermic. (4) Yes. Calcium chloride is used in some hot packs because it releases a substantial amount of heat (82.9 kJ/mole).

4.1.2 HEATS OF DILUTION AND SOLUTION

Discussion: Concentrated sulfuric acid (18 M) is approximately 97% H_2SO_4. It has a heat of dilution of -61.4 kJ/mole. Thus, approximately 5.5 kJ will be released when 5 mL of concentrated sulfuric acid are diluted in 50 mL of water. This may cause a temperature rise of approximately 25° C. The temperature may rise nearly 50° when 10 mL of acid are diluted, and 70° when 15 mL are diluted. The increase in heat is related to the quantity of concentrated sulfuric acid diluted.

The heat of solution *($\Delta H_{solution}$)* is determined by three conditions: the breaking of the solute into its components *(ΔH_1)*; the breaking of intermolecular forces in the solvent to make room for the solute *(ΔH_2)*; and the interaction of the solute and solvent to form a solution *(ΔH_3)*. If the heat given off in step 3 *(ΔH_3)* exceeds the heat consumed in the sum of steps 1 and 2 *(ΔH_1 and ΔH_2)*, then the reaction gives off heat and is said to be exothermic. Lithium chloride and calcium chloride release a significant amount of heat when they dissolve (exothermic), while sodium chloride consumes a slight amount of heat (endothermic). If you do not have the chemicals described in this activity, you may wish to demonstrate heats of solution using some of the substances listed in Table 1. Always use goggles and protective clothing.

Table 1: Heats of Solution (kJ/mole solute)

Endothermic		Exothermic	
$Na_2SO_4 \cdot 10H_2O$ (s)	78.5	HCl(l)	−74.3
$KClO_3$(s)	42.0	H_2SO_4 (l)	−74.3
KNO_3(s)	35.7	$CuSO_4$ (s)	−67.8
NH_4NO_3(s)	25.5	KOH(s)	−54.6
KI(s)	21.4	NaOH(s)	−41.6
$NaNO_3$(s)	21.1	LiCl(s)	−35.0
NaCl(s)	4.3	CO_2(g)	−19.9

Answers: (1) Yes. The more an acid is diluted, the greater the heat produced. (2) Heat is required to break bonds, and heat is released when bonds are formed. A reaction is exothermic whenever the heat released by bond formation is greater than that consumed in bond breaking. (3) Lithium chloride and calcium chloride were exothermic, while sodium chloride was slightly endothermic. (4) $LiCl(s) \xrightarrow{\text{water}} Li^+(aq) + Cl^-(aq) + heat.$

4.1.3 CHEMICAL HAND-WARMER

Discussion: Your students may be familiar with the rusting process, but few may realize that it is the exothermic reaction used in commercial hand-warmers. Make certain they understand that the vermiculite and table salt are not part of the reaction. Vermiculite (a hydrated magnesium-aluminum-iron silicate) is a spongy mineral used in potting soils, and is used here as an insulating material to make the hand-warmer last longer.

The corrosion of iron is an electrochemical reaction. Iron is not uniform, and some portions are more easily oxidized (anodic regions) while others are more easily reduced (cathodic regions). In the anodic regions iron gives up two electrons to form the ferrous ion (Fe^{2+}):

$$Fe \longrightarrow Fe^{2+} + 2e^-$$

Ferrous ions migrate to the cathodic regions where they react with oxygen to form hydrated iron (III) oxide ($Fe_2O_3 \cdot nH_2O$), commonly known as rust:

$$4Fe^{2+}(aq) + O_2(g) + (4+2n)H_2O(l) \longrightarrow 2Fe_2O_3 \cdot nH_2O(s) + 8H^+(aq)$$

Water is essential to the rusting process because it serves as a bridge through which ferrous ions migrate between anodic and cathodic regions. The dissolved salt increases the conductivity of the solution and accelerates the electrochemical corrosion process. Iron powder collects on the surface of the vermiculite where it is exposed to oxygen and the salt water. Make certain that the iron powder is black or gray. Red or brown coloration indicates that the iron has already been oxidized, and therefore will not react with oxygen.

There are a variety of chemical hot packs on the market using a variety of formulations. One uses a supersaturated solution of sodium thiosulfate in an inner pouch that crystallizes when mixed with an outer pouch containing a few seed crystals. The heat of crystallization is substantial and produces a moderate amount of heat. Another type of "hot pack" contains calcium chloride in an outer pouch that, when mixed with water in the inner pouch, produces heat of solution. You may wish to demonstrate these reactions in class.

Answers: (1) Yes. The temperature of the bag rises when air mixes with the contents of the package. (2) Opening the bag allows oxygen to enter and mix with the iron. (3) One of the reactants in the "hand-warmer" is oxygen. If air is removed, the reaction will stop and temperature will decrease. (4) Yes. The hand warmer is much hotter when salt is added, indicating that the oxidation of iron proceeds more rapidly in the presence of salt. (5) Yes. Salt provides electrolytes (Na^+, Cl^-) that facilitate the oxidation (rusting) of the iron frames of automobiles.

4.1.4 HEAT OF REACTION

Discussion: The reaction of calcium oxide with water is known as "slaking." Calcium oxide is commonly known as lime, and calcium hydroxide as slaked lime. Approximately 20 kcal (82 kJ) of heat are liberated per mole of lime consumed. Lime (CaO) is often referred to as quicklime or burnt lime. It is used in the production of glass, cement, brick, and other building materials. In the early days of Rome, lime was mixed with sand to form a stucco plaster that covered mud brick walls.

Answers: (1) Students should obtain a value of approximately 20 kcal/mole (82 kJ/mole). (2) The bonds in calcium hydroxide are stronger than the bonds in calcium oxide. Therefore, energy is released as the reaction proceeds. (3) Lime reacts with water and releases significant heat that may ignite flammable mixtures such as sulfur and pitch.

4.1.5 CALORIC CONTENT OF FOODS

Discussion: Most students are familiar with the term "Calorie" either from discussions of diets or from nutritional panels on food containers (Figure I). Unfortunately, food scientists and nutritionists use the term Calorie for what chemists call a kilocalorie (1000 calories). Although a calorie (with a small "c") is the amount of energy required to raise one gram of water one degree Celsius at 15°C, a Calorie (with a large "C," kilocalorie) is the amount of energy required to raise one thousand grams of water one degree Celsius. Make certain students understand this distinction.

You may wish to introduce the concept of respiration and show how it is similar to combustion. The aerobic respiration of glucose, for example, can be represented as follows:

$$C_6H_{12}O_6 + 6O_2 \longrightarrow 6CO_2 + 6H_2O + 36\,ATP$$

This resembles the exothermic reaction of the combustion of glucose:

$$C_6H_{12}O_6 + 6O_2 \longrightarrow 6CO_2 + 6H_2O + heat$$

The energy released by hydrolysis of ATP is approximately 7.3 kcal/mole. Since 36 ATP are produced for each glucose consumed, aerobic respiration of glucose yields 263 kcal/mole. By contrast, the combustion of glucose yields 670 kcal/mole. Thus, in aerobic respiration, 39% of the available energy in glucose is converted to ATP (263/670) while the remaining 61% is dissipated as heat.

Answers: (1) Answers will vary depending on the foods selected. When fully combusted, a peanut should yield approximately 5.6 Calories (5.6 kilocalories) of energy. Student values will typically be lower than this for the reasons explained in question 5. (2) Students should obtain this value by dividing 750 Calories by the number of Calories per peanut calculated in question 1. (3) Energy released from the metabolism of any food is used to synthesize ATP which is in turn used to drive the endothermic reactions necessary for growth and development. (4) Student answers will vary depending on the cereal selected. They should recommend the cereal with the lowest caloric content per gram for a person on a weight loss diet. (5) This activity will typically yield results lower than the actual values because combustion is rarely complete, and some of the heat energy is lost to the surrounding air and metal.

4.1.6 ENTROPY

Discussion: Entropy was originally defined by the German physicist Rudulf Clausius in 1865. He discovered that in all processes of heat exchanges, useful energy is inevitably lost. He referred to this loss in useful energy as a gain in "entropy." The second law of thermodynamics implies that all processes operate at less than 100% efficiency due to an inevitable increase in entropy. A coal-fired electric power plant may be only 33% efficient, while a car may be only 20% efficient. Such losses in usable energy are due to increases in entropy.

Entropy increases as matter is scattered. Larger and more complex molecules are more orderly and therefore have lower entropy. The first law of thermodynamics states that the energy of the universe is constant, while the second law states that the entropy of the universe is increasing.

Answers: (1) Order is highest and entropy is lowest when the colors are distinct and separate. Entropy increases as molecules of blue dye diffuse into the yellow flask, and molecules of yellow dye diffuse into the blue flask. Entropy (disorder) is greatest when the dye molecules are evenly distributed throughout both flasks so that both appear green. (2) At ordinary temperatures, molecules are in constant random motion. The number of blue dye molecules moving out of the blue flask will exceed the number of blue dye molecules moving in, and the number of yellow dye molecules moving out of the yellow flask will exceed the number of yellow dye molecules flowing in. As a result, the system will move from an orderly (low entropy) state where similar molecules are grouped, to a disorderly state (high entropy) where molecules of both dyes are evenly distributed throughout. (3) An increase in temperature causes an increase in diffusion. At higher temperatures, molecules are moving faster and proceed toward the disordered (high entropy) state more rapidly.

4.1.7 ENTROPY-DRIVEN REACTIONS

Discussion: If ammonium thiocyanate is unavailable, you can substitute 7 grams of ammonium chloride or 11 grams of ammonium nitrate. The equations for these spontaneous endothermic reactions are as follows:

$$Ba(OH)_2 \cdot 8H_2O(s) + 2NH_4NO_3(s) \longrightarrow Ba(NO_3)_2(s) + 2NH_3(aq) + 10H_2O(l)$$

$$Ba(OH)_2 \cdot 8H_2O(s) + 2NH_4Cl(s) \longrightarrow BaCl_2 \cdot 2H_2O(s) + 2NH_3(aq) + 8H_2O(l)$$

All of these reactions result in lower temperatures and are good examples of entropy-driven reactions. Ammonium thiocyanate is hygroscopic (absorbs water from the air), and if you do not have a fresh, dry source, you may wish to substitute one of the other ammonia salts.

Answers: (1) The entropy of gases is greater than liquids which is greater than solids. Solids are more highly organized than liquids, and liquids are more highly organized than gases. For example, the ammonium (NH_4^+) ions in crystalline ammonium thiocyanate are fixed in a regular repeating pattern. Aqueous ammonium, $NH_4^+(aq)$, can move with greater freedom, allowing for a more random distribution. Ammonium gas, $NH_3(g)$, is highly disordered. Like all gases, molecules of ammonia gas rarely interact with each other and display a high level of entropy. (2) Analysis of the reaction shows that a few reactant molecules in the solid state yield numerous molecules in the aqueous and liquid states. The increased number of particles, coupled with the change in state explains the significant increase in entropy. (3) Student answers will vary, and may range from −10°C to −30°C. (4) The components are toxic, and the reaction is quite endothermic and may result in temperatures that could freeze body tissues.

4.1.8 ENTROPY AND ENTHALPY

Discussion: This is an interesting counter-intuitive activity because many students are familiar with the principle of thermal expansion which describes how metals and other substances expand when heated. Rubber, however, contracts when heated to the surprise of many students. Capitalize on this interest when introducing entropy and the Gibbs free energy equation:

$$\Delta G = \Delta H - T\Delta S$$

Answers: (1) The relaxation of the rubber band is spontaneous because it requires no external influence. The ΔG value is negative because the process occurs spontaneously. (2) The stretching of the band is exothermic (heat is produced by the band so your skin feels warm), while the contraction (relaxation) of the band is endothermic (heat is removed from your skin by the band so your skin feels cool). (3) The rubber band shrank when heated. (4) The entropy of the band when stretched is less than when relaxed. This is the same as saying that the molecular order of the band is greater when stretched. (5) Entropy. The increase in entropy accompanying contraction is more significant than the increase in enthalpy. As a result, the relaxation of the rubber band is spontaneous. (6) The contracted band has greater entropy (ΔS). When the temperature is raised, the $T\Delta S$ factor in the Gibbs free energy equation increases. As a result, it surpasses the positive enthalpy value and produces a negative value for ΔG, indicating that the reaction proceeds spontaneously. $\Delta G = \Delta H - T\Delta S$.

Applications to Everyday Life

Ice cream makers (endothermic reactions): Old fashioned ice cream makers rely on crushed ice and salt as a refrigerant. Salt has a heat of solution of 4.3 kilojoules/mole (see Table 1). Therefore, 4.3 kilojoules of energy are removed from the ice water slurry to dissolve each mole of salt, dropping the temperature of the ice cream maker below 0°C.

Living systems (exothermic reactions): All living systems rely on exothermic reactions. Energy released from the metabolism of glucose and other molecules is stored in ATP. As the phosphate bond in ATP is broken, energy is released to fuel the endothermic reactions vital to life.

Energy crisis (exothermic reactions): In the past two centuries the advent of modern medicine has greatly reduced infant mortality, increased human longevity, and contributed to the rapid growth of world population illustrated in Figure O. As human population increases, so does the demand for energy to power homes, industries, and transportation. Today, most of the energy comes from exothermic combustion reactions involving oil, natural gas or coal. Unfortunately, these fossil fuels are limited and nonrenewable and it is only a matter of time before we exhaust Earth's supply.

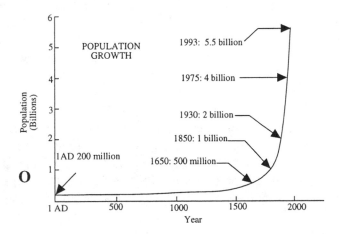

Fossil fuels (exothermic reactions): Most of the energy we use comes from the burning of natural gas, coal and oil. All of these carbon-based "fossil-fuels" release energy in exothermic combustion reactions. Natural gas (methane, CH_4) releases approximately 890 kilojoules of energy per mole when burned:

$$CH_4(g) + 2O_2(g) \longrightarrow CO_2(g) + 2H_2O(l) \qquad \Delta H = -890.3 \text{kJ / mole}$$

Coal is composed primarily of carbon and releases approximately 390 kilojoules per mole:

$$C(s) + O_2(g) \longrightarrow CO_2(g) \qquad \Delta H = -393.5 \text{kJ / mole}$$

Gasoline is made by the distillation of crude oil and contains many alkanes including hexane (C_6H_8), heptane (C_7H_{16}) and octane (C_8H_{18}). Octane releases more than 5400 kilojoules per mole when burned:

$$C_8H_{18}(g) + O_2(g) \longrightarrow 8CO_2(g) + H_2O \qquad \Delta H = -5439kJ$$

An analysis of these reactions shows that they all have a negative enthalpy (ΔH) value, indicating that energy is released. The energy released from such exothermic reactions powers our homes and businesses. For example, water heaters use the heat released by the burning of methane. Many power plants use the energy released from the burning of coal to power the generators that provide our homes and businesses with electricity. The energy released by the burning of the alkanes in gasoline is used to power the internal combustion engines in our automobiles. Exothermic reactions are essential to produce the energy to drive the variety of machines and services we have become accustomed to. In 1991 approximately 346 quadrillion BTU (approximately 365 quintillion joules) of energy were produced by exothermic reactions. Currently, world energy production is increasing at approximately 2.5% per year.

Food pyramid (conservation of energy, entropy): The first law of thermodynamics states that energy can neither be created nor destroyed, but that it can be converted from one form to another. For example, energy from nuclear reactions in the Sun is converted to electromagnetic radiation (visible light, X-rays, radio waves, etc.). This energy is captured in the chloroplasts of plants where it is converted to simple carbohydrates. As herbivores eat these plants, the energy is passed on and incorporated in new molecules within the animals' bodies. As predators eat herbivores, the energy is once again transformed from one form to another. Although energy can be transformed from one form to another, the second law of thermodynamics states that this is always done at a loss of free (usable) energy. In other words, the total entropy increases with each successive transfer of energy, and the amount of available energy continuously decreases. As a result, any given ecosystem can support more producers than herbivores, and more herbivores than carnivores.

Perpetual-motion machine: For centuries, inventors have tried in vain to develop a machine that could operate continuously and supply useful work without requiring a continuous supply of energy. The second law of thermodynamics (the law of entropy) states that any system will run down when left to itself. No processes are 100% efficient, and so the useful energy output from a machine is never sufficient to drive the machine as would be required by a perpetual-motion machine.

4.2 HEAT TRANSFER

The Gila monster *Heloderma suspectum* is a poisonous lizard that inhabits the deserts of the southwestern United States. Hikers often spot these and other interesting reptiles such as rattlesnakes in the cool hours of the morning on top of well-lit rocks, but by afternoon few are seen as they retreat to the shade of desert rocks and shrubs. As night approaches and temperatures fall, Gila monsters and other reptiles seek the shelter of their burrows in the soil, and return to the surface only after the Sun has risen again.

Unlike mammals and birds, reptiles have no internal mechanisms to regulate their body temperature. While the body temperature of a human stays within a few degrees of 37°C (98.6°F), and that of a sparrow stays near 43.5°C (110.3°F), the temperature of a Gila monster or other reptile may vary widely. Mammals and birds are endothermic (inner-heated) and regulate their body temperature by altering their metabolic rates. When temperatures drop, their bodies "burn" food more rapidly to produce the heat necessary to maintain optimal internal body temperature.

By contrast, reptiles like the Gila monster are ectothermic (outer-heated) and are able to regulate their temperature only by positioning themselves appropriately within their environment. At night, Gila monsters seek the warmer temperatures of the soil, but these are often insufficient to maintain optimal temperature, and so shortly after sunrise, they leave their burrows in search of sunlit rocks where they can warm themselves by processes known as conduction and radiation.

Conduction is the flow of heat energy (energy associated with random molecular motion) transferred by molecular collisions. When the lizard is in physical contact with a warm rock, energetic molecules on the surface of the rock vibrate and collide with less energetic molecules on the surface of the lizard's skin, transferring energy and warming the lizard by conduction. The lizard continues to gain heat from the rock as long as the temperature of its skin is lower than that of the rock on which it is positioned. Heat always flows from a region of higher temperature where molecules have a higher average kinetic energy, to a region of lower temperature where molecules have a lower average kinetic energy.

While basking on a sunlit rock, the Gila monster absorbs radiant energy (visible light, ultraviolet, infrared, etc.) from the Sun. Waves transmit energy without transmitting matter, so no physical contact with the radiant source is required for energy to be transferred. Light waves from the Sun transmit energy to the lizard, whose body temperature increases as energy from these waves is absorbed.

If a Gila monster gets too warm, it may move to a shaded location where it receives less energy from conduction and radiation, or to a windy location where it may cool by convection. Convection is the transfer of heat resulting from a transfer of matter. Energetic ("warmer") molecules in the warm boundary layer (a relatively motionless layer of air adjacent to an object) of the lizard are carried away by the wind and are replaced with less energetic ("cooler") molecules. Since heat always flows from a region of higher temperature to lower temperature, the Gila monster loses heat and its temperature drops.

As the Sun sets, the temperature of the dry desert air drops more rapidly than the temperature of the desert soil. Heat is conducted from the ground to the surrounding air. This warm air is less dense than the cool air above it and rises by convection, allowing cool air to sink and replace it. As the night progresses, convective heat loss causes air temperature in dry stream beds and other low spots to become cooler than that of surrounding ridges. To avoid these cool temperatures Gila monsters and other ectothermic animals may seek refuge on the ridges or in their burrows. The soil, which received heat by absorbing radiant energy, now releases this heat to the lizard by the process of conduction.

Ectothermic animals such as the lizard regulate their body temperature by making use of the heat transferring principles of radiation, conduction, and convection. Although we are endothermic and regulate our body temperature largely through changes in metabolism, we also make use of the processes of heat transfer to regulate our body temperature. Can you give examples of how we use conduction, convection, and radiation to maintain optimal body temperature?

The processes of heat transfer are necessary for understanding a wide range of phenomena including continental drift, hang glider navigation, household heating, cookware design, and weather patterns. In the activities that follow you will gain a better understanding for these important processes and how they affect the world around us.

4.2.1 HEAT CONDUCTION IN METALS

Concepts to Investigate: Heat, conduction, energy transfer, conductometers.

Materials: <u>Option 1</u>: Commercial conductometer (Figure A), matches, laboratory burner; <u>Option 2</u>: Paraffin, washer, matches, burner, and aluminum, copper, zinc, iron, nickel and brass wires of similar diameter, as shown in Figure B.

Safety: Wear goggles in this activity and whenever using an open flame.

Principles and Procedures: The flame of a stove heats the metal on the bottom of a cooking pan. As the atoms on the bottom surface of the pan vibrate, they collide with adjacent atoms, conducting heat to the inner surface where the food is cooked. Although the metal surfaces of the pot may be extremely hot, its wooden, plastic or ceramic handle remains cool to the touch. Metals are generally excellent conductors of heat, but woods, plastics and ceramics are not.

  The bases of some expensive cookware are made of copper. The manufacturers of such cookware claim that copper is a better conductor of heat than either steel or aluminum, distributing heat more uniformly and allowing for more even cooking. In this activity you will rank the thermal conductivity of these and other metals to test the validity of this claim.

Option 1: Figure A illustrates a commercial conductometer, consisting of a brass hub with aluminum, copper, zinc, iron, nickel and brass spokes. Place match heads in each of the wells on the spokes of the conductometer and then heat the hub with a laboratory burner. Measure the time required for each match head to burst into flame. The less time required to ignite the match, the higher the thermal conductivity of the metal.

Option 2: If you do not have access to a commercial conductometer, you may make your own as shown in Figure B. Tie one end of each of two or more different metal wires to a washer, and then tie their free ends to ring stands or other supports so the washer is suspended approximately 20 centimeters above the table top. Using molten candle wax, attach paper clips or thumbtacks to each wire at a distance of 20 centimeters from the washer. Make certain that the same amount of wax is used to support each item. Place a lit burner under the washer and record the time when each paper clip falls. Thermal conductivity is

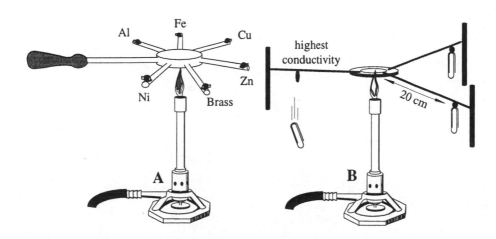

inversely related to the time required to melt the wax. The higher the thermal conductivity, the quicker the wax melts and the sooner the tack or paper clip falls.

Rank the metals from highest to lowest thermal (heat) conductivity. Does copper conduct heat faster than the other metals as manufacturers of cookware claim?

Questions

(1) List the metals tested in order from highest to lowest thermal conductivity.

(2) Backpackers often carry an aluminum cup equipped with a steel rim and handle. This bi-metallic cup allows them to heat the contents of the cup on a small backpacking stove, and then drink from it without burning their hands or lips. Explain.

(3) In the 1970s, many sporting goods stores imported inexpensive cups that appeared similar to those described in the previous question. Although the handles were made of steel, the rims and bottoms were made of aluminum. Explain why many backpackers (including the author) may have burned their lips when using these cups.

(4) Cowboys brand cattle by placing one end of a branding iron in a fire, and then quickly removing it and placing it against the hide of the animal. What would happen to the cowboy's hands if the branding tools were made of copper rather than iron or steel? Explain.

(5) As the space shuttle re-enters the atmosphere, it compresses the air in front of it, transforming it to plasma that can reach temperatures nearly equal to those on the surface of the Sun. To prevent damage to the shuttle and its crew, the surface of the shuttle is covered with ceramic tiles that have extremely low thermal conductivity. Explain.

4.2.2 CONDUCTION AND COMBUSTION

Concepts to Investigate: Conduction, kindling point, heat conductivity, combustion.

Materials: Insulated copper wire, candle, matches.

Safety: Wear goggles in this activity and whenever using an open flame.

Principles and Procedures: The ability to use fire for heating, light, cooking and metal smelting was essential for the development of early civilizations. Modern civilizations continue to rely upon fire to meet ever growing energy demands. Coal, natural gas and oil are burned to produce energy necessary for transportation, industry and homes. Three criteria are required to sustain fire: fuel, oxygen and sufficient temperature. A fire will be extinguished if the fuel is consumed, the oxygen is depleted or the temperature drops below the kindling point (the minimal temperature at which combustion may be sustained). Water is effective in extinguishing many types of fires because it reduces the temperature of the fuel source below the kindling point. (Water has a high specific heat and a high heat of vaporization, and therefore absorbs a great amount of energy as it is heated and boiled.) Is it possible to extinguish or prevent fire using metal rather than water?

Strip the insulation from a 30-cm section of a 40-cm length of copper wire. Wind the bare wire into a coil as shown in Figure C. To extinguish the candle flame, lower the coil over a lit candle. Re-light the candle, and lower the coil over the flame slowly so that the coil is heated by the flame as it is lowered. Is it possible to lower the coil slowly enough that the flame is not extinguished? Allow the coil to cool, and re-light the candle. Heat the coil in the flame of a laboratory burner and then lower it over the candle flame (Figure D). Is the flame extinguished as before? Why or why not?

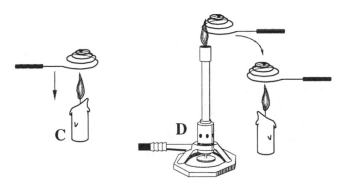

Table 1: Average Thermal and Electrical Conductivities at Room Temperature

	Thermal Conductivity $cal \cdot s^{-1} \cdot cm^{-2}$	*Electrical Conductivity* $ohm^{-1} \cdot cm^{-1}$
copper	0.92	0.59
aluminum	0.50	0.38
zinc	0.27	0.17
brass	0.26	0.13
iron	0.16	0.10
nickel	0.14	0.15
steel	0.12	0.03

Questions

(1) Why is the flame extinguished when a cool coil of copper wire is lowered over it?

(2) Is it possible to lower the coil over the flame in such a manner that the candle remains lit? Explain.

(3) Would it be easier to extinguish the candle if you used iron wire rather than copper wire? Explain (see Table 1).

4.2.3 CONDUCTION: DAVY SAFETY LAMP

Concepts to Investigate: Safety lamp, heat conduction, kindling temperature.

Materials: Laboratory burner, ring stand, wire gauze (copper works best), aluminum screen mesh.

Safety: Wear goggles in this activity and whenever using an open flame.

Principles and Procedures: Department of Labor statistics show that the most hazardous industrial occupation is underground coal mining. Coal miners may be injured by machinery accidents, cave-ins or inhalation of dust and gases, but the principal hazard is explosion. Coal mines contain significant quantities of coal dust and methane that form a potentially explosive mixture. In 1942, more than 1500 coal miners lost their lives in a single explosion in Benxihu, China, making it the worst mining accident in history.

Coal became a popular heating fuel in England during the late Middle Ages and was the primary fuel of the industrial revolution that flourished in the 18th century. The growth of industry in the British Isles created a huge demand for coal, and entrepreneurs developed large mining operations to bring it to market. Because electric lights had not yet been invented, miners had to use kerosene lamps to light the coal mines, despite the great risk of fires and explosions. To reduce such risks, Sir Humphry Davy invented the miner's safety lamp in which a wire mesh was placed around the flame, allowing light to escape, but preventing explosions and fires. How can a simple wire mesh prevent such serious problems?

Part 1: Heat conduction and kindling temperature: *Wear goggles and lab coat.* A material will not burn if it is maintained at a temperature below its kindling point. Water is useful in extinguishing wood fires because it absorbs so much energy (water has a high specific heat and a heat of vaporization) that it conducts heat away from the wood, thereby reducing the temperature below the kindling point of wood. Sir Humphry Davy discovered that a metal mesh or grill can accomplish the same result if placed between a flame and a fuel source. Place a laboratory burner beneath a wire gauze (copper wire works best) as shown in Figure E. Turn the gas on and light the gas above the mesh. The flame burns on top of the mesh, but it doesn't spread through the mesh to the fuel on the bottom. The metal mesh conducts heat away from the flame so that the temperature of the gas below the mesh never reaches its kindling point.

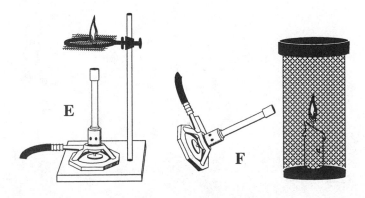

Part 2: Davy safety lamp: *Teacher demonstration only. Perform the following activity in a well-ventilated room. Wear goggles and lab coat.* The apparatus illustrated in Figure F resembles the lamp that Sir Humphry Davy invented. Select a metal lid from a screw-top jar to serve as the top of the lamp. Cut a rectangle from a piece of copper, aluminum or other metal screen. *Do not use screens made of nylon or other synthetic materials because they may be flammable.* Make the rectangle slightly longer than the circumference of the lid. Using staples, attach the screen to form a cylinder as shown in Figure F. Light a candle and secure it to the second lid using melted paraffin from the candle. Place the wire mesh cylinder over the candle. Turn on the gas in the burner and <u>briefly</u> move it around the lamp to show that the gas will not ignite outside the screen.

Questions

(1) Suppose a manufacturer introduced a discount line of Davy safety lamps made using a steel mesh rather than a copper mesh. Would these discount lamps be as safe? Explain.

(2) When you lit the gas under the gauze, did the flame spread to the top of the gauze? Why or why not?

(3) If you place your bare foot on a rug it may feel warm. If you step from the rug to a tile floor at the same temperature it may feel much cooler than the rug. Explain.

4.2.4 CONVECTION IN GASES

Concepts to Investigate: Convection, heat transfer, buoyancy, cold air drainage, chimney design, updrafts (thermals), downdrafts.

Materials: Part 1: Dry cleaning bag (or large, lightweight plastic trash bag), thread, tape, hair drier; Part 2: Commercial smoke box, or box, Plexiglas® or glass tubes, Plexiglas® or glass sheet, electrician's tape, candle, matches, stick of incense.

Safety: Wear goggles in this activity and whenever using an open flame.

Principles and Procedures: In June of 1988, Per Lindstrand of Great Britain ascended in a hot air balloon to a record height of 65,000 feet, over twice the altitude of Mt. Everest, the highest mountain in the world. To accomplish this feat, Lindstrand relied on convection, the same principle that causes smoke to rise from a chimney, warm air to rise to the second story of a house or thunderclouds to form on a hot summer day.

    Unlike conduction, convection does not rely on the transfer of energy between molecules, but rather on the movement of energetic molecules from one location to another. When heated, molecules in a gas move farther apart. The heated gas becomes less dense and more buoyant than the unheated gas surrounding it. Warmer, less dense gases ascend, while cooler, denser gases descend to take their place. Thus, when the propane torch in a hot air balloon is ignited, air within the balloon expands and becomes more buoyant than the cooler, denser air on the outside of the balloon (see 5.1.4).

Part 1: Hot air balloon: Tape five lengths of thread to the lower edges of a dry cleaning bag as shown in Figure G. Tie the loose ends of the threads to a small washer that will serve as the balloon's "basket." While your partner holds the bag up, fill it using hot air from a hair drier as shown. Move the hair drier in circles while heating so that the walls of the bag do not become excessively warm and melt. Continue to heat the air in the bag until it rises to the ceiling. Alternatively, you may wish to make a hot air balloon using tissue paper as specified in section 5.1.4.

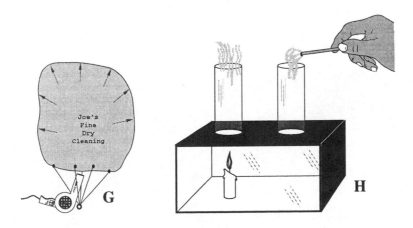

Part 2: Chimney, smoke box: In today's houses, fireplaces are generally installed for aesthetic purposes rather than to meet heating needs. Fireplaces are normally much less

efficient than the natural gas or electric heating systems found in most homes today. Much of the heat that a fire produces escapes out the chimney by convection, while cool air from the outside enters through cracks to replace it. Thus, it is common to feel cool drafts in your home when a fire is blazing in the fireplace. Figure H illustrates a smoke box that can be constructed using a wooden or plastic box. Drill holes in the top and cement two sections of clear tubing (glass or Plexiglas® work well) as shown. Light a candle under one of the chimneys as illustrated, and seal a glass or Plexiglas® sheet across the front of the box with electrician's tape. Light a stick of incense, a sheet of touch paper, or other smoke producing material and hold it over both chimneys. Draw arrows on Figure H to illustrate the movement of smoke.

Questions

(1) In 1709 Father Barolomeu de Gusmao flew the first model hot air balloon. Nearly three centuries later, in 1987, Per Lanstrand and Richard Branson became the first people to cross the Atlantic Ocean in a hot air balloon. What kinds of technological advances occurred during this period to make such a long distance flight possible?

(2) Would convection currents occur in the weightless environments of orbiting spacecraft such as the space shuttle or a space station? Explain.

(3) Describe and explain the smoke patterns seen in the smoke box.

(4) Citrus fruits (oranges, lemons, limes, etc.) are frost sensitive. Would it be better to plant orchards of citrus trees on the sides or floors of small valleys? Explain.

(5) Why is it important to close the chimney damper when the fireplace is not in use?

4.2.5 CONVECTION IN LIQUIDS

Concepts to Investigate: Convection, ocean currents, thermal expansion, buoyancy, heat transfer, seasonal overturn, thermocline, convection currents, density.

Materials: Part 1: Glass tubing, glass "T," flexible tubing, food coloring, burner, ring stand, test tube clamp; Part 2: 2-liter soft drink containers, food coloring, pliers, burner, nail, tape, aquarium or similar container; Part 3: Glass tubing, Erlenmeyer flask, two-hole stopper, glycerin or other lubricant, aquarium or similar container, food coloring.

Safety: Wear goggles in this activity and whenever using an open flame. Only the teacher should insert glass tubing or rods into stoppers. Lubricate the glass with glycerin, hold the tubing or rod with a towel at the base next to the stopper, and twist slowly with minimal pressure. It may be necessary to re-lubricate the glass until it slides freely.

Principles and Procedures: When a pan of water is heated on a stove, the water adjacent to the metal expands and rises by convection. This less dense, warm water carries thermal energy to the cooler regions causing the temperature to remain relatively constant throughout. Convection in liquids is an important process of heat transfer that is useful in understanding a wide variety of phenomena from such things as hot water plumbing to the seasonal overturn in lakes and ponds.

Part 1: Hot water plumbing: You may have noticed that it requires a few moments to obtain hot water in your sink or shower. As heated water stands in pipes between usage, it cools and must be removed before new hot water from the water heater can reach your faucet. The greater the distance between the water heater and the faucet, the greater the time required to obtain hot water. Although this may be a minor nuisance at home, think of the problems it would cause for those in huge buildings like the 110-story World Trade Center towers in New York. In tall buildings, hot water heaters are often many stories below the faucet, yet tenants rarely complain that it requires a long time to get hot water. This is because many tall buildings are equipped with a parallel recirculating pipe system in which water is kept warm by convection. Rather than a single pipe between the hot water heater and the faucet, there are two, one which takes hot water from the heater to the faucets, and the other which takes water that has cooled in the pipes back to the heater to be warmed again. Warm water continually rises in the heated pipe, while cool water returns to the water heater in the other pipe. Thus, there is always warm water a short distance from any faucet. To test this idea, construct the apparatus shown in Figure I. Use short sections of flexible tubing to connect three straight portions of glass tubing, and support as shown. Fill the apparatus with water, and then place a drop of food coloring in the "T" as illustrated. Use a laboratory burner or similar heat source to gently heat one arm of the apparatus. Draw a diagram of your apparatus and indicate the direction of the convection current.

Part 2: Seasonal overturn in lakes: Phytoplankton (tiny, floating algae) are the base of the food chain in most lakes and ponds. Phytoplankton, like all plants, require mineral nutrients, but these nutrients tend to sink to the bottom of lakes because their density is greater than that of water. Convection currents, however, bring these nutrients to the surface where phytoplankton can use them. In temperate and cold climates, water on the surface cools in late autumn and becomes denser than the water below. As a result, it sinks and the water from below rises to the surface, bringing with it many nutrients. This seasonal overturn in lakes and ponds helps increase the production of phytoplankton, and all of the organisms that ultimately depend on them. Perform the following activity to investigate seasonal overturn. Acquire two 2-liter plastic soft-drink containers. Using pliers, heat a nail in the flame of a burner and then melt two holes in each container as shown in Figure J. Attach small paper squares to one end of each of two pieces of adhesive tape. These ends will not stick to the bottle and will serve as handles with which to remove the tape later. Cover the holes with the sticky portion of the tape, and place 10 or more drops of red food coloring in one bottle, and the same number of drops of blue food coloring in the other. Fill the "red" container with warm water, and the "blue" container with ice cold water. Place both bottles in a large container such as an aquarium, and then fill the container with tap water. Grab the paper tabs on the tape and carefully remove from all holes, causing as little disturbance as possible. Note the direction of the cold and warm water. Out of which hole does the red (warm) water come? Out of which hole does the blue (cold) water come? Why?

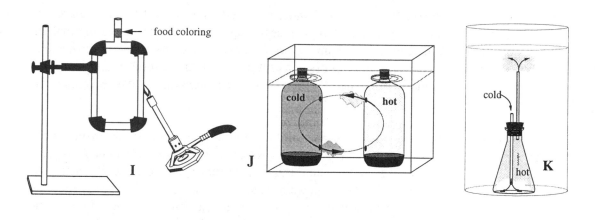

Part 3: Convection currents: Convection currents can be easily observed using the apparatus illustrated in Figure K. Add red food coloring to the flask and fill with hot water. Seal the flask with the stopper assembly so no air remains in the flask. Submerge the apparatus in an aquarium or similar container, and observe the flow of clear (cool) and red (hot) water.

Questions

(1) Using convection, explain the circulation pattern in part 1.

(2) How would you have to change the way in which food is cooked on your stove if convection did not exist?

(3) Using convection, explain the circulation pattern in part 2.

(4) A thermocline is a permanent or temporary boundary layer between warm water above and cold water below. Are thermoclines more stable at higher latitudes where seasons are profoundly different, or near the equator where temperatures are relatively constant all year long? Explain.

(5) Describe and explain the flow patterns of water in part 3.

4.2.6 RADIATION

Concepts to Investigate: Radiation, heat transfer.

Materials: <u>Part 1</u>: Radiometer, bright light source, colored cellophane or filters, electric room heater; <u>Part 2</u>: Thermometers, food coloring, beakers.

Principles and Procedures: The word "radiation" may conjure up the thought of the atomic bomb at Hiroshima or the melt-down of the Chernobyl nuclear power plant. Although radiation is certainly emitted from such sources, it is quite different from other forms of radiation with which we are familiar, namely radio waves, visible light and infrared (heat radiation). Radiant energy transfer involves the flow of energy by electromagnetic waves from one location to another. When you stand next to a campfire on a cold night, you are warmed by infrared radiation. There is a net flow of radiant energy if adjacent objects are at different temperatures.

Your hand feels warm if you place it adjacent to a light bulb. The heating of your hand does not result from conduction, for the light bulb is nearly evacuated, glass is a poor conductor, and the air between you and the bulb is a poor conductor as well. The heating is also not due to convection, or else you would only feel it above the light bulb and not to the side. Heat is transferred from the light bulb filament to your hand, not by conduction or convection, but by radiation. As molecules in your skin absorb light energy, they become excited and the temperature of your skin rises.

Part 1: Radiometer: Sir William Crookes designed a simple instrument to illustrate the transfer of energy by radiation. The radiometer illustrated in Figure L can be purchased from novelty stores and scientific supply houses. It consists of four metal vanes, each of which has a silver side and a black side. The four vanes are attached to a rotor and positioned in a nearly evacuated glass bulb. The black sides of the vanes absorb light and warm up while the silvered sides reflect light and remain cool. When gaseous molecules in the bulb strike the warmer, black side of the vane, they acquire more kinetic (thermal) energy and rebound with greater velocity than when striking the cooler, silvered surface. As molecules rebound from the black surface, the vane is propelled in the opposite direction. Because the radiometer is nearly evacuated, the vanes spin relatively freely, experi-

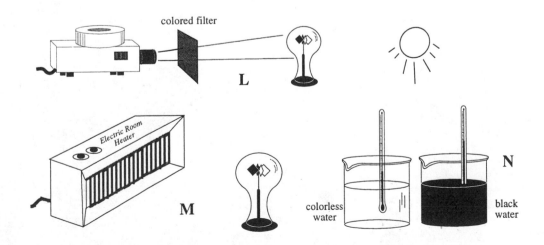

encing virtually no wind resistance. The black surfaces always move away from the light. Position a radiometer in front of a slide projector or other source of intense light. Determine the speed of rotation (revolutions per minute) for various colors of light by placing glass or cellophane filters in front of the light source in a darkened room while keeping the radiometer at the same distance. Are all colors of light as effective in transferring energy to the vanes?

Electric heaters produce invisible infrared light. Can infrared light transfer energy to the vanes even though we cannot see it? In a dimly lit room, place a radiometer in front of a heater as shown in Figure M, and compare the speed of the radiometer to the speed in the various colors of light already tested.

Part 2: Absorption of radiant energy: If you have walked barefoot on a summer day, you have probably noticed that black asphalt (macadam) feels much hotter than white concrete. Both surfaces receive the same amount of radiation, yet the darker surface absorbs more energy than the lighter surface. Is this principle true for other dark and light materials?

Fill two beakers to the same level with tap water. Add a variety of food colorings to one beaker until the water appears black. Place both beakers in sunlight for three to four hours and compare temperatures (Figure N).

Questions

(1) When standing near a campfire, one side of your body may get very warm, while the other remains cold, even though there is very little difference in the distance between both sides of your body and the fire. Explain.

(2) Is the electric heater able to propel the radiometer? Explain.

(3) Which beaker in part 2 has a higher temperature? Explain.

(4) Many ecologists are concerned that the build up of carbon dioxide in the atmosphere resulting from the burning of fossil fuels may create a "greenhouse effect" in which more radiant energy is absorbed by Earth's atmosphere than is re-radiated to space. What effect might this have on global temperatures? Explain.

(5) Would a radiometer spin if the bulb were completely evacuated?

FOR THE TEACHER

4.2.1 HEAT CONDUCTION IN METALS

Discussion: Thermal conductivity is generally measured as the number of calories transmitted per second through a plate one centimeter thick across an area of one square centimeter when the temperature difference is 1°C. Although thermal conductivity changes with temperature, the relative thermal conductivities of different metals remain similar. Table 1 lists the thermal conductivities of the metals used in this activity. Note that good conductors of heat are also good conductors of electricity. The electrical and thermal conductivities of metallic conductors are related by a formula called the Wiedemann-Franz Law.

Answers: (1) Please refer to Table 1. (2) Aluminum is an excellent conductor of heat, so heat from the stove is transferred to the food inside the cup. By contrast, steel is a poor conductor of heat, so heat from the aluminum portion of the cup is not readily transferred to the rim or handle where it might burn the lips or hands of the person using the cup. (3) Relatively little heat is transferred to the steel handle, but much is transferred to the aluminum rim. As a result, the backpacker can hold the cup with no pain, but burns his or her lips when trying to drink from the cup. (The author speaks from experience!) (4) Copper has a much higher thermal conductivity than steel or iron so the cowboy would probably brand his own hand when trying to pick the iron out of the fire! (5) The tiles must have low thermal conductivity, otherwise the shuttle and its passengers would be cooked!

4.2.2 CONDUCTION AND COMBUSTION

Discussion: Copper is an excellent conductor of heat, with a thermal conductivity (0.92 cal·s^{-1}·cm^{-2}) nearly six times that of iron (0.16 cal·s^{-1}·cm^{-2}). Heat is conducted away from the flame as the copper coil is lowered. If the temperature drops below the kindling point of paraffin, the flame is extinguished. Since heat travels from a region of higher temperature to lower temperature, heat will not be removed from the flame if the coil is pre-heated either by a candle or laboratory burner. This explains why the candle flame will not go out when a pre-heated coil is used.

To illustrate how a good heat conductor can be used to prevent combustion, perform the following demonstration. Wrap a thin cotton cloth tightly around a block of wood, and an identical cloth around a block of copper (a pre-1982 copper penny will suffice). Place the end of a smoldering match or splint against both cloths. The cloth wrapped around the copper plate will not scorch as easily as the one wrapped around wood. Copper conducts heat away from the cloth, keeping its temperature below the kindling point. Since wood is a poor conductor of heat, the temperature of the cloth wrapped around the wood may rise to the kindling point and scorch or ignite the cotton.

Answers: (1) Please see discussion. (2) Please see discussion. (3) It would be more difficult to extinguish the flame using iron wire rather than copper wire because iron is a poor conductor of heat compared to copper. As a result, heat will not travel as rapidly from the center of the flame as it would when using copper.

4.2.3 CONDUCTION: DAVY SAFETY LAMP

Discussion: Metals are good heat conductors, and heat from a flame will travel away from the center of the gauze so that the temperature remains below the kindling point, and the gas on the other side is not ignited. If you are performing this activity as a demonstration, you may wish to light the flame on top of the gauze, and then pass a piece of paper between the burner and the gauze. This will extinguish the flame above the gauze by blocking the fuel.

You may wish to perform the simple activity depicted in Figure O as a way of introducing the importance of continuity in heat conduction. Using a slow twisting motion, insert a copper or aluminum rod, lubricated with mineral oil or glycerin, completely through one stopper and into the end of another. Insert a shorter piece of the same material into the opposite end of the second stopper so that students will not see that the rod is discontinuous. Without telling the students the setup, ask for a volunteer to hold both ends of the tubing while heating it in a flame as shown. Ask the student to indicate when an end becomes uncomfortably warm. Students will note that one end (the continuous end) heats up much faster than the discontinuous end, and hopefully will hypothesize the setup illustrated in Figure O.

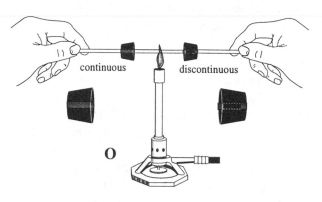

O

Answers: (1) Steel is not a good heat conductor compared to copper. As a result, portions of the steel mesh around a lamp may reach the kindling point for coal dust, and cause an explosion. (2) The flame will probably not spread to the top because heat is conducted away from the flame by the metal gauze, keeping the temperature of the gas below the kindling point. If the gauze is heated sufficiently, however, the flame will spread through the mesh. (3) Tile is a relatively good conductor of heat and transfers energy away from your feet much more rapidly than carpet, which is a relatively poor conductor.

4.2.4 CONVECTION IN GASES

Discussion: Figure P illustrates the flow pattern that will be observed in the smoke box. Commercial versions of the smoke box (Figure H) mentioned in this activity can be purchased from scientific supply companies.

To demonstrate convection currents in the room, attach thin strips of tissue paper to a pencil and hold the pencil above a radiator or other heat source in your classroom. You can trace the convection currents surrounding the heat source by slowly moving the pencil and observing the angle at which the tissue paper is deflected (Figure Q).

Convection results from a difference in density between different portions of a fluid. Denser fluids move down while less dense fluids move up. Archimedes, a third-century BC resident of Sicily, is credited with discovering the natural law of buoyancy and stated that any object submerged or floating in a fluid is buoyed upward by a force equivalent to the weight of the fluid it displaces. A balloon will rise if it has less weight than the air it displaces, and will sink if it has greater weight than the air it displaces.

Answers: (1) Two major technological advances were the development of lightweight, strong synthetic materials for the construction of the balloon, and propane burners to provide a lightweight fuel source to heat the air on the long journey. (2) No. Denser fluids sink and less dense fluids rise. Without gravity, convective flow ceases. (3) Smoke rises with the warm convective updraft above the candle's chimney, and falls with the cool convective downdraft into the other chimney. (4) Citrus growers in temperate climates generally prefer to plant their crops on the sides of valleys rather than in the valley floors. Cool air drains from the sides of the valleys and settles on the valley floors, creating a cooler microclimate in which frosts are more likely to occur. (5) Cold air from outside the house will descend through the chimney and cool the house if the damper is not closed.

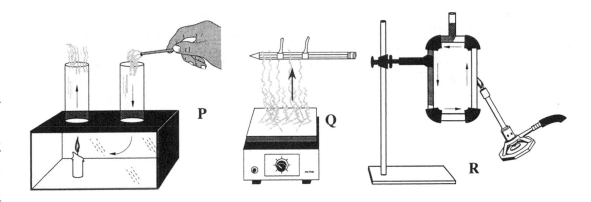

4.2.5 CONVECTION IN LIQUIDS

Discussion: Figure R illustrates the convective flow pattern in a parallel recirculating pipe system. It is possible to observe convection currents in clear water when heated by a hot plate or burner. These currents may be made visible to an entire class by shining light from a slide projector, overhead projector or other bright light source through such a container onto a large screen. Students may notice that these currents resemble the convection currents visible over the hood of a car on a hot day. The optical properties of air, water and other fluids change as they are heated. Light refracts (bends) as it travels through the air of different temperatures, allowing us to visualize convection currents.

Answers: (1) The burner warms water in one arm. As water on this side rises due to convection, cooler water from the other arm sinks to take its place. Thus, the food coloring descends on the unheated side before ascending on the heated side. (2) Without convection, the main method of heat transfer would be conduction. As a result, it would be necessary to stir your food much more often to bring it in contact with the walls of the pot. (3) Warm water in the red bottle rises and exits the top hole. Cold water in the blue bottle sinks and exits the bottom hole. As a result, a current is established in which water flows out of the bottom hole of the cold container and eventually into the bottom hole of the warm container, while warm water eventually exits the top hole of the warm container before entering the top hole of the cold container. (4) Thermoclines are more stable in tropical environments where warm temperatures keep the surface waters warmer, less dense, and thus on top. In cold climates, the surface water may cool below the temperature of the water beneath it, and thus sink, disrupting the thermocline. (5) The hot red water in the flask is less dense than the cooler colorless water outside. The hot water rises to the top of the flask and out the "chimney" into the aquarium. Clear, cooler water flows into the other tubing to replace it.

4.2.6 RADIATION

Discussion: It would be wise to introduce the electromagnetic radiation spectrum illustrated in Figure S to show students the wide range of phenomena we call "radiation." All of these forms of radiation can transfer energy, but infrared radiation is most commonly associated with heat. All objects with a temperature greater than absolute zero emit infrared radiation, and nearly all objects absorb it, causing an increase in temperature.

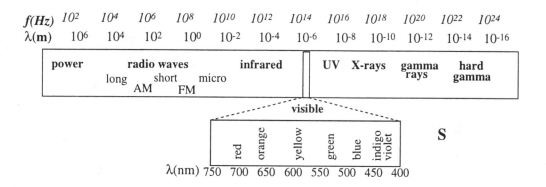

Answers: (1) Most of the heat you feel when standing near a campfire is due to radiation, not convection or conduction. Infrared light from the fire is absorbed by your skin, heating your body. (2) Yes. Although infrared light is invisible, it contains energy that is absorbed preferentially by the black paint on the vanes in the radiometer. As a result, the radiometer spins when placed in white or colored light. (3) The black beaker reaches a higher temperatures since radiant energy from light is absorbed by the dye molecules in the water. (4) Just as the colored water absorbed more energy than the clear water, so air with high concentrations of carbon dioxide will absorb more energy than normal air. As a result, temperatures may rise. Environmental scientists have noted a slight but significant increase in global temperature from the early 1980s to the present. (5) No. The vanes of a radiometer are propelled by excited gas molecules. If all gas molecules are removed, the radiometer will not rotate.

Applications to Everyday Life

Materials engineering: Thermal conductivity is one of the most important factors to consider when selecting materials for specific uses. A brake shoe, for example, must have a very low thermal conductivity, or else heat would be conducted throughout the brake system and cause serious damage to metal components. By contrast, it is important that the core of a car radiator be made of a material with a very high thermal conductivity if heat is to be effectively removed from the cooling system.

Regulation of body temperature: After swimming in cold water, you may have noticed that one of the quickest ways to warm up is to lie on the flat concrete pool deck. The heat from the concrete is conducted to your skin, warming your body. By contrast, you may walk on tip toes when crossing a driveway on a hot day to minimize the burning sensation in your feet. By reducing the surface area of contact between your skin and the ground, you reduce the conduction of heat to your body.

Thunderheads: Summer thunderstorms may arise when moist air is heated over land. Heated air rises by convection. As it rises it cools, and water condenses into tiny droplets that form clouds. Thunderheads are often seen over forest fires, where hot air from the fire rises and eventually cools, allowing water vapor released in combustion to condense in tiny droplets.

Hang-gliding: In recent years, hang-gliding has become a popular sport and enthusiasts continue to set new world records for height and distance. In 1990, Larry Tudor set a world record for distance, traveling over 300 miles from New Mexico to Kansas. Five years earlier he set the record for height gain, ascending more than 14,000 feet above the ground in California's Owen's Valley. Hang-glider pilots like Larry Tudor have an uncanny ability to find thermals, regions of warm air that are rising. Like soaring birds, hang-glider pilots capitalize on these convective currents to take them aloft.

Continental drift: Molten rock, like water or air, expands in response to temperature increases. As a result, it rises and presses against the crust. Many geologists think that convective currents within Earth's mantle are responsible for the movement of the large sections of the crust known as plates, and associated phenomena such as earthquakes and volcanoes.

Geysers: Geysers often occur near volcanoes or other geologically active regions. When ground water comes in contact with molten or hot rock, it expands and rises. Convection may be extremely rapid and continue until the water is expelled from the vent or vaporized as steam.

Greenhouse effect: High energy, short wavelength radiation is absorbed by Earth, and re-radiated as low energy, long wavelength infrared radiation. This radiation is absorbed by water molecules and carbon dioxide in the atmosphere, raising air temperature. Meteorologists believe that global temperatures have been increasing because radiant energy is being absorbed faster than it is re-radiated, due to increasing carbon dioxide pollution. The surface of Venus is hotter than the surface of Mercury, even though it is much farther from the Sun. The atmosphere on Venus is so thick with carbon dioxide and other gases that a much higher percentage of radiant energy is trapped on Venus than on Mercury. The greenhouse effect on Venus is so great that surface temperatures are nearly 500°C higher than those on Mercury!

4.3 CHEMICAL KINETICS

A large rock rests motionless on a hill. A pond of fresh water lies shimmering in the sunlight. A balloon filled with oxygen rests quietly on a table. Although the rock, water and balloon appear motionless, atoms and molecules inside each are in constant motion! Although it is impossible to directly observe the motion of atoms, it is possible to observe the motion of larger particles, and such investigations have led scientists to develop a kinetic theory of matter which asserts that all particles of matter, including molecules, atoms and ions, are in constant and random motion.

Add approximately 20 marbles, ball bearings, "BBs" or other spheres to a clear plastic box, place on an overhead projector, and shake vigorously back and forth (Figure A). You may notice that the spheres engage in three types of motion. Translational motion is movement in a trajectory, such as a bowling ball moving down the gutter of a bowling alley or a baseball moving in a parabolic path when thrown from left field to first base. Rotational motion is movement around a point or axis, such as when an ice skater twirls around her center of mass or when a planet rotates on its axis. Vibrational motion is back and forth movement, such as the up and down motion of a bungee diver or the bouncing motion of a basketball dropped to the floor. An atom, molecule or other object can undergo all three types of motion simultaneously. Each type of motion involves kinetic energy (energy of motion). Temperature is a measure of the average kinetic energy of the particles in a substance. The higher the temperature, the faster molecules and atoms are moving.

A chemical reaction will occur if one atom or molecule strikes and interacts with another, but will not occur if they bounce off each other. You can simulate these types of interaction with marbles. Obtain two marbles and attach a small patch of hooked adhesive Velcro® to one, and smooth Velcro® to the other (Figure B). Place one in the groove of a V-shaped or curved wooden molding such that the marble can roll freely on its sides and without the patches touching the bottom. Place the other marble at one end of the groove and quickly roll it toward the first marble. Moving objects such as these may bounce off one another in an elastic (Figure C) collision, or stick together in an inelastic collision (Figure D). Objects on a much smaller scale, including atoms and molecules, exhibit these same types of collisions.

Collision theory states that the rate of any step in a reaction is proportional to the number of collisions per unit time between reacting particles, and the fraction of these collisions that have sufficient kinetic energy to react. Reaction rates can be increased by increasing the concentration of reactants, by raising the temperature or by adding catalysts. Increasing the concentration of reactants increases the rate of collision, while raising the temperature increases the kinetic energy of colliding particles. Catalysts reduce activation energy, causing more collisions to be effective (in initiating chemical change) at lower kinetic energy. In the activities that follow you will investigate kinetics (reaction rates) and reaction mechanisms.

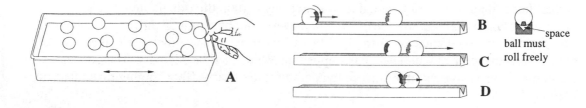

A

B

C

D

space
ball must
roll freely

4.3.1 THE EFFECT OF CONCENTRATION ON REACTION RATE

Concepts to Investigate: Reaction rate, concentration.

Materials: Vinegar, baking soda ($NaHCO_3$), beakers, side arm flasks or flasks fitted with stoppers and tubing.

Principles and Procedures: When baking soda ($NaHCO_3$, sodium hydrogen carbonate) is added to acidic batters (containing acidic foods such as lemon juice, yogurt, vinegar or sour cream), a neutralization reaction occurs that produces carbon dioxide. This carbon dioxide gas gets trapped in the batter and causes it to "rise" during baking. One of the natural acids used in cooking is acetic acid, the acid found in vinegar. Sodium hydrogen carbonate reacts with acetic acid as follows:

$$NaHCO_3(s) + HC_2H_3O_2(aq) \rightarrow NaC_2H_3O_2(aq) + CO_2(g) + H_2O(l)$$

If carbon dioxide is not produced rapidly enough in a pastry or bread product, the product will be flat and dense rather than light and airy. How is the rate of carbon dioxide production related to the concentration of acid? The rate of this neutralization reaction can be estimated by measuring the rate of carbon dioxide production. Construct a gas collection apparatus as illustrated in Figure E. Place 20 g of baking soda ($NaHCO_3$) in the reaction flask. Fill the graduated cylinder with water and invert in a beaker of water with the top of the cylinder covered with a note card so no water escapes. Remove the stopper from the reaction flask, add 100 mL of fresh vinegar (most vinegars are 4 to 6% acetic acid) and immediately replace the stopper. Swirl the flask contents to mix thoroughly. Carbon dioxide production begins instantly. Record the time at which a measurable quantity (e.g., 50 mL or 100 mL) of water has been displaced in the cylinder. Calculate the rate of water displacement by dividing the volume of water displaced by the time required to replace it. We will assume that the rate of water displacement is proportional to the rate of carbon dioxide production. Record the rate of carbon dioxide production for 100% vinegar in Table 1.

Replace the reaction flask with a clean, dry flask and 20 grams of fresh baking soda. Determine the approximate rate of carbon dioxide production (in mL of carbon dioxide gas produced per unit time) using 50%, 25% and 12.5% vinegar (Table 1). Plot the results of your investigation on Figure F.

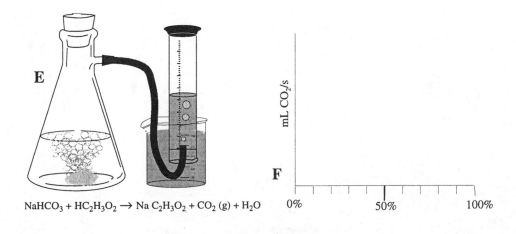

$NaHCO_3 + HC_2H_3O_2 \rightarrow Na\ C_2H_3O_2 + CO_2(g) + H_2O$

Table 1: The Effect of Concentration on Reaction Rate

Vinegar	Water	% Vinegar	mL CO_2/s
100 mL	0 mL	100%	
50 mL	50 mL	50%	
25 mL	75 mL	25%	
12.5 mL	87.5 mL	12.5%	

Questions

(1) Describe the relationship between the concentration of vinegar and the rate of carbon dioxide production.

(2) Explain the relationship between concentration and reaction rate on a molecular basis.

4.3.2 THE EFFECT OF TEMPERATURE ON REACTION RATE

Concepts to Investigate: Reaction rate, temperature.

Materials: <u>Part 1</u>: Vinegar, baking soda (NaHCO$_3$), beakers, side arm flasks or flasks fitted with stoppers and tubing; <u>Part 2</u>: Alka Seltzer® tablets, thermometer, plastic film canisters (optional).

Principles and Procedures:

Part 1: The effect of temperature on neutralization of vinegar: Determine the approximate rate of carbon dioxide production (in mL of carbon dioxide per unit time) as a function of temperature using the apparatus described in 4.3.1 (Figure G). Repeat the investigation using undiluted vinegar at temperatures of approximately 0°C, 15°C, 30°C, 70°C. Use an ice bath or hot plate to achieve the required temperatures. Report your results in Table 2 and plot them in Figure H.

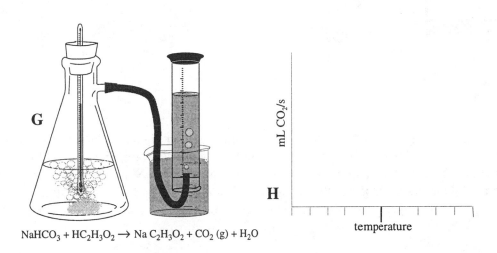

NaHCO$_3$ + HC$_2$H$_3$O$_2$ → Na C$_2$H$_3$O$_2$ + CO$_2$ (g) + H$_2$O

Part 2: The effect of temperature on antacid reactions: Heartburn (acid indigestion, sour stomach) is a common problem associated with anxiety or an acidic diet. An excessively acidic stomach may cause considerable discomfort that can be relieved by neutralization of stomach acids. Numerous products are sold to combat heartburn, one of which is Alka Seltzer®. Alka Seltzer® contains calcium dihydrogen phosphate (Ca(H$_2$PO$_4$)$_2$) and

Table 2: The Effect of Temperature on Reaction Rate

Temperature, C°	Reaction Rate, mL CO$_2$/s

sodium hydrogen carbonate ($NaHCO_3$). When placed in water, these substances react as follows:

$$Ca(H_2PO_4)_2(s) + 2NaHCO_3(s) \longrightarrow$$

$$2CO_2(g) + 2H_2O(l) + Ca^{2+}(aq) + 2HPO_4^{2-}(aq) + 2Na^+(aq)$$

Note that one of the products is carbon dioxide gas. It is this gas that causes you to burp after swallowing a glass of dissolved Alka Seltzer®. When Alka Seltzer® is placed in water it fizzes vigorously. The rate of the above reaction can be gauged by the apparent rate of bubbling. Place a fresh tablet of Alka Seltzer® in ice water, water at room temperature, and water that is near boiling (Figure I.) Which one fizzes fastest?

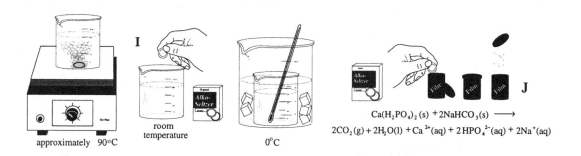

An interesting alternative to this activity is illustrated in Figure J. *Put on goggles and a lab coat.* Fill one plastic film container one third full with ice water, and a second with water at room temperature. Do not use hot water because water may splatter and cause burns! Place an Alka Seltzer® tablet in the canister, seal, *stand back,* and record the time at which the top pops off. Repeat two or three times at each temperature and determine average values.

Questions

(1) Describe your observations of the relationship between temperature and rate of reaction.

(2) What would you predict concerning the rate of reaction if both the concentration and temperature were increased?

(3) Food spoils rapidly at room temperature, but when placed in a refrigerator or freezer, food can be kept for extended periods. Explain.

(4) Explain the difference in the "fizzing" of Alka Seltzer® at different temperatures.

4.3.3 THE EFFECT OF TEMPERATURE AND CONCENTRATION ON REACTION RATE

Concepts to Investigate: Reaction rate, concentration, temperature.

Materials: Beakers, potassium iodate (0.01 M KIO_3), soluble starch, sulfuric acid (1 M H_2SO_4), sodium metabisulfite ($Na_2S_2O_5$), timer, cylinders, distilled water, balance, thermometers.

Principles and Procedures: Those who have worked in the field of chemistry know that color changes accompanying chemical reactions either occur immediately upon the mixing of two chemicals, or gradually with heating, time or other variables. Thus, it came as a great surprise to chemist Vernon Harcourt when he witnessed an abrupt color change occurring 15 to 20 seconds after the mixing of chemicals. The timing of this delayed color change was found to be so regular that the reaction became known as a "clock" reaction. Since Harcourt's time, other clock reactions have been discovered, and although the chemistry of such reactions is not fully understood, they are useful in helping to study chemical kinetics. In the activities that follow, you will study the effect of temperature and concentration on the time required for an abrupt color change. Make a starch solution by mixing approximately 7 grams of soluble starch in a small amount of warm water. Dissolve this starch paste in a liter of boiling water and then allow it to cool to room temperature. Make a 0.01 M solution of potassium iodate by dissolving 2.1 grams of potassium iodate in a liter of warm water.

Part 1: The starch-iodine clock reaction: Place 5 mL of starch solution in a 250 mL or 500 mL beaker. Add 95 mL of distilled water and 0.02 grams of sodium metabisulfite ($Na_2S_2O_5$) and stir until dissolved. Acidify the solution by adding approximately 5 mL of 1.0 M sulfuric acid. Measure out 100 mL of 0.01 M potassium iodate solution and start a stopwatch the moment the solutions are mixed. Record the time when the solution turns black.

Part 2: The effect of temperature on the rate of the starch-iodine clock reaction: Repeat the procedure in part 1 at temperatures of approximately 0°C, 25°C, 50°C. You may cool the solutions in an ice water bath to 0°C, and you may warm them on a hot plate to approximately 50°C. What is the effect of temperature on the rate of the clock reaction?

Part 3: The effect of concentration on the clock reaction: Prepare 100 mL quantities of 0.010, 0.008, 0.006, 0.004, and 0.002 M potassium iodate solutions by adding 100, 80, 60, 40, and 20 mL of 0.01 M potassium iodate from a graduated cylinder to each of five beakers, and filling to 100 mL with distilled water. Repeat the steps in part 1 with each concentration of potassium iodate and plot the time of color change as a function of potassium iodate concentration.

Questions

(1) Why is the starch-iodine reaction called a clock reaction? Why is there a delay before the blue-black color appears?

(2) What is the effect of concentration of iodate on the starch-iodine clock reaction?

(3) What is the effect of temperature on the starch-iodine clock reaction?

(4) How does the presence of HSO_3^- prevent the formation of the blue-black color?

4.3.4 CATALYSTS, REACTION RATES AND ACTIVATION ENERGY

Concepts to Investigate: Reaction rates, catalysts, activation energy, autocatalysts, collision theory.

Materials: Part 1: Hydrogen peroxide (H_2O_2) solution from drug store (higher concentrations are available from chemical supply companies and work better, but must be handled with greater caution), apparatus shown in Figure K, manganese dioxide (MnO_2), activated charcoal, calcium carbonate ($CaCO_3$), potassium permanganate ($KMnO_4$), potassium iodide (KI), spatula; Part 2: Sugar cubes, activated carbon (fireplace ash), tongs, ceramic tile or ash tray, match or burner.

Principles and Procedures: A catalyst is a substance that speeds up the rate of a chemical reaction and can be recovered at the end of the reaction in its original form. Often only a trace of a catalyst is sufficient to accelerate a reaction. A catalyst speeds up a reaction by providing a set of elementary steps with more favorable energetics than those that exist in its absence. Catalysts are classified as heterogeneous when the reactants and catalyst are in different phases (for example, solid catalyst and liquid or gas reactants) or homogeneous when the catalyst is in the same phase as the reactants and products.

Catalysts increase the rates of reactions by decreasing the activation energy required to initiate a reaction. According to the collision theory, in order to react, colliding particles must have a total kinetic energy equal to or greater than the activation energy, the minimum amount of energy required to initiate a chemical reaction. If the minimum energy is not available, the particles remain intact and no change results. If the energy is available, the particles enter a transitional structure called an activated complex that results from an effective collision and that persists while old bonds are breaking and new bonds are forming. Figure L shows the energy relationship among reactants, products, activated complex and catalyzed activated complex. Note that the presence of a catalyst (curved dotted line) reduces the activation energy required. As a result, a larger percentage of the collisions occurring in a catalyzed reaction meet the energy requirements to react, and the reaction proceeds more rapidly. In the reaction illustrated, the products are more stable than the reactants, and the reaction is exothermic and is accompanied by a release of heat ($-\Delta H$). The reverse reaction is endothermic. Heat is absorbed and the reactants are more stable than the products. Note that ΔH is positive in an endothermic reaction.

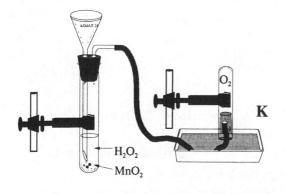

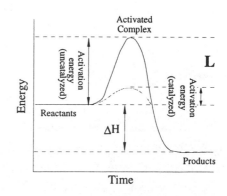

Part 1: Catalysts: Hydrogen peroxide is a colorless liquid used as a rocket propellant, disinfectant, and bleaching agent. You may have used a dilute hydrogen peroxide solution to sterilize a wound. Hydrogen peroxide slowly decomposes into water and oxygen:

$$2H_2O_2(aq) \rightarrow 2H_2O(l) + O_2(g)$$

This process can be accelerated by the addition of numerous substances, particularly salts of such metals as iron, copper, manganese, nickel or chromium. It should be noted that these substances accelerate the decomposition of hydrogen peroxide, but are not consumed in the process. Such substances are known as catalysts.

Set up a gas collection device as illustrated in Figure K. Fill the test tube with water, cover the mouth, and invert into a container of water so no water is lost from the tube. Place three grams of manganese dioxide in a large test tube and clamp to a support as shown. Insert a stopper assembly equipped with a delivery funnel and bent glass tube as illustrated. Add 5 mL of 3% hydrogen peroxide through the delivery funnel. Collect the test tube of gas, stopper, and set aside. Continue collecting gas in additional tubes until the reaction ceases. Now add more hydrogen peroxide and continue until you have collected 5 test tubes of oxygen. Note that the manganese dioxide is not used up in the reaction. It remains visible in the tube, and promotes the decomposition of hydrogen peroxide repeatedly. Manganese dioxide is therefore considered to be a catalyst, and the reaction can be written:

$$2H_2O_2(aq) \xrightarrow{MnO_2} 2H_2O(l) + O_2(g)$$

Note that the manganese dioxide is written above the arrow, indicating that it is not changed, but only catalyzes the reaction. Unstopper the first tube of gas collected, and test for the presence of oxygen by inserting a glowing splint or smoldering match. Test each of the remaining tubes in the same manner. The flame should glow brightest in the final tube because it contains relatively pure oxygen, while the first tubes may contain some air displaced early in the reaction. Decant the hydrogen peroxide from the reaction flask and add fresh hydrogen peroxide to the old manganese dioxide. Does manganese dioxide continue to promote the production of oxygen?

Repeat this activity using 3 grams each of activated charcoal, potassium permanganate, potassium iodide, and calcium carbonate. Record your results in Table 3. Which of the materials appear to be catalysts?

Part 2: Catalysts in combustion: Hold a sugar cube with a pair of tongs above a ceramic tile, ashtray or other fireproof surface, and try to burn it with a match or laboratory burner (Figure M). Since the melting point of sucrose is only 185°C, the sugar cube melts before it

Table 3: Tests for Catalysts

	Rate of Bubbling	*Glowing Splint Test*	*Catalyst?*
manganese dioxide			
activated charcoal			
calcium carbonate			
potassium permanganate			
potassium iodide			

burns. Dip a second cube in very fine powdered activated charcoal (carbon) or ash from a fireplace or ashtray. When a match is brought to this cube, the cube burns readily. The carbon acts as a catalyst in the combustion of sugar.

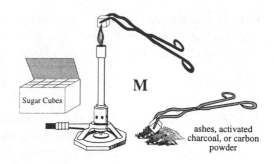

Questions

(1) What is the purpose of a catalyst?

(2) Describe in your own words the meaning of "activation energy" and "activated complex."

(3) Although the heat of formation (ΔH = 285.8 kJ/mol) and the free energy change (ΔG = −237.2 kJ/mol) for the reaction of hydrogen and oxygen to form water are quite high, when hydrogen (H_2) and oxygen (O_2) are mixed at room temperature, they do not combine spontaneously to form water (H_2O). Explain.

(4) A catalyst lowers the activation energy for a reaction. Explain.

4.3.5 ENZYMES

Concepts to Investigate: Reaction rates, enzymes, denaturation.

Materials: Part 1: Test tubes, crackers, Lugol's solution (dissolve 10 g of KI in 100 mL of distilled water and then add 5 g of iodine), Benedict's solution (or Clinitest tablets), white soda crackers, starch suspension (laundry starch from the grocery store diluted 1:10 with water). Benedict's solution may be purchased or prepared as follows: Dissolve 173 grams of sodium citrate and 100 grams of sodium carbonate in 800 mL of warm water and filter. Dissolve 100 grams of copper sulfate in 100 mL of water and add slowly while stirring to the carbonate-citrate solution. Add distilled water to make one liter; Part 2: Potatoes, beef liver, test tubes, 3% hydrogen peroxide (available from a drug store).

Safety: For health reasons, some schools do not allow experiments with saliva. Investigate the policies at your school. Never touch the saliva of another individual. Wear goggles and a lab coat. Do not touch chemicals.

Principles and Procedures: Enzymes are catalysts that dramatically increase the rate of biochemical reactions in living systems while not being consumed. Enzymes, like all catalysts, may be used repeatedly. Since a typical enzyme molecule may convert 1000 substrate molecules per second, only a very small quantity of enzyme is needed to catalyze reactions. Enzymes catalyze all aspects of cellular metabolism, including the digestion of food (in which large nutrient molecules such as proteins, carbohydrates, and fats are broken down into smaller molecules), the transformation of chemical energy, and the construction of large biological molecules from smaller ones. In the first activity you will investigate a digestive enzyme known as amylase. Amylase is secreted in saliva and initiates the breakdown of starch molecules into simple sugars (Figure N). In the second activity you will investigate catalase, an enzyme used to detoxify a metabolic byproduct known as hydrogen peroxide.

Part 1: Amylase, a digestive enzyme: Corn, potato, rice, sorghum, wheat, cassava and other major staple food crops have very high starch content. Starch molecules are glucose polymers linked together by alpha-1,4 and alpha-1,6 glucosidic bonds (as opposed to the beta-1,4 glucosidic bonds found in cellulose, the principal component of wood). In order to make use of the carbon and energy stored in starch, the human digestive system must first break down the polymer into smaller assimilable sugars.

The presence of starch and glucose is detectable with various dyes and solutions, two of which you will use here. Iodine forms a blue-black color when it combines with starch. Benedict's solution forms a yellow, orange or red precipitate when boiled in the presence of glucose. By using both Benedict's and Lugol's solutions it is possible to monitor the breakdown of starch into glucose (Figure O).

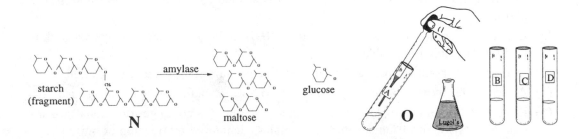

(a) Crush a soda cracker and place it in a test tube with 5 mL of water, add a few drops of Lugol's iodine solution and shake. Is starch present? (b) Salivate and place approximately 5 mL of your saliva into a second test tube, add 5 mL of water and test with Lugol's solution. Does saliva contain starch? (c) Place a fresh soda cracker in your mouth, chew slowly for 10 seconds, and deposit the chewed cracker into the third tube. Add 5 mL of water, a couple of drops of Lugol's solution, and shake. Does it appear as though any starch has been broken down? (d) Place another soda cracker in your mouth, chew slowly for 1 minute, deposit approximately 5 mL of the chewed cracker and saliva into a fourth tube, add five milliliters of water and a couple of drops of Lugol's solution. If the blue-black color is less intense than before, then we may assume that starch is disappearing while being chewed. Does it appear as though starch is broken down by enzymes in the mouth?

Salivary amylase breaks bonds in starch, producing small amounts of glucose and large quantities of the double sugar, maltose. You can test for the presence of glucose using Benedict's solution. Repeat each of the procedures described above, but substitute the Benedict's test, as follows. Add 5 mL of the solution to be tested to a test tube together with approximately 2 mL of Benedict's solution. Heat the mixture to boiling for two to three minutes and re-examine. The appearance of a red, yellow or orange coloration is a positive indicator for the presence of glucose. Does glucose appear in any of the test tubes?

Part 2: Temperature sensitivity of enzymes: Hydrogen peroxide (H_2O_2) is a toxic byproduct of cellular metabolism. Fortunately, living systems are equipped with an enzyme known as catalase which renders hydrogen peroxide harmless by breaking it down into oxygen and water. Catalase is found in many tissues, but most abundantly in those tissues characterized by high metabolic rates. When living tissue is placed in a solution of hydrogen peroxide, bubbles of oxygen form:

$$2H_2O_2(aq) \xrightarrow{\text{catalase}} 2H_2O(l) + O_2(g)$$

Under these conditions high rates of bubble formation are indicative of high concentrations of catalase.

Freeze small samples of liver and allow them to thaw to room temperature. Boil additional samples of liver and potato for at least three minutes and allow them to cool to room temperature. Place small (approximately 3 gram) samples of liver and potato that have been either frozen, boiled or neither frozen nor boiled into separate test tubes containing 10 mL of 3% hydrogen peroxide solution. Make careful observations concerning the rate of bubbling in each test tube. In which tissue is the concentration of catalase apparently greatest? What is the effect of boiling or freezing on the viability of catalase?

Questions

(1) The longer a cracker is chewed, the less it is stained by Lugol's iodine solution. Explain.

(2) Enzymes are quite specific in the reactions they catalyze. Do some library research to find out how this is possible.

(3) Does liver or potato appear to have a greater concentration of catalase? Explain.

(4) Are enzymes more sensitive to freezing or boiling? Explain, using data from part 2.

(5) If the structure of an enzyme has been altered so that it is no longer functional, we say that the enzyme has been denatured. Is catalase denatured by freezing or boiling?

4.3.6 OSCILLATING CHEMICAL REACTIONS

Concepts to Investigate: Kinetics, reaction rates, reaction mechanisms, oscillating reaction, equilibrium.

Materials: Briggs-Rauscher reaction kit; or 6% hydrogen peroxide, potassium iodate, 6 *M* sulfuric acid, malonic acid, manganese sulfate, soluble starch.

Safety: Teacher demonstration only. Wear goggles, gloves, and a lab coat. Carry out in a well-ventilated area. Iodine is produced. The vapor and solid are irritating to the eyes, skin, and mucous membranes. Sulfuric acid, malonic acid, and 30% H_2O_2 (hydrogen peroxide). are strong irritants and hydrogen peroxide is a strong oxidizer. After the activity, reduce the iodine by adding about 10 g of sodium thiosulfate to the mixture and stirring until the mixture becomes colorless. Caution: The reaction between iodine and thiosulfate is exothermic and the mixture may be hot. The cooled, neutralized mixture should be washed down the drain with water.

Principles and Procedures: Teacher demonstration only. Clock reactions, such as illustrated in 4.3.3, are intriguing because color changes occur abruptly and without warning long after reactants are mixed. Oscillating reactions resemble clock reactions except that they repeatedly switch back and forth between two colors! In this activity you will investigate one of the most famous oscillating reactions known as the Briggs-Rauscher reaction, named after the two high school teachers who discovered it.

You may buy the mixtures for the Briggs-Rauscher reaction as a kit, or make them as follows. Solution 1: 6% H_2O_2; solution 2: 4.3 g KIO_3 dissolved in 100 mL distilled H_2O + 1.5 mL 6 *M* H_2SO_4; and solution 3: 1.56 g malonic acid + 0.34 g $MnSO_4 \cdot H_2O$ dissolved in 100 mL H_2O + 3 mL of freshly prepared 1% soluble starch solution. A 1% soluble starch solution may be prepared by mixing 5 mL water together with 1 g of soluble starch until a paste is formed. Add the paste to 95 mL of boiling water and stir until the solution is homogeneous.

Mix 100 mL of solution 1 with 100 mL of solution 2 in a beaker using a magnetic stirring rod or glass rod. Add 100 mL of solution 3, mix briefly, and allow to stand on an overhead projector so students may observe the color oscillations. Within a minute the color will begin to oscillate between light yellow and blue-black. How many color changes does the reaction go through? What is the final color of the solution?

The Briggs-Rauscher reaction may be summarized by the following equation:

$$IO_3^- + 2H_2O_2 + CH_2(CO_2H)_2 + H^+ \longrightarrow ICH(CO_2H)_2 + 2O_2 + 3H_2O$$

It is thought that this reaction is the result of two component reactions (Figure P):

$$(A) \quad IO_3^- + 2H_2O_2 + H^+ \longrightarrow HOI + 2O_2 + 2H_2O$$

$$(B) \quad HOI + CH_2(CO_2H)_2 \longrightarrow ICH(CO_2H)_2 + H_2O$$

Reaction A may proceed by two different processes. Process 1 is faster and is favored by low iodide concentrations, while process 2 is slower and is favored by high iodide concentrations. Thus, when iodide concentrations are low, reaction A–process 1 predominates, producing HOI faster than reaction B can consume it. Thus, the concentration of HOI increases. When the concentration of HOI exceeds that of iodide, then iodide ions combine to form iodine (I_2,

Overall Reaction

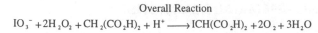

$$IO_3^- + 2H_2O_2 + CH_2(CO_2H)_2 + H^+ \longrightarrow ICH(CO_2H)_2 + 2O_2 + 3H_2O$$

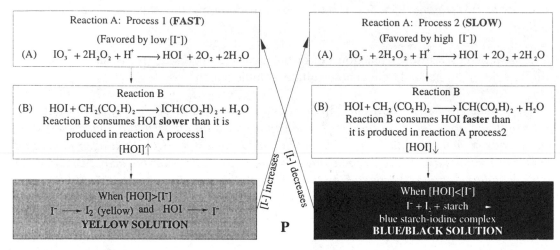

Reaction A: Process 1 (FAST)

(Favored by low [I⁻])

(A) $IO_3^- + 2H_2O_2 + H^+ \longrightarrow HOI + 2O_2 + 2H_2O$

Reaction B

(B) $HOI + CH_2(CO_2H)_2 \longrightarrow ICH(CO_2H)_2 + H_2O$

Reaction B consumes HOI **slower** than it is produced in reaction A process1

[HOI]↑

When [HOI]>[I⁻]

$I^- \longrightarrow I_2$ (yellow) and $HOI \longrightarrow I^-$

YELLOW SOLUTION

Reaction A: Process 2 (SLOW)

(Favored by high [I⁻])

(A) $IO_3^- + 2H_2O_2 + H^+ \longrightarrow HOI + 2O_2 + 2H_2O$

Reaction B

(B) $HOI + CH_2(CO_2H)_2 \longrightarrow ICH(CO_2H)_2 + H_2O$

Reaction B consumes HOI **faster** than it is produced in reaction A process2

[HOI]↓

When [HOI]<[I⁻]

$I^- + I_2 + starch \longrightarrow$ blue starch-iodine complex

BLUE/BLACK SOLUTION

[I⁻] increases   [I⁻] decreases

P

producing the yellow color), and HOI dissociates to produce iodide ions. Increased iodide reactions now favor reaction A–process 2, a slow reaction. The production of HOI drops to rates lower than the rate at which reaction B consumes it. When HOI concentrations drop below iodide concentrations, iodide and iodine bond with starch to produce a noticeable blue/black color. The concentration of iodide drops, creating an environment that once again favors reaction A–process 1, and the cycle is repeated. Thus, reaction A–process 1 combined with reaction B brings about an environment that favors reaction A–process 2, while reaction A–process 2 with reaction B brings about conditions that favor reaction A–process 1. When reaction A–process 1 is favored, the solution turns yellow (the color of iodine), while when process 2 is favored, the solution turns blue-black (the color of the starch-iodine complex). How many oscillations does this reaction go through before it stops?

Questions

(1) What is an oscillating reaction?

(2) In the oscillating reaction you investigated, the solution changed color several times and then finally remained a blue-black color. Explain.

(3) Suppose a net reaction A → D proceeds as follows: A → B; B → C; C → D. Net reaction: A → D. Explain why B and C are referred to as intermediates.

FOR THE TEACHER

4.3.1 THE EFFECT OF CONCENTRATION ON REACTION RATE

Discussion: Atoms or molecules must collide with sufficient energy to produce an activated complex that produces new molecules. The possibility of collisions among these reactants increases as the concentration of reactants increases. Increased collisions provide an opportunity for a greater number of effective collisions to occur, thereby increasing the rate of reaction.

Answers: (1) The production of gas increases with increased concentration of vinegar. (2) See discussion.

4.3.2 THE EFFECT OF TEMPERATURE ON REACTION RATE

Discussion: Temperature is a measure of the average kinetic energy of the atoms and molecules in a substance. Higher temperatures mean that particles (atoms or molecules) are traveling at higher speeds. While two particles colliding at a lower speed may simply rebound, particles at higher speeds may interact and produce new products. Higher temperature increases the number of effective collisions among particles and, therefore, increases the rate of reaction. As a rule of thumb, the rate of a chemical reaction doubles when the temperature is increased 10°C.

A qualitative demonstration of the effect of temperature on reaction rate can be accomplished simply by placing balloons over the mouths of flasks in which the neutralization reaction is occurring. At warmer temperatures, the balloons will fill more readily.

Answers: (1) The higher the temperature, the greater the reaction rate as gauged by the production of carbon dioxide gas. (2) The rate would increase, since both factors increase reaction rate. (3) Chemical reactions, including metabolic reactions in bacteria and fungi that spoil food, as well as oxidation reactions that degrade food, are temperature dependent. At low temperatures, they react slower and cause less damage. (4) An increase in temperature causes an increase in the rate of reaction of the tablet with water, causing a greater degree of fizzing.

4.3.3 THE EFFECT OF TEMPERATURE AND CONCENTRATION ON REACTION RATE

Discussion: The mechanism for the simple iodine clock reaction is not yet completely understood. A probable, simplified sequence of reactions is illustrated.

$$IO_3^- + 3HSO_3^- \rightarrow I^- + 3H^+ + 3SO_4^{2-} \quad (slow)$$

$$IO_3^- + 5I^- + 6H^+ \rightarrow 3I_2 + 3H_2O \quad (slow)$$

$$I_2 + HSO_3^- + H_2O \rightarrow 2I^- + SO_4^{2-} + 3H^+ \quad (fast)$$

$$I_2 + starch \rightarrow starch/iodine\ complex\ (blue - black)$$

IO_3^- reacts with HSO_3^- to form I^-. I^- reacts with IO_3^- to form I_2. I_2 immediately reacts with HSO_3^-. After all the HSO_3^- is consumed, I_2 reacts with starch to form the blue-black colored complex. The first two steps are slow in comparison to the third step. Consequently, as long as bisulfite (HSO_3^-) is present, the rapidity of the third step prevents the accumulation of iodine and the formation of the blue-black starch-iodine complex. However, when the bisulfite is totally consumed, the iodine can no longer be reduced in step three and the starch-iodine complex immediately appears in step four.

There are several variant "clock" reactions, one being the "Old Nassau" reaction in which the color sequence is colorless, orange, blue-black. *This should be performed as an instructor demonstration only. Wear gloves, lab coat and goggles. Avoid contact with all chemicals, particularly the mercury (II) chloride.* Prepare one liter of starch solution as mentioned earlier and add 15 g of $NaHSO_3$. Prepare a mercury (II) chloride solution by dissolving 3 g of $HgCl_2$ in 1 L of distilled water. Prepare one liter of potassium iodate (KIO_3) solution by dissolving 15 g of KIO_3 in 1 L of distilled water. Mix equivalent volumes of all three solutions. After a few seconds the solution turns orange and then quickly turns blue-black. In this reaction, Hg^{2+} and I^- combine to form the precipitate HgI_2 because the solubility of mercuric iodide is exceeded. Shortly after mercuric iodide forms, bisulfite is exhausted, iodine accumulates, and the orange color is masked by the blue-black color of the iodine-starch complex discussed earlier. Refer to local policies for disposal guidelines.

Answers: (1) The time required for the blue-black color to form depends on the concentrations of reactants and the temperature. I_2 is immediately consumed by HSO_3^- to form I^-, but after a certain time the HSO_3^- is consumed and I_2 accumulates and reacts with starch to produce the blue-black color. (2) Increasing the concentration of iodate decreases the time required for the color change to occur. (3) Increasing the temperature decreases the time required for the color change to occur. (4) The HSO_3^- reacts with I_2 to form I^-, leaving no I_2 to react with starch to form the blue-black iodine-starch complex. When all HSO_3^- is consumed, I_2 is available to react with the starch.

4.3.4 CATALYSTS, REACTION RATES AND ACTIVATION ENERGY

Discussion: Table 4 shows the results students should obtain in part 1.

Be certain students understand that catalysts increase the rate of a chemical reaction by lowering the activation energy required for the reaction. That is, a catalyst provides an alternative pathway or reaction mechanism in which the potential-energy barrier between reactants and products is changed. A catalyst is not consumed in the reaction, and equally increases the rate of the forward and reverse reactions, which explains why catalysts do not change the value of the equilibrium constant of a reaction.

Heterogeneous catalysis, in which the reactants and catalyst are in different phases, is very important in industrial chemistry, accounting for the production of millions of tons of important

Table 4: Tests for Catalysts (Results)

	Rate of Bubbling	*Glowing Splint Test*	*Catalyst?*
manganese dioxide	increase	positive	yes
activated charcoal	increase	positive	yes
calcium carbonate	no change	negative	no
potassium permanganate	increase	positive	yes
potassium iodide	increase	positive	yes

chemicals. Heterogeneous catalysts appear to function through a process whereby reactant particles (atoms or molecules) are adsorbed on a surface where the reaction then occurs. In such reactions, gas molecules, for example, may bind to the surface of the catalyst, dissociate, and then recombine forming new products. In homogeneous catalysis, the reactants, products, and catalyst are dispersed in a single phase, usually liquid.

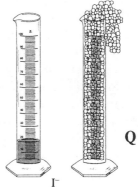

A dramatic *teacher demonstration* of catalysis may be performed as follows (Figure Q). *Put on goggles, gloves and a lab coat.* Pour about 50 mL of 30% hydrogen peroxide into the cylinder. *Use caution since 30% hydrogen peroxide will cause immediate tissue damage.* Add a squirt of dishwashing detergent and approximately 4 grams of solid potassium iodide (KI). The rapid production of oxygen causes foam to form. This foam will fill and probably overflow the cylinder. The two-step decomposition of H_2O_2 is:

$$H_2O_2(aq) + I^-(aq) \longrightarrow H_2O(l) + OI^-(aq)$$

$$H_2O_2(aq) + OI^-(aq) \longrightarrow H_2O(l) + O_2(g) + I^-(aq)$$

Note that iodide (I^-) is found on the reactant side of the first equation, and on the product side of the second equation. It is clear that although iodide undergoes several changes, it is not consumed in the reaction, a characteristic shared by all catalysts.

$$2H_2O_2(aq) \overset{I^-}{\longrightarrow} 2H_2O(l) + O_2(g)$$

Answers: (1) The purpose of a catalyst is to accelerate the rate of a chemical reaction. (2) Activation energy is the energy required to transform reactants into the activated complex. An activated complex is a transitional state that persists while old bonds break and new bonds form. (4) Oxygen and hydrogen exist as diatomic molecules in the atmosphere. The bonds of the molecules must be broken if new bonds between the hydrogen and oxygen are to be formed. Bond breaking is an endothermic process while bond formation is an exothermic process. Before bonds can be broken, the reactants (hydrogen and oxygen) must be supplied with activation energy to get the reaction started. After the reaction begins, the energy released is sufficient to sustain the reaction. (4) A catalyst speeds up a reaction by providing a set of elementary steps with more favorable energetics than those that exist in its absence. That is, a catalyst provides an alternative pathway or reaction mechanism in which the potential-energy barrier between reactants and products is changed. A catalyst may form an alternative activated complex that requires a lower activation energy. The net result is the rate of reaction is increased because more molecules in the catalyzed reaction have sufficient energy to reach the activated state than in the uncatalyzed reaction.

4.3.5 ENZYMES

Discussion: You may wish to extend the experiment by having students analyze the influence of time on enzyme activity. Students should prepare two sets of test tubes, each containing 5 mL of a 0.1 to 1% starch paste suspension and 5 drops of saliva. At timed intervals, remove both samples of the saliva and starch paste mixture and test one with Lugol's solution for the presence of starch and the other with Benedict's solution. Emphasize the need for controls in an experiment by testing both pure saliva and starch with both Lugol's and Benedict's solutions. It should be noted that there is significant variation in the population with respect to the amount of amylase production.

Salivary amylase breaks bonds in starch, producing small amounts of glucose and large quantities of the double sugar maltose. Starches come in several forms, and are a storage form of glucose (dextrose), a simple sugar produced by plants. Cellulose, the principle component of wood, is also composed entirely of glucose, but the glucose units are connected by a different type of bond. Your saliva and pancreatic juices contain enzymes that can break (hydrolyze) the bonds in starches, but not in cellulose, which is why you are able to digest potatoes, but not wood!

Answers: (1) Over time the enzyme amylase in your saliva converts starch into the simple sugar, glucose. When the starch is gone, no blue-black iodine/starch complex forms. (2) An enzyme holds a substrate molecule in the correct position for the reaction to occur. Portions of the enzyme weaken the substrate's bonds, lowering the activation energy required for the reaction to occur. (3) More bubbling is present in the tubes containing liver, indicating that liver has a higher concentration of catalase. This is not surprising, since the liver is known as the "center of metabolism" in the body. (4) Boiling. The three-dimensional structure of enzymes is altered by boiling, causing them to lose their functionality. (5) Catalase, like all enzymes, is denatured by boiling.

4.3.6 OSCILLATING CHEMICAL REACTIONS

Discussion: Your students will be entertained and mystified by this oscillating reaction. It may seem appropriate to use an analogy such as a swinging pendulum when discussing oscillating reactions, but such an analogy is inappropriate because, although the pendulum repeatedly passes through the rest (equilibrium) position, an oscillating reaction cannot repeatedly pass through the equilibrium position. Doing so would violate the second law of thermodynamics which distinguishes the direction of energy transformation in natural processes. Heat flows spontaneously from an object of higher temperature to one of lower temperature. Consequently, a cup of hot chocolate will not extract heat from its cooler surroundings and become hotter! Likewise the second law states that a chemical system at equilibrium cannot deviate from this state spontaneously. So how does the system repeatedly cycle through the colors if it is not repeatedly passing through the equilibrium condition? In an oscillating chemical reaction, the concentrations of some of the species of the reaction mixture repeatedly pass through the same value, accounting for the color changes, while the energy-releasing reaction driving the oscillations continuously proceeds toward completion. Oscillating reactions have a "feedback" loop in which the rate of one step is affected by a product formed in a later step (Figure P).

Answers: (1) An oscillating chemical reaction is one in which a solution alternates between two conditions (e.g., colors, gassing activity, etc.). (2) There is a main reaction which is proceeding toward equilibrium, while other subsidiary reactions proceed in which the concentrations of some reactants and products repeatedly pass through the same concentrations, and it is these subsidiary reactions that account for the color changes. When the main reaction has proceeded to equilibrium, the concentrations of reactants and products remain constant and no further color changes are possible, so the color remains blue-black. (3) A reaction equation (net equation) indicates only what molecular species disappear as a result of the reaction and what species are produced. These equations do not show the pathway by which a reaction proceeds, which means they do not show the step-by-step sequence of reactions by which the overall chemical change occurs. This step-by-step process is called the reaction mechanism, and must first be postulated and then examined by experimental methods. In the example, we know that A produces D. We postulate that A first produces B, that B then produces C, and that C finally produces D. The rate at which the net reaction proceeds is determined by the slowest of the reactions involved. Therefore, if the production of D from A is slow, it might be that this slow rate is caused by the slow production of C from B. The slowest-rate step is called the rate-determining step for the chemical reaction.

Applications to Everyday Life

Cooking and freezing: Raising the temperature of food during cooking increases reaction rates (primarily denaturation reactions) and decreases the time required to prepare food. Low temperatures do not sterilize food, but simply decrease the growth of microorganisms (by reducing the rate of metabolic reactions) and the rate of chemical reactions (primarily oxidation) that cause food deterioration.

Reducing air pollution: To reduce air pollution, automobiles are equipped with devices known as catalytic converters that catalyze the oxidation of toxic CO and unburned hydrocarbons to CO_2 and H_2O, and the conversion of toxic NO and NO_2 to N_2 and O_2.

Chemical production: Catalysts play a major role in the production of important chemicals. A mixture of porous iron and oxides of potassium and aluminum is used to catalyze the production of ammonia from nitrogen gas and hydrogen gas in the Haber process, while a platinum-rhodium mixture is used to catalyze the production of nitric acid from ammonia gas and oxygen gas in the Ostwald process. Sulfuric acid, the most important industrial chemical, is prepared from sulfur and oxygen gas using the surface catalyst vanadium oxide.

Body metabolism: Enzymes are a special class of proteins that catalyze reactions in cells. In general, the reaction between enzyme and substrate can be written as: substrate + enzyme → enzyme-substrate → product + enzyme. Note that the enzyme is not consumed, for the net reaction is simply substrate → product. Pepsin is an enzyme found in the gastric juices of the stomach, and is responsible for the conversion of proteins to peptides and amino acids. Amylase is found in saliva and pancreatic juice and is responsible for the conversion of starch to maltose. Catalase is found in the liver and is responsible for the decomposition of hydrogen peroxide to oxygen and water. Note that the names of enzymes often end in "-ase."

Termites and wood decay: Termites can eat and digest wood, as some homeowners know well, but humans cannot. Termites feed on cellulose but do not produce an enzyme to digest cellulose. The wood-digesting flagellate *Trichonympha* inhabits the gut of a termite and produces the enzyme required to digest cellulose. Neither organism, termite nor *Trichonympha*, can survive without the other. This type of dependency is a symbiotic relationship known as mutualism.

Food preservation: If you examine the contents of a package of salami, Italian sausage, beef sticks or other preserved, dried meat you will probably notice that they contain BHA (butylated hydroxyanisole) and BHT (butylated hydroxytoluene). These chemicals are antioxidants, inhibiting the oxidation and spoiling of food. Sometimes referred to as "negative catalysts," these inhibitors restrain molecules from reacting, and thereby slow processes that contribute to the degradation of foods.

Medicine: A competitive inhibitor is a molecule that competes with the substrate for the active site of an enzyme because its structure closely resembles that of the substrate. When an inhibitor occupies an active site, the substrate of an enzyme cannot undergo a reaction. When a micro-organism such as a bacterium enters the body, a competitive inhibitor may be used to inhibit a bacterial enzyme, and thus disrupt the action of the bacterium. The sulfa drug sulfanilamide fights infections by competing with a substrate in the growth cycle of a bacterium, thus preventing that bacterium from reproducing. It is thought that many other antibiotics, including penicillin, erythromycin and tetracycline operate in a similar manner. The drug dicumarol is used to control blood clotting by interfering with the enzymatic production of prothrombin, a required agent in blood clotting.

4.4 CHEMICAL EQUILIBRIUM

Suppose your school schedules an all-day outing to the beach (Figure A). When you arrive in the morning at 8:00 AM, the weather is cool and no one is in the water. All students are on the beach, and the system (students on the beach and students in the water) is in a state of static equilibrium because the rate of students entering the water (zero) equals the rate of students leaving the water (zero). As the air temperature rises, people enter the water, disrupting the equilibrium. The number of people in the water increases until the air temperature stabilizes at 85°F at 12:00 noon. For the next two hours you notice that the number of students in the water remains constant, although students are continually entering and leaving the water. During this period, the system is said to be in a state of dynamic equilibrium. The rate of students entering the water ($rate_{(in)}$) is equal to the rate of students leaving the water ($rate_{(out)}$), so that the percentage of students in both environments remains constant.

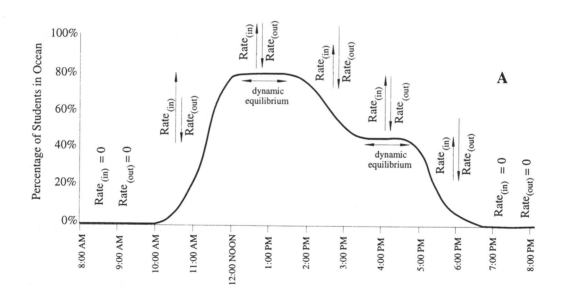

Later in the day, clouds roll in, and as the temperature drops, the rate of students entering the water ($rate_{(in)}$) falls below the rate leaving it ($rate_{(out)}$), and once again equilibrium is disrupted. At approximately 3:00 PM the air temperature stabilizes at 75°F. The percentage of students in the water is less than before, but since the rate of students entering the water once again equals the rate of students leaving the water, the system is again said to be in a state of dynamic equilibrium. It should be noted that equilibrium refers to the rate of student movement (as illustrated by the arrows in Figure A), and not to the actual numbers in one environment or another. For example at 4:00 PM the system is in dynamic equilibrium. Although 55% of the students are on the beach and only 45% are in the water, the rate of students entering the ocean is equal to the rate of students leaving it, and the percentage of students in each environment remains constant.

As evening approaches and the air temperature drops to 65°F, the rate of students leaving the water once again exceeds the rate of students entering the water, and the system is no longer in dynamic equilibrium. At dusk (7:00 PM), all students are on the beach enjoying dinner. Since no students are entering or leaving the water, the system is said to be in a state of static equilibrium.

Dynamic equilibrium is expressed by equal length arrows that point in opposite directions, indicating that opposing processes are balanced. The arrow pointing to the right indicates the direction of the forward process or reaction, and the arrow pointing to the left indicates the direction of the reverse process or reaction. The physical dynamic equilibrium at the beach can be expressed:

$$\text{students on beach} \rightleftarrows \text{students in ocean}$$

The story of an outing at the beach is analogous to what occurs in chemical reactions, with people on the beach representing reactants, people in the ocean representing products, and the rates of movement between the beach and ocean representing the rates of conversion between reactants and products. We may write a generalized chemical reaction as:

$$\text{reactants} \rightleftarrows \text{products}$$

If the rate of conversion of reactants to products is equal to the rate of conversion of products to reactants, the system is said to be in dynamic equilibrium. Dynamic equilibrium refers to an equality of rates, not to an equality in the concentration of reactants and products. Although the concentration of reactants and the concentration of products remain constant during dynamic equilibrium, the concentration of reactants is not necessarily equal to the concentration of products.

Although analogies have limitations, they may help us understand abstract concepts by expressing them in concrete terms. For example, the beach analogy can be used to explain the influence of changing the concentration of reactants or products in a reaction that is in equilibrium. Assume that another bus of students arrives at 1:00 PM. This is analogous to increasing the concentration of reactants. As the students arrive on the beach, equilibrium is disrupted. Many run right to the water, immediately increasing the number of students in the water, but after a few minutes equilibrium is re-established with equal percentages of students in the ocean and on the beach as existed prior to the arrival of the bus. In a similar manner, increasing the amount of a reactant in a reaction vessel increases the amount of product by shifting the reaction toward the product, but when equilibrium is re-established, the relative concentrations of reactants and products are the same as existed prior to the addition of the excess reactant. If, however, the air temperature at the beach increases, a larger percentage of students will flee to the cool waters of the ocean for relief. Not only does the number of people in the ocean increase, but also the percentage of people. In a similar manner, temperature directly affects the percentage of molecules that will be found as reactants or products. From these analogies we can see how changing the concentration of reactants or products disrupts equilibrium but does not change the relative concentrations of reactants or products, while changing the temperature does both. We say that concentration does not affect the equilibrium constant while temperature does. In the activities that follow, you will investigate dynamic chemical equilibrium.

4.4.1 MODELS OF DYNAMIC EQUILIBRIUM

Concepts to Investigate: Reactions, oxidation, reduction, dynamic equilibrium.

Materials: <u>Part 1</u>: None; <u>Part 2</u>: Glass tubing of different diameters or ladles with different capacity, beakers or other clear containers, food coloring.

Principles and Procedures:

Part 1: Classroom model of dynamic equilibrium: Dynamic equilibrium is the state in which two opposing processes occur simultaneously at the same rate so that no overall change occurs. That is, the rate of the forward reaction equals the rate of the reverse reaction. You can model dynamic equilibrium very simply given a room with two exits. One third of the class can stand outside the room, while two thirds remain inside. Every time one student leaves through one door, a student enters through the other door. Note that the number of students inside the room and outside the room remain constant although the students switch places. These parameters describe a state of dynamic equilibrium analogous to what occurs at a molecular level. Add enough table salt to a container of water so a layer of crystals remains on the bottom. The salt crystals are in dynamic equilibrium with the dissolved sodium and chloride ions. Although the system appears to be static, it actually is in a state of dynamic equilibrium. Sodium and chloride ions are dissociating from the salt crystals at the same rate that sodium and chloride ions are depositing on them.

Part 2: Dynamic equilibrium and reaction rates: Fill two beakers half-full with water and add a drop of food coloring to each beaker to improve visibility. Select two glass tubes with significantly different diameters. Label the larger one "forward reaction," and the smaller one "reverse reaction" as illustrated in Figure B. Position the beakers on a table, and label the left one "reactants" and the right one "products." With your left hand place the "forward reaction" tubing in the "reactants" beaker, and with your right hand place the "reverse reaction" tubing in the "products" beaker, as shown. Allow the tubing to fill to the level of the fluid in the beaker, and then seal the tops of each with your index fingers. Transfer fluid from the reactant beaker to the product beaker with the "forward reaction" tubing at the same time you transfer fluid from the products beaker to the reactants beaker using the "reverse reaction." Repeat this process until you reach a state of dynamic equilibrium where the amount of water transferred from the reactants to the products equals the amount transferred

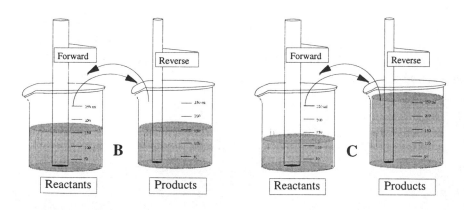

from the products to the reactants and the levels in both containers remain constant (Figure C). Are there more reactants or products when the system reaches equilibrium?

Questions

(1) What is represented by the diameter of the tubing in part 2? Explain.

(2) What do the levels of liquid in the beakers represent in part 2? Explain.

(3) What would happen to the levels at equilibrium if you doubled the size of the larger tubing? Try it.

(4) What would happen to the levels at equilibrium if both pieces of tubing had the same diameter? Try it.

(5) Equilibrium implies that something is equal. On the basis of your observations, what is equal at equilibrium?

4.4.2 DISRUPTION OF EQUILIBRIUM

Concepts to Investigate: Reactions, oxidation, reduction, equilibrium.

Materials: Flask, potassium hydroxide (KOH), methylene blue, glucose.

Principles and Procedures: Many of the activities performed in "magic" shows are based on unusual or dramatic chemical reactions. In this activity you will investigate one commonly known as the "blue bottle reaction," used to entertain audiences for years. In this activity, when a bottle containing a colorless solution is shaken, the solution turns blue, but when allowed to stand, it becomes colorless. At equilibrium the solution is colorless, but when equilibrium is disrupted by the addition of oxygen with shaking, it departs from equilibrium and becomes blue.

In the presence of oxygen the indicator methylene blue (MB) is oxidized and appears blue. When oxygen is removed, methylene blue is reduced and becomes colorless. Prepare the solution for this activity by adding about 8 g of potassium hydroxide (KOH) to 300 mL of water in a flask, cooling the solution, and then dissolving about 10 g of glucose. Use a dropper to add about 2 to 3 drops of methylene blue indicator. Stopper the flask, shake and swirl, and the solution should turn blue (Figure D). After standing, the solution should turn colorless. If necessary, adjust amounts of KOH, glucose and methylene blue until the color changes occur. Place the flask with the solution on your desk (Figure E). After it has turned colorless, remove the stopper, pick it up and shake it. Note that the color of the solution turns blue!

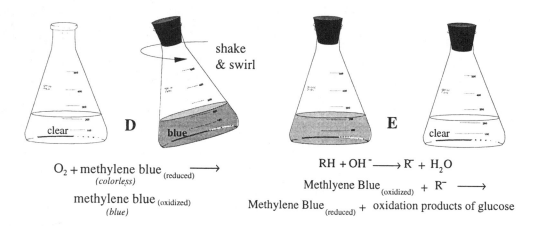

$$O_2 + \text{methylene blue}_{(reduced)} \longrightarrow$$
$$(colorless)$$
$$\text{methylene blue}_{(oxidized)}$$
$$(blue)$$

$$RH + OH^- \longrightarrow R^- + H_2O$$
$$\text{Methylene Blue}_{(oxidized)} + R^- \longrightarrow$$
$$\text{Methylene Blue}_{(reduced)} + \text{oxidation products of glucose}$$

Oxidation and reduction (see chapter 3.3) reactions are responsible for the color changes observed in this "magic trick." Under the conditions prevailing in the classroom, methylene blue is colorless when reduced, but blue when oxidized. In a basic environment, glucose (represented here as RH), is ionized to R^- which then reacts to reduce methylene blue to the colorless state. When the flask is shaken, methylene blue is again oxidized and turns blue.

when shaken : $O_2 + \text{methylene blue}_{(reduced)} \longrightarrow \text{methylene blue}_{(oxidized)}$

upon standing : $RH + OH^- \longrightarrow R^- + H_2O$

$\text{methylene blue}_{(oxidized)} + R^- \longrightarrow \text{methylene blue}_{(reduced)} + \text{oxidation products of glucose}$

If the flask is allowed to rest on a table, equilibrium is reached and the flask remains colorless. When the flask is shaken, oxygen from the atmosphere dissolves into the solution, disrupting equilibrium. LeChâtelier's Principle states that if any of the factors determining an equilibrium are changed, the system will adjust so that the change is minimized. Thus, as oxygen levels rise as a result of shaking, methylene blue is again oxidized and the blue color returns, but as oxygen levels fall with time upon standing, the reduction reaction prevails and the solution returns to its colorless equilibrium state. Will the color changes occur indefinitely? Try it and find out!

Questions

(1) Is the solution blue or colorless at equilibrium? Explain.

(2) Why should you remove the stopper between shakings? What happens if you never remove the stopper?

(3) The blue bottle reaction is an oxidation-reduction reaction. What is the reducing agent in this reaction? What substance is reduced? What is the oxidizing agent in the reaction? What substance is oxidized?

4.4.3 THE EFFECT OF CONCENTRATION ON EQUILIBRIUM

Concepts to Investigate: Reversible reactions, common ion effect, chemical reaction, reactants, products, LeChâtelier's Principle.

Materials: Part 1: Saturated salt (sodium chloride) solution, 6 *M* HCl solution; Part 2: Small test tubes, medium test tubes, test tube racks, medicine droppers, 6 *M* NaOH, 0.2 *M* $Fe(NO_3)_3$, 0.1 *M* KSCN, Na_2HPO_4, distilled water. (Refer to appendices 4.2 and 4.3 for details on making stock solutions.)

Safety: Wear goggles, lab coat and gloves. Use caution when handling 6 M hydrochloric acid or 6 M NaOH since both may cause tissue damage. Store concentrated acids and bases in small vials equipped with droppers. The nontoxic thiocyanate ion (SCN^-) used in this activity should not be confused with the toxic cyanide ion (CN^-). Refer to district polices for disposal standards.

Principles and Procedures: Adding a soluble salt containing an ion common to a slightly soluble salt already in equilibrium alters the position of the equilibrium of the slightly soluble salt system. According to LeChâtelier's Principle, increasing the concentration of the ion shared by both salts (the common ion) places a stress upon the equilibrium of the slightly soluble salt. The equilibrium shifts so as to reduce the concentration of the common ion, which is accomplished by a reduction in the solubility of the slightly soluble salt. This process is known as the common ion effect and allows chemists to change the concentrations of specific ions in systems at equilibrium without changing the temperature or pressure.

Place about 2 mL of the 0.2 *M* $Fe(NO_3)_3$ solution in a 100-mL beaker. Add 2 mL of 0.1 *M* KSCN solution and approximately 50 mL of distilled water to the $Fe(NO_3)_3$ solution and mix well. The ionic equation for the mixture of KSCN and $Fe(NO_3)_3$ is:

$$Fe^{3+}(aq) + NO_3^-(aq) + K^+(aq) + SCN^-(aq) \rightleftarrows NO_3^-(aq) + K^+(aq) + FeSCN^{2+}(aq)$$

Note that the NO_3^- and K^+ ions appear on both sides of the equation, and are not involved in forming any new products. Consequently, we can omit these "spectator ions" from the equation. The equilibrium between undissociated $FeSCN^{2+}$ and the Fe^{3+} and SCN^- ions is:

$$\underset{\text{yellow}}{Fe^{3+}(aq)} + \underset{\text{colorless}}{SCN^-(aq)} \rightleftarrows \underset{\text{red}}{FeSCN^{2+}(aq)}$$

The presence of the $FeSCN^{2+}$ ion is indicated by a red color.

LeChâtelier's Principle states that if a system at equilibrium is subjected to a stress, the system adjusts so as to relieve the stress. A "stress" is any factor that disrupts the equilibrium, such as a change in temperature, pressure or concentration. If, for example, additional $FeSCN^{2+}$ ions are added to the mixture, the reaction proceeds toward the left to relieve the stress of extra $FeSCN^{2+}$ ions. If, however, additional Fe^{3+} ions are added to the solution, the reaction proceeds to the right to relieve the stress of a higher Fe^{3+} concentration and the color becomes redder. Thus, an intensification of the red coloration indicates a shift of the reaction to the right, while a reduction of the red coloration indicates a shift to the left.

If necessary, add water to the mixture so you are able to see writing or other details when looking through the solution. Add 5 mL of this $KSCN/Fe(NO_3)_3$ solution to each of five test tubes. The first tube will serve as the control, so add nothing additional to it. Add 15 drops of the $Fe(NO_3)_3$ solution from a clean dropper to the second test tube, 25 drops of the KSCN solution to the third test tube, 5 drops of 6 M NaOH solution to the fourth test tube, and record the observed colors. Using a spatula, drop one crystal of Na_2HPO_4 into the fifth tube and record your observations. Complete Table 1.

Table 1: LeChâtelier's Principle and the Common Ion Effect

$$Fe^{3+}(aq) + SCN^-(aq) \rightleftarrows FeSCN^{2+}(aq)$$
$$\text{yellow} \qquad \text{colorless} \qquad \text{red}$$

#		*Color*	*Which Way Is Reaction Shifted?*
1	control		
2	15 drops 0.2 M $Fe(NO_3)$		
3	25 drops 0.1 M KSCN		
4	5 drops 6 M NaOH		
5	crystal of Na_2HPO_4		

Questions

(1) Explain the purpose of the $\rightleftarrows$ in chemical equations. What do $\rightarrow$ and $\leftarrow$ indicate?

(2) What are spectator ions and what is their role in forming new products in a reaction?

(3) Why is nothing added to the solution in tube 1, part 2? Explain.

(4) Explain the color changes expressed in Table 1 in terms of LeChâtelier's Principle.

4.4.4 THE EFFECT OF PRESSURE ON EQUILIBRIUM

Concepts to Investigate: Equilibrium, dynamic equilibrium, pressure, LeChâtelier's Principle.

Materials: <u>Part 1</u>: Bottle of carbonated water, lemon-lime soda or other colorless carbonated soda; <u>Part 2</u>: Vacuum pump, bell jar and stand or aspirator, side-arm thick-walled flask, rubber stopper, and thick-walled rubber tubing; phenolphthalein, dilute HCl (0.01 *M*), dilute NaOH (0.01 *M*), saturated solution of sodium bicarbonate (160 g NaHCO₃ per liter of water), medicine dropper.

Principles and Procedures:
Part 1: LeChâtelier's Principle and carbonated soft drinks:
Carefully crack the seal of a new, clear plastic or glass bottle of carbonated water, lemon-lime drink or other colorless carbonated soft drink and observe the formation of gas bubbles throughout the liquid (Figure F). Tighten the cap after a couple of seconds. Does the bubbling stop? Open it slightly once again. Does the bubbling start again? When the cap is secured, internal pressure keeps carbon dioxide gas dissolved in the water. When the seal is broken, the pressure is reduced and carbon dioxide gas leaves the water. LeChâtelier's Principle states that if any of the factors determining equilibrium are changed, the system will adjust so as to minimize that change. Explain the formation of bubbles using LeChâtelier's Principle.

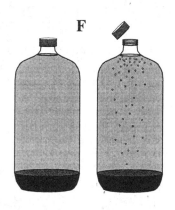

Part 2: LeChâtelier's Principle and pH changes:
Phenolphthalein is a pH indicator that is pink in basic solutions, and colorless in acidic conditions. You can determine the influence of pressure on the pH of a solution to which phenolphthalein has been added by observing color changes as pressure is changed.

Add 130 mL of saturated sodium bicarbonate solution to a small beaker. Sodium bicarbonate (NaHCO₃) partially dissociates into sodium cations, hydroxide ions, and carbon dioxide. Use a medicine dropper to add 1 or 2 drops of phenolphthalein. The solution should be

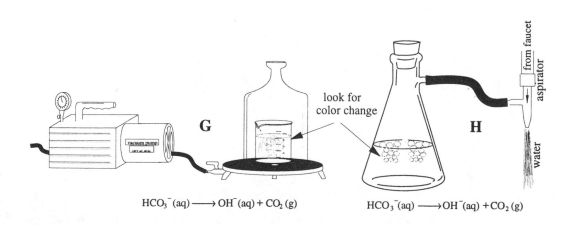

$$HCO_3^- (aq) \longrightarrow OH^- (aq) + CO_2 (g) \qquad\qquad HCO_3^- (aq) \longrightarrow OH^- (aq) + CO_2 (g)$$

slightly pink due to the presence of the hydroxide ions from the sodium bicarbonate. Add dilute HCl (0.01 M) one drop at a time until the color just disappears. If the solution is already colorless, add dilute NaOH (0.01 M) drop by drop until it just turns pink, and then add one drop of dilute HCl to remove the color. Place the beaker in a bell jar as illustrated as Figure G, connect a vacuum pump, and evacuate the air. Alternatively you may connect a thick walled side-arm flask to a vacuum pump or aspirator using thick rubber tubing (Figure H). Notice that bubbles of carbon dioxide gas form throughout the solution as the solution turns pink.

Dissolving $NaHCO_3$ in water results in the following reaction:

$$Na^+(aq) + HCO_3^-(aq) \rightleftarrows Na^+(aq) + OH^-(aq) + CO_2(g)$$

Note that the Na^+ ion (a spectator ion) appears on both sides of the equation and is not involved in the formation of any new products. Consequently, we can remove it and write the simplified equilibrium equation as:

$$HCO_3^-(aq) \rightleftarrows OH^-(aq) + CO_2(g)$$

The OH^- ion is a base and causes phenolphthalein to turn pink. Note that gas is present only on the right side of the equation, so movement to the right causes an increase in pressure. Increased pressure, therefore, shifts the reaction to the left. Use these facts and LeChâtelier's Principle to explain why the solution turns pink when the pressure in the flask is reduced.

Allow air back into the bell jar or vacuum flask. Does the pink color disappear? If not, will the solution turn colorless if the contents of the flask are pressurized? If the solution is not colorless, attach an air pump to the flask or bell jar, increase the pressure and see if it is possible to eliminate the pink color.

Questions

(1) When you open a new bottle of carbonated water, bubbles appear in the liquid and it fizzes. Explain.

(2) Why does a soft drink go "flat" after remaining open for awhile?

(3) Why did the solution in part 2 turn pink when the pressure in the flask was reduced?

(4) Can the pink color of the solution be eliminated if the pressure in the flask is increased? Explain.

(5) The following reaction represents the Haber process used to produce ammonia, a valuable substance used in the synthesis of fertilizers, explosives and many other important compounds.

$$N_2(g) + 3H_2(g) \rightleftarrows 2NH_3(g)$$

Use LeChâtelier's Principle to predict the effect of an increase in pressure on the direction of the reaction and the production of ammonia.

4.4.5 THE EFFECT OF TEMPERATURE ON EQUILIBRIUM

Concepts to Investigate: Equilibrium, dynamic equilibrium, temperature, LeChâtelier's Principle, equilibrium constant (K_{eq}).

Materials: <u>Part 1</u>: Cobalt chloride, concentrated hydrochloric acid; <u>Part 2</u>: 1:20 household ammonia solution (or dilute ammonia made by adding one drop of concentrated ammonium hydroxide to 500 mL of water), phenolphthalein, beaker, hot plate.

Safety: Wear goggles (face mask in part 1), lab coat, and gloves. Part 1 should be performed as an instructor demonstration only because it involves concentrated hydrochloric acid.

Principles and Procedures: For each chemical system there is a relationship among the concentrations of reactants and products that describes the relative proportions of each at equilibrium. A balanced chemical equation for the system is necessary when determining this relationship.

$$aA + bB \rightleftarrows cC + dD$$

The equilibrium constant (K_{eq}) for this generalized reaction may be expressed as:

$$K_{eq} = \frac{[C]^c[D]^d}{[A]^a[B]^b}$$

The quantities written within the brackets represent equilibrium molar concentrations of the reactants and products, and the powers are the stoichiometric coefficients from the equilibrium equation. If K_{eq} is large (much greater than 1) the products are favored and the forward reaction will approach completion, but if K_{eq} is small (much less than 1), the reactants are favored, and the reverse reaction will approach completion. Is the equilibrium constant temperature dependent?

Part 1: Temperature indicators: *Teacher demonstration only. Wear a face mask, lab coat and gloves when working with concentrated hydrochloric acid.* Cobalt chloride is a temperature indicator used in industrial grinding processes where it is not feasible to use standard temperature probes. As temperature rises, pink hexaaquacobalt (II) reacts with chloride ions to form blue tetrachlorocobalt (II) and water.

$$\text{heat} + \underset{\text{pink}}{Co(H_2O)_6^{2+}(aq)} + 4Cl^-(aq) \; \underset{\longleftarrow}{\longrightarrow} \; \underset{\text{blue}}{CoCl_4^{2-}(aq)} + 6H_2O(l)$$

$$K_{eq} = \frac{\left[CoCl_4^{2-}\right]}{\left[Co(H_2O)_6^{2+}\right]\left[Cl^-\right]^4}$$

If the equilibrium constant is greater than one, the products prevail and the solution turns blue, while if the equilibrium constant is less than one, the reactants prevail and the solution remains or turns pink. How do we know that the equilibrium constant for this system is temperature dependent?

Prepare a 0.5 *M* solution of cobalt chloride by dissolving 6.5 grams of cobalt chloride in 100 mL of water. *In a fume hood,* add concentrated hydrochloric acid drop by drop from a glass or disposable pipet until the chloride concentration is great enough to turn the solution purple. Divide the solution equally into three test tubes labeled 1, 2, and 3 (Figure I). Keep tube 1 at room temperature to serve as a control, tube 2 in an ice water bath, and tube 3 on a hot water bath at about 60°C. What colors do the solutions in tubes 2 and 3 turn? Allow tubes 2 and 3 to equilibrate at room temperature, and now place tube 2 in the hot water bath, and tube 3 in the ice water bath. Are color changes reversible? What influence does temperature have on the equilibrium constant of the equation written above?

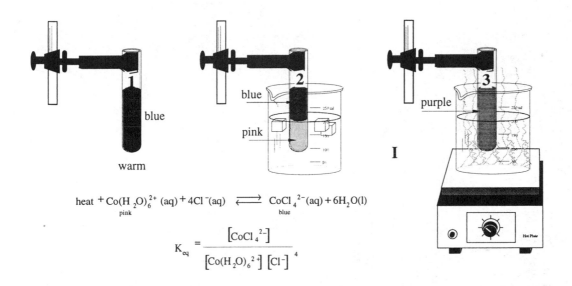

$$heat + Co(H_2O)_6^{2+}(aq) + 4Cl^-(aq) \rightleftarrows CoCl_4^{2-}(aq) + 6H_2O(l)$$
$$\text{pink} \qquad\qquad\qquad\qquad \text{blue}$$

$$K_{eq} = \frac{[CoCl_4^{2-}]}{[Co(H_2O)_6^{2+}][Cl^-]^4}$$

Part 2: The effect of temperature on an equilibrium constant: Ammonia gas reacts with water to form ammonium ions and hydroxide ions:

$$NH_3(aq) + H_2O(l) \rightleftarrows NH_4^+(aq) + OH^-(aq) \qquad\qquad K_{eq} = \frac{[NH_4^+][OH^-]}{[NH_3]}$$

Note that one of the products of this reaction is the hydroxide ion, OH^-, a substance that turns the pH indicator phenolphthalein pink. If the reaction shifts to the right, hydroxide ions are produced, turning the phenolphthalein pink, but if the reaction shifts to the left, hydroxide ions are consumed and the pink color disappears. Does the equilibrium constant get larger (as witnessed by more products and a pinker color) or smaller (as witnessed by fewer products and a paler color) as the temperature is raised? Dilute household ammonia 1 to 20 with water. Add a drop of phenolphthalein and note that the solution turns light pink. If the solution is dark pink, dilute with water until it is a light pink. Gently heat a beaker half-filled with this pink solution and observe any color changes. Does the solution get pinker or less pink? Now cool the beaker and once again observe the colors. Does the solution become pinker or paler when cooled? Does it appear as though the equilibrium constant is temperature dependent?

Questions

(1) What is the color of the cobalt chloride solution at the warmer temperatures? What is the color of the cobalt chloride solution at the cooler temperatures?

(2) Is the equilibrium constant for the reaction in part 1 temperature dependent?

(3) Cobalt chloride is used in hygrometers to indicate the presence of water. Would high humidities turn cobalt chloride pinker or bluer? Add more water to a purple solution of cobalt chloride and determine if your hypothesis was correct.

(4) Is the equilibrium constant for the ammonia/ammonium hydroxide system in part 2 temperature dependent? Explain.

(5) Is this reaction exothermic or endothermic as written? Explain.

FOR THE TEACHER

4.4.1 MODELS OF DYNAMIC EQUILIBRIUM

Discussion: The model in part 1 helps students attain a practical understanding of dynamic equilibrium and relate the principle to areas outside of chemistry. Iodized salt contains a drying agent that does not dissolve. To avoid a cloudy suspension, use rock salt or reagent grade sodium chloride in place of iodized table salt. Students should note that at equilibrium in part 2 the amount of products is not equivalent to the amount of reactants. This helps dispel the common misunderstanding that equilibrium must be a 50:50 situation. Make certain students understand that equilibrium implies equal rates of forward and reverse reactions, and not equal quantities of reactants and products.

Answers: (1) The diameter represents the initial reaction rates. A large diameter tubing will support a large reaction rate as long as the concentration of the substrate molecules is sufficient. (2) The levels of liquid represent the concentration of reactants or products. (3) The "reaction" would go farther to completion and there would be even more product and less reactant at equilibrium. (4) The water level in the reactants beaker (representing concentration of reactants) would be equal to the water level in the products beaker (representing concentration of products). (5) The reaction rates are equal (i.e., the amount of water transferred from the reactants container to the products container equals the amount of water transferred from the products container to the reactants container).

4.4.2 DISRUPTION OF EQUILIBRIUM

Discussion: You may wish to perform this activity as a teacher demonstration. Prepare the materials beforehand and leave the flask sitting on the desk. In the course of your presentation, nonchalantly pick up the flask and swirl it. Students will notice the immediate color change, and you may ask them to generate hypotheses to explain the observed changes. Most students understand that a color change indicates a reaction has occurred, just as the evolution of a gas or the formation of a precipitate indicate that a reaction has occurred. Some students will immediately surmise that the reaction occurs at the gas-liquid interface. Some will also surmise that the liquid is not a pure liquid but is probably a solution. Since nitrogen and oxygen are the major constituents of air, and since nitrogen is relatively inert, some students will suggest that oxygen is involved in the reaction. At this point you can explain that the system involves the reduction of methylene blue by an alkaline solution of glucose (dextrose), and then the re-oxidation of methylene blue by oxygen to yield the blue solution.

Answers: (1) When the flask is allowed to stand for prolonged periods, the solution becomes colorless, indicating that it is colorless at equilibrium. (2) When you remove the stopper, oxygen diffuses into the flask to cause the oxidation of methylene blue. If the stopper is never removed, no new oxygen will diffuse into the flask and the color changes will become less and less dramatic. (3) Ionized glucose, the reducing agent, reduces methylene blue. Oxygen, the oxidizing agent, oxidizes methylene blue.

4.4.3 THE EFFECT OF CONCENTRATION ON EQUILIBRIUM

Discussion: You may wish to perform these activities as a classroom demonstration using Petri dishes placed upon an overhead projector. According to LeChâtelier's Principle, if a closed system at equilibrium is subjected to a stress, processes occur that tend to counteract that stress. A stress can be a change in concentration, pressure, volume or temperature. The results obtained in parts 1 and 2 can be explained in terms of LeChâtelier's Principle. When a salt is dissolved in a solution that already contains one of its ions, its solubility is less than it would be in pure water. For example, AgCl is less soluble in a solution of NaCl than in pure water. The reduction in the solubility in the presence of a common ion, in this case the chloride ion, is called the common ion effect, and is easily explained by LeChâtelier's Principle.

Students investigated the addition of various substances to the equilibrium reaction:

$$\underset{\text{yellow}}{Fe^{3+}(aq)} + \underset{\text{colorless}}{SCN^-(aq)} \quad \rightleftarrows \quad \underset{\text{red}}{FeSCN^{2+}(aq)}$$

The addition of $Fe(NO_3)_3$ increased the concentration of Fe^{3+} ions, shifting the reaction to the right, increasing the concentration of $FeSCN^{2+}$ ions, and resulting in a darker red color. Addition of KSCN causes a stress by increasing the concentration of the SCN^- ion, which shifts the reaction further to the right, resulting in a darker red color. The addition NaOH causes reduction in Fe^{3+} ions by the formation of the precipitate $Fe_3(OH)_3$, thereby shifting the reaction to the left and reducing the intensity of red color. When Na_2HPO_4 crystals are added, they dissociate into Na^+ and HPO_4^{2-} ions. The HPO_4^{2-} ion complexes with Fe^{3+} ions to produce the colorless $FeHPO_4^+$ ion. As Fe^{3+} ions are removed from solution, the reaction shifts to the left and red coloration disappears. The student data table should resemble Table 2.

Table 2: LeChâtelier's Principle and the Common Ion Effect

$$\underset{\text{yellow}}{Fe^{3+}(aq)} + \underset{\text{colorless}}{SCN^-(aq)} \quad \rightleftarrows \quad \underset{\text{red}}{FeSCN^{2+}(aq)}$$

#		*Color*	*Which Way Is Reaction Shifted?*
1	control	red	——
2	15 drops 0.2 *M* Fe(NO$_3$)	dark red	right
3	25 drops 0.1 *M* KSCN	dark red	right
4	5 drops 6 *M* NaOH	light or colorless	left
5	crystal of Na$_2$HPO$_4$	light or colorless	left

Answers: (1) The double arrows ($\rightleftarrows$) indicate that the reaction proceeds in both directions. The right arrow indicates movement in direction of products and the left arrow indicates movement in the direction of reactants. (2) Spectator ions do not undergo any change during the course of a reaction. For example, if we add a solution of sodium chloride to a solution of silver nitrate, the reaction is as follows:

$$Na^+(aq) + Cl^-(aq) + Ag^+(aq) + NO_3^-(aq) \rightleftarrows AgCl(s) + Na^+(aq) + NO_3^-(aq)$$

The precipitate AgCl is formed from the Ag^+ and Cl^- ions. The Na^+ and NO_3^- ions do not undergo any change in the reaction and the same Na^+ and NO_3^- ions are present in the same amounts before and after the reaction. (3) It serves as a control with which to compare other reactions. (4) The addition of Fe^{3+} (test tube 2) or SCN^- ions (test tube 3) creates a stress (increased concentration of reactant ions) which shifts equilibrium to the right, favoring the product ions ($FeSCN^{2+}$), resulting in a more intense red color. The addition of NaOH causes a stress (reduced number of Fe^{3+}) due to the formation of a precipitate ($Fe(OH)_3$) which eliminates Fe^{3+} ions from solution. Equilibrium shifts to the left, favoring the dissociation of $FeSCN^{2+}$ and a decrease in intensity of the red color. When Na_2HPO_4 crystals are added, they dissociate into Na^+ and HPO_4^{2-} ions. The HPO_4^{2-} ion complexes with Fe^{3+} ions to produce the colorless $FeHPO_4^+$ ion. As Fe^{3+} ions are removed from solution, the reaction shifts to the left and red color disappears.

4.4.4 THE EFFECT OF PRESSURE ON EQUILIBRIUM

Discussion: Changes in pressure can affect concentrations of the reactants and products, but cannot affect the equilibrium constant if temperature is not changed. In this activity, pressure is reduced, causing a stress on the equilibrium reaction:

$$HCO_3^-(aq) \rightleftarrows OH^-(aq) + CO_2(g)$$

Phenolphthalein is colorless in acidic solutions and pink in basic (alkaline) solutions. The pump or aspirator reduces the pressure in the system, while at the same time removing CO_2 from the system. This reduction of pressure accompanied by the removal of the product CO_2 causes a stress which drives the reaction to the right, increasing the production of OH^-, making the solution more basic (alkaline), and causing a change from colorless to pink. If the pressure in the flask is increased substantially through use of an air pump, CO_2 combines with OH^- to produce HCO_3^-. Consequently, the solution will turn colorless as the reaction moves from right to left.

Answers: (1) Under pressure carbon dioxide reacts with water to form carbonic acid:

$$CO_2(g) + H_2O(l) \rightleftarrows H_2CO_3(aq)$$

Carbonic acid gives soft drinks their bite. When you remove the cap from the bottle, pressure is reduced substantially, causing a stress that forces the reaction to the left, producing carbon dioxide gas which causes the bubbles and fizzing. If the soda is at a temperature substantially above room temperature when the cap is removed, the results will be more dramatic because an increase in temperature also favors the reverse reaction since gas solubility decreases as temperature increases. (2) Soft drinks are bottled at high pressures, causing carbon dioxide to dissolve into solution. When a cap is removed, carbon dioxide comes out of solution as bubbles. If left uncapped, this process continues. Eventually so much carbon dioxide may leave solution that no more bubbles form and it becomes "flat." (3) Gas appears only on the right side of the following equation:

$$HCO_3^-(aq) \ \rightleftarrows \ OH^-(aq) + CO_2(g)$$

Therefore, a decrease in pressure forces equilibrium to the right, increasing the production of OH^- ions which makes the solution more basic and turns phenolphthalein pink. (4) Yes. Under sufficient pressure the reaction will move significantly to the left, decreasing the concentration of OH^- ions in solution, and changing the appearance to colorless or faint pink. (5) There is a reduction in volume if the reaction moves to the right since one mole of $N_2(g)$ combines with three moles of $H_2(g)$ to produce only two moles of $NH_3(g)$. Consequently, LeChâtelier's Principle predicts that an increase in pressure will drive the reaction to the right favoring the production of ammonia. In commercial processes pressure is maintained between 500 atm and 1000 atm to increase the yield of ammonia.

4.4.5 THE EFFECT OF TEMPERATURE ON EQUILIBRIUM

Discussion: The cobalt chloride solution in part 1 may be used to illustrate LeChâtelier's Principle. According to this principle, the reaction may be shifted to the left and the solution made pinker by removing chloride ions from solution. The chloride ions may be removed from solution by precipitating them as silver chloride, an insoluble salt. Add 0.1 M silver nitrate to a beaker containing purple cobalt chloride solution until the solution turns pink. LeChâtelier's Principle also suggests that the reaction may be shifted to the right and the solution made bluer by removing water. Acetone forms hydrogen bonds with water to effectively decrease the water concentration. The instructor may add a small amount of acetone to a purple cobalt chloride solution until the upper layer turns blue.

A dramatic illustration of the effect of temperature on the equilibrium constant can be shown by immersing the lower half of a heated (blue) test tube in an ice bath (Figure I). The equilibrium constant for the reaction is greater than 1 at warm temperatures (significantly above room temperatures), and less than 1 at cool temperatures (significantly lower than room temperature). Thus, the warmer top portion of the tube remains pink, while the lower, colder portion of the tube turns blue. You may wish to place the bottom half of a cool (blue solution) test tube in a warm water bath and note that the entire solution turns purple as convection currents equalize the temperature throughout.

Explain to your students that physical equilibrium deals with two phases of the same substance (e.g., liquid and gaseous phases of water), while chemical equilibrium deals with different substances (reactants and products) involved in a chemical process. In chemical equilibrium, the net concentrations of reactants and products do not change with time because the forward and reverse rates are equal. In this chapter we have focused on chemical equilibria.

Refer to the activities in chapter 4.3 on reaction rates to help students understand the connection between chemical equilibrium and chemical kinetics. The collision theory of chemical kinetics states that, for a reaction to occur, the reacting molecules must collide with each other. The rate of reaction is proportional to the rate of collisions occurring between the reacting particles Only a small percentage of the collisions are effective in producing a net chemical change, and these effective collisions depend on the nature of the reactants and the temperature. The average kinetic energy of the particles of a substance is proportional to the temperature of the substance. Consequently, as the temperature increases so too does the number of effective collisions among particles in a reaction and, thus, the reaction rate. As a rule of thumb, the rates of many reactions double with a 10°C increase in temperature.

Consider the following reversible reaction:

$$2A + B \rightleftarrows C + D$$

Assume that the reaction occurs via a mechanism consisting of a single process in both directions. The rate of the forward reaction is:

$$rate_f = k_f [A]^2 [B]$$

The rate of the reverse reaction is:

$$rate_r = k_r [C][D]$$

The rate constants, k_f and k_r, are for the forward and reverse reactions, respectively. At equilibrium the rates of the forward and reverse reactions must be equal ($rate_f = rate_r$) and we have:

$$k_f [A]^2 [B] = k_r [C][D]$$

The rate constants are consistent at any given temperature and their ratio is also a constant equal to the equilibrium constant K_{eq} (the ratio of two constants is a constant):

$$\frac{k_f}{k_r} = K_{eq} = \frac{[C][D]}{[A]^2[B]}$$

Since rate constants are temperature dependent, the equilibrium constant is also temperature dependent. In general, regardless of whether a reaction occurs in a single step or in multiple steps, the equilibrium constant for the generalized reaction

$$aA + bB \rightleftarrows cC + dD$$

can be expressed according to the law of mass action as shown in the following equation:

$$K_{eq} = \frac{[C]^c[D]^d}{[A]^a[B]^b}$$

Based on chemical kinetics, the equilibrium constant of a reaction can be expressed as a ratio of the rate constants of the forward and reverse reactions, which clarifies why the value of the equilibrium constant changes with changes in temperature and why it is constant at any given temperature.

Knowledge of the equilibrium constant allows one to predict the direction in which a reaction will proceed and to calculate the concentrations of reactants and products at equilibrium. The equilibrium constant does not depend on the amount of pure liquid or solid present in the reaction as long as some of each is present at equilibrium. When writing equilibrium constant expressions: (1) express the concentrations of reactants and products in mol/L;

(2) do not include the concentrations of pure liquids and solids in the equilibrium constant expressions for heterogeneous equilibria; (3) do not include the concentration of solvents in the equilibrium constant expressions for homogeneous equilibria; (4) express the temperature at which the equilibrium constant was determined; and (5) remember that if a reaction is the sum of two or more reactions, the equilibrium constant for the resultant (overall) reaction is the product of the equilibrium constants for the individual reactions.

Answers: (1) Cobalt chloride is blue at warmer temperatures due to the tetrachlorocobalt (II) complex, and is pink at cool temperatures due the hexaaquacobalt (II) complex. (2) Yes. The equilibrium constant for this reaction increases as the temperature increases, and decreases as the temperature decreases. (3) High humidity means an increase in available water. Water appears on the product side, so an increase in water would shift the reaction toward the pink hexaaquacobalt (II) complex. (4) Yes. At higher temperatures the solution is colorless, indicating an absence of hydroxide ions, while at cooler temperatures the solution is pink, indicating their presence. This indicates that the equilibrium constant decreases as the temperature is raised. (5) It is exothermic as written, because heating the reaction favors the reverse reaction.

Applications to Everyday Life

Altitude sickness: The oxygen concentrations in your blood and tissues are in a state of dynamic equilibrium. If, however, you rapidly move from a low elevation to a much higher elevation where oxygen concentrations are less, you may suffer from a disruption in equilibrium known as altitude sickness (hypoxia), which may cause headaches, fatigue and nausea. Oxygen combines with hemoglobin Hb in the blood according to the simplified reaction: hemoglobin + oxygen $\rightleftarrows$ oxyhemoglobin. When you move from a lower to higher elevation, the partial pressure of oxygen decreases and the reaction shifts to the left (according to LeChâtelier's Principle), reducing the amount of oxyhemoglobin. Lower oxyhemoglobin levels mean less oxygen for body tissues, giving rise to the symptoms associated with altitude sickness.

Acclimation to high elevations: In response to the low oxygen concentrations at high elevations, the body synthesizes more hemoglobin and more red blood cells. An increase in hemoglobin concentration shifts the following reaction to the right, ensuring more oxygen for body tissues: hemoglobin + oxygen $\rightleftarrows$ oxyhemoglobin. Many athletes train at high elevations so that when they return to competition at lower elevations they will have higher hemoglobin concentrations, and be better able to remove oxygen from the air in the midst of stressful physical exercise.

Blood pH: One of the byproducts of respiration is carbon dioxide, CO_2. Carbon dioxide combines with water in the blood to form carbonic acid.

$$CO_2(g) + H_2O(l) \; \rightleftarrows \; \underset{\text{carbonic acid}}{H_2CO_3(aq)}$$

As one exercises, carbon dioxide is produced, shifting the equilibrium to the right, forming more carbonic acid, and lowering the pH. Fortunately, our bodies are equipped with pH sensors (the carotid bodies) that detect low pH and stimulate breathing. As blood enters the alveoli (air sacs) in the lungs, it encounters atmospheric air that has lower levels of carbon dioxide. Carbon dioxide then diffuses from the blood to the air in the alveoli, the equation shifts to the left, and the pH of the blood returns to approximately 7.4. It should be noted that blood contains buffers that prevent significant changes in pH.

Carbonated beverages: You may have had the misfortune of opening a can or bottle of warm soda and been drenched as the soda effervesced. Carbonated beverages are bottled under pressure to ensure a high degree of carbonation.

$$CO_2(g) + H_2O(l) \; \rightleftarrows \; \underset{\text{carbonic acid}}{H_2CO_3(aq)}$$

Note that gas appears only on the left of the equation. According to LeChâtelier's Principle, the addition of pressure at the bottling plant causes gaseous carbon dioxide to combine with water to form carbonic acid. However, the removal of pressure that occurs when the consumer opens the bottle causes a shift in the opposite direction. In addition, it should be noted that gases are less soluble in liquids at higher temperatures than at lower temperatures. Thus, removal of pressure shifts the reaction to the left, causing vigorous bubbling as carbon dioxide rapidly comes out of solution.

The "Bends": Deep sea divers may experience a serious condition known as "the bends" (decompression sickness) if they ascend too rapidly from a depth of more than 15 meters. Nitrogen and other gases dissolve in the blood during the breathing cycle. At high pressures, such as those experienced by a diver deep beneath the surface, the equilibrium for this process is moved to the right:

$$\text{nitrogen(g)} \rightleftarrows \text{nitrogen (dissolved)}$$

As the diver comes to the surface, pressure falls, and equilibrium shifts to the left. If the reduction in pressure is too rapid, nitrogen bubbles form in the blood and other body fluids causing severe abdominal and joint pain, and perhaps even death. To avoid the bends, divers are taught to surface gradually, allowing for the slow equilibration of pressure and a slow release of nitrogen from the blood. It should be noted that this is an example of physical equilibrium, not chemical equilibrium.

Tissue healing: Serious burns often destroy the capillaries that deliver oxygen to the skin. To provide the oxygen necessary for tissue healing in the absence of normal blood supply, patients are sometimes placed in hyperbaric chambers. Inside these chambers, patients are subjected to high pressures that shift the following equilibrium to the right:

$$\text{oxygen(g)} \rightleftarrows \text{oxygen (dissolved)}$$

Oxygen dissolves in the tissue fluids where it is used in the metabolic processes essential for tissue repair and growth. It should be noted that this is an example of physical equilibrium, not chemical equilibrium.

Chemical synthesis: Chemists must understand principles of equilibrium if they are to maximize the yield and minimize the cost of producing various chemicals. Hydrochloric acid is an important industrial acid made by the reaction of hydrogen and chlorine gas:

$$H_2(g) + Cl_2(g) \rightleftarrows 2HCl(g)$$

An analysis of the equation shows that the equilibrium will not be shifted by an increase in pressure because there are the same number of gas molecules on the right as on the left. By contrast, the synthesis of another important industrial chemical, ammonia, occurs as:

$$N_2(g) + 3H_2(g) \rightleftarrows 2NH_3(g)$$

There are twice as many gas molecules on the left as on the right, so increasing the pressure in this reaction causes it to shift to the right. As a result, chemical companies always synthesize ammonia under great pressures.

Gases, Liquids, Solids, and Mixtures

433

5.1 GASES

Of the nine planets in our solar system, Mercury, Venus, Earth and Mars are closest to the Sun and are known as the inner planets, while Jupiter, Saturn, Uranus, Neptune and Pluto are farther from the Sun and are known as the outer planets. The inner planets are also known as the terrestrial or rocky planets and are composed primarily of rock and metal. These planets have relatively high densities, slow rotation, solid surfaces, no rings and few moons. The first four of the outer planets (Jupiter, Saturn, Uranus and Neptune) are known as the jovian or gas planets. The gas planets are composed primarily of hydrogen and helium and generally have low densities, rapid rotation, deep atmospheres, rings and many moons.

The rocky inner planets differ greatly in chemical composition from the gas planets. For example, Earth, one of the inner planets, is made primarily of solid and liquid substances consisting of iron, oxygen, silicon and magnesium (Table 1). By contrast, Jupiter, one of the gas planets, is composed primarily of gaseous and liquid hydrogen and helium. Although gas is a predominant phase of matter on the gas planets, it is rare on the inner planets. Only 0.0000086% of the mass of the Earth is in the gaseous phase, yet despite their rarity, gases are extremely important to the character of the planet and all life forms that inhabit it. Table 1 indicates that our bodies are composed of 65% oxygen, 18% carbon, 10% hydrogen, and 3% nitrogen (by mass). Although these elements may be found in solid form (e.g., most of the Earth's oxygen is bound in mineral oxides), they must at some time be in gaseous form to be of use by us or other organisms. Bacteria fix atmospheric nitrogen to make nitrates that are essential for plant growth. Plants fix atmospheric carbon dioxide into sugars, starches and other products that we ultimately consume as our primary source of carbon, hydrogen and oxygen. Humans and other creatures derive energy from these foods by oxidizing them with atmospheric oxygen. Approximately 60% of our bodies are composed of water, the universal solvent of living systems. Although water in biological systems is primarily in the liquid phase, it must become a gas to enter the atmosphere before it can condense and fall as rain or snow to provide the water necessary to support terrestrial life. Thus, although gases compose only a small percentage of the matter of the inner planets, they are common in the solar system and universe, and are absolutely essential for life on Earth.

Table 1: Percent Composition by Mass

	Earth	*Jupiter*	*Human Body*
iron	34.6%	trace	0.004%
oxygen	29.5%	trace	65%
silicon	15.2%	trace	—
magnesium	12.7%	trace	0.50%
nickel	2.4%	trace	0.25%
sulfur	1.9%	trace	trace
hydrogen	trace	75%	10%
helium	trace	25%	—
carbon	trace	trace	18%
nitrogen	trace	trace	3%
calcium	trace	trace	2%
phosphorous	trace	trace	1%

A gas can be defined as a collection of widely separated molecules, moving about freely, and capable of expanding and being compressed. A substance is known as a gas if it exists in the gaseous state at ordinary temperatures and pressures (25°C and 1 atm pressure). By contrast, a vapor is the gaseous form of any substance that is a liquid or solid at normal temperatures and pressures. For this reason oxygen is considered to be a gas, but steam a vapor. Gases expand to fill the volume of a container regardless of its shape. When two or more gases are mixed in a container, they mix evenly. Gases are very compressible and have a much lower density than liquids or solids.

The atmosphere is an ocean of gases composed of about 78% nitrogen, 21% oxygen, and 1% other gases. Gravitational attraction for the molecules of gas in the atmosphere pulls them toward the Earth's surface, causing the atmosphere to exert pressure. A barometer is a device that measures the pressure exerted by the atmosphere. Pressure is the force pushing on a unit of area and may be measured in several different units including pounds per square inch or newtons per square meter (N/m^2). Normal atmospheric pressure at sea level and 0°C supports a column of mercury 76.0 cm in height and is referred to as one atmosphere (101.325 kilopascals).

According to the kinetic theory, a gas is made of very small particles that are in constant random motion. The particles in a gas are not held together by van der Waals forces as they are in the liquid state, so the gas particles are free to spread apart to fill the volume of any container. The volume of a gas is determined by the number of molecules of gas, the pressure of the gas, and the temperature of the gas. Consequently, when discussing quantities of gases it is necessary to specify the volume, pressure, and temperature. Standard atmospheric pressure (pressure at sea level) is 101.325 kilopascals and standard temperature is 0°C (273 K, the freezing point of water at standard pressure). STP stands for standard temperature and pressure. The force of the collisions of the gas particles on the sides of the container constitute the pressure of the gas. Increasing the temperature of the gas increases the speed of the gas molecules, increasing the force of collisions and the pressure. Increasing the number of molecules of gas will also increase the number of collisions on the sides of the container and increase pressure. In this chapter you will investigate properties of gases as well as the relationships between the quantity, temperature, pressure and volume of gases.

5.1.1 PROPERTIES OF GASES

Concepts to Investigate: Matter, gases, properties of gases, pressure, volume.

Materials: Part 1: Drinking glass or beaker, newspaper, balloon, large container; Part 2: Triple beam balance, and basketball, volleyball, soccer ball or other inflatable ball, bicycle wheel with tire, spring scale; Part 3: See materials section 1.3.9; Part 4: Scented air freshener and materials listed in section 2.3.2; Part 5: See materials list in section 2.4.1; hot air popcorn popper, popcorn, balance.

Principles and Procedures: All gases (1) occupy space, (2) possess mass, (3) are fluid, (4) expand to fill their containers, (5) are approximately one thousandth the density of the liquid state, and (6) are highly compressible. In this section you will investigate these properties of gases. In the remainder of the chapter you will examine relationships between the temperature, pressure, and volume of gases.

Part 1: Gases occupy space: All matter, including gas, has mass and occupies space. Air is a collection of invisible gases consisting primarily of nitrogen (78%) and oxygen (21%). Although we cannot see air or many other gases, we can show that they occupy volume by carrying out the following simple procedure. Place a wad of dry newspaper in the bottom of a tall glass or beaker. Invert the glass and immerse it in a container of water as shown in Figure A so no bubbles escape. Remove the glass or beaker from the container, retrieve the paper and observe that it is dry. The air trapped in the container occupied volume and prevented water from entering. Will the paper remain dry when submerged in a deep pail of water or at the bottom of a swimming pool? If possible, try it and find out!

Fill a small balloon to a diameter of approximately 15 cm. Immerse the balloon and slowly push it to the bottom of a deep container of water. What happens to the diameter of the balloon? What is the effect of pressure on the volume of a gas? If you have a clear container, you can measure the diameter of the balloon while it is under the water. To do this, it is important that the ruler also be submerged to prevent errors in measurement due to refraction of light at the water/glass and glass/air interfaces.

Part 2: Gases have mass: Matter is defined as anything that occupies space and has mass. From the activity in part 1, it is easy to conclude that gas occupies space, but on what basis can you conclude that it has mass? Certainly your bathroom scale or your laboratory balance registers zero when nothing rests on it but air!

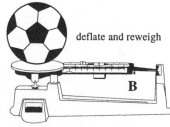

deflate and reweigh

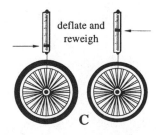

deflate and reweigh

Determine the mass of a fully inflated basketball, soccer ball, volleyball or similar ball using a triple beam or pan balance (Figure B). If you have access to a pressure gauge, measure and record the pressure. Deflate the ball so the pressure is approximately one half its original value and once again determine the mass. Is the mass of the partially inflated ball less than the mass of the fully inflated ball? You may also perform this activity with a bicycle tire (Figure C).

Part 3: Gases do not have definite shape and exhibit high fluidity: A fluid is defined as a substance in which particles flow easily and change their relative position without a separation of mass. Gases fill the shape of a container, as can be easily illustrated by filling a variety of different shaped balloons with your breath. You can demonstrate the fluidity of gases by pouring invisible gaseous carbon dioxide to extinguish a candle according to the procedure described in section 1.3.9.

Part 4: Unconfined gases expand indefinitely: In the absence of external forces, gases expand indefinitely to fill any containers into which they are introduced, regardless of their shape. Stand in the middle of the room, depress the nozzle of a container of scented air freshener for approximately 2 seconds. Students should raise their hands when they first detect the scent of the air freshener. Although the vapors from the air freshener can not be seen, they can be smelled, and eventually all should detect the odor, illustrating that the vapor molecules fill the room. See activity 2.3.2.

Part 5: Gases have low density: Under ordinary conditions, a substance in the gaseous state has a density of approximately only one thousandth its density in the liquid state. This principle is illustrated dramatically in the following activities: *Air Pressure Fountain* (2.4.1 part 2), *Collapsing Can* (2.4.1 part 3), and *Liquid and Gaseous Air* (2.4.1 part 3), and is also demonstrated whenever you pop popcorn! A small amount of liquid water is trapped inside each popcorn kernel. When heated sufficiently, the water becomes steam. The increase in volume and pressure accompanying the phase change

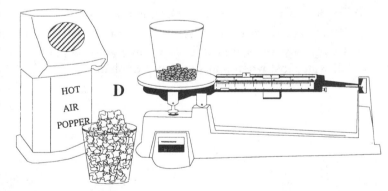

from liquid to gaseous water is evidenced by the expansion and fluffing of popcorn kernels and by the cloud of steam that diffuses from a bag of freshly microwaved popcorn. How much water is lost as vapor when a popcorn kernel pops? Determine the mass of 100 unpopped kernels of popcorn (Figure D). Pop the kernels in a hot-air (no-oil) popcorn popper and once again determine the mass after the kernels have cooled to room temperature. Repeat the process three times and complete Table 2. Calculate the average mass of one kernel of unpopped corn, and the average mass of one kernel of popped corn. How much water is lost as steam per kernel of corn popped? *Do not eat the popcorn or any other food in the laboratory.*

Table 2: Phase Change While Popping Popcorn

	Trial 1	Trial 2	Trial 3	Average
mass of cup				
mass of 100 unpopped kernels and cup				
mass of 100 unpopped kernels				
average mass of one unpopped kernel				
mass of 100 popped kernels and cup				
mass of 100 popped kernels				
average mass of one popped kernel				
average mass of water lost per kernel as steam				

Questions

(1) Does the volume of air trapped in an inverted open container change as the container is pushed deeper in the water (part 1)?

(2) Determine the mass of air in a fully inflated ball by measuring it on a scale and then deflating the ball and remeasuring its mass. What was the mass of air in the ball?

(3) At room temperature, carbon dioxide is a gas with a density greater than air. Describe how these two properties are essential to its use in CO_2-based fire extinguishers.

(4) Mercury, the planet closest to the Sun, is much smaller than Earth and therefore has much less gravity. Energy from the Sun in the form of "solar winds" (plasma ejected from the Sun) blasts atoms off the surface of Mercury to create a very thin atmosphere, but these gaseous molecules rapidly escape from the planet's gravitational field. Why is the atmosphere on Mercury lost, while the atmosphere on Earth remains?

(5) Explain why oxygen used by hospitals and welders is shipped as a liquid, not as a gas.

(6) What percentage of the mass of a popcorn kernel is lost as steam when popcorn pops? How many times greater is the volume of the popped corn than the unpopped corn? Is all water lost when popcorn pops? Explain.

5.1.2 PRESSURE-VOLUME RELATIONSHIP OF GASES (BOYLE'S LAW)

Concepts to Investigate: Boyle's Law, pressure-volume relationship of gases, density, Cartesian diver.

Materials: Part 1: Eyedropper, permanent marker, 2-liter flexible soda container; Part 2: Balloon, bell jar, vacuum pump or water aspirator, syringe, marshmallow; Part 3: Disposable syringe (as large as possible; available at drugstore), five or more wood blocks (or other stackable objects with identical mass), ring stand, clamps.

Principles and Procedures: The pressure exerted by a gas depends on the number of gas molecules present, the volume in which they are contained, and the temperature. If we hold the number of molecules and the temperature of the gas constant, we can investigate the relationship between the pressure of a gas and its volume.

Part 1: Cartesian diver: Use a permanent fine-tipped marker to draw a scale on the eyedropper in 2-millimeter increments. Fill approximately one fourth to one third of the eyedropper with water (dyed with food coloring) and place it in a flexible, plastic soft-drink container that is completely filled with water. Once the eyedropper is floating with its tip down, screw the lid on the bottle and measure the height of the water in the eyedropper (Figure E). Squeeze the walls of the container and observe the descent of the "Cartesian diver" (the diver consists of the rubber bulb, the glass eyedropper, the water in the eyedropper, and the air in the eyedropper). If the diver sinks before pressure is applied, there is too much water in the diver. If it does not descend when pressure is applied to the container, there is not sufficient water in the diver. Determine the length of the air column (the distance between the end of the air chamber in the bulb and the water line in the dropper) in the eyedropper when it floats on top, rests in the middle, or rests on the bottom. Describe the relationship between pressure (how hard you press on the container) and the volume of air in the eyedropper.

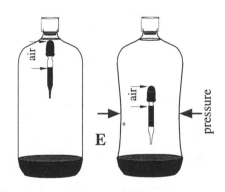

Part 2: Pressure-volume relationships: Pressure-volume relationships can be investigated using a vacuum pump and bell jar as shown in Figure F. Fill a balloon with air until it is the size of your fist and place it under a bell jar attached to a vacuum pump or water aspirator. Turn on the pump to evacuate air from the bell jar and watch the balloon fill the jar. Turn off the pump and open the valve so air may enter the bell jar again. Does the balloon return to its original size? Repeat the procedure with marshmallows and shaving cream. Do these materials return to their original size and appearance when air re-enters the bell jar? Position the plunger in a disposable syringe so it is at one-quarter of full-scale. Seal the end of the syringe with a clamp and place under the bell jar. Which way does the plunger move? If your pump is equipped with a pressure gauge, construct a plot of volume as a function of pressure. Make certain to account for the volume of air before the first graduation.

If you do not have access to a vacuum pump or water aspirator, you may examine the pressure-volume relationship of gases by placing a small fresh marshmallow in the cylinder of a disposable syringe (available at pharmacies and drugstores) and replacing the plunger

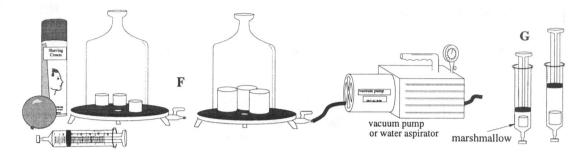

(Figure G). Clamp the end of the syringe and then pull the plunger back. As the volume inside the cylinder increases, the pressure decreases. In response to the lower external pressure, the air bubbles trapped inside the marshmallow expand and the marshmallow grows. Push the plunger in. What happens to the size of the marshmallow?

Part 3: Boyle's Law: Position the plunger of a syringe at the highest graduation. Seal the end with a clamp, or attach a piece of flexible tubing and clamp the tubing. Push the plunger to the 90% full mark and hold for a few seconds. Push to the 80% mark and hold. Continue pushing in 10% volume increments and qualitatively describe the relationship between the pressure on a gas and its volume. What is the smallest volume you can achieve?

Use two buret clamps to attach a disposable syringe to a ring stand as shown in Figure H. Make certain the syringe is positioned vertically. Remove the syringe cap and adjust the plunger so it is positioned at the 100% mark (highest graduation). With no weight on the open plunger, the pressure of the gas in the syringe is the same as atmospheric pressure (1 atm, 760 mm Hg). Seal the end of the syringe with a clamp so no air can escape. Place a block of wood—drilled with a socket to fit the end of the plunger—on top of the plunger as shown in Figure H. Determine the volume in the syringe. (You may substitute books or other equal-massed stackable objects for the blocks specified in this activity.) Add a second block of equal mass on top of the first and record the new volume. Continue to add blocks (a minimum of five), record the resulting volumes (Figure I), and plot your data on Figure J.

In this activity, the pressure applied is directly proportional to the number of equal-massed objects stacked on the plunger. Pressure is the quotient of force (weight) divided by

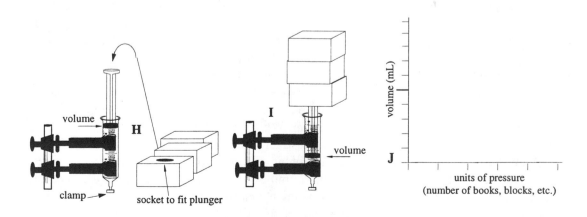

area. Since the cross-sectional area of the plunger remains constant as more blocks are added, the only factor affecting pressure that changes is the weight of the blocks. Since the blocks are equal mass, the pressure applied by the blocks is directly proportional to their number. Thus, two blocks represent twice the pressure of one block. Describe the graph of volume vs. pressure at constant temperature. Is it a straight line or a curve? Does it have a positive or negative slope?

In 1660, English chemist Robert Boyle published findings that are now known as Boyle's Law: At constant temperature, the volume of a gas varies inversely with the pressure exerted upon it. Boyle's Law states that the product of the pressure and volume of a gas is constant: $PV = k$, where k is a constant whose value depends only on the quantity of a gas and its temperature. If the pressure on a gas at constant temperature changes, the volume changes, but the product of pressure and volume remains a constant, k. Thus, at pressure 1, $P_1V_1 = k$, and at pressure 2, $P_2V_2 = k$. Since both products are equal to the same value, we can re-write the equation as:

$$P_1V_1 = P_2V_2$$

Thus, we can calculate a new pressure (P_2) if we know the original pressure (P_1), original volume (V_1), and final volume (V_2):

$$P_2 = P_1V_1/V_2$$

Does this mathematical relationship hold true for your data? Are your data consistent with Boyle's Law?

Questions

(1) Explain why the diver descends when the bottle is squeezed and rises when the squeeze is released.

(2) Describe the operation of a submarine in terms of the Cartesian diver.

(3) Did the balloon, shaving cream and marshmallow return to their original sizes after air was allowed to re-enter the evacuated bell jar? Explain your findings.

(4) When you pressed the plunger in part 2 to successively smaller increments, the volume of gas in the syringe continued to decrease. Explain.

(5) Describe Boyle's Law in your own words. Is your volume vs. pressure graph consistent with Boyle's Law?

(6) How is the density of a gas affected by the pressure on it?

(7) The volume of an inflated automobile tire is 10 liters. If an empty tire is to be inflated to a pressure of 2.5 atm (37 lb/in^2), what volume of air (measured at one atmosphere pressure) will be required?

5.1.3 TEMPERATURE-VOLUME RELATIONSHIP OF GASES (CHARLES'S LAW)

Concepts to Investigate: Charles's Law, pressure, volume, temperature, absolute zero, temperature-volume relationship of gases.

Materials: <u>Part 1</u>: (See Figure K) Erlenmeyer flask, flexible tubing, stopper, glass tubing bent in a "U," food coloring; <u>Part 2</u>: Spherical balloon, ruler, large beakers or similar containers, ice, dry ice, thermometer, tubing, screw clamp; <u>Part 3</u>: 10-mL syringe, beakers, thermometer, hot plate or laboratory burner, ice, isopropyl alcohol, dry ice, gloves, tongs, tubing, screw clamp, graph paper.

Principles and Procedures: The volume of a gas depends on its quantity, temperature, and pressure. To study the influence of temperature on gas volume, it is necessary to hold the quantity and pressure constant. This may be accomplished by sealing the gas in a gas-tight container (sealing the gas ensures a constant quantity of gas) that is flexible so internal pressure may equilibrate with atmospheric pressure (atmospheric pressure is relatively constant over short time intervals). In the following activities we use balloons, syringes and a simple manometer because they meet these criteria. A balloon will enlarge or shrink with changes in pressure, while the plunger of a calibrated sealed syringe will move back and forth, allowing the experimenter to read volume changes.

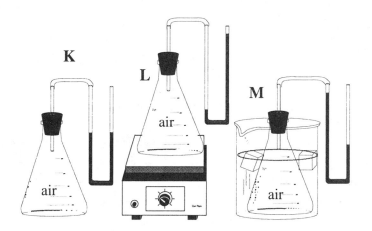

Part 1: Qualitative relationship between the temperature and volume of gases: Attach a "U"-shaped glass tube to an air-filled Erlenmeyer flask as illustrated in Figure K. Fill the U-tube with colored water (use food coloring) as shown, remove the cork and reseal so water levels on both sides of the U-tube are identical. Slowly warm the flask on a hot plate (Figure L). Does the volume of air inside the flask increase, decrease or remain unchanged? Cool the flask in an ice water bath (Figure M). Does the volume of air inside the flask increase, decrease or remain unchanged? Describe, in qualitative terms, the relationship between the temperature and volume of a gas.

Part 2: Quantitative relationship between the temperature and volume of gases: Inflate a small spherical balloon to a diameter of approximately 12 cm. Measure the radius of the

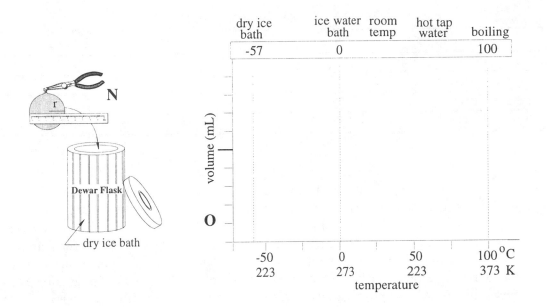

balloon by aligning its diameter at the "equator" with a ruler and dividing by 2 (Figure N). Record the room temperature exactly (approximately 20°C, 293 K) and calculate the approximate volume of the balloon using the formula for the volume of a sphere, $V = (4/3)\pi r^3$, where r represents the radius of the balloon (e.g. volume = 904 cm^3 when radius is 6 cm). Fill a large container with hot tap water and record the temperature. Tie a weight to the balloon with a short piece of string and submerge the balloon in the hot water. Determine the volume after a couple of minutes or when the volume is no longer changing. *Put on insulated gloves, lab coat and goggles.* Remove the balloon from hot water and allow it to equilibrate with room temperature before submerging it first in an ice bath (0°C, 373 K), and then in a dry ice bath (isopropyl alcohol and dry ice; −57°C, 216 K). Record volumes in Table 3 and plot them in Figure O. On the basis of your data, describe the relationship between the temperature and volume of gas at constant pressure.

Part 3: Charles's Law and absolute zero: Data from parts 1 and 2 indicate that the volume of a gas at constant pressure changes directly with temperature. The data plotted in Figure O shows that the relationship between volume and temperature is linear. As the temperature

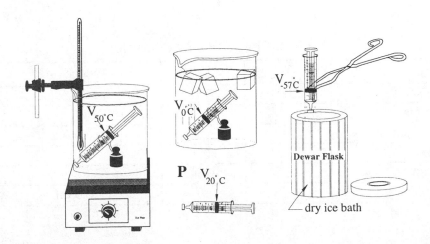

Table 3: Charles's Law (Balloon)

	°C	K	Volume (mL)
hot tap water			
room temperature			
ice water bath	0	273	
dry-ice bath	−57	216	

increases, so does volume, and as temperature decreases, so does volume. If the graph in Figure O is extrapolated to colder temperatures, it eventually crosses the x-axis, at which point the volume is zero. Since it is impossible to have negative volumes, this point represents the lower limit of temperature. In other words, nothing can ever be colder than this temperature. Chemists have designated this lower limit "absolute zero." What is the value of absolute zero in degrees Celsius? To determine this, you will apply similar techniques to those used in part 2, but rather than using a balloon you will use a disposable syringe. By extrapolating to zero volume on a plot of volume versus temperature, you will determine the approximate Celsius temperature of absolute zero.

Fill a 10-mL syringe with 6.0 mL of air and clamp the end with a tubing clamp so no gases can enter or escape (Figure P). Attach a weight to the barrel (not the plunger!) of the syringe with a short piece of string and place in the bottom of a large beaker. Cover the syringe with hot tap water and allow the system to stand for two minutes so temperature equilibrates. Record the temperature and volume below. Remove the syringe and allow it to stand at room temperature for two minutes before placing it in an ice water bath. Finally, place it in a dry-ice bath (rubbing alcohol and dry ice). Complete Table 4.

Construct a plot of volume (y-axis; 0 to 10 mL) versus temperature (x-axis; −300°C to 100°C) on graph paper. Plot the data from Table 3 on the graph and draw the line of best fit through the points. Extend (extrapolate) the line until it intersects the x-axis (volume: 0.0 mL). At what temperature does the line intersect the x-axis? In other words, according to your extrapolation, at what temperature would the volume of gas be zero? This temperature is known as absolute zero, the lowest possible temperature.

Charles's Law states that at constant pressure the volume of a fixed mass of gas varies directly with the Kelvin temperature:

$$V = kT$$

Table 4: Charles's Law (Syringe)

	°C	K	Volume (mL)
boiling water	100	373	
hot tap water			
room temperature			6.0 mL
ice water	0	273	
dry-ice bath	−57	216	
absolute zero		0	0.0 mL

where V is volume, and T is temperature in Kelvin. To convert temperature in degrees Celsius to Kelvin, simply add 273. Plot the volume of gas in the syringe as a function of the Kelvin temperature. Charles's Law indicates that you will obtain a straight line with a positive slope, intercepting at $T = 0$. Are your data consistent with Charles's Law?

Questions

(1) Why do marshmallows initially expand when placed in a cup of hot cocoa?

(2) On the basis the of data from part 2, describe the relationship between temperature and volume.

(3) Charles's Law states that the volume of a fixed quantity of gas maintained at constant pressure is directly proportional to the absolute temperature of the gas $(V = kT)$. Explain.

(4) At atmospheric pressure and $-23°C$, the volume of a sample of air is 2000 mL. Using your findings, what will be the volume of this gas at $27°C$?

(5) To what temperature must 3000 mL of gas at $0°C$ be heated to increase the volume to 5000 mL?

(6) Chemists have determined that absolute zero is $-273.15°C$. What temperature does your extrapolation in part 3 indicate?

5.1.4 HOT AIR BALLOONS: AN APPLICATION OF CHARLES'S LAW

Concepts to Investigate: Charles's Law, hot air balloons, buoyancy, density, temperature-volume relationships in gases, Archimedes' Principle.

Materials: Tissue paper, scissors, glue, construction paper or other heavy paper, hair drier.

Principles and Procedures: Frenchmen Joseph and Étienne Montgolfier are credited with the development of the first practical hot air balloon. In September of 1783 they sent a sheep, a rooster and a duck aloft over Versailles, and two months later sent three men (Jean-François Pilâtre de Rozier, François Laurent, and Marquis d'Arlandes) on a 5.5 mile (approximately 9 km) flight over Paris. Later, hot air balloons were used in the Napoleanic and American Civil Wars to perform reconnaissance of enemy positions and movements. Ballooning is a popular sport today, although propane has replaced hay as a heating fuel, and lightweight nylon and other synthetics have replaced silk, cotton and wool as balloon fabric. In this activity you will employ the principles used by the Montgolfier brothers and modern ballooning enthusiasts in the construction and flight of your own hot air balloon.

Four years after the success of the Mongolfier brothers, fellow countryman Jacques Charles formalized the principle responsible for balloon flight. Charles's Law states that at constant pressure, the volume of a fixed mass of gas is directly proportional to the absolute temperature $(V = kT)$. For example, if the absolute temperature of a fixed mass of gas (at constant pressure) is doubled, the volume doubles and the density is cut in half *(density = mass/volume)*. If the temperature is raised from room temperature (20°C, 68°C, 293 K) to 50°C (122°F, 323 K), the volume of the heated air increases 10% (323K/293K = 1.10). Since a hot-air balloon is an open system at constant pressure, this can be accomplished only if air leaves the balloon. Thus, the mass of air remaining in the balloon decreases, leading to a decrease in the composite density of the balloon (balloon and the air it contains). The balloon rises because it now has a lower density than the air surrounding it.

Figures Q–U show the plans for a pentadecahedronal (15-sided) balloon. Cut five 50 × 130 cm panels of tissue paper and fold each in the middle lengthwise as shown (Figures Q–S). Cut the shaded portions out and place one panel on a large flat surface. Place a second panel over it so all but 3 cm of tissue paper along one border are overlapping (Figure T).

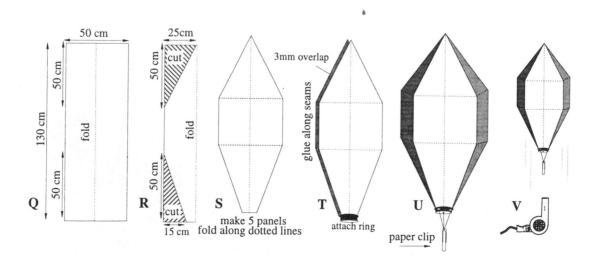

Smear white glue down the margin of the top panel and then fold the border of the bottom panel onto the glue to seal the seam. Repeat this process with all five panels until the pentadecahedron is complete (Figure U). Glue a strip of construction paper or other heavy paper around the base of the balloon. Punch three holes in this paper and suspend a small paper clip by threads as shown (Figure U). One student should steady the balloon while the other heats the air inside with a hair drier (Figure V). You may release the balloon when the top gets quite warm. Compete with other students to see whose balloon goes the highest and stays aloft the longest.

Questions

(1) How high did your balloon travel? How long did it stay aloft?

(2) Will your balloon rise faster on a cool day or a warm day? Explain.

(3) Why does the hot air balloon eventually fall back to earth?

(4) Why does the density of the air in the balloon decrease as it is heated?

5.1.5 TEMPERATURE-PRESSURE RELATIONSHIPS
OF GASES (GAY-LUSSAC'S LAW)

Concepts to Investigate: Gay-Lussac's Law, kinetic theory of gases, temperature-pressure relationships of gases.

Materials: Part 1: Basketball, meter stick or measuring tape; Part 2: Basketball; Part 3: Accurate tire pressure gauge.

Principles and Procedures: Gay-Lussac's Law states that, at constant volume, the pressure (P) of a fixed mass of gas is directly proportional to the absolute $(T,$ Kelvin) temperature: $P = kT,$ where k is a constant that depends on the volume of the sample and the quantity of the gas. Thus, doubling the absolute temperature of a gas doubles the pressure if volume is kept constant.

Part 1: Gaining an intuitive understanding of temperature/pressure relations of gases: The kinetic theory of gases states that gas molecules are always in motion. These molecules collide in elastic collisions (no loss of kinetic energy). The average kinetic energy of gaseous molecules is directly proportional to the Kelvin temperature of the gas. Thus, temperature is a measure of the average kinetic energy of molecules. In the activity that follows, marbles represent gaseous molecules, and the sound the marbles make represents the pressure gaseous molecules exert. Place five marbles in a plastic milk jug or similar container and cap the container. Shake the container slowly at a constant rate and listen to the sound of the marbles bouncing off the walls. Shake the container a little more rapidly at a constant rate and listen. Again increase the frequency of shaking. What can you conclude concerning the relationship between gas pressure and temperature at constant volume?

Part 2: Gay-Lussac's Law and basketball: Leave a basketball outside on a cold night. Early in the morning, drop the basketball from a height of 2 meters and measure the height of the bounce. Repeat at least three times and determine the average. Allow the basketball to warm to room temperature for at least one hour and then repeat the activity. Does the basketball bounce higher when cold or warm? Alternatively, you may start bouncing the basketball after it has been kept out overnight in cold weather. Bouncing the ball causes frictional heating of air within the ball and eventually the temperature will rise significantly above ambient air temperature. Does the basketball bounce higher when it is cold or after it has been heated?

Part 3: Gay-Lussac's Law and tires: How does temperature affect the pressure in automobile or bicycle tires? Using an accurate gauge, measure the tire pressure on a car that has been outside overnight in cold weather. Remeasure the tire pressure after the car has been driven for at least 20 minutes during the warmest part of the day. The temperature of air in the tire increases with driving and with the ambient temperature. Did tire pressure increase, decrease or remain constant after the car was driven?

Questions

(1) Does the basketball bounce higher when the air inside it is cold or warm?

(2) Is the pressure in an automobile tire greater when the tire is cold or hot?

(3) Automobile mechanics recommend that owners check tire pressure routinely during very cold weather. Explain using Gay-Lussac's Law.

(4) Some automotive specialists recommend reducing tire pressure before beginning a long drive through the desert in the summer. Explain using Gay-Lussac's Law.

5.1.6 AVOGADRO'S PRINCIPLE

Concepts to Investigate: Mole, molar volume, Avogadro's Principle (Law), ideal gas law.

Materials: Part 1: Meter stick, tape, scissors, stiff cardboard, basketball, soccer ball, football; Part 2: Dry ice, strong and transparent 13-gallon (49 L) plastic garbage bags, ties, hammer, towel or rags, balance, tongs or insulated gloves.

Safety: Wear goggles, lab coat and insulated gloves or mittens when working with dry ice. Never allow dry ice to touch skin.

Principles and Procedures: Avogadro's Principle states that, at constant pressure and temperature, the volume of a gas is directly proportional to the number of moles of gas present. In other words, equal volumes of any two gases at the same temperature and pressure contain the same number of particles (molecules, or atoms if the gas is monatomic). Avogadro's Law states: if $V_1 = V_2$, then $n_1 = n_2$ where V represents gas volume, and n represents the number of moles. Thus, we may conclude that 1 mole of any gas at STP *(P = 1atm, T = 0°C)* will occupy the same volume as 1 mole of any other gas at STP. One mole of any gas contains the same number (Avogadro's number = 6.022×10^{23}) of particles. The volume of one mole of gas at STP is called the molar volume and has a value of approximately 22.4 L. The molar volume can be determined using the ideal gas equation *(PV = nRT)*. For example, if we have one mole of gas at STP, it will fill a volume of 22.4 L:

$$V = nRT/P = [(1.000 \text{ mol})(0.08206 \text{ L} \cdot \text{atm/K} \cdot \text{mol})(273.2 \text{ K})]/1.000 \text{ atm} = 22.42 \text{ L}$$

Part 1: Visualization of the molar volume of a gas: The volume occupied by a mole of gas at STP is about 22.4 L (22.4 dm³). To visualize this volume, use stiff cardboard and tape to construct a cubical box with volume 22.4 L. First compute the volume of the required box in mL:

$$22.4 \text{ L} \times 1000 \text{ mL/L} = 22,400 \text{ mL}$$

Since 1 mL = 1 cm³, take the cube root of 22,400 cm³ to find the length in centimeters of each side of the cubical box (28.2 cm). Construct the box and compare its volume to that of household items such as a basketball, soccer ball, or toaster. Name a household item that has a volume approximately the same as the molar volume.

Part 2: Estimation of the molar volume of a gas: *Put on goggles, lab coat and insulated gloves.* Use a hammer to break a block of dry ice into small pieces. Wrap these pieces in a towel and use the hammer to pulverize them to make crushed dry ice. *Use caution because dry ice has a temperature of −78°C and can injure the skin.* Measure out a mole (44 g) of crushed dry ice (solid carbon dioxide) on the balance and place the ice in a clear 13-gallon garbage bag. Seal the bag securely with a plastic tie and wait for all the dry ice to sublime to gaseous carbon dioxide. You can decrease the time needed for the dry ice to sublime by resting the bottom part of the bag containing the dry ice in a large container of warm water. After all the dry ice has sublimed, allow the bag and its contents to come to room temperature. Roll the sealed end of the bag until it approaches the turgid state (no major wrinkles), at which point the pressure in the bag is about equal to the pressure outside the bag. Mark this point on the bag with a piece of tape or marking pen. Place the bag in a sink or bucket and add water to it in one liter increments until water occupies the space once held by the carbon dioxide gas. What volume of water was required to fill the bag to the mark? This volume is approximately equal to the molar volume of a gas. Note that your value of molar volume is approximate and is not corrected to STP.

Questions

(1) What is the volume in L of a 22-inch diameter inflated beach ball? Would a mole of gas at STP inflate this ball ($V_{sphere} = (4/3)\pi r^3$)?

(2) How many grams of dry ice would be required to fill a 1-liter plastic bag with carbon dioxide gas at STP?

(3) Automotive air bags inflate on severe impact to prevent passengers from hitting the dashboard or windshield. Air bags contain sodium azide (NaN_3) which decomposes explosively to form solid sodium and nitrogen gas according to the equation: $2NaN_3(s) \rightarrow 2Na(s) + 3N_2(g)$. Compute the volume of nitrogen liberated by 100 g of sodium azide at 25°C and 1 atm pressure.

5.1.7 MEASURING ATMOSPHERIC PRESSURE

Concepts to Investigate: Pressure, atmospheric pressure, barometers, water barometers, weather forecasting, Magdeburg hemispheres.

Materials: <u>Part 1</u>: Vaseline®, plungers (plumbers helpers); <u>Part 2</u>: 12-meter semi-rigid transparent tubing, large bucket, measuring tape, tape or marker, three-story building or bridge.

Principles and Procedures:

Part 1: Atmospheric pressure: We live at the bottom of an ocean of air, which, like an ocean of water, exerts pressure (Figure W). Just as water pressure is caused by the weight of water, atmospheric pressure is caused by the weight of air. Since a square foot contains 144 square inches, and atmospheric pressure at sea level is about 15 pounds per square inch, the atmosphere exerts a force of about one ton on each square foot of the Earth's surface! We are not crushed by this weight because the pressure inside our bodies equals that of the atmosphere. Since there is no net force on our bodies, we do not sense any pressure. You can easily show the enormous pressure of the atmosphere using two plungers. Spread Vaseline® on the rims of two plungers and then place them together to form a tight seal, forcing the air from the plungers while forming the seal (Figure X). Go outside on a lawn and ask for volunteers to try to separate the plungers. *Make certain that nothing is in the way that will cause injury should the spheres separate and the volunteers fall.* Are you able to separate the plungers by pulling? When Otto von Gueicke of Magdeburg, Germany, performed a similar activity using two evacuated copper hemispheres about one-half meter in diameter, two teams of eight horses each were unable to separate the hemispheres!

Part 2: Barometers: Meteorologists have determined that atmospheric (barometric) pressure is very useful in predicting weather, and this is why weather maps (Figure Y) often include pressure readings. A fall in barometric pressure frequently precedes the entrance of a cold front and inclement weather, while a rise in barometric pressure is generally correlated with fair weather. In this section you will make a sensitive barometer for measuring atmospheric pressure and use it to make your own weather predictions.

Copyright © 1999 by John Wiley & Sons, Inc.

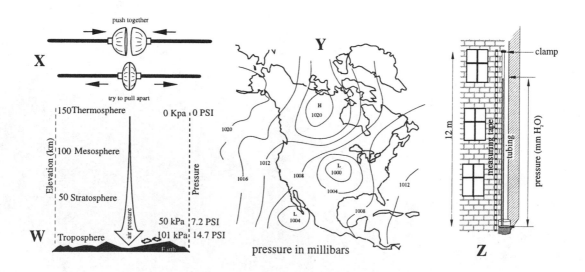

pressure in millibars

Connect one end of a 12-meter (39–40 foot) section of clear, semi-rigid plastic tubing (e.g. Tygon®) to the jet tip of a laboratory water faucet. Immerse the other end of the tubing in a bucket of water, and slowly turn on the faucet. You will know that the tubing is filled with water when no further air bubbles emerge in the bucket. Clamp both ends with screw clamps and hang the tubing out a third story window so the lower end is submerged in a bucket of water (Figure Z). Remove the bottom clamp while the end remains submerged. Do not loosen or remove the upper clamp. Water will drain out of the tubing but stop when water pressure in the tubing reaches equilibrium with atmospheric pressure.

Using a fine tipped permanent marker or a piece of tape, note the location of the meniscus, and measure the height of the water column (from the surface of the water in the bucket to the meniscus in the tube) to the nearest centimeter. This value is the barometric pressure, expressed in centimeters of water. Observe the barometer throughout the month and determine if there is a correlation between barometric pressure and weather patterns. Express barometric pressures in millimeters mercury, millibars, kilopascals, and PSI by using the conversion factors listed in appendix 1.5. Compare your readings with current barometric pressure reported on a weather station or a weather site on the Internet. According to your observations, does it appear as though drops in barometric pressure are correlated with inclement weather and rises with fair weather?

Questions

(1) Mercury is 13.6 times denser than water. Would a mercury barometer need to be taller or shorter than a water barometer? Explain.

(2) The air pressure at the summit of Mount Everest, the highest mountain in the world (29,028 ft.; 8848 m), is only about one third the air pressure at sea level. Explain.

(3) What is the difference between pressure and force? Explain why the diameter of the tube used to make the water barometer does not affect the height of the water column.

FOR THE TEACHER

The expressions for Boyle's, Charles's, and Avogadro's Laws can be combined to form the ideal gas equation which describes the relationship among four variables $(V, P, T$ and $n.)$.

Boyle's Law	$V \alpha 1/P$	$V = k_1 \times 1/P$	$P_1V_1 = P_2V_2$
Charles's Law	$V \alpha T$	$V = k_2 \times T$	$V_1/T_1 = V_2/T_2$
Avogadro's Law	$V \alpha n$	$V = k_3 \times n$	

Combining these three laws, we can express V in terms of P, T and n:

$$V \alpha nT/P \quad \text{or} \quad V = RnT/P$$

where R is the proportionality constant known as the gas constant. The value of R depends on the units used for P, V, T and n. Rearranging, we have the more familiar equation of the ideal gas law:

$$PV = nRT$$

It is important to realize that the ideal gas law is an empirical equation based on experimental measurements of the properties of gases. The ideal gas equation should be regarded as a limiting law, expressing the behavior that real gases approach at low pressures and high temperatures. What often perplexes students when working with the gas equations is the myriad of units in which pressure may be expressed, and the conversions among these units. The SI unit of pressure is the Pascal (Pa) which is defined as 1 N/m². Some typical units and their equivalents in Pa are: kiloPascal (kPa) = 1000 Pa, lb/in² = 6894 Pa, bar = 100,000 Pa, torr = 133.3 Pa, atm = 101,325 Pa, mm Hg = 133.3 Pa.

You may wish to provide your students with a mathematical description of how the kinetic theory explains the ideal gas laws. Ask students to imagine a gas confined in a box. The pressure of the gas is proportional to the number of molecular impacts per unit of wall area per unit time, and is also proportional to the change of momentum (impulse) of these impacts. The number of impacts multiplied by the average change of momentum of the impacts is the total pressure. The number of impacts per unit area per unit time is: (1) directly proportional to N, the number of molecules in the box; (2) inversely proportional to V, the volume of the box; and (3) directly proportional to s, the average speed of the molecules:

Number of impacts per unit area per time α Ns/V

The change in momentum of each impact is: (1) directly proportional to m, the mass of a molecule; and (2) directly proportional to s, the average speed of the molecule:

Change of momentum of each impact α ms

Since the pressure (P) is proportional to the product of the number of impacts and the change of momentum of each impact, we have:

$$P \alpha (Ns/V)(ms) \qquad P \alpha (N/V)(ms^2)$$

Since temperature, T, is a measure of the average kinetic energy $(1/2ms^2)$ of particles (T is proportional to ms^2) we can substitute it in the equation:

$$P \; \alpha \; (N/V) \times T$$

Since the number of molecules, N, is proportional the number of moles, n:

$$P \; \alpha \; (n/V)T$$

The constants of proportionality combine to yield R, the universal gas constant.

$$P = R(n/V)T \qquad or \qquad PV = nRT$$

It is possible to apply the kinetic theory to account for the general properties of gases. Since gas molecules are separated by great distances compared to their size, gases can be easily compressed to occupy smaller volumes. Since the attractive or repulsive forces between gas molecules are minimal, they spontaneously expand to occupy the available volume. The gas laws can also be understood in terms of kinetic theory. Pressure is exerted by gases because molecules collide with the walls of a container, so decreasing the volume of a gas increases the collision rate. Thus, the pressure of a gas is inversely proportional to the volume it occupies as expressed by Boyle's Law $(P \; \alpha \; 1/V)$. The average kinetic energy of gas molecules is proportional to the absolute temperature, so raising the temperature increases the average kinetic energy. At higher temperatures the molecules collide with the walls of the container more frequently and with greater impact, increasing pressure as expressed by Gay-Lussac's Law $(P \; \alpha \; T)$. If, however, the container is expandable (pressure is held constant), the increased pressure results in an increase in volume as expressed by Charles's Law $(V \; \alpha \; T)$.

5.1.1 PROPERTIES OF GASES

Discussion: The activities in this section provide some qualitative information regarding gases. Please read the teacher sections accompanying all referenced activities and make careful note of all safety issues.

The activities referenced in part 5 dramatically contrast the densities of gas and liquid states. In each instance, a small amount of water vapor condenses to liquid, resulting in a dramatic reduction in volume. For example, the mass of water that may have occupied 1000 mL in the vapor phase is reduced to 1 mL in the liquid phase. This shows that the density of water in the gaseous phase is only about one thousandth the density of water in the liquid phase. After conducting the three activities listed in part 5, you may wish to perform the following activity to test for student understanding. *Put on goggles, lab coat and insulated gloves.* Place approximately 10 mL of water in an *un-stoppered* 500-mL flask and heat to boiling (Figure AA). When most (but not all) of the water has boiled off, remove

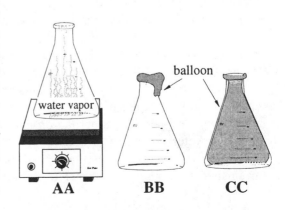

the flask and quickly place a balloon over its mouth as illustrated in Figure BB. It may be necessary to have a student hold the flask with insulated gloves while you put the balloon on. *Be cautious for the flask is hot!* As water vapor cools, it condenses, resulting in approximately a 1000-fold reduction in volume. Air pressure forces the balloon into the flask so that it almost fills it (Figure CC). Place the flask in a prominent location before students enter the room and then ask if they can determine how this was accomplished. You may also wish to see if they can replicate what you have done by allowing them to implement their ideas. Provide a variety of resources including such things as straws, vacuum pumps, glass rods, scoopulas, bicycle pumps, hot plates, and other equipment of your choosing. Students may try to inflate the balloon while it is in the flask with their breath or a tire pump, but to no avail. They may also try to draw air out from around the balloon using a straw or vacuum pump. Hopefully they will eventually realize that they need to use the same principle employed in the three activities mentioned in part 5. *Make certain students abide by all safety regulations while experimenting.*

The popcorn activity (part 5) provides an excellent opportunity for introducing the concept of indirect measurement (see section 1.3). You may wish to have students test kernels that have been sandpapered or scratched. They will note that the kernels do not pop because the coating has been broken, allowing steam to escape before expansive pressures can build.

Answers: (1) Pressure on the trapped air increases as the container is pushed deeper, resulting in compression and a reduction in volume. (2) Student answers will vary. (3) Carbon dioxide flows over and around burning objects, displacing oxygen and thereby extinguishing fires. (4) Unconfined gases expand indefinitely. The gravitational field of Earth is sufficient to prevent gaseous molecules from escaping in large numbers, while the gravitational field of Mercury is too small to retain them. (5) In the liquid state, a substance occupies only one thousandth the volume it occupies in a gaseous state. Thus, it requires much less space to ship materials as liquids. (6) Student answers will vary. Not all of the water is lost when popcorn pops. Some water remains trapped in pockets within the starch-cellulose structure of the popped popcorn kernel.

5.1.2 PRESSURE-VOLUME RELATIONSHIP OF GASES

Discussion: A plot of pressure versus volume shows the familiar inverse relationship, $PV = k$. As pressure increases, volume decreases (Figure DD). If we rearrange this equation, we get: $V = k (1/P)$, which is the equation of a straight line with slope k. You may wish to have students plot V versus $1/P$ to obtain a straight line plot with slope k.

The Cartesian "diver" is useful in illustrating several laws and principles of science. The "diver" is not just the dropper, but rather the dropper and the air and water contained within it. When the plastic bottle is squeezed, pressure is transmitted undiminished throughout the water according to

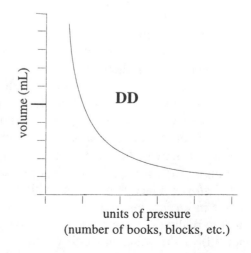

Pascal's principle. Air within the diver is compressed and water enters to fill space this air once occupied. Due to the compression of air and the entrance of water in the diver, the composite density of the diver (eyedropper, air and water) may eventually exceed the density of the surrounding water, causing the diver to descend. When pressure is released all processes work in reverse and the diver ascends. With just the right amount of pressure, the diver can be made to remain at any position in the bottle.

Archimedes' principle may be used to explain the diver. When floating, the diver displaces its own weight of water, the buoyant force of water is equal to the gravitational force and the diver is in equilibrium. When the container is squeezed, more water enters the diver, and at some point the weight of water displaced by the diver is less than the composite weight of the diver and it descends.

Answers: (1) See discussion. (2) When the bottle is squeezed, water enters the eyedropper, increasing the composite density of the diver, and causing it to sink. In a similar manner, submarines take on water in their ballast tanks, increasing their composite density and causing them to dive. When pressure is released from the bottle, water escapes from the dropper, lowering the composite density of the diver, and allowing the diver to rise. In a similar manner, the crew in a submarine may release compressed air into the ballast tanks, causing them to displace water. As water is displaced, the composite density of the submarine decreases, causing it to rise. (3) The balloon returns to its original size, but the shaving cream and marshmallows shrink smaller than their original sizes. The number of gas molecules within the balloon remains relatively constant because the walls allow few gaseous molecules across. By contrast, the air pockets in the shaving cream and marshmallow expand and eventually burst in the evacuated bell jar. When air is allowed to re-enter the jar, shaving cream and marshmallows shrivel under atmospheric pressure because of the lack of trapped air. (4) An increase in pressure on the gas forced the molecules closer together, increasing the density and decreasing the volume. (5) Student answers vary, but should express this concept: At constant temperature, the volume of a gas is inversely proportional to the pressure exerted on it. The volume vs. pressure graph should resemble Figure DD. (6) Increased pressure on a gas decreases the volume of the gas and increases its density. (7) According to Boyle's Law, the product of the initial volume and pressure is equal to the product of the final volume and pressure: $P_1V_1 = P_2V_2$. So (1 atm) × (? L) = (2.5 atm) × (10 L). 25 L of air will be required.

5.1.3 TEMPERATURE-VOLUME RELATIONSHIP OF GASES: CHARLES'S LAW

Discussion: Jacques Charles showed that, at constant pressure, the volume of a gas expands when heated and contracts when cooled, and that the relationship varies linearly with temperature expressed in degrees Celsius. At any given pressure, the plot of volume versus temperature yields a straight line according to the equation:

$$V = c + kT_C$$

where T_C is the temperature in degrees Celsius and c and k are constants. The extrapolation of student graphs to zero volume should yield a temperature of −273.15°C, but student values may vary significantly because the techniques employed are relatively crude.

The equation $V = c + kT_C$ can be simplified by noting that $V = 0$ when $T_C = -273.15$. Thus, $0 = c + k(-273.15)$, or $c = k(273.15)$. Rewriting the equation for volume:

$$V = k(273.15) + kT_C = k(273.15 + T_C)$$

We can further simplify the equation by using the absolute temperature scale in which Kelvin temperature (T_K) is related to Celsius as follows:

$$T_K = T_C + 273.15$$

Substituting Kelvin temperature for Celsius in the first equation, we have:

$$V = kT_K$$

This is Charles's Law, which states that the volume of a fixed amount of gas at constant pressure is directly proportional to the absolute temperature of the gas. Thus, a doubling of the Kelvin temperature doubles the volume of a gas, while tripling the Kelvin temperature triples the volume. Since the constant is the same regardless of the temperature or volume, it is possible to express Charles's Law as:

$$\frac{V_1}{T_1} = \frac{V_2}{T_2}$$

where V_1 and T_1 represent the volume and temperature of a gas at one temperature, and V_2 and T_2 represent their values at another. If any three values are known, the fourth can be determined. Thus, if the volume and temperature of a gas are known, and the temperature is changed, the new volume (V_2) can be calculated as:

$$V_2 = \frac{V_1 T_2}{T_1}$$

The extrapolation of student temperature/volume plots suggests that at a temperature of $-273°C$ the volume of a gas sample would be zero. It is not possible to bring air or any other gas or mixture of gases to absolute zero because their molecules have mass and therefore cannot be reduced to zero volume. In fact, gases condense to a liquid at temperatures above this point and gas behavior can no longer be observed. Oxygen, for example, condenses at $-183°C$, long before the limit of absolute zero is reached. You may wish to demonstrate the condensation of oxygen by submerging a balloon of air in a Dewar flask of liquid nitrogen $(-196°C, 77\ K)$. Approximately 20% of air is oxygen, and this will condense if the balloon remains in liquid nitrogen for a couple of minutes. Using tongs lift the balloon out of the flask and shake it so they students can hear the movement of the liquid oxygen.

Student data in part 3 will be inaccurate if the syringe plunger does not respond readily to changes in pressure. Therefore, select syringes that offer the least resistance to plunger movement. If students already know the value of absolute zero, they may select a "best fit curve" that goes through this point, rather than one that fits their data. To avoid this problem, require students to generate an equation $(y = mx + b)$ for the line where y is volume, x is temperature, and *m* is the slope (volume/temperature). To estimate a value of absolute zero, solve for the x intercept (where $y = 0$).

Answers: (1) Charles's Law states that at constant pressure the volume of a fixed mass of gas varies directly with the Kelvin temperature. The air bubbles trapped inside the marshmallow expand when heated by the hot cocoa. If left too long, however, the marshmallow will dissolve and its volume will decrease. (2) At constant atmospheric pressure, the volume of the gas increases when heated and decreases when cooled. (3) See discussion. (4) 2400 mL. (5) Solve $V_1/T_1 = V_2/T_2$ for T_2 : $T_2 = T_1V_2/V_1$ and substitute known quantities: 273 K × 5000/3000 = 455 K = 182°C. (6) Student answers will vary.

5.1.4 HOT AIR BALLOONS: AN APPLICATION OF CHARLES'S LAW

Discussion: You may wish to sponsor a contest for the highest and longest flight. Height can be measured through construction of a simple sextant as shown in Figure EE. Tape a protractor to a straw and suspend a weight on a string from the point indicated. Look through the barrel of the straw at the balloon and measure the angle (θ) between the hanging string and the dashed perpendicular line. Measure the distance between the viewer and the position directly under the balloon *(d)*. The height *(h)* of the balloon may then be calculated as:

$$h = (d)tan\theta + \textit{the height at which the sextant is being held}$$

Make certain students understand Charles's Law in terms of the kinetic theory of gases. When air in the balloon is heated, molecules of nitrogen, oxygen and other atmospheric gases move more rapidly. These molecules collide with each other and the walls of the balloon, resulting in an increase in local pressure. Since the balloon is open at the base, pressure inside the balloon equilibrates with that outside, as warmer, higher pressure air flows out into the cooler lower pressure air surrounding it. Density is defined as the ratio of mass to volume

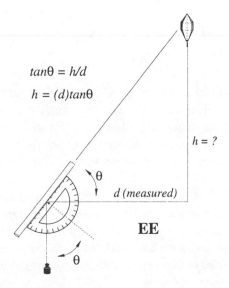

$tan\theta = h/d$

$h = (d)tan\theta$

$h = ?$

d *(measured)*

θ

EE

θ

(d = m/V). As air exits the balloon, the composite density of the balloon drops below that of the surrounding air, and the balloon rises.

You may wish to explain hot air balloons in terms of Archimedes' Principle, which states that any object completely or partially submerged in air, water or other fluid, is buoyed up by a force equal to the weight of the fluid it displaces. The hot air balloon rises because the composite weight of the balloon (balloon and the air it contains) is less than the weight of the outside air it displaces.

Answers: (1) Student answers. On cool days, balloons may ascend a few hundred feet and stay aloft for a few minutes. (2) The balloon will rise faster on a cool day because there will be a greater temperature differential, and thus a greater density differential. (3) The balloon returns to Earth as temperatures, and thus air densities, inside and outside the balloon equilibrate. (4) See discussion.

5.1.5 TEMPERATURE-PRESSURE RELATIONSHIPS OF GASES (GAY-LUSSAC'S LAW)

Discussion: The marble-milk jug activity can also be used to demonstrate the relationship between the number of gaseous molecules and gaseous pressure. Place one marble in a one-gallon plastic milk container and cap the container. Grasp the container in both hands and shake back and forth at a constant rate. Listen to the sound of the marble bouncing off the walls of the container and think of this as an indication of gas pressure. Place another marble in the container and repeat the shaking at the same rate. Repeat the activity with three, four, five and more marbles. Increasing the number of marbles from two to four increases the sound, just as doubling the concentration of gases increases the pressure. This demonstration should help provide students with an intuitive understanding of the kinetic theory of gases and its relationship to gas pressure.

Gay-Lussac's Law applies only when volume is held constant. Boyle's Law holds only when temperature is held constant, and Charles's Law applies only when pressure is held constant. In the real world, however, there are many situations in which two or more variables change simultaneously. By combining all three laws we can write the combined gas law: $PV/T = k$, where k is a constant. This may also be expressed as:

$$\frac{P_1 V_1}{T_1} = \frac{P_2 V_2}{T_2}$$

The subscripts indicate two different sets of conditions. If five variables are known, the sixth can be determined using this equation. The combined equation is very useful in solving problems in gas chemistry. Show students that when temperature is kept constant $(T_1 = T_2)$ we have Boyle's Law $(P_1 V_1 = P_2 V_2)$, when pressure is kept constant we have Charles's Law $(V_1/T_1 = V_2/T_2)$, and when volume is kept constant we have Gay-Lussac's Law $(P_1/T_1 = P_2/T_2)$.

Answers: (1) The basketball bounces higher when it the air inside it is warm. (2) The tire pressure is greater when the tire is hot. (3) Tires deflate as temperature decreases, losing approximately one pound of pressure for every 10°F drop in temperature. (4) Under these conditions tire pressure may rise above recommended values. Motorists have been stranded in the desert when their tires blew out as a result of excessive pressure.

5.1.6 AVOGADRO'S PRINCIPLE

Discussion: The activity in which students construct a cubical box with a volume of 22.4 L provides an opportunity for them to view a molar volume. Students need to see this volume to acquire a perspective of its magnitude and to compare this volume to common objects such as a basketball or soccer ball. Make certain students understand that the pressure of the gas in the inflated basketball, soccer ball, and football is greater than 1 atmosphere. If students are careful in their procedures when estimating molar volume using dry ice and a plastic bag, they can obtain results close to the value of 22.4 L, showing that quantitative results are possible using simple techniques. It is important you emphasize that a mole of any gas will occupy the same volume at STP. Also emphasize the fact that one mole of any gas contains 6.022×10^{23} particles. To check understanding, ask students how many particles are contained in a given volume of gas at STP.

Answers: (1) V_{ball} = 91 L. No. About 4 moles of gas would be required to inflate the beach ball. (2) One mole of dry ice has a mass of 44.0 g, and one mole of gas at STP occupies a volume of 22.4 L. 44.0 g/22.4 L = 1.96 g/L. Hence, approximately 2 grams will be required to fill the plastic bag. (3) From the balanced equation, $2NaN_3(s) \rightarrow 2Na(s) + 3N_2(g)$, 2 moles of NaN_3 produce 3 moles of N_2. The number of moles of N_2 produced by 100 g of NaN_3 is:

$$\text{moles of } N_2 = 100 \text{ g NaN}_3 \times (1 \text{ mol NaN}_3/65.0 \text{ g NaN}_3) \times (3 \text{ mol N}_2/2 \text{ mol NaN}_3)$$
$$= 2.31 \text{ mol N}_2$$
$$V = nRT/P = (2.31 \text{ mol})(0.0821 \text{ L·atm/K·mol})(298K)/1 \text{ atm} = 56.5 \text{ L}$$

5.1.7 MEASURING ATMOSPHERIC PRESSURE

Discussion: If performed at sea level, the water level in the tubing will drop until the column is 10.3 meters (34 feet) high when the lower clamp is removed. The top portion of the tube may or may not collapse depending upon the strength of the walls of the tubing. In general, most maps report values in millibars, but often drop the first two digits. For example, a 1013.3 mb may be reported as 13.3. The water barometer should produce very accurate measures of barometric pressure providing there are no air bubbles in the tube. An interesting variation of this activity is to fill the tube, cap one end, and attach the capped end to the rope of a flag pole. Fill the tubing with brightly colored water, and while keeping the open end of the tube submerged in a bucket, slowly raise the clamped end and watch the water column stop at 34 feet even as the tubing is raised higher.

One of the most confusing aspects about pressure is the wide variety of units used to measure it. It is conceivable some students may have heard pressure referred to in units of torrs (torr), millimeters mercury (mm Hg), millimeters water (mm H_2O), inches mercury (in Hg), inches water (in H_2O), pounds per square inch (PSI), pounds per square foot (lb/ft^2), Pascals (Pa), kilopascals (kPa), millibars (mb), barye (dynes/cm^2), newtons per square meter (N/m^2) or atmospheres (atm). It is no wonder students may be confused when studying pressure! When different units are used to indicate pressure, students may think a different quantity is being measured. It is important students realize all these terms are simply different ways of measuring the same thing, namely the ratio of force to area. The SI unit for pressure is the Pascal (Pa), defined as 1 newton of force per square meter of surface area. Although we encourage use of Pascals or kiloPascals whenever possible, each discipline has its own preferred units and it is therefore important to be familiar with these. Appendix 1.5 compares important units of pressure and their SI equivalents.

Answers: (1) Since mercury is much denser than water, it is not lifted as high by air pressure. As a result, a mercury barometer does not need to be as tall as a water barometer. (2) Air pressure is dependent upon depth within the "sea of air" known as the atmosphere. The higher you are in this sea, the less air above you and the lower the atmospheric pressure. (3) Pressure is force per unit area: $P = F/A$. Note that the force is directly proportional to surface area $(F = PA)$, while pressure is independent of surface area, but dependent on the ratio of force to surface area $(P = F/A)$. If surface area doubles, so does force, causing the force to area ratio (pressure) to remain constant.

Applications to Everyday Life

Convection currents: According to Charles's Law *(V = kT)* heated air expands, resulting in a decrease in density. Warmer, lower density air rises while cooler, higher density air sinks. Birds and hang-glider pilots search for updrafts, warm air convection currents known as thermals, that will lift them to greater heights.

Sea breezes and land breezes: Charles's Law *(V = kT)* helps explain the familiar sea breezes (onshore) and land breezes (offshore) encountered in coastal areas. During the day, solar radiation heats the land surface more than the water surface (water has a high specific heat and changes temperature slowly). Consequently, by late morning on a sunny day the air above land is warmer than the air over water. As the warmer lower density air over the land rises, cooler, denser air from the ocean flows onshore to replace it, thereby creating an onshore or sea breeze. At night, air over land cools more rapidly than air over water. With conditions reversed, air flows from the land to the ocean creating an offshore or land breeze.

Air bags: Substances occupy approximately one thousand times as much volume in the gaseous state as in the solid or liquid state. This fact is used in automobile air bags where a small amount of solid sodium azide is transformed by a chemical reaction into solid sodium and gaseous nitrogen. The dramatic increase in volume accompanying the production of nitrogen gas causes the bag to immediately inflate, protecting the driver or passenger during a collision.

Air conditioning and refrigeration: The temperature of a gas decreases if it is allowed to escape from a highly pressurized environment thorough a small aperture. The kinetic energy of the gas is used to overcome the attractive forces between gaseous molecules in the compressed state, resulting in a temperature reduction. The reduction in temperature accompanying rapid depressurization is known as the Joule-Thompson effect, and is employed to cool gases in air conditioners and refrigerators. Using a pencil, depress the valve in a fully inflated bicycle tire. The air escaping from the tire will feel cooler than surrounding air.

Gases from air: Gases can be liquefied by compressing them, cooling them, and then allowing them to expand so they may cool further, according to the Joule-Thompson effect. During expansion, the molecules of gas work against the attractive forces of their neighbors. This requires energy, and since no outside energy is available, the molecules must use up some of their kinetic energy. Consequently, the average kinetic energy, as measured by the temperature, drops. You have observed Joule-Thompson cooling if you have felt the cooling effect accompanying the release of pressure from an aerosol can.

Internal combustion engines: The "four-stroke" engine is used to propel most automobiles and trucks. The piston moves down the cylinder during the intake stroke (Figure FF), increasing volume and decreasing pressure according to Boyle's Law. A mixture of air and fuel rushes into the cylinder through an intake valve, while the exhaust valve is closed. The second stroke is the compression stroke (Figure GG) during which the piston travels upward while both the intake and exhaust valves are closed. The air and fuel above the piston are squeezed into a small volume and the pressure increases dramatically according to Boyle's Law. On the third stroke, called the power stroke (Figure HH), an electric spark ignites the mixture of air and fuel as the piston reaches the top of its stroke, and the piston is forced down

Internal Combustion Engine

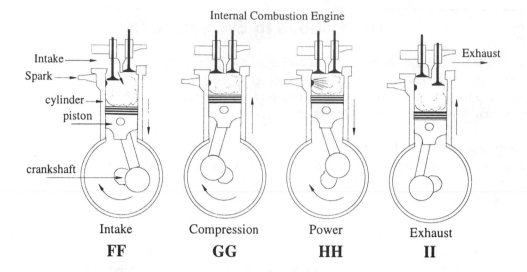

Intake   Compression   Power   Exhaust

FF   **GG**   **HH**   **II**

by the high pressure of the hot burning gases. The power stroke is the only stroke that does work. Finally, in the fourth stroke, known as the exhaust stroke (Figure II), the piston moves up again, increasing pressure according to Boyle's Law, and forcing out combustion products through the exhaust valve while the intake valve remains closed.

Altimeter: The most common method of measuring altitude uses the altimeter, which is generally an aneroid barometer that measures atmospheric pressure. While barometers are calibrated in millibars, altimeters are generally calibrated in meters or feet. A mountain climber or pilot sets the barometer to correspond to a known elevation. As he or she goes up in elevation, the barometer will detect a decrease in pressure which is registered as an increase in elevation. Such altimeters are susceptible to air pressure changes associated with weather changes.

Altitude sickness: Our atmosphere is composed of 21% oxygen. Thus, the partial pressure of oxygen at sea level is 21 kPa (21% of 101.3 kPa). At the top of Mount Whitney, California, the highest peak in the lower 48 states, the barometric pressure is only 60% of the pressure at sea level. Consequently, the partial pressure of oxygen is only 13 kPa (60% of 21.3 kPa). As elevation increases, the external pressure forcing oxygen into blood in the lung capillaries decreases. At sea level, the external oxygen pressure is 21 kPa and the oxygen pressure of blood in the lungs is 5 kPa. Consequently, there is a pressure differential of 16 kPa forcing oxygen into the blood. On top of Mt. Whitney, where the partial pressure of oxygen is only 13 kPa, the pressure differential is only 8 kPa (13 − 5 kPa). Such a reduction in oxygen pressure may cause a reduction in blood oxygen levels leading to the nausea, dizziness and shortness of breath associated with altitude sickness.

Inhaling and exhaling: Inhalation results from a pressure differential that is created by the muscles of the thorax. The brain sends messages which cause the diaphragm, intercostal and levator scapuli muscles to contract so that the volume of the thorax increases. As volume of the thorax increases, the pressure in the lungs decreases according to Boyle's Law. Since atmospheric pressure remains constant, air is pushed into the lungs.

Speech: Phonation, the process of producing voiced sound, is dependent upon air pressure changes in the larynx (voice box). As one exhales, the volume of the lungs decreases, which creates an increase in pressure according to Boyle's Law. This increased air pressure forces the vocal cords in the larynx apart. Simultaneously, according to Bernoulli's Principle, a partial vacuum is created between the vocal cords due to the rapid movement of air past them. The surrounding air is at higher pressure and forces the cords together again. This process is repeated, causing the vocal cords to vibrate and create sounds associated with speech.

5.2 Colloids and Suspensions

In the early 1900s, American novelist Upton Sinclair authored a book entitled *The Jungle* intending to expose the poor working conditions in Chicago's massive meat packing plants. Although the book did help raise concern for the workers, its primary influence was in raising public awareness regarding the impurity of processed foods. Sinclair commented that "I aimed at the public's heart and by accident I hit it in the stomach." Reading *The Jungle,* it is not difficult to see why it produced such an effect. Among other things, Sinclair describes sausage that contained rats killed by poisoned bread, and lard that contained the remains of employees who had fallen into the boiling vats! In response to the public outcry for "pure" foods that resulted from *The Jungle* and other writings, Congress enacted the Pure Food and Drug Act, and formed the Food and Drug Administration (FDA) to establish standards for foods and medicines.

Today's consumers continue to place great emphasis on the purity of foods and medicines. Hot dogs are advertised as "100% pure beef," bottled water as "pure spring water," and breakfast cereal derived from "pure, natural ingredients." Unfortunately, none of these advertisements is correct in a chemical sense. If you examine the labels on food packaging you will note that most "pure foods" contain a wide variety of substances. Even the "pure air" that you breathe on vacation in the mountains is really a complex mixture of gases and particulate matter, and the "pure spring water" you buy at the store is a dilute solution of minerals and gases dissolved in water.

We live in a complex chemical world in which most of the things we deal with are mixtures rather than pure substances. Mixtures such as milk, granite or concrete in which the properties and composition are not uniform throughout a sample are known as "heterogeneous" mixtures. Mixtures such as air or salt water, in which the properties and composition are uniform throughout a sample, are known as "homogeneous" mixtures. Sea water is a complex mixture of mineral ions and water, and yet when you examine it under the most powerful microscope, you only see one phase. Homogeneous mixtures like sea water are known as solutions. By contrast, if you examine a chunk of granite, you will notice that it is composed of three or more minerals that are separate and distinguishable from each other. Granite, like most rocks, is a heterogeneous mixture. In sea water, the particles (dissolved ions) are so small that they cannot be seen, while in granite the mineral particles (quartz, biotite, feldspar, etc.) are large enough to be seen with the unaided eye. Between solutions like sea water, and heterogeneous mixtures like granite, are mixtures that contain dispersed particles so small that the observer may not notice them and mistakenly classify them as solutions. In a solution (like sea water), the size of the dispersed particles is less than 1 nm (1 nanometer = 1 billionth of a meter) in diameter. Mixtures in which the dispersed particles range between 1 nm and 100 nm are generally classified as colloids, and those with particle size in excess of 100 nm are known as suspensions.

When you view a rainbow or the spectrum of light formed by a prism, you will notice there is a continuum of colors from the red through orange, yellow, green, blue, and indigo, to violet. Although you can distinguish one section of the spectrum as red, and another as orange, it is difficult to say where the red ends and the orange begins, because one blends into the other. In the same way, mixtures show a continuum of particle size, and thus a continuum of properties. There are no sharp boundaries between solutions, colloids, and suspensions, but in an effort to discuss the difference in mixtures it is necessary to establish some boundaries.

Table 1: Solutions, Colloids and Suspensions

Property	*True Solutions*	*Colloids*	*Suspensions*
particle size	<1 nm	1 nm – 100 nm	>100 nm
particle composition	single molecules or ions	very large molecules or hundreds to thousands of aggregated molecules	very large aggregates of molecules
stability upon standing	no separation	no separation or very slow separation	separation
filtration through paper	no separation	no separation	separation
filtration through membrane	no separation	separation	separation
Tyndall effect	does not scatter light	scatters light	scatters light
colligative properties	affected	unaffected	unaffected

Table 1 summarizes the accepted definitions of mixtures, and shows that particle size is correlated with characteristics that allow us to classify mixtures as either solutions, colloids or suspensions. In this chapter you will be investigating the properties of these three types of mixtures.

5.2.1 TYNDALL EFFECT

Concepts to Investigate: Tyndall effect, colloids, suspensions, mixtures.

Materials: Powdered dairy creamer, table sugar, table salt, beaker, clay or fine dirt.

Principles and Procedures: Automobile headlights are equipped with low beams, which illuminate the road immediately in front of the car, and high beams, which are aimed farther down the road. When driving on a country road on which there is no opposing traffic, most drivers prefer to use the high beams because they illuminate more of the road. If, however, the car enters a fog bank, most drivers immediately switch to their low beams to avoid the blinding effect of light reflected by the water droplets in the air.

Air is a solution, consisting primarily of nitrogen (21%), oxygen (78%), and small quantities of other gases such as argon, carbon dioxide, and water vapor. Fog, however, is a suspension of tiny water droplets in air. If you watch cars pass by at night, you will not see a beam created by their headlights unless there is sufficient moisture in the air. The suspended water droplets in fog reflect and scatter light beams, making the beam itself visible. The scattering of light by suspended particles in a colloid or suspension is known as the Tyndall effect, and is a standard test for differentiating suspensions (such as fog), from solutions (such as air). A beam of light is visible in a suspension, but not in a solution, because the particles of a suspension are large enough to scatter light whereas the molecules and ions of a solution are not.

Part 1: Classifying mixtures using the Tyndall effect: Add approximately 20 grams of each of the following to separate beakers of water: dairy creamer, sugar (sucrose), table salt (NaCl), and clay (fine dirt will also work). Vigorously stir the contents, allow to stand for one minute, and then shine a flashlight through the mixtures (Figure A). Classify each of the mixtures as suspensions (colloids or coarse suspensions in which a beam is visible) or as solutions (in which no beam is visible)

Part 2: Tyndall effect and smog: The term "smog" was derived from a contraction of "smoke" and "fog" and was originally used to describe the dirty air resulting from the burning of wood, coal and other similar products in humid environments like London. During the 20th century, the meaning of the term broadened to describe any type of air pollution. If you live in a large metropolitan area, you are undoubtedly familiar with smog, and have

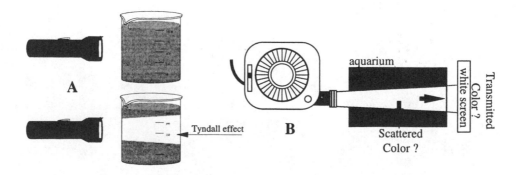

probably noticed that the sky looks less blue while sunsets and sunrises appear redder during smoggy conditions. The change in color of the sky on smoggy days is due to the Tyndall effect caused by tiny particulate matter suspended in the atmosphere. In this activity we will simulate a smoggy environment using a "pollutant" (dairy creamer) in an otherwise clear environment (tap water).

Fill an aquarium or similar container with water. Place a white screen, paper or piece of cardboard as shown in Figure B. Darken the room and shine a bright beam of light from a slide projector or from a flashlight with a focusable beam. Can you see the beam in the water before adding the powdered creamer? Slowly add the creamer and notice the appearance of the beam of light in the water when viewed from the front and from the side. How does the presence of colloids affect the appearance of the "sky" (viewed from the side) and "sunsets or sunrises" (viewed from the end)?

Questions

(1) Which of the mixtures in part 1 are solutions, and which are suspensions? Explain.

(2) Explain the change in appearance of the light beam as more dairy creamer is added to the aquarium.

(3) Explain the change in appearance of the light beam when viewed from the end as more dairy creamer is added to the aquarium.

(4) Explain why the sky generally does not appear as blue in humid climates (like the Eastern United States) as it does in arid climates (like the Southwestern United States).

(5) Explain why the sky often appears bluer following a rain.

5.2.2 CLASSIFICATION OF DISPERSIONS:
SOLUTIONS, COLLOIDS AND SUSPENSIONS

Concepts to Investigate: Dispersions: coarse suspensions, colloidal dispersions, solutions.

Materials: Part 1: Variety of household items listed in the "mixture column" of Table 2. Part 2: Centrifuge.

Principles and Procedures: Table 1 contrasts the properties of solutions, colloids, and suspensions. Each of these properties is dependent on particle size. For example, the particles in solutions (dispersed atoms, ions and molecules) are so small they stay permanently in suspension, dispersed by frequent collisions with molecules of the dispersing media. If particles are large, the influence of collisions with molecules in the dispersing media is insufficient to keep them in suspension, and within a relatively short time, two phases appear. The particle size of col-

Table 2: Classification of Dispersions

Mixture	Preparation (observe each in a 250 = mL beaker)	Does It Separate?	Tyndall Effect?	Classification
		yes	yes	suspension
		no	yes	colloid
		no	no	solution
oil and vinegar salad dressing	shake oil and vinegar salad dressing and observe			
gelatin	prepare a container of Jello® or similar gelatin desert			
sodium borate ($Na_2B_4O_7$) in water	stir 2 g (0.5 tsp) Boraxo® hand cleaner into 200 mL water			
starch in water	cook macaroni or other pasta, decant starch water and observe			
smoke in air	capture smoke from touch paper or incense, and cover with a watch glass			
salt in water	stir in 2 g (0.5 tsp) of noniodized table salt (NaCl) in 200 mL water			
clay in water	stir in 5 g (1.5 tsp) of clay or fine dirt in 200 mL water			
food coloring in water	stir in 5 drops of food coloring in 200 mL water			
carbon dioxide (CO_2) in water	fill container with club soda or similar colorless carbonated drink			
steam in air	using a hot mitt, capture a beaker of steam above boiling water			
table sugar in water (sucrose, $C_{12}H_{22}O_{11}$)	stir 12 g sucrose (3 tsp) in a beaker of water			
homogenized milk	stir 50 mL of regular homogenized milk in 150 mL water			

loids is intermediate, and thus colloidal dispersions are relatively stable, and separate extremely slowly, if at all.

In solutions, the particle sizes are so small that they are incapable of reflecting light. Thus a light beam passes through solutions unhindered, and its pathway is not visible to the observer viewing from the side. By contrast, the particle sizes in colloids and suspensions are sufficiently large to reflect or scatter light, and thus a beam of light is visible when viewed from the side. The scattering of light in a colloid or dispersion is known as the Tyndall effect (see 5.2.1)

On the basis of these two characteristics (separation of phases and Tyndall effect) it is possible to classify the three types of mixtures. As the key at the top of Table 2 indicates, a mixture that does not separate and does not illustrate the Tyndall effect is a solution. One that does not separate but does show the Tyndall effect is a colloid, while one that separates and shows the Tyndall effect is a suspension.

Part 1: Classification of dispersions: Prepare a series of containers with the items listed in the table below. Shake or stir the contents of each mixture and then observe over the next 10 minutes. Darken the room and shine a flashlight beam through the beakers as shown in Figure A. Turn the lights on, and continue to observe each container for signs of phase separation. On the basis of these two criteria (separation and Tyndall effect) classify each of the mixtures listed in Table 2.

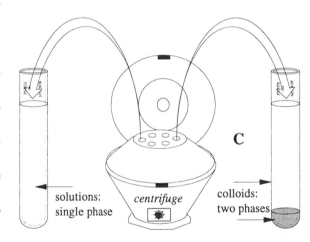

Part 2: Solutions versus colloids and suspensions: Most colloids appear stable (don't separate) during short time spans (one hour or less), but may separate when subjected to greater forces such as those in a rotating centrifuge. Solutions, by contrast, will not separate when exposed to such forces. Thus, stability in a centrifuge can be used to identify solutions (solutions don't sepa-

Table 3: Solutions versus Colloids and Suspensions

	Solution	*Colloid or Suspension*
mayonnaise (egg yokes in vegetable oil)		
tea (tannic acid, $C_{76}H_{52}O_{46}$, in water)		
whole milk (milk fat in milk serum)		
household bleach (sodium hypochlorite, NaClO, in water)		
household ammonia (ammonium hydroxide, NH_4OH, in water)		

rate) from colloids and suspensions (colloids and suspensions separate). Expose each of the following to the highest speed on your centrifuge (Figure C) and classify them as solutions or as colloids and suspensions (Table 3).

Questions

(1) Which of the mixtures were suspensions? Colloids? Solutions?

(2) We selected the Tyndall effect and stability as two criteria to classify mixtures. Could we have used another pair of properties? If so which one(s)?

(3) Some mixtures are more difficult to classify than others because their properties are indistinct. Explain why some mixtures may display characteristics intermediate between those listed in Table 1.

(4) In part 2, which of the liquids appear to be true solutions? Explain.

5.2.3 BROWNIAN MOTION IN COLLOIDS

Concepts to Investigate: Brownian motion, colloids, solutions, suspensions, kinetic theory.

Materials: Homogenized whole milk, microscope (400× or higher magnification), microscope slide, coverslip.

Principles and Procedures: The American dairy industry produces more than 65 billion kilograms of milk each year which is processed into a variety of products including ice cream, yogurt, cheese, butter and a variety of forms of milk (whole, low-fat, nonfat, dried nonfat, condensed, evaporated, etc.). Milk is a complex liquid that arrives at the processing plant as a suspension. If it is allowed to stand undisturbed the suspended globules of milk fat rise to the surface leaving behind a skim milk solution that contains a variety of solutes including lactose (milk sugar) and many minerals, vitamins and proteins. To prevent the separation of milk into different phases, food scientists developed a process known as homogenization in which milk is forced through extremely small holes in a metal plate. The fat globules are sheered by passing through the holes, and then shattered into very small particles when they hit the metal plate on the other side.

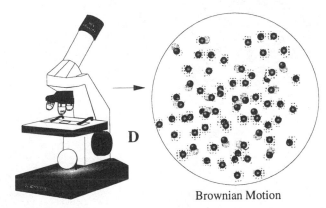

Brownian Motion

Prior to homogenization, fat globules are relatively large, and tend to separate from the suspension to form a layer of cream. After homogenization, fat globules are extremely small and remain suspended in the resulting colloid known as homogenized milk. Although the fat globules in homogenized milk are extremely small, they can be seen using a 400× or 1000× power microscope (Figure D).

Although it is not possible to view the molecules that make up a skim milk solution, it is possible to see the effect of their collisions with the fat globules in homogenized milk. When examining homogenized milk under high power, you will notice that the fat globules appear to vibrate for no apparent reason. This type of movement was first observed by Robert Brown in 1827 when he was observing a suspension of tiny pollen grains. Brownian motion, as it came to be known, was one of the observations that led to the development of the kinetic molecular theory, which states that atoms or molecules are in constant motion. The collision of these molecules with tiny colloidal particles, such as the fat droplets in homogenized milk, is thought to explain the zigzag motion as observed under the microscope. The kinetic theory suggests that the speed of molecules in a gas or liquid is related to the temperature. The higher the temperature, the faster the motion.

Fill three beakers with milk and place one in the refrigerator, one in a hot water bath (approximately 70°C), and leave one at room temperature. Transfer a drop from the cold beaker to a microscope slide and observe the droplets under the highest power (at least 400×) available. Adjust the contrast so that you can see the tiny fat droplets. You should observe that the fat droplets are in constant vibrational movement. Qualitatively describe the movement of the fat droplets, and then repeat the procedure with milk from the other two containers. Make your observations as rapidly as possible before the temperature of the milk equilibrates with the surroundings. Does it appear as though Brownian motion is affected by temperature?

Questions

(1) Why is homogenized milk classified as a colloid rather than a suspension?

(2) Explain why homogenization is sometimes used in the manufacture of paints.

(3) Does the movement of the fat droplets in milk appear to depend on temperature? Explain.

5.2.4 MAKING COLLOIDS

Concepts to Investigate: Emulsifying agents, surfactants, emulsions, gels, sols, foams, aerosols.

Materials: Part 1: Cream; Part 2: Calcium acetate, ethyl alcohol or isopropyl alcohol (rubbing alcohol), matches; Part 3: Powdered laundry detergent, aluminum sulfate, mortar, pestle, baking soda; Part 4: Vegetable oil, vinegar, eggs, salt, mustard (optional), blender; Part 5: Vegetable cooking oil, dishwashing detergent.

Safety: Part 2 should be performed as a teacher demonstration only. Wear goggles and lab coat.

Principles and Procedures: Colloidal systems are classified on the basis of the phases they contain. An emulsion, like the oil in water mixtures found in many cosmetic creams, consists of one liquid dispersed in another. An aerosol, such as smoke or mist, consists of a solid or liquid dispersed in a gas. A gel, such as gelatin dessert, consists of a liquid dispersed in a solid. A foam, such as fire-fighting foam, is a gas dispersed in a liquid. It is also possible to have colloidal systems of solids in solids (like the pigment/glass system in stained glass) or gases in solids (like marshmallows, and some soft soaps). In this activity you will be making and investigating a variety of colloidal systems.

Part 1: Making a solid emulsion (butter) by agitation: Milk is a suspension that separates upon standing as the cream rises to the top, leaving the skim milk behind. The cream is made up primarily of fat globules and water. If this cream is agitated vigorously, a solid emulsion of butter in buttermilk forms. To make butter, fill a container half-full with cream, and then shake the container repeatedly until the butter starts to form. The manufacture of butter became mechanized in the latter part of the 19th century. Prior to that, most was made in churns like the American wood-barreled dash churn with its long handled paddle (Figure E). Why does churning (violent stirring or agitation) of the cream promote the formation of a stable emulsion?

E — dasher

churn

Part 2: Making gels: "canned heat" *(teacher demonstration only):* If you have been to a restaurant that served fondue, or food in a buffet, you may have noticed that the food was being kept warm by Sterno® or another source of "canned heat." "Canned heat" is a gel in which ethyl alcohol (or some other alcohol) is dispersed in a calcium acetate solution. Dissolve 17 g of calcium acetate $Ca(CH_3COO)_2$ in 50 mL of water. Once the calcium acetate is dissolved, add in 8 mL of ethyl alcohol (or isopropyl alcohol). A gel will form almost immediately. A gel is a colloid in which the dispersed phase combines with the dispersion medium to produce a semisolid material. Darken the room and ignite the "canned heat" with a long-stemmed match. The "canned heat" will produce a blue flame that may not be visible when the lights are on. Place a watch glass or other nonflammable lid over the container to extinguish the flame.

Part 3: Making a foam (fire-fighting foam): A foam is a colloidal system in which gas bubbles are dispersed in a liquid. Marshmallows (made from gelatin and sugar and air), and meringues (made from egg white and air), and shaving creams are common household foams. Foams require a stabilizer like a soap or protein to prevent the coalescence of the gas bubbles and the separation of the phases. Albumin, the protein in egg white, is an excellent stabilizer and is used in the production of many edible foams. In this activity you will make carbon-dioxide containing foam that can be used to fight fires. Carbon dioxide is denser than air, and thus the foam lies on the ground, covering and smothering the fire.

Grind approximately 1 gram of powered laundry detergent together with approximately 6 g of aluminum sulfate ($Al_2(SO_4)_3 \cdot 18H_2O$) using a mortar and pestle and then dissolve in 50 mL of water. Dissolve 10 grams of sodium hydrogen carbonate (baking soda, $NaHCO_3$) in the soap solution and stir. The aluminum sulfate produces an acidic environment

$$[Al(H_2O)_x^{3+}(aq) + H_2O(l) \rightarrow H_3O^+(aq) + [Al(OH)(H_2O)_{x-1}]^{2+}(aq)$$

in which sodium hydrogen carbonate produces carbon dioxide

$$HCO_3^-(aq) + H_3O^+(aq) \rightarrow 2H_2O(l) + CO_2(g)$$

which is then captured in the foam that has been stabilized by the laundry detergent. Your instructor may use this foam to extinguish the canned heat made in part 2.

Part 4: Emulsifying agents; making mayonnaise: Oil and vinegar salad dressing (vinaigrette) is an example of a liquid in liquid suspension. When shaken, the oil disperses in the vinegar, but rapidly separates because the hydrophobic oil is repelled by the water in the vinegar (Figure F). In order for the two phases to coexist in a stable mixture, it is necessary to add an emulsifying agent (a surfactant, or surface-active agent) that has lipophilic ("fat-loving") and hydrophilic ("water-loving") ends to act as a "mediator" between the phases and allow them to coexist in the same region. The protein in egg yolk is an excellent emulsifying agent and helps produce the stable emulsion of oil and vinegar in the emulsion commonly known as mayonnaise. In this activity you will make mayonnaise. This activity should be carried out in a kitchen, not in a laboratory, to reduce the opportunity for contamination. Measurements for the recipe are given in customary units because these units are commonly used in cooking.

Mix vegetable oil and vinegar in a container and observe the rapid separation of phases. The oil is hydrophobic and repels the water in the vinegar and coalesces to form a single drop or globule of oil. Now make mayonnaise (a vinegar/oil emulsion) using the proteins in egg yolk as the emulsifier.

Separate the egg yolk (emulsifier) from a raw egg at room temperature, and place it in a bowl with 1/2 teaspoon salt, 1/2 teaspoon mustard and 1 tablespoon of vinegar. Stir the contents rapidly (an electric blender works best) until they are well blended, and then slowly add the oil until it is completed dispersed. The resulting emulsion is mayonnaise. Compare the stability of this emulsion with the oil and vinegar salad dressing suspension. What influence does the emulsifying agent (egg yolk proteins) have on the stability of the system?

Part 5: Emulsifying agents: the "cleansing" power of soap: The American pioneers made soap by boiling grease (animal fat) in a basic solution (made by filtering water through ashes), and used this primitive soap to clean their skin, clothes, and cookware. Although today's soap comes in bright clean packages, it is chemically similar to the pioneer formula, and produces a similar effect. Soaps are excellent surfactants because they have hydrophilic ("water loving") and lipophilc ("fat-loving") ends and thus can act as "mediators" between hydrophobic ("water-hating") oils and water (Figures F–G). How does soap help remove dirt and stains? Pour approximately 200 mL of water and 10 mL of cooking oil into a jar. Seal

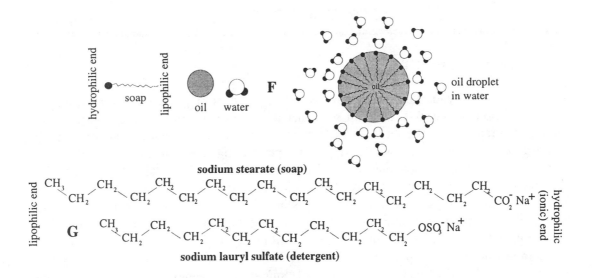

sodium stearate (soap)

G

sodium lauryl sulfate (detergent)

the jar and shake it vigorously. Does the oil stay suspended or does it separate? Now repeat the process, after adding two or three drops of dishwashing soap. Does the oil separate as rapidly? On the basis of these observations, explain how soaps help clean.

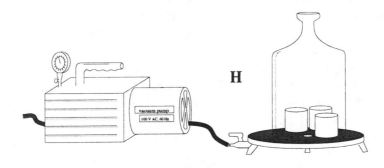

Questions

(1) Butter is a semi-solid emulsion. What are the dispersed particles, and in what are they dispersed?

(2) Why does churning the cream (part 1) promote the formation of a stable emulsion?

(3) The "canned heat" made in part 2 is a gel (a semi-solid colloid). Name some other gels.

(4) A marshmallow is a gas in solid colloid. What do you think would happen to a marshmallow if it were subjected to a vacuum (Figure H)? Try it if you have access to a vacuum pump in your classroom.

(5) What influence does the emulsifying agent (egg yolk protein) have on the stability of the mayonnaise in part 4?

(6) Describe how soaps help clean (part 5).

(7) Read labels of foods, medical creams, and cosmetics to identify ingredients that are used to emulsify and/or stabilize.

FOR THE TEACHER

5.2.1 TYNDALL EFFECT

Discussion: The Tyndall effect explains the brilliant colors of sunrise and sunset, and the blue coloration of the sky. You will note that the beam appears blue after only a small amount of creamer has been added. As more is added, additional light is scattered, and the beam appears progressively whiter. If you are performing a demonstration for the entire class, you may wish to substitute colloidal sulfur for dairy creamer. Colloidal sulfur will be produced if sulfuric acid is mixed with a solution containing sodium thiosulfate. For a 40-liter aquarium, we suggest adding 100 g of sodium thiosulfate (photographers "hypo" used as a fixer in photography), and then slowly adding in 50 mL of 3 *M* hydrochloric acid. During the next 10 to 15 minutes, colloidal sulfur will gradually form, creating a suspension. If the demonstration is set up as shown in Figure B, students will be able to observe the appearance of "blue sky" (side view) and a red "sunset" (end view) caused by the colloidal sulfur.

$$Na_2S_2O_3 + 2HCl \rightarrow 2NaCl + H_2O + S + SO_2$$

Answers: (1) The Tyndall effect occurs when dairy creamer or clay is added to water, indicating that these form suspensions. (2) When viewed from the side, the beam initially appears blue (as in clean air when only the air molecules themselves scatter the light), and subsequently appears lighter and whiter as more and more wavelengths of light are scattered. (3) The end of the beam appears redder as more and more particulate matter is dispersed in the aquarium. The larger particulate matter is capable of reflecting the shorter wavelengths (the blue end of the spectrum), leaving behind the longer wavelengths (the reds in the spectrum) to produce the "red sunset" effect. (4) Moisture scatters light. The more moisture, the more light is scattered and the whiter the sky appears when viewed from the ground. (5) Rain washes particulate matter out of the atmosphere so there are fewer particles to reflect light.

5.2.2 CLASSIFICATION OF DISPERSIONS: SOLUTIONS, COLLOIDS AND SUSPENSIONS

Discussion: Table 4 provides the answers to part 1. You may also choose to use clarity as a discriminating factor when classifying mixtures. Solutions tend to be clear while colloids and suspensions tend to be cloudy (but not always). Clarity was not used in this activity because it is a more subjective measure, and what appears "clear" to one student may appear "slightly cloudy" to another.

Answers: (1) Suspensions: oil and vinegar salad dressing, smoke in air, clay in water, carbon dioxide in water, steam in air; Colloids: gelatin, starch in water, homogenized milk; Solutions: sodium borate in water, salt in water, food coloring in water, table sugar in water. (2) Any set of properties selected from Table 1 may be used to classify mixtures, providing each mixture has a unique set of characteristics with respect to these properties.

Table 4: Classification of Solutions, Colloids and Suspensions

Mixture	*Does It Separate?*	*Tyndall Effect?*	*Classification*
	yes	*yes*	*suspension*
	no	*yes*	*colloid*
	no	*no*	*solution*
oil and vinegar salad dressing	yes	yes	suspension
gelatin	no	yes	colloid
sodium borate ($Na_2B_4O_7$) in water	no	no	solution
starch in water	no	yes	colloid
smoke in air	yes	yes	suspension
salt in water	no	no	solution
clay in water	yes	yes	suspension
food coloring in water	no	no	solution
carbon dioxide (CO_2) in water	yes	yes	solution
steam in air	yes	yes	suspension
table sugar in water (sucrose, $C_{12}H_{22}O_{11}$)	no	no	solution
homogenized milk	no	yes	colloid

(3) The properties of these mixtures are dependent upon particle size. The larger the particle size, the more the mixture's characteristics resemble a suspension, and the smaller the size, the more they resemble a solution. A mixture with particle size intermediate between a solution and a colloid, or between a colloid and a suspension, will exhibit intermediate properties. (4) Tea, ammonia, and bleach are true solutions because they do not separate when exposed to the forces in the centrifuge.

5.2.3 BROWNIAN MOTION IN COLLOIDS

Discussion: If possible, project the image on a screen using a videomicroscope. This will allow the entire class to observe Brownian motion at the same time, so when they perform their own investigations they won't waste time focusing on the dust on the coverslip of the slide as many students do!

Answers: (1) A suspension separates upon standing. The fat droplets in homogenized milk are sufficiently small that they do not separate as they do in non-homogenized milk. (2) Paint is a suspension, and the pigments tend to separate upon standing. After homogenization, the pigment particles are evenly suspended in the paint, creating a colloid that is more consistent and requires little or no stirring prior to application. (3) Yes. The warmer the colloid, the faster the Brownian motion.

5.2.4 MAKING COLLOIDS

Discussion: Most foams (part 3) are stable at atmospheric pressure, but separate when subjected to very low pressures. Place shaving cream, whipped cream or other foams in a bell jar and turn on the vacuum pump. The foams collapse dramatically as the gaseous phase escapes. You may demonstrate a similar phenomenon with "gas in solid" systems like marshmallows (Figure H). Part 4 describes a technique for making a useful gel known as Sterno® or "canned heat." We recommend that this activity be performed as a teacher demonstration because of the use of flammable liquids. There are a variety of common gels like jelly, gelatin (Jello®) and agar (medium for bacterial growth) that can be made by students in the laboratory. The directions for making gelatin and agar are on the package, while for jellies or jams they may be found on the side of a package of pectin (found in the jelly section in the market). In making jams and jellies it is essential to maintain acidic conditions by adding something like lemon juice. Pectin molecules normally repel one another, but in an acidified environment, they bond with each other forming a large network that traps the liquid. If the conditions are not acidified, the pectin bonds will not form and you will end up with a sundae sauce rather than a gel.

Answers: (1) Butter is a dispersion of droplets of an aqueous solution in fat. (2) Churning the cream breaks down the fat globules into very small particles. The protective membranes of fat globules are broken, and the liquid fat released helps cement globules together in a semi-solid mass. (3) Jelly, jam, agar (bacterial growth medium), and gelatin are other common gels. (4) A marshmallow or any other foam will rapidly collapse when subjected to a vacuum. The gases separate from the solid, leaving the shriveled remains of the foam. (5) The egg yolk proteins help stabilize the mayonnaise so the oil and vinegar do not separate. (6) Soap is an excellent emulsifying agent, and stabilizes the oil-in-water emulsion. Oil and grease stains that repel water readily disperse in soapy water, and can be removed by rinsing. (7) Some common emulsifiers in food are carageenan, algin and lecithin. Propylene glycol and glycerin are often used to produce the emulsion creams used in cosmetics.

Applications to Everyday Life

Water purification: One technique used in water purification is sedimentation. Dirty water is a suspension that may contain particles such as viruses, colloids, bacteria, and small fragments of silica and alumina. This suspension slowly separates upon standing, leaving purer water on top. The smallest particles (like viruses) separate so slowly that it is necessary to employ much more powerful force fields, such as those produced in an ultracentrifuge, to separate these from the water.

Detergents: Detergents are surface-active agents (surfactants) that allow the water to penetrate soiled surfaces to remove dirt and grime. The detergents help retain the resulting dirt in a water suspension long enough that it may be removed with rinsing.

Food emulsifiers and stabilizers: FDA (Food and Drug Administration) regulations require that food companies list ingredients on the packaging. Often these lists contain explanations of the food additives in parentheses such as "carageenan (added as a stabilizer)". Carageenan, like algin, agar and other substances derived from algae are used to produce and stabilize emulsions such as ice cream and salad dressing, to keep them from separating, give them a uniform texture, and lengthen shelf life.

Coloration in animals: Before the advent of modern dyes, pigments were extracted from natural sources like flowers, leaves, soil, and animal parts. Those who tried to extract the brilliant blue from bird feathers were disappointed to find that the color disappeared as the feathers were ground. The blue coloration in feathers results, not from a chemical pigment, but from the scattering of light through a colloidal dispersion of tiny fat or protein globules in the feather. Such colloids cause a scattering of light (Tyndall effect) and a reflection of short wavelength blue light toward the eye of the observer.

Cosmetics: Most cosmetics contain a cream or lotion that is an emulsion of oil dispersed in water. Ingredients often include vanishing cream (stearic acid in water) or cold creams (mineral oil dispersed in water). Propylene glycol and glycerin are frequently used as emulsifiers. If you examine the content labels of many cosmetics and medical creams you will see these ingredients listed.

Film: Black and white film contains a gel (often referred to as an emulsion) consisting of minute crystals of light-sensitive silver bromide and silver iodide in a gelatinous base. The gelatin not only holds the crystals (grains) but also greatly increases their sensitivity to light.

Protoplasm: Protoplasm is the complex semi-fluid colloidal substance that is the basic matter in all living cells. It contains proteins, fats and other vital molecules dispersed in water.

5.3 SOLUTES, SOLVENTS, SOLUTIONS

What do tea, maté, coffee and cola have in common? Give up? They are popular beverages made from plants (tea and maté from leaves, and coffee and cola from seeds). They also contain a chemical known as caffeine. Caffeine (trimethylxanthine) is a nitrogenous organic substance (Figure A) that has marked physiological effects. It stimulates the central nervous system, and may reduce fatigue and help you remain awake and alert.

These positive effects may explain the compulsion of many to drink coffee or other caffeine-containing beverages as part of their morning routine. Unfortunately, caffeine may also produce negative effects such as irritability, nervousness, jitteriness, headaches, and insomnia. Although tea, maté, coffee and cola are immensely popular (approximately one-third of the people in the world are coffee-drinkers alone!), consumers have become increasingly concerned about the negative effects of caffeine. To address such concerns, beverage companies have hired chemists to determine ways of eliminating caffeine without otherwise altering the drinks.

A

caffeine

After studying solubility characteristics, chemists learned that when seeds and leaves are soaked in methylene chloride (CH_2Cl_2), the caffeine dissolves, leaving the other compounds behind. This technique enjoyed great popularity until consumers became concerned about possible adverse effects of methylene chloride. Back the chemists went to the laboratory to look for a nontoxic solvent that was just as effective at selectively dissolving caffeine.

Realizing that solutes dissolve readily in solvents with similar chemical properties ("like dissolves like"), chemists sought a nontoxic substance composed of small, nonpolar molecules to dissolve the small, nonpolar caffeine molecules. The best candidate for this process was carbon dioxide, a component of the air we breathe. Unfortunately, carbon dioxide is a gas at atmospheric pressure, and liquefies only under intense pressure. After many trials, chemists perfected a way of subjecting the leaves or seeds to highly pressurized liquid carbon dioxide, and found that this solvent indeed penetrated plant tissues and dissolved the caffeine, while leaving the larger flavor components (carbohydrates and proteins) behind. The liquid carbon dioxide/caffeine solution is readily drained off, and any residual carbon dioxide immediately vaporizes when the pressure is released, leaving behind the flavorful, caffeine-free leaves or seeds.

The carbon dioxide decaffination process is gaining popularity worldwide and is one of many practical applications of solution chemistry. In the following investigations you will explore the solution process in greater detail to understand its many applications to everyday life.

5.3.1 SOLUBILITY (SOLUTE/SOLVENT INTERACTION)

Concepts to Investigate: Polarity, solutes, solvents, solutions, solubility.

Materials: Part 1: Turpentine, test tubes, corks, items listed in column 1 of Table 1; Part 2: 2-liter soda bottle, vegetable oil, food coloring.

Principles and Procedures:

Part 1: Determining polar nature ("like dissolves like"): In the middle of the night of March 24, 1989, the giant oil tanker *Exxon Valdez* veered out of the shipping lanes in Alaska's Prince William Sound and struck a reef. The side of the tanker was ripped open, and 11 million gallons of crude oil flowed out into Alaska's clear blue waters. Because petroleum oil is insoluble in water and less dense, it quickly spread across the surface the way vegetable oil spreads on the surface of vinegar shortly after a vinaigrette salad dressing is shaken. The oil slick eventually covered 10,000 square miles (26,000 km^2), contaminating 1500 miles (2400 km) of shoreline, and causing substantial damage to wildlife, the fishing industry, and the marine environment.

Chemists say that "like dissolves like," meaning that polar solvents tend to dissolve polar solutes, and nonpolar solvents tend to dissolve nonpolar solutes, while nonpolar

Table 1: Polar or Nonpolar?

Items to Be Tested	*In Water (Polar Solvent)*	*In Turpentine (Nonpolar Solvent)*	*Polar or Nonpolar*
paraffin (candle wax, C_nH_{2n+2})			
table salt (NaCl)			
mineral oil (a petroleum distillate)			
isopropyl alcohol ($CH_3CHOHCH_3$)			
"Lite salt" (KCl)			
vegetable oil ((C_nH_{2n+1})COOH)			
baking soda ($NaHCO_3$)			
latex-based paint			
oil-based paint			
glycerol ($C_3H_5(OH)_3$)			
sulfur (S)			

and polar substances are immiscible (do not mix). Because petroleum is nonpolar and water is polar, the oil from the leaking *Exxon Valdez* did not mix with the seawater, but rather spread across its surface.

You may have noticed solubility problems when trying to remove pitch stains from your hands after climbing a pine, spruce, fir, cedar or other coniferous tree. Pitch is a sticky resin produced by cone-bearing trees to protect them against insect and fungal attack. When a limb is broken or the bark ruptured, the tree releases resin to seal the wound. If you tried to remove pitch stains with water, you were probably disappointed, and may have resorted to using turpentine or a similar solvent. Turpentine is a nonpolar solvent derived from pine pitch, and will dissolve pitch and other nonpolar stains not soluble in water.

Knowing that "like dissolves like," it is possible to determine the polar nature of various substances. Polar substances show obvious signs of dissolving in water (a polar solvent), but not in turpentine (a nonpolar solvent), while nonpolar substances do just the opposite. Determine the polar nature of each of the items listed in Table 1 by testing their solubility in these two solvents.

Fill one series of test tubes (as many tubes as you have samples) with 5 mL of water, and a second series with 5 mL of turpentine. *Use caution handling turpentine.* Place a small sample of each of the items to be tested in water and a second sample in turpentine (observe the warnings on the container). Stopper, shake vigorously, and watch for signs of solubility such as disappearance of the solute or color change of the solvent. Record whether each item dissolves or does not dissolve in water and turpentine, and classify each as polar or nonpolar (Table 1).

Part 2: "Wave bottle"; immiscible fluids: Fill half of a clear plastic 2-liter soda bottle with water, and the other half with vegetable oil (Figure B). Place a few drops of food coloring in the container, seal and shake. As the container is allowed to stand, a clear boundary develops, and the food coloring is found in only one phase. Is the food coloring a polar or nonpolar substance? Shake the bottle again and describe the process by which the two distinct phases develop.

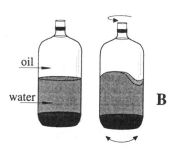

Questions

(1) On the basis of your results in part 1, which of the tested substances are polar, and which are nonpolar?

(2) For centuries sailors used pitch to seal the spaces between the planks on wooden boats. Explain why pitch works well as a sealant.

(3) Turpentine dissolves oil-based paints, but not latex house paints. Explain.

(4) In order to reduce exposure to organic solvents, some art instructors recommend that students clean brushes and hands with a vegetable oil or mineral oil. Would such oils be more effective removing water-based paints or oil-based paints?

(5) Coffee, tea, and soft-drink stains are generally removed in the wash, while stains from candle wax, salad dressing and peanut butter require special treatment. Explain.

(6) On the basis of your observations in part 2, do you believe that the food coloring molecules are polar or nonpolar? Explain.

(7) What chemical property must "sunblock" lotion have if it is "waterproof" (won't wash off when you go swimming)?

5.3.2 SURFACE AREA AND DISSOLUTION RATE

Concepts to Investigate: Dissolution rate, surface area, solvent-solute interaction.

Materials: Sugar (cubes, granulated, powdered), stop watch.

Principles and Procedures: If you go to a home improvement store, you may notice a variety of lawn fertilizers, some of which claim to promote "rapid greening" while others advertise "time-release for long-term growth." Such fertilizers may have the same percentages of nitrogen, phosphorous and potassium (the three major elements in fertilizers) and yet produce different results. When you open these bags of fertilizer, they may look very similar, except that they differ in particle size. How might particle size be related to the effect of the fertilizer on the lawn? After performing the following experiment you should be able to answer this question.

Determine the mass of single sugar cube, and then measure out equivalent masses of powdered and granulated sugar. Place the three forms of sugar in three separate flasks. Pour 50 mL of water in the flask containing the sugar cube, and swirl the flask slowly and constantly. Record the time at which no more sugar can be seen in the flask. Repeat the process using granulated and powdered sugar. Compare the dissolution times for all three forms of sugar. Which form of sugar dissolves the fastest? Why?

Questions

(1) Rank the three forms of sugar in order of the time required for complete dissolution.

(2) The three forms of sugar had the same mass, but different surface areas. Which had the largest surface area, and which had the smallest?

(3) What influence does surface area have on the rate of dissolution? Explain what occurs at a molecular level to produce this effect.

(4) Do you think that large fertilizer particle size will promote "rapid greening" or " long-term growth." Explain.

(5) Many recipes require that you stir while adding a solute (like sugar, powdered milk or salt) to a solvent. Explain the influence of stirring on the dissolution rate.

5.3.3 TEMPERATURE AND DISSOLUTION RATE

Concepts to Investigate: Temperature and solubility, solubility curves.

Materials: Potassium nitrate, ammonium chloride, beakers, burners, ring stands, Celsius thermometers, wire mesh support.

Safety: Wear goggles and lab coat.

Principles and Procedures: Yellowstone National Park in Wyoming is the oldest and best known national park in the United States. The park's thermal basins contain approximately 10,000 hot springs, which surface as steam vents, fumaroles, mud caldrons, hot springs, hot pools, paint pots and geysers. These hot springs produce an astounding variety of colors, formations, and odors, totally unlike the cool springs found in the surrounding mountains. The hot springs in Yellowstone have an abundant supply of minerals, which contribute to the wild array of colors, formations, and odors associated with them. Why are there so many more minerals in the Yellowstone's hot springs than in nearby mountain spring waters? Does temperature affect the solubility of minerals? Are more solutes dissolved in warm water than cold? Perform the following investigations to answer these questions.

Saltpeter is a mineral found in limestone caves like those in Kentucky where it has been deposited by slowly percolating spring water. Saltpeter (potassium nitrate, KNO_3) is a valuable mineral used in the preparation of fertilizers (as a source of nitrogen), as a food preservative, and in fireworks, gunpowder, and other explosives where it provides oxygen. In order to make these products, it is necessary to re-dissolve potassium nitrate in water. How does the solubility of KNO_3 vary with temperature? Using a pipet, place 10 mL of water in each of four test tubes. In the tubes place 16.00 g, 12.00 g, 8.00 g, and 4.00 g of potassium nitrate. Place the four test tubes in a beaker of water, and heat to approximately 90°C. *Gently stir* the test tube containing the 16.00 g of potassium nitrate with a clean, warmed thermometer until all of the potassium nitrate is dissolved. Allow the solution to cool slowly, and watch for the first sign of crystallization. Record the temperature at the time of the first crystals. After recording your data, re-heat the tube and then allow it to cool once again and record the data a second time. Repeat the process for the other three tubes. Record the data in Table 2, and create a graph of temperature versus solubility.

Develop a second solubility curve for ammonium chloride (NH_4Cl) by testing tubes containing 7.00, 6.00, 5.00, and 4.00 grams of ammonium chloride in 10 mL of water.

Table 2: Temperature and Solution Rate

Water	Potassium Nitrate (KNO_3)	Crystallization Temperature of KNO_3 avg.			Ammonium Chloride (NH_4Cl)	Crystallization Temperature of NH_4Cl avg.		
10 mL	16.00 g				7.00 g			
10 mL	12.00 g				6.00 g			
10 mL	8.00 g				5.00 g			
10 mL	4.00 g				4.00 g			

Questions

(1) What is the influence of temperature on the solubilities of potassium nitrate and ammonium chloride?

(2) Which substance, potassium nitrate or ammonium chloride, is more soluble in water? Explain.

(3) Solubility may be expressed as the number of grams of solute that dissolve in a 100 mL of water. According to your data, what are the solubilities of potassium nitrate and ammonium chloride at 50°C?

(4) If the dissolution of a substance is exothermic (gets warmer as it dissolves), will that substance be more or less soluble as the temperature is raised?

(5) Explain why there might usually be more mineral formations surrounding thermal springs than cool mountain springs.

5.3.4 ENTHALPY OF SOLUTION

Concepts to Investigate: Enthalpy of solution (heat of solution), endothermic (endergonic) processes, exothermic (exergonic) processes, LeChâtelier's Principle.

Materials: Part 1: Ammonium chloride, potassium nitrate, calcium acetate, ammonium hydroxide, concentrated hydrochloric acid, test tubes; Part 2: Calcium acetate, potassium nitrate, hot plate.

Safety: Wear goggles and lab coat.

Principles and Procedures: Dissolution requires that solute molecules be separated from each other (an energy-consuming or endothermic process) and surrounded by solvent molecules (an exothermic, energy-producing process). The net process is termed *endothermic* (endergonic) if more energy is required to separate solute molecules than is released when the solvent surrounds them. The process is termed *exothermic* (exergonic) if the reverse is true. The term *enthalpy* is used to describe the total energy or heat content of a system at constant pressure, and a change in enthalpy is easily measured by the amount of heat released or consumed. In this activity you will dissolve various solutes in water and determine whether the enthalpy of solution is positive or negative.

Part 1: Endothermic and exothermic dissolution: Fill four test tubes with 10 mL of water and record the temperature of each. Measure out 5.0 grams of ammonium chloride (NH_4Cl), place in one of the test tubes, and *gently stir* with a clean thermometer (Figure C). Record the temperature at the moment when all of the crystals have completely dissolved. Repeat the process for potassium nitrate (KNO_3), calcium acetate ($Ca(CH_3COO)_2$) and ammonium hydroxide (NH_4OH). Request your instructor to pipet concentrated hydrochloric acid (HCl) into a fifth tube. (Concentrated HCl is hazardous and should be used only under direct supervision of the instructor.) Which dissolution processes are endothermic (consume energy as indicated by a falling temperature), and which are exothermic (produce energy, as indicated by rising temperature)? If the

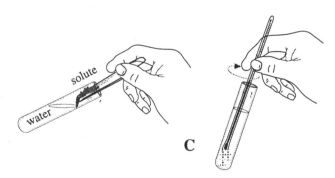

process is exothermic, then it will occur more slowly as the temperature is raised (LeChâtelier's Principle). Will any of the four chemicals tested be less soluble at higher temperatures?

Part 2: LeChâtelier's Principle: LeChâtelier's Principle states that if a "stress" is applied to a system at equilibrium, the system reacts to release or counteract that "stress." A saturated solution in the presence of free solute is at equilibrium. If we "stress" such a solution by adding heat, the solubility will change in a way that absorbs this heat. If the enthalpy of solution is positive (endothermic), the solubility will increase and more solute will dissolve because this process absorbs heat and reduces the "stress." If, however, the enthalpy of solution is negative (exothermic), the solubility will actually decrease and material will come out of solution when heated because the crystallization process absorbs heat and reduces the "stress." Measure out 20 grams of calcium acetate ($Ca(CH_3COO)_2$) and 20 grams of potassium nitrate (KNO_3), and place each in a separate flask containing 50 mL of water. Based on your observations in part 1, predict what will happen if the solutions are warmed. Place them on a hot plate and heat, stirring occasionally. Watch for crystal formation or crystal dissolution. On the basis of your observations, which substance has a positive enthalpy of solution (exothermic) and which has a negative enthalpy of solution (endothermic)?

Questions

(1) Which of the substances tested in part 1 has a positive enthalpy of solution? Explain.

(2) Which of the substances tested in part 1 has a negative enthalpy of solution? Explain.

(3) Does calcium acetate become more or less soluble when heated (part 2)? Does this indicate that it has a positive or negative enthalpy of solution? Explain.

(4) Does potassium nitrate become more or less soluble when heated (part 2)? Does this indicate that it has a positive or negative enthalpy of solution? Explain.

(5) The equation for the dissolution of potassium nitrate follows. According to LeChâtelier's Principle, does the reaction shift to the right or the left if heated? What influence does heating have upon the solubility of potassium nitrate in water?

$$KNO_3(s) + energy \rightleftharpoons K^+(aq) + NO_3^-(aq)$$

(6) Ammonium nitrate is the principal ingredient in some "cold packs" used to reduce swelling after sports injuries. Such "cold packs" contain pouches of water and ammonium nitrate that are broken to allow mixing when needed. Using an equation, explain how these cold packs work.

5.3.5 SOLUBILITY OF GASES IN LIQUIDS

Concepts to Investigate: Henry's Law, gas solubility, differential solubility, Henry's Law constants, gas pressure, LeChâtelier's Principle.

Materials: Part 1: Unopened clear container of club soda or other clear carbonated drink, beaker, hot plate; Part 2: Cylinder of compressed ammonia (or concentrated ammonium hydroxide, sodium hydroxide, and calcium chloride), phenolphthalein, Vaseline®, glassware illustrated in Figure E; Part 3: 2-L unopened soda bottles, materials in Figures H–J.

Safety: Part 2 should be performed only by the instructor. Wear goggles, lab coat and gloves, and perform in a fume hood.

Principles and Procedures: SCUBA (Self-Contained Underwater Breathing Apparatus) diving is a popular sport in many coastal communities. If a SCUBA diver rises rapidly from great depths, dissolved nitrogen in his or her blood and body tissues comes out of solution and forms bubbles known as embolisms. Such a condition is known as "the bends" and may be extremely painful and even fatal since embolisms can stimulate blood clots that may lead to strokes or heart attacks. To prevent the bends, divers are urged to come to the surface slowly so that nitrogen will leave the blood gradually, and not all at once. This gradual release of dissolved nitrogen allows it to be exhaled and prevents the development of dangerous bubbles in the blood. To understand "the bends" and other interesting phenomena, it is important to first have an understanding of the effect of pressure on the solubility of gases.

Part 1: Henry's Law: At the beginning of the 19th century, an English physician, William Henry, noted that the solubility of a gas in a liquid is proportional to the pressure of that gas upon the liquid. Soft drink manufacturers apply Henry's Law when bottling their drinks. After cans or bottles are filled with the drink, they are placed in a chamber in which they are subjected to high carbon dioxide pressure. After carbon dioxide dissolves in the fluid, the cans are sealed and distributed to stores. When you open a soft drink container, the contents are once again exposed to the lower partial pressure of carbon dioxide in the atmosphere, allowing the dissolved carbon dioxide to come out of solution, producing the characteristic "fizz." In this activity you will compare and contrast the formation of carbon dioxide bubbles in a freshly opened soft drink container with the formation of water vapor bubbles in boiling water (Figure D). Obtain a clear plastic bottle of club soda, lemon-lime soda or other clear soft drink. Slowly release the cap and record all of your observations about bubble formation, such as size, abundance,

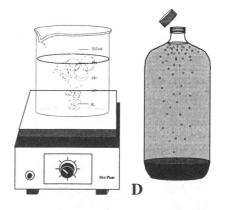

D

distribution, etc. Can you halt the formation of bubbles by quickly resealing the container just after breaking the seal? Place a beaker of water on a hot plate and heat to boiling. Again record all of your observations regarding bubble formation. In what ways is bubble formation in boiling water similar to, and in what ways is it different from the soft drink?

Part 2: Henry's Law constants: ammonia fountain *(teacher demonstration only): This activity produces toxic gaseous ammonia and should only be performed in a fume hood by*

Table 3: Henry's Law Constants *(K)*

Gas	kPa/(mol/liter)	atm/(mol/liter)
He	283,000	2865
N_2	155,000	1600
H_2	121,000	1228
O_2	74,700	757
NH_3	5,690	57

the instructor. Wear goggles, lab coat and gloves. Henry's Law can be expressed as: $p = Kc$, where p is the partial pressure of a gas, c is the molar concentration of the dissolved gas in the liquid (solubility), and K is the Henry's Law constant for that particular gas. Henry's Law constants for various gases are found in Table 3.

The molar solubility *(c)* is equal to the partial pressure of the gas above the solution *(p)* divided by Henry's Law constant *(K)* for that gas: $c = p/K$. Thus helium at one atmosphere pressure has a molar solubility of (1/2865) mol/liter or 0.35 mmol/liter, while ammonia has a solubility of (1/57) mol/liter or 17.5 mmol/liter. Thus, ammonia is very soluble in water compared to helium. This teacher demonstration illustrates the high solubility of ammonia in water.

Invert a flask on a ring-support and place in the fume hood. Fill the flask with ammonia from a bottle of compressed ammonia. If you do not have compressed ammonia, you can prepare dry ammonia in the fume hood by pouring concentrated ammonium hydroxide (NH_4OH) over pellets of sodium hydroxide in an Erlenmeyer flask generator as shown in Figure E. Ammonia will be produced and will flow through the tube containing calcium chloride where water is removed before entering the collection flask. Ammonia is less dense than air, so it will collect in the inverted flask by downward displacement of air. Ammonia is clear, but you can determine its presence because it dissolves in water to form ammonium hydroxide, a base. Place a moistened strip of red litmus paper in the mouth of the flask. When the litmus turns blue, the container has filled with ammonia gas.

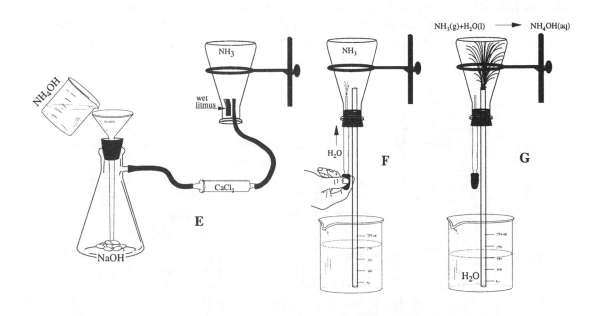

Fill an eyedropper with water and seal the tip with a bit of Vaseline®. (The Vaseline® prevents early contact of water and ammonia, but is easily pushed out of the way when the dropper bulb is squeezed.) Seal the collection flask with a two-holed stopper equipped with a hollow glass tube and the eyedropper filled with water. Position the apparatus such that the lower end of the tube is in a beaker of water as shown in Figure F. Place a couple of drops of phenolphthalein indicator in the beaker. After the apparatus is fully assembled, squeeze the eyedropper to release water into the flask. Ammonia gas is extremely soluble in water and will dissolve in the water. As ammonia dissolves, a partial vacuum is created and air pressure outside the assembly pushes water up the tube from the beaker into the flask to create an "ammonia fountain" (Figure G). The phenolphthalein in the water will turn pink as it enters the flask, indicating the presence of dissolved ammonia (NH_4OH; a base).

Part 3: The effect of temperature on the solubility of gases: Separating solid or liquid solute molecules is an endothermic process, while hydrating them is exothermic. If separation consumes more energy than hydration produces, the process is endothermic, but if hydration releases more energy than separation consumes, the process is exothermic. Because gaseous molecules are already widely spaced, no energy is necessary to separate them, and the only factor to consider is the energy released upon hydration. Therefore, the process of dissolving gases is always exothermic:

$$x(g) \quad \rightleftharpoons \quad x(aq) + energy$$

where $x(g)$ represents the gaseous molecules, and $x(aq)$ represents dissolved molecules. LeChâtelier's Principle states that when a system at equilibrium is subjected to a stress, the system adjusts to relieve the stress. What will happen if heat is applied to a solution containing a dissolved gas? Will the gas become more soluble or less? Perform the following experiment to find out.

Obtain three bottles of a carbonated soft drink. Place one in a refrigerator for a half hour, and leave the other two at room temperature. Fill three graduated cylinders or collection bottles with water, cover with a square cut from an overhead transparency, and invert the cylinders or collection bottles in containers of water. Remove the coverings and brace the cylinders or collection bottles with a ring stand or similar device. Position the end of the delivery tubes in the cylinders filled with water. Remove the cap from the chilled soda, insert the delivery tube apparatus, and place in ice water as shown in Figure H. Repeat the process for the second container, but leave it at room temperature (Figure I). Repeat the process for the third

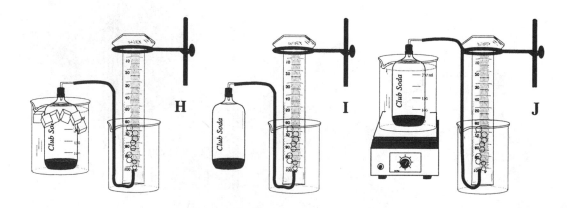

H   I   J

container, but place it in a container of warm water (>50°C; not boiling; Figure J). Allow each to release carbon dioxide gas for 15 minutes. Record the volume of carbon dioxide produced by each. On the basis of your data, does it appear that carbon dioxide is more or less soluble at higher temperatures?

Questions

(1) Do bubbles form on the sides of the beaker before the water boils? If so, are these bubbles any different than those forming at the bottom of the container when the water boils?

(2) Where do the bubbles in the boiling water tend to form? Where do the bubbles in the opened soft drink container tend to form? Explain this difference.

(3) LeChâtelier's Principle states that if a system at equilibrium is disturbed, the system will readjust in such a way as to neutralize the disturbance and restore equilibrium. Explain the formation of carbon dioxide bubbles upon opening a soft drink container in light of this principle.

(4) Use LeChâtelier's Principle to explain the rise of water in the ammonia fountain.

(5) Explain "the bends" (formation of nitrogen bubbles in a rapidly surfacing diver's blood) in terms of Henry's Law.

(6) What does your data from part 3 suggest about the effect of temperature on the solubility of carbon dioxide? Explain.

(7) Fish may die rapidly if you fill their aquarium with distilled water or with water that has been boiled and then cooled. Explain, using information you learned about the influence of temperature on the solubility of gases.

FOR THE TEACHER

5.3.1 SOLUBILITY (SOLUTE/SOLVENT INTERACTIONS)

Discussion: Before introducing this section, you may wish to review the molecular basis of polarity. The polarity of a molecule is determined by the polarity and arrangement of its bonds. If all the bonds in a molecule are nonpolar, then the molecule will be nonpolar like iodine (I_2) (Figure K). If some of the bonds are polar and are positioned such that they do not cancel each other's effect, the molecule will be polar like water (H_2O) (Figure L). Some molecules like carbon tetrachloride (CCl_4) contain polar bonds, but are nonpolar because the bonds are arranged such that they cancel each other's effect (Figure M).

One measure of the polarity of a substance is its dielectric constant. Water has a very high dielectric constant of approximately 90 while turpentine (a complex mixture of organic molecules) has an average dielectric constant of approximately 10. Ionic substances, such as KCl and NaCl, readily dissolve in polar solvents like water, while nonpolar substances, such as iodine, readily dissolve in nonpolar solvents like turpentine.

Many laboratory manuals call for the use of solvents such as benzene and carbon tetrachloride to illustrate solubility principles. While such solvents produce excellent results, we believe that the use of such hazardous materials should be minimized in the school laboratory. In this activity we selected "turpentine" as our nonpolar solvent because it is readily available at hardware stores and is less hazardous than most other organic solvents.

You may wish to illustrate the influence of the length of a hydrocarbon chain upon the polarity of a substance. Ethanol (CH_3CH_2-OH) is hydrophilic, while the longer butanol molecule ($CH_3CH_2CH_2CH_2-OH$) is hydrophobic. Mix equal quantities of ethanol and water in one tube, and equal quantities of butanol and water in another. The butanol/water mixture will display two phases, while the ethanol/water mixture will display just one phase because the smaller, more polar ethanol dissolves completely in water. Add food coloring to both and notice that it diffuses throughout the single ethanol/water phase, but only in the water phase of the butanol/water mix.

Polar solvents dissolve polar solutes because the positive ends of solvent molecules attract the negative ends of the solute molecules, and vice versa. These dipole-dipole forces help separate solute particles from each other. The dissolution of nonpolar solutes in nonpolar solvents is aided by London dispersion forces. These weak forces result from the attraction between the positively charged nuclei of solvent atoms and negatively charged electrons of solute atoms and vice versa.

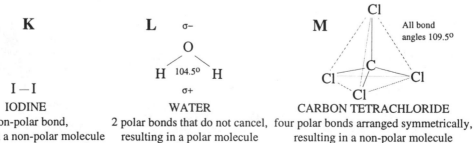

K	**L**	**M**
I−I	σ− O H 104.5° H σ+	Cl, C, Cl, Cl, Cl — All bond angles 109.5°
IODINE	WATER	CARBON TETRACHLORIDE
1 non-polar bond, resulting in a non-polar molecule	2 polar bonds that do not cancel, resulting in a polar molecule	four polar bonds arranged symmetrically, resulting in a non-polar molecule

Answers: (1) Paraffin, mineral oil, iodine, vegetable oil, oil-based paint, and sulfur dissolve readily in turpentine, indicating that they are nonpolar. The rest dissolve in water, indicating they are polar. (2) Pitch is a nonpolar, hydrophobic resin. It sticks to wood in much the same way that it sticks to your hands, and thus serves as a good sealant between the ship's boards. (3) Turpentine is a nonpolar solvent and therefore dissolves nonpolar solutes such as oil, and oil-based products. It is ineffective, however, in dissolving polar, water-based paints. (4) Oils are nonpolar, and therefore are more effective in dissolving oil-based paints. (5) Coffee, tea, and soft-drinks are water-based liquids and contain water-soluble pigments that are relatively easily removed in the washing machine. Salad dressing, peanut butter, and candle wax are nonpolar substances, and are best removed by a nonpolar solvent such as tetrachloroethylene (dry-cleaning fluid) used by professional dry-cleaners. (6) The water (polar) phase takes on the color of the food coloring, while the vegetable oil (nonpolar) does not, indicating that food coloring molecules are polar. (7) The sunblock lotion must contain a nonpolar (hydrophobic; water-insoluble) material.

5.3.2 SURFACE AREA AND SOLUTION RATE

Discussion: Solubility is dependent on the interaction of solvent and solute molecules. The surface area of the sugar cube is only a fraction of the surface area of an equivalent mass of powdered sugar. Initially the solvent (water) comes in contact with many more molecules of the solute (sugar) in the powdered form than it does in the cube form. Since the rate of dissolution is dependent on the rate at which solvent and solute molecules interact, the powdered sugar will dissolve much more rapidly.

This activity can be performed as an instructor demonstration if you use clear glass containers and place them on an overhead projector. If you wish to make the demonstration more colorful, you may substitute copper sulfate for the sugar. Measure three equivalent masses of copper sulfate, and then crush one to an intermediate granule size, and a second sample to a fine powder. The powdered copper sulfate will turn water blue quickly, while the chunks of copper sulfate will turn water blue the slowest.

Answers: (1) The powdered sugar dissolved most rapidly, followed by the granulated sugar, and finally the sugar cube. (2) The powdered sugar had the greatest surface area, followed by the granulated sugar and finally the sugar cube. (3) The higher the surface area to mass ratio, the more rapid the dissolution. See discussion above. (4) The fertilizer with large particle size dissolves much more slowly and probably promotes "long-term growth." The fertilizer with smaller particle size dissolves more rapidly and provides the lawn with nutrients rapidly, causing "rapid greening." (5) As a solute dissolves, the region immediately surrounding the solute particles becomes saturated. Stirring moves the saturated solvent away from the solute particles, and replaces it with solvent that is not saturated so the dissolution process may continue.

5.3.3 TEMPERATURE AND DISSOLUTION RATE

Discussion: Student data should resemble Figure N. In most situations, solubility increases with temperature. If you wish to show this to the entire class using an overhead projector, fill one clear container with hot water, and another with ice water (remove the ice before placing on the overhead to facilitate viewing). Place a sugar cube in each, and have the class observe the time required for total dissolution in both containers. If sugar cubes are not available, you may wish to use aspirin or a bullion cube.

Students may be surprised to learn that the solubilities of some substances (like sodium hydroxide and sulfuric acid) actually decrease with increasing temperature. Explain this phenomenon using LeChâtelier's Principle. One of the products of both sodium hydroxide and sulfuric acid dissolution is heat. According to LeChâtelier's Principle, if a system is subjected to stress, it will react in a manner to relieve the stress. If external heat is added to these solutions, it will be consumed as precipitates form.

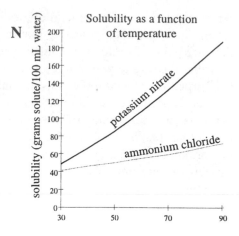

Answers: (1) The solubilities of potassium nitrate and ammonium chloride increase with temperature. (2) Potassium nitrate is more soluble than ammonium chloride as shown in Figure N. (3) The solubility of ammonium chloride is approximately 50 g/100 mL water, while the solubility of potassium nitrate is approximately 80 g/mL water. (4) It will be less soluble at higher temperatures. (5) Most minerals are more soluble in warm water than in cold. As hot water flows through the Earth's crust, minerals dissolve into solution. As water rises to the surface, and then cools or evaporates, minerals are left behind to build the fantastic sculptures commonly associated with hot springs.

5.3.4 ENTHALPY OF SOLUTION

Discussion: You may wish to have your students evaluate their results in light of published data in the *CRC Handbook of Chemistry and Physics* or other similar reference books. At 25°C, the enthalpies of solution for the substances tested are as follows: potassium nitrate (35 kJ/mol), ammonium chloride (15 kJ/mol), sodium hydroxide (−45 kJ/mol), and hydrochloric acid (−75 kJ/mol). You may also wish to have students perform their own calorimetry to determine numeric values for the enthalpies of solution. Figure O illustrates the design for a calorimeter made of Styrofoam cups. Measure a known quantity of water into the calorimeter and record its temperature precisely. Measure a known mass of the solute and determine the number of moles it represents. Stir the solute into the water until it is dissolved and record the highest (or lowest) temperature reached. Knowing that the heat capacity of water (the amount of energy required to raise the temperature of water 1°C) is 4.184 kJ/kg, it is possible to determine the total energy expended. For example, if the temperature of 0.100 kg of water rises 5°C, then approximately 2.1 kJ has been expended. The enthalpy of solution could then be determined by dividing by the number of moles. For example, if the solute in question represented 1 mole, the enthalpy of solution would be

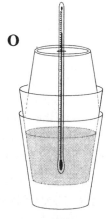

−2.1 kJ/mol. The sign is negative because heat is given off (energy released) when the solute dissolves. This technique does not consider problems such as heat loss to the container and the environment, but may still generate reasonable values and give students excellent experience in experimental technique.

Answers: (1) The solution cools when potassium nitrate or ammonium chloride dissolves, indicating that both have positive enthalpies of solution. (2) The solution warms when sodium hydroxide, calcium acetate or hydrochloric acid dissolves, indicating that all three have negative enthalpies of solution. (3) Calcium acetate became less soluble when heated as evidenced by the increased formation of crystals with rising temperature. This indicates that the enthalpy of solution for calcium is negative (exothermic). (4) Potassium nitrate became increasingly more soluble when heated as indicated by the dissolution of crystals. This shows that the enthalpy of solution for potassium nitrate is positive (endothermic). (5) Energy occurs on the left side of the equation, so if additional energy is applied by heating, it will shift the reaction to the right to release the stress. The solubility of potassium nitrate increases with increasing temperature. (6) The enthalpy of solution for ammonium nitrate is positive (26 kJ/mol), indicating that considerable energy is consumed when it dissolves in water. The equation below shows how heat is absorbed from the environment (in this case the injured tissue) as the pack is activated by mixing the water and ammonium nitrate pouches.

$$heat + NH_4NO_3(s) \xrightarrow{\ water\ } NH_4^+(aq) + NO_3^-(aq)$$

5.3.5 SOLUBILITY OF GASES IN LIQUIDS

Discussion: The solubility of liquid and solid solutes is relatively unaffected by pressure, indicating that Henry's Law is limited to gases. Henry's Law, like the Ideal Gas Law, produces accurate values only at low pressures, but the general relationship holds true for higher pressures as well. Because a substantial vacuum may develop when making the ammonia fountain, you may wish to substitute a round-bottom flask for the Erlenmeyer collection flask. Pressure is more evenly distributed on the wall of a spherical flask and the flask is less likely to shatter when substantial pressure differentials exist. Part 3 illustrates that the value of Henry's Law constant is temperature dependent, increasing with temperature. Thus the solubility of gases decreases with increasing temperature. You may wish to have students examine water heated on a hot plate, and notice that air bubbles form shortly before boiling, indicating that air (nitrogen, oxygen, etc.) is less soluble at high temperatures than at low temperatures.

Answers: (1) Yes, bubbles do form on the side of the beaker before the water boils. These are air bubbles that come out of solution as the water is heated. The bubbles that form on the bottom of the container are made of steam (water vapor) and occur when the water itself undergoes a phase change. (2) The bubbles in boiling water are made of water vapor and tend to form on the bottom of the container nearest the heat source where the water is hot enough to vaporize. The bubbles in the soft drink container form throughout the solution as dissolved carbon dioxide comes out of solution. Bubble formation in boiling water is due to a transition from liquid to gaseous state, while bubble formation in the soft drink results from dissolved (aqueous) carbon dioxide coming out of solution. (3) Gaseous and dissolved carbon dioxide are in equilibrium in a pressurized soft drink can:

$$CO_2(g) + H_2O(l) \rightleftharpoons H_2CO_3(aq)$$

Equilibrium is disturbed when the lid is opened and the partial pressure of carbon dioxide drops. According to LeChâtelier's Principle, a reduction in pressure causes the reaction to shift to the left so as to produce more gas in response to the loss in pressure. As the reaction shifts to the left the soft drink fizzes (carbon dioxide comes out of solution) until equilibrium is re-established. (4) Before water is injected, pressure inside and outside the ammonia-containing flask are in equilibrium. When water is injected, gaseous ammonia immediately dissolves. This results in a dramatic reduction in pressure and disturbs equilibrium. According to LeChâtelier's Principle, when a system at equilibrium is disturbed, the system responds to counter the disturbance until equilibrium is re-established. Since external pressure remains constant at one atmosphere (760 mm Hg), equilibrium will be re-established when the pressure inside the flask returns to one atmosphere. This is accomplished as water fills the flask, pressurizing the gas that remains. (5) According to Henry's Law, the solubility of a gas varies directly with pressure. The pressure at 100 m depth (1082 kPa) is approximately 10 times the pressure of normal atmospheric pressure (101 kPa). As a result, gaseous nitrogen in the lungs dissolves readily in the blood. If the diver resurfaces too rapidly, the external pressure will drop dramatically, and the nitrogen will come out of solution, forming the dangerous bubbles (embolisms) associated with the bends. (6) Students should find that the warm soda releases the most carbon dioxide, followed by room temperature soda and then the cold soda. This indicates that the solubility of gases is inversely related to temperature. (7) When water is distilled or boiled, dissolved air is released. If this water is allowed to cool without shaking, it will remain relatively free of dissolved oxygen. Fish acquire oxygen through their gills, but if the oxygen has been previously removed, the fish die from suffocation.

Applications to Everyday Life

Hypervitaminosis: Vitamins B and C are polar water-soluble molecules, while vitamins A, D, E, and K are nonpolar fat-soluble molecules. It is unlikely one would suffer hypervitaminosis (symptoms due to excessive vitamin intake) from mega-doses of vitamins B and C because these dissolve in the blood and are eliminated in urine after being filtered by the kidneys. It is possible, however, to suffer from excessive amounts of nonpolar fat-soluble vitamins A, D, E and K because these collect in the fat where they will be lost only via chemical breakdown, and not by filtration.

Hydroponics: Hydroponics is a technique for growing plants in water rather than soil. This is possible because all of the essential nutrients for plants are water-soluble and can be added to the solution in which the plants are grown. Hydroponics is used extensively in regions with poor or disease-infested soils.

Ore and mineral formation: Have you ever seen "water spots" on the sides of a container of tap water from which the water has evaporated? The term "water spot" is a misnomer, because these are really residues of minerals that were originally dissolved in the water. After years and years of evaporation, mineral ores may be left behind to form fantastic structures such as the stalactites and stalagmites in caves, "tufa structures" in mineral lakes or terraces around hot springs. Many minerals are slightly water-soluble, and are deposited as the water evaporates. Most minerals are more soluble in the hot waters found deep in the crust than in the cooler waters found near the surface. Thus, minerals dissolve in the deep, high temperature, high pressure waters, and then precipitate in the cooler temperature near the surface. Such mineral deposits are known as "hydrothermal" ores.

Extraction of metals from ores: Most valuable minerals occur in ores where they are found in conjunction with many other minerals. To extract the ores, it may be necessary to subject pulverized ore to solutions in which the desired metal is soluble, but the rest of the ore is not. Gold, for example is soluble in mercury, and therefore gold ore is usually placed in a mercury bath in which the gold and mercury form an amalgam (solution of gold in mercury) that can be separated from the ore. Approximately 70% of the gold in gold ore can be extracted using mercury as a solvent. The remainder is generally solubilized by dilute solutions of sodium cyanide or calcium cyanide.

Food processors and blenders: The larger the surface area to mass ratio between solute and solvent, the greater the solution rate. To reduce the time necessary to produce a solution, cooks often put solute and solvent in a blender to sheer the solute particles, thereby increasing the surface area contact between solute and solvent, and increasing the rate of solution.

Alloys: Not all solutions are liquid or gaseous at room temperature—some are solid! Ancient peoples discovered that bronze (a solution of tin and copper) and brass (a solution of copper and zinc) had desirable qualities unlike their constituent metals. The most important alloys today are steels, solutions containing 3% or less carbon dissolved in iron. Steels are widely used in construction (beams, hardware), manufacturing (machinery, cookware, utensils, appliances), transportation (rails, vehicle parts) and other important industries. Other elements such as chromium, nickel, manganese, molybdenum, silicon, tungsten, vanadium, and boron are used to make a wide variety of steels that have special properties such as corrosion resistance (such as stainless steel containing large amounts of chromium and nickel), strength (chrome-moly steel, containing chromium and molybdenum) magnetizability, ductility, hardness (vanadium steel) or toughness.

The biosphere: Solutions are vital for life! The atmosphere is a complex solution composed of nitrogen 78%, oxygen 21%, argon 0.9%, water vapor 0.1%, carbon dioxide and various other gases. Seawater is a complex solution composed of ions (2.5%; Cl^-, Na^+, SO_4^{2-}, Mg^{2+}, Ca^{2+}, K^+), inorganic and organic molecules, and atmospheric gases dissolved in water.

Solutions in the body: Blood plasma, the liquid component of blood, is a solution consisting of water 90%, proteins 7%, and salts 3%, glucose, amino acids, vitamins, hormones, and waste products of metabolism. Cytosol, the intra-cellular solution surrounding organelles, is a complex solution containing proteins, carbohydrates, nucleic acids, fatty acids, salts and other components dissolved in water.

5.4 Colligative Properties

Throughout history, one of the greatest obstacles to exploration, travel, commerce and the expansion of societies has been an insufficiency of fresh water. Not surprisingly, massive waterless stretches of land like the Gobi and Taklamakan deserts of Asia, the massive Sahara in Northern Africa, and the Great Central Desert of Australia have long discouraged travel and trade. Ironically, the massive oceans and the polar ice caps which together contain 99% of Earth's water supply have also proven to be barriers for the same reason. Explorers like Christopher Columbus and Ferdinand Magellan had to strictly ration water to their crews despite the fact that they were sailing on seas estimated to contain 1.4 billion cubic km of water. Similarly, Peary and Henson's 1908 expedition to the North Pole encountered the constant threat of dehydration as they traveled across thousands of kilometers of the greatest supply of fresh water on Earth!

Although more than 70% of the Earth's surface is covered by water, many communities are in constant threat of running out. The problem is not that there is not enough water on Earth, but simply that there is not enough in a form that we can use. Ninety-seven percent of the Earth's water is sea water, containing high concentrations of mineral salts. Stranded and shipwrecked sailors have often been tempted to drink sea water, but most have known that it would only compound their problems. Drinking sea water actually removes water from the body by a process known as osmosis, and those who consume too much may die of dehydration.

Although most (96.5%) of sea water is H_2O, the relatively small percentage (3.5%) of dissolved solutes render it unfit for consumption, irrigation, cleaning, and many other domestic and industrial applications. Even small concentrations of solutes alter the properties of the solutions into which they are dissolved. Some properties, such as taste, density, conductivity, and appearance, are dependent on the identity of the solute. Other properties, including changes in osmotic pressure, vapor pressure, boiling point, and freezing point, are dependent solely on the concentration of dissolved particles, and not on their identity. Thus solutions of different substances with the same concentration of dissolved particles may have different density, conductivity and appearance, but demonstrate the same osmotic pressure, vapor pressure, boiling point, and freezing point.

It is primarily the heightened osmotic pressure of a sea water solution that makes it unfit for human consumption. In an effort to provide sufficient fresh water to meet the demands of society, chemists have been searching for ways to obtain it from the sea. One of the most promising techniques is "reverse osmosis," a technique that is already used extensively in home water purification systems. Chemists have determined that by applying an external pressure equal to the osmotic pressure of the sea water solution, they are able to force water back through a semi-permeable membrane while leaving dissolved solutes behind. Reverse osmosis has already proven to be more energy efficient than other methods such as distillation or electrodialysis, and is just one of many examples of how an understanding of chemical principles like colligative properties helps in the development of important techniques or processes. In this chapter you will investigate the influence of solute concentration on the colligative properties of solutions, and learn how chemists use such principles to solve real-life problems.

5.4.1 RAOULT'S LAW

Concepts to Investigate: Raoult's Law, vapor pressure, vapor pressure depression, colligative properties.

Materials: Erlenmeyer flasks, glass tubing, flexible tubing, sugar, salt, two-holed stoppers, food coloring.

Principles and Procedures: According to the kinetic theory, molecules in a liquid are in constant motion. Occasionally, molecules on the surface of a liquid break free from intermolecular forces and enter the gaseous phase (Figure A). If a nonvolatile solute is added to a liquid solvent, some solute particles (ions, atoms or molecules) diffuse to the surface layer where they block solvent molecules from escaping (Figure B). Thus, the higher the percentage of nonvolatile solute particles, the lower the percentage of the surface occupied by solvent particles, and the fewer solvent particles that escape into the gaseous phase. Figure B indicates that the vapor pressure of a solution (with a nonvolatile solute) will be less than the vapor pressure of a pure solvent (Figure A).

Raoult's Law states that the vapor pressure of a solution containing a non-volatile, non-electrolyte solute is the product of the vapor pressure of the pure solvent and the mole fraction of the solvent.

$$P_{(solution)} = X_{(solvent)}P_{(solvent)} \qquad \text{where } X_{(solvent)} = \frac{moles\ solvent}{moles\ solvent\ +\ moles\ solute}$$

For example, if only half of the solution is solvent ($X_{solvent} = 0.5$), then the vapor pressure of the solution ($P_{solution}$) will be only 50% of the vapor pressure of the pure solvent ($P_{solvent}$).

If Raoult's Law is accurate, then we should expect vapor pressure to decrease as the quantity of dissolved nonvolatile solute increases. Prepare an apparatus such as illustrated in Figure C. Your instructor can construct the manometer by bending glass tubing in a burner equipped with a flame spreader or simply by mounting clear flexible tubing to cardboard with string or tape such that it assumes a "U" shape. Fill the manometer half-way with water colored with vegetable food coloring. Place approximately 50 grams of salt in a 500 mL flask and add 200 mL of water with as little mixing as possible. Seal the apparatus and record the height in the outer arm of the manometer tube (Figure C). The level will rise above the inside level due to the pressurization that occurs as you press the stopper into the mouth of the flask.

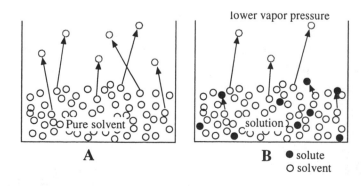

A   B   ● solute
                                            ○ solvent

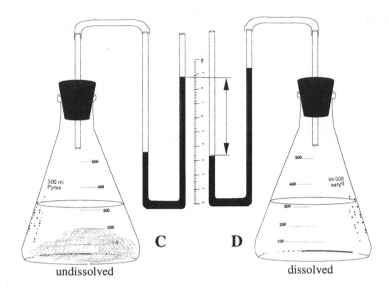

undissolved   dissolved

Swirl the flask for two seconds to promote dissolving the salt, and once again record the height in the outer manometer tube (Figure D). Repeat this process until no further change in the height of the manometer occurs. Does the vapor pressure increase or decrease as solutes dissolve into solution? Is this consistent with Raoult's Law?

Questions

(1) Are your results from part 1 consistent with Rauolt's Law? Explain.

(2) Crude oil is a complex mixture of many hydrocarbons, such as gasoline, kerosene, gas oil, lubricating oil, residual fuel oil, bitumen and paraffin. Would you expect such a mixture to exhibit a vapor pressure equivalent to the most volatile component (gasoline), the least volatile component (paraffin) or somewhere in between? Explain.

(3) The Jordan River flows from the Sea of Galilee (a fresh water lake) to the Dead Sea (highly saline inland sea). Given the same temperature and atmospheric pressure, would you expect more evaporation from the surface of the Sea of Galilee or the Dead Sea?

5.4.2 FREEZING POINT DEPRESSION

Concepts to Investigate: Molality, molarity, freezing point depression, colligative properties.

Materials: Part 1: Cotton string, ice, salt; Part 2: Thermometer, sucrose (table sugar), sodium chloride (non-iodized table salt or rock salt), calcium chloride.

Principles and Procedures: If you have ever lived in a cold climate, you may have noticed road-workers spreading salt on the roads after a snowstorm. Salt, like other nonvolatile solutes, reduces the freezing point of water (Figure E) by interfering with crystal formation. The reduction in the freezing point can be expressed as: $\Delta T_f = K_f m$, where ΔT_f indicates the freezing point depression, K_f represents the freezing point depression constant of the solvent, and m indicates the molality of the solution. It should be noted that molality *(m)* is defined as the number of moles of solute per kilogram of solvent, in contrast to molarity *(M)* which is defined as the number of moles of solute per liter of solution.

Table salt (NaCl) nearly fully dissociates in water to sodium and chloride ions. We say that sodium chloride has a mole number of two because a one molal solution of sodium chloride yields a two molal solution of sodium and chloride ions. When determining the molality of an ionic solution, it is important to know the mole number and the percent dissociation.

Part 1: Freezing point lowering: Place two ice cubes in a Petri dish or other container. Pour salt on one, but not on the other. Carefully record your observations.

Moisten two cotton strings and place upon ice cubes as illustrated in Figure F. Pour salt on one of them. After one minute, pick up the loose end of each string. Which string is frozen to the cube? Why?

Part 2: Solute concentration and freezing point depression: Sucrose ($C_{12}H_{22}O_{11}$, MW 342.3) is a covalent molecule that does not dissociate when it dissolves, while sodium chloride (mole number = 2) nearly fully dissociates into two ions (NaCl $\rightarrow$ Na$^+$ + Cl$^-$) and calcium chloride (mole number = 3) nearly fully dissociates into three (CaCl$_2$ $\rightarrow$ Ca^{+2} + 2Cl$^-$). Therefore, a one molal solution of sodium chloride represents two molal of total ions, while a one molal solution of calcium chloride represents three molal solution of total ions. If equal molal solutions of sucrose, sodium chloride, and calcium chloride are compared, which will have the lowest freezing point?

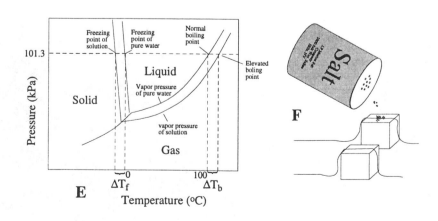

Table 1: Sucrose, Sodium Chloride and Calcium Chloride

	Sucrose	*Sodium Chloride*	*Calcium Chloride*
formula	$C_{12}H_{22}O_{11}$	NaCl	$CaCl_2$
dissociation equation	no dissociation	$NaCl \rightarrow Na^+ + Cl^-$	$CaCl_2 \rightarrow Ca^{+2} + 2Cl^-$
molecular weight (g/mole)	342.3	58.5	111.0
mass of solute (g)	273.8	46.8	88.8
moles of solute (mol)	0.800	0.800	0.800
mass of solvent (kg)	0.400	0.400	0.400
molality (solute)	2.00	2.00	2.00
mole number	1	2	3
molality of particles (m)	2.00	4.00	6.00

Data from 5.4.2 (Freezing Point Depression)

freezing point (°C)			
freezing point depression (°C)			

Data from 5.4.3 (Boiling Point Elevation)

boiling point (°C)			
boiling point elevation (°C)			

Fill each of four beakers with 0.200 kg (200 mL) of ice-cold water (without ice). Add 200 grams of crushed ice to each. Prepare 2 molal solutions by dissolving 273.8 grams of sucrose (table sugar) in the first beaker, 46.8 grams of sodium chloride (table salt) in the second, and 88.8 grams of calcium chloride in the third. Add nothing to the fourth because it serves as a control. Measure the lowest temperature each solution reaches. This temperature is the freezing point of the solution—the point at which solid and liquid phases co-exist. Record your findings in Table 1. Which solution has the greatest freezing point depression?

Questions

(1) Which ice cube (the control or the one with salt) melted faster? Explain.

(2) Why did the string freeze to the ice cube in part 1 after salt was added, but did not freeze to the cube in which no salt was added?

(3) Although ice cream is available in practically every supermarket, some people prefer to make their own. When doing so, they mix the cream in a container that rests within another container that they fill with water, ice, and salt. Explain the purpose of this outer tub.

(4) The freezing point of water decreases as salt is added until it reaches the limit of sodium chloride solubility at −21°C. What are the molarity and molality of the solution at this temperature?

(5) Which solute produced the greatest reduction in freezing point?

(6) What freezing point depressions would you expect for 1 molal, 2 molal, and 3 molal aqueous solutions?

(7) Sodium chloride, potassium chloride, and calcium chloride are all used to de-ice streets. Given equal concentrations of each, which de-ices streets best? Explain.

(8) As water freezes, it expands. This expansive force can fracture rocks and roads when water freezes in existing cracks. Roads tend to degrade more rapidly when salt is used than when nothing is added to de-ice the roads. Offer a possible explanation.

5.4.3 BOILING POINT ELEVATION

Concepts to Investigate: Colligative properties, molarity, molality, boiling point elevation.

Materials: Part 1: 1 large heavy pan, 1 metal tablespoon, 1 baking pan with sides lined with aluminum foil, 1 candy thermometer, 3-3/4 cups of granulated sugar, 1-1/2 cups high fructose corn syrup (e.g. Karo®), 1 cup water, 1 teaspoon of favorite candy flavoring (can be purchased at grocery store), food coloring of choice, powdered sugar; Part 2: Thermometer, sucrose (table sugar), sodium chloride (non-iodized table salt or rock salt), calcium chloride, hot plate.

Safety: Solution temperatures in these activities exceed 100°C and may cause serious burns. Wear goggles, lab coat, and insulated mitts.

Principles and Procedures: The boiling point of a liquid is the temperature at which the vapor pressure of the liquid equals the atmospheric pressure. In activity 5.4.1 you learned that the presence of nonvolatile solute particles lowers the vapor pressure of a solution at any temperature. The higher the mole fraction of nonvolatile solute particles, the lower the vapor pressure of the solution, and the higher the temperature must be raised before the solution will once again boil. Thus, the boiling point of a solution is higher than the boiling point of pure solvent.

Part 1: Boiling point elevation and cooking (rock candy): *This activity should be performed in a kitchen rather than a laboratory. Never eat any food in a laboratory. Mitts and protective eyeware must be used because this activity involves a boiling sugar solution that is very hot.*

Figures C and D show how the addition of nonvolatile solute particles lowers the vapor pressure of a solvent and causes it to boil at a higher temperature. Just how much does the dissolved sugar in a candy recipe raise the boiling point?

Refer to the materials list above for quantities. Place sugar (sucrose; $C_{12}H_{22}O_{11}$, MW 342.3) and high fructose ($C_6H_{12}O_6$) corn syrup into the saucepan, and gently heat while stirring with a tablespoon until the sugar has dissolved. Slowly bring to a boil. What is the current temperature? What is the boiling point elevation? In other words, how high above the normal boiling point of water (100°C) does the solution boil? Allow the solution to boil without stirring for approximately three minutes. Remove from heat, add candy flavoring and food coloring. Pour the solution into a foil-lined baking pan. As the mixture cools, cut with scissors and place in powdered sugar as desired.

Part 2: Solute concentration and boiling point elevation. You may study the influence of molarity and molality on boiling point elevation using the same materials used to study freezing point depression in activity 5.4.2. Prepare solutions as before, only this time determine the boiling point of each by gently raising the temperature of each to boiling. The temperature will plateau at the boiling point and will be easy to read. You may wish to double the molality of your solutions to see a more pronounced effect. Report your results in Table 1.

Questions

(1) What was the highest temperature reached by your solution when making the rock candy in part 1?

(2) Why are confectioners (candy-makers) warned to be extra careful when preparing such treats as "rock candy?"

(3) Which solute produced the greatest increase in the boiling point?

(4) The molal boiling point elevation constant for water is 0.515°C/molal. What boiling point elevations would you expect for 1 molal, 2 molal, and 3 molal aqueous solutions?

(5) A popular brand of automobile radiator antifreeze advertises that their product (ethylene glycol; $C_2H_6O_2$) provides engine protection from temperatures of −84°F to 276°F when mixed with water in a 50%/50% mix. What is the boiling point elevation and freezing point depression provided by such a mixture?

(6) Chemists use the freezing point depression or boiling point elevation equations to determine the molecular weight of various solutes. Explain how this could be done.

(7) A solution was prepared by dissolving 18.00 g of glucose in 150.0 g of water. The boiling point of the solution was 100.34°C at 1 atm pressure. Calculate the molecular weight (MW) of glucose.

5.4.4 OSMOTIC PRESSURE

Concepts to Investigate: Colligative properties, diffusion, osmosis, osmotic pressure.

Materials: Part 1: Small food storage bags (lightweight sandwich bags), iodine solution, starch, beaker; Part 2: 500 mL beakers, salt, celery, balance; Part 3: Large carrots, apple corer, glass tubing, high fructose corn syrup (Karo®), one-holed stoppers, graduated cylinders.

Principles and Procedures: The electric refrigerator was introduced into the consumer market in the 1920s. Before that people had to rely on an ice box or simply eat warm food. Unfortunately, food spoils readily at room temperature due to rapid growth of bacteria and fungi (mold). Refrigeration helps preserve food by slowing or stopping the growth and reproduction of such organisms.

How would your life be different without your refrigerator or freezer? No cold milk on your cereal, no ice cream for those midnight snacks, no frozen pizza to pop in the oven! Prior to the advent of refrigeration, people preserved food by storing it in vinegar (acetic acid solution) or in a heavy sugar or salt solution (brine). Even today some foods such as pickles and some canned fruits are prepared or preserved this way. The process of preserving food in a highly concentrated solution of salt, vinegar, or sugar is known as "pickling." At the cellular level, pickling is simply the process of osmosis.

Osmosis (Figure G) is a special type of diffusion in which a solvent (typically water) diffuses across a semi-permeable membrane (permeable to the solvent, impermeable to the dissolved solutes) from a region of high water (low solute) concentration to a region of low water (high solute) concentration. Thus bacteria and fungi die by osmotic dehydration when placed in brine because water flows from within them (high water, low solute) to the surrounding brine (low water, high solute).

Part 1: Membrane permeability: Synthetic dialysis membrane is often used in osmosis studies because it is uniform, and much simpler to work with than natural membranes. Unfortunately, dialysis tubing is rather expensive, so we suggest that you study osmosis using the inexpensive semi-permeable membranes found in food storage bags.

Fresh fruits and vegetables are made of living tissues that respire according to the following equation:

$$6O_2 + C_6H_{12}O_6 \rightarrow 6CO_2 + 6H_2O + energy$$

If fruits and vegetables are stored in air-tight containers, the oxygen levels will fall, the carbon dioxide levels will rise, respiration will cease, and eventually the tissue will die for lack of available energy (ATP). To address this problem, chemists developed semi-permeable plastic film for food storage bags that allows oxygen in and carbon dioxide out. Carbon dioxide and oxygen pass through these membranes, but will other small molecules like water or iodine or large molecules like starch move freely through these membranes?

Fill a small food storage bag (use the thinnest film available) with water and a 5% starch solution. Mass the bag and its contents to the nearest 0.01 g. Place the bag in a container of pure water and allow it to stand for 24 hours, blot it dry, and re-mass it (Figure H). Was there any change in mass? An increase in mass indicates that water has entered the bag. A decrease in mass indicates that water or starch has exited. What can you conclude from your mass determinations?

(7) Candied fruit is covered with sugar and can last much, much longer than regular fruit. Explain.

(8) Reverse osmosis is a popular technique used to purify household water. Do some research in the library or Internet to determine how it works.

FOR THE TEACHER

5.4.1 RAOULT'S LAW

Discussion: The activity in part 1 is a qualitative investigation that illustrates a drop in pressure accompanying the progressive dissolution of a solute. The drop in the water level in the outer manometer tube is significant and clearly illustrates Raoult's Law.

Equimolal solutions of sodium chloride (mole number = 2) and sucrose (mole number = 2) do not produce the same effect on vapor pressure because sodium chloride dissociates and produces two moles of ions for every mole of salt dissolved. Although twice as many solute particles are in the flask of salt water than in the sugar water, the influence on vapor pressure is not twice as great because this is not an "ideal solution." It is unfortunate that the word "law" (Raoult's "Law") is associated with the relationship between mole fraction and vapor pressure because no real solutions obey this relationship precisely. Raoult's Law describes the relationship in "ideal" solutions in which solute particles do not interact with each other. In reality, the interaction between solute particles can be quite significant and cause large deviations from Raoult's Law.

Answers: (1) Students should find that the vapor pressure of water decreases significantly as solute dissolves, a finding consistent with Raoult's Law. (2) The vapor pressure of crude oil is intermediate between gasoline and paraffin. The vapor pressure of a solution is the sum of the vapor pressures of each component's contribution. If the crude oil is rich in gasoline, the vapor pressure will be higher, and if it is rich in paraffin it will be lower. (3) You would expect more evaporation from the Sea of Galilee because the vapor pressure of pure water is higher than saline water. (4) These are all ionic substances that readily dissociate in water. A solution of calcium chloride will have the lowest vapor pressure since calcium chloride ($CaCl_2$) produces 50% more ions when it dissociates than either of the others.

5.4.2 FREEZING POINT DEPRESSION

Discussion: The freezing point equation predicts that a 2.00 molal solution of sodium chloride (4 molal solution of particles) will freeze at −7.44°C when in fact it freezes at −6.93°C. Such discrepancies occur because the equation holds only for ideal solutions which do not account for intermolecular interactions. In fact, real solutions always involve such interactions. The greater the concentration, the greater the interaction between solute particles, and the greater the deviation from predicted values. The freezing point depression equation applies strictly only for nonvolatile, nonelectrolytic solutes. Therefore, it is not possible to use this equation to predict the freezing point depression associated with ethylene glycol (automobile antifreeze) or other volatile solutes.

Answers: (1) Salt lowers the freezing point of water, and thus the salted cube melts more rapidly than the control. Salts are often spread on icy roads to promote melting. (2) The addition of salt causes some ice to melt. Melting is an endothermic process and absorbs heat from the water in the string until it is cold enough to freeze to the ice. (3) The addition of salt to ice lowers the freezing point. When ice melts (an endothermic process), heat is removed from the environment so the temperature drops. Thus, the outer tub reaches a temperature significantly below 0°C, sufficiently cold that the cream will freeze. (4) The freezing point depression equation is expressed as: $\Delta T_f = K_f m$. A $-21°C$ depression indicates an 11.3 molal (approximately 5.6 M) solution. (5) A 1 M solution of calcium chloride is approximately 3 molal in ions, while a 1 M solution of sodium chloride is approximately only 2 molal in ions and a 1 M solution of sugar is approximately only 1 molal in molecules. Thus, when comparing equimolar concentrations, calcium chloride will produce the greatest effect. (6) $-1.86°C$, $-3.72°C$, $-5.58°C$. (7) Calcium chloride de-ices fastest because it dissociates into three ions rather than just two as in sodium chloride and potassium chloride. (8) The use of a de-icer increases the number of freeze/thaw cycles and thus the number of times that freezing water pushes against the surrounding pavement.

5.4.3 BOILING POINT ELEVATION

Discussion: *Be extremely careful when making the rock candy in part 1. The temperature of the boiling sugar solution is approximately 50°C higher than normal boiling water. Make sure that you use a commercial candy thermometer because these are designed to measure high temperatures.* You may wish to try other molalities, but remember that the more concentrated the solution, the less "ideal" its behavior, and the greater the deviation between empirical data and that predicted by the boiling point elevation equation.

Colligative properties are dependent on the number of particles in solution. The freezing point depression, boiling point elevation, vapor pressure and osmotic pressure are all directly related to the concentration of dissolved particles. Thus, it is possible to determine the concentration of dissolved particles if you know how one of these four values has changed. Chemists can, in turn, use this information to determine the molecular weight of a substance. For example, assume that a solution is prepared by dissolving 18.00 g of glucose in 150.0 g of water, and the resulting solution has a boiling point of 100.34°C at 1 atm. The molecular weight of glucose can be calculated as follows:

$$\Delta T_b = 100.34 - 100 = 0.34°C$$

$$K_b = 0.51°C/m$$

$$\Delta T_b = K_b\, m$$

$$m = \Delta T_b / K_b = 0.34°C/0.51°Cm^{-1} = 0.67\ m = 0.67\ mol_{glucose}/kg_{water}$$

$$m = (18.00\ g\ /\ MW_{glucose})\ /\ 0.1500\ kg_{water}$$

$$MW_{glucose} = 18.00\ g\ /\ \{m\ (\ 0.1500\ kg)\}$$

$$MW_{glucose} = 18.00\ g\ /\ \{(0.67\ mol_{glucose}/kg_{water})\ (\ 0.1500\ kg_{water})\}$$

$$MW_{glucose} = 180\ g\ /mol$$

You may notice that the boiling point elevation in this experiment is much smaller (0.34°C) than most standard equipment would be able to measure accurately. It is possible to obtain larger temperature changes by increasing the solute concentration, but then the relationships become less accurate because the solution becomes less "ideal." Unless you have well calibrated thermocouples and appropriate probeware, we suggest you use a solvent that has a high boiling point elevation constant such as camphor (1,7,7-trimethylbicyclo[2,2,1]heptan-2-one, a natural moth repellent; $K_b = 37.8°C/m$) so that the temperature change will be easy to detect.

Answers: (1) Approximately 154°C, (309°F). (2) The solutions they deal with are often 50°C higher than the temperature of normal boiling water, and scalding is possible. (3) A 1 *M* solution of calcium chloride yields approximately a 3 molal solution of ions, while a 1 *M* solution of sodium chloride yields approximately only a 2 molal solution of ions, and a 1 *M* solution of sugar yields approximately a 1 molal solution of molecules. Thus, when comparing equimolal concentrations, calcium chloride will produce the greatest effect. (4) Approximately 0.5°C, 1.0°C, 1.5°C. (5) The antifreeze causes a freezing point depression of 64°C (116°F) and a boiling point elevation of 36°C (64°F). (6 and 7) Please see discussion.

5.4.4 OSMOTIC PRESSURE

Discussion: Please refer to Chapter 2.3 for additional activities dealing with osmosis and osmotic pressure. Osmosis is an extremely important process for all living systems, and you may wish to examine cellular response to hypotonic (low osmotic pressure), isotonic (same osmotic pressure), and hypertonic (higher osmotic pressure) solutions. If you or your students are confused by these terms, you may wish to review the student and teacher portions of Chapter 2.3.

Place a leaf from an Elodea (*Egeria densa;* Anacharis) or other thin leafed aquarium plant on a microscope slide. Adjust the microscope so cells are clearly seen under the highest power. Place a few drops of highly saline solution at one side of the cover slip, and draw it over the tissue by absorbing water with bilbous paper placed on the other side. Cell membranes will pull away from the cell walls as the cells dehydrate in this solution. If possible, use a videomicroscope to display the image on a monitor or large screen. This will allow the entire class to monitor the process at the same time.

Chemistry teachers often use dialysis tubing (available from scientific supply companies) to study osmosis and osmotic pressure. Although this tubing produces excellent results, we have introduced techniques that use common household semi-permeable membranes such as plastic bags and living tissue in fruits and vegetables. We believe that the use of household items not only saves money, but also helps students develop an understanding of how scientific principles apply to everyday life. In part 1 we suggest using food storage bags. Occasionally manufacturer's specifications change, so you may find a large degree of variability between different products, or even with the same product from year to year. You may wish to compare a variety of food storage bags to see if they all have similar permeability. In part 3 we recommend that you use large, wide carrots because it is possible to develop a good seal with the stopper/tube assembly without using any wax or other sealant. You may, however, wish to experiment with potatoes, sweet potatoes or other large tubers or roots. You may use silicone glue, modeling clay or other sealant if necessary.

The osmotic pressure for solution can be calculated by the equation $\pi = cRT$, where π represents osmotic pressure, R is the universal gas constant, c is the concentration of solute (molarity of solute particles), and T is the temperature in Kelvin. This formula works well only for very dilute solutions. Osmotic pressure is a significant force in the biological world. The osmotic pressure of a 0.020 *M* sugar solution is 0.49 atmospheres, which equates to approximately 16 feet of water. Osmotic pressure (known as root pressure in plants) contributes to the rise of sap in plants.

Answers: (1) Most thin food storage bags are permeable to water and impermeable to starch. Thus a bag containing starch solution will gain water (and weight) when placed in a beaker of tap water. (2) Most food storage bags are permeable to iodine, as indicated by the purple iodine/starch complex inside. By contrast, they are not permeable to starch as indicated by the lack of purple coloration in the water in the beaker. (3) Students should find that celery gains weight after standing in water and loses weight after standing in the salt solution. Water is hypotonic (lower solute concentration, higher water concentration) to the celery, and thus water enters the celery. The salt solution is hypertonic (higher solute concentration, lower water concentration) to the celery, and thus celery loses water (dehydrates). (4) Honey is a very concentrated solution of sugar in water. Consequently, bacteria and fungi landing in honey dehydrate by osmosis and die. (5) Blood cells will enlarge and possibly burst (plasmolyze) when placed in hypotonic (less concentrated) solutions, and will shrink when placed in hypertonic (more concentrated) solutions. (6) The most concentrated solutions rise the highest, indicating that they have the highest osmotic pressure. This is to be expected since osmotic pressure is dependent upon the concentration of dissolved solutes. The higher the concentration of dissolved solutes, the lower the concentration of water and the greater the differential in water concentration between fresh water and the solution, and the greater the osmotic driving force. (7) Bacteria landing on the sugared surface of a candied fruit will dehydrate and die as fluids flow from a region of higher water concentration (the bacteria), to a region of low water concentration (the sugary solution immediately outside). (8) Read section on reverse osmosis in "applications to everyday life."

Applications to Everyday Life

Gram-molecular weight determination: Gram molecular weight is expressed as a ratio of grams per mole. The number of grams of a sample can be determined simply by massing it on a balance. The number of moles can be determined by examining its influence on any of the colligative properties of a solution since such properties are dependent only on the number of particles, and not on their identity. The gram-molecular weight is then determined by dividing the mass of the sample by the number of moles it represents.

Natural antifreeze: Some of the fish and insects that live in cold environments have been shown to contain special blood proteins that act as antifreeze. In some organisms antifreeze proteins (AFPs) may behave colligatively, lowering the freezing points as predicted by the freezing point equation. In other situations AFPs appear to act noncolligatively, lowering the freezing point proportionately more than they raise the osmotic pressure. An understanding of colligative properties has led chemists to surmise that certain AFPs work in a noncolligative manner, perhaps binding to incipient ice crystals, and thereby preventing their growth.

Frost protection: Frost or ice formation can damage sensitive crops, certain foods, preserved organs, and other biological material. Chemists have long known that such material can be kept from freezing by increasing the concentration of dissolved solutes ($\Delta T_{fp} = mK_{fp}$), but the trick has been to find a solute that is safe and does not alter the desired properties of the product. Researchers are currently studying artificial antifreeze proteins (AFPs) similar to those found in cold water fish because they are nontoxic and produce the desired effects. Researchers hope that eventually such proteins could be delivered in a nontoxic spray to save crops, foods and organs or de-ice airplanes and highways!

Cold ocean waters: Ocean temperatures in polar regions are generally about −1.9°C. Such cold temperatures would be impossible if not for the freezing point depression associated with the dissolved solutes.

Disinfectant: Perhaps you have heard people compare a harsh comment to "rubbing salt in a wound." Salt in a wound definitely stings, but it also dehydrates and kills bacteria by the process of osmosis. Tears are relatively salty, and kill pathogens on the eye by osmotic dehydration.

Reverse osmosis and water purification: Osmosis is a statistical phenomenon. It is much more likely for a molecule of water on the fresh side of a semi-permeable membrane to pass through than it is for a water molecule on the solution side to do so, simply because there are more water molecules in contact with the membrane on the pure water side. Since more water molecules flow into the solution, its volume increases. If, however, pressure is applied to the solution side, it will become more probable for the reverse to occur. "Reverse osmosis" reverses the process by forcing molecules back in the other direction. Reverse osmosis is used to purify drinking water.

Dehydration: Minerals are lost when you perspire. For many years people were given salt tablets to replace salts lost through perspiration. Physicians now recommend that such salts be replenished through sports drinks because salt tablets only accelerate dehydration in the intestines through osmosis. Some fish die when they are swept by fast moving rivers into the sea. The osmotic pressure of the ocean is too great, and the fish die of dehydration.

5.5 ACIDS AND BASES

Are you interested in entering politics? Are you planning on going into business? Are you concerned about the environment? If you answered "yes" to any of these questions, then you should study chemistry! Our society depends on the chemical industry for building materials, fuels, pharmaceuticals, agricultural supplies, fabrics and thousands of products in the marketplace. For centuries, wars, business ventures and environmental disasters have revolved around chemical commodities.

One of the most significant environmental issues of our day is "acid rain," a chemical problem with serious implications for business and international relations. Emissions from automobiles, coal and oil burning electric power plants, and certain industrial operations contain significant quantities of sulfur dioxide and nitrogen oxide. These gases combine with water vapor in clouds to form sulfuric and nitric acids. When such acids are present in clouds, the resulting rain is quite acidic and may have pH as low as 2 (7 is neutral on a 0 to 14 scale).

Acid rain causes problems wherever it falls. It damages the foliage of plants by destroying the waxy cuticle of leaves, creating lesions through which fungi and other pathogens may enter. When acidic water percolates through topsoil it kills nitrogen-fixing bacteria that are needed to provide plants with essential nitrogen-based nutrients. Acidic water solubilizes many minerals in the soil, and if rains are frequent, many vital nutrients such as calcium, magnesium and potassium are washed away, leaving infertile soils behind. In addition, acid rain dissolves aluminum, some of which finds its way into lakes and streams where it is highly toxic to fish and other aquatic life.

One of the first locations where the effect of acid rain was clearly seen was in the famous Black Forest of southern Germany. In the early 1970s ecologists began to monitor the slow decline of this beautiful forest. More recently, researchers have linked declining productivity in farm lands and commercial fisheries near major industrial centers to acid rain.

Acid rain becomes an international issue when the air pollution from one nation crosses a border into another, such as occurs along the Canadian/U.S. border in the Great Lakes region. For years, major industrial cities surrounding the lakes have produced emissions that have resulted in acid rain. Farmers and fishermen in southern Canada realized that if pollution from neighboring American cities such as Detroit, Cleveland and Buffalo remained unchecked, their yields of crops and fish would continue to decline. The issue became so serious that a summit was held in which the leaders of the two countries signed an agreement to make strong efforts to reduce emissions in border regions.

Although acid rain is a relatively recent problem, people have known about acids and their counterpart, bases, for a long time. The term "acid" comes from the Latin term *acetum* meaning vinegar, a liquid that has been used for thousands of years as a condiment and preservative. Vinegar is responsible for the sour taste in many foods such as sauerbraten, sourdough bread and vinaigrette dressings. Vinegar (from the French *vinaigre*, meaning "sour wine") is a liquid obtained from the fermentation of alcohol, and in addition to its use in cooking, has been used to change the color of certain dyes (e.g., the litmus dye produced from lichens turns red in vinegar) and as an electrolyte in early batteries.

Long before it was possible to examine the chemical structure of substances, chemists attempted to classify substances according to similar properties. If substances had vinegar-like properties (sour, turned litmus red, and conducted electricity), they were classified as acids.

As our understanding of chemistry expanded, scientists developed theories to explain the nature of acids. The Swedish chemist Svante Arrhenius defined acids as any chemicals that release hydrogen ions (H^+) in solution. In 1923, the Danish chemist J. N. Brønsted offered his own definition, suggesting that acids are substances that donate protons in a chemical reaction. In the same year, the American chemist G. N. Lewis offered yet another definition, stating that acids are electron-pair acceptors. Although these definitions are slightly different, they all attempt to provide a chemical explanation of substances that behave like vinegar.

The counterparts of acids are known as bases. Bases produce a bitter taste *(never use the taste test to identify a substance),* such as is associated with unsweetened baker's chocolate, and generally have a slippery feel *(never use the touch test to identify an unknown substance)* such as soap. Bases change the color of many dyes, but in different ways from acids (e.g., litmus dye turns blue in bases). Bases are electrolytes and produce salts when they react with acids. The traditional chemical definition (Arrhenius) of a base is any substance that releases hydroxide ions (OH^-) in solution, while the Brønsted definition is any substance that acts as a proton acceptor, and the Lewis definition is any substance that serves as an electron-pair donor. These concepts will be explained in greater detail in the activities that follow, as you study the properties of acids and bases and learn about their importance in everyday life, business, politics and the environment.

5.5.1 ACIDS

Concepts to Investigate: Acids, acid properties, acid anhydrides, reactivity, combustion, bone structure, acid rain, rock cycle.

Materials: Part 1: Iron nails, sulfuric acid (or hydrochloric acid), flask, tongs; Part 2: Flask, one-holed stopper, glass tubing, surgical tubing, test tube, mossy zinc, hydrochloric acid; Part 3: Baking soda, vinegar, chalk, marble, sulfuric acid; Part 4: Cooked chicken or turkey leg bone, 1 *M* hydrochloric acid, beaker; Part 5: Child's deciduous tooth (a tooth that has fallen out), colorless soft drink; Part 6: Dry ice, universal indicator, beaker.

Safety: Wear goggles, lab coat and gloves. Only the instructor should dispense strong acids. Neutralize acid spills with baking soda.

Principles and Procedures: For thousands of years people have possessed a rudimentary understanding of what we now call acids and bases. Initially, they realized that foods like pickles, grapefruit, lemons and cranberries all produced the same "sour" sensation, and thus were classified as "acids" because of their similarity to vinegar (*acetum* is the Latin word for vinegar). *Although the "taste test" is a fairly accurate way of identifying acidic foods, it is unsafe and impractical for other substances.*

With time, it was noticed that vinegar and other acids shared other properties in common. In addition to having the same effect on litmus and other indicators (see Activity 5.5.3), they also react with active metals to liberate hydrogen gas, and with carbonates to release carbon dioxide.

Part 1: Reactions with metals: *This should be carried out as a teacher demonstration only. Perform in a fume hood and wear goggles, lab coat and gloves.* Acids contain hydrogen and react with active metals (e.g. Pb, Sn, Ni, Co, Cd, Fe, Cr, Zn, Mn, Al, Mg, Na, Ca, Sr, Ba, K, Rb, and Li) to liberate hydrogen. The stronger and more concentrated the acid, the more rapid the reaction. In the fume hood, submerge a few iron nails in a container of 6 *M* sulfuric acid. Is there any evidence of hydrogen formation? After allowing the container to stand overnight, remove the nails with tongs and then wash with water in the sink. Is there any evidence that sulfuric acid reacted with the iron in the nails? Do you think that there is any long term effect of acid rain upon iron structures?

Part 2: Hydrogen production: Acids react with active metals to produce hydrogen gas. Using a gas collection apparatus as illustrated in Figure A, hydrogen gas can be collected and tested. Submerge test tubes in water and allow the air to escape so that all air is removed. Upright one test tube as shown (base up, mouth down), making certain not to break the surface of the water so no air may enter. Place 5 grams of zinc in the flask and stopper it with the assembly as shown in Figure A. Wrap the flask with a towel for safety, and then add 30 mL of 2 *M* sulfuric acid (or hydrochloric acid) through the funnel. Sulfuric acid will react with the zinc to produce hydrogen gas:

$$H_2SO_4 + Zn \rightarrow Zn^{+2}(aq) + SO_4^{2-}(aq) + H_2(g)$$

Air and hydrogen gas escape from the flask and can be collected in the test tube as the water is displaced. As each tube fills, stopper it, remove it, and place another one in its place. The presence of hydrogen can be tested by holding the tube upside down, removing the stopper,

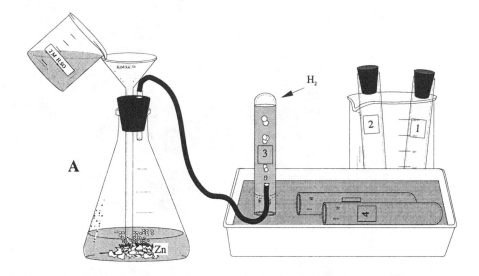

and placing a glowing splint near the mouth. A small explosion ("bark") indicates that the container is filled with oxygen and hydrogen. If the tube is completely filled with hydrogen, it will only burn at the mouth of the tube where oxygen is present:

$$2H_2 + O_2 \rightarrow 2H_2O$$

Which batch contains the purest hydrogen?

Part 3: Reaction with carbonates: Acids react with carbonates to release carbon dioxide. Place approximately 30 grams of sodium hydrogen carbonate (baking soda) in the bottom of a one liter beaker or similar container. Slowly add vinegar (a dilute solution of acetic acid) until most of the bubbling is complete. If carbon dioxide is produced, it will remain primarily in the beaker because it is denser than air. You can test for carbon dioxide by examining the influence of the invisible gas on a flame. Secure a candle stub in an upright position to small can lid using melted paraffin as shown in Figure B. Lower the candle into a beaker, and then light it. Mix vinegar and baking soda as mentioned before, and when the bubbling has stopped, slowly pour the invisible gas over the beaker with the candle. If sufficient carbon dioxide is present, it will fill up the beaker (it is denser than air) and extinguish the flame. Is carbon dioxide produced?

Marble is metamorphic rock that has been used for thousands of years as a building material and as the raw material for sculptors. Such buildings as the Parthenon in Athens, the Coliseum in Rome and the Capitol Building in Washington D.C. are made primarily of marble. Marble is composed mainly of calcium carbonate (calcite) and is similar in nature to chalk and limestone. Since acids react with carbonates, acid rain slowly erodes marble and limestone structures and statues. Historical and cultural preservation societies are very concerned about the problem of acid rain, particularly in regions in central Europe where there are many historic structures, and where pollution is also great. To visualize the effect of acid rain on marble, place a piece of chalk (a less dense version of calcium carbonate) in a container of vinegar or other acid and watch. Is there evidence of carbon dioxide production?

One of the main components of shells and bones is calcium carbonate. When sea creatures die, their skeletons sink to the bottom of the ocean where they collect. With time and pressure, calcium carbonate-based sedimentary rocks form. With continued pressure and

time, limestone forms. Chalk is a fine-grained limestone made from the shells of tiny marine creatures known as *foraminifera, coccoliths,* and *rhabdoliths.* Large-grained limestone generally contains the skeletons and shells of larger creatures. If limestone is exposed to great pressures over a long period of time, it eventually is transformed into marble. Geologists often test for the presence of carbonates by observing the reaction of specimens with acids. Bubbling indicates the presence of carbonates. Use this test to determine if bones, shells, chalk, limestone, and marble may have a similar chemistry. Using a *pipet,* deliver a couple of drops of 6 M sulfuric or hydrochloric acid to samples of each (Figure C). Do they all bubble? Do they all appear to contain carbonates?

Part 4: Solubility in acids ("rubberized" bones and disappearing teeth): Ionic compounds in which component ions are multiply charged generally do not dissolve in water because the intra-crystalline attraction between the multiply charged ions is greater than the forces of hydration. Calcium phosphate ($Ca_3(PO_4)_2$) is insoluble in water, but becomes more soluble in acidic solutions. As the phosphate ion (PO_4^{3-}) combines with the protons (H^+) released by the acid, the net charge on the anion decreases (HPO_4^{2-}, $H_2PO_4^-$) and it becomes more soluble. The two major inorganic components of bone are calcium carbonate, $CaCO_3$, and calcium phosphate, $Ca_3(PO_4)_2$, both of which make the bone rigid and give it strength. The major organic component is a protein known as collagen, that gives bones their flexibility. Calcium carbonate is obviously insoluble in water, otherwise your bones would dissolve because your body is made up primarily of water. What if bones are placed in acid, however? Will the acids dissolve mineral salts ($Ca_3(PO_4)_2$, $CaCO_3$)? Will acids dissolve the organic components?

Obtain a cooked chicken or turkey leg bone or other long slender bone. Place the bone in 1 M hydrochloric acid overnight (Figure D). Using tongs, remove the bone and wash it under a stream of water in the sink. Does the bone look the same? Does it have the same properties? Try bending the bone. If it breaks under stress, it indicates that the flexible proteins have been removed, but if it merely bends, then it indicates that the rigid calcium phosphate and calcium carbonate minerals have been removed. Does the acid seem to increase the solubility of the mineral components or the protein components?

Part 5: Soft drinks and disappearing teeth: Soft drinks contain carbonic and phosphoric acids. What effect do these acids have upon the inorganic compounds (primarily calcium carbonate and calcium phosphate) of which your teeth are composed? Place a deciduous tooth (a "baby tooth" that has fallen out) in colorless soft drink and allow it to stand overnight (Figure E). Does the acid erode the tooth? Is it possible to make the entire tooth disappear by placing it in new soft drink each day? Try it!

Part 6: Preparation of acids from nonmetallic oxides: *Caution: Always use gloves when handling dry ice.*

The label on the side of a soft drink container says that it contains carbonic acid. The news magazine reports that rain around major industrial centers is unusually acidic with sulfurous and sulfuric acid. From where do these acids come?

In general, oxides of the highly electronegative elements react with water to form solutions that are acidic. Such substances are known as acid anhydrides because they are "acids" without water, or better stated, they become acids when they react with water. Sulfur dioxide is an acid anhydride because it combines with water to form sulfurous acid:

$$H_2O + SO_2 \rightarrow H_2SO_3$$

To study this reaction further refer to the activities dealing with acid rain (Section 5.5.5).

Carbon dioxide is an acid anhydride because it combines with water to form carbonic acid:

$$CO_2 + H_2O \rightarrow H_2CO_3$$

$$H_2CO_3 \rightarrow H^+ + HCO_3^-$$

In this activity you will observe the gradual acidification of a solution as the carbon dioxide (an acid anhydride) reacts with water to produce carbonic acid.

Fill a beaker half-full with water and add a couple of drops of universal indicator. Add 0.1 *M* sodium hydroxide solution until the solution turns a deep violet color (pH 9). Slowly add crushed dry ice to the beaker and observe. Universal indicator displays the following colors depending on the pH: violet (pH 9), blue (pH 8), green (pH 7), yellow (pH 6), pale orange (pH 5), orange (pH 4). How acidic can you make the solution by adding carbon dioxide?

Questions

(1) Explain why art and historic building preservationists are quite concerned about acid rain.

(2) Why does the first tube of hydrogen produced in part 2 "bark" while the last ones simply burn?

(3) Write an equation to show how calcium carbonate reacts with sulfuric acid.

(4) Your stomach contains hydrochloric acid. How might this aid the digestive process?

(5) Why might dentists recommend against eating lemons regularly?

(6) How acidic does the carbon dioxide make the solution in part 6?

5.5.2 BASES

Concepts to Investigate: Bases, base anhydride.

Materials: <u>Part 1</u>: Sodium, potassium, calcium, phenolphthalein; <u>Part 2</u>: Calcium oxide, magnesium oxide, Hydrion paper or pH meter, thermometer, phenolphthalein.

Safety: Wear goggles, lab coat and gloves. Part 1 should be performed as a teacher demonstration. Metallic sodium is a flammable, corrosive solid that reacts violently with water and oxidizers, and is spontaneously flammable when heated in air.

Principles and Procedures: Bases are proton acceptors (Bronsted definition), the most common of which is the hydroxide ion (OH^-) which accepts protons (H^+) to form water:

$$OH^- + H^+ \rightarrow H_2O$$

Soluble metal hydroxide solutions (e.g. NaOH, $Ca(OH)_2$, KOH) form the most common basic solutions.

Part 1: The preparation of bases from active metals: *This should be performed as a teacher demonstration only.* Federal law requires that chemical manufacturers include a material safety data sheet (MSDS) with each product they ship. When you receive a chemical shipment, it is important to read the MSDS to know what the safety hazards are. One of the many warnings on the MSDS for metallic sodium, potassium or calcium may read: "Danger: Keep away from water!" Normally we think of water as a relatively harmless substance, so why would such warnings exist?

Fill a beaker one-quarter full of water and add a couple of drops of phenolphthalein (pink color indicates a basic solution). Using a knife or chemical spatula, cut a portion of metallic sodium approximately one quarter the size of a pea, place in the beaker and immediately cover it with a small glass plate (Figure F). This reaction is extremely exothermic and may ignite the hydrogen with a resulting flame or small "bark."

$$2Na(s) + 2H_2O(l) \rightarrow 2NaOH(aq) + H_2(g) + heat$$

Is the resulting solution acidic, basic, or neutral?

Repeat the procedure in clean glassware using a similar size chunk of potassium. Repeat again with fresh calcium turnings.

$$2K(s) + 2H_2O(l) \rightarrow 2KOH(aq) + H_2(g)$$

$$Ca(s) + H_2O(l) \rightarrow Ca(OH)_2(aq) + H_2(g)$$

Part 2: Preparation of bases from metal oxides: Camellias and azaleas are acid-loving flowering shrubs. They are frequently planted around the foundations of homes, but many times die if there is plaster or stucco dust in the soil left over from construction. One of the main ingredients in plaster and stucco is calcium oxide (CaO, lime). What effect does lime have on the soil and the plants growing in it?

Test the pH of dry calcium oxide with Hydrion paper or a pH meter. Test the pH of tap water in the same way. Do they appear to be acidic, neutral or basic? Fill a large test tube

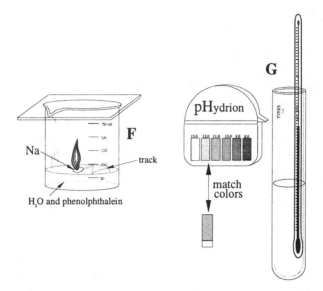

with 5 mL of water and measure the temperature. Add approximately 1 gram of fresh calcium oxide to the test tube containing 5 mL of water, shake for 2 minutes, re-read the temperature, and re-measure the pH (Figure G). Is the hydration of calcium oxide an exothermic or endothermic reaction?

$$CaO(s) + H_2O(l) \rightarrow Ca(OH)_2(aq)$$

Add a drop of phenolphthalein to a tube of fresh water and a tube containing the dissolved calcium oxide. What effect does the calcium oxide have upon the pH of the solution? What impact might this have on the growth of acid-loving plants? Do other metal oxides have a similar effect? Repeat the investigation using magnesium oxide.

Questions

(1) In part 1, bases were made by mixing reactive metals (potassium, sodium, calcium) with water. Explain why these metals are known as base anhydrides.

(2) What effect do metal oxides have upon the pH of a solution?

(3) Write an equation showing the reaction that occurs when magnesium oxide is dissolved in water.

(4) Most textbooks describe bases as substances that "feel slippery" and "taste bitter." Unfortunately, touching or tasting chemicals is a dangerous method of making such determinations. Perhaps, however, you have touched, tasted or smelled the following household substances in the past. If so, try to think back on your experiences and make an educated guess about which are basic: carbonated soft drink, vinegar, ammonia, dishwashing detergent, shampoo, laundry detergent, baking soda, and lemon juice.

5.5.3 pH SCALE

Concepts to Investigate: pH scale, acids, bases, indicators.

Materials: Part 1: Head of red cabbage, transparent plastic cups or glass 250 mL beakers, hot plate, knife and cutting board, large beaker or similar container; items listed in Table 1. You may also wish to test other colorless household solutions such as aspirin, shampoo, dish soap, sugar, milk, bleach, Epsom salts, colorless soft drinks, Alka-Seltzer®, and pickle juice; Part 2: Red cabbage, beaker, filter paper, materials in part 1; Part 3: Grape juice, beets or red onion; materials in part 1.

Safety: This activity uses household chemicals such as drain cleaner and pool acid that are potentially dangerous. Read manufacturer's warnings. Wear goggles, lab coat and gloves.

Principles and Procedures: Each year millions of tourists travel to the woods of New England, upstate New York, Wisconsin, and Canada to witness the appearance of brilliant autumn colors. Sugar maples, red oaks, sumac, birch and other trees and shrubs turn from green to bright red, orange, and yellow. The short, cool days of autumn bring an end to the production of chlorophyll (the green light-gathering pigment). As chlorophyll gradually breaks down, the colors of the more stable carotenoid (yellow/orange) and anthocyanin (red/blue/purple) pigments become visible. Some years the leaves of a particular species are bright yellow, while other years they may appear redder or even purple. Although no one can accurately predict the timing or coloration of each year's show, we do know that there is a chemical basis for it.

Anthocyanins (Figure H) are responsible not only for the red and purplish colors of autumn, but also for similar colors in various summer leaves (red cabbage, red lettuce, red plum tree), flowers (roses, hydrangeas, geraniums, bachelor buttons, dark pansies), fruit (cherries, red apples, grapes, tomato, blackberry, blueberry, plum), roots (beets, radishes), bulbs (red

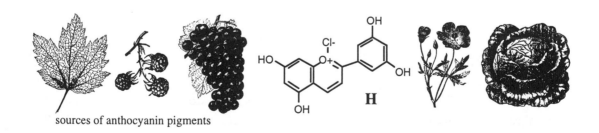

sources of anthocyanin pigments

H

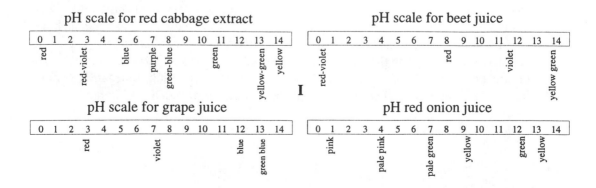

I

onions), and petioles (rhubarb). Anthocyanins are water-soluble and are dissolved in the cell sap rather than bound to the membranes as chlorophyll is. If cell sap in a leaf is quite acidic the anthocyanins impart a bright red color, but if it is less acidic the color may appear purple.

The color of anthocyanin depends on acidity, and thus it may serve as a pH (acid/base) indicator (Figure I). pH is a quantitative measure of the acidity or basicity of solutions. Numerically, the pH of a solution is defined as the negative logarithm (base 10) of the hydronium ion (H_3O^+) concentration. If the pH is less than 7 the solution is acidic, if it is greater than 7 the solution is basic, and if it is 7 the solution is neutral. The higher the pH, the more basic the solution, and the lower the pH, the more acidic the solution. Figure I illustrates the relationship between color and pH for anthocyanin pigments extracted from red cabbage or other sources. In this activity you will determine the pH of numerous household products using this pH scale.

Part 1: Testing the pH of household chemicals using red cabbage juice: *Put on safety goggles and lab coat.* Fill beakers with common household chemicals to be tested according to the specifications in Table 1. Dissolve all solids by stirring until the solution is relatively colorless. Using a knife and cutting board, carefully dice a quarter head of red cabbage and boil for ten minutes in a pan or beaker containing 1000 mL of water (Figure J). Allow the mixture to cool and then pour the contents through a strainer or filter paper and collect in a beaker. The red cabbage extract appears dark purple, the color of anthocyanin at pH 7. Test each of the household chemicals by placing 20 mL of the anthocyanin indicator solution in each beaker (Figure K). Record the color and estimate the pH according to the scale listed in Figure I. Which appears to be the most acidic? Which is the most basic? Do any of the chemicals appear to produce neutral solutions?

Part 2: Making pH paper: You may have noticed that the pH of a solution is often tested with litmus paper, Hydrion paper or other similar pH sensitive paper. To prepare your own anthocyanin pH test paper, soak filter paper in a very concentrated solution of cabbage juice. Remove the paper from the beaker and hang on a clothesline or string to dry. Once dry, cut the paper into strips and test the pH of the solutions listed in Table 1.

Part 3: Other indicators: Anthocyanins may be extracted from virtually any plant that has purple or red coloration. The composition of these extracts differs from the red cabbage extract, so the pH color response may also be expected to vary. Use grape juice or prepare an

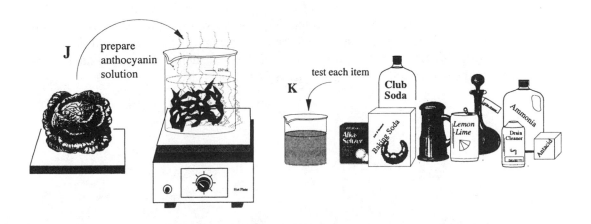

Table 1: pH Scale

	Active Ingredient	*Preparation*	*Color*	*pH (est.)*
antacid (Tums®)	$CaCO_3$	10 g in 100 mL H_2O		
baking soda	$NaHCO_3$	10 g in 100 mL H_2O		
household ammonia	NH_4OH	100 mL		
lemon juice	$C_6H_8O_7$	100 mL		
lye, (Draino® liq. drain cleaner)	$NaOH$	100 mL		
Milk of Magnesia	$Mg(OH)_2$	10 g in 100 mL H_2O		
pool acid (Muriatic acid)	HCl	100 mL		
seltzer water (club soda)	H_2CO_3	100 mL		
table salt	$NaCl$	10 g in 100 mL H_2O		
white vinegar	CH_3COOH	100 mL		

extract from beets or red onions as before. Compare the pH color response to that of the red cabbage extract. Do your anthocyanin extracts produce similar color responses to the cabbage extract?

Questions

(1) Some of the autumn leaves on a tree are bright red, while others are purplish. Which leaves are probably more acidic (lower pH)?

(2) Red cabbage is an ingredient in certain ethnic foods like the German dish sauerbraten. Experienced chefs can tell how sour (acidic) the food is by the color of the cabbage. Explain.

(3) Which of the household chemicals tested have warning labels on them? Where are these chemicals located on the pH scale? Explain.

(4) Which of the substances tested appear to be neutral?

(5) What are the similarities and differences in the pH scales of the various items tested?

(6) On the basis of the comparisons made in part 3, which of the indicators tested in this series of activities produces the most useful (greatest range) color/pH scale?

(7) Oils dissolve best under basic conditions. As a result, many detergents, soaps, cleansers, and shampoos are basic. Unfortunately, bases break the disulfide bonds that hold the polymer chains in hair together. With excessive use of basic shampoos, hair tends to get dull and fracture in a phenomenon commonly known as "split ends." To remedy this situation, shampoo manufacturers also sell shampoo rinses. What do you predict is the chemical nature of such rinses? Explain.

5.5.4 ACID/BASE CONCENTRATION, EQUIVALENCE AND STRENGTH

Concepts to Investigate: Acid concentration, base concentration, acid equivalence, base equivalence, acid strength, base strength, titration, indicators, titration, end point, neutralization.

Materials: 0.1 *M* acetic acid, 0.1 *M* hydrochloric acid, 0.1 *M* sulfuric acid, burets, flasks, phenolphthalein.

Safety: Wear goggles and lab coat.

Principles and Procedures: Although it is one of the strongest acids known, we chlorinate swimming pools with hydrochloric acid (sold as muriatic acid or pool acid) and go swimming later the same day! Acetic acid, however, is a weak acid, and yet the *Merck Manual* warns that ingestion may cause "severe corrosion of mouth and G.I. tract, with vomiting, hematemesis, diarrhea, circulatory collapse, uremia [and/or] death!" How can we swim in a pool containing a strong acid, and yet be killed by ingesting a weak acid?

When discussing acids and bases, it is important to differentiate the following terms: "concentration," "strength," and "equivalence." The concentration is measured in molarity, or the number of moles of acid or base that are dissolved in a liter of solution. Appendix 4.3 shows how to make acid and base solutions with common molarities. A one molar (1 *M*) solution of HCl is made by dissolving a mole of HCl (36.5 g) in a liter of solution.

The equivalence of an acid or base refers to how much titrant (base or acid) is required to neutralize it. The equivalence of an acid depends upon the concentration of the acid, and upon the number of acidic hydrogens it contains. Thus, a 1 *M* solution of phosphoric acid (H_3PO_4) will have three times the equivalence of a 1 *M* solution of hydrofluoric acid (HF) because it has three times as many acidic hydrogens. Thus, a 1 *M* solution of phosphoric acid is 3 *N* (3 normal; 3 equivalents/liter).

The strength of an acid is measured by pH (see section 5.5.3) and depends on the concentration and equivalence of a solution, as well as on the degree of ionization of a particular acid or base.

In this activity you will compare the equivalence and strength of 3 acids that have the same concentration (molarity). Your instructor will prepare 0.1 *M* solutions of acetic, hydrochloric, and sulfuric acids as per the instructions in appendix 4.3. Test the strength of each of the acids using a pH meter or Hydrion paper.

Add 50 mL of 0.1 *M* acetic acid to a flask, and then add a couple of drops of phenolphthalein indicator solution. Repeat the

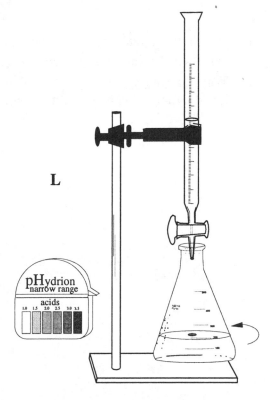

L

Table 2: Acid/Base Concentration, Strength and Equivalence

	Concentration (molarity)	*Strength (pH)*	*Equivalence (mL of titrant)*
acetic acid 50.0 mL $HC_2H_3O_2$	0.1 *M*		
hydrochloric acid 50.0 mL HCl	0.1 *M*		
sulfuric acid 50.0 mL H_2SO_4	0.1 *M*		

procedure with 0.1 *M* solutions of hydrochloric acid and sulfuric acid. Fill a buret with 0.1 *M* NaOH and position in a ring stand as shown in Figure L. Open the stopcock of the buret and while stirring the solution in the beaker, slowly release sodium hydroxide solution until traces of pink color appear (phenolphthalein is colorless under acidic conditions, but pink under basic conditions). Decrease the rate of addition as the pink color persists longer. Add drop by drop until a slight pink color remains even after stirring. The point at which this occurs is known as the end point. At the end point the acid in the beaker has been neutralized by the base added. The equivalence of the acid can be expressed through the mL of 0.1 *M* NaOH needed to reach the end point. All of the acids had the same concentration, but do they all have the same strength and equivalence? Record your findings in Table 2.

Questions

(1) Which of the acids ionizes the least in water? How can you tell?
(2) Which acid is (are) the strongest? Explain.
(3) Why can we swim in a pool containing a strong acid (hydrochloric acid), and yet be killed by ingesting a weak acid (acetic acid)?

5.5.5 ACID RAIN

Concepts to Investigate: Acid anhydrides, acid rain, air pollution.

Materials: Part 1: Sulfur, deflagrating spoon or substitute, Erlenmeyer flask or similar container, universal indicator, wide range pH paper (or pH meter), matches; Part 2: Potassium nitrite or sodium nitrite, sulfuric acid, bromthymol blue indicator (bromocresol green or methyl red may be substituted), plastic pipets, Petri dishes; Part 3: Hydrochloric acid (0.001 M HCl), bromocresol green, granite chips (gravel), marble (calcium carbonate) chips, beakers.

Safety: Wear goggles, lab coat and gloves. Parts 1 and 2 should be performed only by the instructor and only in a fume hood or outdoors.

Principles and Procedures: Acid rain results when either sulfur dioxide (SO_2) or nitrogen oxides (NO_x) dissolve in water. Both of theses gases are considered to be acid anhydrides because the solution becomes acidic when they dissolve. Coal and oil-burning power plants generate approximately two-thirds of the sulfur dioxide pollution, while vehicles with internal combustion engines (e.g., automobiles) generate approximately two-thirds of the nitrogen oxide pollution.

Part 1: Acid rain from sulfur dioxide: *This is an instructor demonstration and should be performed in a fume hood or outside.*

Sulfur is one of the elements commonly found in coal. When coal is burned to generate electricity or to warm a building, the sulfur is oxidized and becomes sulfur dioxide, a gas with a strong suffocating odor:

$$S_8(s) + 8O_2(g) \rightarrow 8SO_2(g)$$

As sulfur dioxide dissolves in water vapor in clouds, sulfurous acid forms:

$$SO_2(g) + H_2O(l) \rightarrow H_2SO_3(aq)$$

Some sulfurous acid reacts with oxygen in the atmosphere to form sulfuric acid:

$$2H_2SO_3(aq) + O_2(g) \rightarrow 2H_2SO_4(aq)$$

Sulfuric and sulfurous acid are highly soluble in water and fall to the earth in rain or snow.

You may illustrate the formation of acid rain by performing the following experiment. Place a couple drops of universal indicator in the bottom of an Erlenmeyer flask and note the color. Measure the pH of the water using a pH probe, universal indicator or wide range Hydrion pH paper. Working in the fume hood, ignite a clump of sulfur the size of a pea in a deflagrating spoon. The sulfur will burn with a deep blue flame. Place the deflagrating spoon in the flask and cover the top with a glass plate as shown (Figure M). Sulfur dioxide fumes will fill the flask and eventually the sulfur will burn out either when the sulfur is consumed or when the oxygen in the flask is exhausted. Seal the flask and swirl and shake it so the water hits all of the upper walls (Figure N). Does the liquid in the flask change color? If so, what does it indicate? Measure the pH once again using a pH meter or Hydrion paper. What effect did the sulfur dioxide have upon the pH of the water in the flask?

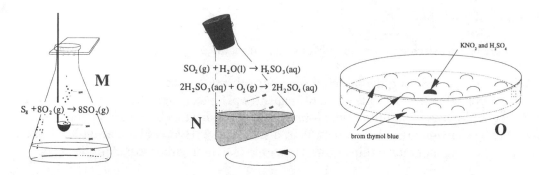

$$S_8 + 8O_2(g) \rightarrow 8SO_2(g)$$

$$SO_2(g) + H_2O(l) \rightarrow H_2SO_3(aq)$$

$$2H_2SO_3(aq) + O_2(g) \rightarrow 2H_2SO_4(aq)$$

KNO$_2$ and H$_2$SO$_4$

brom thymol blue

Part 2: Acid rain from nitrogen oxides: *This is an instructor demonstration and should be performed in a fume hood or outdoors.*

Internal combustion engines develop extremely high pressures and temperatures in which atmospheric nitrogen and oxygen combine to form a variety of nitrogen oxides. In this experiment you will investigate the effect that nitrogen dioxide has on the pH of lakes, ponds and rivers surrounding large metropolitan areas.

Place a drop of approximately 1 *M* potassium nitrite (KNO$_2$) or sodium nitrite (NaNO$_2$) in the middle of a Petri dish. Place small droplets of bromthymol blue indicator in two or three concentric bands around the center as illustrated in Figure O. Place the Petri dish in a fume hood and moisten the potassium nitrite with approximately 2 *M* (4 *N*) sulfuric acid (H$_2$SO$_4$). Immediately replace the cover. Nitrogen dioxide, released as potassium or sodium nitrite, reacts with sulfuric acid. What is the color of the nitrogen dioxide?

As the nitrogen dioxide dissolves in the water droplets, nitric (HNO$_3$) and nitrous acid (HNO$_2$) are formed:

$$2NO_2(g) + H_2O(l) \rightarrow HNO_3(aq) + HNO_2(aq)$$

Bromthymol is blue at or above pH 7.5, and yellow at or below pH 6.0. Between 7.5 and 6.0 bromthymol blue displays intermediate colors. Which drops of bromthymol blue turn color first? Which turn last?

Part 3: Acid rain and lakes: Acid rain can lower the pH of lakes and ponds and dramatically affect the aquatic food web. Surprisingly, however, some lakes seem to show little if any change in pH even though they have been exposed to acid rain for many years. Ecologists have suggested that the differing response of lakes or ponds to acid rain is due, in part, to the geological composition of the lake bed. Some of the lakebeds are composed of granite (or silicate clays made from decomposed granite), while others are made of limestone (or carbonate sands and clays made from decomposed limestone). Which type of lake bed is more effective in neutralizing the effect of acid rain?

Wash granite chips (fine gravel) completely with tap water until no signs of dirt, clay or organic material remain, then rinse twice with distilled water. Repeat with marble (calcium carbonate) chips. Prepare a liter of 0.001 *M* hydrochloric acid solution, and add a couple of drops of bromocresol green indicator solution. The solution should appear yellow. If it does not, add 0.1 *M* hydrochloric acid drop by drop until the solution turns yellow.

Place 100 grams of granite chips in one beaker and 100 grams of marble chips in another. Add the 0.001 *M* hydrochloric acid solution to cover the rocks in both beakers to an equal depth. Swirl the containers and then let the containers stand undisturbed. If the acid is neutralized, the solution will turn green, otherwise it will remain yellow. Does one type of rock have more acid neutralizing capacity than the other?

Questions

(1) What was the effect of the sulfur dioxide gas on the pH of the "rain water" in part 1? Explain.

(2) A large generator in a coal-burning electric power plant can burn 650 tons of coal per hour. If coal is 2% sulfur and all of the sulfur is oxidized, how many tons of sulfur dioxide will be released per hour in the combustion process?

(3) In Part 2 the small droplets of bromthymol blue may represent ponds or lakes surrounding a major city. Which "ponds" are affected first by acid rain? Explain.

(4) Which type of lake bed (granitic or limestone) is more effective in moderating the effect of acid rain? Explain.

FOR THE TEACHER

5.5.1 ACIDS

Discussion: Part 1: If the production of hydrogen is too slow, add a couple of drops of copper (II) sulfate solution as a catalyst. Sulfuric acid reacts with iron to produce hydrogen:

$$H_2SO_4 + Fe \rightarrow Fe^{2+} + SO_4^{2-} + H_2$$

The sulfuric acid etches the surface of the iron nails. Acid rain is obviously very dilute compared with concentrated sulfuric acid, but it produces the same results over a long period of time. You may wish to show that other reactive metals such as zinc, magnesium and aluminum behave in a similar manner when placed in acid. Part 2: The first test tubes collected will contain a mixture of hydrogen and air (nitrogen, oxygen, etc.). Because hydrogen and oxygen are both present, a small bang will occur when ignited by a glowing splint. With time, the hydrogen will displace the remaining air and the tubes will contain only hydrogen and will burn only at the surface of the tube where hydrogen can mix with atmospheric oxygen. Part 3: Students should notice the formation of bubbles on the surface of the chalk as the acid reacts with the calcium carbonate in the chalk to release carbon dioxide:

$$CaCO_3(s) + H_2SO_4(l) \rightarrow Ca^{2+}(aq) + SO_4^{2-}(aq) + H_2O(l) + CO_2(g)$$

Parts 4 and 5: Students are amazed to see the flexible bones produced in this activity. The bones can be saved by placing them in a plastic bag and keeping them in the freezer. Allow the bones to thaw for about 60 minutes before using them in another class. Calcium carbonate is in equilibrium with its ions:

$$CaCO_3(s) \rightleftharpoons Ca^{2+}(aq) + CO_3^{2-}$$

When acidified, free protons (H^+) react with carbonate ions to form carbonic acid, which decomposes to water and carbon dioxide:

$$2H^+(aq) + CO_3^{2-} \rightarrow H_2CO_3(aq) \rightarrow H_2O + CO_2$$

The more acid added, the more carbonate ions are removed from solution. According to LeChâtelier's Principle, more calcium carbonate must be dissolved. This illustrates how acids solubilize carbonates.

Answers: (1) Acid rain slowly erodes many metals (like the iron used in many historic structures) and carbonates (like the marble and limestone used in many statues and buildings). (2) When hydrogen is produced it mixes with the air in the reaction flask, and so the first tube contains a well carbureted mixture of hydrogen and oxygen that "barks." With time, the hydrogen produced displaces all the air so the final tube is composed of pure hydrogen which can only burn at the entrance to the tube where it mixes with oxygen. (3) $CaCO_3(s) + H_2SO_4(l) \rightarrow Ca^{2+}(aq) + SO_4^{2-}(aq) + H_2O(l) + CO_2(g)$. (4) Part 4 shows that hydrochloric acid increases the solubility of ionic compounds. Hydrochloric acid (stomach acid) also denatures proteins so they are more readily attacked by pepsin. (5) Lemons are very sour, which indicates they are acidic. Acids react with the calcium carbonate in teeth, and may accelerate the formation of dental caries (cavities). (6) The pH may drop to 5 or 4 with the addition of carbon dioxide.

5.5.2 BASES

Discussion: *Part 1 is a potentially dangerous demonstration that should be carried out with great care. Do not use more sodium than suggested.* Make certain students stand back and that the container is covered with a watch glass to minimize splattering. Make a transparency photocopy of an actual material safety data sheet (MSDS) for sodium or a similar substance so students become aware of the hazards and regulations surrounding chemical products.

Quicklime (CaO) reacts with water to form slaked lime ($Ca(OH)_2$). You may wish to have students measure the temperature increase that accompanies the slaking process. The heats of reaction for the slaking process are as follows:

$$CaO(s) + H_2O(l) \rightarrow Ca(OH)_2 \text{ (s)} + 65 \text{ kJ/mole}$$

$$CaO(s) + H_2O(l) \rightarrow Ca(OH)_2 \text{ (aq)} + 82 \text{ kJ/mole}$$

It is important that students be able to relate chemistry to everyday life. Oils and fats are insoluble in water, but are soluble in bases. Household cleaning supplies such as ammonia, dishwashing detergent, shampoo, laundry detergent, and baking soda are good examples of bases with which students will be familiar.

Answers: (1) Anhydride means "without water." A base anhydride forms a base when added to water. (2) Metal oxides react with water to produce bases that increase the pH of the solution. (3) $MgO(s) + H_2O(l) \rightarrow Mg(OH)_2(s)$. (4) Ammonia, laundry detergent, and baking soda are basic. Dishwashing detergent and shampoo are often basic, but may be neutral ("pH balanced").

5.5.3 pH SCALE

Discussion: The higher the concentration of hydronium ions (H_3O^+; H^+ exists as H_3O^+ in aqueous solutions), the more acidic the solution. The lower the concentration of hydronium ions, the more basic the solution. In extremely acidic solutions the concentration of hydronium ions can exceed 10 *M,* and in extremely basic solutions, the concentration may be less than 10^{-15} *M.* In normal laboratory conditions, however, the range of hydronium ion concentration generally falls between 1 *M* (10^0 *M*) and 10^{-14} *M.* In an effort to simplify notation, chemists report acidity as the negative logarithm of the hydronium ion concentration.

$$pH = -\log[H_3O^+]$$

The term "pH" comes from the French *pouvoir hydrogène* meaning "hydrogen power." If, for example, the hydronium ion concentration of a solution is 10^{-13} *M,* then the pH would be determined as follows:

$$pH = -\log[H_3O^+] = -\log(10^{-13}) = -(-13) = 13$$

Similarly, the pH of a solution with a hydronium ion concentration of 10^{-4} *M* has a pH of 4, while a solution with a hydronium ion concentration of 10^{-1} *M* has a pH of 1.

Hydronium ions react with hydroxide ions in solution to produce water.

$$H_3O^+ + OH^- \rightarrow 2H_2O$$

The hydroxide ion concentration can be reduced by increasing the hydronium ion concentration. The more hydronium ions in solution, the more common the above reaction. A solution may be made more basic by adding more hydroxide. The hydroxide reacts with the hydronium and removes it from solution, reducing its concentration and raising the pH of the solution. A solution in which the concentration of hydronium ions exceeds the concentration of hydroxide ions is known as an acidic solution, while a solution in which the concentration of hydroxide ions exceed the concentration of hydronium ions is known as a basic solution. A solution is neutral (neither acidic nor basic) when the hydronium ion concentration equals the hydroxide ion concentration. This occurs at pH 7 where the hydronium ion concentration is 10^{-7} *M* and the hydroxide ion concentration is 10^{-7} *M*.

The structure and color of certain molecules such as anthocyanin change with pH. Such molecules may be used as pH indicators. A discussion of indicator chemistry may be used to introduce the common ion effect or LeChâtelier's Principle. Most indicators are weak acids (H*In*) that dissociate slightly to release a proton, H$^+$, and an indicator anion, *In*$^-$.

$$HIn \quad \rightleftharpoons \quad In^- + H^+$$

LeChâtelier's Principle indicates that the above reaction will tend to go from left to right in a basic solution as free protons are consumed by the following reaction:

$$OH^- + H^+ \rightarrow H_2O$$

In reality, "free" protons (H$^+$) are actually bound to water as hydronium ions (H$_3$O$^+$), so we can represent this process more accurately as:

$$H_3O^+ + OH^- \rightarrow 2H_2O$$

Thus, in a basic solution an indicator like anthocyanin will become more highly ionized. In acidic solutions more protons are present and the ionization of the indicator moves in the reverse direction so that less is ionized. When the environment is highly acidic more hydrogen ions are available to bind to anthocyanin molecules than when the environment is basic. All indicators work on the same principle: One form of the indicator differs from another which causes the indicator to absorb light of different wavelengths.

Phenolphthalein (a common indicator) is colorless, while the phenolphthalein anion is red. The addition of a base (OH$^-$) causes more phenolphthalein to dissociate, and thus the solution turns pink. The addition of protons (H$^+$) has just the reverse effect.

Table 3 shows the approximate pH of a number of common household items. You may wish to have your students test some of these substances using the pH paper they made in part 2. Don't be surprised if the results are not very accurate—there are many variables in this activity, not the least of which is that the extracts contain a variety of chemicals in addition to the anthocyanin pigment, and these may confound the results.

Table 3: pH of Common Substances

pH	Substance with This pH
0	hydrochloric acid
1	gastric juices (stomach acids)
2	lemons, vinegar
3	apples, oranges, carbonated soft drinks
4	tomatoes
5	potatoes
6	milk, most bland vegetables
7	pure water, blood, saliva
8	baking soda, eggs
9	
10	Milk of Magnesia
11	ammonia
12	soda ash (sodium carbonate, used to raise swimming pool pH
13	
14	caustic soda (lye, sodium hydroxide based drain cleaner)

In this activity we introduced anthocyanins, a class of flavenoid pigments whose color is pH-dependent. It should be noted that the pH measured with this technique is the pH of the final solution and does not take into account any dilution of the various substances tested.

You may notice that the anthocyanin solutions are relatively cloudy. If you wish to have a clearer indicator, you may prepare an extract using ethanol or isopropyl alcohol. First shred

Table 4: pH and Anthocyanin Colors

Color	pH
cherry red	1–2
cerise	3
plum	4
royal purple	5
blue-purple	6
blue	7
blue-green	8
emerald green	9–10
grass green	10–11
lime green	12–13
yellow	14

the cabbage with a food processor or knife, then soak it in alcohol and filter as before. Table 4 correlates pH and anthocyanin colors.

Answers: (1) The red leaves are more acidic. (2) If red cabbage is red or pink then the food is sour (acidic). If it is purple, the food is neutral. (3) Both highly acidic (pool acid) and highly basic (drain cleaner) products have warning labels because they can damage human tissues. (4) A salt solution is neutral. (5) In general, acidic solutions are more red, and basic solutions are more yellow. None of the three items tested in part 3 exhibits the same range of colors as the anthocyanin pigment in red cabbage. (6) The red cabbage solution produces the most detailed scale because it displays the most colors, and therefore is a relatively useful "universal indicator." (7) Most shampoo rinses are slightly acidic so as to restore hair to an optimal pH.

5.5.4 ACID/BASE CONCENTRATION, EQUIVALENCE AND STRENGTH

Discussion: Your students may ask what it is that makes one acid strong and another acid weak. Why is this base strong while this base is weak? What is neutral? The answer lies in the amount of dissociation which occurs when an acid or base is dissolved in water. In general, acids are molecular substances that produce hydronium ions by reaction with water. For example, hydrogen chloride is an acid because, when it is dissolved in water, it reacts to produce hydronium ion (H_3O^+).

$$HCl + H_2O \rightarrow H_3O^+ + Cl^-$$

If we use H^+ as an abbreviation for H_3O^+ and omit the molecule of water that carries the H^+, we can write the reaction as:

$$HCl \rightarrow H^+ + Cl^-$$

When hydrogen chloride gas (HCl) is dissolved in water, it is completely dissociated (split into H^+ and Cl^-) into hydrogen ions and chloride ions. Because of the large number of hydrogen ions in solution, HCl is a strong acid. In contrast some acids, when dissolved in water, are only partially dissociated and release only a small number of hydrogen ions. These are weaker acids. Acetic acid is a weak acid because only a small fraction of the acid is dissociated into ions (hydrogen ions and acetate ions) when dissolved in water.

When sodium hydroxide (NaOH) is added to water it is completely dissociated (split into Na^+ and OH^-) into sodium ions and hydroxide ions. The large number of hydroxide ions in solution makes the solution strongly basic. In contrast, when ammonia gas is dissolved in water only a small fraction of the NH_3 in the solution is present as NH_4^+ and OH^- at any given instant, and therefore ammonia is considered to be a weak base.

A solution is neutral if the number of hydrogen ions is equal to the number of hydroxide ions. Pure water is neutral. When an equivalent amount of acid is added to an equivalent amount of base, neutralization occurs. A salt solution is the result. For example, if an appropriate amount of sodium hydroxide is added to an appropriate amount of hydrochloric acid we obtain a solution of sodium chloride, which is neutral.

$$NaOH + HCl \rightarrow NaCl + H_2O$$

Student results should resemble those in Table 5. The results indicate that equal concentrations of hydrochloric and sulfuric acid have relatively equal strength (as measured by pH) but that sulfuric acid has twice the equivalence, simply because it has twice the number of acidic protons (HCl is monoprotic, while H_2SO_4 is diprotic). Acetic acid and hydrochloric acid have the same equivalence (same quantity of acidic hydrogens), but hydrochloric acid is stronger (lower pH) because it dissociates more completely.

Acetic acid is considered a weak acid because it does not fully ionize in water.

$$HC_2H_3O_2(aq) + H_2O \rightleftarrows H_3O^+(aq) + C_2H_3O_2^-(aq)$$

The degree of dissociation is measured by a value known as the ionization constant, K_a which is expressed as the product of the concentrations (indicated by brackets [concentration]) of the dissociated products divided by the concentration of the undissociated acid.

$$K_a = \frac{[H_3O^+][C_2H_3O_2^-]}{[HC_2H_3O_2]} = 1.8 \times 10^{-5}$$

If the K_a is significantly greater than one, the acid is mostly dissociated and we refer to it as a strong acid. If the K_a is significantly lower than one (e.g., the K_a of acetic acid is 1.8×10^{-5}) then the acid does not dissociate appreciably (does not donate protons as readily) and is considered to be weak. Thus, a strong acid is one in which the loss of a proton to water is essentially complete, while a weak acid is one in which the loss of a proton is noticeably incomplete. By contrast, the ionization of hydrochloric acid is nearly complete so that its K_a is extremely high.

Students may question why sulfuric acid (a diprotic acid) has the same pH as hydrochloric acid (a monoprotic acid). The ionization of hydrochloric acid is complete:

$$HCl(aq) + H_2O(l) \rightarrow H_3O^+(aq) + Cl^-(aq)$$

and the first ionization of sulfuric acid is complete:

$$H_2SO_4 + H_2O \rightarrow HSO_4^- + H_3O^+$$

but the hydronium ions released from the first ionization of sulfuric acid decrease the second ionization so that it does not approach completion.

$$HSO_4^- + H_2O \rightarrow SO_4^{2-} + H_3O^+$$

Thus, the K_a of the second ionization is only about 2×10^{-2}. This is a good example of LeChâtelier's Principle in action.

Table 5: Acid/Base Concentration, Strength and Equivalence

	Concentration (molarity)	*Strength (pH)*	*Equivalence (mL of titrant)*
acetic acid 50.0 mL $HC_2H_3O_2$	0.1 *M*	3	50 mL
hydrochloric acid 50 mL HCl	0.1 *M*	1	50 mL
sulfuric acid 50.0 mL H_2SO_4	0.1 *M*	1	100 mL

It should be noted that it is necessary to use equal molar concentrations of all acids or bases when determining acid or base strength.

If you wish to investigate bases you may compare the strength and equivalence of equimolar concentrations of common bases such as sodium hydroxide, ammonia, and calcium hydroxide. Sodium hydroxide is a stronger base than ammonia, and calcium hydroxide and barium hydroxide require twice as much acid to neutralize because they are diprotic rather than monoprotic.

Answers: (1) Acetic acid. Although all three acids are made to the same concentration, acetic acid demonstrates a much higher (more neutral) pH, indicating that it does not dissociate as completely as the other two. (2) Sulfuric and hydrochloric acids are stronger than acetic acid. Equimolar concentrations of these acids have similar pH values, indicating that they have relatively equivalent strengths. (3) The strength of an acid is measured by pH and depends on the concentration and equivalence of a solution, as well as on the degree of ionization of a particular acid or base. Concentrated solutions of weak acids may be stronger than dilute solutions of strong acids. A chlorinated swimming pool is a very dilute and harmless solution of hydrochloric acid, while reagent grade acetic acid is concentrated and dangerous.

5.5.5 ACID RAIN

Discussion: If you do not have deflagrating spoons, place sulfur in a small cup fashioned out of aluminum foil. Ignite the pea of sulfur and lower into the flask or Pyrex® jar using tongs. These activities require the use of indicators. You may wish to suggest that students study the effect of acid rain upon living systems as part of a class or science fair project. They can examine the germination and growth of bean or corn seedlings in towels wetted with water of different pH, or examine the growth and reproduction of small aquatic plants such as duckweed *(Lemma)* in containers of water at different pH.

Answers: (1) The sulfur dioxide acidified the rainwater considerably due to the formation of sulfurous and sulfuric acid:

$$SO_2(g) + H_2O(l) \rightarrow H_2SO_3(aq)$$

$$2H_2SO_3(aq) + O_2(g) \rightarrow 2H_2SO_4(aq)$$

(2) Twenty-six tons of sulfur dioxide per hour! Two percent of 650 tons of sulfur is 13 tons of sulfur. Since sulfur (32 g/mole) has only half the mass of sulfur dioxide (64 g/mole), a total mass of 26 tons of sulfur dioxide would be released per hour. (3) Nitrogen oxides are gases that diffuse from the source in the center of the plate ("city") to the surrounding droplets ("ponds"). The closer the droplets, the sooner and more pronounced the acidification process. (4) Limestone. Limestone is composed largely of calcium carbonate, which reacts with acids to release carbon dioxide which diffuses out of solution. The limestone lake bottom thereby buffers against acidification:

$$CaCO_3(s) + H_2NO_3(l) \rightarrow Ca^{2+}(aq) + NO_3^{2-}(aq) + H_2O(l) + CO_2(g)$$

Applications to Everyday Life

Forest damage: Experts agree that worldwide burning of coal, oil, and natural gas has produced a major environmental problem called acid rain. Sulfur dioxide (SO_2) and nitrogen oxides (NO_x) emissions react with atmospheric water to form acids that fall in rain or snow. Acid rain has caused significant damage to the Black Forest in southern Germany, the forests of Sweden, and the forests of the Czech Republic.

Taste: There are four basic tastes to which the human tongue responds: sweet, salty, sour and bitter. The sour taste buds are stimulated by acids such as the citric acid in citrus fruits. The bitter taste buds are stimulated by bases such as exist in unsweetened bakers' chocolate and many medications.

Acids in the body: Many biological processes involve weak organic acids. Fatty acids ($C_nH_{2n+1}COOH$) are used in the synthesis of body fats (lipids). Nucleic acids (adenine, thiamine, guanine, cytosine, uracil) are the building blocks of deoxyribonucleic acid (DNA) and ribonucleic acid (RNA), the genetic material that directs the synthesis of proteins. Many carboxylic acids (citric acid, succinic acid, malic acid, etc.) are involved in the metabolism of sugars to release energy (Krebs citric acid cycle) in the form of ATP. Amino acids (Figure P) are the building blocks of proteins. Ascorbic acid (vitamin C, Figure Q) is necessary for the production of collagen, an essential protein in skin, tendons, bones and healing of wounds.

Synthesis of chemical products: Mineral acids (those that are not carbon-based) such as sulfuric, nitric, hydrochloric, and phosphoric have many important industrial applications. Sulfuric acid, one of the most important of all chemicals, is used in the manufacture of fertilizers, pigments, dyes, drugs, explosives and detergents as well as in petroleum refining and many metallurgical processes.

Batteries: Sulfuric acid serves as the electrolyte in lead-acid storage batteries used in many motor vehicles. Examine the label on your car battery and note the warning regarding the battery acid.

Digestion: Hydrochloric acid is a major component of the gastric juices that aid in the chemical breakdown of food in the stomach. The pH of the stomach is approximately 1–2!

Defense mechanisms: Many organisms defend themselves with acids against pathogens or predators. Acids are secreted on the surface of your skin that make the skin a less hospitable environment for bacteria. The hydrochloric acid in your stomach kills bacteria on ingested foods. Persons who do not produce sufficient stomach acid are susceptible to typhoid fever and other diseases caused by bacteria in the *Salmonella* genus. Sea slugs defend themselves with a stream of sulfuric acid. Formicine ants, which account for approximately 10% of the ants in the world, secrete formic acid as a defense against predators. The estimated 100 trillion formicine ants release approximately 10 billion kg of formic acid into the atmosphere each year!

Swimming pools: Muriatic acid (hydrochloric acid, HCl) is added to swimming pools to kill algae and aquatic pathogens.

Cleaning supplies (bases): Bases solubilize fats and greases and are therefore employed in many cleaning supplies. Household ammonia is a base used to clean glass and other surfaces. Sodium hydroxide (lye) is a major component of oven cleaner and drain cleaner.

5.6 ACID AND BASE REACTIONS

The effects of acid rain are being felt from the tropical rain forests of central Africa to the boreal forests of Scandinavia. Forest ecologists have documented a gradual decline in productivity in many forest lands, and agricultural researchers have noted similar problems in farmlands. Soil scientists have noted that acid rain is slowly leaching out many of the essential nutrients from the soil, leaving the soils too impoverished to support the vegetation that otherwise would grow there. Hydrologists have noted that many of the minerals leached from the soil end up in the streams and rivers where they contaminate the water supply. Limnologists have observed that elevated concentrations of aluminum in pond and lake water can be fatal to fish and other aquatic life.

Limnologists have also noticed that slight changes in the pH of lakes and rivers are correlated with the disappearance of various forms of aquatic life. As the pH of water drops to 6.0, insects, crustaceans, and some plankton species begin to disappear. At a pH of 5.0 many fish species disappear. Below pH 5.0, lakes and streams are generally devoid of fish and the bottoms of the lakes become covered with undecayed materials since the organisms which promote decay are no longer present. As the lake habitat declines, waterfowl and terrestrial animals that depend upon aquatic species for their food also decrease in number.

Scientists have declared numerous lakes and ponds in the northeastern United States and Scandinavia "dead." Where these bodies of water once supported complex communities, they are now sterile. The impact of acid rain upon large areas of the world demonstrates the effect that chemical pollution can have.

When people discuss air or water pollution, they are referring to chemicals that have been added to the environment and are causing adverse effects. To understand and fight pollution, you need to understand chemistry. In recent years, many countries in North America and northern Europe have dedicated resources to dealing with the acid rain problem. Chemists have been employed to study environmental pollution problems, and to suggest ways of dealing with these. Some chemists have focused their attention on the source of pollution and have developed technologies that reduce emissions from cars (e.g., the catalytic converter in automobile engines) and coal burning power plants (e.g., scrubber stacks that remove sulfur dioxide from exhaust fumes.) Other chemists have focused their attention on techniques to repair the damage done to soils and water.

One of the most widely used techniques to combat the acidification of waters and soils is a process known as "liming." Pilots drop calcium oxide (CaO, lime) into lakes and farmers plow it into agricultural fields. Calcium oxide reacts with water to form calcium hydroxide, a base:

$$CaO(s) + H_2O(l) \rightarrow Ca(OH)_2(aq) \rightarrow Ca^{2+}(aq) + 2OH^-(aq)$$

The hydroxide ions (OH^-) produced by liming react with hydronium ions (H_3O^+) in the water or soil to neutralize the pH. Liming is now a common treatment in many parts of the world and has proven to be an effective, although expensive, technique in treating acidic soils and waters.

Bases neutralize acids, and acids neutralize bases. In this chapter you will be examining acid/base reactions and investigating the variety of practical applications of acid/base reactions like the liming process just discussed.

5.6.1 NEUTRALIZATION

Concepts to Investigate: Acids, bases, salts, neutralization, acid-base reactions, Arrhenius acids, Arrhenius bases, Brønsted acids, Brønsted bases, heat of neutralization.

Materials: Part 1: Phenolphthalein, 0.10 *N* sodium hydroxide, 0.10 *N* hydrochloric acid, magnifying glass, table salt (NaCl), evaporating dish, beakers, eyedroppers; Part 2: Fume hood, concentrated (14.8 *M*) ammonium hydroxide, concentrated (12 *M*) hydrochloric acid, Hydrion paper; Part 3: Calcium hydroxide, 6 V DC conductivity meter, beaker.

Safety: Wear goggles and lab coat in these activities, or whenever working with acids or bases. Part 2 should be performed only by the instructor because it involves concentrated hydrochloric acid and concentrated ammonium hydroxide.

Principles and Procedures: Does your teacher wear a lab coat with holes in it? If so, the holes are most likely due to acid spills, and not to normal wear and tear. Sulfuric acid is a very corrosive liquid that has such a high affinity for water that it will extract it from the air as well as many organic substances. This strong "dehydrating" agent can remove hydrogen and oxygen from cotton polymers and leave the fabric permanently damaged.

If sulfuric acid or another strong acid is spilled in the classroom, don't try to wipe it up with a sponge or cloth because it will react with the cellulose in the sponge, the cotton in the cloth or the collagen in your skin in much the same way it reacts with the cotton fibers in a lab coat! Before you can wipe up an acid, you must first neutralize it with a weak base such as sodium bicarbonate (also known as sodium hydrogen carbonate; baking soda; $NaHCO_3$). If you spill a strong base, you must first neutralize it with a weak acid or acidic salt like citric acid, sodium bisulfate or monosodium phosphate.

Neutralization refers to the consumption of an acid by a base or vice versa. Neutralization results in the elimination of both acid and base by the formation of neutral products. When an Arrhenius acid is neutralized by an Arrhenius base, salt and water are produced.

$$acid + base \rightarrow salt + water + heat$$

Note that one of the products of the neutralization process is heat. If a strong base is mixed with a strong acid, the amount of heat released may be so great that the solution may boil and splatter. For this reason, an acid spill should only be neutralized by a weak base, and a base spill should only be neutralized by a weak acid. If the neutralization is complete, no acid or base will remain, and the solution will be indistinguishable from one made simply by dissolving the salt in water.

Part 1: Neutralization and the production of salts; heat of neutralization: *Wear goggles and lab coat.* An Arrhenius acid is a substance that releases hydrogen ions (H^+) in solution. The free hydrogen ions (H^+) combine with water (H_2O) to form hydronium ions (H_3O^+):

$$H_2O + H^+ \rightarrow H_3O^+$$

Although H_3O^+ is the actual species in solution, chemists often use H^+ to represent the H_3O^+ ion. An Arrhenius base releases hydroxide ions (OH^-) in solution, and these may combine with hydronium ions to produce water:

$$H_3O^+ + OH^- \rightarrow 2H_2O$$

Sodium chloride (NaCl, common table salt) is the most common and important salt, and has been used for centuries to flavor and preserve food. Sodium chloride accounts for approximately 80% of all of the dissolved salts in the ocean. Sodium chloride can be reclaimed from salt water simply by evaporation of water, or it can be made by neutralizing hydrochloric acid (HCl) with sodium hydroxide (NaOH):

$$NaOH + HCl \rightarrow NaCl + H_2O$$

and then evaporating the water. If the neutralization process is complete, then it will not be possible to distinguish the salt produced in this fashion from the salt that is left when salt water is allowed to evaporate.

Place 30.0 mL of 0.10 *N* sodium hydroxide in a flask and add a couple of drops of phenolphthalein. Measure the temperature as accurately as possible. Slowly add 30.0 mL of 0.10 *N* hydrochloric acid (Figure A). Swirl the flask and measure the pH (Figure B). It necessary, add a couple more drops of acid or base with an eyedropper until the solution is neutralized (pH 7). Record the final temperature. Does neutralization appear to be an endothermic process (as indicated by drop in temperature) or an exothermic process (as indicated by a rise in temperature)? Is heat of neutralization a positive or negative value?

Place the contents of the flask in an evaporating dish or crucible (Figure C) and carefully boil off the water until the dish is dry. Scrape the crystals from the evaporating dish and examine them using a magnifying lens. Compare these crystals with those of ordinary table salt. Do they appear to have the same shape? *(We recommend against using a "taste test" to*

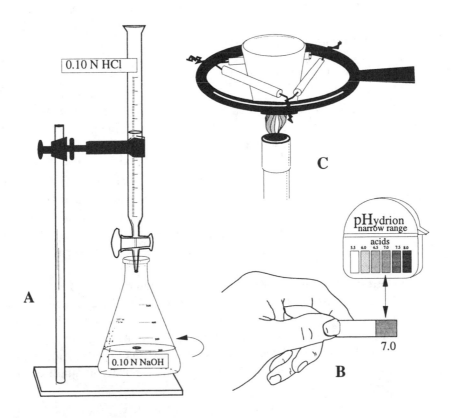

compare the two crystals. It may be hazardous to ingest anything made in the laboratory because of the potential for contamination or mistake.)

Part 2: Neutralization of a Brønsted acid and base: *This should only be performed by the instructor. Wear goggles, lab coat and gloves, and use a fume hood to remove ammonia and hydrogen chloride vapors. Concentrated (12 M) hydrochloric acid is highly toxic by ingestion or inhalation and severely corrosive to skin and eyes. Concentrated (14.8 M) ammonium hydroxide is toxic and vapors are extremely irritating, especially to eyes.*

If you look in your chemical storage room, you may notice a fine white dust on the surface of many chemical bottles, particularly those closest to the bottle of concentrated hydrochloric acid. This dust is not normal household dust, but rather a fine white powder known as ammonium chloride. How does it get there? What causes a crystal to form on the outside of a chemical bottle?

Turn on the exhaust fan of a fume hood. Open a bottle of concentrated (12 *M*) hydrochloric acid. Test the pH of the vapors by holding with tongs a moistened strip of litmus paper. Does the vapor produce an acid or base when dissolved in the water on the litmus paper (litmus turns red in acid and blue in base)? Close the bottle of acid. Open a bottle of concentrated (14.8 *M*) ammonium hydroxide solution and test the pH of its vapor in the same manner. Is the vapor basic (litmus turns blue in basic conditions)? Close the bottle of ammonium hydroxide. What happens if the vapor from an acid combines with the vapor from a base?

Ammonia (a Brønsted base) is a small, volatile molecule and diffuses rapidly through the air. Hydrogen chloride (an acid) is a larger molecule and travels more slowly. What happens if hydrogen chloride vapors contact ammonia vapors? Will they neutralize each other? Place a bottle of concentrated (12 *M*) hydrochloric acid approximately 10 cm from a bottle of concentrated (14.8 *M*) ammonium hydroxide solution in the fume hood. Turn on the exhaust fan and open the bottles. If ammonia and hydrogen chloride vapors combine, a white crystal will form in the air and eventually settle on the bottles.

$$NH_3 + HCl \rightarrow NH_4Cl$$

The longer the bottles are left open, the more ammonium chloride crystals form. Scrape some of this fine white crystal off the surface of the beaker, dissolve in water and test the pH with pH paper. Is it as acidic as hydrochloric acid or as basic as ammonia or relatively neutral?

If the formation of ammonium chloride is too slow, you may wish to construct the apparatus shown in Figure D. *In a fume hood,* place 30% hydrochloric acid in one flask and 30% ammonium hydroxide in the other. Attach the free end of the tubing to a source of compressed air. *Do not attempt to blow on the tube because the vapors are very hazardous.* As air is forced through the solutions, a cloud of ammonium chloride will form.

Part 3: "Blowing out a light bulb": *Wear goggles and lab coat.* Add 5 grams of calcium hydroxide, $Ca(OH)_2$, to a container holding 1 liter of water. Seal the container and shake for one minute and then allow the undissolved materials to settle. Decant the clear solution (lime-water) into a beaker. Place the probes of a 6 V DC conductivity apparatus (Figure E) in this beaker and note that the bulb lights. Lime-water contains dissolved ions (Ca^{2+}, OH^-), and therefore conducts electricity. What will happen to the electrolytic qualities of the solution if it is neutralized?

Oxides of nonmetallic substances yield acids when dissolved in water. If, for example, you exhale into water, carbon dioxide dissolves to form carbonic acid (H_2CO_3) as shown below:

$$CO_2(g) + H_2O(l) \longrightarrow H_2CO_3(aq)$$

The carbonic acid will combine with calcium hydroxide to form calcium carbonate (a relatively insoluble salt) and water:

$$Ca(OH)_2(aq) + H_2CO_3(aq) \longrightarrow CaCO_3(s) + 2H_2O(l)$$

Blow through a straw into the lime-water solution containing the 6 V DC conductivity meter. As you exhale, does the light get brighter, stay the same or get dimmer (Figure F)? Test the pH of the solution and determine the conditions under which the light is brightest and dimmest. Aside from pH, how can you determine when the solution is neutralized?

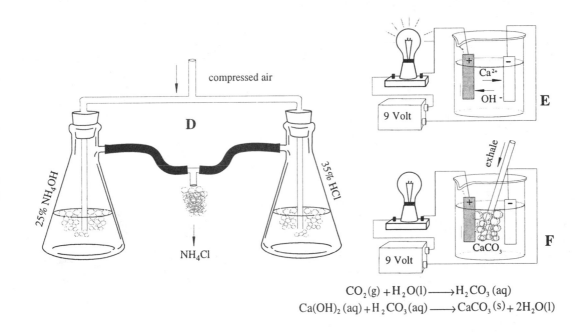

$$CO_2(g) + H_2O(l) \longrightarrow H_2CO_3(aq)$$
$$Ca(OH)_2(aq) + H_2CO_3(aq) \longrightarrow CaCO_3(s) + 2H_2O(l)$$

Questions

(1) Do the crystals formed by the neutralization of sodium hydroxide and hydrochloric acid in part 1 look similar to those from a container of table salt?

(2) The stomach contains hydrochloric acid with a pH of 1–2. As partially digested food leaves the stomach, it enters the intestines where it encounters a small duct from the pancreas and gall bladder that serves as a conduit for bicarbonate. What do you think is the purpose of the bicarbonate?

(3) Milk of magnesia is an antacid containing magnesium hydroxide, which is used to settle sour (acid) stomachs. Write an equation to show how the active ingredient ($Mg(OH)_2$) neutralizes excess hydrochloric acid.

(4) What effect does exhaling have on the intensity of the conductivity tester bulb in part 3?

(5) How can you tell that the calcium carbonate is less soluble than calcium hydroxide?

(6) Under what conditions (acidic, neutral, basic) does the lamp in part 3 glow the least? Explain.

(7) Lime-water is frequently used as a test for the presence of carbon dioxide. Explain.

5.6.2 TITRATION

Concepts to Investigate: pH, hydronium ion concentration, hydroxide ion concentration, Arrhenius acids, Arrhenius bases, Brønsted acids, Brønsted bases, neutrality, neutralization, titration, antacids, percent composition.

Materials: Part 1: Burets, 0.10 *N* hydrochloric acid, sodium hydroxide, phenolphthalein, flask; Part 2: Vinegar, 0.50 *N* sodium hydroxide, buret, flask, phenolphthalein; Part 3: Antacids; (Pepto-Bismo®, Tums®, Rolaids®, Di-Gel®, etc.), 1.0 *N* HCl, mortar and pestle, buret, phenolphthalein.

Safety: Wear goggles and lab coat.

Principles and Procedures: Have you ever purchased a shirt and found a tag that said something like: "This garment inspected by #15"? In the clothing business, companies hire inspectors to ensure the quality of their products. If a shirt has not been sewn correctly, or if the fabric colors do not meet a given standard, the garment is removed and either destroyed or distributed as "irregular" merchandise.

The department in which such inspectors work is often known as "Quality Control." Federal law requires that foods and medicines be inspected and certified according to established standards. Look at the "Nutrition Facts" label (Figure G) on a package of food and note that it specifies the quantity of cholesterol, sodium and other components. As food is being packaged an inspector analyzes random samples from a given lot to ensure that the product falls within specified standards.

Of the variety of techniques used by quality control inspectors to determine the chemical composition of foods, medications and industrial chemicals, perhaps the most common is titration. Titration is a process in which the concentration of an unknown solution is determined by its reaction with a solution of known concentration. A known solution is slowly mixed with an unknown solution until the same number of equivalents of both are present. This point is known as the end point.

Nutrition Facts		
Serving Size 4 Crackers (14 g)		
Servings Per Container about 32		
Amount Per Serving		
Calories 70	Calories from Fat 25	
	% Daily Value*	
Total Fat 3g		5%
Saturated Fat 1g		5%
Cholesterol 0 mg		0%
Sodium 80 mg		3%
Total Carbohydrate 9g		3%
Dietary Fiber Less than 1 g		1%
Sugars 1g		
Protein 1 g		
Vitamin A 0%	Vitamin C 0%	
Calcium 0%	Iron 2%	

G

The end point for acid/base titrations can be determined by use of a pH indicator that turns color when the acid equivalents equal the base equivalents (pH 7, neutrality). Litmus and phenolphthalein, for example, turn color near pH 7, and therefore serve as excellent indicators for acid/base titrations. For purposes of titration, it is best to express concentrations in normality (*N*, equivalents per liter of solution). A 1 normal (1 *N*) solution of acid is capable of neutralizing an equal amount of a 1 normal solution of base. A 1 *M* solution of a monoprotic acid such as HCl is 1 *N* because it has the capacity to neutralize an equal quantity of a 1 *N* base like sodium hydroxide. By contrast, a 1 *M* solution of a diprotic acid like H_2SO_4 is a 2 *N* solution. It can neutralize twice as much base as an equal volume of hydrochloric acid since it has twice as many protons to donate.

The product of the normality (*N;* equivalents per liter) and the volume (*V;* liters) is simply the equivalents. At neutrality the acid equivalents = the base equivalents:

$$N_{acid}V_{acid} = N_{base}V_{base}$$

$$\left(\frac{\text{equivalents}_{(acid)}}{\text{liter solution}_{(acid)}}\right)\left(\text{liters}_{(acid)}\right) = \left(\frac{\text{equivalents}_{(base)}}{\text{liter solution}_{(base)}}\right)\left(\text{liters}_{(base)}\right)$$

$$\text{equivalents}_{(acid)} = \text{equivalents}_{(base)}$$

If the normality of one solution is known, and the volumes of both acid and base necessary to reach the end point are known, then the normality of the unknown solution may be determined. For example, if the normality of the acid is known, then the normality of the titrating base may be determined as follows:

$$N_{base} = \frac{N_{acid}V_{acid}}{V_{base}}$$

Part 1: Determining the normality of an unknown base: Your instructor will prepare a basic solution with an unknown normality between 0.05 N and 0.5 N. You must determine the concentration of this "unknown" by titration with 0.10 N hydrochloric acid. Rinse a buret with 0.10 N hydrochloric acid and then fill it with the same. Rinse a second buret with the unknown base, and then fill it with the same. Determine the initial readings in both burets to the nearest 0.1 mL. Draw off approximately 10 mL of the unknown base into a 250 mL Erlenmeyer flask, and add approximately 30 mL of distilled water and one or two drops of phenolphthalein indicator solution. The solution should appear pink because of the presence of base. Slowly add the acid solution and mix with a swirling motion (Figure H). Occasionally stop adding acid and wash down the sides of the flask with distilled water to make sure that neither acid nor base clings to the walls. The distilled water is neutral and does not affect the results of the titration. As you approach the end point, the color of the solution will fade from dark to light pink. At this point, slowly add the acid drop by drop until the last trace of pink is gone. Calculate the volume of the acid added (V_{acid}) and the volume of the base added (V_{base}), and then calculate the normality of the base using the equation listed earlier. Repeat twice, complete the left-hand portion of Table 1 (Table 1 is used for both parts 1 and 2 of this activity), and calculate your average value for normality of the unknown base. Check with your instructor and determine the percentage error between your value and the actual value.

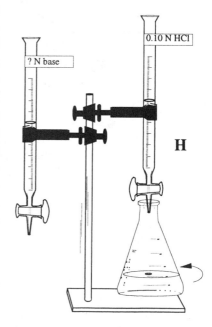

Part 2: Determining the percentage of acetic acid in vinegar: Vinegar companies employ chemical technicians to certify that the vinegar packaged for market has the appropriate concentration of acetic acid. Commercial vinegars generally have a mass percentage between 4 and 6% acetic acid. If the acetic acid content exceeds 6%, the vinegar tastes too sour for

Table 1: Data for Parts 1 and 2

	Part 1: Normality of Base			Part 1: Percentage Acetic Acid		
	1	*2*	*3*	*1*	*2*	*3*
volume of acid	mL	mL	mL	mL	mL	mL
volume of base	mL	mL	mL	mL	mL	mL
normality of acid	0.10 *N*	0.10 *N*	0.10 *N*	*N*	*N*	*N*
normality of base	*N*	*N*	*N*	0.50 *N*	0.50 *N*	0.50 *N*
	avg. *N* of unknown base:		*N*	avg. *N* of unknown acid:		*N*
				percentage acetic acid		%

most consumers. If, however, the acetic acid content is less than 4%, the vinegar tastes too bland. In this activity you will titrate vinegar with a base of known concentration to determine its normality and mass percentage of acetic acid.

Rinse one buret with vinegar and then fill it with vinegar. Rinse a second buret with 0.50 *N* sodium hydroxide and then fill it with sodium hydroxide. Draw off 10 mL of vinegar into a clean flask and add 50 mL distilled water and a drop of phenolphthalein. Slowly add 0.50 *N* sodium hydroxide while swirling the flask until a pink color remains for more than a second. If you go over the end point too rapidly, add drops of vinegar until the color again reverses. The end point is the point at which either one drop of acid (vinegar) or one drop of base (0.50 *N* NaOH) permanently turns the color of the solution. Record the values in the right-hand portion of Table 1 and calculate the normality of vinegar. Repeat the procedure with two more samples and average the value.

Having calculated the normality of the vinegar, you can now determine the mass percentage of acetic acid. The normality of the vinegar represents the number of equivalents of acetic acid per liter of solution (represented by the question mark in the equation below). Since acetic acid has a gram-molecular weight of 60 g/mole, and the density of vinegar is approximately 1000 g/L, the percentage of acetic acid in vinegar may be represented as follows:

$$\% \ HC_2H_3O_2 \ = \ \frac{? \ \text{equivalents}}{L} \ \left| \ \frac{60 \ g \ HC_2H_3O_2}{\text{equivalent}} \ \right| \ \frac{L \ \text{vinegar}}{1000 \ g \ \text{vinegar}} \ \left| \ 100 \ \% \right.$$

What is the percentage of acetic acid in the vinegar you have selected? What is the difference between your value and the value marked on the vinegar container?

Part 3: Analyzing antacids: The terms we use in everyday language are often imprecise. When people complain about a stomach ache, they are generally referring to a pain that arises from the intestines. When they complain about "heartburn" they are generally complaining about a pain arising from the stomach or esophagus. "Heartburn" (acid indigestion, sour stomach) is a common problem, as indicated by the number of medications advertised to relieve it, such as Rolaids®, Maalox®, Tums®, Mylanta®, Di-Gel®, Riopan®, and Alka-Seltzer®. "Heartburn" is actually a burning sensation created when gastric juices in the stomach (primarily hydrochloric acid) splash up on the unprotected coating of the esophagus. Anxiety and other stimuli can cause an excessive secretion of gastric juices which leads to "heartburn" and ulcers. People suffering from heartburn can purchase antacids that contain weak bases like magnesium hydroxide, aluminum hydroxide or sodium hydrogen carbonate. These bases react with and neutralize hydrochloric acid:

$$Mg(OH)_2 + 2HCl \rightarrow MgCl_2 + 2H_2O$$

$$Al(OH)_3 + 3HCl \rightarrow AlCl_3 + 3H_2O$$

Other antacids contain carbonates (generally sodium carbonate or calcium carbonate) that neutralize acids as shown in the following equation:

$$CO_3^{2-}(aq) + 2H^+(aq) \rightarrow H_2O(l) + CO_2(g)$$

The question is, which of the many antacids on the market has the greatest capacity to neutralize excess acids? Refer to the instructions on the antacid containers and measure out equivalent "adult dosages" of each antacid to be tested (generally 1–4 tablets). Grind each using a mortar and pestle, transfer to an Erlenmeyer flask, and dissolve in 200 mL of distilled water. Add two drops of phenolphthalein solution to each antacid solution and then slowly add 1.0 *N* hydrochloric acid from a buret while swirling the flask until the pink color disappears, indicating that the end point has been reached (see parts 1 and 2).

Which antacid seems to be the most effective in neutralizing excess acid? The number of moles of acid neutralized by each acid can be calculated simply by multiplying the normality of the titrating acid by the volume of the acid titrated:

$$N_{acid}V_{acid} = \text{equivalents of acid neutralized}$$

How many moles of acid can a dosage of each antacid neutralize? Examine the contents of each antacid, and write a neutralization reaction.

Questions

(1) Why is titration such a valuable technique in quality control?

(2) How might titration be used when analyzing chemicals left at the scene of a crime?

(3) What was the percentage of acetic acid in the vinegar you tested in part 2?

(4) Would vinegar be more or less sour if water were removed?

(5) Which antacid is able to neutralize the most acid?

(6) How many moles of acid can a dosage of the strongest antacid neutralize?

(7) Explain how the term "heartburn" may have received its three names: heartburn, acid indigestion, and sour stomach.

5.6.3 BUFFERING

Concepts to Investigate: Buffers, acids, bases.

Materials: Part 1: Alka-Seltzer®, 1 *N* HCl, 1 *N* NaOH, burets, flasks, bromthymol blue; Part 2: KH_2PO_4, K_2HPO_4, NaOH, phenolphthalein, and bromcresol green, methyl orange or bromthymol blue.

Safety: Wear goggles and lab coat.

Principles and Procedures: One of the most common pain relievers used today is aspirin (acetylsalicylic acid). Aspirin is a mild, non-narcotic pain reliever that is used to alleviate the pain associated with headaches, and muscle and joint aches. Aspirin, however is an acid and may exacerbate sour stomach or acid indigestion. To deal with this problem, some aspirin manufactures have "buffered" their aspirin (e.g., Bufferin®). In other words, they have added additional chemicals to the aspirin that reduce its acidity in the stomach. A buffer is a solution that resists a change in pH when either acid or base is added by consuming free protons (H^+ or H_3O^+) or hydroxide ions (OH^-). Generally a buffer is a water solution of a weak acid and its conjugate base (the species that remains after the acid has lost a proton) in approximately equal proportions.

Alka-Seltzer® is an aspirin-based analgesic (pain reliever) that contains sodium bicarbonate and citric acid. These react when dissolved in water to produce aqueous sodium citrate and bicarbonate:

$$3\,NaHCO_3(s) + H_3C_3H_5O_7(s) \rightarrow 3Na^+\,(aq) + C_3H_5O_7^{3-}\,(aq) + 3HCO_3^{-}(aq) + 3H^+(aq)$$

The citrate ion is an antacid and absorbs free protons:

$$C_3H_5O_7^{3-}\,(aq) + 3H^+(aq) \rightarrow H_3C_3H_5O_7\,(aq)$$

The bicarbonate ion neutralizes excess protons in acidic conditions,

$$HCO_3^{-}(aq) + H^+(aq) \rightarrow CO_2(g) + H_2O(l)$$

or excess hydroxide ions in basic conditions:

$$HCO_3^{-}(aq) + OH^-(aq) \rightarrow CO_3^{2-}(g) + H_2O(l)$$

Thus, the combination of sodium bicarbonate and citric acid produces a buffer solution that resists a change in pH regardless of whether an acid or a base is added. As long as the amount of acid or base added is relatively small compared with the amount of buffer, it will be consumed with a minimal change in pH.

Part 1: Buffered medicines: Bromthymol blue is an indicator that is green between pH 6.0 and 7.6 (neutral range), yellow below 6.0 (acidic conditions), and blue above 7.6 (basic conditions). Add 100 mL of distilled water to each of two 250 mL flasks. Add equal amounts of bromthymol blue indicator (5–10 drops) to each container. Dissolve an Alka-Seltzer® tablet in one of the flasks. Both flasks should have a green or blue tint. Fill a pipet or buret with 1.0 N HCl and count the minimum number of drops necessary to change the color of both solutions to yellow (Figure I). Once they are yellow, count the number of drops of 1 N NaOH necessary to turn the color to blue (pH 7.6). Does Alka-Seltzer® buffer the solution against pH changes?

I

Unbuffered

Part 2: Natural buffers in the body: For proper functioning of the body, it is necessary to maintain the pH of the blood at pH 7.4. Normal physiological activities produce carbon dioxide which acts to acidify the solution:

$$CO_2(g) + H_2O(l) \rightleftarrows H_2CO_3 \rightleftarrows H^+ + HCO_3^- \rightleftarrows 2H^+ + CO_3^{2-}$$

If blood were not buffered, blood pH would drop with increased respiration (carbon dioxide is a byproduct of respiration), causing many physiological problems. Fortunately, blood contains phosphate and serum protein buffers that prevent acidification. Hydrogen phosphate (HPO_4^{2-}) and hydrogen carbonate (HCO_3^-) ions in blood react with extra protons and protect the body against the carbonic acid produced during respiration:

$$HPO_4^{2-}(aq) + H^+(aq) \rightleftarrows H_2PO_4^-(aq)$$

$$HCO_3^-(aq) + H^+(aq) \rightleftarrows H_2CO_3(aq)$$

Phosphate buffers are commonly used in biological studies. They are mixtures of monobasic phosphates (KH_2PO_4) and a dibasic phosphate (K_2HPO_4). To prepare a pH 7 phosphate buffer, dissolve 6.8 g of KH_2PO_4 in water and add 296 mL of 0.10 N NaOH and dilute to one liter. Add 100 mL of this buffer to a 250 mL flask and 100 mL of tap water to a second. Add 2 or 3 drops of bromcresol green (pH range 3.8–5.4), methyl orange (pH range 3.2–4.4) or bromthymol blue (pH range 6.0–7.4) to each flask. Using a hammer, crush a chunk of dry ice into a fine powder. *Be careful not to touch the dry ice.* Measure 5 grams of dry ice, put in the unbuffered solution, swirl and record the time elapsed before bromcresol green turns from blue to yellow, methyl orange turns from yellow to orange-red or bromthymol blue turns from blue to yellow. Repeat the procedure using the buffered solution and the same indicator. The dry ice sublimes to produce carbon dioxide gas that reacts with water to form carbonic acid. The resulting increase in carbonic acid causes a drop in pH, which then stimulates a change in indicator color. What effect does the buffer appear to have on the pH of the system when acid is added?

An alternative method to study the buffering capacity of solutions is to measure the amount of base or acid required to significantly alter the pH of the solution. Add 100 mL of tap water to one flask and 100 mL of buffer solution to another. Add 2 to 3 drops of phenolphthalein (pH range 8.2–10) to each. From a buret or pipet, slowly add 0.1 N NaOH solution to the flask containing water and measure the volume (or count the number of drops) until a pink color remains (similar setup to Figure I). Repeat the process with the buffered solution. How many times more base must be added to turn the color of the buffered solution than the unbuffered solution?

Add 100 mL of tap water to one flask, 100 mL of buffer solution to another and a couple of drops of bromcresol green (pH range 4–5.6) or methyl orange (pH range 3.2–4.4) to each. Slowly add 0.1 N HCl solution from a buret or pipet to the flask containing water, and measure the volume necessary to change the indicator color (bromcresol green turns from blue to yellow, and methyl orange turns from yellow to orange-red). Repeat the process with the buffered solution. How many times more acid must be added to turn the color of the buffered solution than the unbuffered solution?

Questions

(1) Does Alka Seltzer® buffer a solution? Explain.

(2) Would blood pH be higher or lower than 7.4 if it were unbuffered? Explain.

(3) One of the most important processes in physiology is homeostasis—the ability or tendency of an organism or a cell to maintain optimal internal equilibrium by adjusting its physiological processes. Explain how the buffering system in the blood helps maintain homeostatic equilibrium.

(4) List other chemical factors that you suspect must be maintained in homeostatic equilibrium in the body.

(5) When dipotassium hydrogen phosphate K_2HPO_4 dissolves in water, two phosphate ions are produced: HPO_4^{2-} and $H_2PO_4^-$. Write equations to show how these ions can consume either excess protons (H^+) in an acid environment, or excess hydroxides (OH^-) in a basic environment.

5.6.4 SOIL pH

Concepts to Investigate: Acid anhydrides, base anhydrides, soil pH, acid rain, agricultural chemistry.

Materials: Part 1: Wide-range pH paper or a pH meter, filter paper, funnel, beakers, soil samples; Part 2: CaO, $FeSO_4$, Petri dish, wide-range pH paper; Part 3: 0.1 N H_2SO_4, 2-liter plastic bottle, beaker, ring stand, pH paper or pH meter.

Safety: Wear goggles and lab coat.

Principles and Procedures: Agriculture is the world's oldest and most basic industry. Until relatively recently, the vast majority of people in the world lived and worked on farms, but recent advances in agricultural engineering, soil science and plant breeding have enabled farmers to obtain much greater yields with much less labor. As farming has become more efficient, fewer people are needed to work the land, and more have emigrated to cities in search of other employment (Figure J). New technologies have enabled farmers not only to obtain larger yields on existing farmland, but also to transform marginal lands into productive acreage. As the world's population continues to grow (Figure K), and much of the best farmland in the world gets paved over by rapidly growing cities, it becomes increasingly important to learn how to manage these marginal lands. In many regions the climate is suitable for growing crops, but the soil pH is not. Farmers routinely add chemicals to soils in such regions to create soil conditions suitable for crops.

Part 1: Measuring soil pH: Some plants grow better in slightly acidic environments (pH 4.0–5.0), while others do better in neutral or slightly basic environments (7.0–8.0). The correlation between vegetation and soil pH is so strong that experienced observers can accurately estimate soil pH on the basis of the plants growing there. For example, blueberries,

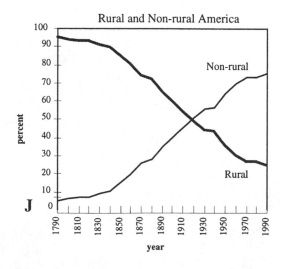

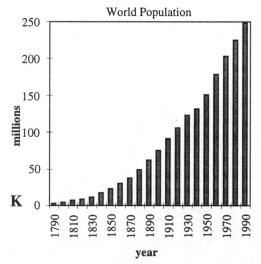

cranberries, mountain ash and spruce are commonly found in soils with a pH of 4–5, while sunflowers, clover, elms, sugar maples and locusts are found in soils with a pH of 6–8. Knowing the pH preferences of various horticultural and agricultural plants is useful, because different types of fertilizers or soil additives can be administered to promote growth of the desired plants.

The pH of moist or boggy soils is often quite different from the pH of agricultural or grassland soils. If possible, collect five or more soil samples from a bog, swamp or other fresh water wetland, and a similar number of samples from a grassland or agricultural region. (If these selections are not possible, you may wish to compare soils from other regions such as coniferous forests, deciduous forests, desert soils, home gardens, etc.) Place 50 grams of soil in a container with 100 mL of distilled water. Stir the soil for one minute and then pour the mud into a funnel fitted with a piece of filter paper. Allow the water to drain through the paper and test its pH using wide range pH paper or a pH meter. Does there appear to be any correlation between vegetation or environment and soil pH?

Part 2 Modifying soil pH: Some soils are too acidic for optimal crop growth, while others are too basic. Farmers have learned to monitor and adjust the pH of soils to maximize crop growth. Two minerals frequently added to soils are lime (calcium oxide, CaO) and iron (II) sulfate ($FeSO_4$). How do these minerals affect soil pH? Place a small quantity of dry lime in a Petri dish or test tube and test the pH using wide range pH paper. Does the lime change the color of the paper? Repeat the process using dry iron (II) sulfate in another dish. Are these dry minerals acidic, basic or neutral? Now add water to each container, stir and re-test. Examine the color chart on the pH paper dispenser to determine the approximate pH of the resulting solutions. Which substance would you recommend that a gardener or farmer add to a soil that is too basic? Too acidic?

Part 3: pH-buffering effects of soil: Coal-burning electric power generation plants release sulfur dioxide into the atmosphere. Sulfur dioxide combines with moisture and falls to the earth as "acid rain." Are soils immediately acidified when this occurs, or is it a slow process? Prepare a container to hold soil by cutting off the bottom of a 2-liter plastic bottle. Fill the bottle with soil and then add 1 liter of distilled water. Allow the water to filter through the container and collect in a beaker below as shown in Figure L. Test the pH of the filtrate using wide range pH paper or a pH meter. This is the normal pH of the soil. Prepare some "acid rain water" by making a 1-liter solution of 0.1 *N* sulfuric acid. *(Always use goggles and a laboratory coat or apron when working with acids!)* Measure the pH of this "rain water" and then mix it with the soil as before. Does soil alter the pH of the water as the water percolates through? Repeat the process with different types of soil such as sand, highly organic soil, etc. Which soil tested serves as the most effective buffer?

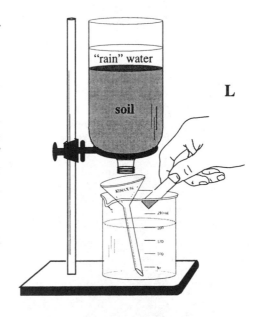

Questions

(1) Was there any correlation between environment/vegetation and soil pH?

(2) Substances that form acids when dissolved in water are known as acid anhydrides, and those that form bases are known as basic anhydrides. SO_2, NO_2, and P_4O_{10} are acid anhydrides, while Na_2O, CaO, and MgO are basic anhydrides. On the basis of these data and your observations in part 2, suggest a relationship between the type of element combined with oxygen and the tendency to form acid or base anhydrides.

(3) Ashes contain metal oxides. Why do gardeners recommend that you not use ashes from your fireplace to fertilize acid-loving plants such as rhododendrons, azaleas, magnolias, and blueberries?

(4) Which of the soils tested in part 3 appear to have the greatest buffering capacity? Which have the least?

5.6.5 pH CONTROL OF RESPIRATION

Concepts to Investigate: Titration, end point, pH, respiration, homeostasis.

Materials: Phenolphthalein, flasks, straws, 0.01 N NaOH solution.

Safety: This activity requires physical exercise and should only be performed by volunteers who are in good health and physical condition. Make certain that no one inhales or sucks through the straw since the solution is mildly hazardous. Students should rinse their mouths with water for 15 minutes if such a mishap occurs.

Principles and Procedures: Your body responds to stimuli to maintain optimal (best) internal conditions. For example, if you are too cold, your muscles spontaneously contract (shiver) to generate frictional heat, but if you are too warm, blood flows to body surfaces where sweat glands are activated and excess heat is removed as water evaporates from your skin. Your body regulates many chemicals as well. For example, the liver converts glucose to glycogen when levels are high, but allows glycogen to be broken down to glucose when glucose levels are low. The ability of an organism or cell to maintain optimal internal conditions by adjusting physiological processes is known as homeostasis (*homeo-,* same; *stasis-,* state).

Organisms maintain optimal internal conditions of oxygen and carbon dioxide. Your breathing pattern is determined by the concentration of carbon dioxide and oxygen in the blood. If carbon dioxide concentrations are too high (oxygen levels too low), the respiratory center in your brain sends additional signals to contract the diaphragm and chest muscles that control breathing. If carbon dioxide levels are too low (oxygen levels too high), the respiratory center sends fewer signals until the levels return to normal. The breathing reflex is automatic, but you can override it. If, for example, you are excited and breathe too much (hyperventilate), you may pass out and the respiratory center will re-establish a respiration rate that restores appropriate levels of carbon dioxide and oxygen. Similarly, if you were to hold your breath (*do not try this!*) you might eventually pass out, and the respiratory center would stimulate breathing until levels of these gases once again reached normal (homeostatic equilibrium).

It is believed that one way your body responds to soaring or falling levels of gases is through the changes in pH that accompany them. If you hold your breath, carbon dioxide concentrations increase and carbonic acid forms:

$$CO_2 + H_2O \rightarrow H_2CO_3$$

Carbonic acid dissociates to release free protons that cause the pH to fall.

$$H_2CO_3 \rightarrow H^+ + HCO_3^-$$

It is thought that chemoreceptors in arteries detect the drop in pH and send signals via nerves to the respiratory centers in the brain, stimulating the breathing response. The reverse holds true when there is insufficient carbon dioxide.

If respiration is mediated by blood pH, then you would expect the breathing rate to increase when blood is acidic (too much carbon dioxide in the blood) and decrease when blood is too basic (too little carbon dioxide in the blood). Because gases are exchanged in the lungs, you would expect more carbon dioxide in your breath when exercising and less when resting.

$$① \; 6O_2 + C_6H_{12}O_6 \xrightarrow{\text{tissue}} 6CO_2 + 6H_2O + 38ATP$$

$$② \; CO_2 \,(\text{blood}) \longrightarrow CO_2 \,(\text{air})$$

$$O_2 \,(\text{air}) \longrightarrow O_2 \,(\text{blood})$$

$$③ \; H_2O + CO_2 \longrightarrow H_2CO_3$$

$$H_2CO_3 \longrightarrow H^+ + HCO_3^-$$

$$H^+ + \text{Phenolphthalein}^-_{(\text{pink})} \longrightarrow \text{Phenolphthalein}_{(\text{colorless})}$$

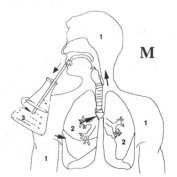

M

You may have noticed that your breathing rate increases significantly when you exercise. This increased respiration rate is necessary to provide the body with more oxygen and remove excess carbon dioxide to restore the body to optimal concentrations of these gases. In this activity you will investigate the influence of exercise on the amount of carbon dioxide in your exhaled breath. Because carbon dioxide diffuses into the lungs from surrounding blood vessels, changes in carbon dioxide concentrations in the blood will be reflected by similar changes in the breath.

Prepare a 0.01 N solution of sodium hydroxide by dissolving 0.4 gram of sodium hydroxide per liter of water. Carefully measure 50 mL of this solution into each of six flasks and dilute with 100 mL of water. Put a couple of drops of phenolphthalein in each flask. Blow steadily through a straw into the first solution while swirling its flask (Figure M), and record the time required to eliminate all pink color (the end point). *(Caution! At no time should you inhale or suck through the straw! If for some reason you do get some solution in your mouth, wash it out with water for 15 minutes.)* Now jog in place for exactly one minute and repeat the process with a second flask. Try to blow at the same rate as before. How much time is required to titrate the solution this time? Record your results in Table 2.

Rest for 5 minutes and then repeat both processes. Rest again and repeat both processes a third time and average your values and compare them with those of your classmates. Does exercise influence the time required to titrate the solution? Does your breath appear to have more carbon dioxide in it after exercising? Compare the effect of different exercises on the amount of carbon dioxide in your breath.

Table 2: Exercise and Carbon Dioxide Production

Exercise	Trial 1	Trial 2	Trial 3	Average Time to Titrate	Rank
resting	s	s	s	s	
jogging	s	s	s	s	
	s	s	s	s	
	s	s	s	s	

Questions

(1) You can add more water to the flask containing the sodium hydroxide solution and it will have no influence on your results. Explain.

(2) Which activity (resting, jogging or other activity) produced the most carbon dioxide? Explain how you determined this.

(3) Oxygen and carbon dioxide levels in the blood are inversely related. In other words, the more oxygen, the less carbon dioxide, and vise versa. Explain this relationship using the respiration equation shown below:

$$6O_2 + C_6H_{12}O_6 \rightarrow 6CO_2 + 6H_2O + 38ATP$$

(4) The carotid body is a small organ (chemoreceptor) that detects blood pH changes and sends impulses to the brain to adjust respiration appropriately. How would one's respiration rate be affected if the carotid body were to detect an abnormally low pH?

FOR THE TEACHER

5.6.1 NEUTRALIZATION

Discussion: Students will probably record a slight increase in temperature as the sodium hydroxide and hydrochloric acids react. The neutralization of hydrogen ions (H^+) and hydroxide ions (OH^-) is exothermic and is easy to observe when neutralizing concentrated solutions of acid and base, but is more difficult when dealing with dilute solutions as in this experiment.

$$H^+(aq)_{6M} + OH^-(aq)_{6M} \rightarrow H_2O(l) + 64 \text{ kJ/mole}$$

If you wish to demonstrate the heat of neutralization more dramatically, slowly mix equal quantities of 6 N NaOH and HCl and watch the temperature climb more than 40°C! This, however, should only be performed as a teacher demonstration.

Answers: (1) Yes. They should appear cubic, the standard shape for sodium chloride crystals. Salts produced by neutralization reactions are indistinguishable from those formed by other means. (2) The stomach has a thick mucus membrane to protect it against the acidic gastric juices. The intestines have thinner walls so that nutrients may be absorbed into the bloodstream. The bicarbonate is introduced to neutralize the acid before it enters the intestines where it could cause serious ulcerations. (3) $Mg(OH)_2 + 2HCl \rightarrow MgCl_2 + 2H_2O$. (4) The carbon dioxide exhaled forms carbonic acid that reacts with the calcium cations in solution to form the insoluble product calcium carbonate. The protons released from carbonic acid combine with the hydroxides of calcium hydroxide to form water. Eventually there are insufficient ions in solution to support a current and the bulb goes out. The light bulb will go out as the solution is neutralized. (5) Calcium carbonate settles out on the bottom of the solution. In addition, a solution of calcium carbonate does not conduct electricity as well as a solution of calcium hydroxide, indicating that it has fewer ions in solution. (6) Neutral. See the answers to questions 4 and 5. (7) A white, insoluble, cloudy precipitate (calcium carbonate) forms in lime-water when calcium hydroxide reacts with carbon dioxide.

5.6.2 TITRATION

Discussion: The procedure in part 1 involves the titration of acid into base, with an end point marked by the disappearance of any trace of pink. Because many students find it easier to note an endpoint marked by the first permanent trace of pink, you may instead wish to titrate base into acid.

Students generally enjoy the "mystery" aspect associated with determining "unknowns." You may wish to embellish their task with a story. For example, you may suggest that they are playing the role of forensic chemists called upon to analyze a substance found at the scene of the crime. You may wish to have students determine which of three suspects left the substance (e.g., poison, blood, cosmetic, etc.) at the scene, and print on the board three possible suspects, each of whom has been linked with a given concentration of the substance in question. Although the task in this situation is simply one of calculating the concentration of an unknown acid or base, it is analogous to much of the analytical forensic work that is performed in police "crime labs" on a daily basis.

The analysis of household products in parts 2 and 3 helps students understand the relevance of chemistry to everyday life, and introduces them to some valuable concepts of quality control. You may wish to have them investigate other products as well. For example, they may determine the amount of ascorbic acid in a vitamin C tablet by titrating with 0.1 N NaOH or the amount of ammonia in household ammonia window cleaner by titrating with 0.50 N hydrochloric acid.

You may wish to provide your students with the following information so that they may understand the principles of acid/base titration more fully.

The product of the hydronium and hydroxide ion concentrations in an aqueous solution is always $10^{-14} M^2$. Thus, if you know the hydronium ion concentration, you can determine the hydroxide ion concentration and vise versa.

$$[H_3O^+][OH^-] = 10^{-14} M^2$$

If the hydronium ion concentration is $10^{-3} M$, then the hydroxide ion concentration must be $10^{-11} M$:

$$[10^{-3}][10^{-11}] = 10^{-14} M^2$$

This helps us predict the pH of laboratory solutions of strong (fully dissociating) acids and strong (fully dissociating) bases. For example, a 0.001 M solution of HCl will produce a hydronium ion concentration of $10^{-3} M$, and a pH of 3, while a 0.00001 M solution will produce a hydronium concentration of $10^{-5} M$ and a pH of 5. By contrast, a 0.01 M solution of sodium hydroxide will produce a solution with a hydroxide ion concentration of $10^{-2} M$, and thus a hydronium ion concentration of $10^{-12} M$ ($[10^{-12} M][10^{-2} M] = 10^{-14} M^2$) and a pH of 12.

Figure H illustrates how pH changes as an acid is added to a base. To help students understand why the relationship is non-linear, you may want to use the "rotating sign analogy." Some stores have rotating signs, and although the sign rotates at a constant speed, the apparent rate of change does not appear constant to the viewer. The rate of change appears to be slowest when one side of the sign is perpendicular to the viewer ("acid"), greatest when it is at right angles ("neutrality"), and then slowest again when the other side ("base") is perpendicular to the viewer. You may make your own teaching tool by painting one side of a piece of cardboard pink (basic color with phenolphthalein) and leaving the other side white (phenolphthalein is colorless in acidic solutions). Mount the sign on a rod that you may rotate at an even rate. The amount of pink visible represents the untitrated base, and the amount of white represents the untitrated acid. The rate of change of pH clearly increases as you reach the end point. You may rotate the board back and forth through the end point to introduce the concept that titration can be performed from the acid side or from the base side.

Answers: (1) It allows them to determine chemical concentrations in company products to make certain that these are within specifications. (2) Titration allows you to determine concentrations of unknown solutions and match them with those associated with other data related to a crime. For example, forensic chemists may need to titrate a bottle of poison from a suspect's home to see if it has the same concentration as one left at the scene of a poisoning. (3) Student answers will most likely be between 4 and 6%. (4) More sour. The sour taste in vinegar is due to the concentration of acetic acid. The more concentrated the solution, the more sour it tastes. (5) This will vary depending upon which ones were tested. (6) 0.01–0.03

moles of HCl. (7) "Heartburn" is a burning sensation in the lower esophagus, just behind the sternum, a location behind the heart. Many people have confused the symptoms of heartburn with heart attacks. Acid indigestion indicates that there is excessive acid present, and sour stomach also indicates excessive acid because acids taste "sour."

5.6.3 BUFFERING

Discussion: When dissolved, Alka-Seltzer® creates a stable buffer system with a pH of approximately 6.6. You may wish to have students compare the buffering capacity of various commercial antacids. If you do not have access to KH_2PO_4 and K_2HPO_4, you may substitute NaH_2PO_4 and Na_2HPO_4.

In part 2 students examine the phosphate buffer system found in the bloodstream. Dry ice is used to simulate respiration because it continuously releases carbon dioxide as it sublimes. You may wish to show your students that the same thing happens (although more slowly) if you exhale through both solutions. As a teacher demonstration, blow through a straw into the solution until the color changes. Be careful never to inhale or suck through the straw!

The phosphate buffer contains two ions (HPO_4^{2-} and $H_2PO_4^-$) that buffer the solution by consuming excess protons or hydroxides:

$$HPO_4^{2-}(aq) + H^+(aq) \rightleftharpoons H_2PO_4^-(aq)$$

$$H_2PO_4^-(aq) + OH^-(aq) \rightleftharpoons HPO_4^{2-}(aq) + H_2O(l)$$

Answers: (1) Yes. It is more difficult to change the pH of a solution when it contains Alka Seltzer®. (2) The pH of the blood would drop below 7.4 due to the build-up of carbonic acid accompanying the production of metabolic carbon dioxide. (3) If weak acids or bases are added to the blood they are neutralized by the phosphate buffering system. (4) Oxygen, water, osmotic pressure, glucose, blood protein levels, nutrient concentrations, etc. (5) HPO_4^{2-} (aq) + H^+(aq) → $H_2PO_4^-$(aq); $H_2PO_4^-$(aq) + OH^- → HPO_4^{2-}(aq) + H_2O(l)

5.6.4 SOIL pH

Discussion: Although soils may buffer the pH of soil moisture, significant changes eventually occur with repeated exposure to certain chemicals. For example, years of acid rain in certain regions may cause a significant degradation in soil quality. Most minerals essential for plant growth (Ca^{2+}, Mg^{2+}, K^+, etc.) are cations and are easily displaced by free protons in acid rainwater. As nutrient minerals are leached away, soils become so impoverished that they are incapable of supporting normal plant growth.

Answers: (1) In general, soils in bogs, swamps, marshes, coniferous forests, and oak forests tend to have a lower pH than soils in deserts, farmlands, and home gardens. Don't be surprised, however, if student data does not corroborate these general trends because their soils are very complex and varied. (2) Oxides of electronegative elements (nonmetals) such as sulfur, nitrogen and phosphorous form acid anhydrides, while oxides of electropositive elements (metals) such as calcium, magnesium, and sodium form base anhydrides. (3) Metal oxides are often base anhydrides that raise soil pH above the optimal level for acidophilic (acid-loving) plants. (4) Student results will vary. Generally sandy soils have a lower buffering capacity than loam or clay-loam soils.

5.6.5 pH REGULATION OF RESPIRATION

Discussion: <u>Instructor demonstration</u>: Students may believe that the pH in the flask changes simply due to the amount of air, not the amount of carbon dioxide rich exhaled breath. Challenge them to develop an experiment to differentiate the effect of inhaled air from exhaled air. Figure N illustrates an apparatus that may be used for this purpose. *Make certain that the tubing is attached as illustrated or you may suck up water from the flasks!* Add 100 mL of water to each flask and add a couple of drops of bromthymol blue (the color of the solution should be a light blue). The instructor will repeatedly inhale and exhale through the attached tube. As you inhale, the pressure in "inhalation flask" drops and air is bubbled through the solution. As you exhale, exhaled air is bubbled through the "exhalation flask" causing the solution to become slightly acidic due to the formation of carbonic acid. Gently inhale and exhale through the tube to make certain that your set up is correct and no fluid is drawn up into the tubes. Repeatedly inhale and exhale into the tube until the solution with the exhaled air becomes acidic and turns yellow, while the solution that has air bubbled through it remains blue.

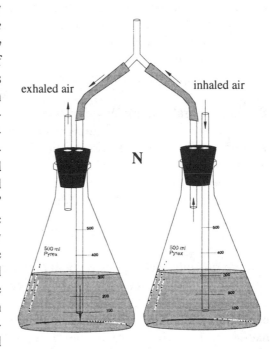

Answers: (1) Titration determines the amount of substance, not its concentration. The water is added to increase the volume so as to promote mixing and viewing. (2) The more vigorous the exercise, the more rapidly the titration will occur. (3) Oxygen oxidizes glucose ($C_6H_{12}O_6$) to produce carbon dioxide. If respiration proceeds rapidly the levels of oxygen will fall and carbon dioxide will rise. (4) Breathing rate will increase.

Applications to Everyday Life

Reclamation of mined land: Mining leaves many scars upon the land, not the least of which is soil pollution. Mine waste often contains minerals that change the pH of the soil. Pyrite (FeS_2), for example, is found in many mine tailings and combines with oxygen and water to form sulfuric acid and other toxic products. Such acidified soils are often neutralized by adding mineral oxides (acid anhydrides) such as are found in limestone.

Reclamation of lakes: Acidic precipitation in much of the northeastern United States, southeastern Canada, and Scandinavia has caused the pH of lake and stream waters to drop too low to support indigenous aquatic life. To combat this problem, limestone (primarily calcium carbonate, $CaCO_3$) is added to the waters. Recent research shows that such treatments are effective in reducing the acidity. Fish and plankton populations return, but they do not always have the original biotic composition.

Baking (neutralization): When baking soda $NaHCO_3$ (sodium hydrogen carbonate) is added to acidic batters (those containing acidic foods such as lemon juice, yogurt, vinegar or sour cream) a neutralization reaction occurs that produces carbon dioxide. This carbon dioxide gas gets trapped in the batter and causes it to "rise" during baking. If insufficient baking soda is added the product will be flat and dense rather than light and airy. Sodium hydrogen carbonate reacts with acetic acid (the acidic ingredient in vinegar) as follows:

$$NaHCO_3 + HC_2H_3O_2 \rightarrow NaC_2H_3O_2 + CO_2\,(g) + H_2O$$

Baking powder: Baking powder will produce carbon dioxide only when mixed into an acidic environment. If a recipe does not include acidic ingredients, then it may be necessary to use baking powder in order to get the batter to rise. Baking powder contains sodium hydrogen carbonate ($NaHCO_3$) and a dry acid such as tartaric acid ($C_4H_6O_6$). When dissolved in the batter, the following neutralization reaction occurs, producing carbon dioxide to cause the batter to rise:

$$2NaHCO_3 + C_4H_6O_6 \rightarrow Na_2C_4H_4O_6 + 2CO_2(g) + 2H_2O$$

Seawater and blood: The rate and equilibrium state of many physiological reactions are pH dependent. The blood contains bicarbonate and phosphate buffers that maintain the blood at an optimal pH of approximately 7.4 as shown in the following two equations:

$$CO_3^{2-}(aq) + H^+(aq) \rightleftharpoons HCO_3^-(aq)$$

$$HPO_4^{2-}(aq) + H^+(aq) \rightleftharpoons H_2PO_4^-(aq)$$

Marine life, like cells in your body, depends on a stable, relatively neutral pH. The ocean is buffered mainly by the bicarbonate system as shown above.

Photographs and archives: To promote long life, photographs and important documents are mounted on "acid free" paper. In the past, acidic anhydrides were used as filler in the manufacture of paper. Under humid conditions acids form and break down the cellulose fibers in the paper.

Stalactites and stalagmites: Rain water is naturally slightly acidic. As it percolates through a basic rock like limestone, minerals are dissolved. These minerals may seep through the ceiling of a cave, and be slowly deposited as hanging spike-like formations (stalactites) where the water drips, or as rising spike-like floor formations (stalagmites) where dripping water lands. If you live in an area with a mineral-rich water supply, you may notice the formation of similar structures around the openings of drinking fountains or faucets.

5.7 CRYSTALS AND CRYSTALLIZATION

The ancient Greeks were impressed with the beauty and symmetry of naturally occurring crystals and gave the name *"crystallos"* ("frozen") to quartz and similar clear crystals because their appearance resembled that of ice. We now use the term "crystal" to refer to any solid body composed of an element or compound that displays regular flat surfaces that intersect each other at specific, predictable angles. In the 17th century, the Dutch scientist Nicolaus Steno postulated that angles between crystal faces on all samples of a given substance are equal. Years of research have confirmed Steno's postulate, and it is now known as the law of the "constancy of interfacial angles" and allows us to identify compounds on the basis of crystal shape. Figures A, B and C show rocks that contain crystals, each with its own unique crystalline structure.

Crystals have many applications in today's world, as a brief discussion of quartz, the most common of all crystals, indicates. As in ancient times, people today value crystals for their beauty. Amethyst (February's birthstone), citrine, ametrine, rose quartz, onyx, agates, and chrysoprase are a few examples of popular quartz gem stones. Although you may not have seen many large quartz crystals before, you are undoubtedly familiar with fractured quartz if you have ever been to the beach. Many of the approximately 5×10^{21} grains of sand on the world's beaches are quartz crystals which have been worn down by abrasive interaction with each other. Because quartz crystals have sharp edges, they are used as abrasives in sandpapers, sandblasting, and for polishing and cutting glass, stone, and metal. Some forms of quartz are transparent and are used for windows that must be exposed to extreme pressure (such as those in deep-sea vessels) or extreme heat (such as those in incinerators and foundries).

Because crystals are composed of regularly arranged atoms or molecules, they vibrate at consistent, predictable frequencies when subjected to an electric field. Look at your watch and you may notice that it says "quartz" on it, indicating that the mechanisms are timed by a vibrating quartz crystal in much the same way a grandfather clock is timed by a swinging pendulum. Quartz crystals are also used to regulate the frequency of radio transmitters and receivers, computer microprocessors, and many telecommunication devices. Because the resonant frequency of a quartz crystal is temperature sensitive, it is used in sensitive thermometers that must detect temperature changes of microkelvins (millionths of Kelvins!). When quartz crystals are squeezed, they generate a voltage, and thus can be used to detect changes in pressure in microphones (where they detect sound waves) and electronic balances (where they detect pressure).

As a brief analysis of quartz has shown, crystals are used in a wide variety of household and industrial applications. In this chapter you will investigate crystals and crystallization, the process by which crystals are formed.

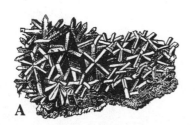

A   B   C

5.7.1 SUPERSATURATION
AND CRYSTALLIZATION

Concepts to Investigate: Supersaturation, seed crystals, crystallization, exothermic reactions, endothermic reactions, heat of crystallization.

Materials: Part 1: Sodium acetate trihydrate, distilled water, beaker, watch glass, hot plate, stirring rod, squeeze water bottle, test tubes; Part 2: Sodium thiosulfate pentahydrate, microspatula, glass wool.

Safety: Wear goggles, lab coat and gloves. Sodium acetate is a skin, eye and respiratory irritant. Handle glass wool with gloves.

Principles and Procedures: Bees produce honey, a thick solution of glucose and fructose, to feed their larva and use as food during months when flowers are not available (Figure D). If you have kept a jar of honey for a long time, you may have noticed that it eventually crystallizes. Why would honey be a free-flowing liquid when you bring it home from the market, but a crystallized mass a few months later?

Honey is an example of a supersaturated solution—a solution that contains more dissolved solutes than would be predicted on the basis of its temperature and pressure. When honey is opened and allowed to stand at room temperature, sugar starts to crystallize out of solution (Figure G). Because most people prefer honey in fluid form, honey processors first heat it to about 66°C (Figure E), then package it in hermetically sealed (air-tight) containers (Figure F). After the honey is opened, water may evaporate, and crystals may form. Once a few crystals form, the rest of the honey crystallizes rather rapidly (Figure G).

A solution is said to be at the saturation point when both the dissolved and undissolved states of the solute exist, and when the rate of dissolution (the rate at which crystals are dissolving) is equivalent to the rate of crystallization (the rate at which crystals are forming). The amount of dissolved solute in a saturated solution at a given temperature and pressure is constant and predictable. No more solute will dissolve when added to a saturated solution if the solute phase is present. It is possible, however, to create a supersaturated solution in

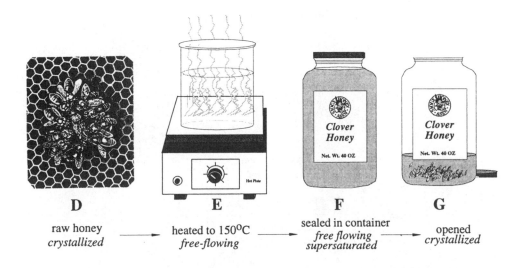

D
raw honey
crystallized

E
heated to 150°C
free-flowing

F
sealed in container
free flowing
supersaturated

G
opened
crystallized

which more solute is dissolved than at the saturation point if the crystallized solute phase is absent.

In most cases, the solubility of a solute increases with temperature. Thus, a hot solution can contain more dissolved solutes than a cool one. If a solution is saturated at high temperatures and then gradually cooled, crystals may not form even at the saturation point. When crystals do begin to form, or when "seed crystals" of the solute are added, crystallization may take place rapidly. In these activities you will investigate rapid crystallization in supersaturated solutions.

Part 1: Sodium acetate trihydrate: Place 25 g of sodium acetate trihydrate in a beaker and add 3 mL of distilled water. Gently heat the beaker to dissolve the crystals. Add water, drop by drop, to the warm mixture to dissolve any crystals in the solution or on the sides of the beaker.

$$CH_3COONa(s) \longrightarrow Na^+(aq) + CH_3COO^-(aq)$$

Cover the beaker and allow it to cool to room temperature. Prepare two clean watch glasses, Petri dishes or glass plates, one with a small pile of approximately 0.3 grams of sodium acetate trihydrate and the other without. Slowly pour a few mL of the solution onto the bare watch glass. Does any crystallization occur? Now pour the solution on the pile of crystals. Do crystals form more rapidly in the presence or absence of existing crystals? If time permits, repeat the procedure that produces crystals the fastest and see how tall you can make a crystal column (Figure H).

$$Na^+(aq) + CH_3COO^-(aq) \longrightarrow CH_3COONa(s)$$

Part 2: Seed crystals: Dissolve approximately 20 g of sodium thiosulfate pentahydrate (hypo, $Na_2S_2O_3 \cdot 5H_2O$) in 10 mL of distilled water that has been heated to just below the boiling point. Stir the solution until no crystals remain. Filter the hot solution through glass wool (to remove crystals or other contamination) into two very clean test tubes. Cover the solutions and allow them to cool to room temperature without disturbance for at least 30 minutes. Add a few crystals of sodium chloride to one test tube and a few crystals of sodium thiosulfate pentahydrate to the other (Figure I). Do crystals form in both? How fast do the crystals form? Feel the test tubes. Is there any change in the temperature of the tubes as the crystals form? Is the crystallization of sodium thiosulfate pentahydrate an endothermic

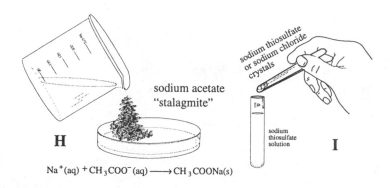

sodium acetate "stalagmite"

H

I

sodium thiosulfate or sodium chloride crystals

sodium thiosulfate solution

$$Na^+(aq) + CH_3COO^-(aq) \longrightarrow CH_3COONa(s)$$

(consumes energy, temperature decreases) or exothermic (produces energy, temperature increases) reaction?

This activity may also be performed by heating test tubes that are half-filled with sodium thiosulfate pentahydrate ($Na_2S_2O_3 \cdot 5H_2O$). With sufficient heating, the bound water is released and the crystals dissolve in the water of hydration. Wash down any crystals on the sides of the tube with a minimal amount of distilled water. Once the crystals are completely dissolved, seal the tubes and allow them to cool in a room-temperature water bath. Hold the tubes in your hand and add a crystal of sodium chloride to one and a crystal of sodium thiosulfate pentahydrate to the other. Which crystallizes faster? Is there any change in temperature? What happens if you shake the test tubes?

Questions

(1) In part 1, did crystals form more rapidly when the supersaturated solution was poured on to clean glass or on to crystals of sodium acetate trihydrate? Explain.

(2) A seed crystal is one that stimulates the crystallization of the solute in a supersaturated solution. Can any crystal serve as a seed crystal, or is it necessary to use a crystal of dissolved solute?

(3) Is the crystallization of sodium thiosulfate (part 2) an endothermic or exothermic process? Explain.

(4) Why is it necessary to fully dissolve all solutes and wash down the sides of the containers in these activities?

5.7.2 CRYSTALLIZATION BY EVAPORATION

Concepts to Investigate: Crystallization, evaporation, nucleation, crystal shape.

Materials: Bare brick or charcoal briquette, salt, laundry bluing ($KFe[Fe(CN)_6]$), household ammonia (NH_4OH), hand lens or dissecting microscope.

Principles and Procedures: Today you may have eaten grapes grown in Chile, worked on a computer made in America, driven a car assembled in Mexico, worn clothes sewn in Thailand, and kept time with a watch made in Switzerland. The robust international trade that allows us to acquire goods from around the world began thousands of years ago with simple commodities such as salt. Traders traveled thousands of miles to exchange salt for other precious commodities such as gold and spices. Salt was, and is, of great value as a flavor enhancer (it adds flavor to bland foods, and masks the flavors of spoiled foods), and as a food preservative (meats and vegetables are preserved in brine). Salt was harvested by trapping seawater behind dikes made in shallow coastal waters. As water evaporated from these basins, salt crystallized and was collected. Such solar evaporation pans are still used to collect salt from inland seas such as the Salton Sea in California and the Dead Sea in Israel. Evaporation is a useful technique to crystallize sodium chloride and many other salts as well.

Part 1: Re-crystallization of salt: Examine table salt (NaCl) crystals using a hand lens or microscope. What is the shape of these crystals? Add 20 to 30 grams of salt to a container and add sufficient water until all is dissolved. Allow the container to sit undisturbed in full sunlight until all the water has evaporated. Examine the salt crystals formed. Do these crystals have the same shape as the original crystals?

Part 2: "Salt garden": Place four or five charcoal briquettes in the bottom of a bowl. Red brick may be substituted if briquettes are not available. Make a solution as follows: one part table salt, one part laundry bluing, one part household ammonia, and two parts water. Place the briquettes in a pan or bowl and pour the solution over them until they are half-submerged as shown in Figure J. After two or three days, add additional solution to the bottom of bowl (don't disturb the crystals forming on the tops of the briquettes) so that the bottom half of the briquettes remain submerged. Solution is drawn up through the porous briquettes via capillary action. As water evaporates from the top surfaces of the briquettes, salt crystals begin to form. The growth of these crystals can be continued by adding more solution to the bowl.

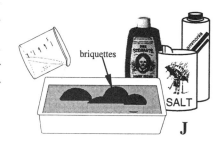

Although the crystals that form upon the surface of the briquettes are salt crystals, they do not appear to have the same shape as those formed in part 1. Laundry bluing is a colloidal suspension containing potassium iron (II) hexacyanoferrate (III) ($KFe[Fe(CN)_6]$). The tiny particles in this suspension provide nuclei on which salt crystals may form.

Questions

(1) In part 1 you examined salt crystals, dissolved them, and then re-examined them. Do they appear to have the same shape upon re-crystallization?

(2) Will a salt crystal garden form more rapidly under humid conditions or arid conditions? Explain.

(3) Particles of laundry bluing served as nuclei to accelerate the formation of salt crystals in part 2. What kinds of particles might accelerate the formation of ice crystals (snow) in the atmosphere?

(4) In 1785 there was a major volcanic eruption in Iceland that released a significant amount of dust into the atmosphere. Climatologists suggest that this caused the exceptionally heavy snowfall that occurred throughout Scandinavia that year. Explain.

5.7.3 GROWING CRYSTALS; CRYSTAL SHAPES

Concepts to Investigate: Crystallization, crystal shape, supersaturation, cubic, tetragonal, orthorhombic, monoclinic, triclinic, rhombohedral, and hexagonal crystals.

Materials: Part 1: Table sugar (sucrose), beaker, hot plate, string or thread, overhead transparency; Part 2: Sodium chloride (table salt, NaCl), ammonium chloride (NH_4Cl), ammonium ferric sulfate ($NH_4Fe(SO_4)_2 \cdot 12H_2O$), copper sulfate pentahydrate ($CuSO_4 \cdot 5H_2O$), magnesium sulfate heptahydrate (Epsom salts, $MgSO_4 \cdot 7H_2O$), aluminum potassium sulfate dodecahydrate (alum, $KAl(SO_4)_2 \cdot 12H_2O$), potassium chloride (KCl), sodium tartrate (Rochelle salt, $KNaC_4H_4O_6$), potassium sulfate (K_2SO_4), sodium bicarbonate (baking soda, $NaHCO_3$), zinc nitrate hexahydrate ($Zn(NO_3)_2 \cdot 6H_2O$).

Safety: Wear goggles and lab coat. Never touch these or any other chemicals. The temperature of the sugar solution in part 1 will rise significantly above 100°C and can cause severe burns.

Principles and Procedures:

Part 1: Sugar crystals: Heat 250 mL of water to boiling. Slowly add 500 mL of table sugar (sucrose, $C_{12}H_{22}O_{11}$), stirring constantly with a glass rod until all sugar is dissolved. Once all sugar has dissolved, remove the beaker from the hot plate. Tie a washer or nut to a cotton string or thread and dip the thread into the hot solution, and then dip it into dry sugar so that some seed crystals of sucrose adhere to the string. Allow the solution to cool to room temperature, cover it with a section of acetate from an overhead transparency through which a small window has been cut, and suspend the string with seed crystals into the solution as shown in Figure K. The nut or washer will weight the string so that it will not float on the surface. Do not disturb the container, and observe and record the growth of the crystals daily. Remove the crystals from the solution after two weeks and examine the crystalline structure with a hand lens or dissecting microscope. Compare the shape of these large crystals with the shape of small sugar crystals used for cooking. Do they have the same shape? Describe the shape of the crystals.

Part 2: Crystallization of mineral salts from supersaturated solutions: Water is a polar molecule and therefore an excellent solvent for polar solutes like most mineral salts. Sodium chloride (table salt) dissociates into sodium cations and chloride anions when dissolved in water. If water in a salt solution is allowed to evaporate, the ions combine once again in an orderly fashion to make ionic crystals. In this experiment you will grow a variety of crystals and compare their shapes.

Fill a test tube or beaker half-full with boiling water and stir in sodium chloride (NaCl, table salt) until no more dissolves. Decant the hot liquid into a clean container. Tie a washer or nut to the end of a length of thread or string, dip the string in the hot solution, and then draw the string through salt crystals so that one or more adhere to the string. Allow the string and salt solution to cool to room temperature, and then suspend the string in the solution as illustrated in Figure K. Allow the container to stand undisturbed for one week, observing and recording crystal growth when possible. Use a magnifying glass to observe and describe the shape of the salt crystals. Repeat the process with the following compounds and compare the shapes of their crystals.

ammonium chloride (NH_4Cl)

ammonium ferric sulfate dodecahydrate ($NH_4Fe(SO_4)_2·12H_2O$)

copper sulfate pentahydrate ($CuSO_4·5H_2O$)

magnesium sulfate heptahydrate (Epsom salts; $MgSO_4·7H_2O$)

aluminum potassium sulfate dodecahydrate (alum, $AlK(SO_4)_2·12H_2O$)

potassium chloride (KCl)

potassium sodium tartrate (Rochelle salt, $KNaC_4H_4O_6$)

potassium sulfate (K_2SO_4)

sodium bicarbonate (baking soda, $NaHCO_3$)

zinc nitrate hexahydrate ($Zn(NO_3)_2·6H_2O$)

To obtain larger crystals you will need to repeat the crystallization process. Select a large crystal from the first activity, or simply allow one of the solutions to evaporate and select a large crystal from the resulting mass. Use a slip knot to tie the crystal with fine cotton thread. Re-dissolve the remainder of the crystals and prepare a supersaturated solution as before. Allow the solution to cool to room temperature and suspend the crystal (Figure K). You may repeat the process until the crystal reaches the desired size. A crystal consists of millions of individual structural units (unit cells) composed of groups of atoms, molecules, or ions. These cells are repeated in all directions to form a distinct geometric shape (Figure L).

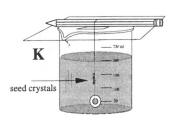

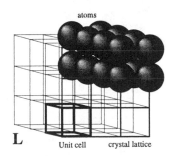

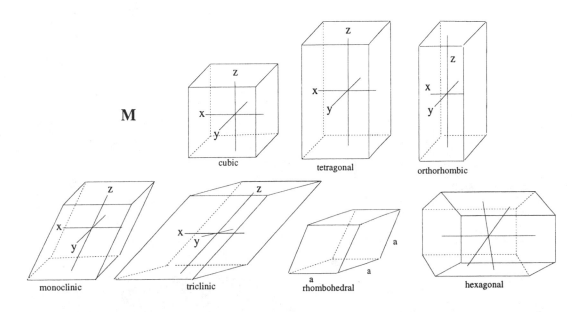

Crystals can be categorized according to shape. In cubic crystals, all three axes (x,y,z) are of equal length and mutually perpendicular, and all faces are square. In tetragonal crystals the axes are mutually perpendicular, but one axis (z) is longer than the other two (x,y). This creates a crystal with two square faces and four equal rectangular faces. Orthorhombic is similar to tetragonal except that all three axes are of different lengths. Each face of the crystal is rectangular, but no two pairs of faces have equal dimensions (Figure M).

In a monoclinic crystal, two axes are perpendicular to each other (creating four rectangular faces) but these axes are not perpendicular to the third (creating two parallelogram faces). In a triclinic crystal, none of the axes are perpendicular to each other and all six faces are parallelograms. A hexagonal crystal has eight faces, two of which are hexagons, and six of which are rectangles. A rhombohedral crystal is like a tilted cube, and all its faces have equal area (Figure M). Classify the crystals you have grown.

It should be noted that crystal growth is often distorted by environmental factors. For example, a crystal growing on the bottom of a container can only grow up and out, but not down, creating an irregular crystal. Contamination and the presence of other crystals will also affect crystal growth and give a distorted appearance.

Questions

(1) Classify the crystals you grew according to their shape.

(2) Why don't your crystals appear as regular as those illustrated in Figure M?

(3) Around which of the following bodies of water would you expect to see the largest accumulation of salt crystals? The numbers in parentheses indicate the concentration in parts per million (ppm) of salt in each body of water. Lake Tahoe (California/Nevada) (70), Lake Michigan (170), Missouri River (360), Ocean (35,000), Dead Sea (250,000). Explain.

(4) The space shuttle has provided scientists the opportunity to perform a variety of experiments in a "weightless" environment. On Earth it is often difficult to grow perfect crystals because they tend to grow faster near the bottom of the crystal than near the top because the supersaturated solution is denser near the bottom than near the top. Would crystals grow more symmetrically in the weightless environment of space? Explain.

5.7.4 METALLIC CRYSTALS

Concepts to Investigate: Crystallization, polycrystalline masses, metallic crystals, rate of crystallization.

Materials: Part 1: Steel wool, iron nail (ungalvanized), copper (II) sulfate pentahydrate ($CuSO_4 \cdot 5H_2O$), beaker, hand lens or microscope; Part 2: Copper wire, 1 *M* silver nitrate ($AgNO_3$) solution.

Safety: Wear goggles, lab coat and gloves. Copper (II) sulfate is a skin and respiratory irritant, and silver nitrate is a corrosive solid. Avoid contact with these and all chemicals.

Principles and Procedures: When we think of crystals, we generally think of large, brilliant gems or minerals that have a clearly recognizable shape and symmetry. Most people would not think that metal, rock or dirt are crystalline. Yet most such solids indeed have a crystalline nature, but the orderliness is on such a small scale that it can often not be seen with the unaided eye. As a molten metal cools, crystals start to form. If the metal cools rapidly, crystals form in numerous locations, forming a polycrystalline mass. Figure N shows three orderly crystalline masses developing as a molten metal cools. If the crystals are extremely small (as when the molten metal is cooled very rapidly) then no crystalline structures will be visible, even with powerful microscopes. It is possible, however, to see some crystalline structure in cast iron or zinc. If possible examine the surface of a chunk of cast iron that has been broken in two, and you may notice detail such as illustrated in Figure O. The small smooth masses in the fractured surface are probably iron crystals that formed as the iron slowly cooled.

In this activity you will investigate the formation of metallic crystals, not as a molten metal cools, but as metallic ions in solution are reduced and align with existing atoms.

Part 1: Growing copper crystals: Prepare a copper sulfate solution by dissolving 5 to 10 grams of copper (II) sulfate pentahydrate ($CuSO_4 \cdot 5H_2O$) in a beaker containing 100 mL of water. Polish an ungalvanized iron nail with steel wool and then suspend in the beaker with thread as shown in Figure P. Iron is a more active metal than copper and displaces copper ions in the aqueous copper sulfate solution as indicated by the following equation:

$$2Fe(s) + 3CuSO_4(aq) \longrightarrow Fe_2(SO_4)_3(aq) + 3Cu(s)$$

Tiny copper crystals should start to grow on the submerged surfaces of the nail. Remove the nail after approximately 10 to 15 minutes and compare the submerged and unsubmerged surfaces. The reddish brown deposit on the nail is copper. Examine the copper deposit using a magnifying lens, dissecting microscope or video microscope. Is the copper an amorphous

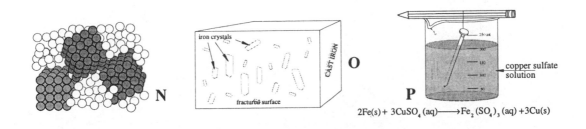

iron crystals

CAST IRON

fractured surface

N   **O**   copper sulfate solution   **P**

$2Fe(s) + 3CuSO_4(aq) \longrightarrow Fe_2(SO_4)_3(aq) + 3Cu(s)$

(without shape) mass, or is it a polycrystalline mass (composed of many small crystals)? Estimate the length of the longest copper crystals if they are visible. Try to grow longer crystals by suspending the nail in the copper sulfate solution for a week. Do you observe any changes in the solution after the nail has been hanging for such a long time?

Part 2: Growing silver crystals:
Polish a section of copper wire using steel wool. Place a one centimeter section of the polished wire on a microscope slide and add a few drops of 1 M silver nitrate solution to one end of the wire. Silver crystals will begin to grow on the wire as the following single replacement reaction occurs:

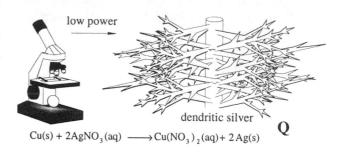

$$Cu(s) + 2AgNO_3(aq) \longrightarrow Cu(NO_3)_2(aq) + 2Ag(s)$$

Observe the crystals using a magnifying lens, a dissecting microscope, or a laboratory microscope set on low power with above-stage lighting (Figure Q). Dilute a small quantity of silver nitrate solution to 0.1 M and repeat. Is the rate of crystal growth related to the concentration of the silver nitrate solution?

Questions

(1) In nature, copper is found in ores as sulfides (chalcocite, chalcopyrite, bornite) and oxides (cuprite, malachite, azurite). The copper is extracted from these ores by crushing the ore, dissolving it in acidic solutions, and then reacting it with scrap iron. Explain the role of the scrap iron in this process.

(2) What is the relationship between solution concentration and the rate of crystal growth (part 2)? Explain.

(3) Silver crystals (Figure Q) have a "dendritic" shape. The root word "dend" is found in many words including dendrite, dendrology, rhododendron, and philodendron. Look these words up in a dictionary and find out what they all have in common and explain why the silver crystals may be described as dendritic.

(4) Large metallic crystals are rarely found in nature. Explain.

5.7.5 SILICATE CRYSTALS

Concepts to Investigate: Silicates, crystal growth, semi-permeable membranes, minerals.

Materials: Magic Rocks® kit, and/or: sodium silicate; distilled water, cobalt (II) chloride ($CoCl_2$), copper (II) chloride ($CuCl_2$), iron (III) chloride ($FeCl_3$), iron (II) sulfate ($FeSO_4$), iron (III) sulfate ($Fe_2(SO_4)_3$), manganese (II) chloride ($MnCl_2$), zinc sulfate ($ZnSO_4$).

Principles and Procedures: Have you ever been to a mineral show and seen some wonderful crystals like those shown in Figures A, B, C and R? Although such specimens are beautiful and attract attention, we should not forget that the dirt we walk on is also composed of minerals. A mineral is any naturally occurring homogeneous solid that has a definite chemical composition and an internal crystalline structure. Examine soil, sand and rock particles under a dissecting microscope and see if you can distinguish small crystals.

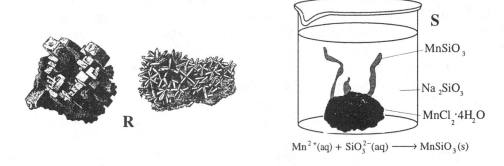

R   S

$MnSiO_3$

Na_2SiO_3

$MnCl_2 \cdot 4H_2O$

$$Mn^{2+}(aq) + SiO_3^{2-}(aq) \longrightarrow MnSiO_3(s)$$

Nearly 95% of the Earth's crust is composed of silicon-based minerals known as silicates. Many of the most common silicates are simply composed of silicon and oxygen (SiO_4, Si_2O_7, Si_6O_{18}, SiO_3, Si_2O_6, Si_2O_5 or SiO_2), while others include metal ions such as Mg^{2+}, Fe^{2+}, Fe^{3+}, Mn^{2+}, Al^{3+}, and Ti^{4+}. Magnesium silicate ($MgSiO_3$), for example, is a common silicaceous mineral (pyroxene) found in many rocks and soils.

Most silicates are insoluble in water, which explains why soil doesn't dissolve when it rains. Sodium silicate (Na_2SiO_3), however, is unusual in that it is water soluble. Dissolved sodium silicate reacts with many mineral salts to form a variety of mineral silicates. For example, when manganese (II) chloride ($MnCl_2 \cdot 4H_2O$) dissolves in an aqueous solution of sodium silicate, it dissociates into manganese (Mn^{2+}) and chloride (Cl^-) ions. These ions react with the silicate ion to form red manganese silicate:

$$Mn^{2+}(aq) + SiO_3^{2-}(aq) \longrightarrow MnSiO_3(s)$$

The formation of manganese silicate at the boundary of the manganese (II) chloride and the sodium silicate solution occurs rapidly. Manganese silicate is insoluble and forms a semi-permeable membrane around a chunk of manganese (II) chloride. Water passes through this membrane by osmosis because the concentration of dissolved solutes inside is greater than it is outside (see sections 2.3.5–6). As water moves in, more manganese (II) chloride dissolves and dissociates. The osmotic pressure inside the membrane increases until the membrane

Table 1: Silicate Crystals

Mineral Salt	Formula	Possible Silicate	Color
cobalt (II) chloride	$CoCl_2 \cdot 6H_2O$		
copper (II) chloride	$CuCl_2 \cdot 2H_2O$		
iron (III) chloride	$FeCl_3 \cdot 6H_2O$		
iron (II) sulfate	$FeSO_4 \cdot 7H_2O$		
iron (III) sulfate	$Fe_2(SO_4)_3 \cdot 5H_2O$		
manganese (II) chloride	$MnCl_2 \cdot 4H_2O$		
zinc sulfate	$ZnSO_4 \cdot 7H_2O$		

bursts and a new, larger membrane forms rapidly. The process is repeated as more water flows in by osmosis, increasing the pressure inside the membrane and causing it to rupture and re-form. As a result, the crystalline membrane grows in a rather rapid and often bizarre fashion (Figure S). In this activity you will investigate the formation of various mineral silicates placed in a sodium silicate solution. If you have grown Magic Rocks® at home then you will be familiar with this activity.

Dilute reagent grade sodium silicate solution by adding two parts distilled water to one part sodium silicate. This will produce a solution with a concentration similar to that used in the commercial Magic Rocks® product. Add sodium silicate solution to a series of test tubes or beakers. Into each container place a small lump (0.5 cm in diameter) of each of the salts listed in Table 1. Record all of your observations about crystal growth. Which minerals cause the fastest growth? Are the colors of the crystals always the same as the colors of the lumps from which they arise? Complete Table 1. Suggest possible silicates that may form.

Questions

   (1) What were the colors of the resulting silicates?

   (2) In which solutions did the silicates grow fastest?

   (3) Why are the silicate structures hollow?

   (4) Sodium silicate is often referred to as "water glass." Explain.

5.7.6 STALACTITES AND STALAGMITES

Concepts to Investigate: Speleothems, stalactites, stalagmites, crystallization, LeChâtelier's Principle.

Materials: Part 1: Magnesium sulfate (Epsom salts, $MgSO_4$), beakers, cotton string or thread; Part 2: Copper (II) sulfate pentahydrate ($CuSO_4 \cdot 5H_2O$), screen mesh, test tubes, household ammonia.

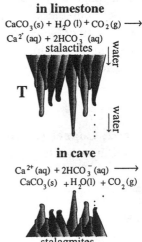

Principles and Procedures: Mammoth Cave is the longest cave in the world, winding for nearly 531 km (330 miles) through limestone in western-central Kentucky! Mammoth Cave, like nearly all limestone caves, displays spectacular speleothems, spire-like formations that grow from both the top and the bottom of caverns (Figure T). The spires that descend from the ceilings are known as stalactites, while those that rise from the floor of the cave are known as stalagmites. Stalactites and stalagmites are formed by the opposite reaction that forms the caverns themselves.

Carbon dioxide, an atmospheric gas, dissolves in water to produce a very dilute solution of carbonic acid:

$$H_2O(l) + CO_2(g) \longrightarrow H_2CO_3(aq)$$

Although this weak acidic solution has virtually no effect on granite and many other rocks, it does react with calcium carbonate found in limestone:

$$H_2CO_3(aq) + CaCO_3(s) \longrightarrow Ca^{2+}(aq) + 2HCO_3^-(aq)$$

Over considerable time, a dilute solution of carbonic acid can slowly erode limestone and create caves like those in Kentucky. The summary equation for this process may be written:

$$CaCO_3(s) + H_2O(l) + CO_2(g) \longrightarrow Ca^{2+}(aq) + 2HCO_3^-(aq)$$

As solutions containing aqueous calcium (Ca^{2+}(aq)) and aqueous bicarbonate ion (HCO_3^-(aq)) slowly percolate through limestone, they may eventually enter an air-filled cavern. Since the carbon dioxide concentration in the cavern is lower than it is in solution, carbon dioxide diffuses from the water into the air. According to LeChâtelier's Principle, the reaction now shifts to the left, and calcium carbonate crystallizes on the surface of the cave.

$$CaCO_3(s) + H_2O(l) + CO_2(g) \longleftarrow Ca^{2+}(aq) + 2HCO_3^-(aq)$$

Calcium carbonate (calcite) forms wherever water drips. Stalactites grow as more and more calcium carbonate crystallizes from solution just as icicles grow when liquid water freezes while running down the outside of an existing spire.

Calcium carbonate also crystallizes at the point on the floor where water drips, causing the formation of cone-shaped structures rising from the ground known as stalagmites. After very long periods of time, the stalactites and stalagmites may eventually grow together to create calcite columns in the cave. Since the formation of calcite speleothems is much too slow to observe, we will investigate a similar phenomena using other chemicals. It must be remembered that these activities are analogous to what occurs in limestone caves, but not the real thing.

Part 1: Magnesium sulfate "stalactites": Fill a container with warm water and dissolve as much magnesium sulfate (Epsom salts, $MgSO_4$) as possible. Use this solution to fill two smaller containers. Soak a cotton string in the solution and then drape the string between the two containers as shown in Figure U. The strings should extend to the bottom of each container and sag below the levels of solution. Allow the string to stand undisturbed for a week or more and measure the rate of "stalactite" formation at the dip in the string.

$$Mg^{2+}(aq) + SO_4^{2-}(aq) \longrightarrow MgSO_4(s)$$

Part 2: Copper (II) hydroxide "stalactites: Copper sulfate ($CuSO_4$) dissociates when dissolved in water to produce copper ions:

$$CuSO_4(s) \longrightarrow Cu^{2+}(aq) + SO_4^{2-}(aq)$$

When such copper ions are placed in a basic ammonia solution (NH_4OH), copper (II) hydroxide ($Cu(OH)_2$ forms.

$$Cu^{2+}(aq) + 2NH_4OH(aq) \longrightarrow Cu(OH)_2(s) + 2NH_4^+(aq)$$

In this activity you will observe the development of stalactite and stalagmite-like copper (II) hydroxide formations. *Put on goggles, lab coat and gloves* and cut a small section of fiberglass screening mesh or cheesecloth and create a small basin in the top of a wide test tube, flask, beaker or other container (Figure V). Fill the container with household ammonia solution until the solution just covers the bottom of the mesh. Place a layer of large copper (II) sulfate pentahydrate crystals in the mesh and observe the formation of copper hydroxide "stalactites." Leave the solution undisturbed for a week. Maintain the level of the ammonia solution as shown in Figure V. Stalagmite-like formations may form if some of the crystals break off and sink to the bottom of the solution. Record the length of the longest "stalactite" after 10 minutes. What is the rate of growth in millimeters per minute? Because of the presence of the dark blue tetra-amine copper (II) complex ion ($Cu(NH_3)_4^{2+}$) it may be necessary to view the forming "speleothems" with a flashlight.

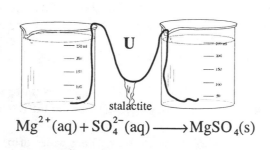

$$Mg^{2+}(aq) + SO_4^{2-}(aq) \longrightarrow MgSO_4(s)$$

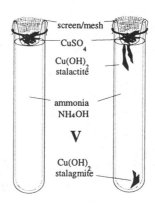

Questions

(1) Speleologists (those who study caves) and park rangers warn tourists not to touch stalactites and stalagmites because the oils from one's hand may hinder the future growth of these structures. Explain.

(2) Many public drinking fountains exhibit a build up of lime where the water exits. Explain.

(3) Do some research in the library or on the Internet to gather pictures of the types of crystal formations that may occur in caves. What are some of their names, and what are they made of?

(4) From a chemical perspective, which of the two reactions (magnesium sulfate crystal formation or copper (II) hydroxide formation) is a better analogy for speleothem formation. Explain.

5.7.7 RATE OF CRYSTALLIZATION AND CRYSTAL SIZE

Concepts to Investigate: Rate of crystallization, crystal size.

Materials: <u>Part 1</u>: Mannitol (mannite, $HOCH_2(CHOH)_4CH_2OH$), hot plate, microscope slide; <u>Part 2</u>: Phenyl salicylate (salsol, $C_6H_4OHCOOC_6H_5$); <u>Part 3</u>: Sulfur, heavy-duty aluminum foil, forceps, burner.

Principles and Procedures: Granite and obsidian are two igneous rocks that have a very similar chemical composition, but very different properties. Granite is generally a white rock containing numerous clearly visible quartz and feldspar crystals. Many mountains, like the famed Half Dome in Yosemite Valley or Mount Everest (the tallest peak in the world, 29,028 ft.; 8848 m), are made of granite. Granite is used for many applications such as counter tops, flooring, monuments (e.g., most of the large monuments in Washington D.C. have large amounts of granite), and facings for buildings. Obsidian (volcanic glass), by contrast, is generally a very dark rock, contains no visible crystals and has many of the properties of common household glass. Native Americans used obsidian for arrow-heads because of its hard, glass-like qualities. Why might two rocks which have nearly the same chemical composition have such different properties? Do the following activities to find out!

Part 1: Mannitol: Place a small amount of mannitol (mannite, $HOCH_2(CHOH)_4CH_2OH$) on a microscope slide and place on a hot plate until the mannitol melts (m.p. 166–168°C). Pick up the slide with forceps, cover with a cover-slip and place on a ceramic plate that has been cooled in a refrigerator. Repeat the process with a second slide, only allow this one to cool slowly on a room-temperature counter top. Observe both slides at low power (40×) and draw pictures of the crystal patterns you see. Note the size, number, and shape of the crystals. Are crystals more noticeable in the sample that cooled quickly or slowly?

Part 2: Phenyl salicylate: Melt a small amount of phenyl salicylate ($C_6H_4OHCOOC_6H_5$, m.p. 41–43°C) on a hot plate adjusted to one of its lowest settings. Once the crystal has melted, place it on a ceramic plate that has been cooled in the refrigerator. If necessary, you may need to add a seed crystal to start the process. Prepare a second sample in a similar way, only allow it to cool slowly by placing on a countertop at room temperature. Examine the crystalline structure of both.

Part 3: Sulfur *Teacher demonstration only*: Fashion two "crucibles" out of heavy-duty aluminum foil by wrapping a square piece around the end of a test tube. Add sulfur to each to a depth of approximately 1 centimeter. In a fume hood melt the sulfur in one "crucible" by holding the tube with tongs in the flame of a laboratory burner. (Note: excessive heating will cause the sulfur to ignite). Once the sulfur has melted, place the "crucible" in cold water, being careful not to allow water to contact the sulfur. Repeat the procedure with a second sample of sulfur, only allow this sample to cool slowly on the counter top. When both samples have cooled to room temperature, open them and examine the structure of the sulfur with a magnifying glass. Do both look the same? Which looks more like obsidian (smooth and glassy)? Which looks more crystalline?

Questions

(1) Compare and contrast the crystal size of the rapidly cooled samples of mannitol, phenyl salicylate, and sulfur with the samples cooled more slowly.

(2) Does rapid cooling promote large or small crystal formation?

(3) Geologists think that large crystal size in igneous rocks indicates that such rocks formed deep underground, while small crystal size indicates they formed near the surface. Explain this reasoning.

(4) Granite includes large crystals of quartz and feldspar, while obsidian, although chemically similar, does not. What might this tell you about the way in which these rocks are formed?

FOR THE TEACHER

5.7.1 SUPERSATURATION AND CRYSTALLIZATION

Discussion: The test tubes containing the "melted" (dissolved in their own water of crystallization) sodium thiosulfate can be used year after year. Seal and store them in a box.

Answers: (1) The crystals form rapidly when they come in contact with the "seed crystals" of sodium acetate. The seed crystals provide a "template" upon which dissolved solute particles align during the rapid crystallization process. (2) Crystals of the same substance as the dissolved solute serve as the best seeds because they provide the ionic bonding patterns required. Other crystals may serve as nuclei upon which crystals may grow. (3) The crystallization of sodium thiosulfate is exothermic as indicated by the observed rise in temperature. (4) It is important to use distilled water to completely dissolve all crystals and to wash down the sides of each container. This ensures that no crystals are present that might act as seeds and confound the results.

5.7.2 CRYSTALLIZATION BY EVAPORATION

Discussion: The "salt garden" is a well-known activity that students may have performed simply as a fun project at home or in grade school. If you wish to make colorful crystals, simply add a couple of drops of food coloring to the top of each briquette. If you elect to add this colorful touch, make sure students understand that the addition of color represents a physical change and not a chemical change. The salt crystal "flowers" that grow have different colors only because of the color of the particles of food coloring trapped inside.

Answers: (1) Yes. Although size varies, both the original and re-crystallized salt crystals are cubic. (2) The solution moves up through the briquette by capillary action following evaporation of water at the surface. The faster the evaporation, the faster the solution is drawn up, and the faster the salt crystallizes. Therefore, salt crystals grow faster under arid conditions. (3) Dust, smoke, airborne bacteria, and other tiny particles may serve as nuclei upon which snow crystals may form. (4) Volcanoes eject a large amount of dust, much of which remains airborne and may serve as nuclei for the formation of snow crystals.

5.7.3 GROWING CRYSTALS; CRYSTAL SHAPES

Discussion: To illustrate why crystal structure is orderly, fill a glass cake pan or other clear container with ball bearings, marbles, copper shot, golf balls or similar spheres. Place the container on the overhead and then gently tap it. The spheres will assume a regular arrangement which can be analogized to the formation of crystals.

Two crystals that typically produce good results for beginners are alum $(AlK(SO_4)_2 \cdot 12H_2O)$ and Rochelle Salt (potassium sodium tartrate, $KNaC_4H_4O_6$). You may wish to start with these substances first and try the others as time permits. The following list identifies the crystalline shapes of the materials tested. Don't be surprised if students have a difficult time classifying these. Crystal irregularity is very common, and students have a difficult time understanding the distinctions between the classifications.

cubic: sodium chloride (NaCl), ammonium chloride (NH_4Cl); ammonium ferric sulfate ($NH_4Fe(SO_4)_2 \cdot 12H_2O$), potassium chloride (KCl)

tetragonal: zinc nitrate hexahydrate ($Zn(NO_3)_2 \cdot 6H_2O$)

orthorhombic: magnesium sulfate heptahydrate (Epsom salts; $MgSO_4 \cdot 7H_2O$), potassium sodium tartrate (Rochelle salt, $KNaC_4H_4O_6$)

monoclinic: sodium bicarbonate (baking soda, $NaHCO_3$)

triclinic: copper sulfate pentahydrate ($CuSO_4 \cdot 5H_2O$)

hexagonal: potassium sulfate (K_2SO_4)

rhombohedral: calcite ($CaCO_3$), chabazite ($(Ca,Na_2)Al_2Si_4O_{12} \cdot 6H_2O$)

Answers: (1) See discussion. (2) Impurities, container walls or other crystals interrupt the growth of a crystal in one direction, changing its ultimate shape. (3) The Dead Sea. The concentration of salts is far greater in the Dead Sea than in any of the other bodies of water mentioned. As a result, crystalline salt will form around the perimeter of the lake as water evaporates in the shallow regions, providing small regions where the water is supersaturated. (4) Yes. In a weightless (microgravity) environment crystals remain suspended in solution, so all sides are available for growth.

5.7.4 METALLIC CRYSTALS

Discussion: You may wish to modify this activity to illustrate the relationship between the speed of crystal formation and the size of the resulting crystals. In general, crystals that form slowly grow larger than those that form rapidly. The rate of crystal formation can be controlled by adjusting the concentration of solution containing the dissolved metal. You can place a nail in a very dilute solution of copper sulfate for a few days. In such a solution, the crystals will form more slowly, and in a more organized fashion. While the tiny dust-like copper crystals formed in concentrated copper sulfate solution can be easily brushed off the nail, the larger copper crystals formed in the dilute solution tend to plate the iron and cannot be as easily removed.

Answers: (1) Iron is a more active metal than copper and will displace copper in aqueous solutions, yielding pure metallic copper. This is clearly seen in the copper sulfate solution in part 1.

$$2Fe(s) + 3CuSO_4(aq) \longrightarrow Fe_2(SO_4)_3(aq) + 3Cu(s)$$

(2) Crystals form more rapidly in concentrated solutions because more ions are available to bond to the growing crystal. (3) The root word *"dend"* means tree. The crystals have a "tree-like" shape. Dendrites are neurons that have a tree-like appearance. Dendrology is the study of trees. Philodendron is a plant that climbs (*philo-*, love) up trees. Rhododendron is a tree-like plant often with beautiful red (*rhod-*, red) flowers. (4) Conditions necessary for large crystal formation are uncommon in the Earth's crust.

5.7.5 SILICATE CRYSTALS

It should be noted that many metal silicates combine with metals to form additional minerals. For example iron silicate combines with other metals to produce these minerals: *actinolite* (calcium magnesium iron silicate hydroxide), *aegirine* (sodium iron silicate), *allanite* (calcium cerium lanthanum yttrium aluminum iron silicate hydroxide), *andradite* (calcium iron silicate), *hedenbergite* (calcium iron silicate), *hypersthene* (magnesium iron silicate).

You may wish to carry out these activities as demonstrations in shallow containers on the overhead. When the silicate arms hit the surface they will branch out across the top, making their growth easily visible to the entire class. You may wish to use the Magic Rocks® kit (available at many hobby stores) to discuss the chemistry of this popular novelty item. You may use this activity to introduce geology from a chemical perspective. Ask your students to bring in rocks they own that contain naturally occurring crystals such as those in Figures (A, B, C, and R). Students can study the regularity of crystalline shape and test the validity of the law of the constancy of interfacial angles (also known as Steno's Law, which states that the angles between two corresponding faces on the crystals of any solid chemical or mineral species are constant and characteristic of the substance). Remind students that impurities and other factors may cause irregular crystal growth.

Table 2: Silicate Crystals

Mineral Salt	*Formula*	*Possible Silicate*	*Color, Names, Uses*
cobalt (II) chloride	$CoCl_2 \cdot 6H_2O$	$CoSiO_3$	blue; used as a blue dye in ceramics
copper (II) chloride	$CuCl_2 \cdot 2H_2O$	$CuSiO_3 \cdot nH_2O$ $Cu_2H_2Si_2O_5(OH)_4$	blue-green; chrysocolla; gemstone, copper ore.
iron (III) chloride	$FeCl_3 \cdot 6H_2O$	$Fe_2(SiO_3)_3$	yellow brown; found in geothermal brines
iron (II) sulfate	$FeSO_4 \cdot 7H_2O$	Fe_2SiO_4	fayalite; grayish-white thought to be a major component in the Earth's mantle
iron (III) sulfate	$Fe_2(SO_4)_3 \cdot 5H_2O$	$Fe_2(SiO_3)_3$	found in geothermal brines
manganese (II) chloride	$MnCl_2 \cdot 4H_2O$	$MnSiO_3$	tephroite; white
zinc sulfate	$ZnSO_4 \cdot 7H_2O$	Zn_2SiO_4	willemite, fluoresces; white

Answers: (1) Refer to Table 2. (2) Student answers may vary, but certain minerals such as iron (III) chloride are associated with fast crystal growth. (3) The silicate forms only at the surface between the sodium silicate rich solution and the mineral rich solution. Once a metal-silicate membrane is formed, the formation of other crystals is slowed because the two solutions are separated from each other until the membrane is once again broken. (4) Sodium silicate is chemically similar to glass (both are silicaceous), is clear, and flows.

5.7.6 STALACTITES AND STALAGMITES

Discussion: It should be stressed that the activities in this section are merely analogies for speleothem formation. For simplicity, we introduced students to only one of the compounds that form in the basic solution in part 2. In addition to copper (II) hydroxide, a mixed crystal containing both copper (II) hydroxide and copper (II) sulfate forms.

Answers: (1) Crystals form when atoms or molecules are attracted to each other and line up in an orderly fashion. Oils on the surface of the crystal provide a barrier to the formation of new layers and thus hinder speleothem growth. (2) In certain areas of the country the water supply contains large quantities of dissolved minerals. Many of these minerals (including calcium carbonate) crystallize as carbon dioxide diffuses out, and as water evaporates from the surface of the fountain. Many commercial products such as "Lime-A-Way®" (sulfamic acid, H_3NO_3S) have been developed to eliminate unwanted calcium carbonate build-up. (3) Hopefully students will find pictures of many wonderful formations, such as Baldacchino canopies, bathtubs, bell canopies, bottlebrushes, columns, conulites, death coral, draperies, folia, gypsum flowers, halite flowers, helictites, pearls, popcorn, mammillaries, raft cones, rimstone, shelfstone, shields, showerheads, soda straws, splattermites, spar, stalactites, stalagmites, and stegamites. Most are made of calcite or aragonite (forms of calcium carbonate), although some are made of sodium chloride, gypsum, and other minerals. (4) The first reaction involves the re-crystallization of dissolved magnesium sulfate, and thus is more similar to the process that occurs in speleothem formation (re-crystallization of copper carbonate) than is the reaction in part 2 which results from the formation of an entirely new compound, copper (II) hydroxide.

5.7.7 RATE OF CRYSTALLIZATION AND CRYSTAL SIZE

Discussion: Mannitol and phenyl salicylate have been selected because they form crystals that are clearly visible under the microscope and because they are relatively nontoxic. If possible, use video-camera with a tele-macro zoom lens to monitor crystal growth under both conditions. Videotape this process by setting up your video equipment as illustrated in Figure W. Feed the video signal from the camera into the "video in" port of a VCR, and the "video out" cable from the VCR to the "video in" portion of your monitor. By pressing the "pause" button while recording, you can eliminate unwanted footage. Many video-microscopes also contain audio input and allow you to narrate while videotaping. Figure X illustrates that slow cooling promotes the growth of larger crystals.

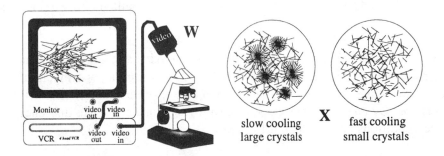

Answers: (1) The rapidly cooled samples display much smaller crystal size than the slowly cooled samples. (2) Rapid cooling promotes small crystal formation. (3) Magma near the Earth's surface cools more rapidly than magma deep beneath the surface. Thus, rocks forming deep beneath the surface tend to exhibit larger crystals than those forming rapidly at the surface. (4) Granite forms more slowly, deep beneath the surface. Obsidian forms more quickly as it cools rapidly near or at the surface.

Applications to Everyday Life

Hand-warmers: Hand-warmers (available in camping stores) consist of a pouch filled with a supersaturated solution of sodium acetate. Snapping a disk inside the pouch stimulates crystallization of the sodium acetate and releases heat. The temperature of the hand pouch reaches approximately 50°C, just right for a cold winter day.

Paleoclimatology: Calcite dissolves more rapidly under warm, humid conditions, and thus more minerals are available for the growth of stalactites and stalagmites under such conditions. By analyzing the cross section of a speleothem, and dating it with radioactive isotopes, geologists can determine periods of rapid growth (indicating warm, moist conditions) as well as periods of slow growth (indicating cool and/or dry conditions). By analyzing many speleothems, paleoclimatologists can determine ancient climatic changes.

Snow and "cloud seeding": At temperatures above −40°C, snow crystals will not form unless foreign particles are present. Generally soil dust, salt dust or particulate air pollution provide nuclei upon which ice crystals form. The nucleation process can be stimulated by seeding the clouds with silver-iodide particles. This process, known as "cloud seeding," has been used with marginal success to stimulate rainfall in arid regions of the world.

Element analysis: The shape of a crystal is dependent upon the manner in which constituent atoms or molecules pack. Many crystals can be identified simply on the basis of their shape, but others require more sophisticated techniques such as X-ray crystallography. When an X-ray beam is directed through a crystal, unique diffraction patterns are revealed. The "fingerprints" (diffraction patterns) of over 200,000 compounds have been identified by X-ray crystallography. X-ray diffraction of single crystals led to the determination of the structure of DNA.

Ductility of metals: Metals are composed of many crystals, the planes of which are aligned with one another like cards in a deck of playing cards. When a force is applied to a metal, crystals slide across each other just as cards in a deck slide when pushed or pulled from the side. As a result, metals are ductile and malleable and can be pulled into wire or pressed into coins.

Snowflakes: Meteorologists and hydrologists have noted that the shape of snowflakes is dependent upon the temperature at which they form. For example, at temperatures of −5 to −3°C, the crystals have a needle-like shape, while at temperatures from −3 to 0° they have a hexagonal shape. By analyzing the shape of a snowflake, one can make inferences about the atmospheric conditions under which it formed.

Geodes: Geodes are hollow spherical rocks that contain layers of inward growing crystals. Geodes are cut open, polished and used in many decorative pieces such as bookends and knickknacks.

Petrified wood: Petrified Forest National Park in Arizona contains the petrified trunks and stumps of many ancient trees. Minerals dissolved in water seeped into the trunks of these trees and crystallized in the tiny pores left by the decaying wood.

Gemstones: Most precious and semi-precious gems are derived from well-formed crystals. Diamonds (crystalline carbon), rubies and sapphires (aluminum oxide), emerald (beryllium-aluminum silicate), and tourmaline (complex borosilicate) are a few of the many crystals that are considered gemstones and are frequently used in jewelry.

Synthetic gems: The science of crystal growth has advanced greatly in recent years, allowing chemists to produce gems that have no natural counterparts. Cubic zirconia is a synthetic gem that so closely resembles diamond in brilliance and color dispersion that often only experts can distinguish the two.

Gout: Gout is a painful form of arthritis that occurs due to formation of monosodium-urate crystals in the joints.

TABLE OF APPENDICES

APPENDIX 1.1 PHYSICAL QUANTITIES AND THEIR SI UNITS

	Symbol	SI Measurement Units	Symbol	Unit Dimensions
distance	d	meter	m	m
mass	m	kilogram	kg	kg
time	t	second	s	s
electric charge*	Q	coulomb	C	C
temperature	T	kelvin	K	K
amount of substance	n	mole	mol	mol
luminous intensity	I	candela	cd	cd
acceleration	a	meter per second squared	m/s^2	m/s^2
area	A	square meter	m^2	m^2
capacitance	C	farad	F	C$^2\cdot$s^2/kg$\cdot$m^2
concentration	$[C]$	molar	M	mol/dm^3
density	D	kilogram per cubic meter	kg/m^3	kg/m^3
electric current	I	ampere	A	C/s
electric field intensity	E	newton per coulomb	N/C	kg$\cdot$m/C$\cdot$s^2
electric resistance	R	ohm	Ω	kg$\cdot$m^2/C$^2\cdot$s
emf	ξ	volt	V	kg$\cdot$m^2/C$\cdot$s^2
energy	E	joule	J	kg$\cdot$m^2/s^2
force	F	newton	N	kg$\cdot$m/s^2
frequency	f	hertz	Hz	s^{-1}
heat	Q	joule	J	kg$\cdot$m^2/s^2
illumination	E	lux (lumen per square meter)	lx	cd/m^2
inductance	L	henry	H	kg$\cdot$m^2/C^2
magnetic flux	ϕ	weber	Wb	kg$\cdot$m^2/C$\cdot$s
potential difference	V	volt	V	kg$\cdot$m^2/C$\cdot$s^2
power	P	watt	W	kg$\cdot$m^2/s^3
pressure	p	pascal (newton per square meter)	Pa	kg/m$\cdot$s^2
velocity	v	meter per second	m/s	m/s
volume	V	cubic meter	m^3	m^3
work	W	joule	J	kg$\cdot$m^2/s^2

* The official SI quantity is electrical current, and the base unit is the ampere. Electrical current is the amount of electrical charge (measured in coulombs) per unit of time.

APPENDIX 1.2 METRIC SYSTEM PREFIXES

Power	Decimal Representation	Prefix	Symbol
10^{18}	1,000,000,000,000,000,000	exa	E
10^{15}	1,000,000,000,000,000	peta	P
10^{12}	1,000,000,000,000	tera	T
10^{9}	1,000,000,000	giga	G
10^{6}	1,000,000	mega	M
10^{3}	1,000	kilo	k
10^{2}	100	hecto	h
10^{1}	10	deka	da
10^{0}	1		
10^{-1}	0.1	deci	d
10^{-2}	0.01	centi	c
10^{-3}	0.001	milli	m
10^{-6}	0.000 001	micro	μ
10^{-9}	0.000 000 001	nano	n
10^{-12}	0.000 000 000 001	pico	p
10^{-15}	0.000 000 000 000 001	femto	f
10^{-18}	0.000 000 000 000 000 001	atto	a

APPENDIX 1.3 SI AND CUSTOMARY UNITS AND CONVERSIONS

Quantity	SI Unit	Symbol	Customary Unit	Symbol	Conversion
length	meter	m	foot	ft	1 m = 3.280 ft
area	square meter	m^2	square foot	ft^2	1 m^2 = 10.76 ft^2
volume	cubic meter	m^3	cubic foot	ft^3	1 m^3 = 35.32 ft^3
speed	meter per second	m/s	foot per second	ft/s	1 m/s = 3.280 ft/s
acceleration	meter per second per second	m/s^2	feet per second per second	ft/s^2	1 m/s^2 = 3.280 ft/s^2
force	newton	N	pound	lb	1 N = 0.2248 lb
work (energy)	joule	J	foot-pound	ft·lb	1 J = 0.7376 ft·lb
power	watt	W	foot-pound per second	ft·lb/s	1 W = 0.7376 ft·lb/s
pressure	pascal	Pa	pound per square inch	lb/in^2	1 Pa = 1.450×10^{-4} lb/in^2
density	kilogram per cubic meter	kg/m^3	pound per cubic foot	lb/ft^3	1 kg/m^3 = 6.243×10^{-2} lb/ft^3

APPENDIX 1.4 COMMON CONVERSIONS

Quantity	Customary Unit	Metric Unit	Customary/Metric	Metric/Customary
length	inch (in)	millimeter (mm)	1 in = 25.4 mm	1 mm = 0.0394 in
	foot (ft)	meter (m)	1 ft = 0.305 m	1 m = 3.28 ft
	yard (yd)	meter (m)	1 yd = 0.914 m	1 m = 1.09 yd
	mile (mi)	kilometer (km)	1 mi = 1.61 km	1 km = 0.621 mi
area	square inch (in^2)	square centimeter (cm^2)	1 in^2 = 6.45 cm^2	1 cm^2 = 0.155 in^2
	square foot (ft^2)	square meter (m^2)	1 ft^2 = 0.0929 m^2	1 m^2 = 10.8 ft^2
	square yard (yd^2)	square meter (m^2)	1 yd^2 = 0.836 m^2	1 m^2 = 1.20 yd^2
	acre (acre)	hectare (ha)	1 acre = 0.405 ha	1 ha = 2.47 acre
volume	cubic inch (in^3)	cubic centimeter (cm^3)	1 in^3 = 16.39 cm^3	1 cm^3 = 0.0610 in^3
	cubic foot (ft^3)	cubic meter (m^3)	1 ft^3 = 0.0283 m^3	1 m^3 = 35.3 ft^3
	cubic yard (yd^3)	cubic meter (m^3)	1 yd^3 = 0.765 m^3	1 m^3 = 1.31 yd^3
	quart (qt)	liter (L)	1 qt = 0.946 L	1 L = 1.06 qt
mass	ounce (oz)	gram (g)	1 oz = 28.4 g	1 g = 0.0352 oz
	pound (lb)	kilogram (kg)	1 lb = 0.454 kg	1 kg = 2.20 lb
	ton (ton)	metric ton (t)	1 ton = 0.907 t	1 t = 1.10 ton
weight	pound (lb)	newton (N)	1 lb = 4.45 N	1 N = 0.225 lb

APPENDIX 1.5 UNITS OF PRESSURE

Unit	Definition	Pascal Equivalents	When It Is Used
pascal (Pa)	N/m^2	1	Standard SI unit. Used when mass is measured in kg and area in meters.
kilopascal (kPa)	1000 N/m^2	1000	Practical metric unit of measuring gaseous, fluid or mechanical pressure (Pa is generally too small).
bar	10,000 N/m^2	100,000	Practical metric unit of measuring atmospheric pressure. One bar is approximately 1 atmosphere.
millibar (mb)	100 N/m^2	100	Weather reports. Note: Some weather maps drop the first two digits (e.g., 1013.3 mb may be reported as 13.3).
barye (dyne/cm²)	0.1 N/m^2	0.1	Standard CGS unit. Used when measurements are made in centimeters and grams.
torr	1/760 of standard atmospheric pressure	133.3	Used when pressure is measured with a mercury manometer or barometer.
mm Hg	Pressure required to support a column of Hg 1 mm in height	133.3	Blood pressure measurements. Normal blood pressure is 120/80 (systolic/diastolic).
cm H_2O	Pressure required to support a column of water 1 cm in height	98.1	Used when pressure is measured using simple water barometer or manometer.
atmosphere (atm)	Atmospheric pressure at sea level	101,325	Used when a comparison to standard atmospheric pressure is desired.
PSI	lb/in²	6894	Common measurement in mechanical and structural engineering. Tire pressures are rated in PSI.

APPENDIX 1.6 VAPOR PRESSURE OF WATER

Temperature °C	Pressure kPa	Temperature °C	Pressure kPa	Temperature °C	Pressure kPa
0	0.6	20	2.3	30	4.2
3	0.8	21	2.5	32	4.8
5	0.9	22	2.6	35	5.6
8	1.1	23	2.8	40	7.4
10	1.2	24	3.0	50	12.3
12	1.4	25	3.2	60	19.9
14	1.6	26	3.4	70	31.2
16	1.8	27	3.6	80	47.3
18	2.1	28	3.8	90	70.1
19	2.2	29	4.0	100	101.3

$1 \text{ mm } H_2O = 0.00981 \text{ kPa}$ $1 \text{ cm } H_2O = 0.0981 \text{ kPa}$

APPENDIX 2.1 WRITING STYLE GUIDELINES

SI UNITS

Le Systéme International des Unités (SI) is an internationally recognized system of measurement adopted in 1960 by the General Conference of Weights and Measures. Scientists are encouraged to express all measurements in SI units so colleagues around the world can interpret them readily.

Fundamental SI Units: A fundamental unit is one that cannot be expressed in simpler terms. It is defined by a physical standard of measurement. The seven fundamental quantities and their SI units are as follows:

Quantity	*Unit*	*Symbol*
length	meter	m
mass	kilogram	kg
time	second	s
temperature	kelvin	K
amount	mole	mol
charge	coulomb	C
luminous intensity	candela	cd

Derived SI Units: A derived unit is one that can be expressed in terms of fundamental units. Volume, for example, is expressed in length cubed, and velocity is expressed in length (distance) per time. Appendix 1.1 lists the seven fundamental SI units and a variety of derived SI units expressed in terms of these fundamental units.

CAPITALIZATION

Unit Names: When written in full, all units begin with a lower case letter.
    Correct: kelvin, farad, newton, joule, hertz, degree
    Incorrect: Kelvin, Farad, Newton, Joule, Hertz, Degree

Symbol: The first letter in a unit symbol is uppercase when the unit name is derived from a person's name. The following is a list of units that are named after famous scientists. Note that the unit name is not capitalized, but the unit symbol is.

ampere	A	André Ampère: discovered basic principles of electrodynamics.
coulomb	C	Charles Coulomb: discovered law of force between charged bodies.
farad	F	Michael Faraday: pioneered research in electricity and magnetism.
henry	H	Joseph Henry: discovered electromagnetic induction and self-induction.
hertz	Hz	Heinrich Hertz: discovered radio waves.
joule	J	James Joule: pioneered research in thermodynamics.
kelvin	K	William Thomson (AKA Lord Kelvin): developed absolute temperature scale.
newton	N	Isaac Newton: pioneered work in calculus, optics and gravitation.
ohm	Ω	Georg Ohm: discovered relationship between current, voltage, and resistance.
pascal	Pa	Blaise Pascal: discovered basic principles of hydrostatics.

tesla	T	Nicola Tesla: developed AC motor and high-voltage transformers.
volt	V	Allesandro Volta: invented first battery.
watt	W	James Watt: developed the steam engine as a practical power source.
weber	Wb	Wilhelm Weber: performed early research in electricity and magnetism.

The following units are not named after people, and therefore their symbols are not capitalized: meter, m; kilogram, kg; second, s; mole, mol; candela, cd; lux, lx; degree, °.

Prefixes: The symbols for all prefixes representing powers less than one million are never capitalized (a,f,p,n,μ,m,c,d,da,h,k). The symbols representing powers greater than or equal to 1 million are always capitalized (M,G,T,P,E).

PERIODS

Periods are never used after a symbol, except at the end of a sentence.

DECIMALS

For numbers less than 1, a zero is written before the decimal point.
    Correct: 0.03256   0.5234
    Incorrect: .03256   .5234

COMPOUND UNITS

A centered dot is used to indicate that a unit is the product of two or more units.
    Correct: N·m   kg·m/s^2
    Incorrect: Nm   kgm/s^2

DIFFERENTIATING QUANTITY SYMBOLS AND UNIT SYMBOLS

By convention, quantity symbols are italicized but unit symbols are not. Quantity symbols represent a physical quantity such as time, mass and length, while unit symbols represent specific measures of those quantities, such as seconds, kilograms, and meters.

Quantity Symbols *(italicized)*	Unit Symbols (not italicized)
time, t	seconds, s
mass, m	kilograms, kg
length, l	meter, m
heat, Q	joule, J

APPENDIX 2.2 ROOT WORDS USED FREQUENTLY IN CHEMISTRY

Root	Origin*	Meaning	Example	Explanation
-ane	—	single covalent bond	alkane, propane	alkanes have only single bonds
-ene	—	double covalent bond	alkene, polypropylene	alkenes have one or more double bonds
-ion	L	process	fusion	the process of combing or fusing nuclei to form a heavier nucleus
-oid	G	like, form	metalloid	some properties are like those of metals
-yne	—	triple covalent bond	alkyne, ethyne	alkynes have one or more triple bonds
-meter	G	measure	calorimeter	measures heats of reactions
a-	G	not, without	amorphous carbon	carbon without crystalline shape
acid	L	sour, sharp	hydrochloric acid	acids stimulate the sour taste buds
alkali	—	soda ash, alkali	alkali lake	alkali lakes have very high mineral content
allo, -io	G	other, different	allotrope	one of the two or more forms of an element that have the same physical state
alpha	G	1st letter of Greek alphabet	alpha particle	designated by the letter "alpha"
amin	N	ammonia	amine, amino acid	an ammonia base in which one or more of the three hydrogens is replaced by an alkyl group
amph, -i, -o	G	double, on both sides	amphoteric, amphibian	amphoteric species react either as acids or bases
anti	G	against, opposite	antiseptic	substance that works against microbes
aqua	L	water	aqueous solution	water-based solution
baro	G	pressure	barometer, bar	barometer measures pressure
beta	G	second letter of Greek alphabet	beta particle	designated by the letter "beta"
bi	L	two	binary compounds	compound made of two elements
bio	G	life	biochemistry	chemistry of living systems
carb, -o, -on	L	coal, carbon	carbohydrate	compound made of carbon, hydrogen, and oxygen $(CH_2O)_n$
chem	G	chemistry	chemical kinetics	the kinetics of a chemical reaction
co, -l, -m, -n	L	with, together	coefficient, colligative	number that appears with a formula in a chemical equation
com	L	with, together	composition reaction	a reaction in which molecules are assembled
conjug	L	joined together	conjugate acid, conjugal	acid formed from its conjugate base by the addition of a proton

APPENDIX 2.2 ROOT WORDS USED FREQUENTLY IN CHEMISTRY *(Continued)*

Root	Origin*	Meaning	Example	Explanation
cosm, -o	G	the world or universe	cosmic rays, cosmos	high-energy rays from space (the cosmos)
cry, -mo, -o	G	cold	crystal	crystals form when solutions are cooled
de	L	down, without, from	decomposition, denature, dehydrate	a reaction in which materials are broken down
dens	L	thick	density, dense	density is a measure of how "thick" a fluid is (how much mass per unit volume)
di	G	separate, double, across	disaccharide	two monosaccharides tied together
dis	G	separate, apart	dissociation	separation of ions when dissolving
duc, -t	L	lead	ductile	able to be pulled or led through a small opening to produce a wire
e	L	out, without, from	evaporation	the process of vapor leaving from
ef	L	out, from, away	effervescence	rapid escape of gas from a liquid in which it is dissolved
electr, -i, -o	G	electrode	electrolyte	dissolves in water to give a solution that conducts an electric current
elem	L	basic	elements	can't be broken down into more basic substances by normal chemical means
empir, -o	G	experienced	empirical	based on experience or observation
en	G	in, into	endothermic	a reaction which takes in heat
equ	L	equal	equilibrium	a dynamic condition in which two opposing reactions occur at equal rates
erg	G	work	energy, erg	energy is the ability to perform work
exo	G	out, outside, without	exothermic	exothermic reactions give heat to the outside environment
ferr, -o	L	iron	ferromagnetism	strongly attracted to a magnet, like iron
fiss, -i, -ur	L	cleft, split	fission	the splitting of nuclei
flu	L	flow	fluids	gases and liquids are fluids because they flow
fract	L	break, broken	fractional distillation	distillation in which the components of a mixture are "broken down" and separated by different boiling points
gamma	G	3rd letter of the Greek alphabet	gamma rays	high-energy electromagnetic waves identified by the Greek letter "gamma"
gen	G	bear, produce, beginning	gene	a section of a DNA chain that codes for a particular protein that the organism can produce

(continued)

APPENDIX 2.2 ROOT WORDS USED FREQUENTLY IN CHEMISTRY *(Continued)*

Root	Origin*	Meaning	Example	Explanation
glyc, -er, -o	G	sweet	glycogen, glycolysis, glycolipid	a sugar (glucose)-based polymer that stores energy in animals
graph, -o, -y	G	write, writing	graphite	form of carbon used in pencils
halo-	G	salt	halogens	halogens (*e.g.* F, Cl, Br) are often found in salts (e.g. NaF, NaCl, KBr)
hetero-	G	other, different	heterogeneous mixture	a mixture in which properties and composition differ from point to point
hom, -eo, -o	G	same, alike	homogeneous mixture	a mixture in which properties and composition are the same throughout
hybrid	L	a mongrel, combination	hybrid orbital	orbitals produced by the combination of two or more orbitals of the same atom
hydr, -a, -i, -o	G	water	hydrolysis	the breaking of bonds using water
hyper	G	over, above, excessive	*(hy)*perchloric acid	the oxidation state of chlorine in perchloric acid is above what it is in chloric acid
hypo	G	under, beneath	hypochlorous acid	the oxidation state of chlorine in hypochlorous acid is below the oxidation state of chlorine in chlorous acid
im	L	not	immiscible	not mutually soluble (not miscible)
in	L	in, into	intrinsic physical properties	properties inherent to a substance, and not on the amount present
iso	G	equal	isomers	compounds that have the same molecular formula but different structures
kilo	G	thousand	kilogram	1000 grams
kine	G	move, moving, movement	kinetic energy	energy of motion
lip, -o	G	fat	lipoprotein	fatty acid combined with protein
liqu, -e, -i	L	fluid, liquid	liquefy	the process of becoming a liquid
lys, -io, -is, -io	G	loose, loosening, breaking	hydrolysis	the breaking apart of a substance by an electric current
macr, -o	G	large, long	macromolecule	macromolecules are large organic molecules
malle, -o, -us	L	hammer	malleable	ability to bend and shape when hit by a hammer
mer, -e, -i,-o	G	a part	dimer	made of two parts
met, -a	G	between, change	metabolism	reactions that change biochemicals from one form to another
meter	G	measure	calorimeter	measures heat energy (calories)
mill, -e, -i, -o	L	one thousand	milliliter	one thousandth of a liter

APPENDIX 2.2 ROOT WORDS USED FREQUENTLY
IN CHEMISTRY *(Continued)*

Root	Origin*	Meaning	Example	Explanation
misc	L	mix	miscible	when two solvents dissolve (mix evenly) in each other
mon, -a, -er, -o	G	single, one	monomer	single molecular units that can join to form a polymer
morph, -a, -o	G	form	amorphous sulfur	sulfur without definite crystals or shape
neo	G	new, recent	neoprene	a synthetic (new) rubber
neutr	L	neither	neutral	neither positive nor negative
nom, -en, -in	G	name	nomenclature	system of assigning names
non	L	not, ninth	nonpolar	does not have polar characteristics
nuc, -ell, -i	L	nut, center	nucleus	center of the atom
oct, -i, -o	L	eight	octet rule	tendency to acquire a total of eight electrons in highest energy level
orbi, -t, -to	L	circle	orbital	electrons travel around the nucleus in patterns known as orbitals
oxid	—	oxygen	oxide	compound containing oxide ion
photo	G	light	photochemical smog	air pollutants transformed by sunlight
polar, -i	L	of the pole, polarity	polar covalent	one pole of the bond has a more negative character, and the other a more positive character
poly	G	many	polymer	many molecules bound together to make a new, longer molecule
pro	G	forward, positive, for, in front of	proton	positively charged particle
quant	L	how much	quantum	refers to a discrete amount of energy
radi, -a, -o,	L	spoke, ray, radius	radioactive	produces rays of electromagnetic energy
sacchar, -o	G	sugar	monosaccharide	single sugar unit
sal, -i	L	salt	salinity	referring to the amount of salt in solution
solu-	L	dissolve	solubility	refers to the tendency to dissolve
spect	L	see, look at	spectator ions	ions that "watch" but are not involved in a reaction
super	L	above, over	superheated	retaining liquid properties beyond the normal boiling point
syn	G	together, with	photosynthesis	molecules are put together with energy derived from light
therm, -o	G	heat	thermochemistry	the study of changes in heat energy accompanying chemical and physical changes
thesis	G	an arranging, statement	hypothesis	a testable statement

(continued)

APPENDIX 2.2 ROOT WORDS USED FREQUENTLY
IN CHEMISTRY *(Concluded)*

Root	Origin*	Meaning	Example	Explanation
tran, -s	L	across, through	transition elements	elements through which you pass when going from the right to left side of the periodic table
un	L	not	unsaturated	bonds that are not saturated
vapor, -i	L	steam, vapor	vaporization	the process of changing a liquid into a vapor
vulcan	L	fire	vulcanized	vulcanized rubber has been treated with heat

* L = Latin
   G = Greek

APPENDIX 2.3 ETYMOLOGY OF THE NAMES OF THE ELEMENTS

Element	Symbol	Z	Year	Meaning
Actinium	Ac	89	1900	Greek: *aktis*, ray
Aluminum	Al	13	1825	Latin: *alumen*, substance with astringent taste
Americium	Am	95	1944	English: *America*
Antimony	Sb	51	1400s	Greek: *antimonos*, opposite to solitude
Argon	Ar	18	1894	Greek: *argos*, inactive
Arsenic	As	33	1200s	Greek: *arsenikon*, valiant
Astatine	At	85	1940	Greek: *astatos*, unstable
Barium	Ba	56	1808	Greek: *barys*, heavy
Berkelium	Bk	97	1949	English: University of California *Berkeley*
Beryllium	Be	4	1797	Greek: *beryllos*, a mineral
Bismuth	Bi	83	1400s	German: *bisemutum*, white mass
Boron	B	5	1808	Arabic: *bawraq*, white, borax
Bromine	Br	35	1826	Greek: *bromos*, a stench
Cadmium	Cd	48	1817	Latin: *cadmia*, calamine, a zinc ore
Calcium	Ca	20	1808	Latin: *calcis*, lime
Californium	Cf	98	1950	English: State and University of *California*
Carbon	C	6	prehistoric	Latin: *carbo*, coal
Cerium	Ce	58	1804	English: The asteroid *Ceres*, discovered 1803
Cesium	Cs	55	1860	Latin: *caesius*, sky blue
Chlorine	Cl	17	1808	Greek: *chloros*, grass green
Chromium	Cr	24	1797	Greek: *chroma*, color
Cobalt	Co	27	1735	Greek: *kobolos*, a goblin
Copper	Cu	29	prehistoric	Latin: *cuprum*, copper
Curium	Cm	96	1944	French: Marie & Pierre *Curie*
Dysprosium	Dy	66	1886	Greek: *dysprositos*, hard to get at
Einsteinium	Es	99	1952	German: *Albert Einstein*
Erbium	Er	68	1843	Swedish: *Ytterby*, town in Sweden where discovered
Europium	Eu	63	1900	English: Europe
Fermium	Fm	100	1953	Italian: Enrico *Fermi*
Fluorine	F	9	1886	Latin: *fluere*, to flow
Francium	Fr	87	1939	French: *France*
Gadolinium	Gd	64	1886	Finnish: Johan *Gadolin*, Finnish chemist
Gallium	Ga	31	1875	Latin: *Gaul*, or France
Germanium	Ge	32	1886	German: Germany
Gold	Au	79	prehistoric	Anglo-Saxon: for gold; symbol from Latin *aurum* for gold
Hafnium	Hf	72	1922	Latin: *Hafnia*, the city of Copenhagen, Denmark
Helium	He	2	1895	Greek: *helios*, the sun
Holmium	Ho	67	1879	Latin: *Holmia*, the city of Stockholm, Sweden
Hydrogen	H	1	1766	Greek: *hydro genes*, water former

(continued)

APPENDIX 2.3 ETYMOLOGY OF THE NAMES
OF THE ELEMENTS *(Continued)*

Element	Symbol	Z	Year	Meaning
Indium	In	49	1863	Latin: *indicum*, produces an indigo-blue spectrum line
Iodine	I	53	1811	Greek: *iodes*, produces a violet-like *spectrum line*
Iridium	Ir	77	1804	Latin: *iridis*, rainbow
Iron	Fe	26	prehistoric	Anglo-Saxon: *iren*, symbol from Latin *ferrum*
Krypton	Kr	36	1898	Greek: *kryptos*, hidden
Lanthanum	La	57	1839	Greek: *lanthanien*, to be concealed
Lawrencium	Lw	103	1961	English: Earnest *Lawrence*, inventor of cyclotron
Lead	Pb	82	prehistoric	Anglo-Saxon: *lead;* symbol from Latin *plumbum*
Lithium	Li	3	1817	Greek: *lithos*, stone
Lutetium	Lu	71	1905	Latin: *Lutetia*, ancient name of Paris
Magnesium	Mg	12	1774	Latin: *magnes*, magnet
Mendelevium	Md	101	1955	Russian: Dmitri *Mendeleev*, devised periodic table
Mercury	Hg	80	prehistoric	Latin: *Mercury*, messenger; symbol *Hydrarygus*, liquid silver
Molybdenum	Mo	42	1782	Greek: *molybdos*, lead
Neodymium	Nd	60	1885	Greek: *neos*, new and *didymos*, twin
Neon	Ne	10	1898	Greek: *neos*, new
Neptunium	Np	93	1940	English: planet *Neptune*
Nickel	Ni	28	1750	German: *kupfernickel*, false copper
Niobium	Nb	41	1801	Greek: *Niobe*, mythological daughter of Tantalus
Nitrogen	N	7	1772	Latin: *nitro*, native soda and *gen*, born
Nobelium	No	102	1957	Swedish: Alfred *Nobel*, discoverer of dynamite
Osmium	Os	76	1804	Greek: *osme*, odor of volatile tetroxide
Oxygen	O	8	1774	Greek: *oxys*, sharp and *gen*, born
Palladium	Pd	46	1803	English: planetoid *Pallas*, discovered 1801
Phosphorus	P	15	1669	Greek: *phosphoros*, light bringer
Platinum	Pt	78	1735	Spanish: *plata*, silver
Plutonium	Pu	94	1940	English: *Pluto* the planet
Polonium	Po	84	1898	Polish: *Poland*, country of co-discoverer Marie Curie
Potassium	K	19	1807	English: *potash;* symbol Latin, *kalium*
Praseodymium	Pr	59	1885	Greek: *Praseos*, leek green and *didymos*, a twin
Promethium	Pm	61	1947	Greek: *Prometheus*, fire bringer in Greek mythology
Protactinium	Pa	91	1917	Greek: *protos*, first
Radium	Ra	88	1898	Latin: *radius*, ray
Radon	Rn	86	1900	Latin: comes from *radium*
Rhenium	Re	75	1924	Latin: *Rhenus*, Rhine province of Germany
Rhodium	Rh	45	1804	Greek: *rhodon*, a rose
Rubidium	Rb	37	1860	Latin: *rubidus*, red
Ruthenium	Ru	44	1845	Latin: *Ruthenia*, Russia
Samarium	Sm	62	1879	Russian: *Samarski*, a Russian engineer

APPENDIX 2.3 ETYMOLOGY OF THE NAMES
OF THE ELEMENTS *(Concluded)*

Element	Symbol	Z	Year	Meaning
Scandium	Sc	21	1879	Scandinavian: *Scandinavia*
Selenium	Se	34	1817	Greek: *selene*, moon
Silicon	Si	14	1823	Latin: *silex*, flint
Silver	Ag	47	prehistoric	Anglo-Saxon, *siolful;* symbol Latin, *argentum*
Sodium	Na	11	1807	Latin: *sodanum* for headache remedy; symbol Latin, *natrium*
Strontium	Sr	38	1808	Scottish: town of *Strontian*, Scotland
Sulfur	S	16	prehistoric	Latin: *sulphur*, sulfur
Tantalum	Ta	73	1802	Greek: *Tantalus* of Greek mythology
Technetium	Tc	43	1937	Greek: *technetos*, artificial
Tellurium	Te	52	1782	Latin: *tellus*, the earth
Terbium	Tb	65	1843	Swedish: *Ytterby*, town in Sweden
Thallium	Tl	81	1862	Greek: *thallos*, a young shoot
Thorium	Th	90	1819	Scandinavian: *Thor* from Scandinavian mythology
Thulium	Tm	69	1879	Latin: *Thule*, northerly part of habitable world
Tin	Sn	50	prehistoric	Latin: Etruscan god, *Tinia*; symbol Latin, *stannum*
Titanium	Ti	22	1791	Greek: Greek mythology, *Titans* first sons of the earth
Tungsten	W	74	1783	Swedish: *tung sten*, heavy stone; symbol German, *worfram*
Uranium	U	92	1789	English: Planet *Uranus*
Vanadium	V	23	1830	Scandinavian: goddess *Vanadis* of Scandinavian mythology
Xenon	Xe	54	1898	Greek: *xenos*, strange
Ytterbium	Yb	70	1905	Scandinavian: *Ytterby*, a town in Sweden
Yttrium	Y	39	1843	Scandinavian: *Ytterby*, a town in Sweden
Zinc	Zn	30	prehistoric	German: *Zink*, akin to *Zinn*, tin
Zirconium	Zr	40	1824	named for the mineral, *zircon*

APPENDIX 2.4 BALANCING EQUATIONS

The following technique is helpful in balancing chemical reactions.

(I) WORD EQUATION (IDENTIFY REACTANTS AND PRODUCTS)

Make sure reactants and products are logical.

(II) SKELETON EQUATION (CHANGE ONLY SUBSCRIPTS)

Use subscripts to balance oxidation states within reactants and products.

(III) BALANCED EQUATION (CHANGE ONLY COEFFICIENTS)

(a) Balance substances in which atoms occur in <u>only one reactant</u> **and** <u>one product first</u>. This establishes ratios which must exist. If no such elements exist, then balance atoms that appear *in only one reactant* **or** *one product first*.
(b) Balance elemental substances (e.g. O_2, H_2, Ag, etc.) last, using fractions if necessary. In general, the following sequence works well:
   [1] Balance metallic atoms.
   [2] Balance polyatomic ions that are not destroyed in the reaction.
   [3] Balance nonmetallic atoms.
   [4] Balance elemental substances like O_2 and H_2 last, <u>using fractions</u> if necessary.
(c) Multiply to remove fractions.

Sample Problem 1: Aluminum nitrate reacts with sulfuric acid.

(I)   Aluminum nitrate reacts with sulfuric acid to produce aluminum sulfate and nitric acid.

(II) $Al^{3+}(NO_3^{1-}) + H^{1+}SO_4^{2-} \rightarrow Al^{3+}(SO_4^{2-}) + H^{1+}NO_3^{1-}$
       $Al(NO_3)_3 + H_2SO_4 \rightarrow Al_2(SO_4)_3 + HNO_3$

(IIIa) $\textbf{2}Al(NO_3)_3 + H_2SO_4 \rightarrow Al_2(SO_4)_3 + HNO_3$

(IIIb) $\textbf{2}Al(NO_3)_3 + \textbf{3}H_2SO_4 \rightarrow Al_2(SO_4)_3 + \textbf{6}HNO_3$

Sample Problem 2: The combustion of paraffin (C_nH_{2n+2} where n ranges between 26 and 30).

(I)   Paraffin combusts in the presence of oxygen to produce carbon dioxide and water.

(II) $C_{30}H_{62} + O_2\ (g) \rightarrow CO_2\ (g) + H_2O\ (g)$

(IIIa) $C_{30}H_{62} + O_2\ (g) \rightarrow \textbf{30}CO_2\ (g) + \textbf{31}H_2O\ (g)$

(IIIb) $C_{30}H_{62} + \dfrac{\textbf{91}}{\textbf{2}}O_2\ (g) \rightarrow \textbf{30}CO_2\ (g) + \textbf{31}H_2O\ (g)$

(IIIc) $\textbf{2}C_{30}H_{62} + \textbf{91}O_2\ (g) \rightarrow \textbf{60}CO_2\ (g) + \textbf{62}H_2O\ (g)$

APPENDIX 3.1 SAMPLE SAFETY CONTRACT

PREPARE FOR LABORATORY WORK

- Study laboratory procedures prior to class.
- Never perform unauthorized experiments.
- Keep your lab bench organized and free of apparel, books, and other clutter.
- Know how to use the safety shower, eye wash, fire blanket and first aid kit.

DRESS FOR LABORATORY WORK

- Tie back long hair.
- Do not wear loose sleeves.
- Wear shoes with tops.
- Wear lab coats during all laboratory sessions.
- Wear safety goggles during all laboratory sessions.
- Wear gloves when using chemicals that irritate or can be absorbed through skin.

AVOID CONTACT WITH CHEMICALS

- Never taste or "sniff" chemicals.
- Never draw materials in a pipet with your mouth.
- When heating substances in a test tube, point the mouth away from people.
- Never carry dangerous chemicals or hot equipment near other people.

AVOID HAZARDS

- Keep combustibles away from open flames.
- Use caution when handling hot glassware.
- When diluting acid, always add acid slowly to water. Never add water to acid.
- Allow teacher to insert glass tubing into stoppers.
- Turn off burners when not in use.
- Do not bend or cut glass unless appropriately instructed by teacher.
- Keep caps on reagent bottles. Never switch caps.

CLEAN UP

- Consult teacher for proper disposal of chemicals.
- Wash hands thoroughly following experiments.
- Leave laboratory bench clean and neat.

IN CASE OF ACCIDENT

- Report all accidents and spills immediately.
- Place broken glass in designated containers.
- Wash all acids and bases from your skin immediately with plenty of running water.
- If chemicals get in your eyes, wash eyes for at least 15 minutes with an eyewash.

I, _____, agree to: (a) follow the teacher's instructions, (b) protect my eyes, face, hands and body during laboratory, (c) conduct myself in a responsible manner at all times in the laboratory, and (d) abide by all of the safety regulations specified above.

Signature _____ Date _____

Parent's (Guardian's) Signature _____ Date _____

APPENDIX 3.2 CHEMICAL STORAGE

NFPA HAZARD CODES

The National Fire Protection Association developed a standard label to display chemical hazard ratings (see Appendix 3.3). The NFPA label is required by many institutions, industries, and municipalities, and is found on most new chemical reagent containers. The left diamond is printed in blue and indicates toxicity (health hazard), the top diamond is printed in red and indicates flammability and the right diamond is printed in yellow and indicates reactivity. The bottom diamond is printed in white and is reserved for special warnings such as radioactivity or reactivity with water.

MATERIAL SAFETY DATA SHEETS (MSDS)

Chemical manufacturers provide material safety data sheets (MSDS) with the chemicals they sell. These sheets include pertinent safety and health information compiled from OSHA (Occupational Safety and Health Administration), the EPA (Environmental Protection Agency) and the National Library of Medicine. Instructors should keep this information in an appropriate location and should be aware of the possible dangers of the chemicals they use.

FIRE AND FIRE EXTINGUISHER CODES

The National Fire Protection Association (NFPA) classifies fires as follows:

> Class <u>A</u> fires involve ordinary combustibles such as wood, paper, cloth, etc. Such fires can be extinguished by the heat absorbing effect of water.
>
> Class <u>B</u> fires involve flammable and combustible liquids, greases, and similar materials. Such fires are best extinguished by smothering them with noncombustible gases like carbon dioxide or halon.
>
> Class <u>C</u> fires involve electrical equipment and should be extinguished with a material that is electrically nonconducting to avoid shock hazard.
>
> Class <u>D</u> fires involve combustible metals like magnesium and must be extinguished by a heat-absorbing material that does not react with the burning metal.

Fire extinguishers are classified by the fires they extinguish. For example, an ABC extinguisher could be used on class A, B and C fires.

CHEMICAL STORAGE CATEGORIES

Explosions, fires, toxic fumes, and other hazards can arise if incompatible chemicals are accidentally mixed. To minimize the possibility of such hazards, the fronts of all chemical storage shelves should be equipped with horizontal bars so chemicals will not fall in the event of an earthquake. To minimize the potential of such hazards, chemicals should be stored with other compatible chemicals and separated by appropriate distances from incompatible chemicals. The following is a storage classification system suggested by the California State Department of Education.

Metals: All metals, except mercury, can be stored together. Metals should be stored separate from all oxidizers, halogens, organic compounds and moisture.

Oxidizers (except ammonium nitrate): Oxidizers include such chemicals as nitrates, nitrites, permanganates, chromates, dichromates, chlorates, perchlorates, and peroxides. They should be separated from metals, acids, organic materials, and ammonium nitrate. They should be separated from flammable liquids by a one-hour fire wall or a distance of eight meters.

Ammonium Nitrate: Ammonium nitrate should be stored in isolation from all other chemicals.

Bases: All strong bases, such as sodium hydroxide or potassium hydroxide should be stored in a dedicated corrosive chemicals cabinet that is coated with corrosion-resistant material.

Acids: All inorganic acids (except nitric acid), and all regulated organic acids should be stored in a cabinet constructed of corrosion-resistant material. Acids may be stored with bases, but fumes from acids and bases may produce an annoying coating of salt crystals on the outside of reagent containers. Nitric acid should be stored separately from acetic acid. Fuming nitric acid should never be used in the school laboratory.

Flammables: Flammables should be stored in a dedicated wooden flammable materials cabinet, eight meters away from all oxidizers. The cabinet should be coated with flame retardant paint and should be appropriately labeled with the notice: FLAMMABLE LIQUID STORAGE. KEEP FIRE AWAY!

Poisons: Highly toxic substances such as cyanides should never be used in a school laboratory. Poisons approved by state and district education boards should be stored in a locked cabinet away from the acids cabinet.

Compressed Gases: Compressed gas cylinders should be strapped to the wall. Oxidizing gases such as oxygen should be stored far away from flammable liquids, gases, and metals. Flammable gases should be separated from oxidizers and oxidizing gases by a one-hour fire wall or a distance of eight meters.

Low-Hazard Chemicals: Many weak bases, oxides, sulfides, indicators, amino acids, sugars, stains and carbonates are classified as low-hazard chemicals. These chemicals may be stored on open shelves with bars to prevent accidental spillage.

STORAGE CODES

Some manufacturers provide color-coded labels to categorize chemicals for storage purposes. Chemicals with a common storage color may be stored together, except when indicated otherwise. Chemicals with different storage color labels should be stored in different areas. The following is a commonly accepted code.

R	Storage code **Red**	**Flammable.** Store in area designated for flammable reagents.
Y	Storage code **Yellow**	**Reactive and oxidizing.** May react violently with air, water or other substances. Store away from flammable and combustible materials.
B	Storage code **Blue**	**Health hazard.** These chemicals are toxic if inhaled, ingested or absorbed through the skin. They should be stored in a locked cabinet.
W	Storage code **White**	**Corrosive.** These chemicals may harm skin, eyes, and mucous membranes. They should be stored away from red-, yellow-, and blue-coded reagents.
G	Storage code **Gray**	**Moderate or minimal hazard.** According to current data, these chemicals do not pose more than a moderate hazard in any category.

APPENDIX 3.3 DISPOSAL OF CHEMICALS

Regulations: It is important that your school is in compliance with all federal, state, local and district regulations pertaining to the handling, storage and disposal of chemical wastes. Consult your local environmental health and safety specialist regarding the policies and regulations in your school, community and state.

Drain Disposal: The National Research Council's Committee on Hazardous Substances in the Laboratory has published a book entitled *Prudent Practices for Disposal of Chemicals from Laboratories* (National Academy Press; Washington DC). This book provides detailed information regarding the handling of chemical waste. The Committee approves compounds of the following low-toxic-hazard cations and anions for disposal down the drain with excess water in quantities up to 100 g at a time. Any strongly acidic or basic substances should be neutralized before disposal down the drain. Always consult local policies and regulations before disposing of chemical wastes in your laboratory drain.

Low-Toxicity Ions

Low-Toxicity Cations		*Low-Toxicity Anions*	
Al^{3+}	Na^+	BO_3^{3-}	OH^-
Ca^{2+}	NH_4^+	$B_4O_7^{2-}$	I^-
Cu^{2+}	Sn^{2+}	Br^-	NO_3^-
$Fe^{2+, 3+}$	Sr^{2+}	CO_3^{2-}	PO_4^{3-}
H^+	$Ti^{3+, 4+}$	Cl^-	SO_4^{2-}
K^+	Zn^{2+}	HSO_3^-	SCN^-
Li^+	Zr^{2+}	OCN^-	
Mg^{2+}			

Trash Disposal: In most areas, nonhazardous solids can be disposed of in the trash. Liquid wastes are generally not allowed in sanitary landfills and should not be placed in the trash. The following types of solid laboratory waste are generally considered nonhazardous or of low toxicity and may be placed in the trash depending on quantities involved. Always consult local policies before disposing of chemical wastes in the trash.

<u>organic chemicals</u>
naturally occurring α-amino acids and salts
citric acid and its Na, K, Mg, Ca, and NH_4 salts
lactic acid and its Na, K, Mg, Ca, and NH_4 salts
sugars and starches

<u>inorganic chemicals</u>
borates: Na, K, Mg, Ca
carbonates: Na, K, Mg, Ca, Sr, NH_4
chlorides: Na, K, Mg
fluorides: Ca
oxides: B, Mg, Ca, Sr, Al, Si, Ti, Mn, Fe, Co, Cu, Zn
phosphates: Na, K, Mg, Ca, Sr, NH_4
sulfates: Na, K, Mg, Ca, Sr, NH_4

<u>laboratory materials</u> NOT contaminated with hazardous materials: chromatographic paper and absorbents, filter paper, filter aids, glassware, and rubber and plastic protective clothing

APPENDIX 3.4 COMMON CHEMICAL HAZARD LABELS

Label	Description of Hazard	Examples
FLAMABLE	Any solid, liquid, vapor or gas that can be ignited readily. Burns so strongly as to create a serious hazard. The Department of Transportation defines a flamable liquid as a liquid with a flash point of less than 141°F (60.5°C).	acetone glacial acetic acid amyl nitrate benzene cyclohexane ethanol methanol isopropyl alcohol
CORROSIVE	A liquid or solid that causes visible destruction of, or irreversible alterations in, living tissue by chemical action at the site of contact; or a liquid that causes a severe corrosion rate on steel or aluminum.	ammonia, aqueous nitric acid phosphoric acid glacial acetic acid hydrochloric acid sodium hydroxide sulfuric acid
NON-FLAMABLE GAS	A pressurized dissolved gas or a gas liquefied by compression or refrigeration. Refrigerated gases may cause frostbite on contact.	argon carbon dioxide chlorine nitrogen sulfur dioxide
Yellow Label **OXIDIZERS**	A chemical that initiates or promotes combustion in other materials, causing fire either by itself or through the release of oxygen or other gases. Oxidizers must be stored away from all flammable materials.	chlorates nitrates nitrites bromates peroxides permanganates
Diborane [3] [W] Ignites spontaneously in moist air.	**US National Fire Protection Association Label** Blue (left): health hazard Red (top): fire hazard Yellow (right): reactivity hazard White (bottom): special hazard	0 = minimal hazard 1 = slight hazard 2 = moderate hazard 3 = serious hazard 4 = severe hazard

APPENDIX 4.1 COMMON AND INEXPENSIVE SOURCES OF CHEMICALS

Many of the chemicals used in this book may be purchased from the market, drug store, pet store or hardware store at dramatically lower prices than are available through scientific supply companies. We believe that students gain a greater appreciation for the applicability of chemistry to everyday life if they are able to use everyday products to conduct their experiments and investigations. Although the products listed on this page are less expensive, it should be noted that they often contain additives. Most of these additives do not affect the performance of the chemicals, but the instructor should always carefully examine the label to note the percent concentration of the desired substance and adjust the quantities used as necessary. It should also be noted that manufacturers sometimes change the composition of their products, so you should always carefully examine the contents label before purchasing. As with all experiments, the instructor should carefully perform all experiments and test for safety prior to classroom experiments or demonstrations.

Chemical	Formula	Source/Description
acetic acid	CH_3COOH	<u>Vinegars</u> vary between 4–5.5% acetic acid; more concentrated acetic acid (28%) may be purchased at photography supply stores.
acetone	CH_3COCH_3	<u>Nail polish remover</u> is generally acetone; <u>fiberglass cleaner</u> is also generally made of acetone and is available at boating supply stores.
aluminum	Al	<u>Aluminum foil</u>; <u>aluminum turnings</u> are available as scrap from machine shops.
potassium aluminum sulfate	$KAl(SO_4)_2 \cdot 12H_2O$	<u>Alum</u> is available at most drug stores. It is used as an astringent to shrink mucus membranes.
ammonia	$NH_3(aq)$; NH_4OH	<u>Household ammonia</u> (ammonium hydroxide) is an aqueous solution of ammonia. Note: This often has additives.
ammonium nitrate	NH_4NO_3	<u>Nitrate of ammonia</u> fertilizer is available at most garden supply stores.
amylose	$(C_6H_9O_5)_n$	<u>Cornstarch</u> is available at most markets and is used extensively in cooking.
anthocyanin	$C_{15}H_{11}OCl$	Anthocyanin solution can be prepared by cutting, boiling and filtering <u>red cabbage.</u>
ascorbic acid	$C_6H_8O_6$	<u>Vitamin C tablets</u> sold at the market are primarily ascorbic acid.
bromthymol blue	$C_{27}H_{28}Br_2O_5S$	<u>Aquarium pH test kits</u> often employ bromthymol blue because it changes color in the 6.0–7.6 range.
butane	C_4H_{10}	The lighter <u>fluid</u> in hand-held <u>fire starters</u> or <u>cigarette lighters</u> is usually liquid butane.
calcium carbonate	$CaCO_3$	<u>Chalk</u>, <u>limestone</u> and <u>marble chips</u> are good sources of solid calcium carbonate; some antacids are largely calcium carbonate.
calcium chloride	$CaCl_2$	Much of the <u>road salt (de-icer)</u> used to de-ice roads in cold climates is calcium chloride.

APPENDIX 4.1 COMMON AND INEXPENSIVE SOURCES OF CHEMICALS *(Continued)*

Chemical	*Formula*	*Source/Description*
calcium hydroxide	$Ca(OH)_2$	Some <u>antacids</u> are primarily calcium hydroxide; <u>slaked lime</u> is calcium hydroxide and is used in <u>lime-softening water treatment</u> and in plastering.
calcium hypochlorite	$Ca(ClO)_2$	<u>Bleaching powder</u> and some <u>swimming pool disinfectants</u> contain calcium hypochlorite. Available from cleaning or swimming pool supply companies.
calcium oxide	CaO	In the past, <u>quicklime</u> was a material plasterers used in making plaster. It is now difficult to obtain from hardware stores.
carbon	C	<u>Charcoal</u> used in cooking, <u>activated charcoal</u> used in fish tank filters and <u>graphite</u> used in pencil leads are good sources of carbon.
carbon dioxide	CO_2	<u>Dry ice</u> is available from party stores, refrigeration supply companies and ice cream companies.
carbonic acid	H_2CO_3	<u>Soda water</u> is simply carbonated water, a dilute solution of carbonic acid.
copper	Cu	<u>Electrical wire</u>, <u>copper pipe</u>, and <u>copper sheeting</u> are available at hardware stores; <u>American pennies</u> (minted 1944–1946, 1962–1982) are 95% copper and 5% zinc.
copper sulfate pentahydrate	$CuSO_4 \cdot 5H_2O$	Basicop® or Bluestone® algaecide used to kill algae and other aquatic pests contain copper sulfate.
ethylene glycol	CH_2OHCH_2OH	Some engine <u>antifreezes</u> are primarily ethylene glycol.
glucose	$C_6H_{12}O_6$	<u>Dextrose</u> (glucose) is available in many drug stores; some specialty throat lozenges are dextrose.
glycerol	$C_3H_8O_3$	<u>Glycerin</u> is an emollient used to soften skin by delaying the evaporation of water. It is available at most drug stores.
gold	Au	Gold <u>jewelry</u> is generally not pure gold. Gold is generally alloyed with other metals to increase strength.
helium	He	<u>Helium</u> can be obtained from party stores or wherever helium balloons are available.
hydrochloric acid	HCl	<u>Muriatic acid</u> (the common name for HCl) is used in swimming pool maintenance. It is also sold as <u>masonry cleaner</u> and is available at the hardware store. Percentage concentrations vary.
hydrogen peroxide	H_2O_2	Hydrogen peroxide antiseptic (3%) is available from the drug store. Clairoxide® hair bleach by Clairol is much more concentrated and is available from beauty supply stores.

(continued)

APPENDIX 4.1 COMMON AND INEXPENSIVE SOURCES OF CHEMICALS *(Continued)*

Chemical	*Formula*	*Source/Description*
iodine	I_2	Tincture of iodine, a topical antiseptic used for treating wounds, is a solution of iodine dissolved in ethyl alcohol. It is available at most drug stores.
iron	Fe	Steel wool, iron nails, iron bolts, nuts and screws are good sources of iron. You can get iron filings by dragging a strong magnet through sand.
ferric oxide	Fe_2O_3	Ceramic rust is used to add a red color to pottery and can be purchased at ceramic stores.
kerosene	C_nH_{2n+1} (n = 12 – 16)	Lamp oil or kerosene is sold in the paint departments of most hardware stores.
lead	Pb	Lead shot and lead sinkers are used by fishermen and are available at sporting goods stores.
magnesium hydroxide	$Mg(OH)_2$	Milk of Magnesia is an antacid used to settle sour (acidic) stomachs. Some antacid tablets also contain magnesium hydroxide.
magnesium silicate	$Mg_3Si_4O_{10}(OH)_2$	Talcum powder comes from talc, the softest of all minerals, and is used as a dusting powder for babies. It is available in the body-care section of the drug store.
magnesium sulfate	$MgSO_4 \cdot 7H_2O$	Epsom salt is sold at most drug stores and is used as a laxative or as an anti-inflammatory soak.
methanol	CH_3OH	Methanol is sold as a solvent in paint supply stores under the names "wood alcohol" or "methyl alcohol."
methylene blue	$C_{16}H_{18}ClN_3S$	Methylene blue (Methidote® antiseptic) is used to treat small injured fish and is available at pet stores.
mineral oil	complex mixture of hydrocarbons	Mineral oil is sold in drug stores as an emollient. Some baby oils are essentially mineral oil and fragrance.
nickel	Ni	Pre-1985 Canadian nickels are made of nickel. Note: American "nickels" are composed of 25% nickel and 75% copper.
oxygen	O_2	Portable welding oxygen tanks are available at welding shops and some hardware stores.
paraffin	CnH_{2n+2} (*n* >19)	Candle wax is made of paraffin. Some grocery stores sell paraffin as a sealant for home canning.
phenolphthalein	$C_{20}H_{14}O_4$	Ex-Lax® laxative contained phenolphthalein prior to 1997. In that year it was determined phenolphthalein might cause cancer, and the ingredients were changed.
phosphoric acid	H_3PO_4	Some pH reducers (available at pet stores) used in fish tanks are simply dilute solutions of phosphoric acid.

APPENDIX 4.1 COMMON AND INEXPENSIVE SOURCES OF CHEMICALS *(Continued)*

Chemical	Formula	Source/Description
potassium bitartrate	$KHC_4H_4O_6$	Cream of tartar is available at the market and is used to stabilize delicate foods like meringue toppings and other baked egg-white products.
potassium carbonate	K_2CO_3	Some agricultural supply companies sell potash to farmers who need to increase the potassium content in their soils.
potassium chloride	KCl	Lite Salt® is used as a salt substitute by people who must limit their sodium intake and is available at most markets.
potassium bromide	KBr	Potassium bromide may be purchased from photography stores where it is used in photographic development.
potassium iron (II) hexacyanoferrate (III)	$KFe[Fe(CN)_6]$	Mrs. Stewart's® liquid <u>laundry bluing</u> is used to whiten clothes and may be found in the detergents section of the market.
potassium nitrate	KNO_3	<u>Saltpeter</u> or <u>quick salt</u> is used to cure homemade sausages and corned beef and may be available at some butcher shops.
potassium permanganate	$KMnO_4$	Clearwater® is a solution of approximately 50% potassium permanganate and is used to remove odors and cloudiness from water to be used in aquariums.
propane	C_3H_8	Gas barbecue fuel is generally made of propane and is available at many gasoline stations or picnic supply stores.
2-propanol	$CH_3CHOHCH_3$	Rubbing alcohol (isopropyl alcohol) is a concentrated solution (generally 70%) of 2-propanol and may be found in most drug stores.
silicon dioxide	SiO_2	Quartz sand is relatively pure silicon dioxide and is available at most building supply stores.
silver	Ag	Older non-clad American dimes, quarters, half dollars and silver dollars are 90% silver and 10% copper.
sodium acetate	$NaC_2H_3O_2$	Re-Heater® and other hand-warmers are available at sporting goods stores.
sodium bicarbonate	$NaHCO_3$	Baking soda is pure sodium bicarbonate and may be found in the baking section of the market.
sodium carbonate	Na_2CO_3	Washing soda is used to treat wool fibers and is available at spinning, weaving, and art supply stores.
sodium chloride	$NaCl$	The table salt used in cooking is sodium chloride. Iodized salt contains a trace of sodium iodide.

(continued)

APPENDIX 4.1 COMMON AND INEXPENSIVE
SOURCES OF CHEMICALS *(Concluded)*

Chemical	Formula	Source/Description
sodium hydroxide	NaOH	Known also as caustic soda and lye, sodium hydroxide is used in many commercial drain cleaners.
sodium hypochlorite	NaClO	Household bleach is generally a 5% solution of sodium hypochlorite.
sodium phosphate	Na_3PO_4	Tri-sodium phosphate, commonly known as TSP, is available at hardware stores and is used to clean walls prior to painting.
sodium tetraborate decahydrate	$Na_2B_4O_7 \cdot 10H_2O$	Borax, such as Twenty Mule Team Borax® Laundry Booster, is sodium tetraborate decahydrate.
sodium thiosulfate	$Na_2S_2O_3$	Photographer's hypo is used in photograph development and is available at photography supply stores.
sucrose	$C_{12}H_{22}O_{11}$	Table sugar is available at grocery stores in large or small bags.
sulfur	S	Flowers of sulfur is sold at some garden stores to treat certain plant diseases.
sulfuric acid	H_2SO_4	Battery acid, also known as oil of vitriol, is sulfuric acid and may be obtained at some auto supply stores.
tungsten	W	The filament in incandescent light bulbs is made of tungsten.
zinc	Zn	Recent American pennies (1982–present) are 97.5% zinc with a 2.5% copper coating.

APPENDIX 4.2 PREPARATION OF STOCK SOLUTIONS AND DILUTIONS

Stock Solutions: Many of the activities in this resource require specific molar concentrations of aqueous stock solutions of soluble inorganic and organic compounds. Molarity is defined as the number of moles of solute per liter of solution. Before making a stock solution, it is necessary to calculate the formula weight (generally written on the side of the container), and then measure out the appropriate mass of solute. For example, to make a 1 *M* solution of NaCl, measure out 58.5 grams of NaCl (NaCl has a formula weight of 58.5 grams/mole) and place in a volumetric flask. Add water slowly while stirring until a solution volume of 1 liter is reached. To make a 2 *M* solution of NaCl, it would be necessary to dissolve 117 grams of NaCl (117 grams represent two moles of NaCl) and add water until the 1 liter mark is reached. Most of the activities in this book are qualitative and do not require precise concentrations. It is therefore often appropriate to use less precise containers, such as graduated cylinders, to prepare stock solutions.

If the formula weight is not printed on the container, it may be calculated by adding the masses (see the Periodic Table, Appendix 6.1) of the component atoms. For example, $NaHCO_3$ is 84 g/mole: 1 sodium (23 g/mole) + 1 hydrogen (1 gram/mole) + 1 carbon (12 grams/mole) + 3 oxygens (16 grams/mole) = 23 + 1 + 12 + 3(16) = 84 grams/mole.

Dilutions: It is often necessary to make dilute solutions from existing solutions. Since a solution is diluted by simply adding more solvent, the moles of solute remain unchanged. In other words, the number of moles before dilution equals the number of moles following dilution. Knowing this, the dilution formula can be derived:

$$M_1 V_1 = M_2 V_2$$

where M_1 is the initial concentration, V_1 is the initial volume, M_2 is the final concentration and V_2 is the final volume. If concentrations are measured in grams equivalents/liter then the equation becomes:

$$N_1 V_1 = N_2 V_2$$

If the concentration *(C)* of the solution is expressed in grams solute/liter solution, the dilution equation becomes:

$$C_1 V_1 = C_2 V_2$$

This equation is derived from the principle that the initial number of grams of solute must equal the final number (conservation of mass).

Sample Dilution Problem (Molarity): Prepare a 100-mL solution of 0.1 *M* NaOH from a stock solution of 1.0 *M* NaOH. Thus, dilute 10 mL of 1 *M* NaOH solution by adding more solute until a final volume of 100 mL is reached:

$M_1 = 1.0$ *M* NaOH (the initial concentration) $V_1 = ?$ (the initial volume of 1 *M* NaOH)
$M_2 = 0.1$ *M* NaOH (the final concentration) $V_2 = 100$ mL (the final volume)

$$V_1 = M_2 V_2 / M_1 = (0.1 \text{ } M \text{ NaOH})(100 \text{ mL})/1.0 \text{ } M \text{ NaOH} = 10 \text{ mL}$$

Sample Dilution Problem (Grams/liter): A solution of sodium chloride contains 20 grams of silver chloride in a liter of solution. Dilute this so the resulting solution contains only 4 grams of sodium chloride per liter of solution. Thus, dilute 1 L of the original solution to a final volume of 5 L.

C_1 = (20 g NaCl)/liter solution $\qquad$ V_1 = 1 liter of the original solution

C_2 = (4 g NaCl)/liter solution $\qquad$ V_2 = ?

$$V_2 = C_1V_1/C_2 = (20 \text{ g/L})(1 \text{ L})/(4 \text{ g/L}) = 5 \text{ L}$$

APPENDIX 4.3 PREPARATION OF ACID AND BASE STOCK SOLUTIONS

WARNINGS

- Perform all acid dilutions in a <u>fume hood or well ventilated area</u>. Acids can irritate the skin and vapors can damage the eyes and respiratory system. Always <u>wear goggles and lab coat</u> when working with acids and bases.
- When diluting, always add acid to water. <u>Never add water to acid</u> because it may splatter. The heat released in the dilution process may be substantial. A small amount of water in a concentrated acid will heat up and may vaporize and cause splattering. A small amount of acid in water will also heat up, but because the specific heat of water is great and there is so much water, it will not vaporize and will not splatter.
- Cover acid spills with baking soda ($NaHCO_3$, sodium hydrogen carbonate) before wiping up with plenty of water
- Place 500 mL of distilled water in the beaker before mixing.
- Always add the acid or base slowly and stir with a glass rod.
- Add distilled water until 1 L of solution has been reached.
- Only instructors should dilute concentrated acids and bases.

To make:	Dissolve this in water to make 1 liter solution:	To make:	Dissolve this in water to make 1 liter solution:
acetic acid $HC_2H_3O_2$	glacial acetic acid (17.5 M)	aqueous ammonia NH_3	concentrated ammonia (15 M)
5 M	286 mL	5 M	333 mL
2 M	114 mL	2 M	132 mL
1 M	57 mL	1 M	67 mL
0.10 M	5.7 mL	0.1 M	6.7 mL
hydrochloric acid (HCl)	concentrated HCl (12 M)	sodium hydroxide NaOH	sodium hydroxide (pellets or powder)
6 M	500 mL	6 M	240 g
2 M	167 mL	2 M	80 g
1 M	83 mL	1 M	40 g
0.1 M	8.3 mL	0.1 M	4.0 g
sulfuric acid H_2SO_4	concentrated sulfuric acid (18 M)	nitric acid HNO_3	concentrated nitric acid (16 M)
2 M	111 mL	2 M	125 mL
1 M	55 mL	1 M	63 mL
0.1 M	5.5 mL	0.1 M	6.3 mL

APPENDIX 5.1 PROPERTIES OF COMMON ELEMENTS

Element	*Symbol*	*Atomic Mass*	*Common Oxidation States*	*Phase 25°C*	*Color*	*Density g/cm³*
aluminum	Al	27.0	+3	s	silver	2.70
antimony	Sb	121.8	−3,+3,+5	s	silver	6.69
arsenic	As	74.9	−3,+3,+5	s	gray	5.73
barium	Ba	137.3	+2	s	silver	3.51
bismuth	Bi	209.0	+3,+5	s	silver	9.75
bromine	Br	79.9	−1,+1,+3,+5,+7	l	red/brown	3.12
calcium	Ca	40.1	+2	s	silver	1.55
carbon (graphite)	C	12.0	+2,+4,−4	s	blk/clear	2.26
chlorine	Cl	35.5	−1,+1,+3,+5,+7	g	grn/yellow	0.0032
chromium	Cr	52.0	+2,+3,+6	s	silver	7.19
cobalt	Co	59.0	+2,+3	s	silver	8.90
copper	Cu	63.5	+1,+2	s	red	8.96
fluorine	F	19.0	−1	g	yellow	0.0017
gold	Au	197.0	+1,+3	s	yellow	19.3
hydrogen	H	1.0	−1,+1	g	none	0.00009
iodine	I	126.9	−1,+1,+3,+5,+7	s	blue/black	4.93
iron	Fe	55.8	+2,+3	s	silver	7.87
lead	Pb	207.2	+2,+4	s	silver	11.4
magnesium	Mg	24.3	+2	s	silver	1.74
manganese	Mn	54.9	+2,+3,+4,+6,+7	s	silver	7.3
mercury	Hg	200.6	+1,+2	l	silver	13.5
nickel	Ni	58.7	+2,+3	s	silver	8.90
nitrogen	N	14.0	−1,+3,+5	g	none	0.0012
oxygen	O	16.0	−2,−1	g	none	0.0014
phosphorous	P	31.0	+3,+5	s	yellow/red	1.82
platinum	Pt	195.1	+2,+4	s	silver	21.4
potassium	K	39.1	+1	s	silver	0.86
silicon	Si	28.1	+2,+4	s	gray	2.33
silver	Ag	107.9	+1	s	silver	10.5
sodium	Na	23.0	+1	s	silver	0.97
strontium	Sr	87.6	+2	s	silver	2.54
sulfur	S	32.1	−2,+4,+6	s	yellow	2.07
tin	Sn	118.7	+2,+4	s	silver	7.31
titanium	Ti	47.9	+2,+3,+4	s	silver	4.54
tungsten	W	183.8	+6	s	gray	19.3
zinc	Zn	65.4	+2	s	silver	7.13

APPENDIX 5.2 COMMON IONS

Common Cations		*Common Anions*	
aluminum	Al^{3+}	acetate	$(C_2H_3O)_2^-$
ammonium	NH_4^+	bromide	Br^-
barium	Ba^{2+}	carbonate	CO_3^{2-}
calcium	Ca^{2+}	chlorate	ClO_3^{2-}
chromium (III)	Cr^{3+}	chloride	Cl^-
cobalt (II)	Co^{2+}	chlorite	ClO_2^-
copper (I)	Cu^+	chromate	CrO_4^{2-}
copper (II)	Cu^{2+}	cyanide	CN^-
hydronium	H_3O^+	dichromate	$Cr_2O_7^{2-}$
iron (II)	Fe^{2+}	fluoride	F^-
iron (III)	Fe^{3+}	hexacyanoferrate (II)	$Fe(CN)_6^{4-}$
lead (II)	Pb^{2+}	hexacyanoferrate (III)	$Fe(CN)_6^{3-}$
magnesium	Mg^{2+}	hydride	H^-
mercury (I)	Hg_2^{2+}	hydrogen carbonate	HCO_3^-
mercury (II)	Hg^{2+}	hydrogen sulfate	HSO_4^-
nickel (II)	Ni^{2+}	hydroxide	OH^-
potassium	K^+	hypochlorite	ClO^-
silver	Ag^+	iodide	I^-
sodium	Na^+	nitrate	NO_3^-
tin (II)	Sn^{2+}	nitrite	NO_2^-
tin (IV)	Sn^{4+}	oxide	O^{2-}
zinc	Zn^{2+}	perchlorate	ClO_4^-
		permanganate	MnO_4^-
		peroxide	O_2^{2-}
		phosphate	PO_4^{3-}
		sulfate	SO_4^{2-}
		sulfide	S^{2-}
		sulfite	SO_3^{2-}

APPENDIX 5.3 STANDARD REDUCTION POTENTIALS

Standard Reduction Potentials at 25°C
For all half-reactions the concentration is 1 M for dissolved
species and the pressure is 1 atm for gases.

Half-Reaction	$E°$ (V)
$Li^+(aq) + e^- \rightarrow Li(s)$	−3.05
$K^+(aq) + e^- \rightarrow K(s)$	−2.92
$Ba^{2+}(aq) + 2e^- \rightarrow Ba(s)$	−2.90
$Ca^{2+}(aq) + 2e^- \rightarrow Ca(s)$	−2.76
$Na^+(aq) + e^- \rightarrow Na(s)$	−2.71
$Mg^{2+}(aq) + 2e^- \rightarrow Mg(s)$	−2.37
$Al^{3+}(aq) + 3e^- \rightarrow Al(s)$	−1.66
$2H_2O + 2e^- \rightarrow H_2(g) + 2OH^-(aq)$	−0.83
$Zn^{2+}(aq) + 2e^- \rightarrow Zn(s)$	−0.76
$Cr^{3+}(aq) + 3e^- \rightarrow Cr(s)$	−0.73
$Fe^{2+}(aq) + 2e^- \rightarrow Fe(s)$	−0.44
$Cd^{2+}(aq) + 2e^- \rightarrow Cd(s)$	−0.40
$Co^{2+}(aq) + 2e^- \rightarrow Co(s)$	−0.28
$Ni^{2+}(aq) + 2e^- \rightarrow Ni(s)$	−0.23
$Sn^{2+}(aq) + 2e^- \rightarrow Sn(s)$	−0.14
$Pb^{2+}(aq) + 2e^- \rightarrow Pb(s)$	−0.13
$2H^+(aq) + 2e^- \rightarrow H_2(g)$	**0.00**
$Cu^{2+}(aq) + e^- \rightarrow Cu^+(aq)$	+0.16
$Cu^{2+}(aq) + 2e^- \rightarrow Cu(s)$	+0.34
$O_2(g) + 2H_2O + 4e^- \rightarrow 4OH^-(aq)$	+0.40
$I_2(s) + 2e^- \rightarrow 2I^-(aq)$	+0.54
$O_2(g) + 2H^+(aq) + 2e^- \rightarrow H_2O_2(aq)$	+0.68
$Fe^{3+}(aq) + e^- \rightarrow Fe^{2+}(aq)$	+0.77
$Hg_2^{2+}(aq) + 2e^- \rightarrow 2Hg(l)$	+0.80
$Ag^+(aq) + e^- \rightarrow Ag(s)$	+0.80
$Hg^{2+}(aq) + 2e^- \rightarrow Hg(l)$	+0.85
$NO_3^-(aq) + 4H^+(aq) + 3e^- \rightarrow NO(g) + 2H_2O$	+0.96
$Br_2(l) + 2e^- \rightarrow 2Br^-(aq)$	+1.09
$O_2(g) + 4H^+(aq) + 4e^- \rightarrow 2H_2O$	+1.23
$Cl_2(g) + 2e^- \rightarrow 2Cl^-(aq)$	+1.36
$MnO_4^-(aq) + 8H^+(aq) + 5e^- \rightarrow Mn^{2+}(aq) + 4H_2O(l)$	+1.51
$Au^{3+} + 3e^- \rightarrow Au$	+1.50
$H_2O_2(aq) + 2H^+(aq) + 2e^- \rightarrow 2H_2O$	+1.78
$F_2(g) + 2e^- \rightarrow 2F^-(aq)$	+2.87

PERIODIC TABLE OF THE ELEMENTS

1	2		3	4	5	6	7	8	9	10	11	12	13	14	15	16	17	18
1 H Hydrogen 1.008																		2 He Helium 4.003
3 Li Lithium 6.941	4 Be Beryllium 9.012												5 B Boron 10.81	6 C Carbon 12.011	7 N Nitrogen 14.007	8 O Oxygen 15.999	9 F Fluorine 18.998	10 Ne Neon 20.179
11 Na Sodium 22.990	12 Mg Magnesium 24.305												13 Al Aluminum 26.981	14 Si Silicon 28.086	15 P Phosphorus 30.974	16 S Sulfur 32.06	17 Cl Chlorine 35.453	18 Ar Argon 39.948
19 K Potassium 39.098	20 Ca Calcium 40.08		21 Sc Scandium 44.956	22 Ti Titanium 47.88	23 V Vanadium 50.942	24 Cr Chromium 51.996	25 Mn Manganese 54.938	26 Fe Iron 55.847	27 Co Cobalt 58.993	28 Ni Nickel 58.69	29 Cu Copper 63.546	30 Zn Zinc 65.39	31 Ga Gallium 69.72	32 Ge Germanium 72.59	33 As Arsenic 74.913	34 Se Selenium 78.96	35 Br Bromine 79.904	36 Kr Krypton 83.80
37 Rb Rubidium 85.468	38 Sr Strontium 87.62		39 Y Yttrium 88.906	40 Zr Zirconium 91.224	41 Nb Niobium 92.906	42 Mo Molybdenum 95.94	43 Tc Technetium (98)	44 Ru Ruthenium 101.07	45 Rh Rhodium 102.906	46 Pd Palladium 106.42	47 Ag Silver 107.868	48 Cd Cadmium 112.41	49 In Indium 114.82	50 Sn Tin 118.71	51 Sb Antimony 121.75	52 Te Tellurium 157.60	53 I Iodine 126.905	54 Xe Xenon 131.29
55 Cs Cesium 132.905	56 Ba Barium 137.33		57 La Lanthanum 138.906	72 Hf Hafnium 178.49	73 Ta Tantalum 180.948	74 W Tungsten 183.85	75 Re Rhenium 186.207	76 Os Osmium 190.2	77 Ir Iridium 192.22	78 Pt Platinum 195.08	79 Au Gold 196.967	80 Hg Mercury 200.59	81 Tl Thallium 204.383	82 Pb Lead 207.2	83 Bi Bismuth 208.980	84 Po Polonium (209)	85 At Astatine (210)	86 Rn Radon (222)
87 Fr Francium (223)	88 Ra Radium 226.025		89 Ac Actinium 227.028	104 Rf Rutherfordium (261)	105 Db Dubnium (262)	106 Sg Seaborgium (263)	107 Bh Bohrium (262)	108 Hs Hassium (265)	109 Mt Meitnerium (266)									

Lanthanide Series

58 Ce Cerium 140.12	59 Pr Praseodymium 140.908	60 Nd Neodymium 144.24	61 Pm Promethium (145)	62 Sm Samarium 150.36	63 Eu Europium 151.96	64 Gd Gadolinium 157.25	65 Tb Terbium 158.925	66 Dy Dysprosium 162.50	67 Ho Holmium 164.930	68 Er Erbium 167.26	69 Tm Thulium 168.934	70 Yb Ytterbium 173.04	71 Lu Lutetium 174.967

Actinide Series

90 Th Thorium 232.038	91 Pa Protactinium 231.036	92 U Uranium 238.029	93 Np Neptunium 237.048	94 Pu Plutonium (244)	95 Am Americium (243)	96 Cm Curium (247)	97 Bk Berkelium (247)	98 Cf Californium (251)	99 Es Einsteinium (252)	100 Fm Fermium (257)	101 Md Mendelevium (258)	102 No Nobelium (259)	103 Lr Lawrencium (260)

Key:

1 — atomic number
H — symbol
Hydrogen — name
1.008 — atomic mass

Index

References to appendices are preceded by the letter "A."